THE LYRIC BOOK

THE Lyric BOOK

ISBN 0-634-02565-1

HAL•LEONARD®
CORPORATION

7777 W. BLUEMOUND RD. P.O. BOX 13819 MILWAUKEE, WI 53213

Visit Hal Leonard Online at
www.halleonard.com

P9-DVN-518

CONTENTS

8

ARTIST INDEX

11

The Lettermen
153 Hurt So Bad
155 I Believe
359 When I Fall in Love

Jerry Lee Lewis
133 Great Balls of Fire

Joe E. Lewis
288 Sam, You Made the Pants Too Long

Liberace
180 I'll Be Seeing You

Abbey Lincoln
314 Story of My Father

Little Anthony & The Imperials
153 Hurt So Bad

Little Eva
223 The Loco-Motion

Dave Loggins
259 Nobody Loves Me Like You Do

Kenny Loggins
116 For the First Time

Guy Lombardo
269 Out of Nowhere

Julie London
86 Cry Me a River

Lonestar
43 Amazed

Jennifer Lopez
193 If You Had My Love

Trini Lopez
191 If I Had a Hammer (The Hammer Song)

Loverboy
143 Heaven in Your Eyes

The Lovin' Spoonful
89 Daydream
92 Do You Believe in Magic
315 Summer in the City

Art Lund
262 On a Slow Boat to China

Jeanette MacDonald
62 Beyond the Blue Horizon

Johnny Maddox
141 Heart and Soul

Mama Cass Elliot
233 Make Your Own Kind of Music

The Mamas and the Papas
89 Dedicated to the One I Love

Melissa Manchester
94 Don't Cry Out Loud

Henry Mancini
361 Where Do I Begin (Love Theme)

Manhattan Transfer
67 The Boy from New York City
207 Java Jive
286 Route 66
342 Tuxedo Junction

Barry Manilow
84 Copacabana (At the Copa)
84 Could it Be Magic
104 Even Now
155 I Am Your Child
178 I Write the Songs
221 Let's Hang On
225 Looks Like We Made It
235 Mandy
306 Somewhere in the Night

Martha & The Vandellas
142 Heatwave

Dean Martin
239 Memories Are Made of This
326 That's Amoré
381 You're Nobody 'til Somebody Loves You

Freddy Martin
186 I've Got a Lovely Bunch of Cocoanuts
262 On a Slow Boat to China

Marilyn Martin
291 Separate Lives

The Marvelettes
276 Please Mr. Postman

Dave Mason
354 We Just Disagree

Matchbox 20
280 Real World
333 3 AM

Johnny Mathis
244 Misty
360 When Sunny Gets Blue

Martina McBride
346 Valentine

Edwin McCain
179 I'll Be

Paul McCartney
101 Ebony and Ivory
237 Maybe I'm Amazed
252 My Love

Maureen McGovern
91 Different Worlds

Tim McGraw
206 It's Your Love

The McGuire Sisters
298 Sincerely

Sarah McLachlan
32 Adia
44 Angel
71 Building a Mystery
176 I Will Remember You
360 When She Loved Me

Don McLean
86 Crying
298 Since I Don't Have You

Meat Loaf
178 I'd Do Anything for Love
(But I Won't Do That)
344 Two Out of Three Ain't Bad

Sergio Mendes
225 The Look of Love

Ethel Merman
97 Down in the Depths
(On the Ninetieth Floor)

The Merry Macs
232 Mairzy Doats

George Michael
96 Don't Let the Sun Go Down on Me

Bette Midler
120 From a Distance
130 God Help the Outcasts

Glenn Miller
216 The Lady's in Love with You
245 Moonlight Becomes You
245 Moonlight Cocktail
254 My Prayer
300 Skylark
325 That Old Black Magic
342 Tuxedo Junction
365 (There'll Be Bluebirds Over)
The White Cliffs of Dover

Jody Miller
297 Silver Threads and Golden Needles

Roger Miller
213 King of the Road

The Mills Brothers
179 I'll Be Around
217 Lazy River

The Mindbenders
135 A Groovy Kind of Love

Kylie Minogue
223 The Loco-Motion

The Miracles
172 I Second That Emotion
322 The Tears of a Clown

Mr. Big
336 To Be with You

Guy Mitchell
299 Singing the Blues

Monica
67 The Boy Is Mine

The Monkees
89 Daydream Believer

Vaughn Monroe
176 I Wish I Didn't Love You So
288 Sam, You Made the Pants Too Long

Bill Monroe & The Blue Grass Boys
65 Blue Moon of Kentucky

John Michael Montgomery
211 The Keeper of the Stars

The Moody Blues
258 Nights in White Satin

Russ Morgan
381 You're Nobody 'til Somebody Loves You

Mountain
243 Mississippi Queen

Gerry Mulligan
231 Lullaby of the Leaves

Anne Murray
84 Could I Have This Dance
259 Nobody Loves Me Like You Do
378 You Needed Me

Music Explosion
222 Little Bit o' Soul

'N Sync
162 I Drive Myself Crazy

Nazareth
135 Hair of the Dog

Willie Nelson
43 Always on My Mind
122 Georgia on My Mind
235 Mammas Don't Let Your Babies Grow Up
to Be Cowboys

Aaron Neville
96 Don't Know Much

The New Vaudeville Band
368 Winchester Cathedral

Anthony Newley
366 Who Can I Turn To
(When Nobody Needs Me)

Juice Newton
45 Angel of the Morning

Olivia Newton-John
168 I Honestly Love You
316 Summer Nights

Stevie Nicks
282 Rhiannon
310 Stand Back

Harry Nilsson
106 Ev'rybody's Talkin' (Echoes)

98 Degrees
324 Thank God I Found You

No Mercy
362 Where Do You Go

Ray Noble
138 Harlem Nocturne
347 The Very Thought of You

Red Norvo
165 I Get Along Without You Very Well

Oasis
371 Wonderwall

Helen O'Connell
48 Arthur Murray Taught Me Dancing
in a Hurry
321 Tangerine

Anita O'Day
105 Ev'ry Time We Say Goodbye
239 Memories of You

112
180 I'll Be Missing You

Roy Orbison
86 Crying
261 Oh, Pretty Woman

Jeffrey Osborne
263 On the Wings of Love

Donny Osmond
129 Go Away, Little Girl

Patti Page
324 Tennessee Waltz

Charlie Parker
312 Stella by Starlight

The Alan Parsons Project
109 Eye in the Sky

The Partridge Family
173 I Think I Love You
177 I Woke Up in Love This Morning

Les Paul
152 How High the Moon

The Penguins
100 Earth Angel

Peter, Paul & Mary
191 If I Had a Hammer (The Hammer Song)
218 Leaving on a Jet Plane
278 Puff the Magic Dragon

Phil Phillips & The Twilights
289 Sea of Love

The Platters
134 The Great Pretender
254 My Prayer
268 Only You (And You Alone)
343 Twilight Time

The Police
 97 Don't Stand So Close to Me
105 Every Breath You Take
105 Every Little Thing She Does Is Magic
212 King of Pain
241 Message in a Bottle
286 Roxanne

Franck Pourcel's French Fiddles
268 Only You (And You Alone)

Elvis Presley
 40 All Shook Up
 47 Are You Lonesome Tonight
 65 Blue Hawaii
 65 Blue Moon of Kentucky
 74 Can't Help Falling in Love
 94 Don't Be Cruel (To a Heart That's True)
131 Good Luck Charm
141 Heartbreak Hotel
196 In the Ghetto (The Vicious Circle)
204 It's Now or Never
207 Jailhouse Rock
227 Love Me Tender
282 Return to Sender
325 That's All Right
346 Until It's Time for You to Go

Billy Preston
260 Nothing from Nothing
367 Will It Go Round in Circles

Lloyd Price
274 (You've Got) Personality

Ray Price
116 For the Good Times
289 Scotch and Soda

Louis Prima
209 Just a Gigolo
325 That Old Black Magic

Procol Harum
365 A Whiter Shade of Pale

Puff Daddy
180 I'll Be Missing You

Queen
 85 Crazy Little Thing Called Love
355 We Will Rock You
381 You're My Best Friend

Bonnie Raitt
158 I Can't Make You Love Me
228 Love Sneakin' Up on You
304 Something to Talk About (Let's Give Them
     Something to Talk About)

Collin Raye
125 The Gift

The Rays
297 Silhouettes

Otis Redding
 94 (Sittin' On) The Dock of the Bay

Helen Reddy
 74 Candle on the Water
154 I Am Woman
374 You and Me Against the World

REO Speedwagon
283 Ridin' the Storm Out

Alvino Rey
 90 Deep in the Heart of Texas

Lionel Richie
103 Endless Love

The Righteous Brothers
307 (You're My) Soul and Inspiration
345 Unchained Melody

Jeannie C. Riley
138 Harper Valley P.T.A.

LeAnn Rimes
 65 Blue
371 Written in the Stars

Tex Ritter
374 You Are My Sunshine

Marty Robbins
299 Singing the Blues
325 That's All Right

Kenny Rogers
 95 Don't Fall in Love with a Dreamer
121 The Gambler
334 Through the Years

Roy Rogers
137 Happy Trails

The Rolling Stones
 57 Beast of Burden
102 Emotional Rescue
242 Miss You
293 Shattered
296 She's So Cold
311 Start Me Up
342 Tumbling Dice
348 Waiting on a Friend

Linda Ronstadt
 91 Different Drum
 96 Don't Know Much

153 Hurt So Bad
297 Silver Threads and Golden Needles
358 What'll I Do?
358 What's New?

The Rooftop Singers
349 Walk Right In

Diana Ross
 35 Ain't No Mountain High Enough
 93 Do You Know Where You're Going To?
103 Endless Love
280 Reach Out and Touch
     (Somebody's Hand)

Shirley Ross
324 Thanks for the Memory

David Lee Roth
209 Just a Gigolo

Run D.M.C.
349 Walk This Way

Todd Rundgren
143 Hello, It's Me

Merilee Rush & The Turnabouts
 45 Angel of the Morning

Buffy Sainte-Marie
346 Until It's Time for You to Go

Sam & Dave
172 I Thank You

The Sandpipers
 82 Come Saturday Morning

Savage Garden
340 Truly, Madly, Deeply

Leo Sayer
377 You Make Me Feel Like Dancing

Neil Sedaka
136 Happy Birthday, Sweet Sixteen

Blossom Seeley
351 'Way Down Yonder in New Orleans

The Shangri-Las
218 Leader of the Pack

Del Shannon
289 Sea of Love

Artie Shaw
152 How Deep Is the Ocean
     (How High Is the Sky)
269 Out of Nowhere
310 Star Dust

George Shearing
179 I'll Be Around

Duncan Sheik
 56 Barely Breathing

The Shirelles
 89 Dedicated to the One I Love
367 Will You Love Me Tomorrow
     (Will You Still Love Me Tomorrow)

Dinah Shore
176 I Wish I Didn't Love You So
181 I'll Get By (As Long as I Have You)
300 Skylark

Simply Red
149 Holding Back the Years

Frank Sinatra
 39 All or Nothing at All
 73 Call Me Irresponsible
 81 The Coffee Song (They've Got an Awful
     Lot of Coffee in Brazil)
 87 Cycles
 88 Day by Day
106 Everything Happens to Me
146 Here's That Rainy Day
152 How Deep Is the Ocean
     (How High Is the Sky)
160 I Didn't Know What Time It Was
173 I Thought About You
177 I Wish I Were in Love Again
180 I'll Be Seeing You
187 I've Got the World on a String
187 I've Got You Under My Skin
197 In the Still of the Night
198 In the Wee Small Hours of the Morning
202 It Was a Very Good Year
214 The Lady Is a Tramp
239 Memories of You
245 Moonlight Becomes You
264 One for My Baby
     (And One More for the Road)
269 Out of Nowhere
292 September Song
312 Stella by Starlight
325 That Old Black Magic
334 Three Coins in the Fountain
358 What'll I Do?
368 Witchcraft

The Skyliners
298 Since I Don't Have You

Kate Smith
365 (There'll Be Bluebirds Over)
     The White Cliffs of Dover

Michael W. Smith
119 Friends
227 Love of My Life

Will Smith
124 Gettin' Jiggy Wit It

"Whispering" Jack Smith
125 Gimme a Little Kiss (Will Ya Huh?)

Sonny & Cher
357 What Now My Love

The Springfields
297 Silver Threads and Golden Needles

Bruce Springsteen
350 War

Jo Stafford
 88 Day by Day
100 Early Autumn
147 Hey, Good Lookin'
196 In the Cool, Cool, Cool of the Evening
200 It Could Happen to You

The Staple Singers
183 I'll Take You There
194 If You're Ready (Come Go with Me)
281 Respect Yourself
340 Touch a Hand, Make a Friend

Kay Starr
296 Side by Side

14

SONGWRITER INDEX

28

Songs from Musicals, Films* and Television**

Abraham, Martin and John
Words and Music by Richard Holler
Copyright © 1968, 1970 (Renewed) by Regent Music Corporation (BMI)

recorded by Dion

Has anybody here seen my old friend Abraham?
Can you tell me where he's gone?
He freed a lotta people,
But it seems the good die young,
But I just looked around and he's gone.

Has anybody here seen my old friend John?
Can you tell me where he's gone?
He freed a lotta people,
But it seems the good die young,
But I just looked around and he's gone.

Has anybody here seen my old friend Martin?
Can you tell me where he's gone?
He freed a lotta people,
But it seems the good die young.
But I just looked around and he's gone.

Didn't you love the things they stood for?
Didn't they try to find some good for you and me?
And we'll be free.
Someday soon;
It's gonna be one day.

Has anybody here seen my old friend Bobby?
Can you tell me where he's gone?
I thought I saw him walkin' up over the hill
With Abraham, Martin and John.

Ac-cent-tchu-ate the Positive
Lyric by Johnny Mercer
Music by Harold Arlen
© 1944 (Renewed) HARWIN MUSIC CO.

from the film *Here Come the Waves*
recorded by Bing Crosby with The Andrews Sisters, and
various other artists

You've got to ac-cent-tchu-ate the positive,
E-lim-my-nate the negative,
Latch on to the affirmative,
Don't mess with Mister In-between.

You've got to spread joy up to the maximum,
Bring gloom down to the minimum,
Have faith or pandemonium
Liable to walk upon the scene.

To illustrate
My last remark
Jonah and the whale.
Noah in the Ark,
What did they do
Just when everything looked so dark?
"Man," they said, "We better...

Ac-cent-tchu-ate the positive
E-lim-my-nate the negative,
Latch on to the affirmative,
Don't mess with Mister In-between."
No! Don't mess with Mister In-between.

Adia
Words and Music by Sarah McLachlan and Pierre Marchand
Copyright © 1997 Sony/ATV Songs LLC, Tyde Music and Pierre J. Marchand
All Rights on behalf of Sony/ATV Songs LLC and Tyde Music Administered by Sony/ATV Music
    Publishing, 8 Music Square West, Nashville, TN 37203

recorded by Sarah McLachlan

Adia, I do believe I failed you.
Adia, I know I've let you down.
Don't you know I tried so hard,
To love you in my way;
It's easy, let it go.

Adia, I'm empty since you left me.
Trying to find a way to carry on;
I search myself and everyone,
To see where we went wrong.
There's no one left to finger,
There's no on here to blame.
There's no one left to talk to honey,
And there ain't no one to buy our innocence;
'Cause we are born innocent.
Believe me, Adia,
We are still innocent.
It's easy, we all falter.
And does it matter?

Adia, I thought that we could make it.
I know I can't change the way you feel.
I leave you with your misery,
A friend who won't betray.
Pull you from your tower,
I take a away your pain.
I show you all the beauty you possess.
If you'd only let yourself believe,
That we are born innocent.
It's easy, we all falter.
And does it matter?

'Cause we are born innocent.
Believe me, Adia,
We are still innocent.
It's easy, we all falter,
Does it matter?
Believe me, Adia,
We are still innocent.
'Cause we are born innocent.
Believe me, Adia,
We are still innocent.
Its easy, we all falter,
Does it matter?

After the Love Has Gone

Words and Music by David Foster, Jay Graydon
and Bill Champlin

recorded by Earth, Wind & Fire

For a while to love was all we could do;
We were young and we knew,
And our eyes were alive.
Deep inside we knew our love was true.
For awhile we paid no mind to the past,
We knew love would last.
Every night
Somethin' right
Would invite us to begin the dance.

Somethin' happened along the way;
What used to be happy was sad.
Somethin' happened along the way
And yesterday was all we had.

Oh, after the love has gone,
How could you lead me on,
And not let me stay around?
Oh, after the love has gone,
What used to be right is wrong.
Can love that's lost be found?

For awhile,
To love each other was all we would ever need.
Love was strong for so long,
Never knew that what was wrong,
Baby, wasn't right.
We tried to find what we had
'Til sadness was all we shared.
We were scared this affair
Would lead our love into...

Somethin' happened along the way;
Yesterday was all we had.
Somethin' happened along the way;
What used to be happy is sad.
Somethin' happened along the way;
What used to be was all we had.
Oh, after the love has gone,
How could you lead me on
And not let me stay around?

Oh, after the love has gone,
What used to be right is wrong.
Can love that's lost be found?

Oh, after the love has gone,
What used to be right is wrong.
Can love that's lost be found?

Against All Odds
(Take a Look at Me Now)

Words and Music by Phil Collins

from the film *Against All Odds*
recorded by Phil Collins

How can I just let you walk away,
Just let you leave without a trace?
When I stand here taking
Every breath with you,
You're the only one
Who really knows me at all.
How can you just walk away from me,
When all I can do is watch you leave.
'Cause we've shared the laughter and the pain,
And even shared the tears.
You're the only one who really knew me at all.

So take a look at me now
'Cause there's just an empty space.
There's nothing left here to remind me,
Just the memory of your face.
So take a look at me now,
There's just an empty space,
And you coming back to me is against the odds,
And that's what I've got to face.

I wish I could just make you turn around,
Turn around and see me cry.
There's so much I need to say to you,
So many reasons why
You're the only one who really knew me at all.

So take a look at me now,
There's just an empty space,
And there's nothing left here to remind me,
Just the memory of your face.
So take a look at me now,
'Cause there's just an empty space.
But to wait for you is all I can do,
And that's what I've got to face.

Take a good look at me now
'Cause I'll still be standing here,
And you coming back to me is against all odds.
That's the chance I've got to take...
Take a look at me now.

Ain't Goin' Down
('Til the Sun Comes Up)
Words and Music by Kim Williams, Garth Brooks
and Kent Blazy

Copyright © 1993 Sony/ATV Tunes LLC, Major Bob Music Co., Inc., No Fences Music, Inc.
and Careers-BMG Music Publishing, Inc.
All Rights on behalf of Sony/ATV Tunes LLC Administered by Sony/ATV Music Publishing,
8 Music Square West, Nashville, TN 37203

recorded by Garth Brooks

Six o'clock on Friday evening,
Mama doesn't know she's leaving
'Til she hears the screen door slamming,
Rubber squealing, gears a-jammin,
Local country station
Just a-blaring on the radio.
Pick him up at seven
And they're heading to the rodeo.
Mama's on the front porch,
Screaming out a warning:
"Girl, you'd better get your red head
Back in bed before the morning."

Nine o'clock, the show is ending,
But the fun is just beginning.
She knows he's anticipating,
But she's gonna keep him waiting.
First a bite to eat,
And then they're heading to the honky-tonk.
But loud crowds and line dancing
Just ain't what they really want.
Drive out to the boondocks
And park down by the creek,
Where it's George Strait
'Til real late
And dancing cheek to cheek.

They ain't going down 'til the sun comes up,
Ain't giving in 'til they get enough.
Going 'round the world in a pick-up truck.
Ain't going down 'til the sun comes up.

Ten 'til twelve it's wine and dancing.
Midnight starts the hard romancing.
One o'clock that truck is rocking.
Two is coming, still no stopping.
Break to check the clock at three.
They're right at where they want to be
And four o'clock get up and going.
Five o'clock that rooster's crowing.
Hey. Yeah, they…

They ain't going down 'til the sun comes up,
Ain't giving in 'til they get enough.
Going 'round the world in a pick-up truck.
Ain't going down 'til the sun comes up.

Six o'clock on Saturday,
Her folks don't know he's on his way.
The stalls are clean, the horses fed.
They say she's grounded 'til she's dead.
Well, here he comes around the bend,
Slowing down. She's jumping in.
Hey, Mom, your daughter's gone.
And there they go again.
Hey.

Twice:
They ain't going down 'til the sun comes up,
Ain't giving in 'til they get enough.
Going 'round the world in a pick-up truck.
Ain't going down 'til the sun comes up.

Ain't Misbehavin'
Words by Andy Razaf
Music by Thomas "Fats" Waller and Harry Brooks
Copyright © 1929 by Mills Music, Inc.
Copyright Renewed, Assigned to Mills Music, Inc., Chappell & Co. and
Razaf Music Co. in the United States
All Rights for Razaf Music Co. Administered by The Songwriters Guild Of America

a standard recorded by various artists
featured in the musical revue *Ain't Misbehavin'*

Verse:
Boy:
Tho's it's a fickle age
With flirting all the rage,
Here is one bird with self-control;
Happy inside my cage.
I know who I love best,
Thumbs down for all the rest,
My love was given, heart and soul
So it can withstand the test.

Refrain:
No one to talk with,
All by myself.
No one to walk with,
But I'm happy on the shelf.
Ain't misbehavin',
I'm savin' my love for you.

I know for certain,
The one I love.
I'm thru with flirtin',
It's just you I'm thinkin' of.
Ain't misbehavin',
I'm savin' my love for you.

Like Jack Horner,
In the corner,
Don't go nowhere.
What do I care?
Your kisses are worth waitin' for;
Believe me.

I don't stay out late,
Don't care to go.
I'm home about eight,
Just me and my radio.
Ain't misbehavin',
I'm saving my love for you.

Verse:
Girl:
Your type of man is rare,
I know you really care.
That's why my conscience never sleeps,
When you're away somewhere.
Sure was a lucky day,
When fate sent you my way,
And made you mine alone for keeps,
Ditto to all you say.

Repeat Refrain

Ain't No Mountain High Enough
Words and Music by Nickolas Ashford
and Valerie Simpson

recorded by Marvin Gaye & Tammi Terrell; also adapted
by Diana Ross

Now, if you need me, call me.
No matter where you are,
No matter how far.
Don't worry baby.
Just call out my name.
I'll be there in a hurry.
You don't have to worry,
'Cause baby there

Refrain:
Ain't no mountain high enough,
Ain't no valley low enough,
Ain't no river wide enough
To keep me from getting to you, babe.

Remember the day I set you free?
I told you could always count on me.
And from that day on,
I made a vow:
I'll be there when you want me,
Some way somehow.
'Cause baby there

Refrain

And no wind,
And no rain or winter's cold
Can stop me, baby.
Oh baby, if you are my goal.
(If you're ever in trouble,
I'll be there on the double.
Just send for me baby!
Oh, baby!)

My love is alive,
Deep down in my heart,
Although we are miles apart.
If you ever need a helping hand,
I'll be there on the double,
Just as fast as I can.
Don't you know that there

Refrain Three Times

Twice:
Ain't no mountain high enough,
Ain't no valley low enough,
Ain't no river wide enough
To keep me from you.

Twice:
Ah.
Nothing can keep me,
Keep me from you.
Ain't no mountain high enough.
Nothing can keep me,
Keep me from you.

Ain't Too Proud to Beg

Words and Music by Edward Holland and
Norman Whitfield

recorded by The Temptations

I know you wanna leave me,
But I refuse to let you go.
If I have to beg, plead for your sympathy,
I don't mind 'cause you mean that much to me.

Refrain:
Ain't to proud to beg and you know it,
Please don't leave me girl, don't you go.
Ain't too proud to plead, baby, baby.
Please don't leave me, girl, don't you go.

Now I've heard a cryin' man
Is half a man with no sense of pride.
But if I have to cry to keep you
I don't mind weepin' if it'll keep you by my side.

Refrain

If I have to sleep on your doorstep all night and day,
Just to keep you from walking away,
Let your friends laugh, even this I can stand,
'Cause I wanna keep you any way I can.

Refrain

Now I've got a love so deep in the pit of my heart,
And each day it grows more and more.
I'm not ashamed to call and plead to you, baby,
If pleading keeps you from walking out that door.

Refrain

The Air That I Breathe

Words and Music by Albert Hammond and
Michael Hazelwood

recorded by The Hollies

If I could make a wish I think I'd pass,
Can't think of anything I need.
No cigarettes, no sleep, no light, no sound,
Nothing to eat, no books to read.

Making love with you
Has left me peaceful warm and tired.
What more could I ask,
There's nothing left to be desired.

Peace came upon me and it leaves me weak.
Sleep, silent angel, go to sleep.

Sometimes,
All I need is the air that I breathe.
And to love you,
All I need is the air that I breathe.
Yes, to love you,
All I need is the air that I breathe.

Peace came upon me and it leaves me weak.
Sleep, silent angel, go to sleep.

Alfie

Words by Hal David
Music by Burt Bacharach

from the Paramount Picture *Alfie*
recorded by Dionne Warwick and various other artists

What's it all about, Alfie?
It is just for the moment we live?
What's it all about when you sort it out, Alfie?
Are we meant to take more than we give,
Or are we meant to be kind?
And if only fools are kind, Alfie,
Then I guess it is wise to be cruel.
And if life belongs only to the strong, Alfie,
What will you lend on an old golden rule?

As sure as I believe there's a heaven above, Alfie,
I know there's something much more,
Something even nonbelievers can believe in.
I believe in love, Alfie.
Without true love we just exist, Alfie.
Until you find the love you've missed,
You're nothing, Alfie.
When you walk let you heart lead the way,
And you'll find love any day, Alfie.
Alfie.

All Alone

Words and Music by Irving Berlin

featured in the musical *Music Box Revue of 1924*
a standard recorded by various artists

Just like a melody that lingers on,
You seem to haunt me night and day.
I never realized till you had gone,
How much I cared about you.
I can't live without you.

All alone,
I'm so all alone.
There is no one else but you.
All alone
By the telephone
Waiting for a ring,
A ting-a-ling.
I'm all alone
Every evening
All alone.
Feeling blue,
Wondering where you are,
And how you are
And if you are
All alone too.

All for Love

Words and Music by Bryan Adams,
Robert John "Mutt" Lange and Michael Kamen

from Walt Disney Pictures' *The Three Musketeers*
recorded by Bryan Adams, Sting & Rod Stewart

When it's love you give
(I'll be a man of good faith.)
Then in love you'll live.
(I'll make a stand. I won't break.)
I'll be the rock you can build on,
Be there when you're old,
To have and to hold.
When there's love inside pain.

(I swear I'll always be strong.)
Then there's a reason why.
(I'll prove to you we belong.)
I'll be the wall that protects you
From the wind and the rain,
From the hurt and pain.

Refrain:
Let's make it all for one and all for love.
Let the one you hold be the one you want,
The one you need,
'Cause it's all for the one for all.
When there's someone that should know,
Then just let your feelings show,
And make it all for one and all for love.

Then it's love you make.
(I'll be the fire in your night.)
Then it's love you take.
(I will defend, I will fight.)
I'll be there when you need me.
When honor's at stake,
This vow I will make:

Repeat Refrain

Don't lay our love to rest
'Cause we could stand up to the test.
We got everything and more than we had planned,
More than the rivers that run the land.
We got it all in our hands.

Now it's all for one and all for love.
(It's all for love.)
Let the one you hold be the one you want,
The one you need.
'Cause when it's all for one it's one for all.
(It's one for all.)
When there's someone that should know,
Then just let your feelings show.
When there's someone that you want,
When there's someone that you need,
Let's make it all, all for one,
And all for love.

All I Ask of You

Music by Andrew Lloyd Webber
Lyrics by Charles Hart
Additional Lyrics by Richard Stilgoe

from the musical *The Phantom of the Opera*

Raoul:
No more talk of darkness,
Forget these wide-eyed fears:
I'm here, nothing can harm you,
My words will warm and calm you.
Let me be your freedom;
Let daylight dry your tears:
I'm here, with you, beside you,
To guard you and to hide you.

Christine:
Say you love me every waking moment;
Turn my head with talk of summertime.
Say you need me with you now and always;
Promise me that all you say is true;
That's all I ask of you.

Raoul:
Let me be your shelter;
Let me be your light.
You're safe;
No one will find you;
Your fears are far behind you.

Christine:
All I want is freedom,
A world with no more night;
And you, always beside me,
To hold me and to hide me.

Raoul:
Then say you'll share with me one love, one lifetime;
Let me lead you from your solitude.
Say you need me with you,
Here beside you.
Anywhere you go, let me go too.
Christine, that's all I ask of you

Christine:
Say you'll share with me one love, one lifetime;
Say the word and I will follow you.

Together:
Share each day with me, each night, each morning

Christine:
Say you love me!

Raoul:
You know I do.

Together:
Love me, that's all I ask of you.
Anywhere you go, let me go too.
Love me, that's all I ask of you.

All in Love Is Fair
Words and Music by Stevie Wonder
© 1973 JOBETE MUSIC CO., INC. and BLACK BULL MUSIC
   c/o EMI APRIL MUSIC INC.

recorded by Stevie Wonder

All is fair in love.
Love's a crazy game.
Two people vow to stay
In love as one they say
But all is changed with time.
The future none can see.
The road you leave behind.
Ahead lies mystery,
But all is fair in love.
I had to go away.
A writer takes his pen,
To write the words again,
That all in love is fair.

All of fate's a chance.
It's either good or bad.
I tossed my coin to say,
In love with me you'd stay,
But all in war is cold.
You either win or lose.
When all is put away,
The losing side I'll play.
But all is fair in love.
I should never have left your side.
A writer takes his pen,
To write the words again,
That all in love is fair.

A writer takes his pen,
To write the words again,
That all in love is fair.

All My Life
Words by Joel Hailey
Music by Joel Hailey and Rory Bennett
© 1997 EMI APRIL MUSIC INC., CORD KAYLA MUSIC and HEE BEE DOOINIT MUSIC
All Rights for CORD KAYLA MUSIC Controlled and Administered by
  EMI APRIL MUSIC INC.

recorded by K-Ci & JoJo

Baby, baby, baby, baby, baby,
Baby, baby, baby, baby, baby, babe.

I will never find another lover sweeter than you,
Sweeter than you.
And I will never find another lover more preious than you,
More precious than you.
Girl, you are close to me,
You're like my mother,
Close to me,
You're like my father,
Close to me,
You're like my sister,
Close to me,
You're like my brother.
You are the only one.
You're my everything
And for you this song I sing.

Refrain:
And all my life
I prayed for someone like you,
And I thank God that I,
That I finally found you.
For all my life
I prayed for someone like you,
And I hope that you
Feel the same way too.
Yes, I pray that you
Do love me too.

I said that you're all that I'm thinking of.
Da, da, da…
Said I promise to never fall in love with a stranger.
You're all I'm thinking of.
I praise the Lord above
For sending me your love.

I cherish every hug.
I really love you.
For …

Refrain

You're all that I ever know.
When you smile on my face,
All I see is a glow.
You turned my life around.
You picked me up when I was down.
You're all that I ever know.

When you smile life is glow.
You picked me up when I was down.
Sayin' you're all that I ever know.
When you smile life is glow.
You picked me up when I was down.
And I hope that you
Feel the same way too.

Repeat Refrain and Fade

All My Loving

Words and Music by John Lennon and Paul McCartney

recorded by The Beatles

Close your eyes and I'll kiss you,
Tomorrow I'll miss you;
Remember I'll always be true.
And then while I'm away,
I'll write home everyday,
And I'll send all my loving to you.

I'll pretend that I'm kissing,
The lips I am missing
And hope that my dreams will come true.
And then while I'm away,
I'll write home everyday,
And I'll send all my loving to you.

All my loving,
I will send to you,
All my loving,
Darling, I'll be true.

Repeat Song

All my loving,
All my loving, oo,
All my loving
I will send to you.

All of You

Words and Music by Cole Porter

from the musical *Silk Stockings*

I love the looks of you, the lure of you.
The sweet of you, the pure of you.
The eyes, the arms, the mouth of you.
The East, West, North and the South of you.
I'd love to gain complete control of you.
And handle even the heart and soul of you.
So love, a least, a small percent of me do.
For I love all of you.

Alternate Verse:
I love the looks of you, the lure of you,
I'd love to make a tour of you
The eyes, the arms, the mouth of you
The east, west, north, and the south of you.
I'd love to gain complete control of you,
And handle even the heart and soul of you,
So love, at least, a small percent of me, do.
For I love all of you.

All or Nothing at All

Words by Jack Lawrence
Music by Arthur Altman

recorded by Frank Sinatra, and various other artists

All or nothing at all!
Half a love never appealed to me.
If your heart never could yield to me,
Then I'd rather have nothing at all!
All or nothing at all!
If it's love, there is no in between.
Why begin,
Then cry for something that might have been.
No, I'd rather have nothing at all.

But, please, don't bring your lips so close to my cheek.
Don't smile, or I'll be lost beyond recall.
The kiss in your eyes,
The touch of your hand makes me weak,
And my heart may grow dizzy and fall.
And if I fell under the spell of your call,
I would be caught in the undertow.
So, you see, I've got to say: No! No!
All or nothing at all!

All Shook Up

Words and Music by Otis Blackwell and Elvis Presley

recorded by Elvis Presley

A-well-a bless my soul, what's wrong with me?
I'm itching like a man on a fuzzy tree.
My friends say I'm actin' queer as a bug.

Refrain:
I'm in love.
I'm all shook up!
Mm, mm, oh, oh, yeah!

My hands are shaky and my knees are weak
I can't seem to stand on my own two feet.
Who do you thank when you have such luck?

Please don't ask what's on my mind,
I'm a little mixed up but I feelin' fine.
When I'm near that girl that I love the best,
My heart beats so it scares me to death!
She touched my hand,
What a chill I got,
Her kisses are like a volcano that's hot!
I'm proud to say she's my buttercup,

Refrain

My tongue gets tied when I try to speak,
My insides shake like a leaf on a tree,
There's only one cure for this soul of mine,
That's to have the girl that I love so fine!
She touched my hand,
What a chill I got,
Her kisses are like a volcano that's hot!
I'm proud to say she's my buttercup,

Refrain Three Times

I'm all shook up!

All This Time

Written and Composed by Sting

recorded by Sting

I looked out across the river today.
Saw a city in the fog and an old church tower
Where the seagulls play.
Saw the sad shire horses walking home
In the sodium light,
Two priests on the ferry.
October geese on a cold winter's night.

All this time the river flowed
Endlessly to the sea.

Two priests came 'round our house tonight,
One young, one old,
To offer prayers for the dying, to serve the final rite.
One to learn, one to teach,
Which way the cold wind blows.
And fussing and flapping in priestly black,
Like a murder of crows.

All this time the river flowed
Endlessly to the sea.
If I had my way,
Take a boat from the river
And I'd bury the old man.
I'd bury him at sea.

Blessed are the poor,
For they shall inherit the earth.
Better to be poor than a fat man in the eye of the needle.
As these words were spoken I swear
I hear the old man laughing,
What good is a used up world?
And how could it be worth having?

All this time the river flowed,
Endlessly, like a silent tear.
All this time the river flowed.

Father, if Jesus exists then how come he never lives here?
Yeah yeah…
Teachers told the Romans built this place.
They built a wall and a temple,
And an edge of the empire,
A garrison town.
They lived and they died.
They prayed to their gods,
But the stone gods did not make a sound.
And their empire crumbled 'til all that was left
Were the stones the workmen found.

All the time the river flowed
In the falling light of a Northern sun.

If I had my way, take a boat from the river.
Men go crazy in congregations,
They only get better one by one.
One by one.
One by one by one.
One by one.

Repeat and Fade:
I looked out across the river today.
Saw a city in the fog and an old church tower
Where the seagulls play.
Saw the sad shire horses walking home
In the sodium light…

All You Need Is Love

Words and Music by John Lennon and Paul McCartney

recorded by The Beatles

Love, love, love
Love, love, love
Love, love, love.

There's nothing you can do that can't be done,
Nothing you can sing that can't be sung.
It's easy.
There's nothing you can make that can't be made,
No one you can save that can't be saved.
Nothing you can do, but you can learn how to be in time.
It's easy.

All you need is love, all you need is love,
All you need is love, love, love is all you need.
Love, love, love, love, love, love, love, love, love.
All you need is love, all you need is love,
All you need is love,
Love, love is all you need.

There's nothing you can know that isn't known.
Nothing you can see that isn't shown.
Nowhere you can be that isn't where you're meant to be.
It's easy.

All you need is love, all you need is love,
All you need is love, love, love is all you need.
All you need is love (all together now),
All you need is love (everybody),
All you need is love, love,
Love is all you need.

Allentown

Words and Music by Billy Joel

recorded by Billy Joel

Well we're living here in Allentown,
And they're closing all the factories down.
Out in Bethlehem they're killing time,
Filling out forms, standing in line.
Well our fathers fought the Second World War,
Spent their weekends on the Jersey shore,
Met our mothers in the U.S.O;
Asked them to dance, danced with them slow.
And we're living here in Allentown,
But the restlessness was handed down.
And it's getting very hard to stay.

Well, we're waiting here in Allentown,
For the Pennsylvania we never found,
For the promises our teachers gave,
If we worked hard, if we behaved.
So the graduations hang on the wall,
But they never really helped us at all.
No they never taught us what was real,
Iron and coke and chromium steel.
And we're waiting here in Allentown,
But they've taken all the coal from the ground.
And the union people crawled away.

Every child had a pretty good shot
To get at least as far as their old man got,
But something happened on the way to that place.
They threw an American flag in our face.

Well I'm living here in Allentown
And it's hard to keep a good man down.
But I won't be getting up today.
And it's getting very hard to stay
And we're living here in Allentown.

Along Comes Mary

Words and Music by Tandyn Almer

recorded by The Association

Every time I think that I'm the only one who's lonely,
Someone calls on me
And every now and then I spend my time at rhyme
And verse and curse the faults in me.
But then along comes Mary,
And does she wanna give me kicks and be my steady chick
And give me pick of memories?
Or maybe rather gather tales
From all the fails and tribulations no on ever sees?

Refrain:
When we met, I was sure out to lunch.
Now my empty cup tastes as sweet as the punch.

The vague desire is the fire in the eyes of chicks
Whose sickness is the games they play
And when the masquerade is played and neighbor folks
Made jokes at who is most to blame today.
And then along comes Mary,
And does she wanna set them free
And make them see realities in which she got her name?
And will they struggle much when told
That such a tender touch of hers will make them not the same?

Refrain

Sweet as the punch.

Alright, Okay, You Win

Words and Music by Sid Wyche and Mayme Watts

recorded by Joe Williams with Count Basie, and various other artists

Well, alright, okay, you win,
I'm in love with you.
Well, alright, okay, you win.
Baby, what can I do?
I'll do anything you say.
It's just gotta be that way.

Well, alright, okay, you win,
I'm in love with you.
Well, alright, okay, you win.
Baby, what can I do?
I'll do anything you say.
As long as it's me and you.

All that I am askin',
All I want from you,
Just love me like I love you.
An' it won't be hard to do!

Well, alright, okay, you win,
I'm in love with you.
Well, alright, okay, you win.
Baby, what can I do?
I'll do anything you say.
Sweet baby take me by the hand.
Well, alright, okay, you win.

Always

Words and Music by Irving Berlin

dropped from the musical *The Cocoanuts*
a standard recorded by various artists

Everything went wrong
And the whole day long
I'd feel so blue.
For the longest while
I'd forget to smile.
Then I met you.

Now that my blue days have passed,
Now that I've found you at last,
I'll be loving you, always
With a love that's true, always
When the things you've planned
Need a helping hand,
I will understand, always,
Always.

Days may not be fair, always.
That's when I'll be there, always,
Not for just an hour,
Not for just a day,
Not for just a year, but
Always.

Dreams will all come true,
Growing old with you,
And time will fly,
Caring each day more
Than the day before,
Till spring rolls by.

Then when the springtime has gone,
Then will my love linger on.
I'll be loving you, always
With a love that's true, always
When the things you've planned
Need a helping hand,
I will understand, always,
Always.

Days may not be fair, always.
That's when I'll be there, always,
Not for just an hour,
Not for just a day,
Not for just a year, but
Always.

Always in My Heart (Siempre en mi corazón)

Music and Spanish Words by Ernesto Lecuona
English Words by Kim Gannon

a standard recorded by various artists

You are always in my heart,
Even though you're far away.
I can hear the music
Of the song of love I sang with you.
You are always in my heart,
And when skies above are gray,
I remember that you care,
And then and there the sun breaks through.

Just before I go to sleep,
There's a rendezvous I keep,
And the dreams I always meet
Help me forget we're far apart.
I don't know exactly when dear,
But I'm sure we'll meet again, dear,
And my darling 'til we do,
You are always in my heart.

Always on My Mind

Words and Music by Wayne Thompson, Mark James and Johnny Christopher

recorded by Willie Nelson

Maybe I didn't treat you
Quite as good as I should have.
Maybe I didn't love you,
Quite as often as I should have;
Little things I should have said and done,
I just never took the time.

You were always on my mind;
You were always on my mind.

Tell me,
Tell me that your sweet love hasn't died.
Give me,
Give me one more chance to keep you satisfied, satisfied.

Maybe I didn't hold you,
All those lonely, lonely times;
And I guess I never told you
I'm so happy that you're mine.
If I made you feel second best,
Girl, I'm sorry I was blind.

You were always on my mind;
You were always on my mind.

Amazed

Words and Music by Marv Green, Chris Lindsey and Aimee Mayo

recorded by Lonestar

Every time our eyes meet,
This feelin' inside me
Is almost more than I can take.
Baby, when you touch me,
I can feel how much you love me,
And it just blows me away.
I've never been this close to anyone or anything.
I can hear your thoughts.
I can see your dreams.

Refrain:
I don't know how you do what you do,
I'm so in love with you.
It just keeps gettin' better.
I wanna spend the rest of my life
With you by my side, forever and ever.
Every little thing that you do,
Baby, I'm amazed by you.

The smell of your skin,
The taste of your kiss,
The way you whisper in the dark.
Your hair all around me;
Baby, you surround me.
You touch every place in my heart.
Oh, it feels like the first time every time.
I wanna spend the whole night in your eyes.

Refrain

Every little thing that you do
I'm so in love with you.
It just keeps gettin' better.
I wanna spend the rest of my life
With you by my side forever and ever.
Every little thing that you do,
Oh, every little thing that you do,
Baby, I'm amazed by you.

And I Love Her

Words and Music by John Lennon and Paul McCartney

recorded by The Beatles

I give her all my love,
That's all I do.
And if you saw my love,
You'd love her too.
I love her.
She gives me everything,
And tenderly.
The kiss my lover brings,
She brings to me.
And I love her.

A love like ours
Could never die,
As long as I
Have you near me.

Twice:
Bright are the stars that shine,
Dark is the sky.
I know this love of mine
Will never die.
And I love her.

And So It Goes

Words and Music by Billy Joel

recorded by Billy Joel

In every heart there is a room,
A sanctuary safe and strong.
To heal the wounds from lovers past,
Until a new one comes along.
I spoke to you in cautious tones;
You answered me with no pretense.
And still I feel I said too much.
My silence is a defense.

And every time I've held a rose,
It seems I only felt the thorns.
And so it goes.
And so it goes.
And so will you soon I suppose.
But if my silence made you leave,
Then that would be my worst mistake.
So I will share this room with you,
And you can have this heart to break.

And this is why my eyes are closed,
It's just as well for all I've seen.
And so it goes.
And so it goes.
And you're the only one who knows.

So I would choose to be with you.
That's if the choice were mine to make.
But you can make decisions too.
And you can have this heart to break.
And so it goes
And so it goes
And you're the only one who knows.

And When I Die

Words and Music by Laura Nyro

recorded by Blood, Sweat & Tears

I'm not scared of dyin' and I don't really care.
If it's peace you find in dyin',
Well, then let the end be near,
Just bundle up my coffin 'cause it's cold way down there.
I hear that it's cold way down there.
Yeah. Crazy cold way down there.

Refrain:
And when I die and when I'm gone,
There'll be one child born in this world to carry on,
To carry on.

Now troubles are many, they're as deep as a well.
I can swear there ain't no heaven,
But I pray there ain't no hell.
Swear there ain't no heaven and I pray there ain't no hell.
But I'll never know by living, only my dyin' will tell.
Yes, only my dyin' will tell.
Yeah. Only my dyin' will tell.

Refrain

Yeah, yeah.
Give me my freedom for as long as I be.
All I ask of livin' is to have no chains on me.
All I ask of livin' is to have no chains on me.
And all I ask of dyin' is to go naturally.
I only wanna go naturally.
Here I go, ha!
Here comes the devil right behind.

Spoken:
Look out children!

Here he come.
Here he come.
Hey, Don't wanna go by the devil.
Don't wanna go by the demon.
Don't wanna go by Satan.
Don't wanna die uneasy,
Just let me go naturally.

And when I die, and when I'm dead, dead and gone,
There'll be one child born in our world to carry on,
To carry on.
Yeah, yeah.

Angel

Words and Music by Sarah McLachlan

recorded by Sarah McLachlan

Refrain:
Spend all your time waiting
For that second chance,
For a break that would make it okay.
There's always some reason
To feel not good enough,
And it's hard at the end of the day.
I need some distraction oh, beautiful release.
Memory seep from my veins.
Let me be empty
Oh and weightless and maybe,
I'll find some peace tonight.

In the arms of the angel.
Fly away from here,
From this dark, cold hotel room,
And the endlessness that you fear.
You are pulled from the wreckage
Of your silent reverie.
You're in the arms of the angel.
May you find some comfort here.

You're so tired of the straight line,
And everywhere you turn
There's vultures and thieves at your back.
Storm keeps on twisting.
Keep on building the lies,
And you make up for all that you lack.
It don't make no difference
Escaping one last time.
It's easier to believe
In this sweet madness,
Oh, this glorious sadness
That brings me to my knees
In the arms of the angel.
Fly away from here,
From this dark, cold hotel room
And the endlessness that you fear.
You are pulled from the wreckage
Of your silent reverie.
You're in the arms of the angel.
May you find some comfort here.

Angel Eyes

Words by Earl Brent
Music by Matt Dennis
Copyright © 1946 (Renewed) by Music Sales Corporation (ASCAP)

from the film *Jennifer*
a standard recorded by various artists

Try to think that love's not around.
Still it's uncomfortably near.
My old heart ain't gainin' no ground
Because my angel eyes ain't here.

Angel eyes that old devil sent,
They glow unbearably bright.
Need I say that my love's misspent,
Misspent with angel eyes tonight.

So drink up all you people,
Order anything you see.
Have fun, you happy people,
The drink and laugh's on me.

Pardon me, but I gotta run,
The fact's uncommonly clear.
Gotta find who's now "Number One"
And why my angel eyes ain't here.
'Scuse me while I disappear.

Angel of the Morning

Words and Music by Chip Taylor
© 1967 (Renewed 1995) EMI BLACKWOOD MUSIC INC.

recorded by Merilee Rush & The Turnabouts;
Juice Newton

There'll be no strings to bind your hands,
Not if my love can't bind your heart.
And there's no need to take a stand,
For it was I who chose to start.
I see no need to take me home
I'm old enough to face the dawn.

Refrain:
Just call me angel of the morning (angel).
Just touch cheek before you leave me, baby.
Just call me angel of the morning (angel).
Then slowly turn away from me.

Maybe the sun's light will be dim,
And it won't matter anyhow.
If morning's echo says we've sinned,
Well, it was what I wanted now.
And if we're victims of the night,
I won't be blinded by the light.

Just call me angel of the morning (angel).
Just touch cheek before you leave me, baby.
Just call me angel of the morning (angel),
Then slowly turn away
I won't beg you to stay with me,
Through the tears of the day, of the years.
Baby, baby, baby.

Just call me angel of the morning (angel).
Just touch my cheek before you leave me, baby.
Just call me angel of the morning (angel)
Just touch my cheek before you leave me, baby.

Annie's Song

Words and Music by John Denver
Copyright © 1974 Cherry Lane Music Publishing Company, Inc. (ASCAP) and
    DreamWorks Songs (ASCAP)
Worldwide Rights for DreamWorks Songs Administered by Cherry Lane Music Publishing
    Company, Inc.

recorded by John Denver

You fill up my senses,
Like a night in a forest,
Like the mountains in springtime,
Like a walk in the rain.
Like a storm in the desert,
Like a sleepy blue ocean.
You fill up my senses,
Come fill me again.

Come let me love you,
Let me give my life to you,
Let me drown in you laughter,
Let me die in your arms.
Let me lay down beside you,
Let me always be with you,
Come let me love you,
Come love me again.

Repeat Verse 1

Another Day in Paradise
Words and Music by Phil Collins
© 1989 PHILIP COLLINS LTD. and HIT & RUN MUSIC (PUBLISHING) LTD.
All Rights Controlled and Administered by EMI APRIL MUSIC INC.

recorded by Phil Collins

She calls out to the man on the street,
"Sir can you help me?"
"It's cold and I've no where to sleep,
Is there somewhere you can tell me?"

He walks on, doesn't look back,
He pretends he can't hear her,
Starts to whistle as he crosses the street,
Seems embarrassed to be there.

Refrain:
Oh, think twice,
'Cause it's another day for you and me in paradise,
Oh, think twice,
'Cause it's another day for you,
You and me in paradise.
Think about it.

She calls out to the man on the street
He can see that she's been crying,
She got blisters on the soles of her feet,
She can't walk, but she's trying.

Refrain

Oh, Lord, is there nothing more anybody can do?
Oh, Lord there must be something you can say.

You can tell from the lines on her face,
You can see that she's been there.
Probably been moved on from every place,
'Cause she didn't fit in there.

Refrain

It's just another day for you and me, in paradise…

Anyone Can Whistle
Words and Music by Stephen Sondheim
Copyright © 1964 by Stephen Sondheim
Copyright Renewed
Burthen Music Company, Inc. owner of publication and allied rights throughout the World
Chappell & Co. Sole Selling Agent

from the musical *Anyone Can Whistle*

Anyone can whistle,
That's what they say,
Easy.
Anyone can whistle,
Any old day,
Easy.
It's all so simple:
Relax, let go, let fly!
So someone tell me why can't I?

I can dance a tango,
I can read Greek,
Easy.
I can slay a dragon
Any old week,
Easy!
What's hard is simple,
What's natural comes hard.
Maybe you could show me
How to let go,
Lower my guard,
Learn to be free.
Maybe if you can whistle,
Whistle for me.

Anytime You Need a Friend
Words and Music by Mariah Carey and Walter Afanasieff
Copyright © 1993 Sony/ATV Songs LLC, Rye Songs, WB Music Corp. and Wallyworld Music
All Rights on behalf of Sony/ATV Songs LLC and Rye Songs Administered by
  Sony/ATV Music Publishing, 8 Music Square West, Nashville, TN 37203
All Rights on behalf of Wallyworld Music Administered by WB Music Corp.

recorded by Mariah Carey

If you're lonely and need a friend,
And troubles seem like they never end,
Just remember to keep the faith,
And love will be there to light the way.

Refrain:
Anytime you need a friend,
I will be here.
You'll never be alone again,
So don't you fear.
Even if you're miles away,
I'm by your side.
So don't you ever be lonely.

Love will make it alright.

When the shadows are closing in,
And your spirit diminishing,
Just remember you're not alone,
And love will be there to guide you home.

Refrain

If you just believe in me,
I will love you endlessly.
Take my hand.
Take me into your heart.
I'll be there forever, baby.
I won't let go,
I'll never let go.

Refrain

It's alright.
It's alright.

Repeat Refrain and Fade

April in Paris
Words by E.Y. Harburg
Music by Vernon Duke

from the film *Walk a Little Faster*
a standard recorded by various artists

April's in the air,
But here in Paris April wears a different gown.
You can see her waltzing down the street.
The tang of wine is in the air,
I'm drunk with all the happiness that Spring can give,
Never dreamed it could be so exciting to live.

April in Paris, chestnuts in blossom,
Holiday tables under the trees.
April in Paris, this is a feeling
No one can ever reprise.
I never knew the charm of Spring,
Never met it face to face.
I never knew my heart could sing,
Never missed a warm embrace,

Till April in Paris
Whom can I run to
What have you done to my heart?

Aquellos ojos verdes (Green Eyes)
Music by Nilo Menendez
Spanish Words by Adolfo Utrera
English Words by E. Rivera and E. Woods

a standard recorded by various artists

Life held no charm, dear, until I met you.
Love always seemed oh, so far away.
Your eyes met mine now I can't forget you.
Dark nights become as bright as the day.

Your green eyes with their soft lights,
Your eyes that promise sweet nights
Bring to my soul a longing,
A thirst for love divine.
In dreams I seem to hold you,
To find you and enfold you.
Our lips meet, and our hearts too,
With a thrill so sublime.

Those cool and limpid green eyes,
A pool where in my love lies
So deep, that in my searching,
For happiness, I fear,
That they will ever haunt me.
All through my life they'll taunt me,
But will they ever want me?
Green eyes make my dreams come true.

Are You Lonesome Tonight?
Words and Music by Roy Turk and Lou Handman

recorded by Elvis Presley

Are you lonesome tonight?
Do you miss me tonight?
Are you sorry we drifted apart?
Does your memory stray
To a bright summer day,
When I kissed you
And called you sweetheart?

Do the chairs in you parlor
Seem empty and bare?
Do you gaze at your doorstep
And picture me there?
Is your heart filled with pain?
Shall I come back again?
Tell me, dear,
Are you lonesome tonight?

Arthur Murray Taught Me Dancing in a Hurry

Words by Johnny Mercer
Music by Victor Schertzinger

from the Paramount Picture *The Fleet's In*
recorded by Helen O'Connell with Jimmy Dorsey, and
various other artists

Life was so peaceful at the drive-in,
Life was so calm and serene.
Life was trés gay, till the unlucky day,
I happened to read that magazine.
Why did I read that advertisement,
Where it said: "Since I Rumba, Jim thinks I'm sublime."
Why, oh why, did I ever try,
When I didn't have the talent
I didn't have the money
And teacher did not have the time.

Arthur Murray taught me dancing in a hurry.
I had a week to spare.
He showed me the ground-work,
The walk around work,
And told me to take it from there.

Arthur Murray then advised me not to worry.
It'd come out all right
To my way of thinkin'
It came out stinkin',
I don't know my left from my right.

The people around me can all sing,
A-one and a-two and a-three.
But any resemblance to waltzing
Is just coincidental with me.
'Cause Arthur Murray taught me dancing in a hurry.
And so I take a chance.
To me it resembles the nine day trembles,
But he guarantees
It's a dance.

As If We Never Said Goodbye

Music by Andrew Lloyd Webber
Lyrics by Don Black and Christopher Hampton,
with contributions by Amy Powers

from the musical *Sunset Boulevard*

I don't know why I'm frightened,
I know my way around here.
The cardboard trees, the painted seas, the sound here.
Yes, a world to rediscover,
But I'm not in any hurry,
And I need a moment.

The whispered conversations in overcrowded hallways,
The atmosphere as thrilling here
As always.
Feel the early morning madness,
Feel the magic in the making.
Why, everything's as if we never said goodbye.

I've spent so many mornings,
Just trying to resist you.
I'm trembling now, you can't know how I've missed you,
Missed the fairytale adventures
In this ever-spinning playground.
We were young together.

I'm coming out of makeup,
The light's already burning.
Not long until the cameras will start turning,
And the early morning madness,
And the magic in the making,
Yes, everything's as if we never said goodbye.

I don't want to be alone,
That's all in the past.
This world's waited long enough,
I've come home at last,

And this time will be bigger,
And brighter than we knew it.
So watch me fly, we all know I can do it.
Could I stop my hand from shaking?
Has there ever been a moment
With so much to live for?

The whispered conversations in over-crowded hallways,
So much to say, not just today, but always.
We'll have early morning madness,
We'll have magic in the making.
Yes, everything's as if we never said goodbye,
Yes, everything's as if we never said goodbye.
We taught the world new ways to dream.

As Long as He Needs Me

Words and Music by Lionel Bart

from the Columbia Pictures - Romulus Motion Picture
Production of Lionel Bart's *Oliver!* (originally a stage musical)

As long as he needs me,
I know where I must be,
I'll cling on steadfastly,
As long as he needs me.

As long as life is long,
I'll love him, right or wrong;
And somehow I'll be strong,
As long as he needs me.

If you are lonely,
Then you will know,
When someone needs you,
You love them so.
I won't betray his trust,
Though people say I must.
I've got to stay true,
Just as long as he needs me.

At Seventeen

Words and Music by Janis Ian

recorded by Janis Ian

I learned the truth at seventeen;
That love was meant for beauty queens,
And high school girls with clear-skinned smiles,
Who married young and then retired.
The valentines I never knew,
The Friday night charades of youth,
Were spent on one more beautiful;
At seventeen, I learned the truth.

And those of us with ravaged faces,
Lacking in the social graces,
Desperately remained at home.
Inventing lovers on the phone,
Who called to say, "Come dance with me,"
And murmured vague obscenities.
It isn't all it seems
At seventeen.

A brown-eyed girl in hand-me-downs,
Whose name I never could pronounce,
Said, "Pity, please, the ones who serve.
They only get what they deserve.
The rich-relationed home town queen
Marries into what she needs,
A guarantee of company
And haven for the elderly."

Remember those who win the game,
Lose the love they sought to gain,
In debentures of quality,
And dubious integrity.
Their small town eyes will gape at you,
In dull surprise when payment due
Exceeds accounts received
At seventeen.

To those of us who know the pain
Of valentines that never came,
And those whose names were never called,
When choosing sides for basketball.
It was long ago and far away.
The world was younger than today,
And dreams were all they gave for free,
To ugly duckling girls like me.

We all play the game and when we dare
To cheat ourselves at solitaire,
Inventing lovers on the phone,
Repenting other lives unknown,
That call and say, "Come dance with me,"
And murmur vague obscenities,
At ugly girls like me;
At seventeen.

Atlantis

Words and Music by Donovan Leitch

recorded by Donovan

Spoken:
The continent of Atlantis was an island,
Which lay before the great flood in the
Area we now call the Atlantic Ocean.
So great an area of land, that from her western shores,
Those beautiful sailors journeyed to the south
And the North Americas with ease,
In their ships with painted sails.
To the east, Africa was a neighbor
Across a short strait of sea miles.
The great Egyptian age is but a remnant
Of the Atlantian culture.

The antedeluvian Kings colonized the world.
All the gods who play in the mythological dramas
In all legends from all lands
Were from fair Atlantis.
Knowing her fate, Atlantis sent out ships
To all corners of the earth.
On board were the twelve;
The poet, the physician, the farmer, the scientist,
The magician, and other so called of our legends.
Tho' gods they were and as the elders of our time
Choose to remain blind,
Let us rejoice and let us sing and dance
And ring in the new.

Hail Atlantis!

Sung,:
Repeat and Fade:
Way down below the ocean
Where I wanna be,
She may be…

Autumn in New York

Words and Music by Vernon Duke
Copyright © 1934 by Kay Duke Music
Copyright Renewed
All Rights Administered by BMG Songs, Inc.

from the musical *Thumbs Up*
a standard recorded by various artists

It's time to end my lovely holiday
And bid the country a hasty farewell.
So on this gray and melancholy day
I'll move to a Manhattan hotel.
I'll dispose of my rose-colored chattels
And prepare for my share of adventures and battles.
Here on the twenty-seventh floor,
Looking down on the city I hate and adore!

Autumn in New York,
Why does it seem so inviting?
Autumn in New York,
It spells the thrill of first knighting.
Glimmering crowds and shimmering clouds
In canyons of steel,
They're making me feel I'm home.
It's autumn in New York,
That brings the promise of new love;
Autumn in New York
Is often mingled with pain.
Dreamers with empty hands
May sigh for exotic lands;
It's autumn in New York,
It's good to be alive again.

Autumn in New York,
The gleaming rooftops at sundown.
Autumn in New York,
It lifts you up when you're run down.
Jaded roués and gay divorcees
Who lunch at the Ritz,
Will tell you that "it's divine!"
This autumn in New York,
Transforms slums into Mayfair.
Autumn in New York,
You'll need no castles in Spain.
Lovers that bless the dark
On benches in Central Park
Greet autumn in New York;
It's good to be alive again.

Autumn Leaves (Les feuilles mortes)

English lyric by Johnny Mercer
French lyric by Jacques Prevert
Music by Joseph Kosma
© 1947, 1950 (Renewed) ENOCH ET CIE
Sole Selling Agent for U.S. and Canada: MORLEY MUSIC CO.,
   by agreement with ENOCH ET CIE

recorded by Roger Williams, and various other artists
Note: The verses have never been translated from French
into English.

The falling leaves drift by the window,
The autumn leaves of red and gold.
I see your lips, the summer kisses,
The sunburned hands I used to hold.
Since you went away the days grow long,
And soon I'll hear old winter's song.
But I miss you most of all my darling,
When autumn leaves start to fall.

Baby, Come to Me
Words and Music by Rod Temperton

recorded by James Ingram & Patti Austin

Thinkin' back in time,
When love was only in the mind,
I realize ain't no second chance;
You've got to hold on to romance.
Don't let it slide.
There's a special kind of magic in the air
When you find another heart that needs to share.

Refrain:
Baby, come to me;
Let me put my arms around you.
This was meant to be,
And I'm oh, so glad I found you.
Need you every day;
Got to have your love around me.
Baby, always stay,
'Cause I can't go back to livin' without you.

Spendin' every dime
To keep you talkin' on the line;
That's how it was,
And all those walks together out in any kind of weather,
Just because.
There's a brand new way of looking at your life,
When you know that love is standing by your side.

Refrain

The night can get cold;
There's a chill to every evening when you're all alone.
Don't talk anymore,
'Cause you know that I'll be here to keep you warm.

Refrain

Baby Grand
Words and Music by Billy Joel

recorded by Billy Joel

Verse:
Late at night, when it's dark and cold,
I reach out for someone to hold.
When I'm blue, when I'm lonely,
She comes through; she's the only one who can;
My baby grand is all I need.

In my time, I've wandered everywhere,
Around this world; she would always be there,
Any day, any hour;
All it takes is the power in my hands.
My baby grand's been good to me.

I've had friends, but they slipped away.
I've had fame, but it doesn't stay.
I've made fortunes, spent them fast enough.
As for women, they don't last with just one man;
My baby grand's gonna stand by me.

They say no one's gonna play this on the radio;
They said melancholy blues were dead and gone.
But only songs like these, played in minor keys,
Keep those memories holding on.
I've come far from the life I strayed in;
I've got scars from those dives I played in.
Now I'm home, and I'm weary in my bones;
Every dreary one-night stand,
My baby grand came home with me.
Ever since this gig began,
My baby grand's been good to me.

Baby, I Love Your Way
Words and Music by Peter Frampton

recorded by Peter Frampton

Shadows grow so long before my eyes,
And they're moving across the page.
Suddenly the day turns into night,
Far away from the city.
Don't hesitate 'cause your love won't wait.

Refrain:
Ooh, baby I love your way.
Wanna tell you I love your way.
Wanna be with you night and day.

Coda:
I can see the sunset in your eyes
Brown and gray and blues besides,
Clouds are stalking islands in the sun,
I wish I could buy one out of season.
Don't hesitate 'cause your love won't wait.

Repeat Refrain

Repeat Coda

Baby, It's Cold Outside

By Frank Loesser

from the Motion Picture *Neptune's Daughter*
a standard recorded by various artists

Note: The song is a duet; the male lines are in parentheses

I really can't stay,
(But baby it's cold outside!)
I've got to go 'way.
(But baby it's cold outside!)
This evening has been
(Been hoping that you'd drop in!)
So very nice.
(I'll hold your hands they're just like ice.)
My mother will start to worry
(Beautiful, what's your hurry?)
And father will be pacing the floor.
(Listen to the fireplace roar!)
So really I'd better scurry,
(Beautiful, please don't hurry.)
Well, maybe just half a drink more.
(Put some records on while I pour.)
The neighbors might think
(But, baby it's bad out there.)
Say, what's in the drink?
(No cabs to be had out there.)
I wish I knew how
(Your eyes are like starlight now)
To break the spell.
(I'll take your hat your hair looks swell.)
I ought to say "No, no, no, Sir!"
(Mind if I move in closer?)
At least I'm gonna say that I tried.
(What's the sense of hurting my pride.)
I really can't stay
(Oh, baby, don't hold out,)
Ah, but it's cold outside.
(Baby, it's cold outside.)

I simply must go.
(But baby it's cold outside!)
The answer is no!
(But baby it's cold outside!)
The welcome has been,
(How lucky that you dropped in!)
So nice and warm.
(Look out the window at that storm.)
My sister will be suspicious,
(Gosh, your lips look delicious.)
My brother will be there at the door.
(Waves upon a tropical shore!)
My maiden aunt's mind is vicious.
(Gosh, your lips are delicious)
Well, maybe just a cigarette more.
(Never such a blizzard before.)
I've got to get home
(But, baby, you'd freeze out there)
Say, lend me a comb.
(It's up to your knees out there.)

You've really been grand,
(I thrill when you touch my hand)
But don't you see.
(How can you do this thing to me.)
There's bound to be talk tomorrow.
(Think of my life-long sorrow.)
At least there will be plenty implied.
(If you caught pneumonia and died.)
I really can't stay
(Get over that old doubt,)
Ah, but it's cold outside.
(Baby, it's cold outside.)

Baby What a Big Surprise

Words and Music by Peter Cetera

recorded by Chicago

Right before my very eyes,
I thought that you were only fakin' it,
And like before my heart was takin' it.
Baby, what a big surprise;
Right before my very eyes, oh, oh, oh.

Yesterday it seemed to me.
My life was nothing more than wasted time.
But here today you softly changed my mind.
Baby, what a big surprise;
Right before my very eyes, oh, oh, oh.

Just to be alone was a little more than I could take,
Then you came to stay. Oo..
Hold me in the morning, love me in the afternoon.
Help me find my way, hey, yeah.
Now and then just like before
I think about the love I've thrown away,
But now it doesn't matter anyway.

Repeat and Fade:
Baby, what a big surprise;
Right before my very eyes, oh, oh, oh.

Back in the High Life Again

Words and Music by Will Jennings and Steve Winwood

recorded by Steve Winwood

It used to seem to me that my life ran on too fast,
And I had to take it slowly
Just to make the good parts last.
But when you're born to run,
It's so hard to just slow down,
So don't be surprised to see me
Back in that bright part of town.

I'll be back in the high life again.
All the doors I closed one time will open up again.
I'll be back in the high life again.
All the eyes that watched me once will smile and take me in.
And I'll drink and dance with one hand free,
Let the world back into me.
And oh, I'll be a sight to see,
Back in the high life again.

You used to be the best to make life be life to me,
And I hope that you're still out there.
And you're like you used to be.
We'll have ourselves a time,
 And we'll dance till the morning sun,
And we'll let the good times come in
And we won't stop until we're done.

Refrain:
We'll be back in the high life again.
All the doors I closed one time will open up again.
We'll be back in the high life again.
All the eyes that watched us once will smile and take us in.
And we'll drink and dance with one hand free,
And have the world so easily.
And oh, we'll be a sight to see,
Back in the high life again.

Repeat Refrain

High life.
Back in the high life.
Oh, we'll be back.

Back in the Saddle Again

Words and Music by Ray Whitley and Gene Autry
Copyright © 1939 (Renewed 1995) by Katielu Music and Western Music Publishing Co.

recorded by Gene Autry

I'm back in the saddle again,
Out where a friend is a friend;
Where the long-horn cattle feed
On the lowly jimson weed,
I'm back in the saddle again.

Ridin' the range once more,
Totin' my old friend forty-four;
Where you sleep out every night,
Where the only law is right,
I'm back in the saddle again.

Whoo-pi-ti-yi-yo, rockin' to and fro,
Back in the saddle again.
Whoo-pi-ti-yi-yay, I go my way,
Back in the saddle again.

Back in the U.S.S.R.

Words and Music by John Lennon and Paul McCartney
Copyright © 1968 Sony/ATV Songs LLC
Copyright Renewed
All Rights Administered by Sony/ATV Music Publishing, 8 Music Square West,
 Nashville, TN 37203

recorded by The Beatles

Flew in from Miami Beach BOAC.
Didn't get to bed last night.
On the way the paper bag was on my knee.
Man I had a dreadful flight.

Refrain:
I'm back in the USSR.
You don't know how lucky you are boy,
Back in the USSR.

Been away so long I hardly knew the place.
Gee it's good to be back home.
Leave it till tomorrow to unpack my case.
Honey disconnect the phone.

Refrain

Back in the US, back in the US,
Back in the USSR.

Well the Ukraine girls really knock me out.
They leave the West behind.
And Moscow girls make me sing and shout.
That Georgia's always on my mind.

Refrain

Show me round your snow peaked mountains
Way down south.
Take me to your daddy's farm.
Let me hear your balalaikas ringing out.
Come and keep your comrade warm.

Refrain

Bad, Bad Leroy Brown

Words and Music by Jim Croce
Copyright © 1972 (Renewed) Time In A Bottle and Croce Publishing (ASCAP)

recorded by Jim Croce

Well the South side of Chicago
Is the baddest part of town,
And if you go down there
You better just beware
Of a man name of Leroy Brown.
Now Leroy more than trouble,
You see he stand 'bout six-foot four;
All the downtown ladies call him "Tree-top" lover
All the men just call him, "Sir."

Refrain:
And he's bad, bad Leroy Brown,
The baddest man in the whole damned town;
Badder than old King Kong
And meaner than a junk-yard dog.

Now Leroy he a gambler,
And he like his fancy clothes.
And he like to wave his diamond rings
In front of everybody's nose.
He got a custom Continental,
He got a Eldorado too;
He got a thirty-two gun
In his pocket for fun,
He got a razor in his shoe.

Refrain

Well, Friday 'bout a week ago,
Leroy shootin' dice.
And at the edge of bar sat a girl name of Doris
And oh, that girl looked nice.
Well, he cast his eyes upon her,
And the trouble soon began,
And Leroy Brown, he learned a lesson
'Bout messin' with the wife of a jealous man.

Refrain

Well, the two men took to fightin',
And when they pulled them from the floor,
Leroy looked like a jig-saw puzzle
With a couple of pieces gone.

Refrain

Yes, you were badder than old King Kong,
And meaner than a junk-yard dog.

Bad Medicine

Words and Music by Desmond Child, Richie Sambora and
Jon Bon Jovi

recorded by Bon Jovi

Refrain 1:
Your love is like bad medicine,
Bad medicine is what I need, whoa.
Shake it up just like bad medicine.

There ain't no doctor that can cure my disease.

I ain't got a fever, got a permanent disease,
And it'll take more than a doctor to prescribe a remedy.
I got lots of money but it isn't what I need;
Gonna take more than a shot to get this poison out of me.
And I got all the symptoms, count 'em 1,2,3.
First you need

Refrain 2:
(That's what you get for falling in love.)
Then you bleed,
(You get a little but it's never enough.)
On your knees,
(That's what you get for falling in love.)
Now this boy's addicted
'Cause your kiss is the drug, whoa.

Refrain 1

There ain't no doctor that can cure my disease.
Bad, bad, medicine.

I don't need no needle to be givin' me a thrill
And I don't need no anesthesia or a nurse to bring a pill.
I got a dirty down addiction that doesn't leave a track;
I got a jones for your affection like a monkey on my back.
There ain't no paramedic gonna save this heart attack.

Refrain 2

Refrain 1

There ain't no doctor that can cure my disease.
Bad, bad medicine is what I want.
Bad, bad medicine. Oh it's what I need.

I need a respirator 'cause I'm running out of breath.
You're an all night generator wrapped in stockings
    and a dress.
When you find your medicine you take what you can get.
'Cause if there's something better baby, well they haven't
    found it yet, whoa.

Refrain 1

There ain't no doctor that can cure my disease.

Refrain 1

Your love's the potions that cure my disease.
Bad, bad medicine, is what I want.
Bad, bad medicine.
Bad, bad medicine.

Bali Ha'i

Lyrics by Oscar Hammerstein II
Music by Richard Rodgers

from the musical *South Pacific*

Most people live on a lonely island,
Lost in the middle of a foggy sea.
Most people long for another island,
One where they know they would like to be.

Bali Ha'i
May call you,
Any night
Any day.
In your heart
You'll hear it call you:
"Come away,
Come away."

Bali Ha'i
Will whisper
On the wind
Of the sea:
"Here am I,
Your special island!
Come to me,
Come to me!"

Your own special hopes,
Your own special dreams,
Bloom on the hillside
And shine in the stream.

If you try,
You'll find me
Where the sky
Meets the sea;
"Here I am,
Your special island!
Come to me,
Come to me!"
Bali Ha'i
Bali Ha'i
Bali Ha'i.

Someday you'll see me,
Floating in the sunshine,
My head sticking out
From a low-flying cloud;
You'll hear me call you,
Singing through the sunshine,
Sweet and clear as can be:
"Come to me,
Here I am,
Come to me!"

Bali Ha'i
Will whisper
On the wind
Of the sea:
"Here am I,
Your special island!
Come to me,
Come to me,"

Bali Ha'i
Bali Ha'i
Bali Ha'i.

The Bare Necessities

Words and Music by Terry Gilkyson

from Walt Disney's *The Jungle Book*

Refrain:
Look for the bare necessities,
The simple bare necessities;
Forget about your worries and your strife.

I mean the bare necessities,
Or Mother Nature's recipes
That bring the bare necessities of life.
Wherever I wander, wherever I roam.
I couldn't be fonder of my big home.
The bees are buzzin' in the tree,
To make some honey just for me.
You look under the rocks and plants
And take a glance at the fancy ants,
Then maybe try a few.
The bare necessities of life will come to you,
They'll come you!

Refrain

I mean the bare necessities,
That's why a bear can rest at ease
With just the bare necessities of life.
When you pick a paw-paw or prickly pear.
And you prick a raw paw, next time beware.
Don't pick the prickly pear by paw,
When you pick a pear, try to use the claw.
But you don't need to use the claw
When you pick a pear of the big paw-paw.
Have I given you a clue?
The bare necessities of life will come to you,
They'll come you!

Refrain

I mean the bare necessities,
Or Mother Nature's recipes
That bring the bare necessities of life.
So just try to relax
(Oh Yeah!)

In my backyard.
If you act like that bee acts,
You're working too hard.
Don't spend you're time just looking around
For something you want that can't be found.
When you find out you can love without it,
And go along not thinkin' about it.
I'll tell you something true.
The bare necessities of life will come to you,
They'll come you!

Barely Breathing
Words and Music by Duncan Sheik

recorded by Duncan Sheik

Well I know what you're doing. I see it all too clear.
I only taste the saline when I kiss away your tears.
You really had me going, wishing on a star.
The black holes that surrounded you are heavier by far.
I believed in your confusion, so completely torn.
It must have been that yesterday was the day that I was born.
There's not much to examine, nothing left to hide.
You really can't be serious, you have to ask me why?
I say goodbye.

Refrain:
'Cause I am barely breathing, and I can't find the air.
Don't know who I'm kidding, imagining you care.
And I could stand here waiting, ooh, for another day.
I don't suppose it's worth the price, it's worth the price,
The price that I would pay.

And everyone keeps asking what's it all about.
It used to be so certain. Now I can't figure us out.
What is this attraction? Don't it fill the day,
And nothing left to reason, and only you to blame.
Will it ever change?

Refrain

But I'm thinking it over anyway.
But I'm thinking it over anyway. Oh.
I come to find I may never know.
A changing mind, is it friend or foe?
I rise above, I sink below,
And every time you come and go.
Please don't come and go.

Refrain

But I'm thinking it over anyway.
But I'm thinking it over anyway.
Oh, and I know what you're doing.
I see it all too clear.

Be Careful, It's My Heart
Words and Music by Irving Berlin

from the film *Holiday Inn*

Sweetheart of mine,
I've sent you a valentine.
Sweetheart of mine,
It's more than a valentine.
Be careful, it's my heart.

It's not my watch you're holding,
It's my heart.
It's not the note I sent you that you quickly burned.
It's not the book I lent you that you never returned.
Remember, it's my heart.
The heart with which so willingly I part.
It's yours to take to keep or break,
But please, before you start,
Be careful, it's my heart.

Be True to Your School
Words and Music by Brian Wilson and Mike Love

recorded by The Beach Boys

When some loud braggart tries to put me down,
And says his school is great,
I tell him right away now what's the matter?
Buddy ain't you heard of my school?
It's number one in the state.

Refrain:
So be true to your school.
Just like you would to your girl or guy.
Be true to your school now,
And let your colors fly.
Be true to your school.

I got a letterman's sweater with the letters in front.
I get from football and track.
I'm proud to wear it now,
When I cruise around the other parts of the town.
I got my decal in back.

Refrain

On Friday we'll be jacked up on the football game,
And I'll be ready to fight.
We're gonna smash 'em now.
My girl will be workin' on her pom-poms now,
And she'll be yellin' tonight.

Refrain

So be true to your school.
So be true to your school.

Beast of Burden

Words and Music by Mick Jagger and Keith Richards

recorded by The Rolling Stones

I'll never be your beast of burden.
My back is broad but it's a-hurtin'.
All I want is for you to make love to me.

I'll never be your beast of burden.
I've walked for miles, my feet are hurtin'.
All I want us for you to make love to me.

Refrain:
Am I hard enough?
Am I rough enough?
Am I rich enough?
I'm not too blind to see.

I'll never be your beast of burden
So let' go home and draw the curtains
Music on the radio
Come on baby make sweet love to me

Refrain

Oh little sister, pretty, pretty, pretty, pretty girl
You're a pretty, pretty, pretty, pretty, pretty girl
Pretty, pretty, such a pretty, pretty, pretty girl
Come on baby please, please, please.

I'll tell ya
You can put me out
On the street.
Put me out
With no shoes on my feet
But, put me out, put me out,
Put me out of misery.

Yeah, all your sickness
I can suck it up.
Throw it at me
I can shrug it off.
There's one thing, baby
That I don't understand
You keep telling me
I ain't your kind of man.

Ain't I rough enough?
Ain't I tough enough?
Ain't I rich enough, in love enough?
Ooh! Ooh! Please

I'll never be your beast of burden.
I've walked for miles and my feet are hurtin'.
All I want is you to make love to me.

I don't need no beast of burden.
I need no fussin',
I need no nursin'.
Never, never, never, never, never, never, never, never be.

Beautiful in My Eyes

Words and Music by Joshua Kadison

recorded by Joshua Kadison

You're my peace of mind
In this crazy world.
You're everything I've tried to find.
Your love is a pearl.
You're my Mona Lisa, you're my rainbow skies,
And my only prayer is that you realize,
You'll always be beautiful in my eyes.

The world will turn
And the seasons will change,
And all the lessons we will learn
Will be beautiful and strange.
We'll have our fill of tears, our share of sighs.
My only prayer is that you realize,
You'll always be beautiful in my eyes.

You will always be beautiful in my eyes.
And the passing years will show
That you will always grow,
Ever more beautiful in my eyes.

When there are lines upon my face,
From a lifetime of smiles.
When the time comes to embrace
For one long last while;
We can laugh about how time really flies.
We won't say goodbye 'cause true love never dies;
You'll always be beautiful in my eyes.

You'll always be beautiful in my eyes.
And the passing years will show
That you will always grow,
Ever more beautiful in my eyes.

The passing years will show
That you will always grow,
More beautiful in my eyes.

Beauty and the Beast

Lyrics by Howard Ashman
Music by Alan Menken

from Walt Disney's *Beauty and the Beast*

Tale as old as time,
True as it can be.
Barely even friends,
Then somebody bends
Unexpectedly.

Just a little change.
Small, to say the least.
Both a little scared,
Neither one prepared.
Beauty and the Beast.

Ever just the same.
Ever a surprise.
Ever as before,
Ever just as sure
As the sun will rise.

Tale as old as time.
Tune as old as song.
Bittersweet and strange,
Finding you can change,
Learning you were wrong.

Certain as the sun
Rising in the East.
Tale as old as time,
Song as old as rhyme.
Beauty and the Beast.

Tale as old as time,
Song as old as rhyme
Beauty and the Beast.

Because
Words and Music by John Lennon and Paul McCartney

recorded by The Beatles

Because the world is round it turns me on.
Because the world is round.
Ah, love is old, love is new,
Love is all, love is you.

Because the wind is high it blows my mind.
Because the wind is high.
Ah, love is old, love is new,
Love is all, love is you.

Because the sky is blue it makes me cry.
Because the sky is blue.
Ah, love is old, love is new,
Love is all, love is you.

Bein' Green
Words and Music by Joe Raposo

from the television show *Sesame Street*

It's not that easy bein' green,
Having to spend each day the color of the leaves.
When I think it could be nicer bein' red or yellow or gold,
Or something much more colorful like that.

It's not easy bein' green,
It seems you blend in with so many other ordinary things,
And people tend to pass you over, 'cause you're not
    standing out
Like flashy sparkles on the water or stars in the sky.

But green is the color of spring,
And green can be cool and friendly like.
And green can be big like an ocean,
Or important like a mountain or tall like a tree.

When green is all there is to be,
It could make you wonder why,
But why wonder, why wonder?
I am green and it'll do fine,
It's beautiful, and I think it's what I want to be.

Being Alive
Music and Lyrics by Stephen Sondheim

from the musical *Company*

Someone to hold you too close,
Someone to hurt you too deep,
Someone to sit in your chair
To ruin your sleep,
To make you aware
Of being alive,
Being alive.

Someone to need you too much,
Someone to know you too well,
Someone to pull you up short,
To put you through hell,
And give you support
Is being alive,
Being alive.

Someone you have to let in,
Someone whose feelings you spare,
Someone who, like it or not,
Will want you to share
A little, a lot,
Is being alive,
Being alive.

Someone to crowd you with love,
Someone to force you to care,
Someone to make you come through,
Who'll always be there
As frightened as you
Of being alive,
Being alive,
Being alive,
Being alive.

Somebody hold me too close,
Somebody hurt me too deep,
Somebody sit in my chair,
And ruin my sleep,
And make me aware
Of being alive.
Being alive.

Somebody need me too much,
Somebody know me too well,
Somebody pull me up short
And put me through hell,
And give me support
For being alive.
Being alive.
Make me alive.
Make me alive.
Make me confused,
Mock me with praise.
Let me be used,
Vary my days.
But alone is alone, not alive.

Somebody crowd me with love,
Somebody force me to care.
Somebody make me come through,
I'll always be here
As frightened as you,
To help us survive,
Being alive,
Being alive,
Being alive.

Ben
Words by Don Black
Music by Walter Scharf

from the film *Ben*
recorded by Michael Jackson

Ben, the two of us need look no more,
We both found what we were looking for.
With a friend to call my own,
I'll never be alone,
And you my friend will see,
You've got a friend in me.

Ben, you're always running here and there,
You feel you're not wanted anywhere.
If you ever look behind,
And don't like what you find,
There's something you should know,
You've got a place to go.

I used to say I and me,
Now it's us, now it's we.
I used to say I and me,
Now it's us, now its we.
Ben, most people would turn you away,
I don't listen to a word they say.
They don't see you as I do,
I wish they would try to.
I'm sure they'd think again if they had a friend like Ben

Like Ben, like Ben, like Ben, like Ben.

Bésame mucho (Kiss Me Much)
Music and Spanish Words by Consuelo Velazquez
English Words by Sunny Skylar

a standard recorded by various artists

Bésame, bésame mucho;
Each time I cling to your kiss I hear music divine;
Bésame mucho,
Hold me, my darling, and say that you'll always be mine.
This joy is something new,
My arms enfolding you,
Never knew this thrill before;
Who ever thought I'd be holding you close to me,
Whispering "It's you I adore;"
Dearest one, if you should leave me,
Each little dream would take wing and my life
  would be through;
Bésame mucho;
Love me forever and make all my dreams come true.

Best of My Love
Words and Music by Maurice White and Al McKay

recorded by Emotion

Doesn't take much to make me happy,
And make me smile with glee.
Never, never will I feel discouraged,
'Cause our love's no mystery.
Demonstrating love and affection,
That you give so openly.
I like the way you make me feel about you baby,
Want the whole wide world to see.
Oh, oh, you've got the best of my love.

Refrain:
Oh, oh, you've got the best of my love.
Flowin' in and out of changes,
The kind that come around each day.
My life has a better meaning,
Love has kissed me in a beautiful way.

Repeat Refrain

Demonstrating sweet love and affection,
That you give so openly, yeah.
The way I feel about you, baby, can't explain it,
Want the whole wide world to see.

Repeat and Fade:
Oh, oh, oh…
You've got the best of my love.

Best of My Love
Words and Music by John David Souther, Don Henley and
Glenn Frey
© 1974 EMI BLACKWOOD MUSIC INC., WOODY CREEK MUSIC
    and RED CLOUD MUSIC

recorded by The Eagles

Every night
I'm lying in bed,
Holdin' you close in my dreams;
Thinkin' about all the things that we said
And comin' apart at the seams.
We try to talk it over
But the words come out too rough;
I know you were tryin'
To give me the best of your love.

Beautiful faces,
Loud empty places
Look at the way that we live,
Wastin' our time
On cheap talk and wine
Left us so little to give.

The same old crowd
Was like a cold dark cloud
That we could never rise above,
But here in my heart
I give you the best of my love.

Oh, sweet darlin',
You get the best of my love,
(You get the best of my love.)
Oh, sweet darlin',
You get the best of my love.
(You get the best of my love.)

I'm goin' back in time
And it's a sweet dream.
It was a quiet night
And I would be alright
If I could go on sleeping.

But every mornin'
I wake up and worry
What's gonna happen today.
You see it your way,
And I see it mine,
But we both see it slippin' away.

You know, we always had each other, baby.
I guess that wasn't enough.
Oh, but here in my heart
I give you the best of my love.
Oh, sweet darlin',
You get the best of my love.
Oh, sweet darlin',
You get the best of my love.

The Best Things Happen While You're Dancing
Words and Music by Irving Berlin
© Copyright 1953 by Irving Berlin
Copyright Renewed

from the Motion Picture *Irving Berlin's White Christmas*

The best things happen while you're dancing.
Things that you would not do at home
Come natur'lly on the floor.
For dancing soon becomes romancing
When you hold a girl in your arms
That you've never held before.
Even guys with two left feet
Come out alright if the girl is sweet,
If by chance their cheeks should meet while dancing,
Proving that the best things happen while you dance.

Better Be Good to Me
Words and Music by Mike Chapman, Nicky Chinn and
Holly Knight
Copyright © 1981 by BMG Songs, Inc.

recorded by Tina Turner

A prisoner of your love,
Entangled in your web.
Hot whispers in the night.
I'm captured by your spell,
Captured.
Oh yes, I'm touched by this show of emotion.
Should I be fractured by your lack of devotion,
Should I, Should I?
Oh, you better be good to me;
That's how it's got to be now,
'Cause I don't have no use
For what you loosely call the truth.
Oh, you better be good to me.
Yes, you better be good.

And I think it's only right
That we don't meet at night.
We stand face to face,
And you present your case.
And I know and I really do want to believe,
But did you think I'd just accept you in blind faith?
Oh, sure babe, anything to please you.
Oh, you better be good to me;
That's how it's got to be now,
'Cause I don't have no time for your over-loaded lines.
Oh you better be good to me.
Yes, you better be good.

Spoken:
And I really don't see why it's so hard to be good to me.
And I don't understand what's your plan
That you can't be good to me.
What I can't feel. I surely cannot see.
Why can't you be good to me?
If it is not real, I do not wish to see,
Why can't you be good to me?

Sung, Repeat and Fade:
Why can't you be good to me?

Between the Devil
and the Deep Blue Sea
Lyric by Ted Koehler
Music by Harold Arlen

introduced in the Cotton Club revue *Rhythmania*
a standard recorded by various artists

I don't want you but I'd hate to lose you,
You've got me between the devil and the deep blue sea.
I forgive you, 'cause I can't forget you,
You've got me between the devil and the deep blue sea.

I ought to cross you off my list,
But when you come knocking at my door,
Fate seems to give my heart a twist,
And I come running back for more.

I should hate you, but I guess I love you,
You've got me between the devil and the deep blue sea.

Bewitched
Words by Lorenz Hart
Music by Richard Rodgers

from the musical *Pal Joey*
a standard recorded by various artists

Note: There are two versions of the song's lyric, an
original show version, and Hart's "standard version."
Both are presented here.

SHOW LYRIC

After one whole quart of brandy,
Like a daisy I awake.
With no Bromo Selzer handy,
I don't even shake.
Men are not a new sensation;
I've done pretty well I think.
But this half-pint imitation
Put me on the blink.

Refrain 1:
I'm wild again, beguiled again,
A simpering, whimpering child again,
Bewitched, bothered and bewildered am I.
Couldn't sleep and wouldn't sleep
Until I could sleep where I shouldn't sleep,
Bewitched, bothered and bewildered am I.
Lost my heart, but what of it?
My mistake, I agree.
He's a laugh, but I love it
Because the laugh's on me.
A pill he is but still he is
All mine and I'll keep him until he is,
Bewitched, bothered and bewildered like me.

Refrain 2:
Seen a lot, I mean a lot
But now I'm like sweet sixteen a lot.
Bewitched, bothered and bewildered am I.
I'll sing to him, each spring to him,
And worship the trousers that cling to him.
Bewitched, bothered and bewildered am I.
When he talks, he is seeking
Words to get off his chest.
Horizontally speaking
He's at his very best.

Vexed again, perplexed again,
Thank God I can be oversexed again,
Bewitched bothered and bewildered am I.

Refrain 3:
Sweet again, petite again,
And on my proverbial seat again,
Bewitched, bothered and bewildered am I.
What am I? Half shot am I.
To think that he loves me so hot am I,
Bewitched bothered and bewildered am I.
Though at first we said, "No sir,"
Now we're two little dears.
You might say we are closer
Than Roebuck is to Sears.
I'm dumb again and numb again,
A rich, ready ripe little plumb again,
Bewitched, bothered and bewildered am I.

Reprise:
Wise at last, my eyes at last
Are cutting you down to your size at last,
Bewitched, bothered and bewildered no more.
Burned a lot, but learned a lot,
And now you are broke, though you earned a lot,
Bewitched, bothered and bewildered no more.
Couldn't eat, was dyspeptic,
Life was so hard to bear;
Now my heart's antiseptic,
Since you moved out of there.
Romance—finis; your chance—finis;
Those ants that invaded my pants—finis,
Bewitched, bothered and bewildered no more.

STANDARD LYRIC

Verse:
He's a fool and don't I know it,
But a fool can have his charms.
I'm in love and don't I show it
Like a babe in arms.
Love's the same old sad sensation,
Lately I've not slept a wink
Since this half-pint imitation
Put me on the blink.

Refrain:
I'm wild again, beguiled again,
A simpering, whimpering child again,
Bewitched, bothered and bewildered am I.
Couldn't sleep and wouldn't sleep
When love came and told me I shouldn't sleep,
Bewitched, bothered and bewildered am I.
Lost my heart, but what of it?
He is cold, I agree.
He's a laugh, but I love it
Although the laugh's on me.
I'll sing to him, each spring to him,
And long for the day when I cling to him,
Bewitched, bothered and bewildered am I.

Beyond the Blue Horizon
Words by Leo Robin
Music by Richard A. Whiting and W. Franke Harling

from the Paramount Picture *Monte Carlo*
recorded by Jeanette MacDonald and various other artists

Beyond the Blue Horizon,
Waits a beautiful day;
Goodbye to things that bore me,
Joy is waiting for me.
I see a new horizon,
My life has only begun;
Beyond the blue horizon
Lies a setting sun.

Beyond the Sea
English Lyrics by Jack Lawrence
Music and French Lyrics by Charles Trenet

recorded by Bobby Darin and various other artists

Somewhere beyond the sea,
Somewhere waiting for me,
My lover stands on golden sands
And watches the ships that go sailing.

Somewhere beyond the sea,
He's (She's) there watching for me.
If I could fly like birds on high,
Then straight to his (her) arms

I'd go sailing.
It's far beyond a star;
It's near beyond the moon.
I know beyond a doubt,
My heart will lead me there soon.

We'll meet beyond the shore:
We'll kiss just as before.
Happy we'll be beyond the sea,
And never again I'll go sailing.

Bibbidi-Bobbidi-Boo
(The Magic Song)
Words by Jerry Livingston
Music by Mack David and Al Hoffman

from Walt Disney's *Cinderella*

Salagadoola menchicka boola
Bibbidi-bobbidi-boo
Put them together and what have you got
Bibbidi-bobbidi-boo.

Salagadoola menchicka boola
Bibbidi-bobbidi-boo.
It'll do magic believe it or not,
Bibbidi-bobbidi-boo.

Salagadoola means menchicka booleroo,
But the thing-a-ma-bob that does the job
Is bibbidi-bobbidi-boo.

Salagadoola menchicka boola
Bibbidi-bobbidi-boo.
Put them together and what have you got?
Bibbidi-bobbidi-boo
Bibbidi-bobbidi-boo
Bibbidi-bobbidi-boo.

Bills, Bills, Bills
Words and Music by Kandi L. Burruss, Kevin Briggs,
Beyonce Knowles, Kelendria Rowland and
LeToya Luckett

recorded by Destiny's Child

At first we started out real cool,
Takin' me places I had never been.
But now you're getting comfortable,
Ain't doin' those things you did no more.
You're slowly makin' me pay for things
Your money should be handling.
And now you ask to use my car.
Drive it all day and don't fill up the tank.
And you have the audacity to even come
And step to me and ask to hold some money from me
Until you get your check next week.

Refrain:
You triflin' good-for-nothin' type of brother.
Silly me,
Why haven't I found another?
A baler,
When times get hard need someone to help me out,
Instead of a scrub like you
Who don't know what a man's about.
Can you pay my bills?
Can you pay my telephone bills?
Do you pay my automobills?
If you did then maybe we could chill.
I don't think you do,
So you and me are through.
Can you pay my bills?
Can you pay my telephone bills?
Do you pay my automobills?
If you did then maybe we could chill.
I don't think you do,
So you and I are through.

Now you've been maxin' out my card,
Gave me bad credit,
Buy me gifts with my own name.
Haven't paid the first bill,
But you're steady headin' to the mall,
Goin' on shoppin' sprees
Perpetratin' to your friends that you should be ballin'
And then you use my cell phone,
Callin, whoever that you think at home.
And then when the bill comes,
All of a sudden you back actin' dumb.
Don't know where none of those calls come from
When your mama's number's here more than once.

Refrain Twice

The Bitch Is Back
Words and Music by Elton John and Bernie Taupin

recorded by Elton John

I was justified when I was five,
Raisin' cane, I spit in your eye.
Times are changin' now, the poor get far,
But the fever's gonna catch you when the bitch gets back.

Eat meat on Friday that's alright,
I even like steak on a Saturday night.
I can bitch the best at your social do's,
I get high in the evening sniffing pots of glue.

Refrain:
I'm a bitch, I'm a bitch, oh the bitch is back;
Stone cold sober as a matter of fact.
I can botch, I can bitch 'cause I'm better than you.
It's the way that I move and the things that I do, oh.

I entertain by picking brains,
Sell my soul by dropping names.
I don't like those!
My God what's that!
Oh, it's full of nasty habits when the bitch gets back.

Refrain

Bitch, bitch, the bitch is back.
Bitch, bitch, the bitch is back…

Black Coffee
Words and Music by Paul Francis Webster and
Sonny Burke

a standard recorded by Peggy Lee, Sarah Vaughan
and Ella Fitzgerald, among other artists

Refrain:
I'm feelin' mighty lonesome,
Haven't slept a wink,
I walk the floor and watch the door
And in between I drink
Black coffee.
Love's a hand-me-down broom.
I'll never know a Sunday,
In this weekday room.

I'm talkin' to the shadows,
One o'clock to four.
And Lord, how slow the moments go
When all I do is pour
Black coffee.
Since the blues caught my eye.

I'm hangin' out on Monday
My Sunday dreams to dry.

Now a man is born to go a-lovin',
A woman's born to weep and fret.
To stay at home and tend her oven,
And drown her past regrets
In coffee and cigarettes!

I'm moonin' all the mornin',
And moonin' all the night,
And in between it's nicotine
And not much heart to fight
Black coffee.
Feelin' low as the ground.
It's drivin' me crazy,
This waitin' for my baby,
To maybe come around.

Blackbird
Words and Music by John Lennon and Paul McCartney

recorded by The Beatles

Blackbird singing in the dead of night
Take these broken wings and learn to fly.
All your life
You were only waiting for this moment to arise.

Blackbird singing in the dead of night
Take these sunken eyes and learn to see.
All your life
You were only waiting for this moment to be free.

Blackbird fly, blackbird fly
Into the light of the dark black night.

Blackbird singing in the dead of night
Take these broken wings and learn to fly.
All your life
You were only waiting for this moment to arise
You were only waiting for this moment to arise
You were only waiting for this moment to arise.

Bless the Beasts and Children
Words and Music by Barry DeVorzon and Perry Botkin, Jr.

from the film *Bless the Beasts and Children*
recorded by The Carpenters

Bless the beasts and the children,
For in this world they have no voice,
They have no choice.
Bless the beasts and the children,
For the world can never be,
The world they see.

Refrain:
Light their way
When the darkness surrounds them;
Give them love, let it shine all around them.
Bless the beasts and the children;
Give them shelter from a storm;
Keep them safe;
Keep them warm.

Refrain

Bless the beasts and the children;
Give them shelter from a storm;
Keep them safe;
Keep them warm.

A Blossom Fell

Words and Music by Howard Barnes, Harold Cornelius
and Dominic John

recorded by Nat "King" Cole

A blossom fell from off a tree
It settled softly on the lips you turned to me.
The gypsies say, and I know why,
A falling blossom only touches lips that lie.

A blossom fell and very soon
I saw you kissing someone new beneath the moon.
I thought you loved me,
You said you loved me,
We planned together to dream forever.

The dream has ended
For true love died
The night a blossom fell
And touched two lips that lied.

Blue

Words and Music by Bill Mack

recorded by LeAnn Rimes

Blue, oh, so lonesome for you.
Why can't you be blue over me?
Blue, oh, so lonesome for you.
Tears fill my eyes till I can't see.

Three o'clock in the morning here am I,
Sitting here so lonely,
So lonesome I could cry.
Blue, oh, so lonesome for you.
Why can't you be blue for me?

Now that it's over, I realized
Those weak words you whispered
Were nothing but lies.
Blue, oh, so lonesome for you.
Why can't you be blue over me?
Why can't you be blue over me?

Blue Hawaii

Words and Music by Leo Robin and Ralph Rainger

from the Paramount Picture *Waikiki Wedding*
recorded by Bing Crosby
Theme from the Paramount Picture *Blue Hawaii*
recorded by Elvis Presley

Night and you and blue Hawaii,
The night is heavenly,
And you are heaven to me.
Lovely you and blue Hawaii,
With all this loveliness there should be love.

Come with me while the moon is on the sea.
The night is young and so are we.
Dreams come true in blue Hawaii
And mine could all come true
This magic night of nights with you.

Blue Moon of Kentucky

Words and Music by Bill Monroe

recorded by Bill Monroe & The Blue Grass Boys,
Elvis Presley, Patsy Cline and others

I said the blue moon of Kentucky,
Keep on shinin',
Shine on the one that's gone and left me blue.
Blue moon of Kentucky keep on shinin',
Shine on the one that's gone and left me blue.
It was on one moonlit night,
Stars shinin' bright,
Whispered on high,
Love said goodbye.
I said:

Refrain:
Blue of Kentucky keep on shinin',
Shine on the one that's gone and left me blue.
Blue moon of Kentucky keep on shinin'.
Shine on the one that's gone and left me blue.
Blue moon of Kentucky keep on shinin'.
Shine on the one that's gone and left me blue.

Well, it was on one moonlit night
Stars shinin' bright,
Whispered on high,
Your lover said goodbye.
I said, blue moon of Kentucky keep on shinin'.
Shine on the one that's gone and left me blue,
Left me blue, left me blue.

The Blue Room

Words by Lorenz Hart
Music by Richard Rodgers

from the musical *The Girl Friend*
a standard recorded by various artitsts

All my future plans,
Dear, will not suit your plans.
Read the little blueprints.
Here's your mother's room.
Here's your brother's room.
On the wall are two prints.
Here's the kiddie's room,
Here's the biddy's room,
Here's a pantry lined with shelves, dear.
Here I've planned for us
Something grand for us,
Where we two can be ourselves, dear.

Refrain:
We'll have a blue room,
A new room,
For two room,
Where every day's a holiday,
Because you're married to me.
Not like a ballroom,
A small room,
A hall room,
Where I can smoke my pipe away
With your wee head upon my knee.
We will thrive on,
Keep alive on,
Just nothing but kisses,
With Mister and Missus
On little blue chairs.
You sew your trousseau,
And Robinson Crusoe
Is not so far from worldly cares
As our blue room far away upstairs.

From all visitors
And inquisitors
We'll keep our apartment.
I won't change your plans—
You arrange your plans
Just the way your heart meant.
Here we'll be ourselves
And we'll see ourselves
Doing all the things we're scheming.
Here's a certain place,
Cretonne curtain place,
Where no one can see us dreaming.

Refrain

Blue Skies

Words and Music by Irving Berlin

from the film *Blue Skies*
from the musical *Betsy*
a standard recorded by various artists

I was blue just as blue as I could be.
Every day was a cloudy day for me.
Then good luck came a-knocking at my door.
Skies were gray but they're not gray anymore.

Blue skies,
Smiling at me.
Nothing but blue skies
Do I see.

Blue birds,
Singing a song
Nothing but bluebirds
All day long,

Never saw the sun shining so bright.
Never saw things going so right.
Noticing the days hurrying by
When you're in love, my how they fly.

Blue days,
All of them gone.
Nothing but blue skies
From now on.

Body and Soul

Words by Edward Heyman, Robert Sour and Frank Eyton
Music by John Green

a standard recorded by Coleman Hawkins and many
various artists

Life's dreary for me,
Days seem to be long as years.
I look for the sun,
But I see none through my tears.

Your heart must be like a stone,
To leave me all alone,
When you could make my life worth living
By simply taking what I'm set on giving.

My heart is sad and lonely,
For you I sigh, for you, dear, only.
Why haven't you seen it?
I'm all for you,
Body and soul.

I spend my days in longing,
And wondering why it's me you're wronging.
I tell you I mean it,
I'm all for you,
Body and soul.

I can't believe it,
It's hard to conceive it,
That you'd turn away romance.

Are you pretending?
It looks like the ending.
Unless I could have one
More chance to prove, dear,

My life a wreck you're making,
You know I'm yours for just the taking;
I'd gladly surrender
Myself to you,
Body and soul.

The Boy from New York City
Words and Music by John Taylor and George Davis

recorded by Manhattan Transfer

Oo-wah, oo-wah, cool, cool Kitty,
Tell us about the boy from New York City.
Oo-wah, oo-wah, come on Kitty,
Tell us about the boy from New York City.

He's kinda tall.
He's really fine.
Some day I hope to make him mine, all mine.
And he's neat,
And oh so sweet.
And just the way he looked at me swept me off my feet.
Oo-ee, you ought to come and see,
How he walks,
And how he talks.

Oo-wah, oo-wah, come on Kitty
Tell us about the boy from New York City.

He's really down.
And he's no clown.
He has the finest penthouse I've ever seen in town.
And he's cute
In his mohair suit.
And he keeps his pockets full of spending loot.
Oo-ee, You ought to come and see
His pretty bar,
And his brand new car.

Every time he says he loves me,
Chills run down my spine.
Every time he wants to kiss me,
Ooh, he makes me feel so fine. Yeah!

Oo-wah, oo-wah, come on Kitty,
Tell us about the boy from New York City.
He can dance,
And make romance.
And that's when I fell in with just one glance.
He was shy,
And so was I.
And now I know we'll never ever say goodbye.

Ooh-ee, you ought to see
He's the most
From coast to coast.

Oo-wah, oo-wah, come on Kitty,
Tell us about the boy from New York City.

The Boy Is Mine
Words and Music by LaShawn Daniels, Japhe Tejeda,
Rodney Jerkins, Fred Jerkins and Brandy Norwood

recorded by Brandy & Monica

Brandy:
Excuse me, can I please talk to you for a minute?
Monica:
Uh huh, sure. You know, you look kind of familiar.
Brandy:
Yeah, you do too. But, um, I just wanted to know,
Do you know somebody named…
You know his name.
Monica:
Oh, yeah, definitely. I know his name.
Brandy:
Well, I just want to let you know that he's mine.
Monica:
Heh, no no. He's mine.

Refrain:
You need to give it up; I've had about enough.
It's not hard to see; The boy is mine.
I'm sorry that you seem to be confused.
He belongs to me; the boy is mine.

Think it's time we got this straight;
We'll sit and talk face to face.
There is no way you could mistake
Him for your man. Are you insane?

You see, I know that you may be
Just a bit jealous of me,
But you're blind if you can't see
That his love is all in me.
See, I tried to hesitate;
I didn't want to say what he told me,
He said without me he couldn't make

It through the day. Ain't that a shame?
But maybe you misunderstood
'Cause I can't see how he could
Want to tell you something that's so good.
For my love is all it took.

Refrain

Must you do the things you do?
You keep on acting like a fool.
You need to know it's me, not you,
And if you didn't know it, girl, it's true.
I think that you should realize
And try to understand why
He is a part of my life.
I know it's killing you inside.
You can say what you wanna say,
What we have you can't take.
From the truth you can't escape.
I can tell the real from the fake.
When will you get the picture?
You're the past and I'm future.
Get away, it's my time to shine.
If you didn't know, the boy is mine.

Refrain Twice

I can be sure it's love I've found,
You simply can't, I won't allow.
The boy is mine without a doubt.
You might as well throw in the towel.
What makes you think that he wants you
When I'm the one that brought him to
The special place that's in my heart?
He was my lover from the start.

Refrain Twice

The Brady Bunch
Words and Music by Sherwood Schwartz and Frank Devol
Copyright © 1969 (Renewed 1997) by Addax Music Company, Inc.

Theme from the Paramount Television Series
The Brady Bunch

Boys:
Here's the story of a lovely lady
Who was bringing up three very lovely girls.
All of them had hair of gold like their mother,
The youngest one in curls.

Girls:
It's the story of a man named Brady
Who was busy with three boys of his own.
They were four men living all together,
Yet they were all alone.

All:
Till the one day when the lady met this fellow,
And they knew that it was much more than a hunch
That this group must somehow form a family.
That's the way we all became the Brady Bunch.
The Brady Bunch, the Brady Bunch.
That's the way we became the Brady Bunch.

Brand New Day
Written and Composed by Sting
© 1999 G.M. SUMNER
Published by MAGNETIC PUBLISHING LTD. and Administered
  by EMI BLACKWOOD MUSIC INC. in the USA and Canada

recorded by Sting

How many of you people out there
Been hurt in some kind of love affair?
And how many times did you swear
That you'd never love again?
How many lonely sleepless nights?
How many lies? How many fights?
And why would you wanna put yourself
Through all of that again?
"Love is pain," I hear you say;
"Love has a cruel and bitter way
Of paying you back for all the faith
You had in your brain."

How could it be that what you need the most
Can leave you feeling just like a ghost?
You never wanna feel so sad and lost again.
One day you could be looking
Through an old book in rainy weather;
You see a picture of her smiling at you
When you were still together.
You could be walking down the street,
And who should you chance to meet
But that same old smile you've been thinking of all day?

Why don't we turn the clock to zero, honey?
I'll sell the stock,
We'll spend all the money.
We're starting up a brand new day.

Turn the clock all the way back.
I wonder if she'll take me back.
I'm thinking in a brand new way.
Turn the clock to zero, sister.
You'll never know how much I missed her.

I'm starting up a brand new day.
Turn the clock to zero, sister.
You'll never know how much I missed her.
I'm starting up a brand new day.

It could happen to you,
Just like it happened to me.
There's simply no immunity,
There's no guarantee.
I say love is such a farce;

If you find yourself in it, babe,
Need sometime for reflection. You say,
"Baby, wait a minute, wait a minute,
Wait a minute, wait a minute,
Wait a minute, wait a minute."

And you can turn back the clock to zero, honey.
I'll sell the stock, we'll spend all the money.
We're starting up a brand new day.
Turn the clock to zero, Mac.
I'm begging her to take me back.
I'm thinking in a brand new way.
Turn the clock to zero boss.
The river's wide, we'll swim across.

We're starting up a brand new day.
Turn the clock to zero, buddy.
Don't wanna be no fuddy duddy.
Starting up a brand new day.

I'm the rhythm in your tune.
I'm the sun and you're the moon.
I'm the bat and you're the cave.
You're the beach and I'm the wave.
(It's a brand new day.)

I'm the plough and you're the land.
You're the glove and I'm the hand.
I'm the train and you're the station.
I'm the flagpole to your nation,
Yeah, yeah, yeah, yeah.

I'm the present to your future.
You're the wound and I'm the suture.
You're the magnet to my pole.
I'm the devil in your soul.

You're the pupil, I'm the teacher.
You're the church and I'm the preacher.
You're the flower, I'm the rain.
You're the tunnel. I'm the train.

Stand up, all you lovers in the world,
Stand up and be counted, every boy and every girl.
Stand up, all you lovers in the world;
We're starting up a brand new day.

You're the crop to my rotation.
You're the sum of my equation.
I'm the answer to your question.
If you follow my suggestion

We can turn this ship around;
We'll go up instead of down.
You're the pan and I'm the handle.
You're the flame and I'm the candle.

Stand up, all you lovers in the world;
Stand up and be counted,
Every boy and every girl.
Stand up (It's a brand new day.)
(It's a brand new day.)

Breathe
Words and Music by Holly Lamar and Stephanie Bentley

recorded by Faith Hill

I can feel the magic floating in the air.
Being with you gets me that way.
I watch the sunlight dance across your face
And I never been this swept away.

All my thoughts just seem to settle on the breeze,
When I'm lyin' wrapped up in your arms.
The whole world just fades away,
The only thing I hear is the beating of your heart.

Refrain:
'Cause I can feel you breathe,
It's washing over me,
And suddenly I'm melting into you.
There's nothing left to prove,
Baby, all we need is just to be
Caught up in the touch,
The slow and steady rush.
Baby, isn't that the way
That love's supposed to be?
I can feel you breathe.
Just breathe.

In a way I know my heart is wakin' up
As all the walls come tumbling down.
Closer than I've ever felt before,
And I know and you know
There's no need for words right now.

Refrain

Caught up in the touch,
The slow and steady rush.
Baby, isn't that the way
That love's supposed to be?
I can feel you breathe.
Just breathe.
I can feel the magic floating in the air.
Bein' with you gets me that way.

Broadway Baby
Words and Music by Stephen Sondheim

from the musical *Follies*

I'm just a Broadway Baby,
Walking off my tired feet,
Pounding Forty Second Street
To be in a show.

Broadway Baby,
Learning how to sing and dance,
Waiting for that one big chance
To be in a show.

Gee, I'd like to be
On some marquee,
All twinkling lights,
A spark to pierce the dark
From Batt'ry Park
To Washington Heights.

Some day maybe,
All my dreams will be repaid.
Heck I'd even play the maid
To be in a show.

Say, Mister producer,
Some girls get the brakes.
Just give me my cue, sir,
I've got what it takes.
Say, Mister producer
I'm talkin' to you sir.
I don't need a lot,
Only what I got,
Plus a tube of greasepaint
And a follow spot!

I'm a Broadway Baby,
Slaving at the five and ten,
Dreaming of the great day when
I'll be in a show.
Broadway Baby,
Making rounds all afternoon,
Eating at a greasy spoon
To save on my dough.

At my tiny flat
There's just my cat,
A bed and a chair.
Still I'll stick it till
I'm on a bill
All over Times Square.

Some day maybe,
If I stick it long enough,
I can get to strut my stuff,
Working for a nice man,
Like a Ziegfeld or a Weissman,
In a big-time Broadway show!

Brush Up Your Shakespeare
Words and Music by Cole Porter

Copyright © 1949 by Cole Porter
Copyright Renewed, Assigned to John F. Wharton, Trustee of the Cole Porter Musical and
   Literary Property Trusts
Chappell & Co. owner of publication and allied rights throughout the world

from the musical *Kiss Me, Kate*

The girls today in society
Go for classical poetry,
So, to win their hearts,
One must quote with ease
Aeschylus and Euripidies.
One must know Homer and believe me, bo,
Sophocles, also Sapho,
Unless you know Shelley and Keats and Pope,
Dainty debbies will call you a dope.
But the poet of them all,
Who will start 'em simply ravin'
Is the poet people call
The bard of Stratford on Avon.

Brush up your Shakespeare,
Start quoting him now.
Brush up your Shakespeare
And the women you will wow.
Just declaim a few lines from "Othella"
And they'll think you're a heck-uv-a fella,
If your blonde won't respond when you flatter 'er
Tell her what Tony told Cleopatterer.
And if still to be shocked she pretends, well,
Just remind her that "All's Well End's Well."
Brush up your Shakespeare
And they'll all kow-tow.

Brush up your Shakespeare,
Start quoting him now.
Brush up your Shakespeare
And the women you will wow.
If your goil is a Washington Heights dream,
Treat the kid to a "A Midsummer Night's Dream,"
With the wide of the British embessida
Try a crack out of "Troilus and Cressida."
If she says she won't buy it or tike* it,
Make her tike it, what's, "As You Like It."
Brush up your Shakespeare
And they'll all kow-tow.

Brush up your Shakespeare,
Start quoting him now.
Brush up your Shakespeare
And the women you will wow.
If you can't be a ham and do Hamlet
They will not give a damn or a damnlet.
Just recite an occasional sonnet,
And your lap'll have Honey upon it.
When your baby is pleading for pleasure
Let her sample your "Measure for Measure."
Brush up your Shakespeare
And they'll all kow-tow.

*Cockney for "take"

Building a Mystery

Words and Music by Sarah McLachlan and
Pierre Marchand

recorded by Sarah McLachlan

You come out at night,
That's when the energy comes
And the dark side' light
And the vampires roam.
You strut your rasta wear
And your suicide poem
And a cross from a faith that died before Jesus came.
You're building a mystery.

You live in a church
Where you sleep with voo-doo dolls,
And you won't give up the search.
For the ghost in the halls.
You wear sandals in the snow
And a smile that won't wash away.
Can you look out the window
Without your shadow getting in the way?
You're so beautiful,
With an edge and a charm,
But so careful when I'm in your arms
'Cause:

Refrain:
You're working building a mystery,
Holding on and holding it in.
Yeah, you're working building a mystery
And choosing so carefully.

You woke up screaming aloud
A prayer from your secret god
To feed off fears
And hold back your tears, oh.
You give us a tantrum
And a know-it-all grin,
Just when you need one
When the evening's thin.
You're a beautiful,
A beautiful, fucked up man.
You're setting up your razor wire shrine
'Cause:

Refrain Three Times

You're building a mystery.

By Myself

Words by Howard Dietz
Music by Arthur Schwartz

from the musical *Between the Devil*
later featured in the film *The Band Wagon*

I'll go by myself.
This is the end of romance.
I'll go my way by myself.
Love is only a dance.

I'll try to apply myself,
And teach my heart how to sing.
I'll go my way by myself,
Like a bird on the wing.

I'll face the unknown,
I'll build a world of my own;
No one knows better than I myself,
I'm by myself, alone.

By the Time I Get to Phoenix

Words and Music by Jimmy Webb

recorded by Glen Campbell

By the time I get to Phoenix she'll be risin'
She'll find the note I left hangin' on her door.
She'll laugh when she reads the part that says I'm leavin',
'Cause I've left that girl so many times before.

By the time I make Albuquerque she'll be working'
She'll probably stop at lunch and give me a call.
But she'll just hear that phone keep on ringin',
Off the wall.

By the time I make Oklahoma she'll be sleepin'
She'll turn softly and call my name out low.
And she'll cry just to think I'd really leave her,
'Tho' time and time I've tried to tell her so,
She just didn't know,
I would really go.

Bye Bye Blackbird

Lyric by Mort Dixon
Music by Ray Henderson

from the musical *Pete Kelly's Blues*
a standard recorded by various artists

Blackbird, blackbird,
Singing the blues all day
Right outside of my door,
Blackbird, blackbird,
Why do you sit and say,
"There's no sunshine in store."
All through the winter you hung around.
Now I begin to feel homeward bound.
Blackbird, blackbird,
Gotta be on my way.
Where's the sunshine galore.

Refrain:
Pack up all my care and woe,
Here I go, singing low.
Bye bye blackbird.
Where somebody waits for me,
Sugar's sweet, so is she,
Bye bye blackbird.
No one here can love and understand me.
Oh, what hard luck stories they all hand me.
Make my bed and light the light,
I'll arrive late tonight,
Blackbird bye bye.

Bluebird, bluebird
Calling me far away
I've been longing for you.
Bluebird, bluebird
Why do you sit and say
"Skies are turning to blue."
I'm like a flower that's fading here
Where every hour is one long tear
Bluebird, bluebird
This is my lucky day
Now my dreams will come true.

Refrain

Cabaret

Words by Fred Ebb
Music by John Kander
Copyright © 1966, 1967 by Alley Music Corp. and Trio Music Company, Inc.
Copyright Renewed

from the musical *Cabaret*

What good is sitting alone in your room?
Come hear the music play;
Life is a cabaret, old chum,
Come to the cabaret.

Put down your knitting, the book and the broom,
Time for a holiday;
Life is a cabaret, old chum,
Come to the cabaret.

Come taste the wine,
Come hear the band.
Come blow the horn, start celebrating,
Right this way your table's waiting.

No use permitting some prophet of doom,
To wipe every smile away;
Life is a cabaret, old chum.
Come to the cabaret.

I used to have a girlfriend known as Elsie,
With whom I shared four sordid rooms in Chelsea.
She wasn't what you'd call a blushing flower,
As a matter of fact she rented by the hour.
The day she died the neighbors came to snicker:
"Well, that's what comes of too much pills and liquor."
But when I saw her laid out like a queen,
She was the happiest corpse I'd ever seen.
I think of Elsie to this very day.
I remember how she'd turn to me and say:

What good is sitting alone in your room?
Come hear the music play;
Life is a cabaret, old chum,
Come to the cabaret.

Put down your knitting, the book and the broom,
Time for a holiday;
Life is a cabaret, old chum,
Come to the cabaret.

And as for me, as for me,
I made my mind up back in Chelsea,
When I go I'm going like Elsie.

Start by admitting from cradle to tomb
Isn't that long a stay;
Life is a cabaret, old chum,
Only a cabaret, old chum
And I love a cabaret.

Call Me

Words by Deborah Harry
Music by Giorgio Moroder
Copyright © 1980 by Ensign Music Corporation and Rare Blue Music, Inc.

from the Paramount Motion Picture *American Gigolo*
recorded by Blondie

Color me your color, baby, color me your car.
Color me your color, darling, I know who you are.
Come up off your color chart,
I know where you're coming from.
Call me on the line,
Call me any, any time.
Call me, I love you,
Can't you call me any day or night.

Call Me Irresponsible

Words by Sammy Cahn
Music by James Van Heusen
Copyright © 1962, 1963 (Renewed 1990, 1991) by Paramount Music Corporation

cut from an abandoned Fred Astaire film
from the Paramount Picture *Papa's Delicate Condition*
a standard recorded by Frank Sinatra, Jack Jones and
various other artists

Call me irresponsible,
Call me unreliable,
Throw in undependable too.

Do my foolish alibis bore you?
Well, I'm not too clever.
I just adore you.

Call me unpredictable,
Tell me I'm impractical,
Rainbows I'm inclined to pursue.

Call me irresponsible,
Yes, I'm unreliable,
But it's undeniably true,
I'm irresponsibly mad for you!

Camelot

Words by Alan Jay Lerner
Music by Frederick Loewe
Copyright © 1960, 1961 by Alan Jay Lerner and Frederick Loewe
Copyright Renewed
Chappell & Co. owner of publication and allied rights throughout the world

from the musical *Camelot*

A law was made a distant moon ago here,
July and August cannot be too hot.
And there's a legal limit to the snow here,
In Camelot.

The winter is forbidden till December,
And exits March the second on the dot.
By order summer lingers through September,
In Camelot.

Camelot! Camelot!
I know it sounds a bit bizarre,
But in Camelot, Camelot,
That's how conditions are.

The rain may never fall till after sundown.
By eight the morning fog must disappear.
In short, there's simply not
A more congenial spot,
For happily-ever-aftering
Than here in Camelot!

The winter is forbidden till December,
And exits March the second on the dot.
By order summer lingers through September,
In Camelot.

Camelot! Camelot!
I know it gives a person pause,
But in Camelot, Camelot,
Those are the legal laws.

The snow may never slush upon the hillside.
By nine P.M. the moonlight must appear.
In short, there's simply not
A more congenial spot
For happily-ever-aftering
Than here in Camelot.

Can You Feel the Love Tonight
Music by Elton John
Lyrics by Tim Rice
© 1994 Wonderland Music Company, Inc.

from Walt Disney Pictures' *The Lion King*
recorded by Elton John

There's a calm surrender
To the rush of the day,
When the heat of the rolling world
Can be turned away.
An enchanted moment,
And it sees me through.
It's enough for this restless warrior
Just to be with you.

Refrain:
And can you feel the love tonight?
It is where we are.
It's enough for this wide-eyed wanderer
That we got this far.
And can you feel the love tonight,
How it's laid to rest?
It's enough to make kings and vagabonds
Believe the very best.

There's a time for everyone,
If they only learn,
That the twisting kaleidoscope
Moves us all in turn.
There's a rhyme and reason
To the wild outdoors,

When the heart of this star-crossed voyager
Beats in time with yours.

Refrain

Can't Help Falling in Love
Words and Music by George David Weiss, Hugo Peretti
and Luigi Creatore
Copyright © 1961 by Gladys Music, Inc.
Copyright Renewed and Assigned to Gladys Music (Administered by Williamson Music)

from the Paramount Picture *Blue Hawaii*
recorded by Elvis Presley

Wise men say only fools rush in,
But I can't help falling in love with you.
Shall I stay?
Would it be a sin?
If I can't help falling in love with you.

Like a river flows,
Surely to the sea.
Darling so it goes,
Some things are meant to be.

Take my hand, take whole life too,
For I can't help falling in love in with you.
For I can't help falling in love with you.

Candle on the Water
Words and Music by Al Kasha and Joel Hirschhorn
© 1976 Walt Disney Music Company and Wonderland Music Company, Inc.

from Walt Disney's *Pete's Dragon*
recorded by Helen Reddy

I'll be your candle on the water,
My love for you will always burn.
I know you're lost and drifting,
But the clouds are lifting,
Don't give up you have somewhere to turn.

I'll be your candle on the water,
'Til every wave is warm and bright,
My soul is there beside you,
Let this candle guide you,
Soon you'll see a golden stream of light.

A cold and friendless tide has found you,
Don't let the stormy darkness pull you down.
I'll paint a ray of hope around you,
Circling in the air lighted by a prayer.

I'll be your candle on the water,
This flame inside of me will grow.
Keep holding on, you'll make it,
Here's my hand so take it,
Look for me reaching out to show
As sure as rivers flow,
I'll never let you go,
I'll never let you go.
I'll never let you go.

Caravan

Words and Music by Duke Ellington, Irving Mills and Juan Tizol

featured in the musical revue *Sophisticated Ladies*
a standard recorded by Duke Ellington, Billy Eckstine and
various other artists

Night and stars above that shine so bright,
The mystery of their fading light,
That shines upon our caravan.

Sleep upon my shoulder as we creep
Across the sands so I may keep,
This memory of our caravan.

This is so exciting
You are so inviting
Resting in my arms
As I thrill to the magic charms of you,

Beside me here beneath the blue
My dream of love is coming true
Within our desert caravan.

Careless Whisper

Words and Music by George Michael and
Andrew Ridgeley

recorded by Wham!

I feel so unsure
As I take your hand,
And lead you to the dance floor.
As the music dies
Something in your eyes
Calls to mind a silver screen,
And you're its sad goodbye.

Refrain:
I'm never gonna dance again,
Guilty feet have got no rhythm.
Though it's easy to pretend,
I know you're not a fool
I should have known better than to cheat a friend.
And waste a chance that I've been given,
So I'm never gonna dance again,
The way I dance with you.

Time can never mend
The careless whisper of a good friend.
To the heart and mind,
Ignorance is kind,
There's no comfort in the truth,
Pain is all you'll find

Refrain

Tonight the music seems so loud,
I wish that we could lose this crowd.
Maybe it's better this way.
If we'd hurt each other with the things we want to say,
We could have been so good together.
We could have lived this dance forever.
But now who's gonna dance with me?
Please dance.

Carolina in My Mind

Words and Music by James Taylor

recorded by James Taylor

Refrain:
In my mind I'm gone to Carolina.
Can't you see the sunshine?
And can't you just feel the moonshine?
And ain't it just like a friend of mine to hit me from behind?
And I'm gone to Carolina in my mind.

Karin she's a silver sun,
You'd best walk her away and watch it shine.
Watch her watch the morning come.
A silver tear appearing
Now I'm crying, ain't I?
I'm gone to Carolina in my mind.

There ain't no doubt in no one's mind
That love's the finest thing around.
Whisper something soft and kind.
And hey, babe, the sky's on fire,
I'm dying, ain't I?
I'm gone to Carolina in my mind.

Refrain

Dark and silent late last night,
I think I might have heard the highway call.
Geese in flight and dogs that bite.
And signs that might be omens say I'm going, going.
I'm gone to Carolina in my mind.

Now with a holy host of others standing 'round me no,
Still I'm on the dark side of the moon.
And it seems like it goes on like this forever,
You must forgive me.
If it's up in...

Refrain Twice

Carry On Wayward Son
Words and Music by Kerry Livgren

recorded by Kansas

Carry on my wayward son;
There'll be peace when you are done.
Lay your weary head to rest;
Don't you cry no more.

Once I rose above the noise and confusion
Just to get a glimpse beyond this illusion.
I was soaring ever higher,
But I flew too high.

Though my eyes could see, I still was a blind man.
Though my mind could think, I still was a mad man.
I hear voices when I'm dreaming.
I can hear them say:

Refrain:
Carry on my wayward son;
There'll be peace when you are done.
Lay your weary head to rest;
Don't you cry no more.

Masquerading as a man with a reason,
My charade is the event of the season.
And if I claim to be a wise man,
It surely means that I don't know.

On a stormy sea of moving emotion,
Tossed about, I'm like a ship on the ocean.
I set a course for winds of fortune,
But I hear the voices say:

Refrain

Carry on; you will always remember.
Carry on; nothing equals the splendor.
Now your life's no longer empty;
Surely heaven waits for you.

Repeat Refrain ad lib.

Catch a Wave
Words and Music by Brian Wilson and Mike Love

recorded by The Beach Boys

Throw me a favor, try the greatest sport around.
Everybody tries it once.
Those who don't just have to put it down.
You paddle out, turn around and raise,
And baby, that's all there is to the coastline craze.
You gotta catch a wave and you're sittin' on top of the world.

Not just a fad 'cause it's been going on so long.
All the surfers going strong.
They said it wouldn't last too long.
They'll eat their words with a fork and spoon,
And watch 'em, they'll hit the road and all be surfin' soon.
And when they catch a wave they'll be sittin' on
   top of the world.

So take a lesson from a top notch surfer boy.
Every Saturday, boy,
But don't you treat it like a toy.
Just get away from the shady turf,
And baby, go catch some rays on the sunny surf.
And when you catch a wave you'll be sittin' on
   top of the world.

Celebrate
Words and Music by Alan Gordon and Garry Bonner

recorded by Three Dog Night

Slippin' away, sittin' on a pillow,
Waitin' for night to fall.
A girl and a dream sittin' on a pillow,
This is the night to go to the celebrity ball.

Satin and lace, isn't it a pity,
Didn't find time to call.
Ready or not, gonna make it to the city,
This is the night to go to the celebrity ball.

Dress up tonight,
Why be lonely?
You'll stay late and you'll be alone,
So why be lonely?

Refrain:
Sittin' alone, sittin' on a pillow,
Waitin' to climb the walls.
Maybe tonight, depending how your dream goes,
She'll open your eyes when she goes to the celebrity ball.

Repeat Refrain

Celebrate, celebrate, dance to the music!
Celebrate, celebrate, dance to the music!

Centerfold
Written by Seth Justman

recorded by J. Geils Band

Does she walk? Does she talk?
Does she come complete?
My homeroom, homeroom angel,
Always pulled me from my seat.

She was pure like snowflakes;
No one could ever stain the memory of my angel,
Could never cause me pain.
The years go by,
I'm lookin' through a girlie magazine,
And there's my homeroom angel
On the pages in between.

Refrain:
My blood runs cold;
My memory has just been sold.
My angel is the centerfold.
Angel is the centerfold.
My blood runs cold;
My memory has just been sold.
Angel in the centerfold.

Slipped me notes under the desk
While I was thinkin' about her dress.
I was shy, I turned away
Before she caught my eye.
I was shakin' in my shoes
Whenever she flashed those baby blues.
Something had a hold on me,
When angel passed close by.
Those soft fuzzy sweaters too magical to touch!
To see her in that negligee is really just too much!

Refrain

It's okay, I understand,
This ain't no never, never land.
I hope that when this issue's gone,
I'll see you when your clothes are on.
Take your car, yes we will,
We'll take your car and drive it.
We'll take it to a motel room and take 'em off in private.
A part of me had been ripped,
The pages from my mind are stripped,
Ay no! I can't deny it.
Oh yeah, I guess I gotta buy it.

Refrain

Na na na na...

Chains
Words and Music by Gerry Goffin and Carole King

recorded by The Cookies; The Beatles

Chains, my baby's got me locked up in chains,
And they ain't the kind that you can see.
Wo, these chains of love got a hold on me, yeah.

Chains, well I can't break away from these chains.
Can't run around, 'cause I'm not free.
Wo, these chains of love won't let me be, yeah.

Chains, my baby's got me locked up in chains,
And they ain't the kind that you can see.

Wo, these chains of love got a hold on me, yeah.
I wanna tell you, pretty baby, I think you're fine.
I'd like to love you, but darling I'm imprisoned by these:

Chains, my baby's got me locked up in chains,
And they ain't the kind that you can see.
Wo, these chains of love got a hold on me, yeah.
Please believe me when I tell you, your lips are sweet.
I'd like to kiss them, but I can't break away from all of these:

Chains, my baby's got me locked up in chains,
And they ain't the kind that you can see.
Wo, these chains of love got a hold on me, yeah.
Chains, chains of love.

Change Partners
Words and Music by Irving Berlin

from the RKO Radio Motion Picture *Carefree*
recorded by Fred Astaire and various other artists

Must you dance every dance
With the same fortunate man?
You have danced with him since the music began.
Won't you change partners and dance with me?

Must you dance quite so close
With your lips touching his face?
Can't you see I'm longing to be in his place?
Won't you change partners and dance with me?

Ask him to sit this one out,
And while you're alone
I'll tell the waiter to tell him
He's wanted on the telephone.

You've been locked in his arms
Ever since heaven knows when.
Won't you change partners, and then
You may never want to change partners again.

Change the World
Words and Music by Wayne Kirkpatrick, Gordon Kennedy
and Tommy Sims

featured on the Motion Picture Soundtrack *Phenomenon*
recorded by Wynonna; Eric Clapton

If I can reach the stars, pull one down for you,
Shine it on my heart so you could see the truth.
Then this love I have inside is everything it seems,
But for now I find it's only in my dreams
That I can change the world.
I will be the sunlight in your universe.

You would think my love was really something good,
Baby, if I could
Change the world.

If I could be king, even for a day,
I'd take you as my queen, I'd have it no other way.
And our love will rule in this kingdom we have made.
'Til then I'd be a fool wishing for the day
That I could change the world.

I would be the sunlight in your universe.
You would think my love was really something good,
Baby, if I could
Change the world.

Baby, if I could
Change the world.

I could change the world.
I would be the sunlight in your universe.
You would think my love was really something good,
Baby, if I could,
Change the world,
Baby, if I could
Change the world,
Baby if I could
Change the world.

Chantilly Lace
Words and Music by J.P. Richardson
Copyright © 1958 by Fort Knox Music Inc., Trio Music Company, Inc. and Glad Music Co.
Copyright Renewed

recorded by Big Bopper

Chantilly lace
And a pretty face
And a pony tail
Hangin' down,
Wiggle in her walk
And a giggle in her talk,
Makes the world go 'round.

Ain't nothin' in this world
Like a big-eyed girl
To make me act so funny,
Make me spend my money,
Make me feel real loose
Like a long-necked goose,
Like a girl.

Spoken:
Oh, baby,
That's-a what I like.

Cheek to Cheek
Words and Music by Irving Berlin
© Copyright 1935 by Irving Berlin
Copyright Renewed

from the RKO Radio Motion Picture *Top Hat*
a standard recorded by Fred Astaire
and various other artists

Heaven, I'm in heaven.
And my heart beats so that I can hardly speak.
And I seem to find the happiness I seek
When we're out together dancing cheek to cheek.

Heaven, I'm in heaven.
And the cares that hung around me through the week
Seem to vanish like a gambler's lucky streak
When we're out together dancing cheek to cheek.

Oh, I love to climb a mountain,
And to reach the highest peak.
But it doesn't thrill me half as much
As dancing cheek to cheek.

Oh I love to go out fishing
In a river or a creek
But I don't enjoy it half as much
As dancing cheek to cheek.

Dance with me.
I want my arm about you.
The charm about you
Will carry me thru to

Heaven, I'm in heaven.
And my heart beats so that I can hardly speak.
And I seem to find the happiness I seek
When we're out together
Dancing cheek to cheek.

Cherish
Words and Music by Terry Kirkman
© 1965, 1966 (Renewed 1993, 1994) BEECHWOOD MUSIC CORP.

recorded by The Association

Cherish is the word I use to describe
All the feeling that I have hiding here for you inside.
You don't know how many times
I've wished that I had told you.
You don't know how many times
I've wished that I could hold you.
You don't know how many times
I've wished that I could mold you into someone
Who could cherish me as much as I cherish you.

Perish is the word that more than applies
To the hope in my heart each time I realize
That I am not gonna be the one
To share your dreams.
That I am not gonna be the one

To share your schemes.
That I am not gonna be the one
To share what seems to be the life
That you could cherish as I do yours.

Oh, I'm beginning to think
That man has never found
The words that could make you want me.
That have the right amount of letters,
Just the right sound,
That could make you hear, make you see
That you are driving me out of my mind.

Oh, I could say I need you,
But then you'd realize
That I want you,
Just like a thousand other guys
Who'd say they loved you
With all the rest of their lies.
When all they wanted was to touch your face, your hands
And gaze into your eyes.

Repeat Verse 1

And I do
Cherish you.
And I do
Cherish you.
Cherish is the word.

Child of Mine
Words and Music by Carole King and Gerry Goffin
© 1970 (Renewed 1998) SCREEN GEMS-EMI MUSIC INC.

recorded by Carole King

Although you see the world
Different from me,
Sometimes I can touch upon
The wonders that you see.
All the new colors
And pictures you've designed.

Refrain:
Oh, yes sweet darling,
So glad you are a child of mine,
Child of mine,
Child of mine,
Oh, yes sweet darling,
So glad you are a child of mine.

You don't need directions,
You know which way to go
And I don't want to hold you back,
I just want to watch you grow.
You're the one who taught me
You don't have to look behind.

Refrain

Nobody's gonna kill your dreams
Or tell you how to live your life.
There'll always be people to make it hard for a while
But you'll change their heads when they see you smile.

The times you were born in
May not have been the best,
But you can make the times to come
Better than the rest,
I know you will be honest
If you can't always be kind,

Refrain Twice

Circle of Life
Music by Elton John
Lyrics by Tim Rice
© 1994 Wonderland Music Company, Inc.

from Walt Disney Pictures' *The Lion King*
recorded by Elton John

From the day we arrive on the planet
And blinking, step into the sun,
There's more to be seen than can ever be seen,
More to do than can ever be done.

Some say, "Eat or be eaten."
Some say "Live and let live."
But all are agreed
As they join the stampede,
You should never take more than you give
In the circle of life.

It's the wheel of fortune.
It's the leap of faith.
It's the band of hope
'Till we find our place
On the path unwinding
In the circle of life.

Some of us fall by the wayside,
And some of us soar to the stars.
And some of us sail through our troubles,
And some have to live with the scars.
There's far too much to take in here,
More to find than can ever be found.
But the sun rolling high
Through the sapphire sky
Keeps great and small on the endless round
In the circle of life.

Refrain Twice

On the path unwinding
In the circle,
The circle of life.

Climb Ev'ry Mountain

Lyrics by Oscar Hammerstein II
Music by Richard Rodgers

from the musical *The Sound of Music*

Climb every mountain,
Search high and low,
Follow every byway,
Every path you know.

Climb every mountain,
Ford every stream,
Follow every rainbow,
Till you find your dream!
A dream that will need all the love you can give,
Every day of your life for as long as you live.

Climb every mountain,
Ford every stream,
Follow every rainbow
Till you find your dream!

Close as Pages in a Book

Words by Dorothy Fields
Music by Sigmund Romberg

from the musical *Up in Central Park*
recorded by Benny Goodman and various artists

We'll be close as pages in a book, my love and I.
So close we can share a single look, share every sigh.
So close that before I hear your laugh, my laugh
 breaks through;
And when a tear starts to appear,
My eyes grow misty too.

Our dreams won't come tumbling to the ground.
We'll hold them fast.
Darling, as the strongest book is bound,
We're bound to last.
Your life is my life and while life beats away in my heart,
We'll be as close as pages in a book.

(They Long to Be) Close to You

Lyric by Hal David
Music by Burt Bacharach

recorded by The Carpenters

Why do birds
Suddenly appear
Every time
You are near?
Just like me
They long to be
Close to you.

Why do stars
Fall down from the sky
Every time
You walk by?
Just like me
They long to be
Close to you.

On the day that you were born
The angels got together
And decided to create a dream come true.
So they sprinkled moon-dust in your hair
And gold and starlight in your eyes of blue.

That is why
All the boys (girls) in town
Follow you all around.
Just like me
They long to be
Close to you.

Just like me
They long to be
Close to you.

The Closer I Get to You

Words and Music by James Mtume and Reggie Lucas

recorded by Roberta Flack & Donny Hathaway

The closer I get to you,
The more you make me see;
By giving me all you've got,
Your love has captured me.
Over and over again,
I try to tell myself that we could never be more
 than friends;
And all the while inside I knew it was real,
The way you make me feel.

Repeat Song and Fade

The Closer You Get

Words and Music by James Pennington and Mark Gray

recorded by Alabama

Refrain:
The closer you get, the further I fall,
I'll be over the edge now in no time at all.
I'm falling faster and faster and faster with no time to stall.
The closer you get, the further I fall.

The things that you say to me,
The look on your face,
Brings out the man in me.
Do I see a trace in your eyes of love?

Refrain

Could I be dreaming?
Is this really real?
'Cause there's something magic
The way I feel in your arms tonight.

Refrain

Keep fallin', oh, yeah, yeah.
Keep fallin',
Mm, fallin', oh, yeah, yeah,
I'm fallin'.

A Cockeyed Optimist

Lyrics by Oscar Hammerstein II
Music by Richard Rodgers

from the musical *South Pacific*

When the sky is a bright canary yellow
I forget every cloud I've ever seen—
So they call me a cockeyed optimist,
Immature and incurably green!

I have heard people rant and rave and bellow
That we're done and we might as well be dead—
But I'm only a cockeyed optimist,
And I can't get it into my head.

I hear the human race
If falling on its face
And hasn't very far to go.
But every whippoorwill
Is selling me a bill
And telling me it just ain't so.

I could say life is more that just a bowl of jello
And appear more intelligent and smart,
But I'm stuck, like a dope,
With a thing called hope,
And I can't get it out of my heart!
Not this heart!

Cocktails for Two

Words and Music by Arthur Johnston and Sam Coslow

from the Paramount Picture *Murder at the Vanities*
recorded by Spike Jones and various other artists

In some secluded rendezvous that overlooks the avenue
With someone sharing a delightful chat,
Of this and that and cocktails for two.
As we enjoy a cigarette,
To some exquisite chansonette
Two hands are sure to slyly meet
Beneath a serviette, with cocktails for two.

My head may go reelin',
But my heart will be obedient
With intoxicating kisses
For the principal ingredient;
Most any afternoon at five
We'll be so glad we're both alive
Then maybe fortune will complete her plan,
That all began with cocktails for two.

The Coffee Song (They've Got an Awful Lot of Coffee in Brazil)

Words and Music by Bob Hilliard and Dick Miles

recorded by Frank Sinatra

'Way down among Brazilians
Coffee beans grow by the billions,
So they've got to find those extra cups to fill.
They've got an awful lot of coffee in Brazil.
You can't get cherry soda
'Cause they've got to sell their quota,
And the way things are I guess they never will.
They've got a zillion tons of coffee in Brazil.

No tea or tomato juice, you'll see no potato juice.
'Cause the planters down in Santos all say No! No! No!
A politician's daughter was accused of drinking water
And he was fined a great fifty dollar bill.
They've got an awful lot of coffee in Brazil.

Colors of the Wind

Music by Alan Menken
Lyrics by Stephen Schwartz

from Walt Disney's *Pocahontas*

You think you own whatever land you land on,
The earth is just a dead thing you can claim;
But I know every rock and tree and creature
Has a life, has a spirit, has name.

You think the only people who are people
Are the people who look and think like you,
But if you walk in the footsteps of a stranger
You'll learn things you never knew.

Have you ever heard the wolf cry to the corn moon
Or asked the grinning bobcat why he grinned?
Can you sing with all the voices of the mountain?
Can you paint with all the colors of the wind?
Can you paint with all the colors of the wind?

Come run the hidden pine trails of the forest,
Come taste the sun-sweet berries of the earth,
Come roll in all the riches all around you,
And for once never wonder what they're worth.

The rainstorm and the river are my brothers,

The heron and the otter are my friends,
And we are all connected to each other,
In a circle in a hoop that never ends.

Have you ever heard the wolf cry to the blue corn moon
Or let the eagle tell you where he's been?
Can you sing with all the voices of the mountain?
Can you paint with all the colors of the wind?
Can you paint with all the colors of the wind?

How high does the sycamore grow?
If you cut it down then you'll never know.
And you'll never hear the wolf cry to the blue corn moon.
For whether we are white or copper–skinned,
We need to sing with all voices of the mountain,
We need to paint with all the colors of the wind.
You can own the earth and still all you'll own is earth until
You can paint with all the colors of the wind.

The Colour of My Love
Words and Music by David Foster and Arthur Janov

from the musical *Scream*
recorded by Celine Dion

I'll paint my mood in shades of blue,
Paint my soul to be with you.
I'll sketch your lips in shaded tones,
Draw your mouth to my own.

I'll draw your arms around my waist
Then all doubt I shall erase.
I'll paint the rain that softly lands
On your windblown hair.

I'll trace a hand to wipe your tears,
A look to calm your fears,
A silhouette of dark and light
While we hold each other, oh, so tight.

I'll paint a sun to warm your heart,
Swearing that we'll never part.
That's the colour of my love.

I'll paint the truth, show how I feel,
Try to make you completely real.
I'll use a brush so light and fine
To draw you close and make you mine.

I'll paint a sun to warm your heart,
Swearing that we'll never, ever part.
That's the colour of my love.
I'll draw the years all passing by,

So much to learn, so much to try.
And with this ring our lives will start,
Swearing that we'll never part.
I offer what you cannot buy,
Devoted love until we die.

Come Rain or Come Shine
Words by Johnny Mercer
Music by Harold Arlen

from the musical *St. Louis Woman*
a standard recorded by various artists

I'm gonna love you like nobody's loved you,
Come rain or come shine.
High as the mountain and deep as the river,
Come rain or come shine.
I guess when you met me
It was just one of those things,
But don't ever bet me
'Cause I'm gonna be true if you let me.

You're gonna love me like nobody's loved me,
Come rain or come shine.
Happy together, unhappy together and won't it be fine.
Days may be cloudy or sunny.
We're in or we're out of the money,
But I'm with you always
I'm with you rain or shine.

Come Saturday Morning
(Saturday Morning)
Words by Dory Previn
Music by Fred Karlin

from the Paramount Picture *The Sterile Cuckoo*
recorded by The Sandpipers

Come Saturday morning,
I'm going away with my friend.
We'll Saturday spend till the end of the day.
Just I and my friend,
We'll travel for miles in our Saturday smiles.
And then we'll move on.
But we will remember,
Long after Saturday's gone.

Come Sunday
By Duke Ellington

from the suite *Black, Brown & Beige*

Refrain:
Lord, dear Lord above,
God Almighty, God of love,
Please look down and see my people through.

I believe that God put sun and moon up in the sky.
I don't mind the gray skies
'Cause they're just clouds passing by.

Refrain

Heaven is a goodness time.
A brighter light on high.

Spoken:
Do unto others as you would have them do unto you,"
And have a brighter by and by.

Refrain

I believe God is now, was then and always will be.
With God's blessing we can make it through eternity.

Refrain

Come Together
Words and Music by John Lennon and Paul McCartney

recorded by The Beatles

Here come old flat top.
He come grooving up slowly.
He got joo joo eyeball.
He one holy roller.
He got hair down to his knee.
Got to be a joker he just do what you please.

He wear no shoe shine.
He got toe jam football.
He got monkey finger.
He shoot Coca-Cola.
He say I know you, you know me.
One thing I can tell you is you got to be free.
Come together right now over me.

He bag production.
He got walrus gumboot.
He got Ono sideboard.
He one spinal cracker.
He got feet down below his knee.
Hold you in his armchair you can feel his disease.
Come together right now over me.

He roller coaster.
He got early warning.
He got Muddy Water.
He one Mojo filter.
He say. "One and one and one is three."
Got to be good looking 'cause he so hard to see.
Come together right now over me.
Come together.

Comedy Tonight
Words and Music by Stephen Sondheim

from the musical *A Funny Thing Happened on the Way to the Forum*

Something familiar, something peculiar,
Something for everyone, a comedy tonight!
Something appealing, something appalling.
Something for everyone, a comedy tonight!

Nothing with kings, nothing with crowns.
Bring on the lovers, liars and clowns!
Old situations, new complications,
Nothing portentous or polite;
Tragedy tomorrow, comedy tonight!

Something convulsive, something repulsive,
Something for everyone, a comedy tonight!
Something esthetic, something frenetic,
Something for everyone, a comedy tonight.

Nothing of Gods, nothing of Fate.
Weighty affairs will just have to wait.
Nothing that's formal, nothing that's normal,
No recitations to recite!
Open up the curtain, comedy tonight.

Consider Yourself
Words and Music by Lionel Bart

from the Columbia Pictures - Romulus Motion Picture Production of Lionel Bart's *Oliver!*
  (originally a stage musical)

Consider yourself at home.
Consider yourself one of the family.
We've taken to you so strong,
It's clear we're going to get along.

Consider yourself well in.
Consider yourself part of the furniture.
There isn't a lot to spare.
Who cares, whatever we've got we share.

If it should chance to be we should see some harder days,
Empty larder days, why grouse?
Always a chance to meet somebody to foot the bill,
Then drinks are on the house.

Consider yourself our mate.
We don't want to have no fuss.
For after some consideration we can state,
Consider yourself one of us.

Copacabana (At the Copa)

Music by Barry Manilow
Lyric by Bruce Sussman and Jack Feldman

recorded by Barry Manilow

Her name was Lola;
She was a show girl,
With yellow feathers in her hair
And a dress cut down to there.
She would Merengue,
And do the Cha-Cha,
And while she tried to be a star,
Tony always tended bar
Across the crowded floor
They workled from eight to four.
They were young and they had each other,
Who could ask for more?

At the Copa, Copacabana,
The hottest spot north of Havana.
At the Copa, Copacabana,
Music and passion were always the fashion,
At the Copa
They fell in love,

His name was Rico;
He wore a diamond,
He was escorted to his chair,
He saw Lola dancing there.
And when she finished,
He called her over.
But Rico went a bit too far,
Tony sailed across the bar.
And then the punches flew
And chairs were smashed in two.
There was blood and a single gunshot,
But just who shot who?

At the Copa, Copacabana,
The hottest spot north of Havana.
At the Copa, Copacabana
Music and passion were always the fashion.
At the Copa
She lost her love.

(Copa, Copacabana,
Like in Havana, have a banana,
Music and passion, always in fashion)

Her name is Lola;
She was a show girl,
But that was thirty years ago,
When they used to have a show.
Now it's a disco, but not for Lola.
Still in the dress she used to wear,
Faded feathers in her hair,

She sits there so refined
And drinks herself half blind.
She lost her youth and she lost her Tony,
Now she's lost her mind!

At the Copa, Copacabana,
The hottest spot north of Havana.
At the Copa, Copacabana,
Music and passion were always the fashion,
At the Copa
Don't fall in love.

Could I Have This Dance

Words and Music by Wayland Holyfield and Bob House

from the film *Urban Cowboy*
recorded by Anne Murray

I'll always remember
The song they were playing
The first time we danced and I knew.

And we swayed to the music
And held to each other,
I fell in love with you.

Refrain:
Could I have this dance for the rest of my life?
Would you be my partner every night?
When we're together it feels so right.
Could I have this dance for the rest of my life?

I'll always remember
That magic moment,
When I held you close to me.
As we moved together,
I knew forever you're all I'll ever need.
You're all I'll ever need.

Refrain

Could It Be Magic

Words and Music by Barry Manilow and
Adrienne Anderson

recorded by Barry Manilow

Spirit move me, every time I'm near you,
Whirling like a cyclone in my mind.
Sweet Melissa, angel of my lifetime,
Answer to all answers I can find;
Baby I love you.

Refrain:
Come, come, come into my arms.
Let me know the wonder of all of you.
Baby, I want you.
Now, now, now and hold on fast.
Could this be the magic at last?

Lady take me high upon a hillside,
High up where the stallion meets the sun.
I could love you; building my world around you,
Never leave you till my life is done;
Baby, I love you.

Refrain

Could it be magic?
Come, come, come into my arms.
Let me know the wonder of all of you.

Count Your Blessings Instead of Sheep
Words and Music by Irving Berlin

from the Motion Picture *Irving Berlin's White Christmas*
recorded by Bing Crosby

When I'm worried and I can't sleep,
I count my blessings instead of sheep.
And I fall asleep
Counting my blessings.

When my bankroll is getting small,
I think of when I had none at all.
And I fall asleep counting my blessings.
I think about a nursery
And I picture curly heads.
And one by one I count them,
As they slumber in their beds.

If you're worried and you can't sleep,
Just count your blessings instead of sheep.
And you'll fall asleep
Counting your blessings.

Crazy
Words and Music by Willie Nelson

recorded by Patsy Cline

Crazy, I'm crazy for feelin' so lonely.
I'm crazy, crazy for feelin' so blue.
I knew you'd love me as long as you wanted,
And then someday you'd leave me for somebody new.

Worry? Why do I let myself worry,
Wonderin' what in the world did I do?

Oh, crazy for thinkin' that my love could hold you.
I'm crazy for tryin' and crazy for cryin'
And I'm crazy for lovin' you!

Crazy Little Thing Called Love
Words and Music by Freddie Mercury

recorded by Queen; Dwight Yoakam

Verse 1:
This thing called love, I just can't handle it.
This thing, called love,
I must get 'round to it, I ain't ready.
Crazy little thing called love.

Verse 2:
A-this thing, (This thing.)
Called love, (Called love.)
It cries (Like a baby.) in a cradle all night.
It swings, (Oo.) it jives, (Oo.)
Shakes all over like a jelly fish,
I kinda like it.
Crazy little thing called love.

There goes my baby, she knows how to rock 'n' roll.
She drives me crazy, she gives me hot 'n' cold fever,
She leaves me in a cool, cool sweat.

Verse 3:
I've gotta be cool, relax,
Get hip, get on my tracks,
Take a back-seat, hitch-hike,
Take a long rise on my motor bike until I'm ready.
Crazy little thing called love.

Repeat Verse 3

A-this thing, called love,
I just can't handle it.
This thing, called love
I must get 'round to it,
I ain't ready.
Crazy little thing called love

Repeat and Fade:
Crazy little thing called love.

Cry Me a River
Words and Music by Arthur Hamilton

recorded by Julie London and various other artists

Now you say you're lonely,
You cry the long night through,
Well, you can cry me a river,
Cry me a river.
I cried over you.

Now you say you're sorry
For bein' so untrue,
Well, you can cry me a river,
Cry me a river.
I cried a river over you.

You drove me,
Nearly drove me out of my head,
While you never shed a tear.
Remember?
I remember all that you said;
Told me love was too plebeian,
Told me you were thru with me, an'

Now you say you love me,
Well, just to prove you do,
Come on an' cry me a river,
Cry me a river.
I cried a river over you.

Cry Myself to Sleep
Words and Music by Paul Kennerly

recorded by The Judds

I've tried so hard, you know I can't do more.
It's the turn of the card, it's the close of the door.
The lies you told, you know they hurt so deep.
So I'll go home and cry myself to sleep.

And day after day you've been treating me bad.
Friends come up and say "Why do you take all that?"
'Cause it's making me moan and it's making me weep.
So I'll go home and cry myself to sleep.

You play at love like a child playing games.
One day I'm in, then I'm out again.
You change the rules and I just can't win.
You've broken me now so I give in, yeah, yeah.

I've been through worse but I don't know what.
Oh, I gave to you every thing that I got.
So take this heart or what's left to keep.
And I'll go home and cry myself to sleep.
So I'll go home and cry myself to sleep.
Cry myself to sleep.

Crying
Words and Music by Roy Orbison and Joe Melson

recorded by Roy Orbison; Don McLean

I was alright for a while
I could smile for a while
But I saw you last night,
You held my hand real tight
As you stopped to say "hello."
Oh, you wished me well,
You couldn't tell,
That I'd been crying over you.
Crying over you.
When you said, "So long"
Left me standing all alone,
Alone and crying,
Crying, crying, crying.
It's hard to understand,
But the touch of your hand
Can start me crying.

I thought that I was over you,
But it's true, so true;
I love you even more than I did before.
But darling, what can I do?
For you don't love me
And I'll always be
Crying over you,
Crying over you.
Yes, now you're gone,
And from this moment on,
I'll be crying
Crying, crying, crying.
It's hard to understand,
But the touch of your hand
Can start me crying,
Yeah, crying, crying over you.

The Crying Game

Words and Music by Geoff Stephens

recorded by Brenda Lee; Boy George
featured in the film *The Crying Game*

Refrain:
I know all there is to know about the crying game.
I've had my share of the crying game.
First, there are kisses, then there are sighs,
And then before you know where you are,
You're saying goodbye.

One day soon,
I'm gonna tell the moon about the crying game.
And if he knows maybe he'll explain,
Why there are heartaches,
Why there are tears,
And how to stop feeling blue
When love disappears.

Refrain

Don't want no more of the crying game.
I don't want no more if the crying game.
Oh!

Cycles

Words and Music by Gayle Caldwell

recorded by Frank Sinatra

So I'm down, and so, I'm out,
But, so are many others.
So, I feel like tryin'
To hide my head 'neath these covers.

Life is like the seasons,
After Winter comes the Spring.
So, I'll keep this smile awhile,
And see what tomorrow brings.

I've been told, and I believe
That life is meant for livin'.
Even when my chips are low,
There's still some left for givin'.

I've been many places;
Maybe not as far as you.
So, I think I'll stay awhile,
And see if some dreams come true.

There isn't much that I have learned
Thru all my foolish years;
Except that life keeps runnin' in cycles;
First there's laughter: Then, there's tears.

But I'll keep my head up high,
Although I'm kind-a tired.
My gal (man) just up and left last week:
Friday, I got fired.

You know it's almost funny,
But, things can't get worse than now.
So, I'll keep on tryin' to sing,
But please, just don't ask me how.

Danny Boy (Londonderry Air)
Words by Frederick Edward Weatherly
Traditional Irish Folk Melody
Copyright © 2001 by HAL LEONARD CORPORATION

recorded by various artists

Oh Danny boy, the pipes, the pipes are calling,
From glen to glen, and down the mountain side.
The summer's gone, and all the roses falling.
It's you it's you must go and I must bide.

But come ye back when summer's in the meadow,
Or when the valley's hushed and white with snow.
'Tis I'll be there in sunshine or in shadow,
Oh, Danny boy, Oh, Danny boy, I love you so.

But if ye come, when all the flowers are dying,
And I am dead, as dead I well may be,
Ye'll come and find the place where I am lying,
And kneel and say an "Ave" there for me;

And I shall hear, tho' soft you tread above me,
And all my dreams will warm and sweeter be.
If you will bend to tell me that you love me,
Then I shall sleep in peace until you come to me!

Day by Day
Words and Music by Sammy Cahn, Axel Stordahl and
Paul Weston
Copyright © 1945 (Renewed 1972, 1973) by Famous Music Corporation and Hanover Music Corp.

Theme from the Paramount Television Series *Day by Day*
a standard recorded by Frank Sinatra, Jo Stafford,
Doris Day and various artists

Day by day,
I'm falling more in love with you,
And day by day
My love seems to grow.
There isn't any end to my devotion,
It's deeper, dear, by far, than any ocean.
I find that day by day
You're making all my dreams come true,
Do come what may,
I want you to know,
I'm yours alone,
And I'm in love to stay,
As we go through the years,
Day by day.

A Day in the Life
Words and Music by John Lennon and Paul McCartney
Copyright © 1967 Sony/ATV Songs LLC
Copyright Renewed
All Rights Administered by Sony/ATV Music Publishing, 8 Music Square West,
   Nashville, TN 37203

recorded by The Beatles

I read the news today, oh boy,
About a lucky man who made the grade.
And though the news was rather sad
Well, I just had to laugh.
I saw the photograph

He blew his mind out in a car
He didn't notice that the lights had changed.
A crowd of people stood and stared,
They'd seen his face before.
Nobody was really sure,
If he was from the House of Lords.

I saw a film today, oh boy,
The English Army had just won the war.
A crowd of people turned away,
But I just had to look,
Having read the book.
I'd love to turn you on.

Woke up, got out of bed
Dragged a comb across my head.
Found my way downstairs and drank a cup
And looking up I noticed I was late.

Found my coat and grabbed my hat,
Made the bus in seconds flat.
Found my way upstairs and had a smoke,
And somebody spoke and I went into a dream.

I heard the news today, oh boy,
Four thousand holes in Blackburn, Lancashire
And though the holes were rather small,
They had to count them all.
Now they know how man holes it takes
To fill the Albert Hall.
I'd love to turn you on.

A Day in the Life of a Fool (Manha de Carnival)
Words by Carl Sigman
Music by Luiz Bonfa
Copyright © 1966 by Les Nouvelles Editions Meridian
Copyright Renewed
All Rights Administered by Chappell & Co.

from the film *Black Orpheus*
recorded by Jack Jones and various other artists

A day in the life of a fool,
A sad and a long, lonely day.
I walk in the avenue
And hope I'll run into
The welcome sight of you on my way.

I stop just across from your door
But you're never home anymore.
So back in my room
And there in the gloom
I cry tears of goodbye.
'Til you come back to me,
That's the way it will be
Every day in the life of a fool.

Day Tripper

Words and Music by John Lennon and Paul McCartney

recorded by The Beatles

Got a good reason for taking the easy way out.
Got a good reason for taking the easy way out, now.
She was a day tripper,
One way ticket, yeah,
It took me so long to find out, and I found out.

She's a big teaser, she took me half the way there.
She's a big teaser, she took me half the way there, now.
She was a day tripper,
One way ticket, yeah,
It took me so long to find out, and I found out.

Tried to please her, she only played one night stands,
Tried to please her, she only played one night stands, now,
She was a day tripper,
Sunday driver, yeah,
It took me so long to find out, and I found out.
Day tripper, yeah.

Daydream

Words and Music by John Sebastian

recorded by The Lovin' Spoonful

What a day for a daydream,
What a day for a daydreamin' boy.
And I'm lost in a daydream,
Dreamin' 'bout my bundle of joy.
And even if time ain't really on my side,
It's one of those days for taking a walk outside.
I'm blowing the day to take a walk in the sun,
And fall on my face on somebody's new mown lawn.

I've been having a sweet dream,
I've been dreamin' since I woke up today.
It's starring me and my sweet dream,
'Cause she's the one makes me feel this way.

And even if time is passing by a lot,
I couldn't care less about the dues you say I got.
Tomorrow I'll pay the dues for dropping my load,
And fall on my face on somebody's sleepy bull-toad.

And you be sure that if you're feelin' right,
A daydream will last till long into the night.
Tomorrow at breakfast you may prick up your ears,
Or you may be daydreamin' for a thousand years.

What a day for a daydream,
Custom made for a daydreamin' boy.
And I'm lost in a daydream,
Dreamin' 'bout my bundle of joy.

Daydream Believer

Words and Music by John Stewart

recorded by The Monkees

Oh, I could hide 'neath the wings
Of the bluebird as she sings;
The six o'clock alarm would never ring.
But it rings and I rise,
Wipe the sleep out of my eyes.
My shaving razor's cold and it stings.

Refrain:
Cheer up, sleepy Jean.
Oh, what can it mean,
To a daydream believer
And a homecoming queen?

You once thought of me
As a white knight on his steed.
Now you know how happy you can be.
Oh, and our good times start and end
Without dollar one to spend,
But how much, baby, do we really need?

Refrain Twice

Dedicated to the One I Love

Words and Music by Lowman Pauling and Ralph Bass

recorded by The Shirelles; The Mamas and The Papas

While I'm far away from you, my baby,
I know it's hard for you, my baby,
Because it's hard for me, my baby.
And the darkest hour is just before dawn.
Each night before you go to bed, my baby,
Whisper a little prayer for me, my baby.
And then tell all the stars above.
This is dedicated to the one I love.

Life can never be exactly like I want it to be,
I could be satisfied knowing you love me.
There's one thing I want you to do especially for me,
And it's something that everybody needs.

While I'm far away from you, my baby,
Whisper a little prayer for me, my baby.
Because it's hard for me, my baby.
And the darkest hour is just before dawn.
There's one thing I want you to do especially for me,
And it's something everybody needs.

Each night before you go to bed, my baby,
Whisper a little prayer for me, my baby.
And then tell all the stars above.
This is dedicated to the one I love.

Repeat and Fade:
Dedicated to the one I love.
Dedicated to the one I love.

Deep in the Heart of Texas
Words by June Hershey
Music by Don Swander

recorded by Alvino Rey and various other artists

The stars at night are big and bright,
Deep in the heart of Texas.
The prairie sky is wide and high,
Deep in the heart of Texas.
The sage in bloom is like perfume,
Deep in the heart of Texas.
Reminds me of the one I love,
Deep in the heart of Texas.

The coyotes wail along the trail.
Deep in the heart of Texas.
The rabbits rush around the brush,
Deep in the heart of Texas.
The cowboys cry, "Ki-yip-pee-yi,"
Deep in the heart of Texas.
The doggies bawl, and bawl and bawl,
Deep in the heart of Texas.

Déjà Vu
Lyrics by Adrienne Anderson
Music by Isaac Hayes

recorded by Dionne Warwick

This is insane;
All you did was say hello, speak my name.
Feeling your love, like a love I used to know, long ago.
How can it be?
You're a different space and time, come to me.
Feeling I'm home, in a place I used to know, long ago.

Refrain:
Déjà vu,
Could you be the dream that I once knew?
Is it you?
Déjà vu, Could you be the dream that might come true?
Shining through?

This is divine;
I've been waiting all my life, filling time.
Looking for you, nights were more than you could know,
  long ago.

Come to me now;
We don't have to dream of love, we know how.
Somewhere before it's as if I love you so long ago.

Refrain

I keep remembering me, I keep remembering you,
Déjà vu.

Repeat Refrain and Fade

Devil in Her Heart
Words and Music by Richard B. Drapkin

recorded by The Beatles

Refrain:
She's got the devil in her heart,
But her eyes, they tantalize.
She's gonna tear your heart apart,
Oh, her lips, they really thrill me.
I'll take my chances
For romance is
So important to me.
She'll never hurt me,
She won't desert me,
She's an angel sent to me.
She's got the devil in her heart,
No, no, this I can't believe.
She's gonna tear your heart apart,
No, no, nay will she deceive.

I can't believe that she'll ever, ever go,
Not when she hugs me and says she loves me so.
She'll never hurt me,
She won't desert me,
Listen, can't you see?

Refrain

Don't take chances
If your romance is
So important to you.
She'll never hurt me,
She won't desert me,
She's an angel; sent to me.

She's got the devil in her heart,
No, no, no, this I can't believe.
She's gonna tear your heart apart,
No, no, no nay will she deceive.

Twice:
She's got the devil in her heart,
But she's an angel sent to me.

Diamonds Are a Girl's Best Friend

Words by Leo Robin
Music by Jule Styne
Copyright © 1949 (Renewed) by Music Sales Corporation (ASCAP)

from the musical *Gentlemen Prefer Blondes*
recorded by Carol Channing

A kiss on the hand may be quite continental,
But diamonds are a girl's best friend.
A kiss may be grand but it won't pay the rental
On your humble flat,
Or help you at the Automat.
Men grow cold as girls grow old
And we all lose our charms in the end.
But square cut or pear-shape,
These rocks don't lose their shape,
Diamonds are a girl's best friend.

There may come a time when a lass needs a lawyer,
But diamonds are a girl's best friend.
There may come a time when a hard-boiled employer
Thinks you're awful nice,
But get that "ice" or else no dice.
He's your guy when stocks are high,
But beware when they start to descend.
It's then that those louses go back to their spouses,
Diamonds are a girl's best friend.

Diary

Words and Music by David Gates
© 1972 (Renewed 2000) COLGEMS-EMI MUSIC INC.

recorded by Bread

I found her diary underneath the tree
And started reading about me.
The words she'd written took me by surprise.
You'd never read them in her eyes.
They said that she had found the love she's waited for.
Wouldn't you know it.
She wouldn't show it.

Then she confronted with the writing there,
Simply pretending not to care.
I passed it off as just in keeping with
Her total disconcerting air.
And tho' she tried to hide
The love that she denied.
Wouldn't you know it,
She wouldn't show it.

And as I go thru my life
I will give to her my wife,
All the sweet things I can find.

I found her diary underneath a tree
And started reading about me.
The words began to stick, then tears to fall.
Her meaning now was clear to see.

The love she's waited for
Was someone else, not me.
Wouldn't you know it,
She wouldn't show it.

And as I go through my life
I will wish for her, his wife,
All the sweet things she can find,
All the sweet things she can find.

Different Drum

Words and Music by Michael Nesmith
© 1965 (Renewed 1993) SCREEN GEMS-EMI MUSIC INC.

recorded by the Stone Poneys featuring Linda Ronstadt

You and I travel to the beat of a different drum.
Oh, can't you tell by the way I run,
Every time you make eyes at me?
Woh, oh, you cry and you moan and say it will work out,
But, honey child, I've got my doubts.
You can't see the forest for the trees.

Verse:
Oh, don't get me wrong, it's not that I'm knockin',
It's just that I'm not in the market for a girl
Who wants to love only me.
Yes, and I ain't sayin' you ain't pretty,
All I'm sayin's I'm not ready for any person,
Place or thing to try and pull the reins in on me.
So goodbye, I'll be leavin'
I see no sense in the cryin' and grievin',
We'll both live a lot longer if you live without me.

Repeat Verse

Different Worlds

Words by Norman Gimbel
Music by Charles Fox
Copyright © 1979 by Bruin Music Company

Theme from the Paramount Television Series *Angie*
recorded by Maureen McGovern

Refrain:
Let the time flow, let the love grow.
Let the rain shower, let the rose flower.
Love, it seeks; and love, it finds
Love it conquers; love it binds.

We come to each other from different worlds;
Drawn to each other by the love inside of us.
We give to each other our different worlds.
Long as we can do it,
Life, we're gonna breeze right through it.

Refrain

Do I Love You Because You're Beautiful?

Lyrics by Oscar Hammerstein II
Music by Richard Rodgers

from the musical *Cinderella*

Do I love you
Because you're beautiful,
Or are you beautiful
Because I love you?
Am I making believe I see you,
A girl too lovely to
Be really true?
Do I want you because you're wonderful?
Or are you wonderful
Because I want you?
Are you the sweet invention of a lover's dream?
Or are you really as beautiful as you seem?

Do Nothin' till You Hear from Me

Words and Music by Duke Ellington and Bob Russell

a standard recorded by Duke Ellington, Stan Kenton,
Woody Herman and various other artists

Do nothin' till you hear from me.
Pay no attention to what's said.
Why people tear the seam of anyone's dream
Is over my head.

Do nothin' till you hear from me.
At least consider our romance.
If you should take the word of others you've heard,
I haven't a chance.

True I've been seen
With someone new.
But does that mean
That I'm untrue?

When we're apart,
The words in my heart
Reveal how I feel about you.

Some kiss may cloud my memory
And other arms may hold a thrill.
But please do nothin' till you hear it from me
And you never will.

Do-Re-Mi

Lyrics by Oscar Hammerstein II
Music by Richard Rodgers

from the musical *The Sound of Music*

Let's start at the very beginning,
A very good place to start.
When you read you begin with—
A, B, C.
When you sing you begin with do re mi.

Do re mi?
Do re mi.
The first three notes just happen to be
Do Re Mi.
Doe—a deer, a female deer,
Ray—a drop of golden sun,
Me—a name I call myself,
Far—a long, long way to run,
Sew—a needle pulling thread,
La—a note to follow sew,
Tea—a drink with jam and bread.
That will bring us back to do!

Do re mi fa so la ti do.

Do You Believe in Magic

Words and Music by John Sebastian

recorded by The Lovin' Spoonful

Do you believe in magic, in a young girl's heart,
How music can free her whenever it starts.
And it's magic if the music is groovy,
It makes you feel happy like an old-time movie.
I'll tell you 'bout the magic and a-free your soul,
But it's like tryin' to tell a stranger 'bout rock and roll.

If you believe in magic don't bother to choose,
If it's jug band music or rhythm and blues.
Just go and listen, it'll start with a smile
That won't wipe off your face no matter how hard you try.
Your feet will start tappin' and you can't seem to find,
How you got there so just blow your mind.

If you believe in magic come along with me,
We'll dance until morning 'til there's just you and me.
And maybe, if the music is right
I'll meet you tomorrow sort of late at night.
And we'll go dancin' baby then you'll see,
How the magic's in the music and music's in me.
Yeah!

Repeat and Fade:
Do you believe like I believe?
Do you believe like I believe?

Do You Know the Way to San Jose

Lyric by Hal David
Music by Burt Bacharach

recorded by Dionne Warwick

Do you know the way to San Jose?
I've been away so long.
I may go wrong and lose my way.
Do you know the way to San Jose?
I'm going back to find some peace of mind in San Jose.

L.A. is a great big freeway.
Put a hundred down and buy a car.
In a week maybe two, they'll make you a star.
Weeks turn into years.
How quick they pass,
And all the stars that never were
Are parking cars and pumping gas.

You can really breathe in San Jose.
They've got a lot of space.
There'll be a place where I can stay.
I was born and raised in San Jose.
I'm going back to find some peace of mind in San Jose.

Fame and fortune is a magnet.
It can pull you far away from home.
With a dream in your heart you're never alone.
Dreams turn into dust and blow away,
And there you are without a friend.
You pack your car and ride away.
I've got lots of friends in San Jose.

Repeat and Fade:
Do you know the way to San Jose?
Can't wait to get back to San Jose.

Do You Know What It Means to Miss New Orleans

Lyric by Eddie De Lange
Music by Louis Alter

from the movie *New Orleans*
recorded by Louis Armstrong, Billie Holiday and various
other artists

Do you know what it means to miss New Orleans
And miss it each night and day?
I know I'm not wrong, the feelin's gettin' stronger
The longer I stay away.

Miss the moss covered vines, the tall sugar pines
Where mockin' birds used to sing.
And I'd like to see the lazy Mississippi
A-hurryin' into spring.

The moonlight on the bayou,
A Creole tune that fills the air;
I dream about magnolias in June
And soon I'm wishin' that I was there.

Do you know what it means to miss New Orleans
When that's where you left your heart?
And there's something more:
I miss the one I care for more than I miss New Orleans.

Do You Know Where You're Going To?

Words by Gerry Goffin
Music by Mike Masser

Theme from the film *Mahogany*
recorded by Diana Ross

Refrain:
Do you know
Where you're going to?
Do you like the things that life is showing you?
Where are you going to?
Do you know?

Do you get
What you're hoping for?
When you look behind you there's no open door.
What are you hoping for,
Do you know?

Once we were standing still in time,
Chasing the fantasies that filled our minds.
And you knew
How I loved you but my spirit was free,
Laughing at the questions that you once asked of me.

Refrain

No looking back at all we planned,
We let so many dreams just slip through our hands.
Why must we wait so long before we see
How sad the answers to those questions can be?

Refrain

(Sittin' On) The Dock of the Bay

Words and Music by Steve Cropper and Otis Redding

recorded by Otis Redding

Sittin' in the morning sun,
I'll be sittin' when the evenin' come.
Watchin' the ships roll in,
Then I watch 'em roll away again.
Yeah, I'm sittin' on the dock of the bay,
Watchin' the tide roll away.
Ooh, I'm just sittin' on the dock of the bay,
Wastin' time.

I left my home in Georgia,
Headed for the Frisco bay.
I have nothin' to live for,
Look like nothin's gonna come my way.
So I'm just gonna sit on the dock of the bay,
Watchin' the tide roll away.
Ooh, I'm just sittin' on the dock of the bay,
Wastin' time.

Looks like nothin's gonna change;
Everything still remains the same.
I can't do what ten people tell me to do,
So I guess I'll remain the same.

Sittin' here restin' my bones,
And this loneliness won't leave me alone.
Two thousand miles I roam,
Just to make this dock my home.
Now I'm just gonna sit at the dock of the bay,
Watchin' the tide roll away.
Ooh, I'm just sittin' on the dock of the bay,
Wastin' time.

Don't Be Cruel (To a Heart That's True)

Words and Music by Otis Blackwell and Elvis Presley

recorded by Elvis Presley

Don't be cruel to a heart that's true.
Don't be cruel to a heart that's true.
I don't want no other love.
Baby, it's just you I'm thinking of.

You known I can be found
Sitting all alone.
If you can't come around,
At least please telephone.
Don't be cruel to a heart that's true.

Baby, if I made you mad
For something I might have said,
Please, let's forget the past
'Cause the future looks bright ahead.
Don't be cruel to a heart that's true.

I don't want no other love,
Baby, it's just you I'm thinking of.
Well don't stop thinkin' of me.
Don't make me feel this way.
Come on over here and love me.
You know I wanna say.
Don't be cruel to a heart that's true.

Why should we be apart?
I really, really love you,
Baby, cross my heart.
Let's walk up to the preacher
And let us say, "I do."
And then you'll know you have me,
And I'll know I have you too.

Don't be cruel to a heart that's true.
Why should we be apart?
I don't want no other love.
Baby, it's just you I'm thinking of.

Don't Cry Out Loud

Words and Music by Carole Bayer Sager and Peter Allen

recorded by Melissa Manchester

Baby cried the day the circus came to town,
'Cause she didn't like parades just passing by her.
So she painted on a smile and took up with some clown,
And she danced without a net up on the wire.
I know a lot about it 'cause you see,
Baby is an awful lot like me.

Refrain:
We don't cry out loud,
We just keep it inside,
Learn how to hide out feelings.
Fly high and proud.
And if you should fall,
Remember you almost had it all.

Baby cried the day they pulled the big top down,
They left behind her dreams among the litter.
And the different kind of love she thought she found,
Was nothing more than sawdust and some glitter.
But baby can't be broken 'cause you see,
She had the finest teacher, that's me.

I taught her don't cry out loud,
Just keep it inside,
Learn how to hide your feelings.
Fly high and proud.
And if you should fall,
Remember you almost had it all.

Refrain

Don't Fall in Love with a Dreamer

Words and Music by Kim Carnes and Dave Ellingson

recorded by Kenny Rogers with Kim Carnes

Just look at you sittin' there,
You never looked better than tonight.
And it'd be so easy to tell you I'd stay,
Like I've done so many times.

I was so sure this would be the night,
You'd close the door and wanna stay with me.
And it's be so easy to tell you I'd stay,
Like I've done so many times.

Don't fall in love with a dreamer,
'Cause he'll always take you in;
Just when you think you've really changed him,
He'll leave you again.

Don't fall in love with a dreamer,
'Cause he'll break you every time;
So, put out the light and just hold on,
Before we say goodbye.

Now it's morning and the phone rings,
And ya say you've gotta get your things together.
You just gotta leave before you change your mind.
And if you knew what I was thinkin', girl,
I'd turn around, if you'd ask me one more time.

Don't fall in love with a dreamer,
'Cause he'll always take you in.
Just when you think you've really changed him,
He'll leave you again.

Don't fall in love with a dreamer,
'Cause he'll break you every time;
So put out the light and just hold on,
Before we say goodbye,
Before we say goodbye, goodbye.

Don't Fear the Reaper

Words and Music by Donald Roeser

recorded by Blue Oyster Cult

All our times have come.
Here but now they're gone.
Season don't fear the reaper,
Nor do the wind, the sun or the rain.
We can be like they are.
Come on baby, don't fear the reaper.
Baby take my hand.
Don't fear the reaper.
We'll be able to fly.
Don't fear the reaper.
Baby, I'm your man.
La, la…

Valentine is done.
Here but now they're gone.
Romeo and Juliet are together in eternity.
Forty thousand men and women every day.
Forty thousand men and women every day.
Another forty thousand coming every day.
Come on, baby.
Baby, take my hand.
We'll be able to fly.
Baby, I'm your man.
La, la, la…

Love of two is one.
Here but now they're gone.
Came the last night of sadness,
And it was clear she couldn't go on.
And the door was open and the wind appeared.
The candles blew and then disappeared.
The curtains flew and then appeared.

Said don't be afraid.
Come on baby. And she had no fear.
And she ran to him.
They looked backward and said goodbye.
She had taken his hand.
Come on, baby.
Don't fear the reaper.

Don't Get Around Much Anymore

Words and Music by Duke Ellington and Bob Russell

a standard recorded by Duke Ellington and various other artists

Missed the Saturday dance.
Heard they crowded the floor.
Couldn't bear it without you,
Don't get around much anymore.

Thought I'd visit the club,
Got as far as the door.
They'd have asked me about you.
Don't get around much anymore.

Darling I guess
My mind's more at ease,
But never-the-less
Why stir up memories.

Been invited on dates
Might have gone what for,
Awfully different without you
Don't get around much anymore.

Don't Know Much

Words and Music by Barry Mann, Cynthia Weil
and Tom Snow

recorded by Linda Ronstadt & Aaron Neville

Look at this face,
I know the years are showing.
Look at this life,
I still don't know where it's going.

Refrain:
I don't know much,
But I know I love you,
And that may be
All I need to know.

Look at these eyes,
They've never seen what matters.
Look at these dreams,
So beaten and so battered.

Refrain

So many questions
Still left unanswered.
So much I've never broken through.
And when I feel you near me
Sometimes I see so clearly
The only truth I've ever known is me and you.

Look at this man,
So blessed with inspiration.
Look at this soul,
Still searching for salvation.

Refrain Twice

And that may be all there is to know.

Don't Let Me Be Lonely Tonight

Words and Music by James Taylor

recorded by James Taylor

Do me wrong, do me right.
Tell me lies but hold me tight.
Save your goodbyes for the mornin' light,
But don't let me be lonely tonight.

Say goodbye and say hello.
Sure 'nuf good to see you but it's time to go.
Don't say yes, but please don't say no,
I don't want to be lonely tonight.

Go away then damn ya,
Go on and do as you please, yeah,
You ain't gonna see me gettin' down on my knees.
I'm undecided and your heart's been divided,
You've been turnin' my world upside down.

Do me wrong, do me right, right now, baby.
Go on and tell me lies but hold me tight.
Save your goodbyes for the mornin' light,
But don't let me be lonely tonight.
I don't want to be lonely tonight no, no
I don't want to be lonely tonight.

Don't Let the Sun Go Down on Me

Words and Music by Elton John and Bernie Taupin

recorded by Elton John; George Michael

I can't light
No more of your darkness.
All my pictures
Seem to fade to black and white.
I'm growing tired
And time stands still before me.
Frozen here,
On the ladder of my life.
Too late
To save myself from falling.
I took a chance
And hanged your way of life.
But you misread

My meaning when I met you.
Closed the door
And left me blinded by the light.

Don't let the sun go down on me.
Although I search myself,
It's always someone else I see.
I'd just allow a fragment of you life
To wander free.
But losing everything,
Is like the sun going down on me.

I can't find
Oh the right romantic line.
But see me once
And see the way I feel.
Don't discard me
Just because you think I mean you harm.
But these cuts I have,
Oh, they need love
To help them heal.

Don't let the sun go down on me.
Although I search myself,
It's always someone else I see.
I'd just allow a fragment of your life
To wander free.
But losing everything
Is like the sun going down on me.

Don't Stand So Close to Me

Written and Composed by Sting

recorded by The Police

Young teacher, the subject of school girl fantasy.
She wants him so badly, knows what she wants to be.
Inside her there's longing.
The girl's an open page.
Books marking, she's so close now.
This girl is half his age.

Don't stand so, don't stand so close to me.

Her friends are so jealous: you know how bad girls get.
Sometimes it's not so easy to be the teacher's pet.
Temptation, frustration so bad it makes him cry.
Wet bus stop, she's waiting, his car is warm and dry.

Don't stand, don't stand so, don't stand so close to me.
Don't stand, don't stand so, don't stand so close to me.

Loose talk in the classroom, to hurt they try and try.
Strong words in the staff room, the accusations fly.
It's no use, he sees her. He starts to shake and cough
Just like the old man in that book by Nabokov.

Repeat and Fade:
Don't stand, don't stand so, don't stand so close to me.

Don't You Worry 'Bout a Thing

Words and Music by Stevie Wonder

recorded by Stevie Wonder

Everybody's got a thing,
But some don't know how to handle it.
Always reachin' out in vain,
Accepting the things not worth having.
But don't you worry 'bout a thing,
Don't you worry 'bout a thing, mama.
'Cause I'll be standin' on the side when you check it out.

They say your style of life's a drag,
And that you must go other places.
But just don't you feel too bad
When you get fooled by smiling faces.

But don't you worry 'bout a thing,
Don't you worry 'bout a thing, mama.
'Cause I'll be standin' on the side when you check it out,
When you get off your trip.
Don't you worry 'bout a thing.

Ba bum ba…

Don't you worry 'bout a thing,
Don't you worry 'bout a thing, mama.
'Cause I'll be standin' on the side when you check it out,
When you get off your trip.

Everybody needs a change,
A chance to check out the new.
But you're the only one to see
The changes you take yourself through.
But don't you worry 'bout a thing,
Don't you worry 'bout a thing, pretty mama.
'Cause I'll be standin' in the wings when you check it out.

Repeat and Fade:
Don't you worry 'bout a thing,
Don't you worry 'bout a thing.

Down in the Depths
(On the Ninetieth Floor)

Words and Music by Cole Porter

from the musical *Red, Hot and Blue!*
recorded by Ethel Merman

Manhattan—I'm up a tree,
The one I've most adored
Is bored
With me.
Manhattan, I'm awfully nice,
Nice people dine with me,
And even twice.
Yet the only one in the world I'm mad about

Talks of somebody else
And walks out.

With a million neon rainbows burning below me
And a million blazing taxis raising a roar,
Here I sit, above the town
In my pet pailletted gown.
Down in the depths on the ninetieth floor.
While the crowds at El Morocco punish the parquet,
And at "21" the couples clamor for more,
I'm deserted and depressed
In my regal eagle nest
Down in the depths on the ninetieth floor.
When the only one you wanted wants another
What's the use of swank and cash in the bank galore?
Why, even the janitor's wife
Has a perfectly good love life
And here am I
Facing tomorrow
Alone with my sorrows
Down in the depths on the ninetieth floor.

Dream a Little Dream of Me
Words by Gus Kahn
Music by Wilbur Schwandt and Fabian Andree
TRO - © Copyright 1930 (Renewed) and 1931 (Renewed) Essex Music, Inc.,
    Words and Music, Inc., New York, NY, Don Swan Publications, Miami, FL and
    Gilbert Keyes Music, Hollywood, CA

recorded by Frankie Laine, Mama Cass and various
other artists

Stars shining bright above you,
Night breezes seem to whisper, "I love you,"
Birds singing in the sycamore tree,
"Dream a little dream of me."

Say "Nightie-night" and kiss me,
Just hold me tight and tell me you'll miss me;
While I'm alone and blue as can be,
Dream a little dream of me.

Stars fading, but I linger on, dear,
Still craving your kiss;
I'm longing to linger till dawn, dear,
Just saying this:

Sweet dreams till sunbeams find you,
Sweet dreams that leave all worries behind you,
But in your dreams whatever they be,
Dream a little dream of me.

A Dream Is a Wish
Your Heart Makes
Words and Music by Mack David, Al Hoffman
and Jerry Livingston
© 1948 Walt Disney Music Company
Copyright Renewed

from Walt Disney's *Cinderella*

When I was a little girl, my father used to say,
If trouble ever troubles you,
Just dream your cares away.

A dream is a wish your heart makes
When you're fast asleep.
In dreams you will lose your heartaches;
Whatever you wish for you keep.
Have faith in your dreams and someday
Your rainbow will come smiling thru,
No matter how your heart is grieving,
If you keep on believing,
The dream that you wish will come true.

Dream On
Words and Music by Steven Tyler
Copyright © 1973 Daksel LLC
All Rights Administered by Sony/ATV Music Publishing, 8 Music Square West,
    Nashville, TN 37203

recorded by Aerosmith

Every time that I look in the mirror,
All these lines on my face gettin' clearer.
The past is gone; it went by like dusk to dawn.
Isn't that the way everybody's got their dues in life to pay?
I know nobody knows where it comes and where it goes.
I know it's everybody's sin;
You got to lose to know how to win.

Half my life's in books' written pages
Lived and learned from fools and from sages.
You know it's true,
All these things come back to you.
Sing with me, sing for the years,
Sing for the laughter 'n' sing for the tears.
Sing with me if it's just for today,
Maybe tomorrow the good Lord will take you away.

Twice:
Dream on, dream on, dream on,
Dream yourself a dream come true.

Dream on, dream on, dream on, dream on.
Dream on, dream on, dream on, ah.

Twice:
Sing with me, sing for the years,
Sing for the laughter 'n' sing for the tears.
Sing with me if it's just for today,
Maybe tomorrow the good Lord will take you away.

Dreams
Words and Music by Stevie Nicks
Copyright © 1977 Welsh Witch Music
All Rights Administered by Sony/ATV Music Publishing, 8 Music Square West,
    Nashville, TN 37203

recorded by Fleetwood Mac

Now, here you go again.
You say you want your freedom.
Well who am I to keep you down?
It's only right that you should play the way you feel it.
But listen carefully to the sound of your loneliness,
Like a heart-beat, drives you mad,
In the stillness of remembering what you had
And what you lost and what you had and what you lost.

Refrain:
Oh, thunder only happens when it's raining.
Players only love you when their playing.
Say, women, they will come and they will go.
When the rain washes you clean, you'll know.
You'll know.

Now, here I go again.
I see the crystal vision.
I keep my visions to myself.
It's only me who wants to wrap around your dreams.
And have you any dreams you'd like to sell.
Dreams of loneliness, like a heart-beat, drives you mad,
In the stillness of remembering what you had
And what you lost and what you had and what you lost.

Refrain

You will know.
Oh, you will know.

Drive My Car
Words and Music by John Lennon and Paul McCartney
Copyright © 1965 Sony/ATV Songs LLC
Copyright Renewed
All Rights Administered by Sony/ATV Music Publishing, 8 Music Square West,
   Nashville, TN 37203

recorded by The Beatles

Asked a girl what she wanted to be,
She said, baby can't you see?
I wanna be famous, a star of the screen,
But you can do something in between.

Refrain:
Baby, you can drive my car.
Yes I'm gonna be a star.
Baby you can drive my car and maybe I'll love you.

I told the girl that my prospects were good.
She said, baby, it's understood
Working for peanuts is all very fine,
But I can show you a better time.

Refrain

Beep beep mm, beep beep yeh!

Refrain

I told that girl I could start right away,
And she said, listen, babe, I've got something to say.
Got no car, and it's breaking my heart,
But I've found a driver and that's a start.

Refrain

Beep beep mm, beep beep yeh!

Duke of Earl
**Words and Music by Earl Edwards, Eugene Dixon and
Bernice Williams**
Copyright © 1961, 1968 (Renewed) by Conrad Music, a division of Arc Music Corp. (BMI)

recorded by Gene Chandler

Intro and Verse Underscore:
Duke Duke Duke Duke of Earl
Duke Duke Duke of Earl
Duke Duke Duke of Earl
Duke Duke Duke...

As I walk through this world,
Nothing can stop the Duke of Earl!
And you, you are my girl,
And no one can hurt you, oh no.

Refrain:
Yes I, oh, I'm gonna love you.
Oh, oh, come on, let me hold you, darlin'
'Cause I'm the Duke of Earl.
Yeah, yeah, yeah, yeah, yeah.
Oo oo, Oh, oh….

And when I hold you
You'll be my duchess,
Duchess of Earl!
We'll walk through my dukedom
And paradise we will share

Refrain

Repeat Intro

Dust in the Wind
Words and Music by Kerry Livgren
© 1977, 1978 EMI BLACKWOOD MUSIC INC. and DON KIRSHNER MUSIC
All Rights Controlled and Administered by EMI BLACKWOOD MUSIC INC.

recorded by Kansas

I close my eyes
Only for a moment, and the moment's gone.
All my dreams
Pass before my eyes, a curiosity.
Dust in the wind.
All they are is dust in the wind.

Same old song.
Just a drop of water in an endless sea.
All we do
Crumbles to the ground though we refuse to see.
Dust in the wind.
All we are is dust in the wind.

Don't hang on.
Nothing lasts forever but the earth and sky.
It slips away.
All your money won't another minute buy.
Dust in the wind.
All we are is dust in the wind.
All we are is dust in the wind.
Dust in the wind.
Everything is dust in the wind.
Everything is dust in the wind.

Early Autumn

Words by Johnny Mercer
Music by Ralph Burns and Woody Herman

recorded by Stan Getz, Jo Stafford, and various other
artists

When an early autumn walks the land and chills the breeze
And touches with her hand the summer trees,
Perhaps you'll understand what memories I own.
There's a dance pavilion in the rain all shuttered down.
A winding country lane all russet brown,
A frosty window pane shows me a town grown lonely.

That spring of ours started so April-hearted
Seemed made for a boy and girl.
I never dreamed, did you,
Any fall could come in view so early, early?
Darling, if you care please let me know,
I'll meet you anywhere I miss you so.
Let's never have to share another early autumn.

Earth Angel

Words and Music by Jesse Belvin

recorded by The Crew-Cuts, The Penguins

Earth angel, earth angel,
Will you be mine,
My darling, dear, love you all the time.
I'm just a fool, a fool in love with you.

Earth Angel, earth angel,
The one I adore, love you forever and evermore.
I'm just a fool, a fool in love with you.

I fell for you,
And I knew the vision of your love's loveliness,
I hope and I pray
That someday I'll be the vision of your happiness.

Earth angel, earth angel,
Please be mine, my darling dear, love you all the time.
I'm just a fool, a fool in love with you.

Easter Parade

Words and Music by Irving Berlin

from the musical revue *As Thousands Cheer*
featured in the Motion Picture Irving Berlin's
Easter Parade

Never saw you look quite so pretty before.
Never saw you dressed quite so lovely, what's more.
I could hardly wait
To keep our date
This lovely Easter morning.

And my heart beat fast
As I came through the door for:

In your Easter bonnet,
With all the frills upon it,
You'll be the grandest lady
In the Easter Parade.

I'll be all in clover
And when they look you over
I'll be the proudest fellow
In the Easter Parade.

On the Avenue,
Fifth Avenue,
The photographers
Will snap us.
And you'll find that you're
In the rotogravure.

Oh, I could write a sonnet
About your Easter bonnet
And of the girl I'm taking to the Easter Parade.

Easy

Words and Music by Lionel Richie

recorded by The Commodores

Know it sounds funny, but I just can't stand the pain;
Girl, I'm leaving you tomorrow.
Seems to me, girl, you know I've done all I can.
You see, I begged, stole, and I borrowed, yeah.

Refrain:
Ooh, that's why I'm easy.
I'm easy like Sunday morning.
That's why I'm easy.
I'm easy like Sunday morning.

Why in the world would anybody put chains on me?
I've paid my dues to make it.
Everybody wants me to be what they want me to be.
I'm not happy when I try to fake it, no.

Refrain

I wanna be high, so high.
I wanna be free to know the things I do are right.
I wanna be free, just me, oh, babe.

Repeat and Fade:
That's why I'm easy.
I'm easy like Sunday morning.
That's why I'm easy.
I'm easy like Sunday morning.

Ebony and Ivory

Words and Music by McCartney

recorded by Paul McCartney & Stevie Wonder

Refrain:
Ebony and ivory
Live together in perfect harmony,
Side by side on my piano keyboard,
Oh Lord, why don't we?

We all know that people are the same wherever you go.
There is good and bad in everyone,
We learn to live,
We learn to give each other what we need to survive,
Together alive.

Refrain

Ebony and ivory
Living together in perfect harmony.

Edelweiss

Lyrics by Oscar Hammerstein II
Music by Richard Rodgers

from the musical *The Sound of Music*

Edelweiss,
Edelweiss,
Every morning you greet me.
Small and white,
Clean and bright,
You look happy to meet me.

Blossom of snow,
May you bloom and grow,
Bloom and grow forever

Edelweiss,
Edelweiss,
Bless my homeland forever.

Eight Days a Week

Words and Music by John Lennon and Paul McCartney

recorded by The Beatles

Ooh I need your love babe, guess you know it's true,
Hope you need my love babe, just like I love you,
Hold me, love me,
Hold me, love me.
Ain't got nothin' but love babe,
Eight days a week.

Love you every day girl, always on my mind.
One thing I can say girl, love you all the time.
Hold me, love me,
Hold me love me.
Ain't got nothin' but love babe,
Eight days a week.

Eight days a week
I love you.
Eight days a week
Is not enough to show I care.

Ooh I need your love babe, guess you know it's true,
Hope you need my love babe, just like I love you,
Hold me, love me,
Hold me, love me.
Ain't got nothin' but love babe,
Eight days a week.

Eight days a week
I love you.
Eight days a week
Is not enough to show I care.

Love you every day girl, always on my mind.
One thing I can say girl, love you all the time.
Hold me, love me,
Hold me, love me.
Ain't got nothin' but love babe, eight days a week.

Eight days a week.
Eight days a week.

Eleanor Rigby

Words and Music by John Lennon and Paul McCartney

recorded by The Beatles

Ah, look at all the lonely people.
Ah, look at all the lonely people.

Eleanor Rigby,
Picks up the rice in the church where a wedding has been.
Lives in a dream.
Waits at the window,
Wearing a face that she keeps in a jar by the door.
Who is it for?

All the lovely people, where do they all come from?
All the lonely people, where do they all belong?

Father McKenzie,
Writing the words of a sermon that no-one will hear.
No-one comes near.
Look at him working,
Darning his socks in the night when there's nobody there.
What does he care?

All the lonely people, where do they all come from?
All the lonely people, where do they all belong?

Ah, look at all the lonely people.
All look at all the lonely people.

Eleanor Rigby
Died in the church and was buried along with her name.
Nobody came.
Father McKenzie,
Wiping the dirt from his hands as he walks from the grave.
No-one was saved.

All the lonely people, where do they all come from?
All the lonely people, where do they all belong?

Emotional Rescue
Words and Music by Mick Jagger and Keith Richards

recorded by The Rolling Stones

Is there nothing I can say, nothing I can do
To change your mind?
I'm so in love with you.
You're too deep in, you can't get out.
You're just a poor girl in a rich man's house.
Oo oo oo…

Spoken:
Yeah, baby, I'm crying over you.

Don't you know promises were never meant to keep?
Just like the night, they dissolve up in sleep.

Refrain:
I'll be your savior, steadfast and true.
I'll come to your emotional rescue.
I'll come to your emotional rescue.
Oo oo oo…

Yeah, the other night, cry, cry, yeah, I'm crying.
Yes, I'm cryin', babe,
I'm like a child, babe.
Like a child, yeah, I was crying,
Crying like a child,

You think you're one of a special breed.
You think that you're his pet Pekinese.

Refrain

I was dreaming last night,
Last night I was dreaming, how you'd be mine.
But I was crying like a child,
Yeah, I was crying, like a child.
You will be mine, mine, mine, mine, mine, all mine.
You could be mine, could be mine, mine all mine.

I come to you so silent in the night,
So stealthy, so animal quiet.

Refrain

Yeah, you should be mine, mine, oo.

Repeat and Fade:
You will be mine, you will be mine, all mine.

Emotions
Lyrics by Mariah Carey
Music by Mariah Carey, David Cole and Robert Clivilles

recorded by Mariah Carey

Refrain:
You've got me feeling emotions,
Deeper than I've ever dreamed of.
Woh, oh.
You've got me feeling emotions,
Higher than the heavens above.

I feel good, I feel nice.
I never felt so satisfied.
I'm in love, I'm alive.
Intoxicated, flying high.
It feels like a dream,
When you touch me tenderly.
I don't know if it's real,
But I like the way I feel inside.

Refrain

In the morning when I rise,
You are the first thing on my mind.
And in the middle of the night
I feel you heartbeat next to mine.
It feels like a dream
When you love me tenderly.
I don't know if you're for real
But I like the way I feel.

Refrain

You know the way to make me lose control.
When you're looking into my eyes
You make me feel so high!

Refrain, Repeat ad lib

Last time:
You've got me feeling higher.

End of the Road

Words and Music by Babyface, L.A. Reid and
Daryl Simmons

from the Paramount Motion Picture *Boomerang*
recorded by Boyz II Men

Spoken:
Girl, you know we belong together.
I don't have no time for you to be playin' with my heart
  like this.
You'll be mine forever, baby, you just see.

Sung:
We belong together
And you know that I'm right.
Why do you play with my heart?
Why do you play with my mind?
You said we'd be forever,
Said it's never die.

How could you love and leave me and never
Say goodbye?
Well, I can't sleep at night without holding you tight.
Girl, each time I try I just break down and cry.
Pain in my head, oh, I'd rather be dead,
Spinnin' around and around.

Refrain:
Although we've come
To the end of the road,
Still I can't let you go.
It's unnatural.
You belong to me,
I belong to you.
Come to the end of the road,
Still I can't let you go.
It's unnatural.
You belong to me,
I belong to you, oh.

Girl, I know you really love me,
You just don't realize.
You've never been there before,
It's only your first time.
Maybe I'll forgive you,
Maybe you'll try.
We should be happy together forever, you and I.
Could you love me again like you loved me before?
This time I want you to love me much more.
This time instead, just come to my bed
And, baby, just don't let me down.

Refrain

Refrain

Spoken:
Girl, I'm here for you.
All those times at night when you just hurt me,
And just ran out with that other fellow,
Baby, I knew about it.
I just don't understand how much I love you, do you?
I'm here for you.
I'm not out to go out there
And cheat all night just like you did, baby.
But that's alright, huh, I love you anyway.
And I'm still gonna be here for you
'Til my dyin' day baby.
Right now, I'm just in so much pain, baby.
'Cause you just won't come back to me, will you?
Just come back to me.

Yes, baby, my heart is lonely.
My heart hurts, baby, yes, I feel pain too.
Baby please…

Endless Love

Words and Music by Lionel Richie

from the film *Endless Love*
recorded by Diana Ross & Lionel Richie;
Mariah Carey & Luther Vandross

My love,
There's only you in my life,
The only thing that's right.
My first love,
You're every breath that I take,
You're every step I make.
And I,
I want to share all my love with you,
No one else
Will do.
And your eyes,
They tell me how much you care.
Oh yes,
You will always be
My endless love.

Two hearts,
Two hearts that beat as one,
Our lives have just begun.
Forever
I hold you close in my arms
I can't resist your charms.
And love,
I'd be a fool for you.
I'm sure you know
I don't mind,
'Cause you
You mean the world to me.
Oh I know
I found in you
My endless love.

The Entertainer

Words and Music by Billy Joel
© 1974, 1975 JOEL SONGS

recorded by Billy Joel

I am the entertainer and I know just where I stand,
Another serenader and another long-haired band.
Today I am your champion, I may have won your hearts,
But I know the game you'll forget my name,
And I won't be here in another year,
If I don't stay on the charts.

I am the entertainer and I've had to pay my price,
The things I did not know at first I learned by doing twice.
But still they come to haunt me, still they want their say,
So I've learned to dance with a hand in my pants
I let them rub my neck and I write 'em a check
And they go their merry way.

I am the entertainer, been all around the world,
I've played all kinds of palaces and laid all kinds of girls.
I can't remember faces, I don't remember names,
But what the hell, you know it's just as well
'Cause after a while and a thousand miles,
It all become the same.

I am the entertainer, I bring to you my songs,
I'd like to spend a day or two but I can't stay that long.
I got to meet expenses, I got to stay in line,
Got to get those fees to the agencies
And I'd love to stay but there's bills to pay
So I just don't have the time.

I am the entertainer, I've come to do my show,
You've heard my latest record, it's on the radio.
It took me years to write it,
They were the best years of my life,
If you're gonna have a hit you gotta make it fit
So they cut it down to 3:05.

I am the entertainer, the idol of my age,
I make all kinds of money when I go on the stage.
You see me in the papers, I've been in the magazines,
But if I go cold, I won't get sold,
I get put in the back in the discount rack
Like another can of beans.

I am the entertainer and I know just where I stand,
Another serenader and another long-haired band.
Today I am your champion, I may have won your hearts.
But I know the game, you'll forget my name,
I won't be here in another year
If I don't stay on the charts.

Eternal Flame

Words and Music by Billy Steinberg, Tom Kelly and
Susanna Hoffs

recorded by The Bangles

Close your eyes
Give me your hand, darling.
Do you feel my heart beating?
Do you understand?
Do you feel the same?
Am I only dreaming?
Is this burning an eternal flame?

I believe it's meant to be, darling.
I watch you when you are sleeping.
You are sleeping.
You belong to me.
Do you feel the same?
Am I only dreaming?
Is the burning an eternal flame?

Refrain:
Say my name,
Sun shines through the rain,
A whole life so lonely,
And then come and ease the pain.
I don't wanna lose this feeling, oh.

Repeat Refrain

Verse 1 Twice

Even Now

Lyric by Marty Panzer
Music by Barry Manilow

recorded by Barry Manilow

Even now when there's someone else who cares,
When there's someone home who's waiting just for me.
Even now I think about you as I'm climbing up the stairs,
And I wonder what to do so she won't see...

That even now I know it wasn't right,
And I've found a better life than what we had.
Even now I wake up crying in the middle of the night,
And I can't believe it still could hurt so bad.

Even now when I have come so far,
I wonder where you are,
I wonder why it's still so hard without you,
Even now when I come shining through,
I swear I think of you, and how much I wish you knew
Even now.

Even now when I never hear your name,
And the world has changed so much since you've been gone.
Even now I still remember and the feeling's still the same,
And the pain inside of me goes on and on.
Even now.

Repeat Verse 3

Every Breath You Take
Written and Composed by Sting

recorded by The Police

Every breath you take,
Every move you make,
Every bond you break,
Every step you take,
I'll be watching you.
Every single day,
Every word you say,
Every game you play,
Every night you stay,
I'll be watching you.

Refrain:
Oh, can't you see
You belong to me.
How my poor heart aches
With every step you take.
Every move you make
Every vow you break,
Every smile you fake
Every claim you stake.
I'll be watching you.

Since you've been gone I been lost without a trace,
I dream at night I can only see your face.
I look around but it's you I can't replace,
I feel so cold and I long for your embrace.
I keep crying baby, baby please.

Refrain

Every move you make
Every step you take,
I'll be watching you.
I'll be watching you.

Every Little Thing She Does Is Magic
Written and Composed by Sting

recorded by The Police

Though I've tried before to tell her
Of the feelings I have for her in my heart,
Every time that I come near her
I just lose my nerve as I've done from the start.

Refrain:
Every little thing she does is magic,
Everything she does just turns me on.
Even though my life before was tragic,
Now I know my love for her goes on.

Do I have to tell the story
Of a thousand rainy days since we first met.
It's a big enough umbrella
But it's always me that ends up getting wet.

Refrain

I resolved to call her up a thousand times a day
And ask her if she'll marry me in some old-fashioned way.
But my silent fears have gripped me
Long before I reach the phone,
Long before my time has tripped me,
Must I always be alone?

Repeat Refrain and Fade

Ev'ry Time We Say Goodbye
Words and Music by Cole Porter

from the musical *Seven Lively Arts*
a standard recorded by Benny Goodman, Anita O'Day
and various other artists

Ev'ry time we say goodbye
I die a little
Ev'ry time we say goodbye
I wonder why a little,
Why the gods above me
Who must be in the know
Think so little of me
They allow you to go

When you're near there's such an air
Of Spring about it,
I can hear a lark somewhere
Begin to sing about it,
There's no love song finer,
But how strange the change from major to minor
Ev'ry time we say goodbye.
Ev'ry single time
We say goodbye.

Everybody Has a Dream
Words and Music by Billy Joel
© 1971 (Renewed 1999), 1978 IMPULSIVE MUSIC

recorded by Billy Joel

While in these days of quiet desperation
As I wander through the world in which I love.
I search everywhere for some new inspiration
But it's more than cold reality can give.
If I need a cause for celebration,
Or a comfort I can use to ease my mind,
I rely on my imagination
And I dream of an imaginary time.

Refrain:
Whoa, now I know that everybody has a dream,
Everybody has a dream,
Everybody has a dream
This is my dream, my own,
Just to be at home and to be in love with you.

If I believe in all the words I'm saying,
And if a word from you can bring a better day,
Then all I have are these games that I've been playing
To keep my hope from crumbling away.
So let me lie and let me go on sleeping,
And I will lose myself in palaces of sand.
And all the fantasies I have been keeping
Will make the empty house easier to stand.

Refrain

Repeat Refrain and Fade

Ev'rybody's Somebody's Fool (Everybody's Somebody's Fool)
Words and Music by Jack Keller and Howard Greenfield
© 1960 (Renewed 1988) COLGEMS-EMI MUSIC INC. and
   CAREERS-BMG MUSIC PUBLISHING, INC.

recorded by Connie Francis

The tears I cried for you could fill and ocean,
But you don't know how many tears I cry;
And though you only lead me on and hurt me,
I couldn't bring myself to say goodbye.

Refrain:
'Cause ev'rybody's somebody's fool,
Ev'rybody's somebody's plaything,

And there are no exceptions to the rule.
Yes, everybody's somebody's fool.

I told myself it's best that I forget you,
Though I'm a fool at least I know the score;
But, darling, I'd be twice as blue without you.
It hurts, but I'd come running back for more.

Refrain

Some day you'll find someone to really care for,
And if her love should prove to be untrue;
You'll know how much this heart of mine is breaking,
You'll cry for her the way I cried for you. Yes…

Refrain

Ev'rybody's Talkin' (Echoes)
Words and Music by Fred Neil
Copyright © 1967 Coconut Grove Music (a division of Third Story Music, Inc.)
Copyright Renewed

from the film *Midnight Cowboy*
recorded by Harry Nilsson

Everybody's talkin' at me.
I don't hear a word they're sayin',
Only the echoes of my mind.
People stoppin' starin'.
I can't see the faces,
Only the shadows of their eyes.

I'm goin' where the sun keeps shinin'
Thru the pourin' rain.
Goin' where the weather suits my clothes.
Bankin' off the northeast wind.
Sailin' on a summer breeze.
Skippin' over the ocean like a stone.

Everybody's talkin' at me.
I don't hear a word they're sayin',
Only the echoes of my mind.
And I won't let you leave my love behind.

Repeat Last Line and Fade.

Everything Happens to Me
Words by Tom Adair
Music by Matt Dennis
Copyright © 1941 (Renewed) Dorsey Brothers Music,
   A Division of Music Sales Corporation (ASCAP)

a standard recorded by Frank Sinatra and various other
artists

I make a date for golf and you can bet your life it rains,
I try to give a party and the guy upstairs complains.
I guess I'll go through life just catchin' colds and
   missin' trains.
Everything happens to me.

106

I never miss a thing, I've had the measles and the mumps,
And every time I play an ace my partner always trumps.
I guess I'm just a fool who never looks before he jumps.
Everything happens to me.

At first my heart thought you could break this jinx for me,
That love would turn the trick to end despair.
But now I just can't fool this head that thinks for me.
I've mortgaged all my castles in the air.

I've telegraphed and phoned, I sent an
  "Air-mail Special" too,
Your answer was "Goodbye," and there was even
  postage due.
I fell in love just once and then it had to be with you.
Everything happens to me.

Everything I Own

Words and Music by David Gates

recorded by Bread

You sheltered me from harm,
Kept me warm, kept me warm.
You gave my life to me, set me free.

The finest years I ever knew
Were all the years I had with you.
And I would give anything I own,
Give up my life, my heart, my home.
I would give everything I own
Just to have you back again.

You taught me how to love,
What it's of what it's of.
You never said too much,
But still you showed the way,
And I knew from watching you.

Nobody else could ever know
The part of me that can't let go.
And I would give everything I own,
Give up my life, my heart, my home.
I would give everything I own
Just to have you back again.

Is there someone you know,
You're loving them so,
But taking them all for granted.
You may lose them one day,
Someone takes them away
And they don't hear the words you long to say.

And I would give everything
Give up my life, my heart, my home.
I would give everything I own
Just to have you back again.
Just to touch you once again.

Everything's Coming Up Roses

Words by Stephen Sondheim
Music by Jule Styne

from the musical *Gypsy*

I had a dream,
A dream about you, Baby!
It's gonna come true, Baby!
They think that we're through,
But Baby.

You'll be swell,
You'll be great,
Gonna have the whole world on a plate.
Starting here,
Starting now,
Honey, everything's coming up roses!

Clear the decks,
Clear the tracks,
You got nothing to do but relax,
Blow a kiss,
Take a bow,
Honey, everything's coming up roses!

Now's your inning,
Stand the world on its ear!
Set it spinning,
That'll be just the beginning!

Curtain up,
Light the lights,
You got nothing to hit but the heights!
You'll be swell,
You'll be great!
I can tell, just you wait!
That lucky star I talk about is due!
Honey, everything's coming up roses for me and for you!

You can do it,
All you need is a hand.
We can do it,
Momma is gonna see to it!

Curtain up!
Light the lights!
We got nothing to hit but the heights!
I can tell,
Wait and see,
There's the bell,
Follow me!
And nothing's gonna stop us till we're through!
Honey, everything's coming up roses and daffodils,
Everything's coming up sunshine and Santa Claus,
Everything's gonna be bright-lights and lollipops.
Everything's coming up roses for me and for you.

Everytime I Close My Eyes

Words and Music by Babyface

recorded by Babyface

Girl, it's been a long, long time comin',
But I know that it's been worth the wait.
Yeah.
It feels like springtime in winter.
It feels like Christmas in June.
It feels like heaven has opened up its gates
For me and you.

Refrain:
And every time I close my eyes,
I thank the Lord that I've got you
And you've got me too.
And every time I think of it,
I pinch myself 'cause I don't believe it's true
That someone like you loves me too.

Girl, I think that you're truly somethin',
And I, I know that it's been worth the wait.
With you, babe it never rains, and it's no wonder
The sun always shines when I'm near you.

It's just a blessing that I have found somebody like you.

Refrain

To think of all the nights I've cried myself to sleep.
You really ought to know how much you mean to me.
It's only right that you be in my life right here with me.
Oh, baby, baby, yeah.

Refrain

Everytime You Go Away

Words and Music by Daryl Hall

recorded by Paul Young

Hey, if we can't solve any problems,
Then why do we lose so many tears?
Oh, so you go again, when the leading man appears.
Always the same theme;
Can't you see we've got everything
Going on and on and on.

Refrain:
Every time you go away,
You take a piece of me with you.
Every time you go away,
You take a piece of me with you.

Go on and go free,
Maybe you're too close to see.
I can feel your body move,
Doesn't mean that much to me.
I can't go on singing the same theme;
'Cause can't you see we've got everything, baby,
Even though you know,

Refrain

I can't go on singing the same theme,
'Cause baby, can't you see
We got everything going on and on and on.

Refrain

Exactly Like You

Words by Dorothy Fields
Music by Jimmy McHugh

from the musical *International Revue*
featured in the musical *Sugar Babies*

I know why I've waited, know why I've been blue,
Prayed each night for someone exactly like you.
Why should we spend money on a show or two.
No one does those love scenes exactly like you.

You make me feel so grand.
I want to hand the world to you.
You seem to understand,
Each foolish little scheme I'm scheming,
Dream I'm dreaming.
Now I know why mother taught me to be true.
She meant me for someone exactly like you.

Exhale (Shoop Shoop)

Words and Music by Babyface

from the Original Soundtrack Album *Waiting to Exhale*
recorded by Whitney Houston

Verse 1:
Everyone falls in love sometimes.
Sometimes it's wrong
And sometimes it's right.
For every win
Someone must fail,
But there comes a point when,
When we exhale, yeah, yeah.

Refrain:
Say,
Shoop shoop shoop shoo be doo.
Shoop shoop shoop shoo be doo.
Shoop shoop shoop shoo be doo.
Shoop shoop shoop shoo be doo.
Shoop shoop shoop shoo be doo.
Shoop shoop shoop shoo be doo.
Shoop shoop shoop shoo be doo.

Verse 2:
Sometimes you'll laugh,
Sometimes you'll cry.
Life never tells us the whens or whys.
When you've got friends
To wish you well,
You'll find a point when
You will exhale, yeah, yeah.

Refrain

Hearts are often broken
When there are words unspoken.
In your soul there's answers to your prayers.
If you're searching for a place you know,
A familiar face, somewhere to go,
You should look inside your soul,
You're halfway there.

Repeat Verse 2

Repeat Refrain

Eye in the Sky

Words and Music by Alan Parsons and Eric Woolfson

recorded by The Alan Parsons Project

Don't think sorry's easily said.
Don't try turning tables instead.
You've taken lots of chances before,
But I ain't gonna give any more.
Don't ask me, that's how it goes;
'Cause part of me knows what you're thinking.

Don't say words you're gonna regret.
Don't let the fire rush to your head.
I've heard the accusation before,
And I ain't gonna take it anymore.
Believe me, the sun in your eyes
Made some of the lies worth believing.

Refrain:
I am the eye in the sky,
Looking at you; I can read your mind.
I am the maker of rules
Dealing with fools, I can cheat you blind.
And I don't need to see anymore
To know that I can read your mind.

Don't leave false illusions behind.
Don't cry 'cause I ain't changing my mind.
So find another fool like before,
'Cause I ain't gonna take it anymore.
Believing some of the lies
While all of the signs are deceiving.

Refrain

Repeat Refrain

Falling in Love Again (Can't Help It)

Words by Sammy Lerner
Music by Frederick Hollander

ffrom the Paramount Picture *The Blue Angel*
recorded by Marlene Dietrich

I'm much too sentimental,
My heart is never free;
Perhaps it's accidental
That love should come to me.
Some little thing within me
Protects me for awhile,
'Til someone comes to win me
With only a smile.

Falling in love again,
Never wanted to.
What am I to do?
Can't help it!
Love's always been my game,
Play it how I may,
I was made that way;
Can't help it!
Men cluster to me like moths around a flame;
And if their wings burn, I know I'm not to blame.
Falling in love again,
Never wanted to,
What am I to do?
Can't help it!

Falling in Love with Love

Words by Lorenz Hart
Music by Richard Rodgers

from the musical *The Boys from Syracuse*

I weave with brightly colored strings
To keep my mind off other things;
So, ladies, let your fingers dance,
And keep your hands out of romance.
Lovely witches,
Let the stitches
Keep your fingers under control.
Cut the thread, but leave
The whole heart whole.
Merry maids can sew and sleep;
Wives can only sew and weep!

Refrain:
Falling in love with love
Is falling for make-believe.
Falling in love with love
Is playing the fool.
Caring too much is such
A juvenile fancy.
Learning to trust is just
For children in school.
I fell in love with love
One night when the moon was full.
I was unwise, with eyes
Unable to see.
I fell in love with love,
With love everlasting,
But love fell out with me.

Fantasy

Lyrics by Mariah Carey, Tina Weymouth and Chris Frantz
Music by Mariah Carey, Dave Hall, Tina Weymouth,
Chris Frantz, Adrian Belew and Stephen Stanley

recorded by Mariah Carey

Shu du du du dit du dit du...

Oh, when you walk by every night
Talking sweet and looking fine,
I get kinda hectic inside.
Baby, I'm so into you.
Darling, if you only knew
All the things that flow through my mind.

Refrain:
But it's just a sweet, sweet fantasy, baby,
When I close my eyes you come and take me.
(On and on and on.)
It's so deep in my day dreams,
But it's just a sweet, sweet fantasy, baby.

Shu du du du dit du dit du...

Images of rapture
Creep into me slowly
As you're going to my head.
And my heart beats faster
When you take me over
Time and time again.

Refrain

Shu du du du dit du dit du...

Refrain

I'm in heaven with my boyfriend,
My laughing boyfriend.
There's no beginning and there is no end.
Feels like I'm dreaming, but I'm not sleeping.

Refrain

Fast Car
Words and Music by Tracy Chapman

recorded by Tracy Chapman

You got a fast car.
I want a ticket to anywhere.
Maybe we make a deal.
Maybe together we can get somewhere.
Anyplace is better.
Starting from zero got nothing to lose.
Maybe we'll make something.
Me, myself I've got nothing to prove.

You got a fast car.
I got a plan to get us out of here.
Been working at the convenience store.
Managed to save just a little bit of money.
Won't have to drive too far,
Just cross the border and into the city.
You and I can both get jobs and
Finally see what it means to be living.

See my old man's problem.
He live with the bottle, that's the way it is.
He says his body's too old for working.
His body's too young to look like his.
My mama went off and left him.
She wanted more from life than he could give.
I said somebody's got to take care of him.
So I quit school and that's what I did.

You got a fast car.
Is it fast enough so we could fly away?
We gotta make a decision,
Leave tonight or live and die this way.

Refrain:
I remember when we were driving,
Driving in your car,
Speed so fast I felt like I was drunk,
City lights lay out before us
And your arms felt nice wrapped 'round my shoulder,
And I had a feeling that I belonged.
I had a feeling I could be someone,
Be someone, be someone.

You got a fast car.
We go cruising, entertain ourselves.
You still ain't got a job
And I work in the market as a check-out girl.
I know things will get better.
You'll find work and I'll get promoted.
We'll move out of the shelter,
Buy a big house and live in the suburbs.

Refrain

You got a fast car.
I got a job that pays all our bills.
You stay out drinking late at the bar,
See more of your friends than you do of your kids.
I'd always hoped for better,
Thought maybe together you and me'd find it.
I got no plans, I ain't going nowhere;
So take your fast car and keep on driving.

Refrain

You got a fast car.
Is it fast enough so you could fly away?
You gotta make a decision,
Leave tonight or live and die this way.

Feelings (¿Dime?)
English Words and Music by Morris Albert and Louis Gaste
Spanish Words by Thomas Fundora

recorded by Morris Albert

Feelings,
Nothing more than feelings,
Trying to forget my
Feelings of love.

Teardrops
Rolling down on my face,
Trying to forget my
Feelings of love.

Feelings,
For all my life I'll feel it.
I wish I'd never met you, girl;
You'll never come again.

Feelings,
Wo wo wo feelings.
Wo wo wo feel you
Again in my arms.

Feelings,
Feelings like I've never lost you,
And feelings like I'll never have you
Again in my heart.

Feelings,
For all my life I'll feel it.
I wish I'd never met you, girl;
You'll never come again.

Feelings,
Feelings like I've never lost you,
And feelings like I'll never have you
Again in my life.

Feelings,
Wo wo wo feelings,
Wo wo wo feelings,
Again in my arms.

Fever
Words and Music by John Davenport and Eddie Cooley

recorded by Peggy Lee, and various other artists

Never know how much I love you,
Never know how much I care.
When you put your arms around me,
I get fever that's so hard to bear.

Refrain:
You give me fever
When you kiss me,
Fever when you hold me tight.
Fever in the morning,
Fever all through the night.

Sun lights up the daytime,
Moon lights up the night.
I light up when you call my name,
And you know I'm gonna treat you right.

Refrain

Everybody's got the fever
That is something you all know.
Fever isn't such a new thing,
Fever started long ago.

Romeo loved Juliet,
Juliet, she felt the same,
When he put his arms around her, he said,
"Julie, baby, you're my flame."

Thou givest fever, when we kisseth
Fever with thy flaming youth,
Fever—I'm afire
Fever, Yea, I burn forsooth.

Captain Smith and Pocahontas
Had a very mad affair,
When her Daddy tried to kill him, she said,
"Daddy-o, don't you dare."

Give me fever, with his kisses,
Fever when he holds me tight.
Fever—I'm his Missus
Oh Daddy won't you treat him right.

Now you've listened to my story
Here's the point that I have made:
Chicks were born to give you fever
Be it Fahrenheit or centigrade.

They give you fever when you kiss them,
Fever if you live and learn.
Fever—till you sizzle
What a lovely way to burn.

Fields of Gold
Written and Composed by Sting

recorded by Sting

You'll remember me
When the west wind moves
Upon the fields of barley.
You'll forget the sun
In his jealous sky
As we walk in fields of gold.

So she took her love
For to gaze awhile
Upon the fields of barley.
In his arms she fell
As her hair came down
Among the fields of gold.

Will you stay with me,
Will you be my love
Among the fields of barley?
We'll forget the sun
In his jealous sky
As we lie in fields of gold.

See the west wind move
Like a lover so
Upon the fields of barley.
Feel her body rise
When you kiss her mouth
Among the fields of gold.
I never made promises lightly
And there have been some that I've broken,
But I swear in the days still left
We'll walk in fields of gold.
We'll walk in fields of gold.

Many years have passed
Since those summer days
Among the fields of barley.
See the children run
As the sun goes down
Among the fields of gold.

You'll remember me
When the west wind moves
Upon the fields of barley.
You can tell the sun
In his jealous sky
When we walked in fields of gold.
When we walked in fields of gold.

Fire and Ice

Words and Music by Tom Kelly, Scott Sheets
and Pat Benatar

recorded by Pat Benatar

Ooo, you're givin' me the fever tonight,
I don't wanna give in,
I'd be playin' with fire.
You forget, I've seen you work before,
Take 'em straight to the top,
Leave 'em cryin' for more.
I've seen you burn 'em before.

Refrain:
Fire and ice,
You come on like a flame,
Then you turn a cold shoulder.
Fire and ice,
I wanna give you my love,
But you'll just take a little piece of my heart.

You'll just tear it apart.

Movin' in for the kill tonight,
You got every advantage
When they put out the lights.
It's not so pretty when it fades away,
'Cause it's just an illusion
In this passion play.
I've seen you burn 'em before.

Refrain

So you think you got it all figured out,
You're an expert in the field without a doubt.
But I know your methods inside and out
And I won't be taken in by fire and ice.

Refrain...

Fire and Rain

Words and Music by James Taylor

recorded by James Taylor

Just yesterday morning they let me know you were gone,
Susan the plans they made put an end to you.
I walked out this morning and I wrote down this song,
I just can't remember who to send it to.

Refrain:
I've seen fire and I've seen rain.
I've seen sunny days that I thought would never end.
I've seen lonely times when I could not find a friend,
But I always thought that I'd see you again.

Won't you look down upon me Jesus,
You've got to help me make a stand.
You've just got to see me through another day.
My body's aching and my time is at hand,
And I won't make it any other way.

Refrain

Now I'm walking my mind to an easy time,
My back turned toward the sun.
Lord knows when the cold wind blows
It'll turn your head around.
There's hours of time on the telephone lines,
To talk about things to come.
Sweet dreams and flying machines in pieces on the ground.

Refrain

Thought I'd see you one more time again,
There's just a few things coming my way this time around,
Thought I'd see you,
Thought I'd see you one more time.
Fire and rain now...

The First Time Ever I Saw Your Face

Words and Music by Ewan MacColl

recorded by Roberta Flack

The first time
Ever I saw your face,
I thought the sun
Rose in your eyes,
And the moon and the stars
Were the gifts you gave
To the dark
And the end of the skies.

The first time
Ever I kissed your mouth,
I felt the earth
Move in my hand,
Like the trembling heart
Of a captive bird
That was there
At my command,

The first time
Ever I lay with you
And felt your heart
So close to mine,
And I knew our joy
Would fill the earth
And last
Till the end of time,
My love.

The first time
Ever I saw
Your face.

The Flower That
Shattered the Stone
Words and Music by John Jarvis and Joe Henry

recorded by John Denver

The earth is our mother, just turning around,
With her trees in the forest and roots underground.
Our father above us whose sigh is the wind,
Paint us a rainbow without any end.

Refrain:
As the river runs freely, the mountain does rise.
Let me touch with my fingers and see with my eyes.
In the hearts of the children, a pure love still grows,
Like a bright star in heaven that lights our way home,
Like the flower that shattered the stone.

Sparrows find freedom beholding the sun.
In the infinite beauty we're all joined in one.
I reach out before me and look to the sky.
Did I hear someone whisper?
Did I hear something pass by?

Refrain

Like a bright star in heaven that lights our way home,
Like the flower that shattered the stone.

Fly Away
Words and Music by John Denver

recorded by John Denver

All of her days have gone soft and cloudy.
All of her dreams have gone dry.
All of her nights have gone sad and shady,
She's getting ready to fly.

Refrain 1:
Fly away.
Fly away.
Fly away.

Life in the city can make you crazy
For sounds of the sand and the sea.
Life in a highrise can make you hungry
For things that can't even see.

Refrain 1

Refrain 2:
In this whole world
There's nobody as lonely as she.
There's nowhere to go,
And there's nowhere that she'd rather be.

She's looking for lovers and children playing,
She's looking for signs of the spring.
She listens for laughter and sounds of dancing,
She listens for any old thing.

Refrain 1

Refrain 2

Repeat Verse 1

Fly Me to the Moon
(In Other Words)
Words and Music by Bart Howard

featured in the Motion Picture *Once Around*
a standard recorded by various artists

Fly me to the moon,
And let me play among the stars;
Let me see what spring
Is like on Jupiter and Mars.
In other words,
Hold my hand!
In other words
Darling, kiss me!

Fill my heart with song,
And let me sing forever more;
You are all I long for
All I worship and adore.
In other words,
Please be true.
In other words,
I love you!

The Fool on the Hill
Words and Music by John Lennon and Paul McCartney

recorded by The Beatles

Day after day, alone on a hill,
The man with the foolish grin is keeping perfectly still;
But nobody wants to to know him,
They can see that he's just a fool,
And he never gives an answer.
But the fool on the hill sees the sun going down,
And the eyes in his head see the world spinning round.

Well on the way, head in a cloud,
The man of a thousand voices talking perfectly loud;
But nobody ever hears him,
Or the sound he appears to make,
And he never seems to notice.
But the fool on the hill sees the sun going down
And the eyes in his head see the world spinning round.

And nobody seems to like him,
They can tell what he wants to do,
And he never shows his feelings.
But the fool on the hill sees the sun going down
And the eyes in his head see the world spinning round.

He never listens to them,
He knows that they're the fools.
They don't like him.
The fool on the hill sees the sun going down
And the eyes in his head see the world spinning round.

For All We Know
Words by Sam M. Lewis

a standard recorded by various artists

Sweetheart, the night is growing old,
Sweetheart, my love is still untold,
A kiss that is never tasted
Forever and ever is wasted.

Refrain:
For all we know we may never meet again,
Before you go make this moment sweet again.
We won't say goodnight until the last minute;
I'll hold out my hand and my heart will be in it.
For all we know this may only be a dream;
We come and go like a ripple on a stream.
So love me tonight, tomorrow was made for some,
Tomorrow may never come, for all we know.

Why should we waste a night like this?
Why should we waste a single kiss?
Why can't we laugh at tomorrow?
Tomorrow will pay what we borrow.

Refrain

For Once in My Life
Words by Ronald Miller
Music by Orlando Murden

recorded by Stevie Wonder

Goodbye, old friend,
This is the end
Of the man I used to be.
'Cause there's been a strange
And welcome change in me.

For once in my life I have someone who needs me,
Someone I've needed so long.
For once, unafraid I can go where life leads me
And somehow I know I'll be strong.
For once I can touch what my heart used to dream of
Long before I knew.
Someone warm like you
Would make my dream come true.
For once in my life
I won't let sorrow hurt me, not like it's hurt me before.
For once I have something I know won't desert me,
I'm not alone anymore.
For once I can say this is mine, you can't take it,
Long as I know I have love, I can make it.

First Ending:
For once in my life
I have someone who needs me.

Repeat Song

Second Ending:
For once I can feel
That somebody's heard my plea.
For once in my life
I have someone who needs me.

For the First Time

Words and Music by James Newton Howard,
Jud Friedman and Allan Rich

from the film One Fine Day
recorded by Kenny Loggins

Are those your eyes?
Is that your smile?
I've been looking at you forever,
Yet I never saw you before.
Are these your hands
Holding mine?
Now I wonder how
I could have been so blind.

Refrain:
And for the first time,
I am looking in your eyes.
For the first time,
I'm seeing who you are.
I can't believe how much I see
When you're looking back at me.
Now I understand what love is,
Love is
For the first time.

Can this be real?
Can this be true?
Am I the person I was this morning,
And are you the same you?
It's all so strange.
How can it be?
All along this love
Was right in front of me.

Refrain

Such a long time ago,
I had given up
On finding this emotion
Ever again
But you're here with me now.
Yes, I found you somehow,
And I've never been so sure.

Refrain:
And for the first time,
I am looking in your eyes.
For the first time,
I'm seeing who you are.
I can't believe how much I see
When you're looking back at me.
Now I understand what love is,
Love is
For the first time.

For the Good Times

Words and Music by Kris Kristofferson

recorded by Ray Price

Don't look so sad
I know it's over;
But life goes on
And this old world
Will keep on turning.
Let's just be glad
We had some time
To spend together.
There's no need
To watch the bridges
That we're burning.

Refrain:
Lay your head
Upon my pillow,
Hold your warm and tender body
Close to mine.
Hear the whisper of the raindrops
Blowing soft against the window
And make believe you love me
One more time
For the good times.

I'll get along;
You'll find another;
And I'll be here
If you should find
You ever need me.
Don't say a word
About tomorrow
Or forever.
There'll be time enough
For sadness
When you leave me.

Refrain

For You, for Me, for Evermore

Music and Lyrics by George Gershwin and Ira Gershwin

from the film *The Shocking Miss Pilgrim*

Paradise cannot refuse us;
Never such a happy pair.
Everybody must excuse us,
If we walk on air.
All the shadows now will lose us.
Lucky stars are everywhere.

As a happy being,
Here's what I'm foreseeing
For you, for me, for evermore.
It's bound to be for evermore.

It's plain to see,
We found, by finding each other,
The love we waited for.
I'm yours, you're mine and in our hearts
The happy ending starts.

What a lovely world this world will be
With a world of love in store
For you, for me, for evermore.

For Your Love
Words and Music by Graham Gouldman

recorded by The Yardbirds

For your love.
For your love.
For your love.
I'd give you everything and more and that's for sure.
(For your love.)
I'd give you diamond rings and things right to your door.
(For your love.)

Refrain:
To thrill you with delight,
I'd give you diamonds bright.
There'll be things that will excite,
To make you dream of me at night.
For your love,
For your love.

For your love.
For your love.
I'd give the moon if it were mine to give.
(For your love.)
I'd give that star and the sun above 'fore I live.
(For your love.)

Refrain

For your love,
For your love.
I would give you the stars above.
For your love,
For your love.
I would give you all I could.

Repeat Verse 1 and Refrain

For your love,
For your love.

Forever Young
Words and Music by Rod Stewart, Jim Cregan,
Kevin Savigar and Bob Dylan

recorded by Rod Stewart

May the good Lord be with you
Down every road you roam.
And may sunshine and happiness
Surround you when you're far from home.

And may you grow to be proud,
Dignified and true.
And do unto others
As you'd have done to you.
Be courageous and be brave.
And in my heart you'll always stay

Refrain:
Forever young,
Forever young.

May good fortune be with you,
May your guiding light be strong,
Build a stairway to heaven
With a prince or a vagabond.
And may you never love in vain.
And in my heart you will remain

Refrain

Forever young.
Forever young.

And when you finally fly away,
I'll be hoping that I served you well.
For all the wisdom of a lifetime,
No one can ever tell.
But whatever road you choose,
I'm right behind you win or lose

Refrain

Forever young.
Forever young.

Fortress Around Your Heart
Written and Composed by Sting

recorded by Sting

Under the ruins of a walled city,
Crumbling towers in beams of yellow light.
No flags of truce, no cries of pity;
The siege guns had been pounding through the night.
It took a day to build the city.

We walked through its streets in the afternoon.
As I returned across the fields I'd known,
I recognized the walls that I once made.
Had to stop in my tracks for fear
Of walking on the mines I'd laid.

Refrain:
And if I've built this fortress around your heart,
Encircled you in trenches and barbed wire,
Then let me build a bridge,
For I cannot fill the chasm,
And let me set the battlements on fire.

Then I went off to fight some battle
That I'd invented inside my head.
Away so long for years and years,
You probably thought or even wished that I was dead.
While the armies are all sleeping
Beneath the tattered flag we'd made,
I had to stop in my tracks for fear
Of walking on the mines I'd laid.

Refrain

This prison has now become your home,
A sentence you seem prepared to pay.
It took a day to build the city.
We walked through its streets in the afternoon,
As I returned across the lands I'd known,
I recognized the fields where I once played.
I had to stop in my tracks for fear
Of walking on the mines I'd laid.

Refrain

4 Seasons of Loneliness
Words and Music by James Harris III and Terry Lewis
© 1997 EMI APRIL MUSIC INC. and FLYTE TYME TUNES INC.
All Rights Controlled and Administered by EMI APRIL MUSIC INC.

recorded by Boyz II Men

I long for the warmth of days gone by
When you were mine.
And now those days are memories in time.

Life's empty without you by my side.
My heart belongs to you no matter what I try.
When I get the courage up to love somebody new,
It always falls apart 'cause they just can't compare to you.
You're the one that leads me around under ball and chain,
Reminiscing our love as I watch four seasons change.

Refrain:
Here comes the winter breeze
That chills the air and drifts the snow.
And I imagine kissing you under the mistletoe.
When springtime makes its way here,
Lilac blooms remind me of the scent of your perfume.
When summer burns with heat
I always get the hots for you.

Go skinny dippin' in the ocean
Where we used to do.
When autumn sheds the leaves
The trees are bare when you're not here.
It doesn't feel the same.
Doesn't feel the same.

Remember the nights when we closed our eyes,
And vowed that you and I would be in love for all time?
Anytime I think about these things I share with you,
I break down and cry 'cause I get so emotional.
Until you release me, I'm bound under ball and chain,
Reminiscing our love as I watch four seasons change.

Refrain

This loneliness has cursed my heart.
Please let me love again
'Cause I need your love to comfort me and ease my pain,
All four seasons will bring the loneliness again.

Refrain

Remember the warmth of days gone by.

Free as a Bird
Original Version:
Words and Music by John Lennon
© 1977, 1985 LENONO.MUSIC
All Rights Controlled and Administered by EMI BLACKWOOD MUSIC INC.
Beatles Version:
Words and Music by John Lennon, Paul McCartney,
George Harrison and Ringo Starr
© 1977, 1985, 1995 LENONO.MUSIC
All Rights Controlled and Administered by EMI BLACKWOOD MUSIC INC.

recorded by The Beatles

Verse 1:
Free as a bird,
It's the next best thing to be
Free as a bird.

Verse 2:
Home, home and dry,
Like a homing bird I fly,
As a bird on wings.

Refrain:
Whatever happened to
The life that we once knew?
Can we really live without each other?
Where did we lose touch
That seemed to mean so much?
It always made me feel so

Repeat Verse 1

Whatever happened to
The life that we once knew?
Always made me feel so free.

Free as a bird,
It's the next best thing to be
Free as a bird,
Free as a bird,
Free as a bird.

Free Ride

Words and Music by Dan Hartman

recorded by The Edgar Winter Group

The mountain is high, the valley is low,
And you're confused on which way to go.
So I've come here to give you a hand
And lead you into the promised land.

Refrain:
So, come on and take a free ride,
(Free ride.)
Come on and sit here by my side.
Come on and take a free ride.

All over this country I've seen it the same;
Nobody's winning at this kind of game.
We've gotta do better, it's time to begin.
You know all the answers must come from within.

Refrain

Repeat Refrain

Come on and take a free ride.
Yeah, yeah, yeah, yeah.
Come on and take a free ride…

Friends

Words and Music by Michael W. Smith and
Deborah D. Smith

recorded by Michael W. Smith

Packing up the dreams God planted
In the fertile soil of you;
Can't believe the hopes he's granted
Means a chapter in your life is through.

Refrain 1:
But we'll keep you close as always;
It won't even seem you've gone,
'Cause our hearts in big and small ways
Will keep the love that keeps us strong.

Refrain 2:
And friends are friends forever
If the Lord's the Lord of them.
And a friend will not say "never"
'Cause the welcome will not end.
Though it's hard to let you go,
In the Father's hands we know

That lifetime's not too long
To live as friends.

With the faith and love God's given
Springing from the hope we know,
We will pray the joy you'll live in
Is the strength that now you show.

Refrain 1

Refrain 2

Repeat Refrain 2

No, a lifetime's not too long
To live as friends.

Friends in Low Places

Words and Music by Dewayne Blackwell and Earl Bud Lee

recorded by Garth Brooks

Blame it all on my roots.
I showed up in boots
And ruined your black-tie affair.
The last one to know;
The last one to show;
I was the last one you thought you'd see there.

And I saw the surprise
And the fear in his eyes
When I took his glass of champagne
And I toasted you,
Said, "Honey, we may be through
But you'll never hear me complain

Refrain:
'Cause I've got friends in low places
Where whiskey drowns
And the beer chases blues away.
And I'll be okay.
Yeah, I'm not big on social graces.
Think I'll slip on down to the oasis.
Oh, I've got friends in low places.

Well, I guess I was wrong.
I just don't belong,
But then I've been there before.
Ev'rything's alright.
I'll just say goodnight
And I'll show myself to the door.

Hey, I didn't mean
To cause a big scene
Just give me an hour and then,
Well I'll be as high
As that ivory tower
That you're livin' in.

Refrain Twice

From a Distance

Words and Music by Julie Gold

recorded by Bette Midler

From a distance the world looks blue and green,
And the snow-capped mountains white.
From a distance the ocean meets the stream
And the eagle takes to flight.

From a distance there is harmony,
And it echoes through the land.
It's the voice of hope, it's the voice of peace
It's the voice of every man.

Refrain:
God is watching us,
God is watching us,
God is watching us
From a distance.

From a distance we all have enough,
And no one is in need.
There are no guns, no bombs, no diseases,
No hungry mouths to feed.

From a distance we are instruments,
Marching in a common band.
Playing songs of hope, playing songs of peace,
They're the songs of every man.

Refrain

From a distance you look like my friend,
Even though we are at war.
From a distance I can't comprehend
What all this war is for.

From a distance there is harmony,
And it echoes through the land.
It's the voice of hopes, it's the love of loves,
It's the heart of every man.

It's the hope of hopes,
It's the love of loves,
It's the song of every man.

From This Moment On

Words and Music by Cole Porter

from the musical *Out of This World*
a standard recorded by various artists

Now that we are close,
No more nights morose,
Now that we are one,
The beguine has just begun.
Now that we're side by side,
The future looks so gay,
Now we are alibied
When we say:

Refrain:
From this moment on,
You for me, dear,
From this moment on,
From this happy day,
No more blue songs,
Only whoop-dee-doo songs,
From this moment on.
For you've got the love I need so much,
Got the skin I love to touch,
Got the arms to hold me tight,
Got the lips to kiss me good night.
From this moment on,
You and I, babe,
We'll be ridin' high, babe,
Every care is gone
From this moment on.

Interlude:
My dear one, my fair one,
My sunbeam, my moonbeam,
My bluebird, my lovebird,
My dreamboat, my cream puff,
My ducky, my wucky,
My poopsy, my woopsy
My tootsy, my wootsy,
My cooky, my wooky,
My piggy, my wiggy,
My sugar, my sweet,
No wonder we rewonder,
We rewonder, we repeat:

Repeat Refrain

Galileo

Words and Music by Emily Saliers

recorded by Indigo Girls

Galileo's head was on the block,
The crime was looking up the truth.
And as the bomb-shells of my daily fears explode,
I try to trace them to my youth.

And then you had to bring up reincarnation
Over a couple of beers the other night.
And now, I'm serving time for mistakes
Made by another in another lifetime.

Refrain:
How long till my soul gets it right?
Can any human being ever reach that kind of light?
I call on the resting soul of Galileo,
King of night vision, king of insight.

And then I think about my fear of motion
For which I never could explain.
Some other fool across the ocean,
Years ago must have crashed his little airplane.

Refrain

I'm not making a joke.
You know me,
I take everything so seriously.
If we wait for the time till all souls get it right,
Then at least I know there'll be no
Nuclear annihilation in my lifetime.
I'm still not right.

I offer thanks to those before me.
That's all I've got to say.
'Cause maybe you squandered
Big bucks in your lifetime.
Now, I have to pay.
But then again it feels like some sort of inspiration
To let the next life off the hook.
Or she'll say,
"Look what I had to overcome in my last life.
I think I'll write a book."

How long till my soul gets it right?
Can any human being ever reach the highest light?
Except for the resting soul of Galileo,
King of night vision, king of insight.

How long?
How long?
How long?

The Gambler

Words and Music by Don Schlitz

recorded by Kenny Rogers

On a warm summer's evenin'
On a train bound for nowhere,
I met up with the gambler.
We were both too tired to sleep.
So we took turns a starin'
Out the window at the darkness
'Til boredom overtook us,
And he began to speak.
He said, "Son, I've made a life
Out of readin' people's faces,
And knowin' what their cards were,
By the way they held their eyes.
And if you don't mind my sayin',
I can see you're out of aces.
For a taste of your whiskey
I'll give you some advice."

So I handed him my bottle
And he drank down my last swallow.
Then he bummed a cigarette,
And he asked me for a light.
And the night got deathly quiet,
And his face lost all expression.
Said, "If you're gonna play the game, boy,
Ya gotta learn to play it right.

Refrain:
You got to know when to hold 'em,
Know when to fold 'em,
Know when to walk away,
And know when to run.
You never count your money
When you're sittin' at the table,
There'll be time enough for countin'
When the dealin's done.

Every gambler knows
That the secret to survivin'
Is knowin' what to throw away
And knowin' what to keep.
'Cause every hand's a winner
And every hand's a loser,
And the best that you can hope for
Is to die in your sleep."
And when he'd finished speakin',
He turned back towards the window,
Crushed out his cigarette,
And faded off to sleep.
And somewhere in the darkness,
The gambler, he broke even.
But in his final words,
I found an ace that I could keep.

Refrain Twice

Genie in a Bottle

Words and Music by Steve Kipner, David Frank
and Pam Sheyne

recorded by Christina Aguilera

Oh ooh oh mm.

I feel like I've been locked up tight
For a century of lonely nights
Waiting for someone to release me.
You're lickin' your lips
And blowin' kisses my way.
But that don't mean
I'm gonna give it away,
Baby, baby, baby.

Refrain:
Oh.
Spoken:
My body's saying let's go.
Oh.
Spoken:
But my heart is saying no, no.
Sung:
If you wanna be with me,
Baby, there's a price to pay.
I'm a genie in a bottle;
You gotta rub me the right way.
If you wanna be with me,
I can make your wish come true.

You gotta make a big impression.
Gotta like what you do.
I'm a genie in a bottle, baby.
You gotta rub me the right way, honey.
I'm a genie in a bottle, baby.
Come, come, come on and let me out.

Music's playing and the light's down low.
Just one more dance and then we're good to go,
Waiting for someone who needs me.
Hormones racing at the speed of light.
But that don't mean it's gotta be tonight,
Baby, baby, baby.

Refrain

Just come and set me free, baby,
And I'll be with you.
I'm a genie in a bottle, baby.
You gotta rub me the right way, honey.
I'm a genie in a bottle, baby.
Come, come, come on and let me out.
I'm a genie in a bottle, baby.
You gotta rub me the right way, honey.
I'm a genie in a bottle, baby.
come, come, come on and let me out.

Refrain

You gotta make a big impression.
Gotta like what you do.

Refrain

Just come and let me free, baby,
And I'll be with you.
I'm a genie in a bottle, baby.
Come, come, come on and let me out.

Gentle on My Mind

Words and Music by John Hartford

recorded by Glen Campbell

It's knowing that your door is always open,
And your path is free to walk,
That makes me tend to leave my sleeping bag,
Rolled up and stashed behind your couch.

And it's knowing I'm not shackled,
By forgotten words and bonds,
And the ink stains that have dried upon some line;
That keeps you in the back-roads
By the rivers of my memory,
That keeps you gentle on my mind.

Georgia on My Mind

Words by Stuart Gorrell
Music by Hoagy Carmichael

a standard recorded by Ray Charles, Willie Nelson and
various other artists

Georgia, Georgia, the whole day through,
Just an old sweet song keeps
Georgia on my mind.
(Georgia on my mind.)

Georgia, Georgia, a song of you,
Come as sweet and clear as moonlight through the pines.
Other arms reach out to me;
Other eyes smile tenderly;
Still in peaceful dreams I see
The road leads back to you,
Georgia, Georgia, no peace I find,
Just an old sweet song keeps
Georgia on my mind.

Get Back

Words and Music by John Lennon and Paul McCartney

recorded by The Beatles

Jojo was a man who thought he was a loner,
But he knew it couldn't last.
Jojo left his home in Tucson Arizona,
For some California grass.

Get back, get back,
Get back to where you once belonged.
Get back, get back,
Get back to where you once belonged.

Get back Jojo. Go home.
Get back, get back,
Back to where you once belonged.
Get back, get back,
Back to where you once belonged.
Get back Jo.

Sweet Loretta Martin thought she was a woman,
But she was another man.
All the girls around her say she's got it coming,
But she gets it while she can.

Get back, get back,
Get back to where you once belonged.
Get back, get back,
Get back to where you once belonged.

Get back Loretta. Go home.
Get back, get back,
Get back to where you once belonged.
Get back, get back,
Get back to where you once belonged.

Get back Loretta
Your mother's waiting for you,
Wearing her high-heeled shoes,
And her low necked sweater.
Get on home Loretta.
Get back, get back,
Get back to where you once belonged.

Get Me to the Church on Time

Words by Alan Jay Lerner
Music by Frederick Loewe

from the musical *My Fair Lady*

I'm getting married in the morning.
Ding! Dong! The bells are gonna chime.
Pull out the stopper;
Let's have a whopper;
But get me to the church on time!

I gotta be there in the morning;
Spruced up and looking in my prime.
Girls, come out and kiss me;
Show how you'll miss me,
But get me to the church on time!

If I am dancing,
Roll up the floor!
If I am whistling,
Whewt me out the door!
For I'm getting married in the morning.
Ding! Dong! The bells are gonna chime.
Kick up a rumpus,
But don't lose the compass,
And get me to the church,
Get me to the church,
For Gawd's sake,
Get me to the church on time.

Get Out of Town

Words and Music by Cole Porter

from the musical *Leave It to Me!*
a standard recorded by various artists

The farce was ended,
The curtains drawn.
And I at least pretended
That love was dead and gone.
But now from nowhere,
You come to me as before,
To take my heart,
And break my heart
Some more.

Get out of town,
Before it's too late, my love,
Get out of town,
Be good to me, please.
Why wish me harm?
Why not retire to a farm,
And be contented to charm
The birds off the trees?

Just disappear,
I care for you much too much.
And when you are near,
Close to me, dear,
We touch too much.
The thrill when we meet
Is so bitter sweet
That darling, it's getting me down.
So on your mark, get set,
Get out of town.

Gettin' Jiggy Wit It

Words and Music by Nile Rodgers, Bernard Edwards,
Will Smith, Samuel J. Barnes and J. Robinson

recorded by Will Smith

Bring it.
Whoo!
Unh, unh, unh, unh
Hoo cah cah.
Hah hah, hah hah.
Bicka bicka bow bow bow,
Bicka bow bow bump bump.
What, what, what, what?
Hah hah hah hah.

On your mark, ready, set let's go.
Dance floor pro, I know you know
I go psycho when my new joint hit.
Just can't sit.
Gotta get jiggy wit it.
Ooh, that's it.
Now, honey, honey, come ride,
DKNY all up in the eye.
You gotta Prada bag with alotta stuff in it,
Give it to your friend, let's spin.
Everybody lookin' at me,
Glancin' the kid,
Wishin' they was dancin' a jig
Here with this handsome kid.
Ciga-cigar right from Cuba-Cuba,
I just bite it.
It's for the look, I don't light it.
Ill-way the an-may on the ance-day oor-flay,
Givin' up jiggy, make it feel like foreplay.
Yo, my car-dee-o is Infinit-
Ha, ha.
Big Willie Style's all in it,
Gettin' jiggy wit it.

Refrain Three Times:
Na na na na na na na nana
Na na na na nana.
Gettin' jiggy wit it.

What? You wanna ball with the kid?
Watch your step, you might fall,
Trying to do what I did.
Mama-unh, mama-unh, mama come closer,
In the middle of the club with the rub-a-dub, uhn.
No love for the haters, the haters,
Mad cause I got floor seats at the Lakers.
See me on the fifty yard line with the Raiders.
Met Ali, he told me I'm the greatest.
I got the fever for the flavor of a crowd pleaser.
DJ, play another
For the prince of this.

Your highness,
Only mad chicks ride in my whips.
South to the west to the east to the north,
Bought my hits and watch 'em go off, a-go off.
In the winter or the (Summertime),
It makes it hot
Gettin' jiggy wit it.

Refrain

Eight-fifty I.S.; if you need a lift,
Who's the kid in the drop?
Who else, Will Smith,
Livin' that life some consider a myth.
Rock from South Street to One Two Fifth.
Women used to tease me,
Give it to me now nice and easy
Since I moved up like George and Wheezy.
Cream to the maximum, I be askin' 'em,
Rather play ball with Shaq and um,
Flatten' 'em,
Psyche.
Kiddin',
You thought I took a spill
But I didn't.
Trust the lacy of my life, she hittin'.
Hit her with a drop top with the ribbon,
Crib for my mom on the outskirts of Philly.
You, trying to flex on me?
Don't be silly,
Gettin' jiggy wit it.

Refrain

Getting to Know You

Lyrics by Oscar Hammerstein II
Music by Richard Rodgers

from the musical *The King and I*

It's a very ancient saying,
But a true and honest thought,
That "if you become a teacher
By your pupils you'll be taught."
As a teacher I've been learning
(You'll forgive me if I boast)
And I've now become an expert
On the subject I like most:

Getting to know you.
Getting to know all about you,
Getting to like you,
Getting to hope you like me.
Getting to know you—
Putting it my way, but nicely,
You are precisely
My cup of tea!

Getting to know you,
Getting to feel free and easy;
When I am with you,
Getting to know what to say—
Haven't you noticed?
Suddenly I'm bright and breezy
Because of
All the beautiful and new
Things I'm learning about you,
Day by day.

The Gift

Words and Music by Tom Douglas and Jim Brickman

recorded by Jim Brickman featuring Collin Raye and
Susan Ashton

Female:

Winter snow is falling down,
Children laughing all around,
Lights are turning on,
Like a fairy tale come true.
Sitting by the fire we made,
You're the answer when I prayed
I would find someone
And baby, I found you.

All I want is to hold you forever.
All I need is you more every day.
You saved my heart from being broken apart.
You gave your love away,
And I'm thankful every day for the gift.

Male:

Watching as you softly sleep,
What I'd give if I could keep
Just this moment,
If only time stood still.
But the colors fade away,
And the years will make us gray,
But, baby, in my eyes, you'll still be beautiful.

Both:

All I want is to hold you forever.
All I need is you more every day.

Male:

You saved my heart from being broken apart.

Female:

You gave your love away.

Male:

And I'm thankful every day.

Both:

For the gift.

Both:

All I want is to hold you forever.
All I need is you more every day.

Male:

You saved my heart from being broken apart.

Female:

You gave your love away.

Male:

I can't find the words to say.

Female:

That I'm thankful every day.

Both:

For the gift.

Gimme a Little Kiss (Will Ya Huh?)

Words and Music by Roy Turk, Maceo Pinkard and
Jack Smith

a standard recorded by "Whispering" Jack Smith,
Gene Krupa, Deanna Durbin and various other artists

Gimme a little kiss.
Will ya huh?
What are you gonna miss?
Will ya, huh?
Gosh, oh gee!
What do you refuse?
I can't see what you've got to lose.
Aw, gimme a little squeeze.
Will ya, huh?
Why do you wanna make me blue?
I wouldn't say a word if I were asking for the world.
But what's a little kiss between a feller and his girl?
Aw, gimme a little kiss.
Will ya, huh?
And I'll give it right back to you.

Gimme a little kiss.
Will ya huh?
Must I go on like this?
Will ya, huh?
Once again, a plea I'm gonna make.
Tell me when do I get a break.
Aw, say that you're givin' in.
Will ya, huh?
Anything that you ask I'll do.
I'll take you for a little ride where we can be alone.
And once you kiss me you will never think of walking home.
Aw, gimme a little kiss.
Will ya, huh?
Or I'll steal about ten from you.

Girl Talk

Words by Bobby Troup
Music by Neal Hefti

from the Paramount Picture *Harlow*
a standard recorded by various artists

They like to chat about the dresses they will wear tonight.
They chew the fat about their tresses and the neighbor's
  fight;
Inconsequential things that men don't really care to know
Become essential things that women find so "appropo."
But that's a dame they're all the same;
It's just a game. They call it girl talk, girl talk.

They all meow about the ups and down of all their friends;
The "who," the "how," the "why," they dish the dirt, it
  never ends.
The weaker sex, the speaker sex, we mortal males behold,
But tho' we joke, we wouldn't trade you for a ton of gold.
So baby stay and gab away,
But hear me say, that after girl talk, talk to me.

Repeat Song

The Girl That I Marry

Words and Music by Irving Berlin

from the Stage Production *Annie Get Your Gun*

The girl that I marry will have to be
As soft and as pink as a nursery.
The girl I call my own,
Will wear satin and laces and smell of cologne.

Her nails will be polished and in her hair,
She'll wear a gardenia. And I'll be there
'Stead of flittin' I'll be sittin'
Next to her and she'll purr like a kitten.

A doll I can carry,
The girl that I marry must be.

Girls Just Want to Have Fun

Words and Music by Robert Hazard

recorded by Cyndi Lauper

I come home in the morning light.
My mother ways, "When you gonna live your life right?"
Oh, Mother dear, we're not the fortunate ones.
And girls, they just want to have fun.
Oh, girls just want to have fun.

The phone rings in the middle of the night.
My father yells, "What you gonna do with your life?"
Oh, Daddy dear, you know you're still number one.
But girls just want to have…
That's all they really want:
Some fun.
When the working day is done,
Oh, girls, they want to have fu-un.
Oh, girls just want to have fun.

Some boys take a beautiful girl
And hide her away from the rest of the world.
I want to be the one to walk in the sun.
Oh, girls just want to have…
That's all they really want:
Some fun.
When the working day is done,
Oh, girls, they want to have fu-un.
Oh, girls just want to have fun.

They just wanna,
They just wanna.
They just wanna,
Girls, girls just want to have fu-un.

Give Me Love
(Give Me Peace on Earth)

By George Harrison

recorded by George Harrison

Give me love, give me love,
Give me peace on earth.
Give me light, give me life,
Keep me free from birth.
Give me hope, help me cope
With this heavy load.
Trying to touch and reach you with heart and soul.
Oh, my Lord.
Please take hold of my hand
That I might understand you.
Won't you please.
Oh, won't you:

Refrain:
Give me love, give me love,
Give me peace on earth.
Give me light, give me life,
Keep me free from birth.
Give me hope, help me cope
With this heavy load.
Trying to touch and reach you with heart and soul.
Oh, my Lord. Won't you please.
Oh won't you:

Refrain

Give me love, give me love,
Give me peace on earth.
Give me light, give me life,
Keep me free from birth.
Give me hope, help me cope
With this heavy load.
Trying to touch and reach you with heart and soul.
Oh, my Lord.

Give Me One Reason
Words and Music by Tracy Chapman

recorded by Tracy Chapman

Refrain:
Give me one reason to stay here,
And I'll turn right back around.
Give me one reason to stay here,
And I'll turn right back around.
Said I don't want to leave you lonely;
You got to make me change my mind.

Baby, I got your number.
Oh, and I know that you got mine.
But you know that I called you.
I called too many times.
You can call me, baby.
You can call me anytime.
But you got to call me.

Refrain

I don't want no one to squeeze me.
They might take away my life.
I don't want no one to squeeze me.
They might take away my life.
I just want someone to hold me,
Oh, and rock me through the night.

This youthful heart can love you,
Yes, and give you what you need.
I said this youthful heart can love you,
Oh, and give you what you need.
But I'm too old to go chasing you around,
Wasting my precious energy.

Refrain

Baby, give me just one reason.
Oh, give me just one reason why.
Baby, just give me one reason.
Oh, give me just one reason why I should stay.
Said I told you that I loved you,
And there ain't no more to say.

Give Me the Night
Words and Music by Rod Temperton

recorded by George Benson

Whenever dark is fallin',
You know the spirit of the party starts to come alive.
Until the day is dawnin',
You can throw out all the blues and hit the city lights,

Refrain:
'Cause there's music in the air,
And lots of lovin' everywhere,
So give me the night.
Give me the night.

You need the evenin' action,
A place to dine, a glass of wine, a little romance.
It's a chain reaction,
We'll see the people of the world comin' out to dance.

Refrain

Instrumental Verse

Refrain

And if we stay together,
We'll feel the rhythm of the evening takin' us up high.
Never mind the weather,
We'll be dancin' in the street until the morning light.

Refrain

Give My Regards to Broadway
Words and Music by George M. Cohan

from the musical *Little Johnny Jones*
a standard recorded by various artists

Give my regards to Broadway.
Remember me to Herald Square.
Tell all the gang at Forty Second Street
That I will soon be there.
Whisper of how I'm yearning,
To mingle with the old-time throng.
Give my regards to old Broadway
And say that I'll be there 'ere long.

Glad to Be Unhappy

Words by Lorenz Hart
Music by Richard Rodgers

from the musical *On Your Toes*

Look at yourself.
If you had a sense of humor,
You would laugh to beat the band.
Look at yourself.
Do you still believe the rumor
That romance is simply grand?
Since you took it right on the chin,
You have lost that bright toothpaste grin.
My mental state is all a jumble.
I sit around and sadly mumble.

Refrain:

Fools rush in, so here I am,
Very glad to be unhappy.
I can't win, but here I am,
More than glad to be unhappy.
Unrequited love's a bore,
And I've got it pretty bad.
But for someone you adore,
It's a pleasure to be sad.
Like a straying baby lamb
With no mammy and no pappy,
I'm so unhappy, But oh, so glad.

Glory of Love

Words and Music by David Foster, Peter Cetera and
Diane Nini

Theme from *Karate Kid Part II*
recorded by Peter Cetera

Tonight it's very clear,
As we're both standing here,
There's so many things I want to say.
I will always love you,
I will never leave you alone.

Sometimes I just forget,
Say things I might regret,
It breaks my heart to see you crying.
I don't want to lose you,
I could never make it alone.

Refrain:

I am a man
Who would fight for your honor,
I'll be the hero you're dreaming of.
We'll live forever,
Knowing together,
That we did it all
For the glory of love.

You keep me standing tall,
You help me through it all,
I'm always strong
When you're beside me.
I have always needed you,
I could never make it alone.

Refrain

Just like the a knight in shining armor,
From a long time ago,
Just in time I will save the day,
Take you to my castle far away.

I am the man
Who will fight for your honor,
I'll be the hero that you're dreaming of.
We're gonna live forever,
Knowing together,
That we did it all
For the glory of love.

We'll live forever,
Knowing together,
That we did it all
For the glory of love.
We did it all for love.

The Glory of Love

Words and Music by Billy Hill

a standard recorded by various artists
featured in the films *Guess Who's Coming to Dinner?*
and *Beaches*

You've got to give a little, take a little
And let your heart break a little,
That's the story of,
That's the glory of love.

You've got to laugh a little,
Cry a little,
Before the clouds roll by a little,
That's the story of,
That's the glory of love.

As long as there's the two of us
We've got the world and all its charms,
And when the world is through with us
We've got each other's arms.

You've got to win a little,
Lose a little,
And always have the blues a little,
That's the story of,
That's the glory of love.

Go Away, Little Girl

Words and Music by Gerry Goffin and Carole King

recorded by Steve Lawrence, Donny Osmond

Go away, little girl,
Go away, little girl,
I'm not supposed to be alone with you.
I know that your lips are sweet,
But our lips must never meet.
I belong to someone else and I must be true.

Oh, go away, little girl,
Go away, little girl.
It's hurting me more each minute that you delay.
When you are near me like this,
You're much too hard to resist.
So go away, little girl,
Before I beg you to stay.

Repeat Song

Go the Distance

Music by Alan Menken
Lyrics by David Zippel

from Walt Disney Pictures' *Hercules*
recorded by Michael Bolton

I have often dreamed of a far-off place,
Where a hero's welcome
Would be waiting for me;
Where the crowds will cheer,
When they see my face,
And a voice keeps saying,
This is where I'm meant to be.
I'll be there someday.

I can go the distance.
I will find my way,
If I can be strong.
I know every mile
Will be worth my while.
When I go the distance,
I'll be right where I belong.

Down an unknown road,
To embrace my fate;
Though that road may wander,
It will lead me to you.
And a thousand years would be worth the wait.
It might take a lifetime,
But somehow I'll see it through.
And I won't look back.
I can go the distance.
And I'll stay on the track.
No, I won't accept defeat.
It's an uphill slope,
But I won't lose hope,
Till I go the distance,
And my journey is complete.

Oh, yeah.
But to look beyond the glory,
Is the hardest part,
For a hero's strength is measured,
By his heart.

Like a shooting star,
I will go the distance.
I will search the world.
I will face its harms.
I don't care how far.
I can go the distance,
Till I find my hero's welcome,
Waiting in your arms.

I will search the world.
I will face its harms,
Till I find my hero's welcome,
Waiting in your arms.

God Bless' the Child

Words and Music by Arthur Herzog Jr. and Billie Holiday

a standard recorded by Billie Holiday and
various other artists
featured in the Motion Picture *Lady Sings the Blues*

Them that's got shall get,
Them that's not shall lose,
So the Bible said,
And still it is news;
Mama may have,
Papa may have,
But God bless' the child that's got his own!
That's got his own.

Yes, the strong gets more,
While the weak ones fade,
Empty pockets don't ever make the grade.
Mama may have,
Papa may have,
But God bless' the child that's got his own!
That's got his own.

Money, you got lots o' friends,
Crowdin' 'round the door.
When you're gone and spendin' ends,
They don't come no more.

Rich relations give,
Crust of bread, and such,
You can help yourself,
But don't take too much!
Mama may have,
Papa may have,
But God bless' the child that's got his own!
That's got his own.

God Help the Outcasts

Music by Alan Menken
Lyrics by Stephen Schwartz
© 1996 Wonderland Music Company, Inc. and Walt Disney Music Company

from Walt Disney's *The Hunchback of Notre Dame*
recorded by Bette Midler

I don't know if You can hear me, or if You're even there.
I don't know if You will listen to a humble prayer.
They tell me I am just an outcast; I shouldn't speak to You.
Still I see Your face and wonder: were You once an
  outcast too?

God help the outcasts, hungry from birth.
Show them the mercy they don't find on earth.
The lost and forgotten, they look to You still.
God help the outcasts or nobody will.

I ask for nothing, I can get by.
But I know so many less lucky than I.
God help the outcasts, the poor and downtrod.
I thought we all were the children of God.

I don't know if there's a reason
Why some are blessed, some not.
Why the few You seem to favor,
They fear us, flee us,
Try not to see us.

God help the outcasts, the tattered, the torn,
Seeking an answer to why they were born.
Winds of misfortune have blown them about.
You made the outcasts; don't cast them out.

The poor and unlucky, the weak and the cold;
I thought we all were the children of God.

God Only Knows

Words and Music by Brian Wilson and Tony Asher
Copyright © 1966 IRVING MUSIC, INC.
Copyright Renewed

recorded by The Beach Boys

I may not always love you,
But long as there are stars above you;
You never need to doubt it,
I'll make you so sure about it,
God only knows what I'd be without you.

If you should ever leave me,
Oh, life would still go on believe me;
The world could show nothing to me,
So what good would living do me?
God only knows what I'd be without you,
God only knows what I'd be without you,
God only knows.

Gonna Build a Mountain

Words and Music by Leslie Bricusse and Anthony Newley
© Copyright 1961 (Renewed) TRO Essex Music Ltd., London, England
TRO - Ludlow Music, Inc., New York, controls all publication rights for the U.S.A. and Canada

from the Musical Production *Stop the World—I Want to Get Off*

Gonna build a mountain from a little hill.
Gonna build a mountain, least I hope I will.
Gonna build a mountain; gonna build it high.
I don't know how I'm gonna do it;
Only know I'm gonna try.

Gonna build a daydream from a little hope.
Gonna push that daydream up the mountain slope.
Gonna build a daydream; gonna see it through.
Gonna build a mountain and a daydream;
Gonna make 'em both come true.

Gonna build a heaven from a little hell.
Gonna build a heaven and I know darn well.
If I build my mountain with a lot of care.
And take my daydream up the mountain
Heaven will be waiting there.

When I've built that heaven, as I will someday,
And the Lord sends Gabriel to take me away,
Wanna a fine young son to take my place.
I'll leave a son in my heaven on earth,
With the Lord's good grace.

With a fine young son to take my place
I'll leave a son in my heaven on earth
With the Lord's good grace.

Good Day Sunshine

Words and Music by John Lennon and Paul McCartney
Copyright © 1966 Sony/ATV Songs LLC
Copyright Renewed
All Rights Administered by Sony/ATV Music Publishing, 8 Music Square West,
  Nashville, TN 37203

recorded by The Beatles

Good day sunshine, good day sunshine,
Good day sunshine.
I need to laugh, and when the sun is out,
I've got something I can laugh about.
I feel good in a special way,
I'm in love and it's a sunny day.

Good day sunshine, good day sunshine,
Good day sunshine.
We take a walk, the sun is shining down,
Burns my feet as they touch the ground.

Good day sunshine, good day sunshine,
Good day sunshine.
And then we lie beneath a shady tree,
I love her and she's loving me.
She feels good, and she knows she's looking fine.
I'm so proud to know that she is mine.

Good day sunshine, good day sunshine,
Good day sunshine.
Good day sunshine, good day sunshine.

Good Luck Charm
Words and Music by Aaron Schroeder and Wally Gold

recorded by Elvis Presley

Don't want a four leaf clover;
Don't want an old horse shoe.
Want your kiss 'cause I just can't miss
With a good luck charm like you.

Refrain:
Come on and be my little good luck charm.
Uh-huh-huh, you sweet delight.
I want a good luck charm a-hangin' on my arm
To have, to hold, to hold tonight.

Don't want a silver dollar,
Rabbit's foot on a string.
The happiness in your warm caress
No rabbit's foot can bring.

Refrain

If I found a lucky penny,
I'd toss it across the bay.
Your love is worth all the gold on earth;
No wonder that I say;

Refrain

A Good Man Is Hard to Find
Words and Music by Eddie Green

a standard recorded by Alberta Hunter, Sophie Tucker and
various other artists

My heart's sad and I am all forlorn,
My man's treating me mean.
I regret the day I was born
And that man of mine I've ever seen.
My happiness, it never lasts a day;
My heart is almost breaking while I say;

A good man is hard to find,
You always get the other kind.
Just when you think that he is your pal,
You look for him and find him
Fooling 'round some other gal.
Then you rave;
You even crave
To see him laying in his grave.

So, if your man is nice,
Take my advice
And hug him in the morning,
Kiss him every night,
Give him plenty of lovin',
Treat him right,
For a good man now-a days
Is hard to find.

Good Morning Heartache
**Words and Music by Dan Fisher, Irene Higginbotham and
Ervin Drake**

a standard recorded by Billie Holiday and
various other artists

Good morning heartache,
You old gloomy sight.
Good morning heartache,
Thought we said goodbye last night.
I tossed and turned until it seemed you had gone,
But here you are with the dawn.

Wish I'd forget you
But you're here to stay.
It seems I met you when my love went away.
Now every day I start by saying to you,
Good morning heartache, what's new?

Stop haunting me now.
Can't shake you no-how.
Just leave me alone.
I've got those Monday blues straight thru Sunday blues.

Good morning heartache,
Here we go again.
Good morning heartache,
You're the one who knew me when.
Might as well get used to you hangin' around.
Good morning heartache sit down!

Good Vibrations
Words and Music by Brian Wilson and Mike Love

recorded by The Beach Boys

I love the clothes she wears,
And the way the sunlight plays upon her hair.
I hear the sound of a gentle word,
On the wind that lifts her perfume through the air.

Refrain:
I'm picking up good vibrations,
She's giving me excitations.
Good, good, good, good vibrations.

Close my eyes. She's somehow closer now,
Softly smile, I know she must be kind.
Then I look in her eyes,
She goes with me to a blossom world.

Refrain

Goodbye to Love

Words and Music by Richard Carpenter and John Bettis
Copyright © 1972 HAMMER AND NAILS MUSIC and ALMO MUSIC CORP.
Copyright Renewed
All Rights Administered by ALMO MUSIC CORP.

recorded by The Carpenters

I'll say goodbye to love.
No one ever cared if I should live or die.
Time and time again the chance for love has passed me by,
And all I know of love is how to live without it.
I just can't seem to find it.
So I've made my mind up I must live my life alone.
And tho' it's not the easy way,
I guess I've always known I'd say

Goodbye to love.
There are no tomorrows for this heart of mine.
Surely time will lose these bitter memories and I'll find,
That there is someone to believe in and to live for.
Something I could live for.
All the years of useless search have finally reached an end,
And loneliness and empty days will be my only friend.
From this day love is forgotten and I'll go on as best I can.

What lies in the future is a mystery to us all,
No one can predict the wheel of fortune as it falls,
There may come a time when I will see that I've been wrong.
But for now this is my song.
And it's goodbye to love,
I'll say goodbye to love.

Goodnight, My Someone

By Meredith Willson
© 1957 (Renewed) FRANK MUSIC CORP. and MEREDITH WILLSON MUSIC

from Meredith Willson's *The Music Man*

Goodnight my someone, goodnight my love.
Sleep tight, my someone, sleep tight, my love.
Our star is shining its brightest light
For goodnight, my love for goodnight.

Refrain:
Sweet dreams be yours, dear, if dreams there be;
Sweet dreams to carry you close to me.
I wish they may and I wish they might.
Now goodnight, my someone goodnight.

True love can be whispered from heart to heart,
When lovers are parted they say.
But I must depend on a wish and a star,
As long as my heart doesn't know who you are.

Refrain

Goodnight Saigon

Words and Music by Billy Joel
© 1981, 1982 JOEL SONGS

recorded by Billy Joel

We met as soul mates,
On Paris Island.
We left as inmates,
From an asylum,
And we were sharp,
As sharp as knives,
And we were so gung ho
To lay down our lives.

We came in spastic,
Like tame-less horses.
We left in plastic,
As numbered corpses.
And we learned fast,
To travel light.
Our arms were heavy,
But our bellies were tight.

We had no home front,
We had no soft soap.
They sent us Playboy,
They gave us Bob Hope.
We dug in deep,
And shot on sight,
And prayed to Jesus Christ
With all of our might.

We had no cameras,
To shoot the landscape.
We passed the hash pipe,
And played our Doors tapes.
And it was dark,
So dark at night,
And we held on to each other,
Like brother to brother.

We promised our mothers we'd write,
And we would all go down together.
We said we'd all go down together.
Yes, we would all go down together.

Remember Charlie?
Remember Baker?
They left their childhood
On every acre.
And who was wrong?
And who was right?
It didn't matter in the thick of the fight.
We held the day
In the palm of our hand.
They ruled the night,
And the night
Seemed to last:

As long as six weeks
On Paris Island.
We held the coastline,
They held the highlands.

And they were sharp,
As sharp as knives.
They heard the hum of motors,
They counted the rotors,
And waited for us to arrive.

And we would all go down together.
We said we'd all go down together.
Yes, we would all go down together.

Got My Mind Set on You
Words and Music by Rudy Clark

recorded by George Harrison

I got my mind set on you,
I got my mind set on you,
I got my mind set on you,
Got my mind set on you.
But it's gonna take money.
A whole lotta spending money.
It's gonna take plenty of money
To do it right, child.

It's gonna take time,
A whole lotta precious time.
It's gonna take patience and time
To do it,
To do it,
To do it,
To do it,
To do it,
To do it right, child.

I got my mind set on you,
I got my mind set on you,
I got my mind set on you,
I got my mind set on you.
And this time I know it's real
The feeling that I feel.
I know if I put my mind to it,
I know that I really can do it.
I got my mind set on you, set on you.

Got to Get You into My Life
Words and Music by John Lennon and Paul McCartney

recorded by The Beatles; Earth, Wind & Fire

I was alone, I took a ride,
I didn't know what I would find there.
Another road where maybe I
Could see another kind of mind there.
Ooh, then suddenly I see you,
Ooh, did I tell you I need you
Every single day of my life?

You didn't run, you didn't lie,
You knew I just wanted to hold you.
And had you gone, you knew in time
We'd meet again for I had told you.
Ooh, you were meant to be near me,
Ooh, and I want you to hear me
Say we'll be together every day.

Got to get you into my life.
What can I do, what can I be?
When I'm with you I want to stay there.
If I'm true I'll never leave,
And if I do I know the way there.
Ooh, then I suddenly see you.
Ooh, did I tell you I need you
Every single day of my life?

Got to get you into my life.
Got to get you into my life.
I was alone, I took a ride,
I didn't know what I would find there.
Another road where maybe I
Could see another kind of mind there.
Ooh, then suddenly I see you,
Ooh, did I tell you I need you
Every single day of my life?
What are you doing to my life?

Great Balls of Fire
Words and Music by Otis Blackwell and Jack Hammer

recorded by Jerry Lee Lewis

You shake my nerves and you rattle my brain.
Too much love drives a man insane.
You broke my will,
But what a thrill.
Goodness gracious, great balls of fire!

I laughed at love 'cause I thought it was funny.
You came along and you moved me, honey.
I changed my mind,
Love's just fine.
Goodness gracious, great balls of fire!

Kiss me, baby.
Woo, it feels good.
Hold me, baby.
Girl just let me love you like a lover should.
You're fine, so kind,
I'm gonna tell the world that you're mine, mine, mine.

I chew my nails and I twiddle my thumb.
I'm nervous but it sure is fun.
Come on, baby, you're driving me crazy.
Goodness gracious, great balls of fire.

The Great Pretender

Words and Music by Buck Ram

recorded by The Platters

Oh, yes I'm the great pretender,
Pretendin' I'm doin' well;
My need is such, I pretend too much,
I'm lonely but no one can tell.

Oh yes, I'm the great pretender,
Adrift in a world of my own;
I play the game but, to my real shame,
You've left me to dream alone,
Too real is this feeling of make believe,
Too real when I feel what my heart can't conceal;
Oh, yes, I'm the great pretender,
Just laughin' and gay like a clown;
I seem to be what I'm not, you see,
I'm wearin' my heart like a crown;
Pretendin' that you're still aroun'.

Green-Eyed Lady

Words and Music by Jerry Corbetta, J.C. Phillips and
David Riordan

recorded by Sugarloaf

Green-eyed lady, lovely lady.
Strolling slowly towards the sun.
Green-eyed lady, ocean lady.
Soothing every raging wave that comes.

Refrain:
Green-eyed lady passions lady.
Dressed in love, she lives for life to be.
Green-eyed lady feels life, I never see,
Setting suns and lovely lovers free.

Green-eyed lady, wind swept lady.
Rules the night, the waves, the sand.
Green-eyed lady, ocean lady.
Child of nature, friend of man.

Refrain

Green Green Grass of Home

Words and Music by Curly Putman

recorded by Porter Wagoner, Tom Jones

It's good to touch the green, green grass of home.

The old home town looks the same
As I step down from the train,
And there to meet me is my mama and papa.

Down the road I look and there runs Mary,
Hair of gold and lips like cherries.
Its good to touch the green, green grass of home.

Refrain:
Yes, they'll all come to meet me,
Arms reaching, smiling sweetly;
It's good to touch the green, green grass of home.

The old house is still standing
Tho' the paint is cracked and dry,
And there's that old oak tree that I used to play on.

Down the lane I walk with my sweet Mary,
Hair of gold and lips like cherries.
It's good to touch the green, green grass of home.

Refrain

Spoken:
Then I awake and look around me
At four gray walls that surround me
And I realize that I was only dreaming.

For there's a guard and there's a sad old padre,
Arm in arm we'll walk at daybreak.
Again I'll touch the green, green grass of home.

Yes, they'll all come to see me,
In the shade of that old oak tree
As they lay me 'neath the green, green grass of home.

Groovin'

Words and Music by Felix Cavaliere and Edward Brigati, Jr.

recorded by The Young Rascals

Refrain:
Groovin'
On a Sunday afternoon.
Really
Couldn't get away too soon.

I can't imagine anything that's better,
The world is ours whenever we're together.
There ain't a place I'd like to be instead of

Groovin'
Down a crowded avenue
Doin'
Anything we'd like to do.

There's always lots of things that we could see,
We could be anyone we'd like to be.
And all those happy people we could meet just

Refrain

No, no, no, no.

We'll keep on spendin' sunny days this way.
We're gonna talk and laugh our times away.
I feel it comin' closer day by day.
Life would be ecstasy
You and me endlessly

Refrain

No, no, no, no.
Groovin'
Groovin'...

A Groovy Kind of Love

Words and Music by Toni Wine and Carole Bayer Sager
© 1966 (Renewed 1994) SCREEN GEMS-EMI MUSIC INC.

recorded by The Mindbenders, Phil Collins

When I'm feelin' blue,
All I have to do
Is take a look at you,
Then I'm not so blue.
When you're close to me
I can feel your heart beat
I can hear you breathing in my ear.

Refrain:
Wouldn't you agree,
Baby, you and me
Got a groovy kind of love.
We got a groovy kind of love.

Anytime you want to
You can turn me on to
Anything you want to,
Any time at all.
When I taste your lips,
Oh, I start to shiver,
Can't control the quivering inside.

Refrain

When I'm in your arms
Nothing seems to matter
If the world would shatter
I don't care.

Refrain

Grow Old with Me

Words and Music by John Lennon
© 1982 LENONO.MUSIC
All Rights Controlled and Administered by EMI BLACKWOOD MUSIC INC.

recorded by John Lennon, Mary Chapin Carpenter

Grow old along with me.
The best is yet to be,
When our time has come,
We will be as one.

Refrain:
God bless our love,
God bless our love.

Grow old along with me.
Two branches of one tree,
Face the setting sun,
When the day is done.

Refrain

Spending our lives together,
Man and wife together,
World without end,
World without end.

Grow old along with me.
Whatever fate decrees,
We will see it through,
For our love is true.

Refrain

Guilty

Words and Music by Barry Gibb, Robin Gibb and
Maurice Gibb
Copyright © 1980 by Gibb Brothers Music
All Rights Administered by Careers-BMG Music Publishing, Inc.

recorded by Barbra Streisand & Barry Gibb

Shadows falling, baby,
We stand alone
Out on the street anybody you meet
Got a heartache of their own.
Make it a crime to be lonely or sad
You got a reason for living
You battle on
With the love you're livin' on you gotta be mine.
We take it away.
It's gotta be night and day
Just a matter of time.

Refrain:
And we got nothing to be guilty of
Our love will climb any mountain
Near or far, we are
And we never let it end.
We are devotion
And we got nothing to be sorry for
Our love is one in a million.
Eyes can see that we got a highway to the sky.
I don't want to hear your goodbye.

Pulse's racing, darling,
How grand we are.
Little by little we meet in the middle
There's danger in the dark.
Make it a crime to be out in the cold.
You got a reason for livin'
You battle on
With the love you're buildin' on you gotta be mine.
We take it away.
It's gotta be night and day
Just a matter of time.

Refrain
Don't wanna hear your goodbye.
I don't wanna hear your—
And we got nothing,

Refrain

Hair of the Dog

Words and Music by Dan McCafferty, Darrell Sweet,
Pete Agnew and Manuel Charlton

recorded by Nazareth

I'll break the soul shaker.
I've been told about you.
She rode up, then I showed her,
What they've been sayin' must be true.

Refrain:
Red hot mama, love that charmer;
Just got to pay your dues.
Now you're messin' with a, a son of a bitch.
Now you're messin' with a son of a bitch.
Now you're messin' with a son of a bitch.
Now you're messin' with a son of a bitch.

Talkin' to her with poison ivy,
You ain't gonna cling to me.
Man taker, bone finger,
I ain't so blind I can't see.

Refrain

Now you're messin' with a, a son of a bitch.
Now you're messin' with a son of a bitch.
Now you're messin' with a son of a bitch.
Now you're messin' with a son of a bitch.

Hands of Time

Words by Alan Bergman and Marilyn Bergman
Music by Michel Legrand

Theme from the Screen Gems Television Production
Brian's Song

If the hands of time
Were hands that I could hold,
I'd keep them warm and in my hands
They'd not turn cold.

Hand in hand we'd choose
The moments that should last.
The lovely moments that
Should have no future and no past.

The summer from the top of the swing,
The comfort in the sound of a lullaby,
The innocence of leaves in the spring,
But most of all the moment
When love first touched me!

All the happy days
Would never learn to fly,
Until the hands of time
Would choose to wave "Goodbye."

Happy Birthday Sweet Sixteen

Words and Music by Howard Greenfield and Neil Sedaka

recorded by Neil Sedaka

Tonight's the night I've waited for,
Because you're not a baby anymore.
You've turned into the prettiest girl I've ever seen.
Happy Birthday, sweet sixteen.

What happened to that funny face?
My little tomboy now wears satins and lace.
I can't believe my eyes; you're just a teenage dream.
Happy birthday sweet sixteen.

If I should smile with sweet surprise,
It's just that you've grown up before my very eyes,
You've turned into the prettiest girl I've ever seen.
Happy Birthday, sweet sixteen.

When you were only six, I was your big brother;
Then when you were ten, we didn't like each other.
When you were thirteen, you were my funny valentine.
But since you've grown up your future is sewn up,
From now on, you're gonna be mine.

Repeat Song

Happy Together

Words and Music by Garry Bonner and Alan Gordon

recorded by The Turtles

Imagine me and you, I do.
I think about you day and night,
It's only right
To think about the girl you love,
And hold her tight,
So happy together.

If I should call you up,
Invest a dime,
And you say you belong to me
And ease my mind
Imagine how the world would be,
So very fine,
So happy together.

I can see me lovin' nobody but you
For all my life.
When you're with me baby, the skies will be blue
For all of my life.
Me and you and you and me,
No matter how they toss the dice,
It has to be.

The only one for me is you,
And you for me,
So happy together,
So happy together.

Happy Trails
Words and Music by Dale Evans

from the Television Series *The Roy Rogers Show*
recorded by Roy Rogers & Dale Evans

Happy trails to you until we meet again.
Happy trails to you, keep smilin' until then.
Who cares about the clouds when we're together?
Just sing a song and bring the sunny weather.
Happy trails to you, till we meet again.

A Hard Day's Night
Words and Music by John Lennon and Paul McCartney

from the film *A Hard Day's Night*
recorded by The Beatles

Refrain:
It's been a hard day's night,
And I've been working like a dog.
It's been a hard day's night,
I should be sleeping like a log.
But when I get home to you,
I find the things that you do,
Will make me feel alright.

You know I work all day,
To get you money to buy you things.
And it's worth it just to hear you say,
You're gonna give me everything.
So why on earth should I moan,
'Cause when I get you alone,
You know I feel okay.

When I'm home
Everything seems to be right.
When I'm home,
Feeling you holding me tight, tight, yeah.

Refrain

So why on earth should I moan,
'Cause when I get you alone,
You know I feel okay.

When I'm home
Everything seems to be right.
When I'm home,
Feeling you holding me tight, tight, yeah.

Refrain

Hard Habit to Break
Words and Music by Stephen Kipner and
John Lewis Parker

recorded by Chicago

I guess I thought you'd be here forever,
Another illusion I chose to create.
You don't know what you got until it's gone,
And I found out a little too late.

I was acting as if
You were lucky to have me,
Doin' you a favor
(I hardly knew you were there.)
But then you were gone,
And it all was wrong,
Had no idea how much I cared.

Refrain:
Now being without you
Takes a lot of getting used to,
Should learn to live with it
But I don't want to.
Being without you
Is all a big mistake,
Instead of getting easier,
It's the hardest thing to take.
I'm addicted to you, babe,
You're a hard habit to break.

You found someone else, you had every reason,
You know I can't blame you for runnin' to him.
Two people together but livin' alone,
I was spreading my love too thin.

After all of these years
I'm still try'n to shake it,
Doin' much better.
(They say that it just takes time.)
But deep in the night,
It's an endless fight,
I can't get you out of my mind.

Refrain

Can't go on,
Just can't go on, on.
Can't go on,
Just can't go on, on.

Refrain

Hard to Say I'm Sorry

Words and Music by Peter Cetera and David Foster

recorded by Chicago

Everybody needs a little time away,
I heard her say,
From each other.
Even lovers need a holiday,
Far away
From each other.
Hold me now.
It's hard for me to say I'm sorry.
I just want you to stay.

After all that we've been through,
I will make it up to you.
I'll promise to.
And after all that's been said and done
You're just the part of me I can't let go.

Couldn't stand to be kept away,
Just for the day,
From your body.
Wouldn't wanna be swept away,
Far away,
From the one that I love.
Hold me now.
It's hard for me to say I'm sorry.
I just want you to know.
Hold me now.
I really want to tell you I'm sorry.
I could never let you go.

After all that we've been through,
I will make it up to you.
I'll promise to.
And after all that's been said and done
You're just the part of me I can't let go.
After all that we've been through,
I will make it up to you.
I'll promise to.
You're gonna be the lucky one.

Harlem Nocturne

Music by Earle Hagen
Words by Dick Rogers

a standard recorded by Ray Noble, Herbie Fields,
The Viscounts and various other artists

Deep music fills the night, deep in the heart of Harlem
And tho' the stars are bright, the darkness is taunting me.
Oh! what a sad refrain, a nocturne is born in Harlem,
That melancholy strain, forever is haunting me.

The melody clings around my heart strings
It won't let me go. When I'm lonely
I hear it in my dreams and somehow it seems
It makes me weep and I can't sleep.

An indigo tune it sings to the moon,
The lonesome refrain of a lover.
The melody sighs it laughs and it cries,
A moan in the blue that wails the long night thru.

Tho' with the dawn it's gone.
The melody lives ever
For lonely hearts to learn
Of love in a Harlem nocturne.

Harper Valley P.T.A.

Words and Music by Tom T. Hall

recorded by Jeannie C. Riley

I want to tell you all a story
'Bout a Harper Valley widowed wife
Who had a teenage daughter
Who attended Harper Valley Junior High.
Well her daughter came home one afternoon,
And didn't even stop to play;
She said, "Mom I got a note here
From the Harper Valley P.T.A."

The note said, "Misses Johnson
You're wearing your dresses way too high;
It's reported you've been drinking
And a-runnin' 'round with men and goin' wild:
And we don't believe you ought to be
A-bringing up your little girl this way."
It was signed by the secretary.
Harper Valley P.T.A.

Well, it happened that the P.T.A.
Was gonna meet that very afternoon;
They were sure surprised when Misses Johnson
Wore her mini-skirt into the room.
And as she walked up to the blackboard,
I still recall the words she had to say;
She said, "I'd like to address this meeting
Of the Harper Valley P.T.A."

Well there's Bobby Taylor sittin' there,
And seven times he's asked me for a date;
Misses Taylor sure seems to use a lot of ice
Whenever he's away.

And Mister Baker, can you tell us
Why your secretary had to leave this town,
And shouldn't Widow Jones be told
To keep her window shades all pulled completely down?"

Well Mister Harper couldn't be here
'Cause he stayed too long at Kelly's bar again,
And if you smell Shirley Thompson's breath,
You'll find she's had a little nip of gin.

Then you have the nerve to tell me
You think that as a mother I'm not fit,
Well, this is just a little Peyton Place,
And you're all Harper Valley hypocrites."

No I wouldn't put you on because it really did,
It happened just this way,
The day my Mama socked it to
The Harper Valley P.T.A.
The day my Mama socked it to
The Harper Valley P.T.A.

Have You Ever Really Loved a Woman?
Words and Music by Bryan Adams, Michael Kamen and Robert John Lange

from the Motion Picture *Don Juan DeMarco*
recorded by Bryan Adams

To really love a woman
To understand her, you gotta know her deep inside;
Hear every thought, see every dream,
'N' give her wings when she wants to fly.
Then when you find yourself lyin' helpless in her arms,
Ya know ya really love a woman.

Refrain:
When you love a woman you tell her that she's really wanted.
When you love a woman you tell her that she's the one.
'Cause she needs somebody to tell her
That it's gonna last forever.
So tell me,
Have you ever really, really, really ever loved a woman?

To really love a woman,
Let her hold you 'til ya know how she needs to be touched.
You've gotta breathe her, really taste her,
'Til you can feel her in your blood.
'N' when you can see you unborn children in her eyes,
Ya know ya really love a woman.

Refrain

You got to give her some faith, hold her tight.
A little tenderness, gotta treat her right.
She will be there for you, takin' good care of you.
Ya gotta love your woman…

Have You Met Miss Jones?
Words by Lorenz Hart
Music by Richard Rodgers

from the musical *I'd Rather Be Right*
a standard recorded by various artists

It happened, I felt it happen.
I was awake, I wasn't blind.
I didn't think, I felt it happen.
Now I believe in matter over mind.
And you see we mustn't wait.
The nearest moment that we marry is too late!

Refrain:
"Have you met Miss Jones?"
Someone said as we shook hands.
She was just Miss Jones to me.
Then I said, "Miss Jones,
You're a girl who understands
I'm a man who must be free."
And all at once I lost my breath.
And all at once was scared to death.
And all at once I owned the earth and sky!
Now I've met Miss Jones
And we'll keep on meeting till we die,
Miss Jones and I.

He Ain't Heavy... He's My Brother
Words and Music by Bob Russell and Bobby Scott

recorded by The Hollies, Neil Diamond

The road is long
With many a winding turn
That leads us to
Who knows where, who knows where.
But I'm strong
Strong enough to carry him.
He ain't heavy,
He's my brother.

So on we go.
His welfare is my concern.
No burden is he to bear.
We'll get there.
For I know
He would not encumber me.
He ain't heavy,
He's my brother.

If I'm laden at all,
I'm laden with sadness
That everyone's heart
Isn't filled with the gladness
Of love for one another.

It's a long, long road
From which there is no return.
While we're on our way to there,
Why not share?
And the load doesn't weigh
Me down at all.
He ain't heavy,
He's my brother.

He Thinks He'll Keep Her

Words and Music by Mary Chapin Carpenter
and Don Schlitz

recorded by Mary Chapin Carpenter

She makes his coffee, she makes his bed,
She does the laundry, she keeps him fed.
When she was twenty-one, she wore her mother's lace,
She said forever with a smile upon her face.

She does the carpool, she P.T.A.'s,
Doctors and dentists, she drives all day.
When she was twenty-nine she delivered number three,
And every Christmas card showed a perfect family.

Refrain:
Everything runs right on time, years of practice and design.
Spit and polish 'til it shines, he thinks he'll keep her.
Everything is so benign, the safest place you'll ever find,
God forbid you'd change your mind, he thinks he'll keep her.

She packs his suitcase, she sits and waits,
With no expression upon her face.
When she was thirty-six she met him at their door,
She said, "I'm sorry, I don't love you anymore."

Refrain

For fifteen years she had a job and not one raise in pay,
Now she's in the typing pool at minimum wage.

Refrain

(At least until you change your mind.)

He Was Too Good to Me

Words by Lorenz Hart
Music by Richard Rodgers

from the musical *Simple Simon*

There goes my young intended.
The thing is ended.
Regrets are vain.
I'll never find another half so sweet
And we'll never meet again.

I was a good sport,
Told him
Goodbye.
Eyes dim,
But why complain?

Refrain:
He was too good to me
How can I get along now?
So close he stood to me
Everything seems all wrong now.
He would have brought me the sun.
Making me smile,
That was his fun.
When I was mean to him,
He'd never say, "Go 'way now."
I was a queen to him.
Who's goin' to make me gay now?
It's only natural I'm blue.
He was too good to be true.

He's Sure the Boy I Love

Words and Music by Barry Mann and Cynthia Weil

recorded by The Crystals

Spoken:
I always dreamed the boy I loved would come along
And he'd be tall and handsome, rich and strong.
Now the boy I love has come to me.
But he sure ain't the way I thought he'd be.

Sung:
He doesn't look like a movie star,
He doesn't drive a Cadillac car,
He sure ain't the boy I've been dreamin' of,
But he's sure the boy I love.

Let me tell ya now,
He'll never be a big business man,
He always buys on the installment plan,
He sure ain't the boy I've been dreamin' of,
But he's sure the boy I love.

'Cause when he holds me tight,
Everything's right, crazy as it seems,
I'm his, whatever he is,
And I forgot all of my dreams.
Now everybody knows
That he doesn't hang diamonds 'round my neck,
And all he's got's an unemployment check.
He sure ain't the boy I've been dreamin' of,
But he's sure the boy I love.

Heart and Soul

Words by Frank Loesser
Music by Hoagy Carmichael
Copyright © 1938 (Renewed 1965) by Famous Music Corporation

from the Paramount Short Subject *A Song Is Born*
a standard recorded by Eddy Duchin, Johnny Maddox,
The Cleftones, Jan & Dean and various other artists

I've let a pair of arms enslave me oft time before,
But more than just a thrill you gave me,
Yes more, much more.

Heart and soul,
I fell in love with you.
Heart and soul,
The way a fool would do
Madly,
Because you held me tight
And stole a kiss in the night.

Heart and soul,
I begged to be adored.
Lost control
And tumbled overboard
Gladly
That magic night we kissed
There in the moon-mist.

Oh! But your lips were thrilling, much too thrilling.
Never before were mine so strangely willing.

But now I see
What one embrace can do.
Look at me,
It's got me loving you
Madly;
That little kiss you stole
Held all my heart and soul.

Heartache Tonight

Words and Music by John David Souther, Don Henley,
Glenn Frey and Bob Seger
© 1979 EMI BLACKWOOD MUSIC INC., WOODY CREEK MUSIC, RED CLOUD MUSIC
    and GEAR PUBLISHING CO.

recorded by The Eagles

Somebody's gonna hurt someone
Before the night is through.
Somebody's gonna come undone;
There's nothin' we can do.
Everybody wants to touch somebody,
If it takes all night.
Everybody wants to take a little chance,
Make it come out right.
There's gonna be a heartache tonight,
A heartache tonight, I know.
Lord, I know.

Some people like to stay out late.
Some folks can't hold out that long.
But nobody wants to go home now;
There's too much goin' on.
The night is gonna last forever.
Last all, last all summer long.
Sometime before the sun comes up
The radio is gonna play that song.
There's gonna be a heartache tonight,
A heartache tonight, I know.

There's gonna be a heartache tonight,
A heartache tonight, I know.
Lord, I know.
There's gonna be a heartache tonight,
The moon's shinin' bright,
So turn out the light, and we'll get it right.
There's gonna be a heartache tonight,
A heartache tonight, I know.

Somebody's gonna hurt someone
Before the night is through.
Somebody's gonna come undone;
There's nothin' we can do.
Everybody wants to touch somebody,
If it takes all night.
Everybody wants to take a little chance,
Make it come out right.
There's gonna be a heartache tonight,
A heartache tonight, I know.

Let's go.
We can beat around the bushes;
We can get down to the bone;
We can leave it in the parkin' lot,
But either way, there's gonna be a heartache tonight,
A heartache tonight, I know.
Oh, I know.
There'll be a heartache tonight,
A heartache tonight, I know.

Heartbreak Hotel

Words and Music by Mae Boren Axton, Tommy Durden
and Elvis Presley
Copyright © 1956 Sony/ATV Songs LLC
Copyright Renewed
All Rights Administered by Sony/ATV Music Publishing, 8 Music Square West,
    Nashville, TN 37203

recorded by Elvis Presley

Well, since my baby left me,
Well I found a new place to dwell,
Down at the end of Lonely Street,
At Heartbreak Hotel.
I'm so lonely,
I'm so lonely,
I'm so lonely that I could die.

And though it's overcrowded
You can still find some room
For broken hearted lovers
To cry there in the gloom,
And be so lonely,

Oh, so lonely,
Oh, so lonely they could die.

The bell hop's tears are flowing,
The clerk's dressed in black.
They've been so long in Lonely Street
They never will go back.
And they're so lonely,
Oh, they're so lonely,
They're so lonely they pray to die.

So if your baby leaves you
And you have a tale to tell,
Just take a walk down Lonely Street
To Heartbreak Hotel
Where you'll be so lonely,
And I'll be so lonely,
We'll be so lonely
That we could die.

Heat Wave

Words and Music by Irving Berlin

from the Stage Production *As Thousands Cheer*
featured in the films *Alexander's Ragtime Band,
Blue Skies, There's No Business Like Show Business*

A heat wave blew right into town last week.
She came from the Island of Martinique.
The can-can she dances will make you fry.
The can-can is really the reason why.

Refrain:
We're having a heat wave,
A tropical heat wave.
The temperature's rising,
It isn't surprising.
She certainly can can-can.
She started a heat wave
By letting her seat wave.
And in such a way that
The customers say that
She certainly can can-can.
Gee her anatomy
Made the mercury
Jump to ninety three.
Yes sir!
We're having a heat wave
A tropical heat wave,
The way that she moves
That thermometer proves
That she certainly can can-can.

Repeat Refrain

Patter:
It's so hot the weather man
Will tell you a record's been made.
It's so hot a coat of tan
Will cover your face in the shade.
It's so hot the coldest maiden
Feels just as warm as a bride.
It's so hot a chicken laid an
Egg on the street and it fried.

Refrain

Heatwave
(Love Is Like a Heatwave)

Words and Music by Edward Holland, Lamont Dozier and
Brian Holland

recorded by Martha & The Vandellas

Whenever I'm with him
Something inside
Starts to burnin'
And I'm filled with desire.
Could it be
A devil in me?
Or is this the way
Love's supposed to be?

Refrain:
It's like a heatwave
Burnin' in my heart.
I can't keep from cryin'
It's tearin' me apart.

Whenever he calls my name
Soft, low, sweet and plain,
I feel, yeah, yeah,
Well I feel that burnin' flame.
Has high blood pressure
Got a hold on me
Or is this the way
Love's supposed to be?

Refrain

Sometimes I stare into space,
Tears all over my face.
I can't explain it, don't understand it.
I ain't never felt like this before.
Now that funny feelin'
Has me amazed.
I don't know what to do,
My head's in a haze.

Refrain

Yeah, yeah, yeah, yeah, yeah,
Yeah, whoa ho.
Yeah, yeah, yeah,
Yeah ho.
Don't pass up this chance,
This time it's true romance,

Refrain

Heaven in Your Eyes

Words and Music by Paul Dean, Mike Reno, John Dexter and Mae Moore

from the Paramount Motion Picture *Top Gun*
recorded by Loverboy

I can tell by the look in your eyes you've been hurting;
You know I'll never let you down, oh no.
And I'll try anything to keep it working.
You gave me time to find out what my heart was looking for
And what I'm feeling inside.

Refrain:
I want to see your love again in your eyes;
I never want this feeling to end.
It took some time to find the light,
But now I realize
I can see the heaven in your eyes.

Can't you see I'm finding it hard to let go?
All the heartaches we've been through.
I never really thought I'd see this love grow.
But you helped me to see;
I know what my heart's been looking for
And what I'm feeling inside.

Refrain

We've been living on the edge,
Where only the strong survive.
We've been living on the edge,
And it's something that we just can't hide.
Oh, this feeling inside.

Refrain

Oh, yeah, I can see the heaven in your eyes.
(Heaven in your eyes.)
I can see the heaven in your eyes.

Hello, Goodbye

Words and Music by John Lennon and Paul McCartney

recorded by The Beatles

You say yes,
I say no,
You say stop,
I say go go go.
Oh no.
You say goodbye and I say hello
Hello hello,
I don't know why you say goodbye I say hello.
Hello hello,
I don't know why you say goodbye I say hello.

I say high,
You say low.
You say why
And I say I don't know.
Oh no.
You say goodbye and I say hello.
Hello hello,
I don't know why you say goodbye I say hello.
Hello hello,
I don't know why you say goodbye I say hello.

Why, why, why
Why, why, why
Why do you
Say goodbye, goodbye, bye, bye?
Oh no.
You say goodbye and I say hello.
Hello hello,
I don't know why you say goodbye I say hello.
Hello hello,
I don't know why you say goodbye I say hello.

You say yes,
I say no,
(I say yes
But I may mean no)
You say stop,
And I say go go go.
(I can stay till it's time to go)
Oh, oh no.
You say goodbye and I say hello.
Hello hello,
I don't know why you say goodbye I say hello.
Hello hello,
I don't know why you say goodbye I say hello.
Hello hello,
Hello, hello, hello
Hello, hello, hello
Hela, heba helloa.

Hello, It's Me

Words and Music by Todd Rundgren

recorded by Todd Rundgren

Hello, it's me, I've thought about us for a long, long time.
Maybe I think too much but something's wrong.
There's something here that doesn't last too long.
Maybe I shouldn't think of you as mine.

Seeing you, or seeing anything as much as I do,
I take for granted that you're always there.
I take for granted that you just don't care.
Sometimes I can't help seeing all the way through.

Refrain:
It's important to me that you know you are free,
'Cause I never want to make you change for me.
Think of me.

You know that I'd be with you if I could.
I'll come around to see you once in awhile,
Or if I ever need a reason to smile,
And spend the night if you think I should.

Sometimes I thought it wasn't so bad.

Hello, Young Lovers

Lyrics by Oscar Hammerstein II
Music by Richard Rodgers

from the musical *The King and I*

When I think of Tom
I think about a night
When the earth smelled of summer
And the sky was streaked with white,
And the soft mist of England
Was sleeping on a hill,
I remember this
And I always will.
There are new lovers now
On the same silent hill
Looking on the same blue sea,
And I know Tom and I
Are a part of them all
And they're all a part of Tom and me.

Hello, young lovers,
Whoever you are,
I hope your troubles are few
All my good wishes go with you tonight
I've been in love like you.
Be brave, young lovers, and follow your star,
Be brave and faithful and true.
Cling very close to each other tonight
I've been in love like you.

I know how it feels
To have wings on your heels,
And to fly down a street in a trance
You fly down a street
On a chance that you'll meet,
And you meet
Not really by chance.

Don't cry young lovers,
Whatever you do,
Don't cry because I'm alone.
All of my memories are happy tonight!
I've had a love of my own,
I've had a love of my own like yours,
I've had a love of my own.

Help!

Words and Music by John Lennon and Paul McCartney

from the film *Help!*
recorded by The Beatles

Help, I need somebody.
Help, not just anybody.
Help, you know I need somebody.
Help!

When I was younger
So much younger than today,
I never needed anybody's help in any way.
But now these days are gone,
I'm not so self assured,
Now I find I've changed my mind I've opened up the doors.

Refrain:
Help me if you can I'm feeling down
And I do appreciate you being around.
Help me get my feet back on the ground
Won't you please, please help me.

And now my life has changed
In oh so many ways.
My independence seems to vanish in the haze.
But every now and then I feel so insecure,
I know that I just need you like I've never done before.

Refrain

When I was younger
So much younger than today,
I never needed anybody's help in any way.
But now these days are gone,
I'm not so self assured,
Now I find I've changed my mind I've opened up the doors.

Refrain

Help me!
Help me!

Here and Now

Words and Music by Terry Steele and David Elliot

recorded by Luther Vandross

One look in your eyes,
And there I see
Just what you mean to me.
Here in my heart I believe

Your love is all I ever need.
Holding you close through the night,
I need you. Yeah.

I look in your eyes and there I see
What happiness really means.
The love that we share makes life so sweet.
Together we'll always be.
This pledge of love feels so right,
And ooh, I need you. Yeah.

Refrain:
Here and now,
I promise to love faithfully.
You're all I need.
Here and now,
I vow to be one with thee.
Your love is all I need.

Stay.

When I look in your eyes
And there I see
All that a love should really be.
And I need you more and more each day.
Nothing can take your love away.
More than I dare to dream.
I need you.

Refrain

Starting here.
Ooh, and I'm starting now.
I believe (I believe)
Starting here.
I'm starting right here.
Starting now.
Right now because I believe in your love,
So I'm glad to take the vow.
Here and now, oh,
I promise to love you faithfully.
You're all I need.
Here and now,
I vow to be one with thee.
Your love is all I need.

Here Comes the Sun

Words and Music by George Harrison

recorded by The Beatles

Here comes the sun.
Here comes the sun.
And I say it's all right.

Little darling,
It's been a long cold lonely winter.
Little darling,
It feels like years since it's been here.

Here comes the sun.
Here comes the sun.
And I say it's all right.

Little darling,
The smiles returning to their faces.
Little darling,
It seems like years since it's been here.

Here comes the sun.
Here comes the sun.
And I say it's all right.

Sun, sun, sun, here it comes,
Sun, sun, sun, here it comes,
Sun, sun, sun, here it comes,
Sun, sun, sun, here it comes.

Little darling,
I feel that ice is slowly melting.
Little darling,
It seems like years since it's been clear.

Here comes the sun.
Here comes the sun.
And I say it's all right.

Here in My Arms

Words by Lorenz Hart
Music by Richard Rodgers

from the musical *Dearest Enemy*

He:
I know a merry place
Far from intrusion.
It's just the very place
For your seclusion.
There you can while away.
It's not a mile away
But it's new to you.

Refrain:
Here in my arms it's adorable.
It's deplorable
That you were never there.
When little lips are kissable
It's permissible
For me to ask my share.
Next to my heart it is ever so lonely,
I'm holding only air,
While here in my arms it's adorable!
It's deplorable
That you were never there.

She:
I know a pretty place
At your command, sir.
It's not a city place,

Yet near at hand, sir.
Here, if you loll away,
Two hearts can toll away.
You'd never stroll away,
If only you knew.

Refrain

Reprise:
Your pretty words were adorable.
It's deplorable
That they were only lies.
Still you will find that I'm affable.
It was laughable
That I believed your eyes.
Next to my heart it is ever so lonely,
I'm holding only air,
While here in my arms it's adorable!
It's deplorable
You will never be there.

Here, There and Everywhere
Words and Music by John Lennon and Paul McCartney

recorded by The Beatles

To lead a better life
I need my love to be here.

Here, making each day of the year,
Changing my life with a wave of her hand.
Nobody can deny that there's something there.
There, running my hands through her hair,
Both of us thinking how good it can be.
Someone is speaking, but she doesn't know he's there.

Refrain:
I want her everywhere
And if she's beside me I know I need never care.
But to love her is to need her everywhere,
Knowing that love is to share;
Each one believing that love never dies,
Watching her and hoping I'm always there.

Repeat Refrain

I will be there
And everywhere,
Here, there and everywhere.

Here's That Rainy Day
Words by Johnny Burke
Music by Jimmy Van Heusen

from the musical *Carnival in Flanders*
a standard recorded by Frank Sinatra, Tony Bennett, and
various other artists

Maybe I should have saved those left-over dreams;
Funny, but here's that rainy day.
Here's that rainy day they told me about,
And I laughed
At the thought that it might turn out this way.
Where is the worn out wish that I threw aside,
After it brought my lover near?
Funny how love becomes a cold, rainy day.
Funny that rainy day is here.

Hero
Words and Music by Mariah Carey and Walter Afanasieff

recorded by Mariah Carey

There's a hero
If you look inside your heart.
You don't have to be afraid
Of what you are.
There's an answer
If you reach into your soul
And the sorrow that you know
Will melt away.

Refrain:
And then a hero comes along
With the strength to carry on
And you cast your fears aside
And you know you can survive.
So, when you feel like hope is gone
Look inside you and be strong
And you'll finally see the truth
That a hero lies in you.

It's a long road
When you face the world alone.
No one reaches out a hand
For you to hold.
You can find love
If you search within yourself
And the emptiness you felt
Will disappear.

Refrain

Lord knows
Dreams are hard to follow,
Don't let anyone tear them away.
Hold on,
There will be tomorrow.
In time you'll find the way.

Refrain

Hey, Good Lookin'

Words and Music by Hank Williams

recorded by Hank Williams, Frankie Laine & Jo Stafford

Refrain:
Hey, hey, good loookin'
Whatcha got cookin'
How's about cookin' somethin' up with me

Hey, sweet baby,
Don't you think maybe
We could find is a brand new recipe?

I got a hot rod and a Ford and a two dollar bill
And I know a spot right over the hill.
There's soda pop and the dancin's free,
So if you wanna have fun come along with me.

Refrain

I'm free and ready
So we can go steady.
How's about savin' all your time for me.

No more lookin'
I know I've been tooken.
How's about keepin' steady company?

I'm gonna throw my date book over the fence
And find me one for five or ten cents;
I'll keep it 'til it's covered with age
'Cause I'm writin' your name down on every page.

Refrain

Hey Jude

Words and Music by John Lennon and Paul McCartney

recorded by The Beatles

Hey Jude, don't make it bad,
Take a sad song and make it better.
Remember to let her into your heart,
Then you can start to make it better.

Hey Jude, don't be afraid.
You were made to go out and get her.
The minute you let her under your skin,
Then you begin to make it better.

And anytime you feel the pain,
Hey Jude refrain,
Don't carry the world upon your shoulders,
For well you know that it's a fool who plays it cool
By making the world a little colder.

Hey Jude, don't let me down,
You have found her now go and get her.
Remember (Hey Jude) to let her into your heart
Then you can start to make it better.

So let it out and let it in,
Hey Jude begin,
You're waiting for someone to perform with,
And don't you know that it's just you.
Hey Jude, you'll do.
The movement you need is on your shoulder.

Hey Jude, don't make it bad,
Take a sad song and make it better.
Remember to let her under your skin,
Then you begin to make it better.
Better, better, better …

Hi-De-Ho (That Old Sweet Roll)

Words and Music by Gerry Goffin and Carole King

recorded by Blood, Sweat & Tears

Refrain:
Hi-de-ho, Hi-de-ho,
Gonna get me a piece of the sky,
Gonna find me some o' that old sweet roll,
Singin' hi-de-hi-de-ho-de-hi-de-ho.

I been down so low bottom looked like up.
Once I thought that second saves was enough to fill my cup.
Now I understand all I had,
But it ain't no way to live,
Bein' taken by the ones who got the least amount to give.

Refrain

Once I met the devil and he was mighty slick.
Tempted me with worldly goods and said,
"You can have your pick."
But when he laid that paper on me
And showed me where to sign,
I said "Thank you very kindly,
But I'm in too great a need of mine."

Refrain

Higher Ground
Words and Music by Stevie Wonder

recorded by Stevie Wonder

People keep on learnin'.
Soldiers keep on warrin',
World keep on turnin'
'Cause it won't be too long.
Powers keep on lyin',
While you people keep on dyin'.
World keep on turnin'
'Cause it won't be too long.

Refrain:
I'm so darn glad he let me try it again,
'Cause my last time on earth I lived a whole world of sin.
I'm so glad that I know more than I knew then,
Gonna keep on tryin' till I reach the highest ground.

Lovers keep on lovin',
Believers keep on believin'.
Sleepers just stop sleepin'
'Cause it won't be too long.

Refrain

Repeat and Fade:
Till I reach my highest ground.
No one's gonna bring me down.

Higher Love
Words and Music by Will Jennings and Steve Winwood

recorded by Steve Winwood

Think about it, there must be higher love,
Down in the heart or hidden in the stars above.
Without it, life is wasted time.
Look inside your heart, I'll look inside mine.

Refrain:
Things look so bad everywhere.
In this whole world what is fair?
We walk blind and we try to see,
Falling behind in what could be.
Bring me a higher love,
Bring me a higher love, whoa.
Bring me a higher love.

Where's that higher love I keep thinking of.

Worlds are turning and we're just hanging on,
Facing our fear and standing out there alone.
A yearning, and it's real to me.
There must be someone who's feeling for me.

Refrain
I could rise above on a higher love.

I will not wait for it.
I'm not too late for it.
Until then, I'll sing my song
To cheer the night along.
Bring it.

I could light the night up with my soul on fire.
I could make the sunshine from pure desire.
Let me feel that love come over me.
Let me feel how strong it could be.

Repeat and Fade:
Bring me a higher love,
Bring me a higher love, whoa.
Bring me a higher love,
Bring me a higher love.

Hit Me with Your Best Shot
Words and Music by Eddie Schwartz

recorded by Pat Benatar

Well, you're a real tough cookie
With a long history
Of breaking little hearts
Like the one in me.
That's O.K.
Let's see how you do it.
Put up your dukes.
Let's get down to it.

Refrain:
Hit me with your best shot.
Why don't you
Hit me with your best shot?
Hit me with your best shot.
Fire away.

You come on with a come on.
You don't fight fair.
But that's O.K.
See if I care.
Knock me down.
It's all in vain.
I'll get right back on
My feet again.

Refrain

Well, you're a real tough cookie
With a long history
Of breaking little hearts
Like the one in me.
Before I put another notch
In my lipstick case,
You better make sure
You put me in my place.

Refrain

Hit the Road to Dreamland

Words by Johnny Mercer
Music by Harold Arlen
Copyright © 1942 (Renewed 1969) by Famous Music Corporation

from the Paramount Picture *Star Spangled Rhythm*

Twinkle, twinkle, twinkle, twinkle
Goes the star,
Twinkle, twinkle, twinkle, twinkle
There you are.
Time for all good children to hit the hay.
Cock-a-doodle, doodle, doodle
Brother it's another day
We should be on our way!

Bye, bye, baby
Time to hit the road to dreamland
You're my baby
Dig you in the land of nod.
Hold tight baby
We'll be swinging up in dreamland
All night baby
Where the little cherubs trod.
Look at that knocked out moon,
Been a blowin' his top in the blue.
Never saw the likes of you;
What an angel.
Bye, bye, baby
Time to hit the road to dreamland.
Don't cry baby
It was divine but the rooster has finally crowed
Time to hit the road.

Hold My Hand

Words and Music by Darius Carlos Rucker, Everett Dean
Felber, Mark William Bryan and James George Sonefeld
© 1994 EMI APRIL MUSIC INC. and MONICA'S RELUCTANCE TO LOB
All Rights Controlled and Administered by EMI APRIL MUSIC INC.

recorded by Hootie & The Blowfish

With a little love,
And some tenderness,
We'll walk upon the water,
We'll rise above the mess.
With a little peace,
And some harmony,
We'll take the world together,
We'll take 'em by the hand.
'Cause I got a hand for you.
I wanna run with you.

Yesterday,
I saw you standing there.
Your head was down,
Your eyes were red,
No comb had touched your hair.
I said, "Get up
And let me see you smile.
We'll take a walk together,
Walk the road a while."

'Cause I got a hand for you.
Won't you let me run with you?

Refrain 1:
Hold my hand.
Want you to hold my hand.
Hold my hand.
I'll take you to a place where you can be
Anything you wanna be because
I wanna love you the best that,
The best that I can.

See, I was wasted
And I was wasting time.
'Til I thought about your problem,
I thought about your crime.
Then I stood up
And I screamed aloud,
"Don't wanna be part of your problem,
Don't wanna be part of your crowd."
'Cause I got a hand for you.
Won't you let me run with you?

Refrain 2:
Hold my hand.
Want you to hold my hand.
Hold my hand.
I'll take you to the promised land.
Maybe we can't change the world, but
I wanna love you the best that,
The best that I can.

Refrain 1

Refrain 2

Holding Back the Years

Words by Mick Hucknall
Music by Mick Hucknall and Neil Moss
© 1985 SO WHAT LTD.
All Rights Controlled and Administered by EMI APRIL MUSIC INC.

recorded by Simply Red

Holding back the years,
Thinking of the fear I've had so long
When somebody hears,
Listen to the fear that's gone.
Strangled by the wishes of Pater,
Hoping for the arms of Mater,
Get to meet her sooner or later.
I'll keep holding on. I'll keep holding on.

Holding back the years,
Chance for me to escape from all I've known.
Holding back the tears,
'Cause nothing here has grown.
I've wasted all my tears,
Wasted all those years.
Nothing had the chance to be good,
Nothing ever could.

Refrain:
I'll keep holding on.

Well I've wasted all my tears,
Wasted all of those years.
And nothing had a chance to be good,
'Cause nothing ever could.

Refrain

Honesty
Words and Music by Billy Joel

recorded by Billy Joel

If you search for tenderness,
It isn't hard to find.
You can have the love you need to live.
And if you look for truthfulness
You might as well be blind
It always seems to be so hard to give.

Refrain:
Honesty
Is such a lonely word.
Everyone is so untrue.
Honesty
Is hardly ever heard,
But mostly what I need from you.

I can always find someone
To say they sympathize
If I wear my heart out on my sleeve.
But I don't want some pretty face
To tell me pretty lies.
All I want is someone to believe.

Refrain

I can find a lover,
I can find a friend,
I can have security
Until the bitter end.
Anyone can comfort me
With promises again
I know
I know.

When I'm deep inside of me
Don't be too concerned
I won't ask for nothin' while I'm gone.
When I want sincerity,
Tell me, where else can I turn?
Cause you're the one that I depend upon.

Refrain

Honeysuckle Rose
Words by Andy Razaf
Music by Thomas "Fats" Waller

featured in the musical revue *Ain't Misbehavin'*
a standard recorded by various artists

Every honey bee fills with jealousy
When they see you out with me.
I don't blame them, goodness knows,
Honeysuckle Rose.

When you're passin' by,
Flowers droop and sigh,
And I know the reason why;
You're much sweeter, goodness knows.

Don't buy sugar, you just have to touch my cup.
You're my sugar, it's sweet when you stir it up.
When I'm takin' sips from your tasty lips,
Seems the honey fairly drips.
You're confection, goodness knows,
Honeysuckle Rose.

Hopelessly
Words and Music by Rick Astley and Rob Fisher

recorded by Rick Astley

I walk the wire every night.
I can't decide between wrong and right.
I've lost control over the things I wanna do,
'Cause I'm hopelessly fallin' in love with you.

Now the one who never took a chance
Becomes a victim of circumstance.
I've lost my way, now I'm so confused,
'Cause I'm hopelessly fallin' in love with you.

All my dreams are far behind me.
They don't matter anymore.
I don't care about the things I could lose,
'Cause I'm hopelessly fallin' in love with you.

Now the one who always played it safe
Becomes another who's lost his way.
I can't believe it though I know it's true,
'Cause I'm hopelessly fallin' in love with you.

And all my dreams begin to blind me,
And I was so confused.
And I don't care about the things I could lose,
'Cause I'm hopelessly fallin' in love with you.

I'm not gonna fight it.
I'm gonna choose to hopelessly fall,
Ooh, yeah, you know I'll hopelessly
Fall in love with you.

How Am I Supposed to Live Without You

Words and Music by Michael Bolton and Doug James

recorded by Michael Bolton

I could hardly believe it
When I heard the news today.
I had to come and get it straight from you.
They said you are leavin'
Someone's swept your heart away.
From the look upon your face
I see it's true.
So tell me all about it
Tell me 'bout the plans you makin',
Oh, tell me one thing more
Before I go.

Refrain:
Tell me how am I
Supposed to live without you,
Now that I've
Been lovin' you so long?
How am I
Supposed to live without you?
And how am I
Supposed to carry on
When all that I've
Been living for is gone?

I'm too proud for crying,
Didn't come here to break down.
It's just a dream of mine is comin' to an end.
And how can I blame you
When I built my world around
The hope that one day we'd be
So much more than friends?
I don't want to know the price
I'm gonna pay for dreamin'
Oh, even now
It's more than I can take.

Refrain

Now I don't wanna know the price
I'm gonna pay for dreamin'
Oh, now that your dream has come true.

Refrain

How Are Things in Glocca Morra

Words by E.Y. Harburg
Music by Burton Lane

from the musical *Finian's Rainbow*

I hear a bird,
Londonderry bird,
It well may be he's bringing me a cheering word.
I hear a breeze,
A River Shannon breeze,
It well may be it's followed me across the seas.
Then tell me please:

How are things in Glocca Morra?
Is that little brook still leaping there?
Does it still run down to Donny cove?
Through Killy begs, Kilkerry and Kildare?
How are things in Glocca Morra?
Is that willow tree still weeping there?
Does that laddie {lassie} with the twinklin' eye
Come whistlin' {smiling'} by
And does he {she} walk away,
Sad and dreamy there not to see me there?
So I ask each weepin' willow
And each brook along the way,
And each lad {lass}
That comes a-whistlin' {a-sighin'} Tooralay:
How are things in Glocca Morra this fine day?

How Can You Mend a Broken Heart

Words and Music by Barry Gibb and Robin Gibb

recorded by The Bee Gees

I can think of younger days when living for my life
Was everything a man could want to do.
I could never see tomorrow,
I was never told about the sorrow.

Refrain:
And how can you mend a broken heart?
How can you stop the rain from falling down?
How can you stop the sun from shining?
What makes the world go 'round?
How can you mend this broken man?
How can a loser ever win?
Please help me mend my broken heart
And let me live again.

I can still feel the breeze that rustles through the trees
And misty memories of days gone by.
We could never see tomorrow;
No one said a word about the sorrow.

Refrain

How Deep Is the Ocean
(How High Is the Sky)

Words and Music by Irving Berlin
© Copyright 1932 by Irving Berlin
Copyright Renewed

a standard recorded by Bing Crosby, Coleman Hawkins,
Peggy Lee, Artie Shaw, Frank Sinatra and various
other artists

How much do I love you?
I'll tell you no lie,
How deep is the ocean,
How high the sky?

How many times a day do I think of you?
How many roses are sprinkled with dew?

How far would I travel
To be where you are?
How far is the journey
From here to a star?

And if I ever lost you,
How much would I cry?
How deep is the ocean,
How high the sky?

How Deep Is Your Love

Words and Music by Barry Gibb, Maurice Gibb and
Robin Gibb
Copyright © 1977 by Gibb Brothers Music
All Rights Administered by Careers-BMG Music Publishing, Inc.

from the Motion Picture *Saturday Night Fever*
recorded by The Bee Gees

I know your eyes in the morning sun.
I feel you touch me in the pouring rain.
And the moment that you wander far from me,
I wanna feel you in my arms again.
And you come to me on a summer breeze;
Keep me warm in your love,
Then you softly leave.

Refrain:
And it's me you need to show
How deep is your love?
How deep is your love?
How deep is your love?
I really mean to learn.
'Cause we're living in a world of fools,
Breaking us down
When they all should let us be.
We belong to you and me.

I believe in you.
You know the door to my very soul.
You're the light in my deepest, darkest hour;
You're my savior when I fall.
And you may not think I care for you
When you know down inside
That I really do.

Refrain

How High the Moon

Words by Nancy Hamilton
Music by Morgan Lewis
Copyright © 1940 by Chappell & Co.
Copyright Renewed

from the musical *Two for the Show*
a standard recorded by Benny Goodman, Les Paul and
Mary Ford, Ella Fitzgerald and various other artists

Somewhere there's music,
How faint the tune!
Somewhere there's heaven,
How high the moon!
There is no moon above
When love is far away too,
Till it comes true
That you love me as I love you.

Somewhere's there's music,
It's where you are,
Somewhere there's heaven,
How near, how far!
The darkest night would shine
If you would come to me soon,
Until you will,
How still my heart,
How high the moon!

How Will I Know

Words and Music by George Merrill, Shannon Rubicam
and Narada Michael Walden
Copyright © 1985 IRVING MUSIC, INC., WB MUSIC CORP. and GRATITUDE SKY MUSIC

recorded by Whitney Houston

There's a boy I know, he's the one I dream of.
Looks into my eyes; takes me into the clouds above.

Oh, I lose control; can't seem to get enough.
When I wake from dreamin'; tell me, is it really love?

How will I know?
(Girl, trust your feelings.)
How will I know?
How will I know?
(Love can be deceivin'.)
How will I know?

Refrain:
How will I know if he really loves me?
I say a prayer with every heartbeat.
I fall in love whenever we meet.
I'm askin' you, 'cause you know about these things.
How will I know if he's thinkin' of me?
I try to phone, but I'm too shy.
(Can't speak.)
Falling in love is so bittersweet.
This love is strong.
Why do I feel weak?

Oh, wake me, I'm shakin'; wish I had you near me now.
Said there's no mistakin'; what I feel is really love.

How will I know?
(Girl, trust your feelings.)
How will I know?
How will I know?
(Love can be deceiving.)
How will I know?

Refrain

If he loves me;
If he loves me not.
If he loves me;
If he loves me not.
If he loves me;
If he loves me not. Oh,

Repeat Refrain and Fade

Hurdy Gurdy Man
Words and Music by Donovan Leitch
Copyright © 1968 by Donovan (Music) Ltd.
Copyright Renewed
All Rights Administered by Peer International Corporation

recorded by Donovan

Thrown like a star in my vast sleep,
I open my eyes to take a peep,
To find that I was by the sea,
Gazing with tranquility.
'Twas then when the hurdy gurdy man
Came singing songs of love,
Then when the hurdy gurdy man
Came singing songs of love.

Refrain, Three Times:
Hurdy gurdy hurdy gurdy hurdy gurdy, gurdy he sang.

Histories of ages past
Unenlightened shadows cast,
Down through all eternity,
The crying of humanity.
'Tis then when the hurdy gurdy man
Comes singing songs of love,
Then when the hurdy gurdy man
Comes singing songs of love.

Refrain

Repeat and Fade:
Hurdy gurdy hurdy gurdy hurdy gurdy, gurdy he sang.
Here comes the roly poly man and he's singing songs of love.
Roly poly roly poly roly poly poly roly poly he sang.

Hurt So Bad
Words and Music by Teddy Randazzo, Bobby Weinstein
and Bobby Hart
Copyright © 1965 (Renewed) by Embassy Music Corporation (BMI) and
   Universal - Songs Of PolyGram International, Inc.

recorded by Little Anthony & The Imperials,
The Lettermen, Linda Ronstadt

I know you don't know what I'm going through,
Standing here looking at you.
Well let me tell you that it hurt so bad.
It makes me feel so bad.
It makes me hurt so bad to see you again,
Like needles and pins.

People say you've been makin' out O.K.
She's in love; don't stand in her way.
But let me tell you that it hurt so bad.
It makes me feel so bad.
It's gonna hurt so bad if you walk away.

Why don't you stay and let me make it up to you?
Stay, I'll do anything you want me to.
You loved me before, please love me again.
I can't let you go back to him.
Please don't go, please don't go.

Twice:
It hurt so bad.
Come back, it hurt so bad.
Don't make me hurt so bad,
I'm beggin' you please.
Please don't go.

153

I Am the Walrus

Words and Music by John Lennon and Paul McCartney

recorded by The Beatles

I am he
As you are he
As you are me
And we are all together.
See how they run?
Like pigs from a gun,
See how they fly?
I'm crying.

Sitting on a cornflake,
Waiting for the van to come.
Corporation T-shirt.
Stupid bloody
Tuesday man you been a naughty boy.
You let your face grow long.
I am the eggman oh,
They are the eggmen.
Oh I am the walrus.
Goo goo g'joob.

Mr. City policeman sitting
Pretty little policemen in a row.
See how they fly.
Like Lucy in the sky.
See how they run.
I'm crying.
I'm crying.
I'm crying.

Yellow matter custard
Dripping from a dead dog's eye.
Crabalocker fishwife pornographic priestess
Boy, you been a naughty girl,
You let your knickers down.
I am the eggman oh,
They are the eggmen.
Oh I am the walrus.
Goo goo g'joob.

Sitting in an English garden
Waiting for the sun to come.
If the sun doesn't come
You get a tan from
Sitting in the English rain.
I am the eggman oh
They are the eggmen.
Oh I am the walrus.
Goo goo g'joob.

Expert texpert choking smokers
Don't you think the joker laughs at you.
Ha ha ha,
See how they smile.
Like pigs in a sty
She how they snied.
I' crying.
Semolina pilchard
Climbing up the Eiffel Tower.
Elementary penguin,
Singing Hare Khrishna,
Man you should have seen them
Kicking Edgar Allen Poe.

I am the eggman,
Oh, they are the eggmen,
Oh I am the walrus,
Goo goo g'joob…

I Am Woman

Words by Helen Reddy
Music by Ray Burton

recorded by Helen Reddy

I am woman, hear me roar,
In numbers too big to ignore,
And I know too much to go back to pretend.
'Cause I've heard it all before,
And I've been down there on the floor,
No one's ever gonna keep me down again.

Refrain:
Oh, yes I am wise, but it's wisdom born of pain.
Yes, I paid the price, but look how much I gained.
If I have to I can do anything.
I am strong, I am invincible,
I am woman.

You can bend but never break me,
'Cause it only serves to make me,
More determined to achieve my final goal.
And I come back even stronger,
Not a novice any longer,
'Cause you've deepened the conviction in my soul.

Refrain

I am woman!
I am woman!

I Am Your Child

Lyric by Marty Panzer
Music by Barry Manilow

recorded by Barry Manilow

I am your child.
Wherever you go,
You take me, too.
Whatever I know,
I learn from you.
Whatever I do,
You taught me to do.
I am your child.
And I am your chance.
Whatever will come,
Will come from me.
Tomorrow is won
By winning me.
Whatever I am,
You taught me to be.
I am your hope,
I am your chance,
I am your child.

I Believe

Words and Music by Jeffrey Pence, Eliot Sloan and
Matt Senatore

recorded by Blessid Union of Souls

Walk blindly to the light
And reach out for his hand.
Don't ask any questions
And don't try to understand.
Open up your mind
And then open up your heart,
And you will see that you and me
Aren't so very far apart.
'Cause

Refrain:
I believe that love is the answer.
I believe that love will find a way.
I believe that love is the answer.
I believe that love will find a way.

Violence has spread world wide
And there's families on the street.
We sell drugs to children now.
Oh, why can't we just see
That all we do is eliminate our future
With the things we do today?
Money is our incentive now,
So that makes it okay.
But

Refrain

I've been seeing Lisa now
For a little over a year.
She says she'd never been so happy,
But Lisa lives in fear
That one day daddy's gonna find out she's
In love with a singer from the streets.
Oh, how he would lose it then,
But she's still here with me.
'Cause

She believes that love will see it through
And they'll understand.
He'll see me as a person
And not just a black man.

'Cause I believe that love is the answer.
I believe that love will find a way.
I believe, I believe, I believe,
I believe that love is the answer.
I believe love will find a way.
Love will find a way.
Love will find a way.
Love will find a way.

I Believe

Words and Music by Ervin Drake, Irvin Graham,
Jimmy Shirl and Al Stillman

a standard recorded by Jane Froman, Frankie Laine,
The Lettermen and various other artists

I believe for every drop of rain that falls,
A flower grows.
I believe that somewhere in the darkest night,
A candle glows.
I believe for everyone who goes astray,
Someone will come
To show the way.
I believe.

I believe above the storm the smallest prayer
Will still be heard.
I believe that someone in the great somewhere
Hears every word.
Every time I hear a new-born baby cry
Or touch a leaf,
Or see the sky
I believe
Then I know why
I believe!

I Believe in Music

Words and Music by Mac Davis

recorded by Gallery, Mac Davis

Well, I could just sit around
Makin' music all day long.
Long as I'm makin' music
I know I can't do nobody wrong.
And who knows, maybe someday
I'll come up with a song.
That makes people wanna stop their fussin' and fightin'
Just long enough to sing along.

I believe in music.
I believe in love.

Music is love, love is music,
If you know what I mean.
People who believe in music
Are the happiest people I ever seen.
So clap your hands, stomp your feet,
Shake your tambourine.
Lift your voices to the sky.
God loves you when you sing.

Refrain:
I believe in music. I believe in love.
Sing it to the children.
I, I believe in music.
Lord knows that I,
I believe in love.

Music is the universal language
And love is the key
To brotherhood and peace and understanding
To livin' in harmony.
So take you brother by the hand
And sing along with me.
And find out what it really means
To be young and rich and free.

Refrain

I Believe in You

By Frank Loesser

from the musical *How to Succeed in Business
Without Really Trying*
recorded by Bill Evans and various other artists

You have the cool clear eyes
Of a seeker of wisdom and truth,
Yet, there's that up turned chin
And the grin of impetuous youth.
Oh, I believe in you,
I believe in you.

I hear the sound of good
Solid judgment whenever you talk,
Yet, there's the bold, brave spring
Of the tiger that quickens your walk.
Oh, I believe in you,
I believe in you.

And when my faith in my fellow man
All but falls apart,
I've but to feel your hand grasping mine
And I take heart,
I take heart.

To see the cool clear eyes
Of a seeker of wisdom and truth,
Yet there's that slam bang tang
Reminiscent of gin and vermouth.
Oh, I believe in you,
I believe in you.

I Believe in You and Me

Words and Music by David Wolfert and Sandy Linzer

from the Touchstone Motion Picture *The Preacher's Wife*
recorded by Whitney Houston

I believe in you and me.
I believe that we will be
In love eternally.
Well, as far as I can see,
You will always be
The one for me,
Oh, yes, you will.

And I believe in dreams again.
I believe that love will never end.
And like the river finds the sea,
I was lost, now I'm free
'Cause I believe in you and me.

I will never leave your side.
I will never hurt your pride.
When all the chips are down,
Babe, then I will always be around.
Just to be right where you are, my love.
You know I love you, boy.
I'll never leave you out.
I will always let you in, boy,
Oh, baby, to places no one's ever been.
Deep inside, can't you see
That I believe in you and me.

Maybe I'm a fool to feel the way I do.
I would play the fool forever
Just to be with you forever.
I believe in miracles
And love's a miracle,
And yes, baby, you're my dream come true.
I, I was lost, now I'm free,
Oh baby,
'Cause
I believe, I do believe in you and me.
See, I'm lost, now I'm free
'Cause I believe in you and me.

I Cain't Say No

Lyrics by Oscar Hammerstein II
Music by Richard Rodgers
Copyright © 1943 by WILLIAMSON MUSIC
Copyright Renewed

from the musical *Oklahoma!*

It ain't so much a question of not knowin' what to do,
I knowed whut's right and wrong since I been ten.
I heard a lot of stories, and I reckon they are true,
About how girls're put upon by men.
I know I mustn't fall into the pit,
But when I'm with a feller—I forgit!

I'm jist a girl who cain't say no,
I'm in a terrible fix.
I always say, "Come on let's go!"
Jist when I orta say nix!
When a person tries to kiss a girl
I know she orta give his face a smack.
But as soon as someone kisses me
I somehow sorta wanta kiss him back.
I'm jist a fool when lights are low.
I cain't be prissy and quaint.
I ain't the type that c'n faint.
How c'n I be whut I ain't?
I cain't say no!

Whut you goin' to do when a feller gits flirty
And starts to talk purty?
Whut you goin' to do?
S'posin' 'at he says 'at yer lips're like cherries,
Er roses, er berries?
Whut you goin' to do?

S'posin' 'at he says 'at you're sweeter'n cream
And he's gotta have cream er die?
Whut you goin' to do when he talks thet way?
Spit in his eye?

I'm jist a girl who cain't say no,
Cain't seem to say it at all.
I hate to disserpoint a beau
When he is payin' a call.
Fer a while I ack refined and cool,
A-settin' on the velveteen settee.
Nen I think of thet ol' golden rule,
And do fer him whut he would do fer me.
I cain't resist a Romeo
In a sombrero and chaps.
Soon as I sit on their laps
Somethin' inside of me snaps—
I cain't say no!

I'm jist a girl who cain't say no.
Kissin's my favorite food.
With er without the mistletoe
I'm in a holiday mood.
Other girls arc coy and hard to catch,
But other girls ain't havin' any fun.
Every time I lose a wrestlin' match
I have a funny feelin' that I won.
Though I c'n feel the undertow,
I never make a complaint
Till it's too late for restraint.
Then when I want to I cain't
I cain't say no.

I Can See for Miles

Words and Music by Peter Townshend
© Copyright 1967 (Renewed) Fabulous Music Ltd., London, England
TRO - Essex Music, Inc., New York, controls all publication rights for the U.S.A. and Canada

recorded by The Who

I know you've deceived me,
Here's a surprise.
I know that you have,
'Cause there's magic in my eyes.
I can see for miles and miles and miles
And miles and miles. Oh, yeah.

If you think that I don't know
About the little tricks you play,
And never see you
When deliberately you put things in my way.
Well, here's a poke at you.
You're gonna choke on it too.
You're gonna lose that smile.

Refrain:
Because all the while,
I can see for miles and miles.
I can see for miles and miles.
I can see for miles and miles and miles
And miles and miles. Oh, yeah.

You took advantage of my trust in you
When I was so far away.
I saw you holdin' lots of other guys,
And now you've got the nerve to say
That you still want me.
Well, that's as may be, but you gotta stand trial.

Refrain

Repeat Verse 1

Refrain

The Eiffel Tower and the Taj Mahal
Are mine to see on clear days.
You thought I would need a crystal ball
To see right through the haze.

Well, here's a poke at you.
You're gonna choke on it too.
You're gonna lose that smile.

Repeat Refrain and Fade

I Can't Get Started with You
Words by Ira Gershwin
Music by Vernon Duke

from the musical *Ziegfeld Follies* (1936)
a standard recorded by Bunny Berigan and various other
artists

I've flown around the world in a plane;
I've settled revolutions in Spain;
The North Pole I have charted,
But I can't get started with you.

Around the golf course I'm under par,
And all the movies want me to star;
I've got a home, a showplace,
But I get no-place with you.

You're so supreme,
Lyrics I write of you, scheme,
Just for a sight of you, dream,
Both day and night of you
And what good does it do?

In nineteen twenty-nine I sold short,
In England I'm presented at court,
But you've got me down-hearted
'Cause I can't get started with you.

I do a hundred yards in ten flat;
The Prince of Wales has copied my hat;
With queens I've a-la carted,
But can't get started with you.

The leading tailors follow my styles,
And toothpaste ads all feature my smiles;
The Astor-bilts I visit,
But say, what is it with you?

When we first met,
How you elated me! Pet,
You devastated me! Yet,
Now you've deflated me
'Til you're my Waterloo.

I've sold my kisses at a bazaar
And after me they've named a cigar;
But lately how I've smarted,
'Cause I can't get started with you.

I Can't Give You Anything but Love
Words by Dorothy Fields
Music by Jimmy McHugh

from the musical *Blackbirds of 1928*
featured in the films *Bringing Up Baby, True to the Army,
Stormy Weather, Jam Session, So This Is Paris, The Helen
Morgan Story*

I can't give you anything but love, Baby,
That's the only thing I've plenty of, Baby.
Dreamin' a while,
Schemin' a while,
You're sure to find,
Happiness an' I guess,
All those things you've always pined for.
Gee, I'd like to see you lookin' swell, Baby,
Diamond bracelets Woolworth doesn't sell, Baby.
Till that lucky day you know darn well.
I can't give you anything but love.
I can't give you anything but love.

I Can't Make You Love Me
Words and Music by Mike Reid and Allen Shamblin

recorded by Bonnie Raitt

Turn down the lights, turn down the bed,
Turn down these voices inside my head.
Lay down with me, tell me no lies.
Just hold me close, don't patronize.
Don't patronize me.

Refrain:
'Cause I can't make you love me if you don't.
You can't make your heart feel something it won't.
Here in the dark in these final hours,
I will lay down my heart and I'll feel the power.
But you won't, no, you won't.
'Cause I can't make you love me if you don't.

I'll close my eyes, then I won't see
The love you don't feel when you're holdin' me.
Mornin' will come and I'll do what's right.
Just give me till then to give up this fight.
And I will give up this fight.

Refrain

I Concentrate on You
Words and Music by Cole Porter

from the film *Broadway Melody of 1940*

Whenever skies look gray to me
And trouble begins to brew,
Whenever the winter winds
Become too strong,
I concentrate on you.

When fortune cries "nay, nay!" to me
And people declare "You're through."
Whenever the blues become
My only song,
I concentrate on you.

On your smile so sweet, so tender,
When at first my {your} kiss you {I} decline,
On the light in your eyes,
When you {I} surrender
And once again our arms intertwine.

And so when wise men say to me
That love's young dream never comes true,
To prove that even wise men can be wrong,
I concentrate on you.
I concentrate,
And concentrate
On you.

I Could Have Danced All Night
Words by Alan Jay Lerner
Music by Frederick Loewe

from the musical *My Fair Lady*

I could have danced all night!
I could have danced all night!
And still have begged for more.
I could have spread my wings
And done a thousand things
I've never done before.

I'll never know what made it so exciting.
Why all at once my heart took flight.
I only know when he began to dance with me
I could have danced and danced all night.

I Could Write a Book
Words by Lorenz Hart
Music by Richard Rodgers

from the musical *Pal Joey*

Verse 1:
A B C D E F G
I never learned to spell,
At least not well.
1 2 3 4 5 6 7
I never learned to count
A great amount.
But my busy mind is burning
To use what learning I've got.
I won't waste any time,
I'll strike while the iron is hot.

Refrain:
If they asked me, I could write a book
About the way you walk and whisper and look.
I could write a preface on how we met
So the world would never forget.
And the simple secret of the plot
Is just to tell them that I love you a lot.
Then the world discovers as my book ends
How to make two lovers of friends.

Verse 2:
Used to hate to go to school.
I never cracked a book;
I played the hook.
Never answered any mail;
To write I used to think
Was wasting ink.
It was never my endeavor
To be too clever and smart.
Now I suddenly feel
A longing to write in my heart.

Refrain

I Didn't Know What Time It Was

Words by Lorenz Hart
Music by Richard Rodgers

from the musical *Too Many Girls*
a standard recorded by Frank Sinatra and various other
artists

Once I was young
Yesterday, perhaps
Danced with Jim and Paul
And kissed some other chaps.
Once I was young,
But never was naïve.
I thought I had a trick or two
Up my imaginary sleeve.
And now I know I was naïve.

Refrain:
I didn't know what time it was,
Then I met you.
Oh, what a lovely time it was,
How sublime it was, too!
I didn't know what day it was.
You held my hand.
Warm like the month of May it was,
And I'll say it was grand.
Grand to be alive, to be young,
To be mad, to be yours alone!
Grand to see your face, feel your touch,
Hear your voice say I'm all your own.
I didn't know what year it was.
Life was no prize.
I wanted love and here it was
Shining out of your eyes.
I'm wise,
And I know what time it is now.

Once I was old
Twenty years or so
Rather well preserved
The wrinkles didn't show.
Once I was old,
But not too old for fun.
I used to hunt for little girls
With my imaginary grin.
But now I aim for only one!

Refrain

(Everything I Do) I Do It for You

Words and Music by Bryan Adams, Robert John Lange
and Michael Kamen

from the Motion Picture *Robin Hood: Prince of Thieves*
recorded by Bryan Adams

Look into my eyes,
You will see what you mean to me.
Search your heart, search your soul,
And when you find me there,
You will search no more.
Don't tell me it's not worth trying for.
You can't tell me it's not worth dying for.
You know it's true,
Everything I do,
I do it for you.

Look into your heart,
You will find there's nothing there to hide.
So, take me as I am, take my life,
I would give it all, I would sacrifice.
Don't tell me it's not worth fighting for.
I can't help it, there's nothing I want more.
You know it's true,
Everything I do,
I do it for you.

There's no love like your love,
And no other could give more love.
There's no way, unless you're there,
All the time, all the way, yeah.

Oh, you can't tell me it's not worth trying for.
I can't help it, there's nothing I want more.
Yeah, I would fight for you,
I'd lie for you, walk the wire for you,
Yeah, I'd die for you.
You know it's true,
Everything I do,
Oh, oh, I do it for you.

I Don't Know Why (I Just Do)

Lyric by Roy Turk
Music by Fred E. Ahlert

recorded by Russ Columbo and various other artists

All day long you're asking me what I see in you.
All day long I'm answering, but what good does it do?
I have nothing to explain
I just love you, love you,
And I'll tell you once again:

I don't know why I love you like I do,
I don't know why, I just do.
I don't know why you thrill me like you do,
I don't know why, you just do.

Refrain:
You never seem to want my romancing.
The only time you hold me is when we're dancing.
I don't know why I love you like I do.
I don't know why, I just do.

Repeat Refrain

I Don't Want to Set the World on Fire
Words and Music by Sol Marcus, Bennie Benjamin and Eddie Seiler

a standard recorded by The Ink Spots, Donna Wood,
The Don Juans and various other artists

I don't want to set the world on fire,
I just want to start
A flame in your heart.
In my heart I have but one desire,
And that one is you
No other will do.

I've lost all ambition
For worldly acclaim,
I just want to be the one you love;
And with your admission
That you feel the same
I'll have reached the goal I'm dreaming of.
Believe me!

I don't want to set the world on fire,
I just want to start
A flame in your heart.

I Don't Want to Wait
Words and Music by Paula Cole

recorded by Paula Cole

Refrain 1:
So open up your morning light
And say a little prayer for I.
You know that if we are to stay alive,
Then see the peace in every eye.

She had two babies, one was six months,
One was three, in the war of forty-four.
Every telephone ring, every heartbeat stinging
When she thought it was God calling her.
Oh, would her son grow to know his father?

Refrain 2:
I don't want to wait
For our lives to be over.
I want to know right now,
What will it be?
I don't want to wait
For our lives to be over.
Will it be yes,
Or will it be sorry?

He showed up all wet on the rainy front step
Wearing shrapnel in his skin.
And the war he saw lives inside him still.
It's so hard to be gentle and warm.
The years pass by and now he has grand-daughters.

Repeat Refrain 2

Oh, so you look at me from across the room.
You're wearing your anguish again.
Believe me, I know the feeling;
It sucks you into the jaws of anger.

Oh, so breathe a little more deeply, my love.
All we have is this very moment,
And I don't want to do what his father,
And his father and his father did.
I want to be here right now.

Repeat Refrain 1

Repeat Refrain 2

Repeat Refrain 1

I Dreamed a Dream
Music by Claude-Michel Schönberg
Lyrics by Herbert Kretzmer
Original Text by Alain Boublil and Jean-Marc Natel

from the musical *Les Misérables*

I dreamed a dream in days gone by
When hope was high and life worth living.
I dreamed that love would never die.
I dreamed that God would be forgiving.
Then I was young and unafraid
And dreams were made and used and wasted.
There was no ransom to be paid,
No song unsung, no wine untasted.
But the tigers come at night
With their voices soft as thunder.
As they tear your hope apart,
As they turn your dream to shame.
He slept a summer by my side.
He filled my days with endless wonder.
He took my childhood in his stride.
But he was gone when autumn came.

And still I dreamed he'd come to me,
That we would live the years together.
But there are dreams that cannot be,
And there are storms we cannot weather.
I had a dream my life would be
So different from this hell I'm living,
So different now from what it seemed.
Now life has killed the dream I dreamed.

I Drive Myself Crazy
Words and Music by Rick Nowels, Ellen Shipley and
Allan Rich

recorded by 'N Sync

Lying in you arms
So close together,
Didn't know just what I had.
Now I toss and turn
'Cause I'm without you.
How I'm missing you so bad.
Where was my head? Where was my heart?
Now I cry alone in the dark.

Refrain:
I lie awake.
I drive myself crazy.
Drive myself crazy thinking of you.
Made a mistake when I let you go,
Baby, I drive myself crazy
Wanting you the way I do.

I was such a fool.
I couldn't see it,
Just how good you were to me.
You confessed your love
And dying devotion,
I confessed my need to be free.
And now I'm left with all this pain.
I've only got myself to blame.

Refrain

Why didn't I notice?
(How much I love you, baby.)
Why couldn't I show it
(If I had only told you.)
When I had the chance?
Oh, I had the chance.

Oh, oh.
La la la…
I drive myself crazy.
Ah ah ah…
Oh so crazy.
La la la la oh oh.

Refrain Twice

I Enjoy Being a Girl
Lyrics by Oscar Hammerstein II
Music by Richard Rodgers

from the musical *Flower Drum Song*

I'm a girl and by me that's only great!
I am proud that my silhouette is curvy,
That I walk with a sweet and girlish gait,
With my hips kind of swively and swervy.
I adore being dressed in something frilly
When my date comes to get me at my place.
Out I go with my Joe or John or Billy,
Like a filly who is ready for the race!

When I have a brand new hair-do,
With my eyelashes all in curl,
I float as the clouds on air do,
I enjoy being a girl!

When men say I'm cute and funny,
And my teeth aren't teeth, but pearl,
I just lap it up like honey,
I enjoy being a girl!

I flip when a fellow sends me flowers,
I drool over dresses made of lace,
I talk on the telephone for hours
With a pound and a half of cream upon my face!

I'm strictly a female female,
And my future, I hope, will be
In the home of a brave and free male
Who'll enjoy being a guy,
Having a girl like me!

When men say I'm sweet as candy
As around in a dance we whirl,
It goes to my head like brandy,
I enjoy being a girl!

When someone with eyes that smoulder,
Says he loves every silken curl
That falls on my ivory shoulder,
I enjoy being a girl!

When I hear the complimentary whistle
That greets my bikini by the sea,
I turn and I glower and I bristle
But I'm happy to know the whistle's meant for me!

I'm strictly a female female,
And my future, I hope, will be
In the home of a brave and free male
Who'll enjoy being a guy,
Having a girl like me.

I Fall to Pieces
Words and Music by Hank Cochran and Harlan Howard

recorded by Patsy Cline

I fall to pieces
Each time I see you again.
1 fall to pieces.
How can I be just your friend?
You want me to act like we've never kissed.
You want me to forget,
Pretend we've never met,
And I've tried and I've tried,
But I haven't yet.
You walk by,
And I fall to pieces.

I fall to pieces
Each time someone speaks you name.
I fall to pieces.
Time only adds to the flame.
You tell me to find someone else to love.
Someone who'll love me, too,
The way you used to do,
But each time I go out with someone new,
You walk by, and I fall to pieces.
You walk by,
And I fall to pieces.

I Feel Fine
Words and Music by John Lennon and Paul McCartney

recorded by The Beatles

Baby's good to me you know,
She's happy as can be you know,
She said so.
I'm in love with her and I feel fine.

Baby says she's mine you know,
She tells me all the time you know,
She said so.
I'm in love with her and I feel fine.

I'm so glad she's telling all the world,
That her baby buys her things you know.
He buys her diamond rings you know,
She said so.
She's in love with me and I feel fine.

Baby says she's mine you know,
She tells me all the time you know,
She said so.
I'm in love with her and I feel fine.

I'm so glad that she's my little girl.
She's so glad she's telling all the world
That her baby buys her things you know,
He buys her diamond rings you know,
She said so.
She's in love with me and I feel fine.

I Feel the Earth Move
Words and Music by Carole King

recorded by Carole King

Refrain:
I feel the earth move under my feet;
I feel the sky come tumbling down;
I feel my heart start to tremblin'
Whenever you're around.

Ooh, baby, when I see your face
Mellow as the month of May,
Oh, darlin', I can't stand it
When you look at me that way.

Refrain

Ooh, darlin' when I'm near you
And you tenderly call my name,
I know that my emotions
Are something I just can't tame.
I just got to have you, baby.
Aah! Aah! Yeah,

Repeat and Fade:
I feel the earth move under my feet;
I feel the sky come tumbling down.

I Finally Found Someone
Words and Music by Barbra Streisand, Marvin Hamlisch,
R.J. Lange and Bryan Adams

from the film *The Mirror Has Two Faces*
recorded by Barbra Streisand & Bryan Adams

He: I finally found someone
Who knocks me off my feet.
I finally found someone
Who makes me feel complete.

She: It started over coffee.
We started out as friends.
It's funny how from simple things
The best things begin.

He: This time it's different.
It's all because of you.
It's better than it's ever been
'Cause we can talk it through.

She: My favorite line
Was, "Can I call you sometime?"
It's all you had to say
To take my breath away.

Both: This is it,
Oh, I finally found someone,
Someone to share my life.
I finally found the one
To be with every night.

She: 'Cause whatever I do,
He: It's just got to be you.

Both: My life has just begun.
I finally found someone.

He: Did I keep you waiting?
She: I didn't mind.
He: I apologize.
She: Baby, that's fine.
He: I would wait forever
Both: Just to know you were mine.
He: You know, I love your hair

She: Are you sure it looks right?
He: I love what you wear.
She: Isn't it too tight?
He: You're exceptional.
Both: I can't wait for the rest of my life.

This is it.
Oh, I finally found someone,
Someone to share my life.
I finally found someone
To be with every night.

She: 'Cause whatever I do,
He: It's just got to be you.

Both: My life has just begun.
I finally found someone.

She: And whatever I do,
He: It's just got to be you.
She: My life has just begun.
Both: I finally found someone.

I Found a Million Dollar Baby (In a Five and Ten Cent Store)
Lyric by Billy Rose and Mort Dixon
Music by Harry Warren

from the musical *Crazy Quilt*
featured in the film *Funny Lady*
recorded by Fanny Brice, Bing Crosby

Verse:
Love comes along like a popular song,
Anytime or anywhere at all.
Rain or sunshine, spring or fall,
You never know when it may say hello
In a very unexpected place
For example, take my case:

Refrain 1:
It was a lucky April shower,
It was the most convenient door;
I found a million dollar baby
In a five and ten cent store.

Refrain 2:
The rain continued for an hour,
I hung around for three or four,
Around a million dollar baby
In a five and ten cent store.

Refrain 3:
She was selling china
And when she made those eyes
I kept buying china
Until the crowd got wise.

Refrain 4:
Incidentally, if you run into a shower,
Just step inside my cottage door
And meet the million dollar baby
From the five and ten cent store!

Love used to be quite a stranger to me
Didn't know a sentimental word,
Thoughts of kissing seemed absurd.
Then came a change, and you may think it strange,
But the world became a happy tune
Since that April afternoon.

Repeat Refrains

I Get Along Without You
Very Well (Except Sometimes)
Words and Music by Hoagy Carmichael
Inspired by a poem written by J.B. Thompson

a standard recorded by Red Norvo, Larry Clinton, Karen
Chandler and various other artists

I get along without you very well,
Of course I do,
Except when soft rains fall
And drip from leaves, then I recall
The thrill of being sheltered in you arms,
Of course I do,
But I get along without you very well.

I've forgotten you, just like I should,
Of course I have,
Except to hear your name
Or someone's laugh that is the same,
But I've forgotten you just like I should.
What a guy!
What a fool am I
To think my breaking heart could kid the moon;
What's in store.
Should I phone once more?
No it's best that I stick to my tune.

I get along without you very well,
Of course I do,
Except perhaps in spring
But I should never think of spring
For that would surely break my heart in two.

I Get Around
Words and Music by Brian Wilson and Mike Love

recorded by The Beach Boys

Refrain:
I get around from town to town
I'm a real cool head,
I'm makin' real good bread.

I'm gettin' bugged, drivin' up an' down the same ol' strip.
I gotta find a new place where the kids are hip.
My buddies and me are gettin' real well known,
Yeah, the bad guys know us and they leave us alone.

Refrain

We always take my car 'cause it's never been beat.
And we've never missed yet with the girls we meet.
None of the guys go steady 'cause it wouldn't be right,
To leave your best girl home on a Saturday night.

Repeat Refrain and Fade

I Go to Rio
Words and Music by Peter Allen and Adrienne Anderson

recorded by Peter Allen

When my baby, when my baby smiles at me,
I go to Rio de Janeiro.
Me, oh, me, oh, I go wild,
And then I have to do the Samba and La Bamba.
Now I'm not the kind of person,
With a passionate persuasion for dancin' or romancin'.
But I give in to the rhythm,
And my feet follow the beating of my heart.

Refrain:
Whoa, when my baby, when my baby smiles at me,
I go to Rio de Janeiro.
I'm a Salsa fellow.
When my baby smiles at me the sun lights up my life,
And I feel free at last, what a blast.

When my baby, when my baby smiles at me,
I feel like Tarzan of the Jungle.
Then on the hot sand and in a bungalow,
While monkeys play above-a, we'll make love-a.
Now I'm not the type,
To let vibrations trigger my imagination easily.
You know that's just not me.
But I turn into a tiger every time I get beside the one I love.

Refrain

Repeat Ad Lib and Fade:
When my baby,
When my baby smiles at me.
I go to Rio de Janeiro.
It's when I go to Rio,
Rio de Janeiro.

I Got It Bad and That Ain't Good
Words by Paul Francis Webster
Music by Duke Ellington

a standard recorded by Duke Ellington, Benny Goodman,
Peggy Lee, Ella Fitzgerald and various other artists

The poets say that all who love are blind
But I'm in love and I know what time it is!
The Good Book says, "Go seek and ye shall find."
Well, I have sought and my what a climb it is!

My life is just like the weather,
It changes with the hours.
When he's near I'm fair and warmer
When he's gone I'm cloudy with showers.
In emotion, like the ocean
It's either sink or swim.
When a woman loves a man like I love him.

Never treats me sweet and gentle
The way he should.
I got it bad and that ain't good!
My poor heart is sentimental,
Not made of wood.
I got it bad and that ain't good!

But when the weekend's over
And Monday rolls aroun'
I end up like I start out
Just cryin' my heart out.
He don't love me like I love him,
Nobody could.
I got it bad and that ain't good!

Like a lonely weeping willow
Lost in the wood.
I got it bad and that ain't good!
And the things I tell my pillow
No woman should.
I got it bad and that ain't good!

Tho' folks with good intentions
Tell me to save my tears.
I'm glad I'm mad about him.
I can't live without him.
Lord above me make him love me
The way he should.
I got it bad and that ain't good!

I Got the Sun in the Morning
Words and Music by Irving Berlin

from the Stage Production *Annie Get Your Gun*

Taking stock of what I have and what I haven't,
What do I find?
The things I've got will keep me satisfied.

Checking up on what I have and what I haven't,
What do I find?
A healthy balance on the credit side.

Got no diamond,
Got no pearl,
Still I think I'm a lucky girl.
I got the sun in the morning and the moon at night.

Got no mansion,
Got no yacht,
Still I'm happy with what I've got.
I got the sun in the morning and the moon at night.

Sunshine
Gives me a lovely day.
Moonlight
Gives me the Milky Way.

Got no check books,
Got no banks,
Still I'd like to express my thanks.
I got the sun in the morning and the moon at night.

And with the sun in the morning
And the moon in the evening,
I'm all right.

I Had Myself a True Love
Words by Johnny Mercer
Music by Harold Arlen

from the musical *St. Louis Woman*

I had myself a true love,
A true love who was somethin' to see
I had myself a true love,
At least that's what I kept on tellin' me,

First thing in the mornin'
I still try to think up a way to be with him,
Some part of the evenin'
An' that's the way I live thru the day.
She had herself a true love,
But now he's gone an' left her for good.

Lord knows, I done heard those backyard whispers
Goin' 'round the neighborhood.
There may be a lot of things I miss,
A lot of things I don't know, but I do know this:
Now I ain't got no love
An' once upon a time I had a true love

In the evening!
In the doorway,
While I stand there and wait for his comin'.
With the house swept,
And the clothes hung,
An' the pot on the stove there a-hummin',
Where is he, while I watch the risin' moon?
With that gal in that damn ol' saloon?

No! That ain't the way that it used to be.
No! An' everybody keeps tellin' me,
There may be a lot o' things I miss.
A lot o' things I don't know, but I do know this:
Now I ain't got no love
An' once upon a time I had a true love.

I Have Dreamed
Lyrics by Oscar Hammerstein II
Music by Richard Rodgers

from the musical *The King and I*

I have dreamed that your arms are lovely.
I have dreamed what a joy you'll be.
I have dreamed every word you'll whisper
When you're close, close to me.

How you look in the glow of evening,
I have dreamed and enjoyed the view.
In these dreams I've loved you so
That by now I think I know
What it's like to be loved by you.
I will love being loved by you.

I Hear a Symphony
Words and Music by Edward Holland, Lamont Dozier and Brian Holland

recorded by The Supremes

You've given me a true love
And every day I thank you love,
For a feeling that's so new,
So inviting, so exciting.
Whenever you are near,
I hear a symphony,
A tender melody pulling me closer,
Closer to your arms.

Then suddenly, ooh, your lips are touching mine.
A feeling so divine 'til I leave the past behind.
I'm lost in a world made for you and me.
Ooh love me. Whenever you are near I hear a symphony
Play sweet and tenderly every time your lips meet mine baby.

Baby, baby, I feel a joy within.
Don't let this feeling end.
Let it go on and on and on now baby.

Baby, baby, those tears that fill my eyes,
I cry not for myself
But for those who've never felt the joy we've felt.
Whenever you are near, I hear a symphony
Each time you speak to me
I hear a tender rhapsody of love, love.

Baby, baby, as you stand up holding me
Whispering how much you care,
A thousand violins fill the air now.

Baby, baby, don't let this moment end,
Keep standing close to me,
Ooh so close to me, baby baby.

Baby, baby, I hear a symphony,
A tender melody, ah it goes on and on
And on and on…

I Hear Music

Words by Frank Loesser
Music by Burton Lane

from the Paramount Picture *Dancing on a Dime*
a standard recorded by Billie Holiday and various other
artists

I hear music, mighty fine music,
The murmur of a morning breeze up there,
The rattle of the milkman on the stair.
Sure that's music, mighty fine music,
The singing of a sparrow in the sky,
The perking of the coffee right near-by.

There's my favorite melody,
You, my angel, phoning me.
I hear music, mighty fine music,
And anytime I think my world is wrong,
I get me out of bed and sing this song.

I Heard It Through the Grapevine

Words and Music by Norman J. Whitfield and
Barrett Strong

recorded by Marvin Gaye, Gladys Knight & The Pips

I bet you're wonderin' how I knew
'Bout your plans to make me blue,
With some other guy you knew before.
Between the two of us guys
You know I loved you more.
It took me by surprise I must say
When I found out yesterday.
Don't you know that:

Refrain:
I heard it through the grapevine
Not much longer would you be mine.
Oh, I heard it through the grapevine.
Oh, I'm just about to lose my mind.
Honey, honey oh yeah.

Ooh. I know a man ain't supposed to cry,
But these tears I can't hold inside.
Losin' you would end my life you see,
'Cause you mean that much to me.
You could have told me yourself
That you loved someone else.
Instead:

Refrain

People say believe half of what you see,
Son, and none of what you hear.
But I can't help but be confused.
If it's true, please tell me dear.
Do you plan to let me go
For the other guy you loved before?
Don't you know that:

Refrain

I Honestly Love You

Words and Music by Peter Allen and Jeff Barry

recorded by Olivia Newton-John

Maybe I hang around here a little more than I should.
We both know I got somewhere else to go.
But I got somethin' to tell you that I never thought I
would,
But I believe you really ought to know.
I love you.
I honestly love you.

You don't have to answer, I see it in your eyes.
Maybe it was better left unsaid.
But this is pure and simple and you must realize,
That it's comin' from my heart and not my head.
I love you.
I honestly love you.

I'm not tryin' to make you feel uncomfortable
I'm not tryin' to make you anything at all.
But this feeling doesn't come along every day,
And you shouldn't blow the chance,
When you've got the chance to say:
I love you.
Spoken:
I love you.
Sung:
I honestly love you.

If we both were born in another place and time,
This moment might be ending with a kiss.
But there you are with yours and here I am with mine,
So I guess we'll just be leaving it at this:
I love you.
I honestly love you.
I honestly love you.

I Just Called to Say I Love You

Words and Music by Stevie Wonder

recorded by Stevie Wonder

No New Year's Day
To celebrate;
No chocolate-covered candy hearts
To give away.
No first of spring;
No song to sing.
In fact here's just another ordinary day.

No April rain;
No flowers bloom;
No wedding Saturday within
The month of June.
But what it is
Is something true,
Made up of these three words
I must say to you.

Refrain:
I just called to say I love you.
I just called to say how much I care.
I just called to say I love you.
And I mean it from the bottom of my heart.

No summer's high;
No warm July;
No harvest moon to light
One tender August night.
No autumn breeze;
No falling leaves;
Not even time for birds to fly
To southern skies.

No Libra sun;
No Halloween;
No giving thanks to all
The Christmas joy you bring.
But what it is,
Though old so new
To fill your heart like no
Three words could ever do.

Refrain Twice

I Left My Heart in San Francisco

Words by Douglass Cross
Music by George Cory

recorded by Tony Bennett

The loveliness of Paris
Seems somehow sadly gay,
The glory that was Rome
Is for another day.
I've been terribly alone
And forgotten in Manhattan.
I'm going home
To my city by the bay.

I left my heart
In San Francisco.
High on a hill,
It calls to me.
To be where little cable cars
Climb half-way to the stars!
The morning fog
May chill the air
I don't care!

My love waits there
In San Francisco,
Above the blue and windy sea.
When I come home to you,
San Francisco,
Your golden sun
Will shine for me!

I Let a Song Go Out of My Heart

Words and Music by Duke Ellington, Henry Nemo,
John Redmond and Irving Mills

a standard recorded by Duke Ellington and various other artists

I let a song go out of my heart,
It was the sweetest melody,
I know I lost heaven
'Cause you were the song.

Since you and I have drifted apart
Life doesn't mean a thing to me,
Please come back sweet music.
I know I was wrong.

Am I too late to make amends?
You know that we are meant to be
More than just friends, just friends.
I let a song go out of my heart,
Believe me, darling when I say
I won't know sweet music
Until you return someday.

I Love a Piano

Words and Music by Irving Berlin

from the Stage Production *Stop! Look! Listen!*
featured in the film *Easter Parade*

As a child,
I went wild
When a band played.
How I ran
To the man
When his hand swayed.
Clarinets
Were my pets,
And a slide trombone
I thought was simply divine.
But today
When they play
I could hiss them.
Every bar
Is a jar
To my system.
But there's one musical instrument
That I call mine.

When a green
Tetrazine
Starts to warble,
I grow cold
As an old
Piece of marble.
I allude
To the crude
Little party singer,
Who don't know when to pause.
At her best
I detest
The soprano,
But I run
To the one
At the piano.
I always love the accomp'niment
And that's because,

I love a piano
I love a piano.
I love to hear somebody play
Upon a piano
A grand piano.
It simply carries me away.

I know a fine way
To treat a Steinway.
I love to run my fingers o'er the keys
The ivories.
And with a pedal

I love to meddle
Not only music from Broadway.
I'm so delighted
If I'm invited
To hear a long-haired genius play.
So you can keep your fiddle
And you bow.
Give me a p-i-a-n-o. Oh, Oh
I love to stop right
Beside an upright
Or high toned baby grand.

I Love Lucy

Lyric by Harold Adamson
Music by Eliot Daniel

from the Television Series *I Love Lucy*

I love Lucy and she loves me,
We're as happy as two can be.
Sometimes we quarrel but then,
How we love making up again.

Lucy kisses like no one can.
She's my missus and I'm her man;
And life is heaven you see
'Cause I love Lucy, yes,
I love Lucy
And Lucy loves me.

I Remember It Well

Words by Alan Jay Lerner
Music by Frederick Loewe

from the film *Gigi*

He: We met at nine.
She: We met at eight.
He: I was on time.
She: No, you were late.
He: Ah yes! I remember it well.
He: We dined with friends.
She: We dined alone.
He: A tenor sang.
She: A baritone.
He: Ah yes! I remember it well.

He: That sizzling April moon!
She: There was none that night,
And the month was June.
He: That's right! That's right!
She: It warms my heart to know that you

Remember still the way you do.
He: Ah yes! I remember it well.

He: How often I've thought of that Friday
She: Monday night,
He: When we had our last rendezvous.
And somehow I've foolishly wondered if you might
By some chance be thinking of it too?

He: That carriage ride.
She: You walked me home.
He: You lost a glove.
She: I lost a comb.
He: Ah yes! I remember it well..
The brilliant sky.
She: We had some rain.
He: Those Russian songs
She: From sunny Spain?
He: Ah yes! I remember it well.

He: You wore a gown of gold.
She: I was all in blue.
He: Am I getting old?
She: Oh no! Not you!
How strong you were, how young and gay;
A prince of love in every way.
He: Ah yes! I remember it well.

I Saw Her Standing There
Words and Music by John Lennon and Paul McCartney

recorded by The Beatles

Well, she was just seventeen,
You know what I mean,
And the way she looked was way beyond compare.
So how could I dance with another,
Oh when I saw her standing there.

Well she looked at me,
And I, I could see,
That before too long I'd fall in love with her.
She wouldn't dance with another,
Oh when I saw her standing there.

Well my heart went zoom
When I crossed that room,
And I held her hand in mine.
Oh we danced the night,
And we held each other tight,
And before too long I fell in love with her.
Now I'll never dance with another,
Oh when I her standing there.

I Say a Little Prayer
Lyric by Hal David
Music by Burt Bacharach

recorded by Dionne Warwick, Aretha Franklin

The moment I wake up
Before I put on my make-up
I say a little prayer for you.
While combing my hair now
And wondering what dress to wear now
I say a little prayer for you.

Refrain:
Forever, forever you'll stay in my heart
And I will love you forever and ever.
We never will part.
Oh, how I'll love you.
Together, together, that's how it must be
To live without you
Would only mean heartbreak for me.

I run for the bus, dear,
While riding I think of us, dear.
I say a little prayer for you.
At work I just take time
And all through my coffee break time
I say a little prayer for you.

Refrain

My darling, believe me,
For me there is no one but you.
Please love me too.
I'm in love with you
Answer my prayer.
Say you love me too.

(I Scream-You Scream-We All Scream For) Ice Cream
Words and Music by Howard Johnson, Billy Moll and Robert King

recorded by Fred Waring & The Pennsylvanians and various other artists

I scream, you scream, we all scream for ice cream,
Rah! Rah! Rah!
Tuesdays, Mondays we all scream for Sundaes
Siss! Boom! Bah!
Boola Boola Sasparoola
If you've got chocolet we'll take vanoola.
I scream, you scream, we all scream for ice cream,
Rah! Rah! Rah!

I scream, you scream, we all scream for ice cream,
Rah! Rah! Rah!
Frosted, malted, or peppered and salted,
Siss! Boom! Bah!
Oh! Spumoni
Oh! Tortoni and confidentially,
Oh! Oh! Baloney.
I scream, you scream, we all scream for ice cream.
Rah! Rah! Rah!

Spoken:
Alpha, Beta, A frozen to-may-tuh,
Yes! Oh! Yes!
Ham and egg-a for Lamda Omega S.O.S.
A.B.C.ses
X.Y.Z ses but in the winter time no B.V.D.ses.
Ketchup, mustard on fresh cherry custard
Ice Cream Pi.

I Second That Emotion
Words and Music by William "Smokey" Robinson and Alfred Cleveland

recorded by The Miracles

Maybe you'll wanna give me kisses sweet,
But only for one night with no repeat.
And maybe you'll go away and never call,
And a taste of honey's worse than none at all.

Refrain:
Oh, little girl, in that case I don't want no part.
I do believe that that would only break my heart.
Oh, but if you feel like lovin' me,
If you got the notion, I second that emotion.
So if you fell like giving me a lifetime of devotion,
I second that emotion.

Maybe you think that love will tie you down
And you don't have the time to hang around.
Or maybe you think that love will make us fools,
And so it makes you wise to break the rules.

Refrain Twice

I Started a Joke
Words and Music by Barry Gibb, Maurice Gibb and Robin Gibb

recorded by The Bee Gees

I started a joke, which started the whole world crying.
But I didn't see that the joke was on me.

I started to cry which started the whole world laughing;
Oh, if I'd only seen that the joke was on me.

I looked at the skies, running my hands over my eyes,
And I fell out of bed, hurting my head from things that I said.

Till I finally died, which started the whole world living;
Oh, if I'd only seen that the joke was on me.
Oh, no, that the joke was on me.

I Thank You
Words and Music by Isaac Hayes and David Porter

recorded by Sam & Dave

You didn't have to love me like you did,
But you did, but you did, and I thank you.
You didn't have to love me like you did,
But you did, but you did, and I thank you.

Then you took your love to someone else.
I wouldn't know what it meant to be loved to death.
You made me feel like I've never felt.
Kisses so good I had to holler for help.

You didn't have to squeeze, but you did, but you did,
But you did, and I thank you.
You didn't have to hold me, but you did,
But you did, but you did and I thank you.

Every day was something new.
You put on your bag and your fine to-do.
You got me tryin' new things too,
Just so I can keep up with you.

You didn't have to shake it, but you did,
But you did, but you did, and I thank you.
You didn't have to make it like you did,
But you did, but you did, and I thank you.

All my life, I been short-changed.
Wipeout your love, baby, it's a cryin' shame.
But now that I know what the fellows talkin' about
When they say that they been turned out.
I wanna thank you.
I wanna thank you.

I Think I Love You

Words and Music by Tony Romeo
© 1970 (Renewed 1998) SCREEN GEMS-EMI MUSIC INC.

featured in the Television Series *The Partridge Family*
recorded by The Partridge Family

Bah bah bah bah…

I'm sleeping
And right in the middle of a good dream
I call out once I wake up
From something that keeps knocking in my brain.
Before I go insane I hold my pillow to my head
And spring up in my bed screaming out the words I dread.
I think I love you. I think I love you.

This morning
I woke up with this feeling
I didn't know how to deal with.
And so I just decided to myself I'd hide it to myself
And never talk about it, and did not go and shout it
When you walked into the room. I think I love you.

(I think I love you.)
I think I love you. So what am I so afraid of?
I'm afraid that I'm not sure of a love there is no cure for.
I think I love you. Isn't that what life is made of?
Though it worries me to say that I'd never felt this way.

I don't know what I'm up against.
I don't know what it's all about.
I got so much to think about.
Hey, I think I love you.
So what am I so afraid of?
I'm afraid that I'm not sure of a love there is no cure for.

I think I love you. Isn't that what life is made of?
So it worries me to say I never felt this way.
Believe me you really don't have to worry.
I only wanna make you happy
And if you say hey go away I will.
But I think better still I better stay around and love you.
Do you think I have a case?
Let me ask you to your face,
Do you think you love me?
Oh, I think I love you.

I Thought About You

Words by Johnny Mercer
Music by Jimmy Van Heusen
Copyright © 1939 (Renewed) by Music Sales Corporation (ASCAP) and Commander Music

a standard recorded by Benny Goodman, Frank Sinatra
and various other artists

Seems that I read, or somebody said
That out of sight is out of mind,
Maybe that's so but I tried to go
And leave you behind,
What did I find?

I took a trip on the train and I thought about you.
I passed a shadowy lane and I thought about you.
Two or three cars parked under the stars,
A winding stream,
Moon shining down on some little town,
And with each beam,
Same old dream.
At every stop that we made,
Oh, I thought about you.

But when I pulled down the shade,
Then I really felt blue.
I peeked thru the crack and looked at the track,
The one going back to you.
And what did I do?
I thought about you.

I Walk the Line

Words and Music by John R. Cash
© 1956 (Renewed 1984) HOUSE OF CASH, INC. (BMI)/Administered by BUG MUSIC

recorded by Johnny Cash

I keep a close watch on this heart of mine.
I keep my eyes wide open all the time.
I keep the ends out for the tie that binds.
Because you're mine,
I walk the line.

I find it very, very easy to be true.
I find myself alone when each day is through.
Yes, I'll admit that I'm a fool for you.
Because you're mine,
I walk the line.

As sure as night is dark and day is light,
I keep you on my mind both day and night.
And happiness I've known proves that it's right.
Because you're mine,
I walk the line.

You've got a way to keep me on your side.
You give me a cause for love that I can't hide.
For you I know I'd even try to turn the tide.
Because you're mine,
I walk the line.

I keep a close watch on this heart of mine.
I keep my eyes wide open all of the time.
I keep the ends out for the tie that binds.
Because you're mine,
I walk the line.

I Wanna Dance with Somebody

Words and Music by George Merrill
and Shannon Rubicam

recorded by Whitney Houston

The clock strikes upon the hour,
And the sun begins to fade.
There's still enough time to figure out,
How to chase my blues away.
I've done alright up till now;
It's the light of day that shows me how.
But when the night falls, loneliness calls.

Refrain:
Oh I wanna dance with somebody.
I wanna feel the heat with somebody.
Yeah, I wanna dance with somebody,
With somebody who loves me.

I've been in love and lost my senses,
Spinning through the town.
Sooner or later the fever ends,
And I wind up feeling down.
I need a man who'll take a chance,
On a love that burns hot enough to last.
So when the night falls,
My lonely heart calls.

Refrain

I need a man who'll take a chance,
On a love that burns hot enough to last.
So when the night falls,
My lonely heart calls.

Refrain

I Want to Know What Love Is

Words and Music by Mick Jones

recorded by Foreigner

I've gotta take a little time,
A little time to think things over.
I better read between the lines
In case I need it when I'm older.

Now, this mountain I must climb
Feels like the world upon my shoulders.
Through the clouds I see love shine.
It keeps me warm as life grows colder.

Refrain:
In my life
There's been heartache and pain.
I don't know if I can face it again.
Can't stop now.
I've traveled so far
To change this lonely life.
I want to know what love is.
I want you to show me.
I want to feel what love is.
I know you can show me.

I've gotta take a little time,
A little time to think things over.
I better read between the lines
In case I need it when I'm older.

I'm gonna take a little time,
A little time to look around me.
I've got nowhere left to hide.
It looks like love has finally found me.

Refrain

I want to know what love is.
I want you to show me.
I want to feel what love is.
I know you can show me.

I Want to Spend My Lifetime Loving You

Music by James Horner
Lyric by Will Jennings

from the TriStar Motion Picture *The Mask of Zorro*
recorded by Marc Anthony & Tina Arena

Male:
Moon so bright,
Night so fine,
Keep your heart here with mine.
Life's a dream we are dreaming.

Female:
Race the moon,
Catch the wind,
Ride the night to the end.
Seize the day, stand up for the light.

Refrain:
Both:
I want to spend my lifetime loving you
If that is all in life I ever do.
Male:
Heroes rise, heroes fall.
Rise again, win it all.
Female:
In your heart, can't you feel the glory?
Through our joy, through our pain,
Both:
We can move worlds again.
Take my hand, dance with me.
Male:
Dance with me.

Both:
I want to spend my lifetime loving you
If that is all in life I ever do.
I will want nothing else to see me through
If I can spend my lifetime loving you.

Male:
Though we know we will never come again,
Where there is love,
Both:
Life begins over and over again.
Save the night, Save the day.
Save the love come what may.
Love is worth everything we pay.

I want to spend my lifetime loving you
If that is all in life I ever do.
I want to spend my lifetime loving you.
If that is all in life I ever do.
I will want nothing else to see me through
If I can spend my lifetime loving you.

I Whistle a Happy Tune
Lyrics by Oscar Hammerstein II
Music by Richard Rodgers

from the musical *The King and I*

Whenever I feel afraid
I hold my head erect
And whistle a happy tune,
So no one will suspect
I'm afraid.

While shivering in my shoes
I strike a careless pose
And whistle a happy tune,
And no one ever knows
I'm afraid.

The result of this deception
Is very strange to tell,
For when I fool the people I fear
I fool myself as well!

I whistle a happy tune,
And every single time
The happiness in the tune
Convinces me that I'm
Not afraid!

Make believe you're brave
And the trick will take you far;
You may be as brave
As you make believe you are.
You may be as brave
As you make believe you are.

I Will
Words and Music by John Lennon and Paul McCartney

recorded by The Beatles

Who knows how long I've loved you,
You know I love you still.
Will I wait a lonely lifetime,
If you want me to I will.

For if I ever saw you,
I didn't catch your name.
But it never really mattered,
I will always feel the same.

Love you forever and forever,
Love you with all my heart.
Love you when we're together,
Love you when we're apart.

And when at last I find you,
Your song will fill the air.
Sing it loud so I can hear you,
For the things you do
Endear you to me.
You know I will,
I will.

I Will Be Here

Words and Music by Steven Curtis Chapman

recorded by Steven Curtis Chapman

Tomorrow mornin' if you wake up
And the sun does not appear,
I, I will be here
If in the dark we lose sight of love,
Hold my hand and have no fear
'Cause I, I will be here.

I will be here
When you feel like bein' quiet.
When you need to speak your mind,
I will listen, and I will be here.
When the laughter turns to cryin'
Through the winnin', losin' and tryin',
We'll be together,
'Cause I will be here.

Tomorrow mornin' if you wake up
And the future is unclear,
I, I will be here.
As sure as seasons are made for change,
Our lifetimes are made for years,
So I, I will be here.

I will be here,
And you can cry on my shoulder.
When the mirror tells us we're older,
I will hold you.
And I will be here
To watch you grow in beauty
And tell you all the things you are to me.
I will be here.

I will be true
To the promise I have made
To you and to the One
Who gave you to me.

I, I will be here.
And just as sure
As seasons are made for change,
Our lifetimes are made for years.

So I,
I will be here.
We'll be together.
I will be here.

I Will Remember You

Words and Music by Sarah McLachlan, Seamus Egan and Dave Merenda

Theme from the film *The Brothers McMullen*
recorded by Sarah McLachlan

Refrain:
I will remember you.
Will you remember me?
Don't let your life pass you by.
Weep not for the memories.

Remember the good times that we had.
We let them slip away from us when things got bad.
Clearly I first saw you smilin' in the sun.
Wanna feel your warmth upon me. I wanna be the one.

Refrain

I'm so tired but I can't sleep.
Standin' on the edge of something much too deep.
It's funny how I feel so much but I cannot say a word.
We are screaming inside or we can't be heard.

Refrain

I'm so afraid to love you, more afraid to lose,
Clinging to a past that doesn't let me choose.
Well once there was a darkness, a deep and endless night.
You gave me everything you had, oh, you gave me light.

Refrain Twice

Weep not for the memories.

I Wish I Didn't Love You So

Words and Music by Frank Loesser

from the Paramount Picture *The Perils of Pauline*
a standard recorded by Vaughn Monroe, Dinah Shore and
various other artists

I wish I didn't love you so,
My love for you should have faded long ago,
I wish I didn't need your kiss.
Why must your kiss torture me as long as this?
I might be smiling by now with some new tenor friend,
Smiling by now with my heart on the mend.
But when I try, something in that heart says
"No," you're still there.
I wish I didn't love you so.

I Wish I Were in Love Again

Words by Lorenz Hart
Music by Richard Rodgers

from the musical *Babes in Arms*
a standard recorded by Frank Sinatra and various other
artists

You don't know that I felt good
When we up and parted.
You don't know I knocked on wood,
Gladly broken-hearted.
Worrying is through,
I sleep all night,
Appetite and health restored.
You don't know how much I'm bored.

Refrain 1:
The sleepless nights,
The daily fights,
The quick toboggan when you reach the heights
I miss the kisses and I miss the bites.
I wish I were in love again!
The broken dates,
The endless waits,
The lovely loving and the hateful hates,
The conversation with the flying plates
I wish I were in love again!
No more pain,
No more strain,
Now I'm sane but…
I would rather be gaga!
The pulled-out fur
Of cat and cur,
The fine mis-mating of a him and her
I've learned my lesson, but I wish I were
In love again!

Refrain 2:
The furtive sigh,
The blackened eye,
The words "I'll love you till the day I die,"
The self-deception that believes the lie
I wish I were in love again.
When love congeals
It soon reveals
The faint aroma of performing seals,
The double-crossing of a pair of heels.
I wish I were in love again!
No more care.
No despair.
I'm all there now,
But I'd rather be punch-drunk!
Believe me, sir,
I much prefer
The classic battle of a him and her.
I don't like quiet and I wish I were
In love again.

I Woke Up in Love This Morning

Words and Music by Irwin Levine and
Lawrence Russell Brown

recorded by The Partridge Family

Last night, I turned out the light,
Lay down and thought about you.
I thought about the way that it could be.
Two o'clock,
Wondering what I'm doin' here alone without you.
So, I close my eyes and dream you here to me.

Refrain:
And I woke up in love this mornin'.
I woke up in love this mornin'.
Went to sleep with you on my mind.
I woke up in love this mornin'.
I woke up in love this mornin'.
Went to sleep with you on my mind.

Hello girl, yes, it's five-o'clock, I know,
But just you listen.
There something that I've got to let you know.
This is you,
This pillow that I'm hugging and I'm kissing.
And one more thing before I let you go.

Refrain

Do dreams come true? Well, if they do,
I'll have you, not for just a night,
But for my whole life through.
Oh,

Repeat Refrain and Fade

I Won't Last a Day Without You

Words and Music by Paul Williams and Roger Nichols

recorded by The Carpenters

Day after day,
I must face a world of strangers where I don't belong.
I'm not that strong,
It's nice to know,
That there's someone I can turn to who will always care,
You're always there,

Refrain:
When there's no getting over that rainbow,
When my smallest of dreams won't come true,
I can take all the madness the world has to give,
But I won't last a day without you.

So many times,
When the city seems to be without a friendly face,
A lonely place,
It's nice to know,
That you'll be there if I need you and you'll always smile,
It's all worthwhile,

Refrain

Touch me and I end up singing,
Troubles seem to up and disappear,
You touch me with the love you're bringing,
I can't really lose when you're near.

When you're near my love,
If all my friends have forgotten half their promises
They're not unkind, just hard to find.
One look at you,
And I know that I could learn to live without the rest,
I found the best.

Refrain Twice

I Write the Songs
Words and Music by Bruce Johnston

recorded by Barry Manilow

I've been alive forever,
And I wrote the very first song.
I put the words and the melodies together,
I am music, and I write the songs.

Refrain:
I write the songs that make the whole world sing;
I write the songs of love and special things.
I write the songs that make the young girls cry;
I write the songs, I write the songs.

My home lies deep within you
And I've got my own place in your soul.
Now, when I look out through your eyes
I'm young again, even though I'm very old.

Refrain

Oh, my music makes you dance
And gives you a second chance,
And I wrote some rock 'n' roll
So you can move.

Music fills your heart,
Well, that's a real fine place to start.
It's from me, it's for you,
It's from you, it's for me
It's a world-wide symphony.

Refrain

I'd Do Anything for Love
(But I Won't Do That)
Words and Music by Jim Steinman

recorded by Meat Loaf

And I would do anything for love.
I'd run right into hell and back.
I would do anything for love.
I'll never lie to you and that's a fact.
But I'll never forget the way you feel right now
Oh, no, no way.
And I would do anything for love,
But I won't do that.
No I won't do that.

Some days it don't come easy,
Some days it don't come hard.
Some days it don't come at all
And these are the days that never end.

Some nights you're breathing fire,
Some nights you're carved in ice.
Some nights are like nothing
I've ever seen before or ever will again.

Maybe I'm crazy,
But it's crazy and it's true.
I know you can save me.
No one else can save me now but you.

As long as the planets are turning,
As long as the stars are burning,
As long as your dreams are coming true,
You better believe it
That I would do anything for love.
Oh, I would do anything for love.
Oh, I would do anything for love,
But I won't do that.
No I won't do that.

Refrain:
I would do anything for love,
Anything you've been dreaming of,
But I just won't do that.

Repeat Refrain

Some days I pray for silence,
Some days I pray for soul.
Some days I just pray to the God
Of Sex and Drums and Rock 'n' Roll.

Maybe I'm lonely,
And that's all I'm qualified to be.
There's just one and only,
The one and only promise I can keep.
As long as the wheels are turning,
As long as the fires are burning,
As long as your prayers are coming true,
You better believe it
That I would do anything for love
And you know it's true and that's a fact.
I would do anything for love,
And there'll never be no turning back.

But I'll never do it better than I do it with you.
So long, so long.
And I would do anything for love.
Oh. I would do anything for love.
I would do anything for love,
But I won't do that,
No, no, no, I won't do that.

Girl:
Will you raise me up,
Will you help me down?
Will you get me tight out
Of the God forsaken town?
Will you make it all a little less cold?

Boy:
I can do that,
Oh, no I can do that.

Girl:
Will you cater to every fantasy I got?
Will you hose me down
With holy water if I get too hot?
Will you take me places I've never gone?

Boy:
I can do that,
Oh, no I can do that.

Girl:
I know the territory.
I've been around.
It'll all turn to dust
And we'll all fall down.
Sooner or later you'll be screwing around.

Boy:
I won't do that.
No, I won't do that.

Girl:
Anything for love,
But I won't do that.

I'll Be
Words and Music by Edwin McCain
© 1997 EMI APRIL MUSIC INC. and HARRINGTON PUBLISHING
All Rights Controlled and Administered by EMI APRIL MUSIC INC.

recorded by Edwin McCain

The strands in your eyes
That color them wonderful
Stop me and steal my breath.
And emeralds from mountains
Thrust toward the sky,
Never revealing their depth.

Refrain 1:
And tell me that we belong together.
Dress it up with the trappings of love.
I'll be captivated,
I'll hang from your lips
Instead of the gallows of heartache
That hang from above.

Refrain 2:
I'll be your cryin' shoulder,
I'll be love suicide.
And I'll be better when I'm older,
I'll be the greatest fan of your life.

And rain falls angry on the tin roof
As we lie awake in my bed.
And you're my survival,
You're my living proof
My love is alive and not dead.

Refrain 1

Refrain 2

And I've dropped out, I've burned up.
I fought my way back from the dead.
I've tuned in, turned on, remembered the thing that you said.

Refrain 2 Twice

I'll Be Around
Words and Music by Alec Wilder
TRO - © Copyright 1942 (Renewed) Ludlow Music, Inc., New York, NY

a standard recorded by The Mills Brothers, Cab Calloway,
George Shearing and various other artists

I'll be around
No matter how you treat me now,
I'll be around from now on.
Your latest love can never last,
And when it's past,
I'll be around when he's gone.

Goodbye again,
And if you find a love like mine,
Just now and then drop a line
To say you're feeling fine.
And when things go wrong,
Perhaps you'll see you're meant for me,
So, I'll be around when he's gone.

I'll Be Missing You

Written and Composed by Sting

recorded by Puff Daddy & Faith Evans (Featuring 112)

Spoken:
This right here goes out to everyone
That has lost someone that they truly love.
Check it out.

Rap 1:
Seems like yesterday we used to rock the show.
I laced the track, you locked the flow.
So far from hangin' on the block for dough.
Notorious, they got to know that life ain't always what it
Seemed to be. Words can't express what you mean to me.
Even though you're gone, we still a team.
Through your family, I'll fulfill your dreams.

Rap 2:
In the future, can't wait to see if you open up the gates for me.
Reminisce sometime the night they took my friend.
Try to black it out but it plays again.
When it's real, feelin's hard to conceal.
Can't imagine all the pain I feel.
Give anything to hear half your breath.
I know you're still livin' your life after death.

Refrain 1:
Sung:
Every step I take,
Every move I make,
Every single day,
Every time I pray,
I'll be missing you.
Thinking of the day
When you went away,
What a life to take,
What a bond to break.
I'll be missing you.

Rap 3:
It's kinda hard with you not around.
Know you're in heaven smilin' down
Watchin' us while we pray for you.
Every day we pray for you.
Till the day we meet again,
In my heart is where I keep you, friend.
Memories give me the strength I need to proceed,
Strength I need to believe.

Rap 4:
My thoughts, Big, I just can't define.
Wish I could turn back the hands of time,
Us and a six, shop for new clothes and kicks,
You and me take in flicks.
Make a hit, stages they receive you on.
Still can't believe you're gone.
Give anything to hear half your breath.
I know you're still livin' your life after death.

Refrain 1

Somebody tell me why.
On that morning, when this life is over,
I know I'll see your face.
Every night I pray,
I'll see your face.
Every night I pray,

Refrain 2:
Every step I take,
Every move I make,
Every single day.
Every night I pray,
Every single step I take,
Every move I make.

Every single day.
Every night I pray,

Refrain 2

We miss you.

Refrain 1

I'll Be Seeing You

Lyric by Irving Kahal
Music by Sammy Fain

from the musical *Right This Way*
a standard recorded by Frank Sinatra, Liberace and various
other artists

Cathedral bells were tolling
And our hearts sang on,
Was it the spell of Paris
Or the April dawn?
Who knows,
If we shall meet again?
But when the morning chimes ring sweet again:

I'll be seeing you
In all the old familiar places
That this heart of mine embraces all day thru:
In that small café,
The park across the way,
The children's carrousel,
The chestnut trees, the wishing well.

I'll be seeing you
In every lovely summer's day,
In everything that's light and gay,
I'll always think of you that way.
I'll find you in the morning sun;
And when the night is new,
I'll be looking at the moon
But I'll be seeing you!

I'll Be There

Words and Music by Berry Gordy, Hal Davis,
Willie Hutch and Bob West

recorded by The Jackson 5, Mariah Carey

You and I must make a pact.
We must bring salvation back.
Where there is love,
I'll be there.
(I'll be there.)
I'll reach out my hand to you,
I'll have faith in all you do.

Refrain:
Just call my name
And I'll be there.
(I'll be there.)
I'll be there to comfort you,
Build my world of dreams around you.
I'm so glad I found you.
I'll be there with a love so strong.
I'll be your strength,
You know I'll keep holding on.

Let me fill your heart with joy and laughter.
Togetherness, well it's all I'm after.
Just call my name
And I'll be there.
(I'll be there.)

I'll be there to protect you
With an unselfish love that respects you.

Refrain

If you should ever find someone new,
I know she'd better be good to you,
'Cause if she doesn't,
Then I'll be there (I'll be there.)
Don't you know, baby.
I'll be there, I'll be there.
Just call my name and I'll be there.
I'll be there, I'll be there.
Just call my name and I'll be there.

I'll Follow the Sun

Words and Music by John Lennon and Paul McCartney

recorded by The Beatles

One day you'll look to see I've gone
For tomorrow may rain so I'll follow the sun.
Some day you'll know I was the one
But tomorrow may rain so I'll follow the sun.

And now the time has come and so my love I must go
And though I lose a friend in the end you will know.
Oh, one day you'll look to see I've gone
For tomorrow may rain so I'll follow the sun.

And now the time has come and so my love I must go
And though I lose a friend in the end you will know.
Oh, one day day you'll look to see I've gone
For tomorrow may rain so I'll follow the sun.

I'll Get By
(As Long as I Have You)

Lyric by Roy Turk
Music by Fred E. Ahlert

a standard recorded by Dinah Shore and various other
artists

This old world was just as sad a place for me
As could be,
I was lonely and blue.
This old world then changed to paradise for me
Suddenly.
Why? Because I met you.
Although wealth and power I may never find,
Still as long as I have you, dear, I won't mind.

Refrain:
For I'll get by
As long as I have you.
Though there be rain
And darkness too,
I'll not complain,
I'll laugh it through.
Poverty may come to me
That's true.
But what care I?
Say, I'll get by
As long as I have you.

Since we met my life is full of happiness,
And I guess,
It will always be so.
Just as long as I can feel your fond caress,
I'll confess,
Cares and sorrows must go.
You have turned each frown of mine into a smile.
It's your love alone that guides me all the while.

Refrain

I'll Make Love to You

Words and Music by Babyface

recorded by Boyz II Men

Close you eyes, make a wish,
And blow out the candlelight
For tonight is just your night.
We're gonna celebrate
All through the night.

Pour the wine, light the fire.
Girl, your wish is my command.
I submit to your demands.
I will do anything.
Girl, you need only ask.

Refrain:
I'll make love to you
Like you want me to
And I'll hold you tight,
Baby, all through the night.
I'll make love to you
When you want me to
And I will not go
Till you tell me to.

Girl, relax,
Let's go slow.
I ain't got nowhere to go.
I'm just gonna concentrate on you.
Girl, are you ready?
It's gonna be a long night.

Throw your clothes
On the floor
I'm gonna take my clothes off too.
I made plans to be with you.
Girl, whatever you ask me,
You know I could do.

Refrain

Baby, tonight
Is your night
And I will do you right.
Just make a wish
On your night,
Anything that you ask.
I will give you the love of your life,
Your life, your life.

Refrain

Repeat Refrain

I'll Never Fall in Love Again

Lyric by Hal David
Music by Burt Bacharach

from the musical *Promises, Promises*
recorded by Dionne Warwick

What do you get when you fall in love,
A girl {guy} with a pin to burst your bubble,
That's what you get for all your trouble,
I'll never fall in love again.
I'll never fall in love again.

What do you get when you kiss a girl {guy},
You get enough germs to catch pneumonia,
After you do, she'll {he'll} never phone you;
I'll never fall in love again.

Refrain:
I'll never fall in love again.
Don't tell me what it's all about,
'Cause I've been there and I'm glad I'm out;
Out of those chains, those chains that bind you,
That is why I'm here to remind you.
What do you get when you fall in love,
You only get lies and pain and sorrow,
So for at least until tomorrow,
I'll never fall in love again,
I'll never fall in love again.

What do you get when you give your heart,
You get it all broken up and battered,
That's what you get, a heart that's tattered;
I'll never fall in love again.

Refrain

What do you get when you need a guy {girl},
You get enough tears to fill an ocean,
That's what you get for your devotion;
I'll never fall in love again.

Refrain

I'll Never Love This Way Again

Words and Music by Richard Kerr and Will Jennings

recorded by Dionne Warwick

You looked inside my fantasies and made each one come true,
Something no one else had ever found a way to do.
I've kept the memories one by one, since you took me in.

Refrain:
I know I'll never love this way again.
I know I'll never love this way again,
So I keep holdin' on before the good is gone.
I know I'll never love this way again,
Hold on, hold on, hold on.

A fool will lose tomorrow reaching back for yesterday.
I won't turn my head in sorrow if you should go away.
I'll stand here and remember just how good it's been.
And…

Refrain

I know I'll never love this way again,
So I keep holdin' on before the good is gone.
I know I'll never love this way again,
Hold on, hold on, hold on.

I'll Take Romance
Lyrics by Oscar Hammerstein II
Music by Ben Oakland
Copyright © 1937 by WILLIAMSON MUSIC and BOURNE CO.
Copyright Renewed

from the film *I'll Take Romance*

I'll take romance,
While my heart is young and eager to fly,
I'll give my heart a try,
I'll take romance.

I'll take romance,
While my arms are strong and eager for you,
I'll give my arms their cue,
I'll take romance.

So my lover when you want me,
Call me in the hush of the evening,
When you call me,
In the hush of the evening,
I'll rush to my first real romance,
While my heart is young and eager and gay,
I'll give my heart away,
I'll take romance,
I'll take my own romance.

I'll Take You There
Words and Music by Alvertis Isbell
Copyright © 1972 IRVING MUSIC, INC.
Copyright Renewed

recorded by The Staple Singers

Male:
I know a place, ya'll,
Ain't nobody cryin', no, ain't nobody worried.
Oh, ain't no smiling faces lying to the races.
I said ain't no smiling faces,
No smiling faces lying to the races.
Ain't nobody crying, no more crying.
If you're ready now come on, come on,
I'll take you there.

Female:
Lord have mercy.
Male:
Say if your ready I'll take you there. Oh, yeah.
Help me. Help me, I'll take you there. (Come on.)
Female:
Help me.
Male:
I said come on I'll take you there.

Female:
If you're ready now.
If you're ready now.
Oh, I, oh, I know a place ya'll.
Oh, there ain't nobody crying.
(Say ain't no) Ain't nobody crying.
I said, I said ain't nobody worried yeah.
Ain't no smiling faces.
No smiling faces lying to the races, help me now.
I'll take you there.
I said if you're ready I'll take you there.
I said I'll take you there.
Come on get ready.
I'll take you there.

Repeat and Fade:
Come, go with me.

I'm Beginning to See the Light
Words and Music by Don George, Johnny Hodges,
Duke Ellington and Harry James
Copyright © 1944 by Chappell & Co.
Copyright Renewed

a standard recorded by Duke Ellington, Harry James,
Ella Fitzgerald and various other artists

I never cared much for moon-lit skies,
I never wink back at the fire-flies.
But now that the stars are in your eyes,
I'm beginning to see the light.

I never went in for after glow,
Or candlelight on the mistletoe.
But now when you turn the lamp down low
I'm beginning to see the light.

Used to ramble thru the park,
Shadow boxing in the dark.
Then you came and caused a spark,
That's a four alarm fire now.

I never made love by lantern shine,
I never saw rainbows in my wine.
But now that your lips are burning mine,
I'm beginning to see the light.

I'm Glad There Is You (In This World of Ordinary People)

Words and Music by Paul Madeira and Jimmy Dorsey

a standard recorded by Jimmy Dorsey, Dennis Day and various other artists

In this world of ordinary people, extraordinary people,
I'm glad there is you.
In this world of overrated pleasures, of underrated treasures,
I'm glad there is you.

I'll live to love,
I'll love to be with you beside me.
This role so new, I'll muddle thru' with you to guide me.
In this world where many, many people play at love,
And hardly any stay in love,
I'm glad there is you.
More than ever,
I'm glad there is you.

I'm Gonna Sit Right Down and Write Myself a Letter

Lyric by Joe Young
Music by Fred E. Ahlert

from the musical revue *Ain't Misbehavin'*
a standard recorded by Fats Waller and various other artists

I'm gonna sit right down and write myself a letter
And make believe it came from you.
I'm gonna write words, oh so sweet,
They're gonna knock me off my feet.
A lot of kisses on the bottom,
I'll be glad I got 'em.
I'm gonna smile and say, "I hope you're feeling better"
And close "with love" the way you do.
I'm gonna sit right down and write myself a letter
And make believe it came from you.

I'm Henry VIII, I Am

Words and Music by Fred Murray and R.P. Weston

recorded by Herman's Hermits

I'm Henery the Eighth, I am!
Henery the Eighth, I am, I am!
I got married to the widow next door.
She's been married seven times before
And everyone was a Henery.
She wouldn't have a Willie or a Sam.

I'm her eighth old man named Henery,
Henery the eighth I am!

Spoken:
Second verse same as the first!

Repeat Verse

H-E-N-R-Y Henery, Henery,
Henery the eighth I am, I am!
Henery the eighth I am!

I'm Just a Lucky So and So

Words by Mack David
Music by Duke Ellington

a standard recorded by Duke Ellington and various other artists

As I walk down the street, seems everyone I meet
Gives me a friendly hello.
I guess I'm just a lucky so and so.
The birds in every tree
Are all so neighborly
They sing wherever I go.
I guess I'm just a lucky so and so.

If you should ask me the amount in my bank account,
I'd have to confess that I'm slippin'.
But that don't worry me,
Confidentially,
I've got a dream that's a pipin'.
And when the day is through
Each night I hurry to
A home where love waits, I know.
I guess I'm just a lucky so and so.

I'm Popeye the Sailor Man

Words and Music by Sammy Lerner

Theme from the Paramount Cartoon *Popeye the Sailor*

Refrain:
I'm Popeye the sailor man;
I'm Popeye the sailor man.
I'm strong to the "fin-ich"
'Cause I eats me spinach;
I'm Popeye the sailor man.

I'm one tough gazookus
Which hates all palookas
Wot ain't on the up and square.
I biffs 'em and buffs 'em
And always out-roughs 'em,
An' none of 'em gits nowhere.

If anyone dasses to risk my "fisk,"
It's "boff" an' it's "wham," un'erstan'?
So keep good behavior,
That's your one life-saver
With Popeye the sailor man.

Refrain

I'm Putting All My Eggs in One Basket
Words and Music by Irving Berlin

from the Motion Picture *Follow the Fleet*

I've been a roaming Romeo {Juliet},
My Juliets {Romeos} have been many.
But now my roaming days have gone.
Too many irons in the fire
Is worse than not having any.
I've had my share and from now on

I'm putting all my eggs in one basket.
I'm betting everything I've got on you.
I'm giving all my love to one baby.
Lord help me if my baby don't come through.
I've got a great big amount
Saved up in my love account,
Honey, and I've decided
Love divided in two won't do.
So I'm putting all my eggs in one basket.
I'm betting everything I've got on you.

I'm So Lonesome I Could Cry
Words and Music by Hank Williams

recorded by Hank Williams and various other artists

Hear that lonesome whippoorwill,
He sounds too blue to fly.
The midnight train is whining low.
I'm so lonesome I could cry.
I've never see a night so long,
When time goes crawling by.
The moon just went behind a cloud
To hide its face and cry.

Did you ever see a robin weep
When leaves began to die.
That means he's lost the will to live.
I'm so lonesome I could cry.
The silence of a falling star
Lights up a purple sky.
And as I wonder where you are
I'm so lonesome I could cry.

I'm Still Here
Words and Music by Stephen Sondheim

from the musical *Follies*

Note: The lyrics have been revised in subsequent versions;
these are the original show lyrics.

Good times and bum times,
I've seen them all and, my dear,
I'm still here.
Plush velvet sometimes,
Sometimes just pretzels and beer,
But I'm here.
I've stuffed the dailies in my shoes,
Strummed ukuleles, sung the blues,
Seen all my dreams disappear,
But I'm here.

I've slept in shanties,
Guest of the W.P.A.
But I'm here.
Danced in my scanties,
Three bucks a night was the pay,
But I'm here.
I've stood on breadlines with the best,
Watched while the headlines did the rest.
In the depression was I depressed?
Nowhere near.
I met a big financier and I'm here.

I've been through Ghandi,
Windsor and Wally's affair,
And I'm here.
Amos 'n' Andy
Mahjongg and platinum hair,
And I'm here.
I got through Abie's Irish Rose,
Five Dionne babes, Major Bowes,
Had heebie jeebies for Beebe's Bathysphere.
I lived through Brenda Frazier, and I'm here.

I've gotten through Herbert and J. Edgar Hoover,
Gee, that was fun and a half.
When you've been through Herbert and J. Edgar Hoover,
Anything else is a laugh.

I've been through Reno,
I've been through Beverly Hills,
And I'm here.
Reefers and vino,
Rest cures, religion and pills,
And I'm here.
Been called a pinko Commie tool,
Got through it stinko by my pool.
I should have gone to an acting school,
That seems clear.
Still, someone said, "She's sincere,"
So I'm here.

Black sable one day,
Next day it goes into hock.
But I'm here.
Top billing Monday,
Tuesday you're touring in stock,
But I'm here.
First you're another sloe-eyed vamp,
Then someone's mother,
Then you're camp.
Then you career from career to career.
I'm almost through my memoirs
And I'm here.

I've gotten through "Hey lady aren't you whoozis?
Wow! What a looker you were."
Or better yet, "Sorry, I thought you were whoozis,
Whatever happened to her?"

Good times and bum times,
I've seen 'em all my dear,
I'm still here.
Plush velvet sometimes,
Sometimes just pretzels and beer,
But I'm here.
I've run the gamut, A to Z.
Three cheers and dammit, c'est la vie.
I got through all of last year.
And I'm here.
Lord knows, at least I was there,
And I'm here!
Look who's here!
I'm still here!

I'm Still in Love with You
Words and Music by Al Green, Willie Mitchell
and Al Jackson, Jr.
Copyright © 1972 IRVING MUSIC, INC. and AL GREEN MUSIC
Copyright Renewed

recorded by Al Green

Spending my days thinking about you girl;
Being here with you, being here with you,
I can't explain myself, why I feel like I do,
'Tho it hurt me so to let you know.

And I look into your eyes,
And you let me know how you feel,
Let me know that love is really real.
And it seems to me,
That I'm wrapped up in your love.
Don't you know that I'm still in love,
Sho-nuff in love with you?
Well I know that I'm still in love,
Sho-nuff in love with you.

When I look into your eyes all the years.
How I see me loving you and you loving me.
It seems to me that I'm wrapped up in your love.
Don't you know that I'm still in love,
Sho-nuff in love with you?
I, I, don't you know that I'm still in love,
Sho-nuff in love with you?

I've Got a Lovely Bunch of Cocoanuts
Words and Music by Fred Heatherton
© 1944, 1948 IRWIN DASH MUSIC CO. LTD.
© Renewed 1972, 1976 IRWIN DASH MUSIC CO. LTD.
© 1949 (Renewed 1977) WAROCK CORP.
All Rights for Western Hemisphere Exclusively Controlled by WAROCK CORP. by arrangement
   with BOX AND COX (PUBLICATIONS) LTD.

recorded by Freddy Martin, Danny Kaye and various
other artists

I've got a loverly bunch of cocoanuts,
There they are a-standing in a row.
Big ones, small ones, some as big as your head,
Give 'em a twist, a flick of the wrist,
That's what the showman said.

I've got a loverly bunch of cocoanuts,
Every ball you throw will make me rich.
There stands me wife, the idol of me life,
Singing roll or bowl a ball a penny a pitch.
Roll or bowl a ball, roll or bowl a ball,
Singing roll or bowl a ball a penny a pitch.

I've Got My Love to Keep Me Warm
Words and Music by Irving Berlin
© Copyright 1936, 1937 by Irving Berlin
© Arrangement Copyright 1948 by Irving Berlin
Copyright Renewed

from the 20th Century Fox Motion Picture *On the Avenue*
a standard recorded by various artists

The snow is snowing,
The wind is blowing,
But I can weather the storm.
What do I care how much it may storm?
I've got my love to keep me warm.

I can't remember
A worse December;
Just watch those icicles form.
What do I care if icicles form?
I've got my love to keep me warm.

Off with my overcoat,
Off with my glove.
I need no overcoat,
I'm burning with love.

My heart's on fire,
The flame grows higher.
So I will weather the storm.
What do I care how much it may storm?
I've got my love to keep me warm.

I've Got the World on a String

Lyric by Ted Koehler
Music by Harold Arlen

from the revue *Cotton Club Parade*
a standard recorded by Bing Crosby, Frank Sinatra and
various other artists

I've got the world on a string,
Sittin' on a rainbow,
Got the string around my finger,
What a world,
What a life,
I'm in love!

I've got a song that I sing,
I cannot make the rain go,
Anytime I move my finger,
Lucky me,
Can't you see,
I'm in love?

Life is a beautiful thing,
As long as I hold the string,
I'd be a silly so and so,
If I should ever let go.
I've got the world on a string,
Sittin' on a rainbow,
Got the string around my finger,
What a world, what a life, I'm in love.

I've Got You Under My Skin

Words and Music by Cole Porter

from the film *Born to Dance*
a standard recorded by Frank Sinatra and various other
artists

I've got you
Under my skin,
I've got you
Deep in the heart of me,
So deep in my heart,
You're really a part of me.
I've got you
Under my skin,
I tried so
Not to give in.
I said to myself,
"This affair never will go so well."
But why should I try to resist when, darling,
I know so well?
I've got you
Under my skin.

I'd sacrifice anything,
Come what might,
For the sake of having you near,
In spite of a warning voice
That comes in the night
And repeats and repeats in my ear:
"Don't you know, little fool,
You never can win?
Use your mentality,
Wake up to reality."
But each time I do,
Just the thought of you
Makes me stop before I begin,
'Cause I've got you
Under my skin.

I've Grown Accustomed to Her Face

Words by Alan Jay Lerner
Music by Frederick Loewe

from the musical *My Fair Lady*

I've grown accustomed to her face
She almost makes the day begin.
I've grown accustomed to the tune,
She whistles night and noon,
Her smiles, her frowns,
Her ups, her downs
Are second nature to me now;
Like breathing out and breathing in.
I was serenely independent
And content before we met;
Surely, I could always
Be that way again and yet,
I've grown accustomed to her looks;
Accustomed to her voice
Accustomed to her face.

I've grown accustomed to her face
She almost makes the day begin.
I've gotten used to hear her say:
"Good morning" every day,
Her joys, her woes,
Her highs, her lows
Are second nature to me now;
Like breathing out and breathing in.
I'm very grateful she's a woman
And so easy to forget
Rather like a habit
One can always break and yet,
I've grown accustomed to the trace
Of something in the air;
Accustomed to her face.

I've Heard That Song Before

Lyric by Sammy Cahn
Music by Jule Styne

from the Motion Picture *Youth on Parade*
recorded by Harry James and various other artists

Music helps me to remember,
It helps remind me of things behind me.
Tho' I'm better off forgetting
I try in vain each time I hear that strain:

It seems to me
I've heard that song before;
It's from an old familiar score,
I know it well, that melody,
It's funny how a theme
Recalls a favorite dream
A dream that brought you so close to me.

I know each word because
I've heard that song before,
The lyric said "Forever more."
Forever more's a memory.
Please have them play it again,
And I'll remember just when
I heard that lovely song before.

I've Just Seen a Face

Words and Music by John Lennon and Paul McCartney

recorded by The Beatles

I've just seen a face, I can't forget
The time or place where we met.
She's just the girl for me
And I want all the world to see we've met.

Had it been another day
I might have looked the other way
And I'd have never been aware.
But as it is I'll dream of her tonight.

Refrain:
Falling,
Yes I am falling,
And she keeps calling
Me back again.

I have never known the like of this,
I've been alone
And I have missed things and kept out of sight.
For other girls were never quite like this.

Refrain

Repeat Verse 1

Refrain Three Times

I've Never Been in Love Before

By Frank Loesser

from the musical *Guys and Dolls*

I've never been in love before,
Now all at once it's you.
It's you forever more.

I've never been in love before.
I thought my heart was safe,
I thought I knew the score.

But this is wine that's all too strange and strong.
I'm full of foolish song, and out my song must pour.
So please forgive this helpless haze I'm in.
I've really never been in love before.

If

Words and Music by David Gates

recorded by Bread

If a picture paints a thousand words,
Then why can't I paint you?
The words will never show
The you I've come to know.
If a face could launch a thousand ships,
Then where am I to go?
There's no one home but you,
You're all that's left me to.
And when my love for life is running dry,
You come and pour yourself on me.

If a man could be two places at one time,
I'd be with you;
Tomorrow and today,
Beside you all the way.
If the world should stop revolving,
Spinning slowly down to die,
I'd spend the end with you.
And when the world was through,
Then one by one, the stars would all go out.
Then you and I would simply fly away.

If Ever I Would Leave You

Words by Alan Jay Lerner
Music by Frederick Loewe

from the musical *Camelot*

If ever I would leave you
It wouldn't be in summer.
Seeing you in summer
I never would go.
Your hair streaked with sunlight,
Your lips red as flame,
Your face with a luster
That puts gold to shame!

But if I'd ever leave you,
It couldn't be in autumn,
How I'd leave in autumn
I never will know.
I've seen how you sparkle
When fall nips the air.
I know you in autumn
And I must be there.

And could I leave you running merrily through the snow?
Or on a wintry evening when you catch the fire's glow?

If ever I would leave you,
How could it be in springtime,
Knowing how in spring I'm bewitched by you so?
Oh, no! Not in springtime,
Summer, winter or fall!
No, never could I leave you at all.

If Ever You're in My Arms Again

Words and Music by Michael Masser, Tom Snow
and Cynthia Weil

recorded by Peabo Bryson

It all came so easily, all the lovin' you gave me;
The feelings we shared.
And I can still remember how you touched me so tender.
It told me you care.

We had a once in a lifetime,
But I just couldn't see until it was gone.
A second once in a lifetime
May be too much to ask.
But I swear from now on;

Refrain:
If ever you're in my arms again,
This time I'll love you much better.
If ever you're in my arms again,
This time I'll hold you forever.
This time will never end.

Now I'm seein' clearly how I still need you near me;
The feelings we shared.
There's something between us that won't ever leave us.
There's no letting go.

We had a once in a lifetime,
But I just didn't know it till my life fell apart.
A second once in a lifetime
Isn't too much to ask.
'Cause I swear from now on;

Refrain

Never end.

The best of romancin' deserves second chances.
I'll get to you somehow.
'Cause I promise now;

Repeat Refrain Ad Lib and Fade

If I Could

Lyrics by Ron Miller
Music by Kenny Hirsch and Marti Sharron

recorded by Regina Belle, Barbra Streisand

If I could,
I'd protect you from the sadness in your eyes,
Give you courage in a world of compromise.
Yes, I would.
If I could,
I would teach you all the things I never learned.
And I'd help you cross the bridges that I burned.
Yes, I would.

If I could,
I would try to shield your innocence from time,
But the part of life I gave you isn't mine.
I watched you grow
So I could let you go.

If I could,
I would help you make it through the hungry years,
But I know that I can never cry your tears.
But I would
If I could.

If I live
In a time and place
Where you don't want to be,
You don't have to walk along this road with me.
My yesterday
Won't have to be your way.

If I knew,
I'd have tried to change the world I brought you to,
Through there wasn't very much that I could do.
But I still would
If I could.

If, if I could,
I would try to shield your innocence from time,
But the part of life I gave you isn't mine.
I watched you grow
So I could let you go.

If I could,
I would help you make it through the hungry years,
But I know that I can never cry your tears.
But I would
If I could.

Yes, I would.
Yes, I would
If I could.

If I Ever Lose My Faith in You
Written and Composed by Sting

recorded by Sting

You could say I lost my faith in science and progress.
You could say I lost my belief in the holy church.
You could say I lost my sense of direction.
You could say all of this and worse, but:

Refrain:
If I ever lose my faith in you
There'd be nothing left for me to do.

Some would say I was a lost man in a lost world.
You could say I lost my faith in the people on TV
You could say I lost my belief in our politicians.
They all seem like game show hosts to me.

Refrain

Hey, hey.
I could be lost inside their lies without a trace.
But every time I close my eyes I see your face.
I never saw no miracle of science
That didn't go from a blessing to a curse.
I never saw no military solution
That didn't always end up as something worse,
But, let me say this first:

If I ever lose my faith in you
If I ever lose my faith in you
There'd be nothing left for me to do.
There'd be nothing left for me to do.
If I ever lose my faith,
If I ever lose my faith,
If I ever lose my faith,
If I ever lose my faith in you...

If I Fell
Words and Music by John Lennon and Paul McCartney

recorded by The Beatles

If I fell in love with you
Would you promise to be true
And help me understand.
'Cause I've been in love before
And I found that love was more
Than just holding hands.

If I give my heart to you
I must be sure
From the very start that you
Would love me more than her.

If I trust in you, oh please
Don't run and hide.
If I love you too, oh please,
Don't hurt my pride like her.

'Cause I couldn't stand the pain
And I would be sad
If our new love was in vain.

So I hope you see that I
Would love to love you.
And that she will cry
When she learns that we are two.

'Cause I couldn't stand the pain
And I would be sad
If our new love was in vain.

So I hope you see that I
Would love to love you
And that she will cry
When she learns that we are two.
If I fell in love with you.

If I Had a Hammer
(The Hammer Song)

Words and Music by Lee Hays and Pete Seeger

recorded by The Weavers, Peter, Paul & Mary, Trini Lopez

If I had a hammer,
I'd hammer in the morning,
I'd hammer in the evening
All over this land;
I'd hammer out danger,
I'd hammer out a warning,
I'd hammer out love between
All of my brothers,
All over this land.

If I had a bell,
I'd ring it in the morning,
I'd ring it in the evening
All over this land;
I'd ring out danger,
I'd ring out a warning,
I'd ring out love between
All of my brothers,
All over this land.

If I had a song,
I'd sing it in the morning,
I'd sing it in the evening
All over this land;
I'd sing out danger,
I'd sing out a warning,
I'd sing out love between
All of my brothers,
All over this land.

Well, I got a hammer,
And I've got a bell,
And I've got a song
All over this land;
It's the hammer of justice,
It's the bell of freedom,
It's the song about love between
All of my brothers,
All over this land.

If I Loved You

Lyrics by Oscar Hammerstein II
Music by Richard Rodgers

from the musical *Carousel*

If I loved you,
Time and again I would try to say
All I'd want you to know.
If I loved you,
Words wouldn't come in an easy way,
'Round in circles I'd go.

Longin' to tell you, but afraid and shy,
I'd let my golden chances pass me by!
Soon you'd leave me,
Off you would go in the mist of day,
Never, never to know
How I loved you,
If I loved you.

If I Ruled the World

Words by Leslie Bricusse
Music by Cyril Ornadel

from the musical *Pickwick*

If I ruled the world
Every day would be the first day of spring,
Every heart would have a new song to sing
And we'd sing of the joy every morning would bring.

If I ruled the world
Every man would be as free as a bird,
Every voice would be a voice to be heard.
Take my word we would treasure each day that occurred.

My world would be a beautiful place
Where we would weave such wonderful dreams.
My world would wear a smile on its face
Like the man in the moon has when the moon beams.

If I ruled the world
Every man would say the world was his friend.
There'd be happiness that no man could end.
No, my friend, not if I ruled the world.
Every head would be held up high.
There'd be sunshine in everyone's sky
If the day ever dawned when I ruled the world.

If I Were a Bell

By Frank Loesser

from the musical *Guys and Dolls*

Ask me how do I feel,
Ask me now that we're cozy and clinging.
Well sir, all I can say is
If I were a bell I'd be ringing.
From the moment we kissed tonight
That's the way I've just got to behave.
Boy, if I were a lamp I'd light
Or if I were a banner I'd wave.

Ask me how do I feel,
Little me with my quiet upbringing.
Well sir, all I can say is
If I were a gate I'd be swinging.
And if I were a watch I'd start popping my spring.
Or if I were a bell I'd go ding dong ding dong ding.

Ask me how do I feel
From this chemistry lesson I'm learning.
Well sir, all I can say is
If I were a bridge I'd be burning.
Yes, I knew my morale would crack
From the wonderful way you looked.
Boy, if I were a duck I'd quack
Or if I were a goose I'd be cooked.

Ask me how do I feel,
Ask me now that we're fondly caressing.
Pal, if I were a salad
I know I would be splashing my dressing.
Or if I were a season I'd surely be spring.
Or if I were a bell I'd go ding dong ding dong ding.

If Loving You Is Wrong
I Don't Want to Be Right

Words and Music by Homer Banks, Carl Hampton and
Raymond Jackson

recorded by Luther Ingram

If loving you is wrong, I don't want to be right.
If being right means being without you,
I'd rather live a wrong-doing life.
Your momma and daddy say it's a shame,
It's a down-right disgrace,
But, long as I got you by my side
I don't care what your people say.
Your friends tell you it's no future in loving a married man.
If I can't see you when I want, I'll see you when I can.

If loving you is wrong, I don't wanna be right.

Am I wrong to fall so deeply in love with you,
Knowing I got a wife and two little children
Depending on me too?
And am I wrong
To hunger for the gentleness of your touch,
Knowing I got someone else at home
Who needs me just as much?
And are you wrong to give your love to a married man?
And am I wrong to hold on to the best thing I ever had?

If loving you is wrong, I don't wanna be right.

Are you wrong to give your love to a married man?
And am I wrong for tryin' to hold on to the best thing I
  ever had?
If loving you is wrong, I don't wanna be right.
If loving you is wrong, I don't wanna be right.

Repeat and Fade:
I don't wanna be right, if it means being without you.
I don't wanna be right if it means sleeping at night.

If Tomorrow Never Comes

Words and Music by Kent Blazy and Garth Brooks

recorded by Garth Brooks

Sometimes late at night, I lie awake and watch her sleeping.
She's lost in peaceful dreams, so I turn off the lights,
And lay there in the dark.
And the thought crosses my mind,
If I never wake up in the morning,
Would she ever doubt the way I feel about her in my heart.

Refrain:
If tomorrow never comes,
Will she know how much I loved her?
Did I try in every way, to show her every day,
That she's my only one?
And if my time on earth were through,
And she must face this world without me,
Is the love I gave her in the past
Gonna be enough to last?
If tomorrow never comes?

'Cause I've lost loved ones in my life,
Who never knew how much I loved them.
Now I live with the regret,
That my true feelings for them were never revealed.
So I made a promise to myself,
To say each day how much she means to me,
And avoid that circumstance,
Where there's no second chance to tell how I feel.

Refrain

So tell someone that you love,
Just what you're thinking of,
If tomorrow never comes.

If We Only Have Love
(Quand on n'a que l'amour)

French Words and Music by Jacques Brel
English Words by Mort Shuman and Eric Blau

featured in the musical *Jacques Brel Is Alive and Well and
Living in Paris*

If we only have love, then tomorrow will dawn;
And the days of our years will rise on that morn.
If we only have love, to embrace without fears;
We will kiss with our eyes, we will sleep without tears.
If we only have love, with our arms opened wide;
Then the young and the old will stand at our side.
If we only have love, love that's falling like rain;
Then the parched desert earth will grow green again.
If we only have love, for the hymn that we shout;
For the song that we sing, then we'll have a way out.

Then with nothing at all, but the little we are
We'll have conquered all time, all space, and the stars.

If we only have love, we can reach those in pain;
We can heal all our wounds, we can use our own names.
If we only have love, we can melt all the guns;
And then give the new world to our daughters and sons.
If we only have love, then Jerusalem stands;
And then death has no shadow, there are no foreign lands.
If we only have love, we will never bow down;
We'll be tall as the pines, neither heroes nor clowns.
If we only have love, then we'll only be men;
And we'll drink from the Grail, to be born once again.

Then with nothing at all, but the little we are
We'll have conquered all time, all space, and the stars.

If You Go Away

French Words and Music by Jacques Brel
English Words by Rod McKuen
Copyright © 1959, 1966 by Edward B. Marks Music Company
Copyright Renewed

recorded by Jacques Brel and various other artists

If you go away on this summer day,
Then you might as well take the sun away;
All the birds that flew in the summer sky,
When our love was new and our hearts were high;
When the day was young and the night was long,
And the moon stood still for the night-bird's song.

Refrain:
If you go away,
If you go away,
If you go away,
If you go away.

But if you stay,
I'll make you a day
Like no day has been,
Or ever will be again;
We'll sail the sun,
We'll ride on the rain,
We'll talk to the trees
And worship the wind.
Then if you go,
I'll understand,
Leave me just enough love
To fill up my hand.

Refrain

If you go away, as I know you will,
You must tell the world to stop turning till
You return again, if you ever do,
For what good is love without loving you;
Can I tell you now, as you turn to go,
I'll be dying slowly 'til the next hello.

Refrain

But if you stay,
I'll make you a night,
Like no other night has been
Or will be again;
I'll sail on your smile,
I'll ride on your touch,
I'll talk to your eyes,
That I love so much.
But if you go,
Go, I won't cry,
Though the good is gone
From the world "goodbye."

Refrain

If you go away, as I know you must
There'll be nothing left in the world to trust;
Just an empty room, full of empty space,
Like the empy look I see on your face;
I'd have been shadow of your shadow
If I thought it might have kept me by your side.

Refrain

If You Had My Love

Words and Music by Rodney Jerkins, LaShawn Daniels,
Cory Rooney, Fred Jerkins and Jennifer Lopez
© 1999 EMI BLACKWOOD MUSIC INC., RODNEY JERKINS PRODUCTIONS INC., EMI
APRIL MUSIC INC., LASHAWN DANIELS PRODUCTIONS INC., SONY/ATV SONGS
LLC, CORI TIFFANI PUBLISHING, FRED JERKINS PUBLISHING, ENSIGN MUSIC
CORPORATION and NUYORICAN PUBLISHING
All Rights for RODNEY JERKINS PRODUCTIONS INC. Controlled and Administered by
EMI BLACKWOOD MUSIC INC.
All Rights for LASHAWN DANIELS PRODUCTIONS INC. Controlled and Administered by
EMI APRIL MUSIC INC.
All Rights for SONY/ATV SONGS LLC and CORI TIFFANI PUBLISHING Administered by
SONY/ATV MUSIC PUBLISHING, 8 Music Square West, Nashville, TN 37203
All Rights for FRED JERKINS PUBLISHING Controlled and Administered by
ENSIGN MUSIC CORPORATION

recorded by Jennifer Lopez

Refrain:
If you had my love and I gave you all my trust
Would you comfort me?
And if somehow you knew
That your love would be untrue
Would you lie to me and call me "baby"?

Now if I give you me,
This is how it's got to be:
First of all, I won't take you cheating on me.
Tell me who can I trust if I can't trust in you?
And I refuse to let you play me for a fool.
You said, we could possibly spend eternity.
See, that's what you told me, that's what you said.
But if you want me you have to be fulfilling all my dreams.

You said you want my love and you've got to have it all.
But first there are some things you need to know.
If you wanna live with all I have to give
I need to feel true love or it's got to end, yeah.
I don't want you tryin' to get with me and I end up unhappy.
I don't need the hurt and I don't need the pain.
So before I do give myself to you,
I'll have to know the truth.
If I spend my life with you.

Refrain Three Times

If You Leave Me Now

Words and Music by Peter Cetera
Copyright © 1976 by BMG Songs, Inc. and Big Elk Music

recorded by Chicago

If you leave me now,
You'll take away the biggest part of me.
Ooh, no, baby please don't go.
And if you leave me now,
You'll take away the very heart of me.
Ooh girl, I just want you to stay.

A love like ours is love that's hard to find.
How could we let it slip away?
We've come too far to leave it all behind.
How could we end it all this way?

When tomorrow comes,
Then we'll both regret the things we said today.

If you leave me now,
You'll take away the biggest part of me.
Ooh, no, baby please don't go.

Repeat Song

Repeat and Fade:
Ooh, girl, I just want to have you by my side.
Ooh, no, baby please don't go.

If You Love Somebody
Set Them Free

Written and Composed by Sting
© 1985 G.M. SUMNER
Published by MAGNETIC PUBLISHING LTD. and Administered by
   EMI BLACKWOOD MUSIC INC. in the USA and Canada

recorded by Sting

Free, free, set them free.
Free, free, set them free.
If you need somebody, call my name.
If you want someone, you can do the same.
If you want to keep something precious,
Got to lock it up and throw away the key.
You want to hold on to your possessions,
Don't even think about me.

Refrain:
If you love somebody, If you love someone,
If you love somebody, If you love someone,
Set them free.

If it's a mirror you want, just look into my eyes,
Or a whipping boy, someone to despise.
Or a prisoner in the dark
Tied up in chains you just can't see,
Or a beast in a gilded cage;
That's all some people ever want to be.

Refrain

You can't control an independent heart,
(Can't love what you can't keep.)
Can't tear the one you love apart.
(Can't love what you can't keep.)
Forever conditioned to believe we can't live,
We can't live here and be happy with less.
With so many riches, so many souls,
With everything we see that we want to possess.

Repeat Verse 1

Refrain

If You Really Love Me

Words and Music by Stevie Wonder and Syreeta Wright
© 1970 (Renewed 1998) JOBETE MUSIC CO., INC. and BLACK BULL MUSIC
   c/o EMI APRIL MUSIC INC.

recorded by Stevie Wonder

Refrain:
If you really love me, if you really love me,
If you really love me won't you tell me?
Then I won't have to be playing around.

You call my name, oh, so sweet.
To make your kiss incomplete,
When your mood is clear, you quickly change your ways.
Then you say I'm untrue, what am I supposed to do,
Be a fool who sits alone waiting for you?

I see the light of your smile,
Calling me all the while,
You are saying, baby, it's time to go.
First the feeling's all right, then it's gone from sight,
So I'm taking out this time to say:

Refrain

If You're Ready
(Come Go with Me)

Words and Music by Homer Banks, Carl Hampton and
Raymond Jackson
Copyright © 1972 IRVING MUSIC, INC.
Copyright Renewed

recorded by The Staple Singers

If you're ready come go with me.
If you're ready come go with me.
If you're ready come go with me.
Come go with me. Come go with me.
No hatred. Come go with me.
We'll be tolerated. Come go with me.
Peace and love. Come go with me;
Go between the races. Come go with me.
Love is the only transportation,
To where there's communication.

If you're ready come go with me.
If you're ready come go with me.
If you're ready come go with me.
If you're ready come go with me.
No hate. Come go with me,
Will ever enter there. Come go with me.
No one. Come go with me,
Will ever be sad. Come go with me.
No economical exploitation.
No political domination.

If you're ready come go with me.
If you're ready come go with me.
If you're ready come go with me.
If you're ready come go with me.
You citizens. Come go with me,
You'd better get ready. Come go with me.
Haters. Come go with me,
You'd better get ready. Come go with me.
Back stabbers. Come go with me,
You'd better get ready. Come go with me.
Come on get ready.

Repeat and Fade:
If you're ready come go with me.
If you're ready come go with me.

Imagine

Words and Music by John Lennon

recorded by John Lennon

Imagine there's no heaven.
It's easy if you try.
No hell below us,
Above us only sky.
Imagine all the people
Living for today.

Imagine there's no countries.
It isn't hard to do.
Nothing to kill or die for
And no religion, too.
Imagine all the people
Living life in peace.

You may say I'm a dreamer.
But I'm not the only one.
I hope someday you'll join us
And the world will be as one.

Imagine no possessions.
I wonder if you can.
No need for greed or hunger,
A brotherhood of man.
Imagine all the people
Sharing all the world.

You may say I'm a dreamer.
But I'm not the only one.
I hope someday you'll join us
And the world will live as one.

The Impossible Dream (The Quest)

Lyric by Joe Darion
Music by Mitch Leigh

from the musical *Man of La Mancha*

To dream the impossible dream,
To fight the unbeatable foe,
To bear with unbearable sorrow,
To run where the brave dare not go.

To right the unrightable wrong,
To love pure and chaste from afar,
To try when your arms are too weary,
To reach the unreachable star!

This is my quest,
To follow that star,
No matter how hopeless,
No matter how far;
To fight for the right
Without question or pause.
To be willing to march into hell for a heavenly cause!

And I know,
If I'll only be true
To this glorious quest,
That my heart
Will lie peaceful and calm,
When I'm laid to my rest,

And the world will be better for this;
That one man, scorned and covered with scars,
Still strove with his last ounce of courage,
To reach the unreachable stars.

In a Sentimental Mood

Words and Music by Duke Ellington, Irving Mills and Manny Kurtz

a standard recorded by Duke Ellington and various other artists

In a sentimental mood,
I can see the stars come through my room,
While your loving attitude
Is like a flame that lights the gloom.

On the wings of every kiss
Drifts a melody so strange and sweet.
In this sentimental bliss
You make my paradise complete.

Rose petals seem to fall,
It's all like a dream to call you mine.
My heart's a lighter thing
Since you made this night a thing divine.

In a sentimental mood,
I'm within a world so heavenly,
For I never dreamt that you'd
Be loving sentimental me.

In My Life

Words and Music by John Lennon and Paul McCartney

recorded by The Beatles

There are places I'll remember,
All my life, though some have changed.
Some forever, not for better.
Some have gone and some remain.
All these places had their moments,
With lovers and friends I still can recall.
Some are dead and some are living,
In my life I've loved them all.

But of all these friends and lovers,
There is no one compared with you.
And these memories lose their meaning,
When I think of love as something new.
Though I know I'll never ever lose affection,
For people and things that went before.
I know I'll often stop and think about them,
In my life I'll love you more.

In My Room

Words and Music by Brian Wilson and Gary Usher

recorded by The Beach Boys

There's a room where I can go and tell my secrets to,
In my room, in my room.
In my room.

In this world I lock out all my worries and my cares,
In my room, in my room.
In my room.

Do my dreaming, and my scheming, lie awake and pray.
Do my crying and my sighing, laugh at yesterday.

Now it's dark and I'm alone but I won't be afraid;
In my room, in my room, in my room
In my room, in my room, in my room,
In my room.

In the Cool, Cool, Cool of the Evening

Words by Johnny Mercer
Music by Hoagy Carmichael

from the Paramount Picture *Here Comes the Groom*
recorded by Bing Crosby and Jane Wyman, Frankie Laine
& Jo Stafford

In the cool, cool, cool of the evenin' tell them I'll be there,
In the cool, cool, cool of the evenin' better save a chair.
When the part's gettin' a glow on, 'n' singin' fills the air,
In the shank 'o' the night, when the doin's are right,
You can tell 'em I'll be there.

In the Ghetto (The Vicious Circle)

Words and Music by Mac Davis

recorded by Elvis Presley

As the snow flies
On a cold and grey Chicago mornin',
A poor little baby child is born
In the ghetto.
And his mama cries.
'Cause if there's one thing she don't need
It's another hungry mouth to feed
In the ghetto.

People, don't you understand
The child needs a helping hand
Or he'll grow to be an angry young man some day.
Take a look at you and me
Are we too blind to see?
Or do we simply turn our heads
And look the other way?

Well, the world turns
And a hungry little boy with a runny nose
Plays in the street as the cold wind blows
In the ghetto.
And his hunger burns.

So he starts to roam the streets at night
And he learns how to steal and he learns how to fight
In the ghetto.
And then one night in desperation,
A young man breaks away

He buys a gun, steals a car
Tries to run but he don't get far
And his mama cries.

And a crowd gathers 'round an angry young man
Face down in the street with a gun in his hand
In the ghetto.
As her young man dies
On a cold and gray Chicago morning,
Another little baby child is born
In the ghetto
And his mama cries.

In the Still of the Night

Words and Music by Cole Porter

from the film *Rosalie*
a standard recorded by Frank Sinatra and various other
artists

In the still of the night,
As I gaze from my window,
At the moon in its flight,
My thoughts all stray to you.

In the still of the night,
While the world is in slumber,
Oh, the times without number,
Darling, when I say to you:

Do you love me
As I love you?
Are you my life to be,
My dream come true?

Or will this dream of mine
Fade out of sight
Like the moon
Growing dim
On the rim
Of the hill
In the chill,
Still
Of the night?

In the Still of the Nite (I'll Remember)

Words and Music by Fred Parris

recorded by The Five Satins, Boyz II Men

(Shoo doop doo be doo,
Shoo doop shoo be doo,
Shoo doop shoo be doo.
Shoo doop shoo be wah.)

In the still of the nite
I held you, held you tight.
Oh, I love, love you so,
Promise I'll never let you go
In the still of the nite.
(In the still of the nite.)

I remember that nite in May
That the stars were bright up above.
I'll hope and I'll pray
To keep your precious love.

So, before the light,
Hold me again with all of your might
In the still of the nite.
(In the still of the nite.)

(Shoo wop shoo wah,
Shoo wop shoo wah,
Shoo wop shoo wah,
Shoo wop shoo wah.)

So before the light,
Hold me again
With all of your might
In the still of the nite.

(In the still of the nite.)

In the still of the nite.
(Shoo doop shoo be doo,
Shoo doop shoo be doo,
Shoo doop shoo be doo,
Shoo doop shoo be wah.)…

In the Wee Small Hours of the Morning

Words by Bob Hilliard
Music by David Mann

recorded by Frank Sinatra and various other artists

When the sun is high in the afternoon sky,
You can always find something to do.
But from dusk till dawn as the clock ticks on,
Something happens to you.

Refrain:
In the wee small hours of the morning,
While the whole wide world is fast asleep,
You lie awake and think about the girl {boy},
And never ever think of counting sheep.
When your lonely heart has learned its lesson
You'd be hers {his} if only she {he} would call.
In the wee small hours of the morning
That's the time you miss her {him} most of all.

Repeat Refrain

An Innocent Man

Words and Music by Billy Joel

recorded by Billy Joel

Some people stay far away from the door
If there's a chance of it opening up.
They hear a voice in the hall outside and hope
That it just passes by.
Some people live with the fear of a touch
And the anger of having been a fool.
They will not listen to anyone
So nobody tells them a lie.

I know you're only protecting yourself
I know you're thinking of somebody else.
Someone who hurt you.
But I'm not above
Making up for the love
You've been denying you could ever feel.
I'm not above doing anything to restore your faith if I can.

Some people see through the eyes of the old
Before they ever get a look at the young.
I'm only willing to hear you cry because
I am an innocent man.
I am an innocent man.
Oh yes I am.

Some people say they will never believe
Another promise they hear in the dark.
Because they only remember too well
They heard somebody tell them before.
Some people sleep all alone every night
Instead of taking a lover to bed.

Some people find that it's easier to hate
Than to wait anymore.

I know you don't want to hear what I say,
I know you're gonna keep turning away.
But I've been there and if I can survive
I can keep you alive
I'm not above going through it again.
I'm not above being cool for a while
If you're cruel to me I'll understand.

Some people run from a possible fight
Some people figure they can never win.
And although this is a fight I can lose
The accused is an innocent man.
I am an innocent man.
Oh yes I am.

You know you only hurt yourself out of spite.
I guess you'd rather be a martyr tonight.
That's your decision.

But I'm not below anybody I know
If there's a chance of resurrecting a love.
I'm not above going back to the start
To find out where the heartache began.
Some people hope for a miracle cure,
Some people just accept the world as it is.
But I'm not willing to lay down and die
Because I am an innocent man.
I am an innocent man.
Oh, yes I am,
I am an innocent man.

Instant Karma

Words and Music by John Lennon

recorded by John Lennon

Instant karma's gonna get you,
Gonna knock you right on the head.
You better get yourself together.
Pretty soon you're gonna be dead.
What in the world you thinking of?
Laughing in the face of love?
What on earth you tryin' to do?
It's up to you, yeah, you.

Instant karma's gonna get you,
Gonna look you right in the face.
You better get yourself together.
Join the human race.
How in the world you gonna see?
Laughin' at fools like me?
What on earth d'you think you are?
A superstar?
Well, alright, you are.

Refrain:
Well, we all shine on,
Like the moon and the stars and the sun.
Well, we all shine on.
Everyone, come on.

Instant karma's gonna get you,
Gonna knock you off your feet.
Better recognize your brothers,
Everyone you meet.
Why in the world are we here?
Surely not to live in pain and fear.
Why on earth are you there
When you're everywhere?
Come and get your share.

Refrain Three Times, then Repeat and Fade

Iris
Words and Music by John Rzeznik
© 1998 EMI VIRGIN SONGS, INC. and SCRAP METAL MUSIC
All Rights Controlled and Administered by EMI VIRGIN SONGS, INC.

from the Motion Picture *City of Angels*
recorded by Goo Goo Dolls

And I'd give up forever to touch you
'Cause I know that you feel me somehow.
You're the closest to heaven that I'll ever be
And I don't wanna go home right now.

And all I could taste is this moment,
And all I can breathe is your life.
And sooner or later it's over.
I just don't wanna miss you tonight.

Refrain:
And I don't want the world to see me
'Cause I don't think that they'd understand.
When everything's made to be broken
I just want you to know who I am.

And you can't fight the tears that ain't coming,
Or the moment of truth in your lies.
When everything feels like the movies,
Yeah, you bleed just to know you're alive.

Refrain Twice

Isn't It Romantic?
Words by Lorenz Hart
Music by Richard Rodgers
Copyright © 1932 (Renewed 1959) by Famous Music Corporation

from the Paramount Picture *Love Me Tonight*

Verse:
I've never met you,
Yet never doubt, dear,
I can't forget you
I've thought you out, dear.
I know your profile and I know the way you kiss:
Just the thing I miss
On a night like this.

If dreams are made of
Imagination,
I'm not afraid of
My own creation.
With all my heart,
My heart is here for you to take.
Why should I quake?
I'm not awake.

Refrain:
Isn't it romantic?
Music in the night
A dream that can be heard.
Isn't it romantic?
Moving shadows write
The oldest magic word.

I hear the breezes playing
In the trees above,
While all the world is saying,
"You were meant for love."

Isn't it romantic?
Merely to be young
On such a night as this.
Isn't it romantic.
Every note that's sung
Is like a lover's kiss.

Sweet symbols in the moonlight,
Do you mean that I will fall
In love, perchance?
Isn't it romance?

Verse 2 (from the film): *
My face is glowing,
I'm energetic,
The art of sewing,
I found poetic.
My needle punctuates the rhythm of romance!
I don't give a stitch
If I don't get rich.

*In the film, the song is passed from character to character.

A custom tailor
Who has no custom,
Is like a sailor,
No one will trust 'em.
But there is magic in the music of my shears;
I shed no tears.
Lend me your ears!

Refrain 2 (from the film):
Isn't it romantic?
Soon I will have found
Some girl that I adore.
Isn't it romantic?
While I sit around,
My love can scrub the floor.

She'll kiss me every hour,
Or she'll get the sack.
And when I take a shower
She can scrub my back.

Isn't it romantic?
On a moon-lit night
She'll cook me onion soup.
Kiddies are romantic
And if we don't fight,
We soon will have a troupe!

We'll help the population,
It's a duty that we owe
To dear old France.
Isn't it romance?

Isn't She Lovely
Words and Music by Stevie Wonder

recorded by Stevie Wonder

Isn't she lovely, isn't she wonderful?
Isn't she precious, less than one minute old?
I never thought through love we'd be
Making one as lovely as she.
But isn't she lovely, made from love.

Isn't she pretty, truly the angels' best?
Boy, I'm so happy,
We have been heaven blessed.
I can't believe what God has done;
Through us He's given life to one.
But isn't she lovely, made from love.

Isn't she lovely, life and love are the same.
Life is Aisha, the meaning of her name.
Londie, it could not have been done
Without you who conceived the one
That's so very lovely, made from love.

It Could Happen to You
Words by Johnny Burke
Music by James Van Heusen

from the Paramount Picture *And the Angels Sing*
a standard recorded by Jo Stafford, Bing Crosby and
various other artists

Do you believe in charms and spells,
In mystic words and magic wands
And wishing wells?
Don't look so wise,
Don't show your scorn;
Watch yourself,
I warn you.

Hide your heart from sight,
Lock your dreams at night.
It could happen to you.
Don't count stars or you might stumble,
Someone drops a sigh,
And down you tumble.

Keep an eye on spring,
Run when church bells ring.
It could happen to you.
All I did was wonder how your arms would be
And it happened to me!

It Don't Matter to Me
Words and Music by David Gates

recorded by Bread

It don't matter to me
If you really feel that you need some time to be free,
Time to go out searching for yourself
Hoping to find, time to go find.

And it don't matter to me
If you take up with someone who's better than me,
'Cause your happiness is all I want
For you to find peace, your peace of mind.

Lotta people have an ego hang-up
'Cause they want to be the only one.
How many came before?
It really doesn't matter just as long as you're the last,
Everybody runnin' 'round
And try'n' to find out what's been missin' in the past.

It don't matter to me
If your search brings you back together with me,
'Cause there'll always be an empty room waiting for you.
An open heart waiting for you,
Time is on my side,
'Cause it don't matter to me.

It Might as Well Be Spring

Lyrics by Oscar Hammerstein II
Music by Richard Rodgers
Copyright © 1945 by WILLIAMSON MUSIC
Copyright Renewed

from the film *State Fair*

I'm as restless as a willow in a windstorm.
I'm as jumpy as a puppet on a string!
I'd say that I had spring fever,
But I know it isn't spring.
I am starry-eyed and vaguely discontented,
Like a nightingale without a song to sing.
Oh, why should I have spring fever
When it isn't even spring?

I keep wishing I were somewhere else,
Walking down a strange new street,
Hearing words that I have never heard
From a man I've yet to meet.

I'm as busy as a spider, spinning daydreams,
I'm as giddy as a baby on a swing.
I haven't seen a crocus or a rosebud
Or a robin on the wing,
But I feel so gay, in a melancholy way,
That it might as well be spring…
It might as well be spring.

It Must Be Him

(Original French Title: "Seul sur son etoile")
Words and Music by Gilbert Becaud and Maurice Vidalin
English Adaptation by Mack David
Copyright © 1966 by Editions Rideau Rouge and BMG Music Publishing France
Copyright Renewed
All Rights in the U.S. Administered by BMG Songs, Inc.

recorded by Vicki Carr

I tell myself, what's done is done.
I tell myself don't be a fool,
Play the field, have a lot of fun,
It's easy when you play it cool.
I tell myself, don't be a chump,
Who cares? Let him stay away.
That's when the phone rings, and I jump.
And as I grab the phone I pray.

Refrain:
Let it please be him, oh! Dear God,
It must be him. It must be him,
Or I shall die, or I shall die.
Oh! Hello, hello my dear God,
It must be him, but it's not him.
And then I die,
That's when I die.

After a while I'm myself again.
I pick the pieces off the floor,
Put my heart on the shelf again,
He'll never hurt me anymore.
I'm not a puppet on a string,
I'll find somebody new someday,
That's when the phone begins to ring,
And once again I start to pray.

Refrain

Again I die, again I die.

It Never Entered My Mind

Words by Lorenz Hart
Music by Richard Rodgers
Copyright © 1940 by Williamson Music and The Estate Of Lorenz Hart in the United States
Copyright Renewed
All Rights on behalf of The Estate Of Lorenz Hart Administered by WB Music Corp.

from the musical *Higher and Higher*

I don't care if there's powder on my nose.
I don't care if my hairdo is in place.
I've lost the very meaning of repose.
I never put a mudpack on my face.
Oh who'd have thought
That I'd walk in a daze now?
I never go to shows at night,
But just to matinees now.
I see the show
And home I go.

Refrain 1:
Once I laughed when I heard you saying
That I'd be playing solitaire,
Uneasy in my easy chair,
It never entered my mind.
Once you told me I was mistaken,
That I'd awaken with the sun
And order orange juice for one.
It never entered my mind.
You have what I lack myself,
And now I even have to scratch my back myself.
Once you warned me that if you scorned me
I'd sing the maiden's prayer again
And wish that you were there again
To get into my hair again.
It never entered my mind.

Refrain 2:
Once you said in your funny lingo
I'd sit at bingo day and night
And never get the numbers right.
It never entered my mind.
Once you told me I'd stay up Sunday
To read the Monday-morning dirt
And find you're merging with some skirt.
It never entered my mind.
Life is not so sweet alone.

The man who came to dinner lets me eat alone.
I confess it, I didn't guess it,
That I would sit and mope again
And all the while I'd hope again.
It never entered my mind!

It Was a Very Good Year
Words and Music by Ervin Drake

recorded by Frank Sinatra and various other artists

When I was seventeen, it was a very good year.
It was a very good year for small-town girls
And soft summer nights.
We'd hide from the lights on the village green
When I was seventeen.

When I was twenty-one, it was a very good year.
It was a very good year for city girls
Who lived up the stair,
With perfumed hair that came undone
When I was twenty-one.

When I was thirty-five, it was a very good year.
It was a very good year for blue-blooded girls
Of independent means.
We'd ride in limousines their chauffeurs would drive
When I was thirty-five.

But now the days are short, I'm in the autumn of the year.
And now I think of my life as a vintage wine
From fine old kegs.
From the brim to the dregs it poured sweet and clear.
It was a very good year.

It's a Most Unusual Day
Words by Harold Adamson
Music by Jimmy McHugh

from the film *A Date with Judy*

I woke up singing this morning,
Got out of the right side of the bed.
I woke up singing this morning
And wondering what was ahead.
I took one good look at the sun
And was I the luckiest one.

It's a most unusual day,
Feel like throwing my worries away
As an old native-born Californian would say,
It's a most unusual day.

There's a most unusual sky,
Not a sign of a cloud passing by,
And if I want to sing, throw my heart in the ring,
It's a most unusual day.

There are people meeting people,
There is sunshine everywhere.
There are people greeting people
And a feeling of spring in the air.

It's a most unusual time.
I keep feeling my temperature climb.
If my heart won't behave in the usual way,
Well there's only one thing to say.
It's a most unusual,
Most unusual,
Most unusual day.

It's De-Lovely
Words and Music by Cole Porter

from the musical *Red, Hot and Blue!*

He:
I feel a sudden urge to sing
The kind of ditty that invokes the spring,
So control your desire to curse
While I crucify the verse.
She:
This verse you've started seems to me
The Tin-Pantithesis of melody,
So spare me, please, the pain,
Just skip the damn thing and sing the refrain.
He:
Mi, mi, mi, mi,
Re, re, re, re,
Do, sol, mi do, la, si.
She:
Take it away.

Refrain:
The night is young, the skies are clear,
So if you want to go walking, dear,
It's delightful, it's delicious, it's de-lovely.
I understand the reason why
You're sentimental, 'cause so am I,
It's delightful, it's delicious, it's de-lovely.
You can tell at a glance
What a swell night this is for romance,
You can hear dear Mother Nature murmuring low,
"Let yourself go."
So please be sweet, chickadee,
And when I kiss you, just say to me,

"It's delightful, it's delicious,
It's delectable, it's delirious,
It's dilemma, it's delimit, it's deluxe,
It's de-lovely."

She:
Oh, charming sir the way you sing
Would break the heart of Missus Crosby's Bing,
For the tone of your tra la la
Has that certain je ne sais quoi.
He:
O, thank thee kindly, winsome wench,
But 'stead of falling into Berlitz French
Just warble to me, please,
The beautiful strain in plain Brooklynese.
She:
Mi, mi, mi, mi,
Re, re, re, re,
Do, sol, mi, do, la, si.
He:
Take it away.

Time marches on and soon it's plain
You've won my heart and I've lost my brain,
It's delightful, it's delicious, it's de-lovely.
Life seems so sweet that we decide
It's in the bag to get unified,
It's delightful, it's delicious, it's de-lovely.
See the crowd in that church,
See the proud parson plopped on his perch,
Set the sweet beat of that organ, sealing our doom,
"Here goes the groom, boom!"
How they cheer and how they smile
As we go galloping down the aisle.
"It's divine, dear, it's diveen, dear,
It's de-wunderbar, it's de victory,
It's de vallop, it's de vinner, it's de voika,
It's de-lovely."

The knot is tied and so we take
A few hours off to eat wedding cake,
It's delightful, it's delicious, it's de-lovely.
It feels so fine to be a bride,
And how's the groom? Why he's slightly fried,
It's delightful, it's delicious, it's de-lovely.
To the pop of champagne,
Off we hop in a plush little plane
Till a night light through the darkness cozily calls,
"Niagara Falls"
All's well, my love, our day's complete,
And what a beautiful bridal suite,
"It's de-reamy, it's de-rowsy,
It's de-reverie, it's de-rhapsody,
It's de-regal, it's de-royal, it's de-Ritz,
It's de-lovely."

We settle down as man and wife
To solve the riddle called "married life,"
It's delightful, it's delicious, it's de-lovely.
We're on the crest, we have no cares,
We're just a couple of honey bears,
It's delightful, it's delicious, it's de-lovely.
All's as right as right can be

Till, one night, at my window I see
An absurd bird with a bundle hung on his nose—
"Get baby clothes."
Those eyes of yours are filled with joy
When Nurse appears and cries, "It's a boy,
He's appalling, he's appealing
He's a pollywog, he's a paragon,
He's a Popeye, he's a panic, he's a pip,
He's de-lovely."

It's Easy to Remember
Words by Lorenz Hart
Music by Richard Rodgers

from the Paramount Picture *Mississippi*
from the musical *Higher and Higher*

With you I owned the earth.
With you I ruled creation.
No you, and what's it worth?
It's just an imitation.

Refrain:
Your sweet expression,
The smile you gave me,
The way you looked when we met
It's easy to remember,
But so hard to forget.
I hear you whisper,
"I'll always love you,"
I know it's over, and yet
It's easy to remember,
But so hard to forget.
So I must dream
To have your hand caress me,
Fingers press me tight.
I'd rather dream
Than have that lovely feeling
Stealing through the night.
Each little moment
Is clear before me,
And though it brings me regret
It's easy to remember
And so hard to forget.

It's Going to Take Some Time
Words and Music by Carole King and Toni Stern

recorded by The Carpenters

I really fell out of line this time
I really missed the gate.
The birds on the telephone line, (next time)
Are cryin' out to me, (next time)
And I won't be so blind next time,
And I'll find some harmony.

But it's going to take some time this time,
And I can't make demands.
But like the young trees in the winter time,
I'll learn how to bend.
After all the tears we've spent,
How could we make amends?
So it's one more round for experience
And I'm on the road again,
And it's going to take some time this time!

Going to take some time this time,
No matter what I've planned.
And, like the young trees in the winter time,
I'll learn how to bend.
After all the tears we've spent,
How could we make amends?
So, it's one more round for experience
And I'm on the road again,
And it's going to take some time this time.

It's Impossible (Somos novios)
English Lyric by Sid Wayne
Spanish Words and Music by Armando Manzanero

recorded by Perry Como and various other artists

It's impossible,
Tell the sun to leave the sky.
It's just impossible.
It's impossible.
Ask a baby not to cry,
It's just impossible.
Can I hold you closer to me
And not feel you going through me?
Split the second that I never think of you?
Oh how impossible.

Can the ocean keep from rushing to the shore?
It's just impossible.
If I had you
Could I ever want for more?
It's just impossible.
And tomorrow, should you
Ask me for the world
Somehow I'd get it.
I would sell my very soul and not regret it.
For to live without your love
Is just impossible,
Impossible,
Impossible.

It's My Party
Words and Music by Herb Wiener, Wally Gold and John Gluck, Jr.

recorded by Lesley Gore

Nobody knows where my Johnny has gone,
But Judy left the same time.
Why was he holding her hand,
When he's supposed to be mine?

Refrain:
It's my party and I'll cry if I want to,
Cry if I want to,
Cry if I want to.
You would cry too, if it happened to you.

Play all my records, keep dancing all night,
But leave me alone for awhile.
'Til Johnny's dancing with me,
I've got no reason to smile.

Refrain

Judy and Johnny just walked through the door,
Like a queen and her king.
Oh, what a birthday surprise,
Judy's wearing his ring.

Refrain

It's Now or Never
Words and Music by Aaron Schroeder and Wally Gold

recorded by Elvis Presley

Refrain:
It's now or never
Come hold me tight.
Kiss me, my darlin'
Be mine tonight.
Tomorrow will be too late.
It's now or never,
My love won't wait.

When I first saw you
With your smile so tender,
My heart was captured
My soul surrendered.
I've spent a lifetime
Waiting for the right time.
Now that you're near
The time is here at last.

Refrain

Just like a willow
We could cry an ocean,
If we lost true love
And sweet devotion.
Your lips excite me
Let your arms invite me.
For who knows when
We'll meet again this way.

Refrain

It's Only a Paper Moon
Lyric by Billy Rose and E.Y. Harburg
Music by Harold Arlen

from the musical *Take a Chance*
featured in the film *Paper Moon*
a standard recorded by Ella Fitzgerald, King Cole Trio and
various other artists

I never feel a thing is real,
When I'm away from you.
Out of your embrace,
The world's a temporary parking place.
A bubble for a minute,
You smile, the bubble has a rainbow in it.

Say, it's only a paper moon,
Sailing over a cardboard sea,
But it wouldn't be make believe,
If you believed in me.

Yes, it's only a canvas sky,
Hanging over a muslin tree,
But it wouldn't be make believe,
If you believed in me.

Without your love,
It's a honky-tonk parade,
Without your love,
It's a melody played in a penny arcade.

It's a Barnum and Bailey world,
Just as phony as it can be,
But it wouldn't be make believe
If you believed in me.

It's Only Make Believe
Words and Music by Conway Twitty and Jack Nance

recorded by Conway Twitty, Glen Campbell

People see us everywhere, they think you really care,
But myself I can't deceive I know it's only make believe.
My one and only prayer, is that someday you'll care.

My hopes, my dreams come true, my one and only you,
No one will ever know, how much I love you so,
My only prayer will be, someday you'll care for me,
But it's only make believe.

My hopes, my dreams come true, my life I'd give for you,
My heart, a wedding ring, my all, my everything.
My heart I can't control, you rule my very soul,
My plans, my hopes, my schemes, you are my everything,
But it's only make believe.

My one and only prayer is that someday you'll care,
My hopes, my dreams come true, my one and only you.
No one will ever know, just how much I love you so,
My only prayer will be that someday you'll care for me
But it's only make believe.

It's Still Rock and Roll to Me
Words and Music by Billy Joel

recorded by Billy Joel

What's the matter with the clothes I'm wearing?
"Can't you tell that your tie's too wide?"
Maybe I should buy some old tab collars?
"Welcome back to the age of jive.
Where have you been hidin' out lately honey?
You can't dress trashy till you spend a lot of money."
Everybody's talkin' 'bout the new sound.
Funny, but it's still rock and roll to me.

What's the matter with the car I'm driving?
"Can't you tell that it's out of style?"
Should I get a set of white wall tires?
"Are you gonna cruise the miracle mile?
Now a-days you can't be too sentimental.
Your best bet's a true baby blue continental."
Hot funk, cool punk, even if it's old junk,
It's still rock and roll to me.

Oh, it doesn't matter what they say in the papers
'Cause it's always been the same old scene.
There's a new band in town
But you can't get the sound
From the story in a magazine
Aimed at your average teen.

How about a pair of pink side-wingers
And a bright orange pair of pants?
"Well you could really be a Beau Brummel,
Baby, if you just give it half a chance.
Don't waste your time on a new set of speakers.
You get more mileage from a cheap pair of sneakers."
Next phase, new wave dance craze, anyways,
It's still rock and roll to me.

Oh, it doesn't matter what they say in the papers
'Cause it's always been the same old scene.

There's a new band in town
But you can't get the sound
From the story in a magazine
Aimed at your average teen.

What's the matter with the crowd I'm seeing?
"Don't you know that they're out of touch?"
Should I try to be a straight A student?
"If you are, then you think too much."
"Don't you know about the new fashion honey?
All you need are looks and whole lot of money."
It's the next phase, new wave dance craze, anyways,
It's still rock and roll to me.

Everybody's talkin' 'bout the new sound.
Funny, but it's still rock and roll to me.

It's Too Late

Words by Toni Stern
Music by Carole King

recorded by Carole King

Stayed in bed all mornin' just to pass the time.
There's somethin' wrong here, there can be no denyin'.
One of us is changin' or maybe we've just stopped tryin'.

Refrain:
And it's too late, baby now, it's too late,
Though we really did try to make it.
Somethin' inside has died and I can't hide
And I just can't fake it.

It used to be so easy living here with you.
You were light and breezy and I knew just what to do.
Now you look so unhappy and I feel like a fool.

Refrain

There'll be good times again for me and you,
But we just can't stay together, don't you feel it too?
Still I'm glad for what we had and how I once loved you.

Refrain

It's too late, baby, it's too late
Now, darlin', it's too late.

It's Your Love

Words and Music by Stephony E. Smith

recorded by Tim McGraw with Faith Hill

Male:
Dancin' in the dark,
Middle of the night.
Takin' your heart
And holdin' it tight.
Emotional touch
Touchin' my skin,
And askin' you to do
What you've been doin' all over again.

Refrain:
Oh, it's a beautiful thing
Don't think I can keep it all in.
I just gotta let you know
What it is that won't let me go.
Both:
It's your love.
It just does somethin' to me
It sends a shock right through me.
I can't get enough.
And if you wonder
About the spell I'm under,
It's your love.
Male:
Better than I was,
More than I am,
And all of this happened
By takin' your hand.
And who I am now
Is who I wanted to be.
Both:
And now that we're together,
I'm stronger than ever.
I'm happy and free.
Oh, it's a beautiful thing,
Don't think I can keep it all in.
Male:
Oh, did you ask me why I've changed?
All I gotta do is say your sweet name.
Both:
It's your love.
It just does something' to me.
It sends a shock right through me.
I can't get enough.
And if you wonder
About the spell I'm under,
It's your love.

It's a beautiful thing.

Jailhouse Rock

Words and Music by Jerry Leiber and Mike Stoller

from the film *Jailhouse Rock*
recorded by Elvis Presley

The warden threw a party in the county jail.
The prison band was there and they began to wail.
The band was jumpin' and the joint began to swing.
You should've heard those knocked-out jailbirds sing.

Refrain:
Let's rock!
Everybody, let's rock!
Everybody in the whole cell block
Was a-dancin' to the Jailhouse Rock.

Spider Murphy played the tenor saxophone.
Little Joe was blowin' on the slide trombone.
The drummer boy from Illinois went crash, boom, bang:
The whole rhythm section was the Purple Gang.

Refrain

Number Forty-Seven said to Number Three:
You're the cutest little jailbird I ever did see.
I sure would be delighted with your company.
Come on and do the Jailhouse Rock with me.

Refrain

The sad sack was a-sittin' on a block of stone,
Way over in the corner weeping all alone.
The warden said: "Hey buddy, don't you be no square.
If you can't find a partner use a wooden chair!"

Refrain

Shifty Henry said to Bugs: "For heaven's sake,
No one's lookin'; now's our chance to make a break."
Bugsy turned to Shifty and he said: "Nix, nix;
I wanna stick around awhile and get my kicks."

Refrain

Java Jive

Words and Music by Milton Drake and Ben Oakland

recorded by The Ink Spots, Manhattan Transfer, and
various other artists

I love coffee, I love tea,
I love the java jive and it loves me.
Coffee and tea and the java and me,
A cup, a cup, a cup, a cup, a cup!

I love java, sweet and hot,
Whoops! Mister Moto, I'm a coffee pot.
Shoot me a pot and I'll pour me a shot,
A cup, a cup, a cup, a cup, a cup!

Refrain 1:
Oh, slip me a slug
From that wonderful mug,
And I'll cut a rug,
'Till I'm snug in the jug.

A slice of onion and a raw one.
Draw one.
Waiter, waiter percolator!

Refrain 2:
I love coffee, I love tea,
I love the java jive and it loves me.
Coffee and tea and the jivin' and me,
A cup, a cup, a cup, a cup, a cup.

Boston bean, soy bean,
Lima bean, string bean.
I'm not keen for a bean
Unless it is a cheery coffee bean:

Repeat Verses 1 and 2

Refrain 1

Drop me a nickel in my pot, Joe,
Takin' it slow
Waiter, waiter percolator!

Refrain 2

Jive Talkin'

Words and Music by Barry Gibb, Maurice Gibb and
Robin Gibb

from the film *Saturday Night Fever*
recorded by The Bee Gees

It's just your jive talkin',
You're tellin' me lies, yeah;
Jive talkin',
You wear a disguise.
Jive talkin', so misunderstood, yeah;
Jive talkin', you're really no good.

Oh, my child, you'll never know
Just what you mean to me.
Oh, my child, you got so much;
You're gonna take away my energy
With all your jive talkin',
You're tellin' me lies, yeah.
Good lovin' still gets in my eyes.
Nobody believes what you say;
It's just your jive talkin'
That gets in the way.

Oh, my love, you are so good,
Treating me so cruel.
There you go with your fancy lies,
Leavin' me lookin' like a dumbstruck fool
With all your jive talkin',
You're tellin' me lies, yeah.
Jive talkin';
You wear a disguise.
Jive talkin', so misunderstood, yeah;
Jive talkin', you just ain't no good.

Love talkin' is all very fine, yeah;
Jive talkin' just isn't a crime.
And if there's somebody you'll love till you die,
Then all that jive talkin' just gets in your eye.

Do be lu bu loop
Do be lu bu loop
Do do do do doot doot
Do be lu bu loop
Do be lu bu loop
Do doot do
Jive talkin'

The Joint Is Jumpin'
Words by Andy Razaf and J.C. Johnson
Music by Thomas "Fats" Waller

featured in the musical revue *Ain't Misbehavin'*

They have a new expression along old Harlem way,
That tells you when a party is ten times more than gay.
To say that things are jumpin' leaves not a single doubt,
That everything is in full swing when you hear a body shout:
Spoken: (Here 'tis)

The joint is jumpin',
It's really jumpin'.
Come in cats an' check your hats,
I mean this joint is jumpin'.

The piano's thumpin',
The dancers bumpin'.
This here spot is more than hot,
In fact the joint is jumpin'.

Check your weapons at the door,
Be sure to pay your quarter.
Burn your leather on the floor,
Grab anybody's daughter.

The roof is rockin',
The neighbor's knockin'.
We're all bums when the wagon comes.
I mean this joint is jumpin'.
Spoken: (Let it beat!)

The joint is jumpin',
It's really jumpin'.
Every Mose is on his toes,
I mean the joint is jumpin'.

No time for talkin',
It's time for walkin'. (Yes!)
Grab a jug and cut the rug,
I mean this joint is jumpin'.

Get your pig feet, beer and gin,
There's plenty in the kitchen.
Who is that that just came in?
Just look at the way he's switchin'.

Don't mind the hour,
'Cause I'm in power.
I got bail if we go to jail.
I mean the joint is jumpin'.

The joint is jumpin',
It's really jumpin'.
We're all bums when the wagon comes,
I mean this joint is jumpin'.

Spoken: (Don't give your right name. No, No, No!)

Josephine Please No Lean on the Bell
Words and Music by Ed G. Nelson, Harry Pease and
Duke Leonard

Josephine and Joe and were so in love,
Oh, so in love, so much in love.
In the hall for hours they would stay,
When Josephine came in she'd hear her mother say:

Refrain:
Josephine please no lean on the bell.
When you moosh,
Please no poosh,
On the bell.

I heard Missus Caruso telling Missus O'Flynn,
Somebody keeps ringing but nobody comes in.
You can squeeze all you please, that's alright,
But don't keep us from sleep every night,
When you kiss in the hall,
Stay away from the wall,
Josephine please no lean on the bell.

Refrain

I heard Missus Calingo say she'd call the police,
The landlord he say he's gonna break-a the lease.
Hold the hand that's-a grand and delish,
Tell this guy I guess I no capish,
You eat garlic so strong,
How can he kiss so long,
Josephine please no lean on the bell.

Patter:
You come-a from work and you want-a the sup',
I'm-a cook-a the nice mac-a-ron',
Then you make-a sit down then you make the get up,
For your feller he call on the phone.
You go to the park and you sit in the dark,
And you make what they call-a the pet,
It's-a lip-a stick here and a lip-a stick there,
You no get it from eatin' spagett!

You-a say-a goodnight about 'leven o'clock,
That's-a what-a good gal-a should do,
But you take-a too long when you say the goodnight,
You no finish till half-a past two.
Say why you no bring-a your feller upstairs,
Ravioli with peppers I cook,
You can make-a the love with the kiss and the hug,
And the mom and pop they no look.

Don't I bring-a you up and I make-a you fat,
With the soup and the pasta fazool?
Now you stay-a up late and it make-a you thin,
What's-a the matter with you make-a me fool?
Why no you get marriage and raise-a the fam'?
Then I make-a you promise I keep,
I'll-a buy you the furnish' and pay for your rent,
Then we all-a can get-a the sleep.

Refrain

I heard Missus Caruso telling Missus O'Flynn,
Somebody keeps ringing but nobody comes in.
You can squeeze all you please,
That's alright,
But don't keep us from sleep every night,
When you kiss in the hall,
Stay away from the wall,
Josephine please no lean on the bell.

Joy to the World
Words and Music by Hoyt Axton
Copyright © 1970 IRVING MUSIC, INC.
Copyright Renewed

recorded by Three Dog Night

Jeremiah was a bullfrog,
Was a good friend of mine.
Never understood a single word he said,
But I helped him drink his wine.
Yes, he always had some mighty fine wine.
Singing:

Refrain:
Joy to the world.
All the boys and girls now.
Joy to the fishes in the deep blue sea,
Joy to you and me.

If I were the king of the world,
Tell you what I'd do.

Throw away the cars and the bars and the wars,
And make sweet love to you.
Yes, I'd make sweet love to you.
Singing:

Refrain

You know I love the ladies,
Love to have my fun.
I'm a high night flyer and a rainbow rider,
A straight shootin' son-of-a-gun.
Yes a straight-shootin' son-of-a-gun.

Refrain Three Times and Fade

Just a Gigolo
Original German Text by Julius Brammer
English Words by Irving Caesar
Music by Leonello Casucci
Copyright © 1930 by Chappell & Co. and Irving Caesar Music Corp.
Copyright Renewed
All Rights for Irving Caesar Music Corp. Administered by WB Music Corp.

recorded by Louis Prima, David Lee Roth, and various
other artists

'Twas in a Paris café that first I found him,
He was a French-man, a hero of the war,
But war was over, and here's how peace had crowned him,
A few cheap medals to wear, and nothing more.
Now every night in this same café you'll find him,
And as he strolls by the ladies hear him say,
If you admire me, please hire me,
A gigolo who knew a better day.

I'm just a gigolo,
Everywhere I go,
People know the part I'm playing,
Paid for every dance,
Selling each romance
Every night some heart betraying,
There will come a day,
Youth will pass away,
Then, what will they say about me,
When the end comes I know they'll say,
Just a gigolo,
As life goes on without me.

Just in Time
Words by Betty Comden and Adolph Green
Music by Jule Styne
Copyright © 1956 by Betty Comden, Adolph Green and Jule Styne
Copyright Renewed
Stratford Music Corporation, owner of publication and allied rights throughout the world
Chappell & Co., Administrator

from the musical *Bells Are Ringing*
a standard recorded by various artists

I was resting comfortably, face down in the gutter.
Life was serene, I knew where I was at.
"There's no hope for him,"
My dearest friends would mutter.
I was something dragged in by the cat.
Then…

Just in time,
I found you just in time.
Before you came
My time was running low.

I was lost,
The losing dice were tossed,
My bridges were all crossed,
Nowhere to go.

Now you're here
And now I know just where I'm going,
No more doubt or fear,
I've found my way.

For love came just in time.
You found me just in time,
And changed my lonely life,
That lovely day.

Just My Imagination (Running Away with Me)

Words and Music by Norman J. Whitfield and
Barrett Strong

recorded by The Temptations

Each day through my window I watch her as she passes by.
I say to myself: "You are such a lucky guy."
To have a girl like her is truly a dream come true.
Out of all the fellows in the world, she belongs to me.

Refrain:
But it was just my imagination
Runnin' away with me.
It was just my imagination
Runnin' away with me.

Soon, soon we'll be married and raise a family.
A cozy little home out in the country with children,
Maybe three.
I tell you I can visualize it all.
This couldn't be a dream, for too real it all seems.

Refrain

Every night on my knees I pray
"Dear Lord, hear my plea.
Don't ever let another take her love from me,
Or I would surely die."

Her love is heavenly.
When her arms enfold me,
I hear a tender Rhapsody.
But in reality,
She doesn't even know me.

Just my imagination
Runnin' away with me.
It was just my imagination
Runnin' away with me...

Just Once

Words by Cynthia Weil
Music by Barry Mann

recorded by Quincy Jones featuring James Ingram

I did my best,
But I guess my best wasn't good enough;
'Cause here we are,
Back where we were before.
Seems nothing ever changes,
We're back to being strangers,
Wondering if we ought to stay
Or head out the door.

Just once,
Can't we figure out what we keep doing wrong;
Why we never last for very long.
What are we doing wrong?
Just once,
Can't we find a way to finally make it right;
To make magic last for more than just one night?
If we could get to it,
I know we could break through it.

I gave it my all,
But I think my all may have been too much;
'Cause Lord knows we're not getting anywhere.
It seems we're always blowin'
Whatever we've got goin'.
And it seems at times with all we've got,
We haven't got a prayer.

Just once,
Can't we figure out what we keep doing wrong;
Why we never last for very long?
What are we doin' wrong?
Just once,
Can't we find a way to finally make it right?
To make the magic last for more than just one night?
I know we could get through it,
If we could just get to it.

Just once,
I want to understand;
Why it always comes back to goodbye.
Why can't we get ourselves in hand,
And admit to one another
We're no good without each other.
Take the best and make it better.
Find a way to stay together.

Just once,
Can't we find a way to finally make it right;
Oh, to make the magic last for more than just one night?
I know we could break through it,
If we could just get to it, just once.
Whoa, we can get to it, just once.

Just One More Chance

Words by Sam Coslow
Music by Arthur Johnston

Copyright © 1931 (Renewed 1958) by Famous Music Corporation

recorded by Bing Crosby and various other artists

We spend our lives in groping for happiness,
I found it once and tossed it aside.
I've paid for it with hours of loneliness;
I've nothing to hide, I'd bury my pride for…

Just one more chance,
To prove it's you alone I care for,
Each night I say a little prayer for
Just one more chance.

Just one more night,
To taste the kisses that enchant me,
I'd want no others if you'd grant me
Just one more chance.

I've learned the meaning of repentance;
Now you're the jury at my trial.
I know that I should serve my sentence;
Still I'm hoping all the while you'll give me…

Just one more word.
I said that I was glad to start out,
But know I'm back to cry my heart out,
For just one more chance.

Just the Way You Are

Words and Music by Billy Joel

© 1977, 1978 IMPULSIVE MUSIC

recorded by Billy Joel

Don't go changing to try and please me,
You never let me down before.
Don't imagine you're too familiar,
And I don't see you anymore.

I would not leave you in times of trouble,
We never could have come this far.
I took the good times, I'll take the bad times,
I'll take you just the way you are.

Don't go trying some new fashion,
Don't change the color of your hair.
You always have my unspoken passion,
Although I might not seem to care.

I don't want clever conversation,
I never want to work that hard.
I just want someone that I can talk to,
I want you just the way you are.

I need to know that you will always be
The same old someone that I knew.
Oh, what will it take till you believe in me,
The way that I believe in you.

I said I love you and that's forever,
And this I promise from the heart.
I could not love you any better,
I love you just the way you are.

I don't want clever conversation,
I never want to work that hard.
I just want someone that I can talk to,
I want you just the way you are.

The Keeper of the Stars

Words and Music by Karen Staley, Danny Mayo and
Dickey Lee

Copyright © 1994 by Careers-BMG Music Publishing, Inc., Sixteen Stars Music, Murrah Music
   Corporation, Universal - Songs Of PolyGram International, Inc. and Pal Time Music

recorded by John Michael Montgomery

It was no accident, me finding you.
Someone had a hand in it long before we ever knew.
Now I just can't believe you're in my life.
Heaven's smiling down on me as I look at you tonight.

I tip my hat to the keeper of the stars.
He sure knew what he was doin'
When he joined these two hearts.
I hold everything when I hold you in my arms.
I've got all I'll ever need, thanks to the keeper of the stars.

Soft moonlight on your face, oh, how you shine.
It takes my breath away just to look into your eyes.
I know I don't deserve a treasure like you.
There really are no words to show my gratitude.

So I tip my hat to the keeper of the stars.
He sure knew what he was doin'
When he joined these two hearts.
I hold everything when I hold you in my arms.
I've got all I'll ever need, thanks to the keeper of the stars.

It was no accident, me finding you.
Someone had a hand in it long before we ever knew.

Keeping the Faith

Words and Music by Billy Joel
© 1983 JOEL SONGS

recorded by Billy Joel

If it seems like I've been lost in let's remember;
If you think I'm feeling older,
And missing my younger days,
Oh, then you should have known me much better;
'Cause my past is something that never
Got in my way.
Oh no.

Still I would not be here now
If I never had the hunger.
And I'm not ashamed to say the wild boys were my friends.
Oh, 'cause I never felt the desire,
'Til their music set me on fire.
And then I was saved, yeah.
That's why I'm keeping the faith.
Yeah, yeah, yeah, yeah,
Keeping the faith.

We wore matador boots
Only Flagg Brothers had them with a Cuban heel;
Iridescent socks with the same color shirt,
And a tight pair of chinos.
Oh, I put on my shark jacket,
You know the kind,
With the velvet collar, and ditty-bop shades.
Oh yeah.

I took a fresh pack of Luckies and mint called Sen-Sen.
My old man's Trojans and his Old Spice after shave.
Oh, combed my hair in a pompadour,
Like the rest of the Romeos,
Wore a permanent wave.

Refrain:
Yeah, we were keeping the faith.
Yeah, yeah, yeah, yeah,
Keeping the faith.

You can get just so much from a good thing,
You can linger too long in your dreams.
Say goodbye to the oldies but goodies.
'Cause the good ole days weren't always good,
And tomorrow ain't as bad as it seems.

Learned stick ball as a formal education
Lost a lot of fights but it taught me how to lose O.K.
Oh, heard about sex but not enough.
I found you could dance and still look tough anyway.
Oh yes I did.

I found out a man ain't just being macho.
Ate an awful lot of late drive-in food;
Drank a lot of take-home pay.
I thought I was the Duke of Earl
When I made it with a red-haired girl in the Chevrolet.
Oh...

Refrain

Oh...You know the good ole days weren't always good
And tomorrow ain't as bad as it seems.

Now I told you my reasons for the whole revival
Now I'm going outside to have an ice-cold beer in the shade.
Oh, I'm gonna listen to my forty-fives.
Ain't it wonderful to be alive,
When the rock and roll plays.
Yeah, when memory stays.
Yeah, I'm keeping the faith.

Refrain

King of Pain

Written and Composed by Sting
© 1983 G.M. SUMNER
Published by MAGNETIC PUBLISHING LTD. and Administered by EMI BLACKWOOD
    MUSIC INC. in the USA and Canada

recorded by The Police

There's a little black spot on the sun today
It's the same old thing as yesterday
There's a black hat caught in the high tree-top
There's a flag-pole rag and the wind won't stop
I have stood here before inside the pouring rain
With the world turning circles running 'round my brain.
I guess I'm always hoping that you'll end this reign
But it's my destiny to be the King of Pain.

There's a little black spot on the sun today;
That's my soul up there.
It's the same old thing as yesterday;
That's my soul up there.
There's a black hat caught in a high tree-top;
That's my soul up there.
There's a flag pole rag and the wind won't stop;
That's my soul up there.

Refrain:
I have stood here before inside the pouring rain
With the world turning circles running 'round my brain.
I guess I'm always hoping that you'll end this reign
But it's my destiny to be the King of Pain.

There's a fossil that's trapped in a high cliff wall;
That's my soul up there.
There's a dead salmon frozen in a waterfall;
That's my soul up there.
There's a blue whale beached by a spring tide's ebb;
That's my soul up there.
There's a butterfly trapped in a spider's web;
That's my soul up there.

Refrain

There's a king on a throne with his eyes torn out,
There's a blind man looking for a shadow of doubt;
There's a rich man sleeping on a bed,
There's a skeleton choking on a crust of bread.

There's a red fox torn by a huntsman's pack;
That's my soul up there.
There's a little black spot on the sun today;
It's the same old thing as yesterday.

Refrain

King of the Road
Words and Music by Roger Miller

recorded by Roger Miller

Trailer for sale or rent,
Room to let, fifty cents.
No phone, no pool, no pets,
I ain't got no cigarettes.
Ah, but two hours of pushing broom,
Buys an eight by twelve, four bit room.
I'm a man of means by no means,
King of the road.

Third box car midnight train,
Destination Bangor, Maine.
Old worn out suit and shoes,
I don't pay no union dues.
I smoke old stogies I have found,
Short but not big around.
I'm a man of means by no means,
King of the road.

I know every engineer on every train,
All of the children and all of their names,
And every handout in every town,
And every lock that ain't locked when no one's around.

I sing trailer for sale or rent,
Rooms to let, fifty cents.
No phone, no pool, no pets,
I ain't got no cigarettes.
Ah, but two hours of pushing broom,
Buys an eight by twelve four bit room.
I'm a man of means by no means,
King of the road.

L-O-V-E
Words and Music by Bert Kaempfert and Milt Gabler

recorded by Nat "King" Cole and various other artists

L is for the way you look at me.
O is for the only one I see.
V is very, very extraordinary.
E is even more than anyone that you adore can.

Love is all that I can give to you,
Love is more than just a game for two.
Two in love can make it.
Take my heart and please don't break it,
Love was made for me and you.

Repeat Song

(That's almost true)
For me and you.

The Ladies Who Lunch
Music and Lyrics by Stephen Sondheim

from the musical *Company*

Here's to the ladies who lunch—
Everybody laugh.
Lounging in their caftans and planning a brunch
On their own behalf.
Off to the gym
Then to a fitting
Claiming they're fat.
And looking grim
'Cause they've been sitting choosing a hat.

Spoken:
Does anyone still wear a hat?

I'll drink to that.

Here's to the girls who stay smart.
Aren't they a gas?
Rushing to their classes in optical art,
Wishing it would pass.
Another long, exhausting day,
Another thousand dollars.
A matinee:
A Pinter play,
Perhaps a piece of Mahler's.
I'll drink to that—
And one for Mahler.

Here's to the girls who play wife.
Aren't they too much?
Keeping house, but clutching a copy of *Life*—
Just to keep in touch.
The ones who follow the rules
And meet themselves at the schools—
Too busy to know that they're fools.
Aren't they a gem?
I'll drink to them!
Let's all drink to them!

Here's to the girls who just watch.
Aren't they the best?
When they get depressed, it's a bottle of Scotch—
Plus a little jest.
Another chance to disapprove,
Another brilliant zinger.
Another reason not to move,
Another vodka stinger.

Scream:
Aaah…

I'll drink to that.

So here's to the girls on the go,
Everybody tries.
Look into their eyes and you'll see what they know:
Everybody dies.
A toast to that invincible bunch,
The dinosaurs surviving the crunch,
Let's hear it for the ladies who lunch:
Everybody rise!
Rise! Rise!
Rise! Rise!
Rise! Rise!
Rise!

Lady in Red
Words and Music by Chris DeBurgh

recorded by Chris DeBurgh

I've never seen you looking so lovely as you did tonight;
I've never seen you shine so bright.
I've never seen so many men ask you if you wanted to dance.
They're looking for a little romance,
Given half a chance.
I have never seen that dress you're wearing,
Or the highlights in your hair that catch your eyes.
I have been blind.

Refrain:
The lady in red is dancing with me,
Cheek to cheek.
There's nobody here, it's just you and me.
It's where I wanna be.
But I hardly know this beauty by my side.
I'll never forget the way you look tonight.

I've never seen you looking so gorgeous as you did tonight;
I've never seen you shine so bright.
You were amazing.
I've never seen so many people
Want to be there by your side,
And when you turned to me and smiled,
It took my breath away.
I have never had such a feeling,
Such a feeling of complete and utter love
As I do tonight.

Refrain

I never will forget the way you look tonight.
The lady in red. The lady in red. The lady in red.
My lady in red.
Spoken: I love you.

The Lady Is a Tramp
Words by Lorenz Hart
Music by Richard Rodgers

from the musical *Babes in Arms*
a standard recorded by Frank Sinatra, Lena Horne and
various other artists

I've wined and dined on Mulligan stew
And never wished for turkey
As I hitched and hiked and grifted too,
From Maine to Albuquerque.
Alas, I missed the Beaux Arts Ball,
And what is twice as sad,
I was never at a party
Where they honored Noël Ca'ad.
But social circles spin too fast for me.
My hobohemia is the place for me

I get too hungry for dinner at eight.
I like the theatre, but never come late.
I never bother with people I hate.
That's why the lady is a tramp.
I don't like crap games with barons and earls.
Won't go to Harlem in ermine and pearls.
Won't dish the dirt with the rest of the girls.
That's why the lady is a tramp.
I like the free, fresh wind in my hair,
Life without care.
I'm broke—it's oke.
Hate California—it's cold and damp.
That's why the lady is a tramp.

I go to Coney—the beach is divine.
I go to ball games—the bleachers are fine.
I follow Winchell and read every line.
That's why the lady is a tramp.
I like a prizefight that isn't a fake.
I love the rowing on Central Park Lake.
I go to operas and stay wide awake.
That's why the lady is a tramp.
I like the green grass under my shoes.
What can I lose?
I'm flat! That's that!
I'm all alone when I lower my lamp.
That's why the lady is a tramp.

Don't know the reason for cocktails at five.
I don't like flying—I'm glad I'm alive.
I crave affection, but not when I drive.
That's why the lady is a tramp.
Folks go to London and leave me behind.
I missed the crowning, Queen Mary won't mind.
I don't play Scarlett in *Gone with the Wind.*
That's why the lady is a tramp.
I like to hang my hat where I please.
Sail with the breeze.
No dough—heigh-ho!
I love La Guardia and think he's a champ.
That's why the lady is a tramp.

Girls get massages, they cry and they moan.
Tell Lizzie Arden to leave me alone.
I'm not too hot, but my shape is my own.
That's why the lady is a tramp!
The food at Sardi's is perfect, no doubt.
I wouldn't know what the Ritz is about.
I drop a nickel and coffee comes out.
That's why the lady is a tramp!
I like the sweet, fresh rain in my face.
Diamonds and lace,
No got—so what?
For Robert Taylor I whistle and stamp.
That's why the lady is a tramp!

Lady Madonna
Words and Music by John Lennon and Paul McCartney

recorded by The Beatles

Lady Madonna children at your feet
Wonder how you manage to make ends meet.
Who finds the money when you pay the rent?
Did you think that money was heaven sent?

Friday night arrives without a suitcase
Sunday morning creeping like a nun.
Monday's child has learned to tie his bootlace
See how they'll run.

Lady Madonna baby at your breast
Wonder how you manage to feed the rest
See how they'll run.

Lady Madonna lying on the bed
Listen to the music playing in you head.
Tuesday afternoon is never ending
Wednesday morning papers didn't come,
Thursday night your stockings needed mending,
See how they'll run.

Lady Madonna children at your feet
Wonder how you manage to make ends meet.

Lady Marmalade
Words and Music by Bob Crewe and Kenny Nolan

recorded by Patty LaBelle

He met Marmalade down in ol' New Orleans,
Struttin' her stuff on the street.
She say "Hello, hey Joe, ya wanna give it a go?"

Refrain:
Get cha get cha ya ya da da.
Get cha get cha ya ya here.
Mocha chocolata ya ya.
Creole Lady Marmalade.
Voulez vous coucher avec mois ce soir?
Voulez vous coucher avec mois?

Stayed in her boudoir while she freshened up.
That boy drank all that magnolia wine.
On her black satin sheets, I swear he started to freak...

Refrain

Seein' her skin feelin' silky smooth,
Color of café au lait;
Made the savage beast inside roar
Until it cried more, more, more.
Now he's back home doin' nine to five,
Livin' his gray flannel life.
But when he turns off to sleep,
Old memories keep...
More, more, more.

Refrain

Repeat and Fade:
Get cha get cha ya ya da da.
Get cha get cha ya ya here.

The Lady's in Love with You

Words by Frank Loesser
Music by Burton Lane

from the Paramount Picture *Some Like It Hot* (1939)
a standard recorded by Gene Krupa, Glenn Miller, Benny
Goodman, Tony Bennett and various other artists

If there's a gleam in her eye
Each time she straightens your tie,
You'll know the lady's in love with you.

If she can dress for a date
Without that waiting you hate,
It means the lady's in love with you.

And when your friends ask you over to join their table
But she picks that far away booth for two,
Well, sir, here's just how it stands,
You've got romance on your hands
Because the lady's in love with you.

Last Child

Words and Music by Steven Tyler and Brad Whitford

recorded by Aerosmith

I'm dreaming tonight, I'm leaving back home.

Take me back to South Tallahassee,
Down 'cross the bridge to my sweet sassafrassy.
Can't stand up on my feet in the city,
Got to get back to the real nitty gritty.
Yes sir, no sir, don't come any closer to my
Home sweet home,
Can't catch no dose from a hot tail poontang sweetheart
Sweathog ready to make a silk purse from a
J. Pal Getty and his ear
With a face in a beer.
Home sweet home.

Get out on the field, put the mule in the stable,
Ma, she's a-cookin' put the eats on the table.
Hate's in the city and my love's in the meadow,
Hand's on the plough and my feet's in the ghetto.
Stand up, sit down, don't do nothin',
It ain't no good when boss man's
Stuffin' it down their throats for paper notes
And their babies cry while cities lie at their feet
When you're rockin' in the streets.
Home sweet home.
Mama, take me home sweet home.

Repeat and Fade:
I was the last child, just a punk in the streets.

The Last Night of the World

Music by Claude-Michel Schönberg
Lyrics by Richard Maltby Jr. and Alain Boublil
Adapted from original French Lyrics by Alain Boublil

from the musical *Miss Saigon*

Chris:
In a place that won't let us feel,
In a life where nothing seems real
I have found you,
I have found you.

Kim:
In a world that's moving too fast,
In a world where nothing can last,
I will hold you,
I will hold you.

Chris:
Our lives will change when tomorrow comes.
Kim:
Tonight our hearts dream the distant drums.
Chris:
And we have music alright tearing the night.
A song played on a solo saxophone.
A crazy sound, a lonely sound,
Both:
A cry that tells me love goes on and on.
Played on a solo saxophone,
It's telling me to hold you tight,
And dance like it's the last night of the world.

Chris:
On the other side of the earth,
There's a place where life still has worth.
I will take you.
Kim:
I'll go with you.
Chris:
You won't believe all the things you'll see.
I know 'cause you'll see them all with me.

Both:
If we're together, well then,
We'll hear it again,
A song played on a solo saxophone.
A crazy sound, a lonely sound.
A cry that tells us love goes on and on.
Played on a solo saxophone.
It's telling me to hold you tight
And dance like it's the last night of the world.

Kim:
Dreams were all I ever knew.
Chris:
Dreams you won't need when I'm through.
Both:
Anywhere we may be I will sing with you our song.
So stay with me and hold me tight
And dance like it's the last night of the world.

Layla
Words and Music by Eric Clapton and Jim Gordon

recorded by Derek & The Dominos

What will you do when you get lonely
With nobody waiting by your side?
You've been running and hiding much too long.
You know it's just your foolish pride.

Refrain:
Layla, you got me on my knees, Layla,
I'm begging darling please, Layla,
Darling won't you ease my worried mind.

Tried to give you consolation,
Your old man won't let you down.
Like a fool I fell in love with you,
Turned the whole world upside down.

Refrain

Let's make the best of the situation
Before I finally go insane.
Please don't say we'll never find a way
And tell me all my love's in vain.

Refrain

Repeat and Fade:
Layla, you've got me on my knees, Layla,
I'm begging darling, please...

Lazy Afternoon
Words and Music by John Latouche and Jerome Moross

from the musical *The Golden Apple*

It's a lazy afternoon
And the beetle bugs are zoomin'
And the tulip trees are bloomin'
And there's not another human
In view
But us two.
It's a lazy afternoon
And the farmer leaves his reapin',
In the meadow cows are sleepin'
And the speckled trout stop leapin' upstream
As we dream.

A fat pink cloud hangs over the hill,
Unfoldin' like a rose.
If you hold my hand and sit real still
You can hear the grass as it grows.
It's a hazy afternoon
And I know a place that's quiet
'Cept for daisies running riot
And there's no one passing by it to see.
Come spend this lazy afternoon with me.

Lazy River
Words and Music by Hoagy Carmichael and Sidney Arodin

a standard recorded by Hoagy Carmichael, The Mills Brothers, Benny Goodman, Bobby Darin and various other artists

Up a lazy river by the old mill run,
That lazy river in the noon-day sun,
Linger in the shade of a kind old tree;
Throw away your troubles, dream a dream with me

Up a lazy river where the robin's song,
Awakes a bright new morning, we can loaf along,
Blue skies up above, everyone's in love,
Up a lazy river, how happy you can be.
Up a lazy river with me.

Leader of the Pack

Words and Music by George Morton, Jeff Barry and
Ellie Greenwich

recorded by The Shangri-Las

Spoken:
Is she really going out with him?
There she is, let's ask her.
Betty, is that Jimmy's ring you're wearing?
Mm Hm.
Gee, it must be great riding with him.
Is he picking you after school today?
Unh uh.
By the way, where'd you meet him?

Sung:
I met him at the candy store,
He turned around and smiled at me,
You get the picture?
Spoken:
Yes, we see.
Sung:
That's when I fell for the leader of the pack.

My folks were always putting him down.
They said he came from the wrong side of town.
They told me he was bad,
But I know he was sad,
That's why I fell for the leader of the pack.

One day my dad said find someone new.
I had to tell my Jimmy we were through.
He stood there and asked me why,
But all I could do was cry,
I'm sorry I hurt you, the leader of the pack.

Spoken:
He sort of smiled and kissed me goodbye,
But the tears were beginning to show
As he drove away on the rainy night.
I begged him to go slow but whether he heard,
I'll never know.

Sung:
I felt so helpless, what could I do?
Remembering all the things we'd been through.
In school they all stop and stare,
I can't hide the tears, but I don't care.
I'll never forget him, the leader of the pack.

Leave a Tender Moment Alone

Words and Music by Billy Joel

recorded by Billy Joel

Even though I'm in love,
Sometimes I get so afraid
I'll say something wrong
Just to have something to say.
I know the moment isn't right
To tell the girl a comical line
To keep conversation light.
I guess I'm just frightened out of my mind
But if that's how I feel
Then it's the best feeling I've ever known.
It's undeniably real,
Leave a tender moment alone.

Yes, I know I'm in love,
But just when I ought to relax,
I put my foot in my mouth
'Cause I'm just avoiding the facts.
If the girl gets too close
If I need some room to escape,
When the moment arose
I'd tell her it's all a mistake.
But that's not how I feel
No, that's not the woman I've known
She's undeniably real
So leave a tender moment alone.

But it's not only me breaking down
When tension gets high.
Just when I'm in a serious mood
She is suddenly quiet and shy.
I know the moment isn't right
To hold my emotions inside,
To change the attitude tonight.
I've run out of places to hide,
And if that's how I feel
Then it's the best feeling I've ever known.
It's undeniably real,
Leave a tender moment alone.

Leave a tender moment alone.
Leave a tender moment alone.

Leaving on a Jet Plane

Words and Music by John Denver

recorded by Peter, Paul & Mary

All my bags are packed, I'm ready to go,
I'm standing here outside your door,
I hate to wake you up to say goodbye.

But the dawn is breakin', it's early morn,
The taxi's waitin', he's blowin' his horn.
Already I'm so lonesome I could cry.

Refrain:
So kiss me and smile for me,
Tell me that you'll wait for me,
Hold me like you'll never let me go.
'Cause I'm leavin' on a jet plane,
Don't know when I'll be back again.
Oh babe, I hate to go.

There's so many times I've let you down;
So many times I've played around,
I tell you now they don't mean a thing.
Every place I go I'll think of you,
Every song I sing I'll sing for you
When I come back I'll bring {wear} your wedding ring.

Refrain

Now the time has come to leave you,
One more time let me kiss you,
Then close your eyes, I'll be on my way.
Dream about the days to come,
When I won't have to leave alone.
About the times I won't have to say:

Refrain

'Cause I'm leavin' on a jet plane,
Don't know when I'll be back again…

Let It Be
Words and Music by John Lennon and Paul McCartney

recorded by The Beatles

When I find myself in times of trouble
Mother Mary comes to me
Speaking words of wisdom
Let it be.

And in my hour of darkness
She is standing right in front of me
Speaking words of wisdom
Let it be.

Let it be, let it be, let it be, let it be
Whisper words of wisdom
Let it be.

And when the broken hearted people
Living in the world agree
There will be an answer
Let it be.

For though they may be parted there is
Still a chance that they will see
There will be an answer
Let it be.

Let it be, let it be, let it be, let it be
There will be an answer
Let it be.

And when the night is cloudy
There is still a light that shines on me
Shine until tomorrow
Let it be.

I wake up to the sound of music
Mother Mary comes to me
Speaking words of wisdom
Let it be.

Let it be, let it be, let it be, let it be
There will be an answer
Let it be.

Let it be, let it be, let it be, let it be
Whisper words of wisdom
Let it be…

Let It Rain
Words and Music by Eric Clapton and Bonnie Bramlett

recorded by Eric Clapton

The rain is falling
Through the mist of sorrow that surrounded me.
The sun could melt the fog away,
The mist that may surround me.

Refrain:
Let it rain; let it rain.
Let your love rain down on me.
Let it rain; let it rain.
Let it rain, rain, rain.

My life was like a desert flower,
Burning in the sun.
Until I found the way to love,
The heart was sad and done.

Refrain

Now I know the secret;
There is nothing that I lack.
If I give my love to you,
Be sure to give it back.

Refrain

Let It Ride

Words and Music by Randy Bachman and Charles Turner

recorded by Bachman-Turner Overdrive

Goodbye, hard life, don't cry. Would you let it ride?
Goodbye, hard life, don't cry. Would you let it ride?

You can't see the mornin',
But I can see the light.
Ride, ride, ride, let it ride.
While you've been out runnin'
I've been waiting half the night.
Ride, ride, ride, let it ride.

Refrain:
And would you cry if I told you that I lied,
And would you say goodbye or would you let it ride.

Babe, my life is not complete;
I never see you smile.
Ride, ride, ride, let it ride.
Baby you want the forgivin' kind
And that's just not my style.
Ride, ride, ride, let it ride.

Refrain

I've been doin' things worthwhile
And you've been bookin' time.

Refrain

Four Times:
Would you let it ride?

Five Times:
Ride, ride, ride, let it ride.

Four Times:
Would you let it ride?

Let There Be Love

Lyric by Ian Grant
Music by Lionel Rand

a standard recorded by Sammy Kaye, Pearl Bailey and
various other artists

Let there be you
And let there be me,
Let there be oysters
Under the sea.

Let there be wind
An occasional rain,
Chile con carne
And sparkling champagne.

Let there be birds
To sing in the trees,
Someone to bless me
Whenever I sneeze.

Let there be cuckoos,
A lark and a dove
But first of all,
Please let there be love.

Let Your Soul Be Your Pilot

Written and Composed by Sting

recorded by Sting

Let your soul be your pilot.
Let your soul guide you,
He'll guide you well.

When the doctors failed to heal you,
When no medicine chest can make you well.
When no counsel leads to comfort,
When there are no more lies they can tell.

No more useless information
And the compass spins,
The compass spins between heaven and hell.

Let your soul be your pilot,
Let your soul guide you,
He'll guide you well.
And your eyes turn towards the window pane
To the lights upon the hill.
This distance seems so strange to you now,
And the dark room seems so still.

Let your pain be my sorrow.
Let your tears be my tears too.
Let your courage be my model,
That the north you find will be true.

When there's no information
And the compass turns to nowhere,
To nowhere that you know well.
Let your soul be your pilot.
Let your soul guide you,
Let your soul guide you,
Let your soul guide you upon your way.
(Let your soul guide you along the way.)
(Let your soul guide you along the way.)

Repeat and Fade:
Let your soul guide you.
(Let your soul guide you along the way.)

Let's Face the Music and Dance

Words and Music by Irving Berlin

from the Motion Picture *Follow the Fleet*

There may be trouble ahead.
But while there's moonlight and music
And love and romance,
Let's face the music and dance.

Before the fiddlers have fled,
Before they ask us to pay the bill,
And while we still have the chance,
Let's face the music and dance.

Soon
We'll be without the moon,
Humming a different tune,
And then there may be tear drops to shed.
So while there's moonlight and music
And love and romance,
Let's face the music and dance, dance.
Let's face the music and dance.

Let's Hang On

Words and Music by Bob Crewe, Denny Randell and
Sandy Linzer

recorded by The Four Seasons, Barry Manilow

There ain't no good in our goodbyein'.
True love takes a lot of tryin'.
Oh, I'm cryin'.

Refrain:
Let's hang on to what we got.
Don't let go, girl, we got a lot.
Got a lot of love between us.
Hang on, hang on, hang on to what we got.

You say you're gonna go and call it quits,
Gonna chuck it all and break our love to bits.
I wish you never said it.
No, no, we'll both regret it.
That little chip of diamond on your hand
Ain't a fortune, baby,
But you know its stands.

A love to tie and bind us,
We just can't leave behind us.
Baby, baby, baby, stay...

Refrain

There isn't anything I wouldn't do.
I'd pay any price to get in good with you.
Give me a second turnin'.
Don't cool off while I'm burnin'.
You got me cryin', dyin' at your door.
Don't shut me out,
Let me in once more.
Your arms I need to hold to.
Your heart, oh girl, I told you,
Baby, baby, baby, stay.

Refrain

Let's Live for Today

Words and Music by Guido Cenciarelli, Giulio Rapetti and
Norman David

recorded by The Grass Roots

When I think of all the worries people seem to find,
And how they're in a hurry to complicate their mind.
By chasing after money and dreams that can't come true
I'm glad that we are different, we've better things to do.
May others plan their future, I'm busy lovin' you…
1-2-3-4:

Refrain:
Sha-la-la-la-la-la, live for today,
Sha-la-la-la-la-la, live for today,
And don't worry about tomorrow, hey, hey, hey
Sha-la-la-la-la-la, live for today,
Live for today.

We were never meant to worry the way that people do,
And I don't need to hurry as long as I'm with you.
We'll take it nice and easy and use my simple plan.
You'll be my lovin' woman, and I'll be your lovin' man.
We'll take the most from living,
Have pleasure while we can…
2-3-4:

Refrain

Baby, I need to feel you inside of me
I got to feel you deep inside of me
Baby, please come close to me
I got to have you now, please, please, please;
Gimme some-a lovin', gimme some lovin',
Gimme some-a lovin', gimme some lovin',
Baby, gimme some lovin',
Gimme some lovin' I need all your lovin'
Gimme some lovin' I need all your lovin',
Gimme some love, now,
I need all your lovin'.
Sha-la-la-la-la-la

Refrain

Let's Stay Together

Words and Music by Al Green, Willie Mitchell and Al Jackson, Jr.

recorded by Al Green

I'm, I'm so in love with you.
Whatever you want to do is alright with me.
'Cause you make me feel so brand new,
And now I want to spend my life with you.

Let me say since, baby, since we've been together,
Lovin' you forever is what I need.
Let me be the one you come running to,
And I'll never be untrue.

Oh, baby, let's stay together,
Loving you whether times are good or bad,
Happy or sad.
Baby times are good or bad, happy or sad.

Why, why people break up
Turn around and make up I just can't see.
You'd never do that to me,
Being around you is all I see.

It's why I beg you, let's stay together,
Loving you whether times are good or bad,

Repeat and Fade:
Babe, let's stay together.

Lift Ev'ry Voice and Sing

Words by James Weldon Johnson
Music by J. Rosamond Johnson

Note: This is unofficially known as the African-American national anthem.

Lift every voice and sing,
Till earth and heaven ring,
Ring with the harmonies of Liberty;
Let our rejoicing rise
High as the listening skies,
Let it resound loud as the rolling sea.

Sing a song full of the faith
That the dark past has taught us
Sing a song full of the hope
That the present has brought us;
Facing the rising sun of our new day begun,
Let us march on till victory is won.

Stony the road we trod,
Bitter the chastening rod,
Felt in the days when hope unborn had died;
Yet with a steady beat,
Have not our weary feet
Come to the place for which our fathers sighed?

We have come over a way
That with tears has been watered.
We have come, treading our path
Thro' the blood of the slaughtered,
Out from the gloomy past, till now we stand at last
Where the white gleam of our bright star is cast.

God of our weary years,
God of our silent tears,
Thou who hast brought us thus far on the way;
Thou who hast by Thy might,
Led us into the light,
Keep us forever in the path, we pray.

Lest our feet stray from the places,
Our God, where we met Thee;
Lest our hearts,
Drunk with the wine of the world, forget Thee;
Shadowed beneath Thy hand, may we forever stand,
True to our God, true to our native land.

Little Bit o' Soul

Words and Music by John Shakespeare and Kenneth Lewis

recorded by Music Explosion

Now when you're feelin' low and the fish won't bite,
You need a little bit o' soul to put you right.
You gotta make like you can kneel and pray,
And then a little bit o' soul will come your way.

Now when your girl has gone and you're broke in two,
You need a little bit o' soul to see you through.
And when you raise the roof with your rock and roll,
You'll get a little more kicks with a little bit o' soul.

And if you party falls 'cause there's nobody groovin',
A little bit o' soul and it really starts movin'.

Now when you're in a mess and you feel like cryin',
Just remember this little song of mine.
And as you walk through life tryin' to reach your goal,
Remember what I say 'bout a little bit o' soul.

Repeat and Fade:
A little bit o' soul, a little bit o' soul.

Little Girl Blue

Words by Lorenz Hart
Music by Richard Rodgers

from the musical *Jumbo*

Verse 1:
Sit there and count your fingers,
What can you do?
Old girl you're through.
Sit there and count your little fingers,
Unlucky little girl blue.

Verse 2:
Sit there and count the raindrops
Falling on you.
It's time you knew,
All you can count on is the raindrops
That fall on little girl blue.

No use, old girl,
You may as well surrender.
Your hope is getting slender,
Why won't somebody send a tender
Blue boy to cheer a little girl blue?

When I was very young
The world was younger than I.
As merry as a carousel
The circus tent was strung
With every star in the sky
Above the ring I love as well.

Now the young world has grown old,
Gone are the tinsel and gold.

Repeat Verses 1 and 2

Livin' on a Prayer

Words and Music by Desmond Child, Jon Bon Jovi and
Richie Sambora

recorded by Bon Jovi

Tommy used to work on the docks, union's been on strike.
He's down on his luck, it's tough, so tough.
Gina works the diner all day working for her man.
She brings home her pay, for love, for love.
She says:

Refrain:
We've got to hold on to what we've got.
It doesn't make a difference if we make it or not.
We've got each other and that's a lot for love.
We'll give it a shot.
Whoa, we're halfway there.
Whoa, livin' on a prayer.

Take my hand, we'll make it, I swear.
Whoa, livin' on a prayer.

Tommy's got his six string in hock,
Now he's holding in what he used to make it talk.
So tough, it's tough.
Gina dreams of runnin away;
When she cries in the night, Tommy whispers:
Baby, it's O.K. someday.

Refrain

Oh, we've got to hold on, ready or not,
You live for the fight when it's all that you've got.

Repeat and Fade:
Whoa, we're halfway there.
Whoa, livin' on a prayer.
Take my hand and we'll make it, I swear.
Whoa, livin' on a prayer.

The Loco-Motion

Words and Music by Gerry Goffin and Carole King

recorded by Little Eva, Grand Funk Railroad,
Kylie Minogue

Everybody's doin' a brand new dance now.
(C'mon, baby, do the Locomotion.)
I know you'll get to like it if you give it a chance now.
(C'mon, baby, do the Locomotion.)
My little baby sister can do it with ease,
Its easier than learnin' your A-B-C's.
So come on, come on, do the Locomotion with me.
You gotta swing your hips now.
Come on, baby, jump up, jump back.
Oh, well, I think you got the knack.

Now that you can do it, let's make a chain now.
(C'mon, baby, do the Locomotion.)
A chug-a chug-a motion like a railroad train now.
(C'mon, baby, do the Locomotion.)
Do it nice and easy now, don't lose control,
A little bit of rhythm and a lot of soul.
Come on, come on and do the Locomotion with me.
(C'mon, baby, do the Locomotion.)

Move around the floor in a locomotion.
(C'mon, baby, do the Locomotion.)
Do it holdin' hands if you get the notion.
(C'mon, baby, do the Locomotion.)
There's never been a dance that's so easy to do.
It even makes you happy when you're feelin' blue.
So, come on, come on, do the Locomotion with me.
(C'mon, baby, do the Locomotion.)
(C'mon, baby, do the Locomotion.)

The Logical Song

Words and Music by Rick Davies and Roger Hodgson

recorded by Supertramp

When I was young, it seemed that life was so wonderful,
A miracle, oh it was beautiful, magical.
And all the birds in the trees, well they'd sing so happily,
Joyfully, playfully watching me.

But then they sent me away to teach me how to be sensible,
Logical, responsible, practical.
And they showed me a world where I could be so dependable,
Clinical, intellectual, cynical.

There are times when all the world's asleep,
The questions run too deep for such a simple man.
Won't you please, please tell me what we've learned.
I know it sounds absurd, but please tell me who I am.

Now watch what you say or they'll be calling you a radical.
Liberal, fanatical, criminal.
Won't you sign up your name, we'd like to feel you're
Acceptable, respectable, presentable, a vegetable!

At night, when all the world's asleep,
The questions run so deep for such a simple man.
Won't you please tell me what we've learned.
I know it sounds absurd, but please tell me who I am.

The Long and Winding Road

Words and Music by John Lennon and Paul McCartney

recorded by The Beatles

The long and winding road that leads to your door,
Will never disappear, I've seen that road before.
It always leads me here, leads me to your door.

The wild and windy night that the rain washed away,
Has left a pool of tears crying for the day.
Why leave me standing here, let me know the way.

Many times I've been alone and many times I've cried,
Anyway, you'll never know the many ways I've tried.
But still they lead me back to the long and winding road.

You left me standing here a long, long time ago.
Don't leave me waiting here, lead me to you door.
Da da, da da …

Long Cool Woman
(In a Black Dress)

Words and Music by Allan Clarke, Roger Cook and Roger Greenaway

recorded by The Hollies

Saturday night I was downtown
Working for the F.B.I.
Sitting in a nest of bad men,
Whiskey bottles piling high.
Bootlegging boozer on the west-side
Full of people who are doing wrong.
Just about to call up the D.A. man
When I heard this woman singing a song.

A pair of forty-fives made me open my eyes,
My temperature started to rise.
She was a long cool woman in a black dress.
Just a five-nine beautiful tall.
With just one look I was a bad mess
'Cause that long cool woman had it all.

I saw her head up to the table.
Well, a tall walking big black cat.
When Charlie said, "I hope that you're able."
Boy, I'm telling you she knows where it's at.
Suddenly we heard the sirens,
And everybody started to run.
Jumpin' out of doors and tables
When I heard somebody shooting a gun.

Well, the D.A. was pumping my left hand
And she was holding my right.
Well, I told her don't get scared
'Cause you're gonna be spared.
Well, I'm gonna be forgiven
'Cause I wanna spend my living
With a long cool woman in a black dress.
Just a five-nine beautiful tall.
With just one look I was a bad mess
'Cause that long cool woman had it all.
Had it all.
Had it all…

Longer

Words and Music by Dan Fogelberg

recorded by Dan Fogelberg

Longer than there've been fishes in the ocean,
Higher than any bird ever flew,
Longer than there've been stars up in the heavens,
I've been in love with you.

Stronger than any mountain cathedral,
Truer than any tree ever grew,
Deeper than any forest primeval,
I am in love with you.

I'll bring
Fires in the winters;
You'll send
Showers in the springs.
We'll fly
Through the falls and summers
With love on our wings.

Through the years as the fire starts to mellow,
Burning lines in the book of our lives.
Though the binding cracks and pages start to yellow,
I'll be in love with you.
I'll be in love with you

Repeat Verse 1

I am in love with you.

The Look of Love
Words by Hal David
Music by Burt Bacharach
© 1967 (Renewed 1995) COLGEMS-EMI MUSIC INC.

from the film *Casino Royale*
recorded by Sergio Mendes & Brasil '66

The look of love is in your eyes,
A look your smile can't disguise.
The look of love, it's saying so
Much more than just words could ever say
And what my heart has heard,
Well, it takes my breath away.
I can hardly wait to hold you,
Feel my arms around you,
How long I have waited,
Waited just to love you,
Now that I have found you

You've got the look of love
It's on your face,
A look that time can't erase.
Be mine tonight, let this be just
The start of so many nights like this
Let's take a lover's vow
And then seal it with a kiss.
I can hardly wait to hold you,
Feel my arms around you,
How long I have waited,
Waited just to love you,
Now that I have found you
Don't ever go,
Don't ever go,
I love you so.

Looks Like We Made It
Words and Music by Richard Kerr and Will Jennings
Copyright © 1976 RONDOR MUSIC (LONDON) LTD. and IRVING MUSIC, INC.

recorded by Barry Manilow

There you are,
Lookin' just the same as you did the last time I touched you.
And here I am,
Close to gettin' tangled up inside the thought of you.
Do you love him as much as I love her?
And will that love be strong when old feelings start to stir?
Looks like we made it.

Refrain:
Left each other on the way to another love.
Looks like we made it,
Or I thought so till today, until you were there, everywhere,
And all I could taste was love the way we made it.

Love's so strange,
Playing hide and seek with hearts and always hurting.
And we're the fools,
Standing close enough to touch those burning memories.
And if I hold you for the sake of all those times
Love made us lose our minds,
Could I ever let you go?
Oh no, we've made it.

Refrain

Oh, we made it.
Looks like we made it.
Looks like we made it.

Losing My Mind
Words and Music by Stephen Sondheim
Copyright © 1971 by Range Road Music Inc., Quartet Music Inc., Rilting Music, Inc. and
   Burthen Music Co., Inc.
Copyright Renewed

from the musical *Follies*

The sun comes up,
I think about you.
The coffee cup,
I think about you.
I want you so,
It's like I'm losing my mind.

The morning ends,
I think about you.
I talk to friends,
I think about you.
And do they know?
It's like I'm losing my mind.

Refrain:
All afternoon,
Doing every little chore.
The thought of you stays bright.
Sometimes I stand in the middle of the floor,
Not going left,
Not going right.
I dim the lights
And think about you,
Spend sleepless nights
To think about you.
You said you loved me,
Or were you just being kind?
Or am I losing my mind?

I want you so,
It's like I'm losing my mind.
Does no one know?
It's like I'm losing my mind.

Repeat Refrain

Lost in the Stars
Words by Maxwell Anderson
Music by Kurt Weill

from the Musical Production *Lost in the Stars*

Before Lord God made the sea and the land,
He held all the stars in the palm of His hand,
And they ran through his fingers like grains of sand,
And one little star fell alone.

Then the Lord God hunted through the wide night air
For the little dark star on the wind down there
And he started and promised he'd take special care
So it wouldn't get lost again.

Now a man don't mind if the stars grow dim
And the clouds blow over and darken him,
So long as the Lord God's watching over them,
Keeping track how it all goes on.

But I've been walking through the night and day
Till my eyes get weary and my head turns gray,
And sometimes it seems maybe God's gone away,
Forgetting the promise that we heard him say
And we're lost out here in the stars.

Little stars, big stars, blowing through the night,
And we're lost out here in the stars,
Little stars, big, stars, blowing through the night,
And we're lost out here in the stars.

Love Is Just Around the Corner
Words and Music by Leo Robin and Lewis E. Gensler

from the Paramount Picture *Here Is My Heart*

Love is just around the corner, any cozy little corner,
Love is just around the corner, when I'm around you.
I'm a sentimental mourner, and I couldn't be more forlorner.
When you keep me on a corner just waiting for you.

Venus de Milo was not noted for her charms.
But strictly between us, you're cuter than Venus
And what's more you've got arms.
So let's go cuddle in a corner, any cozy little corner,
Love is just around the corner, and I'm around you.

Love Me Do
Words and Music by John Lennon and Paul McCartney

recorded by The Beatles

Refrain:
Love, love me do,
You know I love you;
I'll always be true,
So please,
Love me do.
Wo ho.
Love me do.

Repeat Refrain

Someone to love,
Somebody new,
Someone to love,
Someone like you.

Repeat Refrain

Love Me or Leave Me
Lyrics by Gus Kahn
Music by Walter Donaldson

from the musical *Whoopee*
featured in the film *Love Me or Leave Me*
a standard recorded by Ruth Etting, Benny Goodman,
Doris Day, Lena Horne and various other artists

Love me or leave me, and let me be lonely;
You won't believe me, and I love you only;
I'd rather be lonely,
Than happy with somebody else.

You might find the night-time, the right time for kissing;
But night-time is my time for just reminiscing,
Regretting, instead of forgetting
With somebody else.

There'll be no one unless that someone is you,
I intend to be independently blue.
I want your love, but I don't want to borrow,
To have it today, and to give back tomorrow;
For my love is your love,
There's no love for nobody else!

Love Me Tender

Words and Music by Elvis Presley and Vera Matson

from the film *Love Me Tender*
recorded by Elvis Presley

Love me tender, love me sweet;
Never let me go.
You have made me life complete,
And I love you so.

Refrain:
Love me tender, love me true
All my dreams fulfill.
For, my darlin', I love you,
And I always will.

Love me tender, love me long;
Take me to your heart.
For it's there that I belong,
And we'll never part.

Refrain

Love me tender, love me dear;
Tell me you are mine.
I'll be yours through all the years,
Till the end of time.

Refrain

Love Me with All Your Heart (Cuendo calienta el sol)

Original Words and Music by Carlos Rigual and Carlos A. Martinoli
English Words by Sunny Skylar

recorded by the Ray Charles Singers, The Bachelors and various other artists

Love me with all your heart,
That's all I want, love.
Love me with all of your heart or not at all.

Just promise me this:
That you'll give me all your kisses,
Every winter every summer every fall.

When we are far apart
Or when you are near me,
Love me with all of your heart as I love you.
Don't give me your love for a moment or an hour,
Love me always as you loved me from the start,
With every beat of your heart.

Love of a Lifetime

Words and Music by Bill Leverty and Carl Snare

recorded by Firehouse

I guess the time was right for us to say
We'd take our time and live our lives together day by day.
We'll make a wish and send it on a prayer.
We know our dreams can all come true,
With love that we can share.

With you I never wonder,
"Will you be there for me?"
With you I never wonder.
You're the right one for me.

Refrain:
I finally found the love of a lifetime,
A love to last my whole life through.
I finally found the love of a lifetime forever in my heart.
I finally found the love of a lifetime.

With every kiss, our love is like brand new
And every star up in the sky was made for me and you.
Still, we both know that the road is long,
But we know that we will be together
Because our love is strong.

Refrain Twice

I finally found the love of a lifetime...

Love of My Life

Words and Music by Jim Brickman and Tom Douglas

recorded by Jim Brickman with Michael W. Smith

I am amazed.
When I look at you,
I see you smiling back at me.
It's like all my dreams come true.

I am afraid.
If I lost you girl,
I'd fall through the cracks and lose my track
In this crazy, lonely world.

Sometimes it's so hard to believe,
When the nights can be so long,
And faith gave me the strength
And kept me holding on.

Refrain:
You are the love of my life,
And I'm so glad you found me.
You are the love of my life.
Baby, put your arms around me.
I guess this is how it feels
When you finally find something real.
My angel in the night,
You are my love
The love of my life.

Now here you are,
With midnight closing in.
You take my hand as our shadows dance,
With moonlight on your skin.

I look in your eyes.
I'm lost inside your kiss.
I think if I'd never met you
About all the things I'd missed.

Sometimes it's so hard to believe
When a love can be so strong
And faith gave me the strength
And kept me holding on.

Refrain Twice

Love Sneakin' Up on You
Words and Music by Jimmy Scott and Tom Snow
Copyright © 1994 Sony/ATV Tunes LLC, Lapsed Catholic Music and Snow Music
All Rights on behalf of Sony/ATV Tunes LLC and Lapsed Catholic Music Administered by
   Sony/ATV Music Publishing, 8 Music Square West, Nashville, TN 37203

recorded by Bonnie Raitt

Rainy night, I'm all alone,
Sitting here waiting for your voice on the phone.
Fever turns to cold, cold sweat,
Thinking about the things we ain't done yet.

Tell me now I've got know.
Do you feel the same?
Do you just light up at the mention of my name?

Refrain:
Don't worry, baby.
It ain't nothing new.
That's just love sneakin' up on you.
If your whole world is shakin'
And you feel like I do,
That's just love sneakin' up on you.
Hey, hey.

Nowhere on earth for your heart to hide
Once love comes sneakin' up on your blind side,
And you might as well try to stop the rain,
Or stand in the tracks of a runaway train.

You just can't fight it,
When a thing is meant to be,
So come on, let's finish what you started with me.

Refrain Six Times

Love Takes Time
Words and Music by Mariah Carey and Ben Margulies
Copyright © 1990 Sony/ATV Songs LLC, Vision Of Love Songs, Inc. and Been Jammin' Music
All Rights on behalf of Sony/ATV Songs LLC and Vision Of Love Songs, Inc. Administered by
   Sony/ATV Music Publishing, 8 Music Square West, Nashville, TN 37203

recorded by Mariah Carey

I had it all but I let it slip away.
Couldn't see I treated you wrong.
Now I wander around feeling down and cold,
Trying to believe that you're gone.

Refrain:
Love takes time to heal
When you're hurting so much.
Couldn't see that I was blind to let you go.
I can't escape the pain inside,
'Cause love takes time.
I don't want to be here.
I don't want to be here alone.

Losing my mind from this hollow in my heart.
Suddenly I'm so incomplete, yeah.
Lord, I'm needing you now.
Tell me how to stop the rain.
Tears are falling down endlessly.

Refrain

You might say that it's over.
You might say that you don't care.
You might say you don't miss me.
You don't need me.
But I know that you do
And I feel that you do inside.

Refrain

Love the One You're With

Words and Music by Stephen Stills

recorded by Stephen Stills

If you're down and confused,
And you don't remember who you're talkin' to
Concentration slips away,
'Cause your baby is so far away.
Well,

Refrain:
There's a rose in the fisted glove
And the eagle flies with the dove,
And if you can't be with the one you love,
Honey, love the one you're with.
Love the one you're with.
Love the one you're with.
Love the one you're with.

Don't be angry, don't be sad,
And don't sit cryin' over good times you've had.
There's a girl right next to you,
And she's just waitin' for something to do.
And,

Refrain

Dit dit dit…

Turn your heartache right into joy,
She's a girl, and you're a boy.
Well, get it together make it nice,
You ain't gonna need any more advice.
And,

Refrain

Dit dit dit…

Love Will Keep Us Together

Words and Music by Neil Sedaka and Howard Greenfield

recorded by Captain & Tenille

Love will keep us together;
Think of me, babe, whenever
Some sweet-talkin' guy comes along,
Singin' his song.
Don't mess around;
You gotta be strong.

Refrain:
Just stop,
'Cause I really love ya;
Stop, I'll be thinkin' of ya.
Look in my heart and let love
Keep us together.

You, you belong to me now;
Ain't gonna set you free now.
When those guys start hangin' around,
Talkin' me down,
Hear with your heart
And you won't hear a sound.

Refrain

…Whatever.
Young and beautiful,
But someday your looks will be gone.
When others turn you off,
Who'll be turning you on?
I will, I will, I will.

I will be there to share forever;
Love will keep us together.
Said it before and I'll say it again,
While others pretend,
I need you now and I'll need you then.

Refrain

… Whatever.

Love, Look Away

Lyrics by Oscar Hammerstein II
Music by Richard Rodgers

from the musical *Flower Drum Song*

Love, look away!
Love, look away from me.
Fly when you pass my door,
Fly and get lost at sea.

Call it a day.
Love, let us say we're through.
No good are you for me.
No good am I for you.
Wanting you so, I try too much.
After you go, I cry too much.

Love, look away.
Lonely though I may be,
Leave me and set me free,
Look away, look away, look away from me.

Lover, Come Back to Me

Lyrics by Oscar Hammerstein II
Music by Sigmund Romberg

from the musical *The New Moon*

You went away, I let you,
We broke the ties that bind;
I wanted to forget you
And leave the past behind.
Still, the magic of the night I met you
Seems to stay forever in my mind.

The sky was blue
And high above
The moon was new
And so was love.
This eager heart of mine was singing:
"Lover, where can you be?"

You came at last,
Love had its day,
That day is past,
You've gone away.
This aching heart of mine is singing:
"Lover, come back to me!"

When I remember every little thing you used to do,
I'm so lonely,
Every road I walk along I've walked along with you,
No wonder I am lonely.

The sky is blue,
The night is cold,
The moon is new,
But love is old,
And, while I'm waiting here,
This heart of mine is singing:
"Lover, come back to me!"

Luck Be a Lady

By Frank Loesser

from the musical *Guys and Dolls*

They call you Lady Luck but there is room for doubt;
At times you have a very unladylike way of running out.
You're on a date with me the pickings have been lush,
And yet before this evening is over,
You might give me the brush.
You might forget your manners, you might refuse to stay,
And so the best that I can do is pray.

Luck be a lady tonight.
Luck be a lady tonight.
Luck, if you've ever been a lady to begin with,
Luck be a lady tonight.

Luck, let a gentleman see,
How nice a dame you can be.
I know the way you've treated other guys you've been with,
Luck be a lady with me.

A lady doesn't leave her escort;
It isn't fair,
It isn't nice!
A lady doesn't wander all over the room
And blow on some other guy's dice.

So, let's keep the party polite,
Never get out of my sight.
Stick with me baby I'm the fellow you came in with.
Luck be a lady, luck be a lady,
Luck be a lady tonight.

Lucy in the Sky with Diamonds

Words and Music by John Lennon and Paul McCartney

recorded by The Beatles, Elton John

Picture yourself in a boat on a river
With tangerine trees and marmalade skies.
Somebody calls you, you answer quite slowly
A girl with kaleidoscope eyes.

Cellophane flowers of yellow and green
Towering over your head.
Look for the girl with the sun in her eyes
And she's gone.

Refrain:
Lucy in the sky with diamonds.
Lucy in the sky with diamonds.
Lucy in the sky with diamonds.
Ah…

Follow her down to a bridge by a fountain
Where rocking horse people eat marshmallow pies.
Everyone smiles as you drift past the flowers
That grow so incredibly high.

Newspaper taxis appear on the shore
Waiting to take you away.
Climb in the back with your head in the clouds
And you're gone.

Refrain

Picture yourself on a train in a station
With plasticine porters with looking glass ties.
Suddenly someone is there at the turnstile
The girl with kaleidoscope eyes.

Refrain

Lullaby of the Leaves

Words by Joe Young
Music by Bernice Petkere

a standard recorded by Art Tatum, Gerry Mulligan,
Dizzy Gillespie and various other artists

Cradle me where southern skies
Can watch me with a million eyes,
Oh, sing me to sleep,
Lullaby of the leaves.
Cover me with heaven's blue
And let me dream a dream or two,
Oh, sing me to sleep,
Lullaby of the leaves.

I'm breezing along, along with the breeze,
I'm hearing a song, a song through the trees,
Ooh, ooh...
The pine melody caressing the shore,
Familiar to me, I've heard it before,
Ooh, ooh ooh ooh,
That's southland, don't I feel it in my soul,
And don't I know I've reached my goal,
Oh, sing me to sleep,
Lullabye of the leaves.

Lullabye (Goodnight, My Angel)

Words and Music by Billy Joel

recorded by Billy Joel

Goodnight, my angel, time to close your eyes,
And save these questions for another day.
I think I know what you've been asking me.
I think you know what I've been trying to say.
I promised I would never leave you,
And you should always know
Wherever you may go,
No matter where you are,
I never will be far away.

Goodnight, my angel, now it's time to sleep,
And still so many things I want to say.
Remember all the songs you sang for me
When we went sailing on an emerald bay.
And like a boat out on the ocean,
I'm rocking you to sleep.
The water's dark and deep inside this ancient heart
You'll always be a part of me.

Goodnight, my angel, now it's time to dream,
And dream how wonderful your life will be.
Someday your child may cry,
And if you sing this lullaby,
Then in your heart there will always be a part of me.

Someday we'll all be gone
But lullabyes goes on and on.
They never die, that's how you and I will be.

Lush Life

Words and Music by Billy Strayhorn

a standard recorded by Nat "King" Cole and various other
artists

I used to visit all the very gay places,
Those come what may places,
Where one relaxes
On the axis
Of the wheel of life
To get the feel of life from jazz and cocktails.

The girls I knew had sad and sullen gray faces,
With distingué traces,
That used to be there.
You could see where they'd been washed away
By too many through the day
Twelve o'clock tails.

Then you came along with your siren song
To tempt me to madness.
I thought for a while
That your poignant smile
Was tinged with sadness
Of a great love for me.
Ah, yes I was wrong,
Again I was wrong!

Life is lonely again,
And only last year
Everything seemed so sure.
Now life is awful again,
A troughful
Of hearts could only be a bore.

A week in Paris
Will ease the bite of it.
All I care is
To smile in spite of it.
I'll forget you, I will,
While you are still burning inside my brain.
Romance is mush,
Stifling those who strive,
I'll live a lush life
In some small dive,
And there I'll be,
While I rot with the rest
Of those whose lives are lonely too.

Maggie May

Words and Music by Rod Stewart and Martin Quittenton

recorded by Rod Stewart

Wake up, Maggie,
I think I got something to say to you.
It's late September
And I really should be back at school.
I know I keep you amused,
But I feel I'm being used.
Oh, Maggie, I couldn't have tried any more.
You led me away from home
Just to save you from being alone.
You stole my heart,
And that's what really hurts.

The morning sun, when it's in your face,
Really shows your age.
But that don't worry me none.
In my eyes you're everything.
I laughed at all of your jokes.
My love you didn't need to coax.
Oh, Maggie, I couldn't have tried any more.
You led me away from home
Just to save you from being alone.
You stole my heart,
And that's a pain I can do without.

All I needed was a friend
To lend a guiding hand.
But you turned into a lover,
And, mother, what a lover!
You wore me out.
All you did was wreck my bed,
And, in the morning, kick me in the head.
Oh, Maggie, I couldn't have tried any more.
You led me away from home
'Cause you didn't want to be alone.
You stole my heart.
I couldn't leave you if I tried.

I suppose I could collect my books
And get on back to school.
Or steal my daddy's cue
And make a living out of playing pool.
Or find myself a rock 'n' roll band
That needs a helping hand.
Oh, Maggie, I wish I'd never seen your face.
You made a first-class fool out of me.
But I'm as blind as a fool can be.
You stole my heart,
But I love you anyway.

Mairzy Doats

Words and Music by Milton Drake, Al Hoffman and Jerry Livingston

recorded by Al Trace, The Merry Macs

I know a ditty nutty as a fruitcake,
Goofy as a goon and silly as a loon.
Some call it pretty, others call it crazy,
But they all sing this tune:

Mairzy doats and dozy doats
And liddle lamzy divey,
A kiddley divey too, wouldn't you?

Yes! Mairzy doats and dozy doats
And liddle lamzy divey,
A kiddley divey too, wouldn't you?

If the words sound queer,
And funny to your ear,
A little bit jumbled and jivey,
Sing "Mares eat oats and does eat oats
And little lambs eat ivey."

Oh! Mairzy doats and dozey doats
And liddle lamzy divey,
A kiddley divey too, wouldn't you?
A kiddley divey too, wouldn't you?

Make Someone Happy

Words by Betty Comden and Adolph Green
Music by Jule Styne

from the musical *Do Re Mi*

The sound of applause is delicious.
It's a thrill to have the world at your feet.
The praise of the crowd is exciting,
But I've learned that is not what makes a life complete.

There's one thing you can do
For the rest of your days
That's worth more than applause,
The screaming crowd, the bouquets.

Refrain:
Make someone happy.
Make just one someone happy.
Make just one heart the heart you sing to.
One smile that cheers you,
One face that lights when it nears you,
One man you're everything to.

Fame, if you win it,
Comes and goes in a minute.
Where's the real stuff in life to cling to?
Love is the answer,
Someone to love is the answer.
Once you've found him,
Build your world around him.
Make someone happy,
Make just one someone happy,
And you will be happy too.

Make Your Own Kind of Music
Words and Music by Barry Mann and Cynthia Weil

recorded by Mama Cass Elliot

Nobody can tell ya;
There's only one song worth singin'.
They may try and sell ya,
'Cause it hangs them up to see someone like you.
But…

Refrain:
You've gotta make your own kind of music,
Sing your own special song.
Make your own kind of music
Even if nobody else sings along.

You're gonna be knowing
The loneliest kind of lonely.
It be may be rough goin',
Just to do your thing's the hardest thing to do.

So if you cannot take my hand,
And if you must be goin', I will understand.
You gotta:

Refrain

Makin' Whoopee!
Lyrics by Gus Kahn
Music by Walter Donaldson

from the musical *Whoopee*
a standard recorded by various artists

Ev'rytime I hear that march from *Lohengrin*,
I am always on the outside looking in.
Maybe that is why I see the funny side,
When I see a fallen brother take a bride.
Weddings make a lot of people sad.
But if you're not the groom, they're not so bad.

Another bride,
Another June,
Another sunny
Honeymoon.
Another season,
Another reason,
For makin' whoopee!

A lot of shoes
A lot of rice,
The groom is nervous
He answers twice.
It's really killing
That he's so willing
To make whoopee!

Picture a little love-nest,
Down where the roses cling.
Picture the same sweet love-nest,
Think what a year can bring.

He's washing dishes,
And baby clothes,
He's so ambitious,
He even sews.
But don't forget folks,
That's what you get, folks,
For makin' whoopee!

Another year,
Or maybe less.
What's this I hear?
Well, can't you guess?
She feels neglected,
And he's suspected,
Of makin' whoopee!

She sits alone,
'Most ev'ry night.
He doesn't phone her,
He doesn't write.
He says he's "busy"
But she says "is he?"
He's makin' whoopee!

He doesn't make much money,
Only five thousand per.
Some judge who thinks he's funny,
Says "you'll pay six to her."

He says, "Now judge,
Suppose I fail?"
The judge says, "Budge
Right into jail."
You'd better keep her,
I think it's cheaper,
Than makin' whoopee!

Mambo No. 5 (A Little Bit Of...)

Original Music by Dámaso Pérez Prado
Words by Lou Bega and Zippy

originally recorded by Pérez Prado
lyric added for the recording by Lou Bega

Spoken:
Ladies and gentlemen, this is Mambo Number Five.

Sung:
One, two, three, four, five.
Everybody in the car.
So, come on, let's ride
To the liquor store around the corner.
The boys say they want some gin and juice,
But I really don't wanna.
Beer bust like I had last week
I must stay deep 'cause talk is cheap.
I like
Spoken:
Angela, Pamela, Sandra and Rita
Sung:
And as I continue you know they're gettin' sweeter.
So, what can I do?
I really beg you my Lord.
To me flirtin' is just like a sport.
Anything fly, it's all good.
Spoken:
Let me dump it, please set in the trumpet.

Refrain, Sung:
A little bit of Monica in my life,
A little bit of Erica by my side,
A little bit of Rita's all I need.
A little bit of Tina's what I see.
A little bit of Sandra in the sun,
A little bit of Mary all night long,
A little bit of Jessica, here I am,
A little bit of you
Spoken:
Makes me your man.

Sung:
Jump
Spoken:
Up and down
And move it all around.
Shake your head to the sound,
Put your hands on the ground.
Take one step left and one step right,
One to the front and one to the side.
Clap your hands one and clap your hands twice
And if it looks like this then you doin' it.

Refrain, Sung

Spoken:
Trumpet,
(Mambo Number Five.)
The trumpet.
Trumpet,
(Mambo Number Five.)
The trumpet.

Refrain, Sung

I do all I do to fall in love with a girl like you
'Cause you can't run and you can't hide.
You and me gonna touch the sky.

Spoken:
Mambo Number Five.

Mame

Music and Lyric by Jerry Herman

from the musical *Mame*

You coax the blues right out of the horn, Mame,
You charm the husk right off of the corn, Mame.
You've got the banjoes strummin'
And plunkin' out a tune to beat the band,
The whole plantation's hummin'
Since you brought Dixie back to Dixieland.

You make the cotton easy to pick, Mame.
You give my old mint julep a kick, Mame.
You make the old magnolia tree
Blossom at the mention of your name,
You've made us feel alive again,
You've given us the drive again,
To make the South revive again, Mame.

You've brought the cakewalk back into style, Mame.
You make the weepin' willow tree smile, Mame.
Your skin is Dixie satin,
There's rebel in your manner and your speech.
You may be from Manhattan,
But Georgia never had a sweeter peach.

You make our black-eyed peas and our grits, Mame,
Seem like the bill of fare at the Ritz, Mame.
You came, you saw, you conquered
And absolutely nothing is the same.
Your special fascination 'll
Prove to be inspirational,
We think you're just sensational,
Mame.

Mammas Don't Let Your Babies Grow Up to Be Cowboys

Words and Music by Ed Bruce and Patsy Bruce

recorded by Waylon Jennings & Willie Nelson
featured in the film *The Electric Horseman*

Refrain:
Mammas don't let your babies grow up to be cowboys.
Don't let 'em pick guitars and drive them old trucks.
Make 'em be doctors and lawyers and such.
Mammas don't let your babies grow up to be cowboys,
'Cause they'll never stay home,
And they're always alone,
Even with someone they love.

A cowboy ain't easy to love and he's harder to hold.
And it means more to him to give you a song
Than silver or gold.
Budweiser buckles and soft faded Levis
And each night begins a new day.
If you can't understand him
And he don't die young,
He'll probably just ride away.

Refrain

A cowboy loves smoky ole pool rooms
And clear mountain mornings.
Little warm puppies, and children, and girls of the night.
Them that don't know him won't like him,
And them that do sometimes won't know how to take him.
He's not wrong, he just different
And his pride won't let him
Do things to make you think he's right.

Refrain

The Man That Got Away

Lyric by Ira Gershwin
Music by Harold Arlen

from the Motion Picture *A Star Is Born* (1954)
recorded by Judy Garland and various other artists

The night is bitter,
The stars have lost their glitter,
The winds grow colder,
And suddenly your older,
And all because of the man that got away.
No more his eager call;
The writing's on the wall,
The dreams you dreamed have all gone astray.

The man that won you,
Has run off and undone you.
That great beginning
Has seen the final inning.
Don't know what happened,
It's all a crazy game!

No more that all-time thrill,
For you've been through the mill,
And never a new love will
Be the same.
Good riddance! Good bye!
Every trick of his you're on to.
But, fools will be fools,
And where's he gone to?

The road gets rougher,
It's lonelier and tougher,
With hope you burn up,
Tomorrow he may turn up.
There's just no let-up
The live-long night and day!

Ever since this world began
There is nothing sadder than
A one man woman
Looking for the man that got away.

Mandy

Words and Music by Scott English and Richard Kerr

recorded by Barry Manilow

I remember all my life
Raining down as cold as ice.
Shadows of a man,
A face through a window,
Cryin' in the night,
The night goes into…

Morning's just another day;
Happy people pass my way.
Looking in their eyes,
I see a memory
I never realized
How happy you made me.

Refrain:
Oh, Mandy,
Well, you came and you gave without taking.
But I sent you away.
Oh, Mandy,
Well, you kissed me and stopped me from shaking,
And I need you today.
Oh, Mandy!

I'm standing on the edge of time;
I've walked away when love was mine.
Caught up in a world of up-hill climbing,
The tears are in my mind
And nothin' is rhyming,

Refrain

Yesterday's a dream,
I face the morning.
Crying on a breeze
The pain is calling.

Refrain

Oh, Mandy,
Well, you came and you gave without taking,
But I sent you away.
Oh, Mandy,
Well, you kissed me and stopped me from shaking,
And I need you.

Manhattan
Words by Lorenz Hart
Music by Richard Rodgers

from the Broadway musical *The Garrick Gaieties*
a standard recorded by various artists

Verse:
Summer journeys to Niagara
And to other places aggra-
Vate all our cares.
We'll save our fares!
I've a cozy little flat in
What is known as Manhattan,
We'll settle down
Right here in town!

Refrain:
We'll have Manhattan
The Bronx and Staten Island too.
It's lovely going through the zoo.
It's very fancy
On old Delancey Street, you know.
The subway charms us so
When balmy breezes blow
To and fro.
And tell me what street
Compares with Mott Street in July?
Sweet pushcarts gently gliding by.
The great big city's a wondrous toy
Just made for a girl and boy.
We'll turn Manhattan
Into an isle of joy.

We'll go to Greenwich,
Where modern men itch to be free;
And Bowling Green you'll see with me.
We'll bathe at Brighton;
The fish you'll frighten when you're in,
Your bathing suit so thin
Will make the shellfish grin
Fin to fin.
I'd like to take a
Sail on Jamaica Bay with you.
And fair Canarsie's Lake we'll view.
The city's bustle cannot destroy
The dreams of a girl and boy.
We'll turn Manhattan
Into an isle of joy.

We'll go to Yonkers
Where true love conquers in the wilds.
And starve together, dear, in Childs.
We'll go to Coney
And eat baloney on a roll.
In Central Park we'll stroll
Where our first kiss we stole,
Soul to soul.
Our future babies
We'll take to *Abie's Irish Rose*.
I hope they'll live to see it close.
The city's clamor can never spoil
The dreams of a boy and goil.
We'll turn Manhattan
Into an isle of joy.

We'll have Manhattan,
The Bronx and Staten Island too.
We'll try to cross Fifth Avenue.
As black as onyx
We'll find the Bronnix Park Express.
Our Flatbush flat, I guess,
Will be a great success,
More or less.
A short vacation
On Inspiration Point we'll spend,
And in the station house we'll end.
But Civic Virtue cannot destroy
The dreams of a girl and boy.
We'll turn Manhattan
Into an isle of joy.

Martha My Dear

Words and Music by John Lennon and Paul McCartney

recorded by The Beatles

Martha my dear, though I spend my days
In conversation,
Please,
Remember me,
Martha my dear.

Refrain:
Hold your head up, you silly girl, look what you've done.
When you find yourself in the thick of it,
Help yourself to a bit of what is all around you,
Silly girl.

Take a good look around you.
Take a good look you're bound to see,
That you and me were meant to be for each other,
Silly girl.

Refrain

Martha my dear, you have always been
My inspiration.
Please,
Be good to me, Martha my love.
Don't forget me,
Martha my dear.

Maybe Baby

By Norman Petty and Charles Hardin

recorded by Buddy Holly & The Crickets

Maybe, baby, I'll have you.
Maybe, baby, you'll be true.
Maybe, baby, I'll have you for me.

It's funny, honey, you don't care.
You never listen to my prayer.
Maybe, baby, you will love me someday.

Well, you are the one that makes me sad,
And you are the one that makes me glad.
When someday you want me
I'll be there. Just wait and see.

Maybe, baby, I'll have you.
Maybe, baby, you'll be true.
Maybe, baby, I'll have you for me.

Maybe I'm Amazed

Words and Music by Paul McCartney

recorded by Paul McCartney

Baby, I'm amazed at the way you love me all the time,
And maybe I'm afraid of the way I love you.
Baby, I'm amazed at the way you pulled me out of time.
You hung me on a line.
Baby I'm amazed at the way I really need you.

Refrain:
Baby, I'm a man,
Maybe I'm a lonely man,
Who's in the middle of something
That he doesn't really understand.
Baby, I'm a man,
And maybe you're the only woman
Who could ever help me.
Baby, won't you help me to understand.

Repeat Refrain

Maybe I'm amazed at the way you're with me all the time.
Maybe I'm afraid of the way I need you.
Baby, I'm amazed at the way you help me sing my song,
Right me when I'm wrong.
Baby I'm amazed at the way I really need you.

Maybe This Time

Words by Fred Ebb
Music by John Kander

from the musical *Cabaret*

Maybe this time,
I'll be lucky.
Maybe this time he'll stay.
Maybe this time,
For the first time,
Love won't hurry away.
He will hold me fast.
I'll be home at last.
Not a loser anymore,
Like the last time and the time before.

Everybody
Loves a winner
So nobody loved me.
Lady Peaceful.
Lady Happy

That's what I long to be.
All the odds are
In my favor
Something's bound to begin.
It's got to happen,
Happen sometime;
Maybe this time I'll win.

Repeat Verse 2

Maybe Tomorrow

Words and Music by Berry Gordy, Alphonso J. Mizell,
Frederick J. Perren and Dennis Lussier

recorded by The Jackson 5

I don't know how many stars there are
Up in the heavenly sky.
I only know my heaven is here on earth
Each time you look into my eyes,
The way you do, baby.
Thank you, thank you, baby.

Refrain 1:
My beautiful bird, you have flown away.
I held you too tight, I can see.
You're all I need to get by.
No one else could make me cry,
The way you do, baby.
'Cause,

Refrain 2:
You are the book that I read each day.
You are the song that I sing.
Gonna sing it to you.
You are the four seasons of my life.
But maybe tommorow you'll change your mind, girl.
Maybe tomorrow, you'll come back to my arms, girl.

Maybe she won't.

Refrain 1

Refrain 2

Me and Bobby McGee

Words and Music by Kris Kristofferson and Fred Foster

recorded by Janis Joplin

Busted flat in Baton Rouge,
Headin' for the trains;
Feelin' nearly faded as my jeans,
Bobby thumbed a diesel down
Just before it rained;
Took us all the way to New Orleans.

I took my harpoon out of my dirty red bandanna
And was blowin' sad while Bobby sang the blues;
With them windshield wipers slappin' time
And Bobby clappin' hands
We finally sang up every song that driver knew.

Freedom's just another word for nothin' left to lose,
Nothin' ain't worth nothin' but it's free;
Feelin' good was easy, Lord,
When Bobby sang the blues;
And feelin' good was good enough for me,
Good enough for me and Bobby McGee.

From the coal mines of Kentucky
To the California sun,
Bobby shared the secrets of my soul;
Standin' right beside me, Lord,
Through everything I done,
And every night she kept from the cold.

Then somewhere near Salinas, Lord,
I let her slip away
Lookin' for the home I hope she'll find;
And I'd trade all of my tomorrows
For a single yesterday,
Holdin' Bobby's body next to mine.

Freedom's just another word for nothin' left to lose,
Nothin' left is all she left for me;
Feelin' good was easy, Lord,
When Bobby sang the blues;
And buddy, that was good was good enough for me,
Good enough for me and Bobby McGee.

Mellow Yellow

Words and Music by Donovan Leitch

recorded by Donovan

I'm just mad about Saffron,
Saffron's mad about me.
I'm just mad about Saffron,
She's just mad about me.

Refrain:
They call me Mellow Yellow.
(*Spoken:* Quite rightly.)
They call me Mellow Yellow.
(*Spoken:* Quite rightly.)
They call me Mellow Yellow.

I'm just mad about Fourteen,
Fourteen's mad about me.
I'm just mad about Fourteen,
She's just mad about me.

Refrain

Born high forever to fly,
Wind velocity: nil.
Born high forever to fly,
If you want your cup I will fill.

Refrain

He's so mellow,
He's so mellow,

Electrical banana,
Is gonna be a sudden craze.
Electrical banana
Is bound to be the very next phase.

Refrain

Memories Are Made of This

Words and Music by Richard Dehr, Frank Miller and Terry Gilkyson

recorded by Dean Martin, Gale Storm

Take one fresh and tender kiss.
Add one stolen night of bliss.
One girl, one boy:
Some grief, some joy.
Memories are made of this.

Don't forget a small moonbeam.
Fold in lightly with a dream.
Your lips and mine,
Two sips of wine.
Memories are made of this.

Then add the wedding bells,
One house where lovers dwell,
Three little kids for the flavor.
Stir carefully thru the days;
See how the flavor stays,
These are the dreams you will savor.

With the blessings from above,
Serve it generously with love.
One man, one love, thru life,
Memories are made of this.

Memories of You

Lyric by Andy Razaf
Music by Eubie Blake

a standard recorded by Ethel Waters, Glen Gray, Bud Freeman, Benny Goodman, Frank Sinatra, Anita O'Day and various other artists

Why can't I forget like I should?
Heaven knows I would if I could,
But I just can't keep you off my mind.
Tho' you've gone and love was in vain,
All around me you still remain;
Wonder why fate should be so unkind.

Refrain:
Waking skies
At sunrise,
Every sunset, too,
Seems to be
Bringing me
Memories of you.
Here and there,
Everywhere,
Scenes that we once knew,
And they all
Just recall
Memories of you.
How I wish I could forget those happy yesteryears,
That have left a rosary of tears.
Your face beams
In my dreams,
Spite of all I do,
Everything
Seems to bring
Memories of you.

Repeat Refrain

Memory

Music by Andrew Lloyd Webber
Text by Trevor Nunn after T.S. Eliot

from the musical *Cats*

Midnight.
Not a sound from the pavement.
Has the moon lost her memory?
She is smiling alone.
In the lamp-light
The withered leaves collect at my feet
And the wind
Begins to moan.

Memory.
All alone in the moonlight
I can smile at the old days,
I was beautiful then.
I remember
The time I knew what happiness was,
Let the memory
Live again.

Ev'ry street lamp seems to beat
A fatalistic warning.
Someone mutters
And a street lamp gutters
And soon it will be morning.

Daylight.
I must wait for the sunrise.
I must think of a new life
And I mustn't give in.
When the dawn comes
Tonight will be a memory too
And a new day
Will begin.

Burnt out ends of smoky days
The stale cold smell of the morning;
The street lamp dies
Another night is over,
Another day is dawning.

Touch me.
It's so easy to leave me
All alone with the memory
Of my days in the sun.
If you touch me
You'll understand what happiness is.
Look, a new day
Has begun.

Mercy, Mercy Me (The Ecology)

Words and Music by Marvin Gaye

recorded by Marvin Gaye

Woo, ah,
Mercy, mercy me.
Ah, things ain't what they used to be.
No, no, where did all the blue skies go,
Poison is the wind that blows
From the north and south and east.

Wo, mercy, mercy me.
Ah, things ain't what they used to be, no, no
Oil wasted on the ocean and upon
Our seas' fish full of mercury, Ah.

Oh, mercy, mercy me.
Ah things ain't what they used to be.
No, no, no, radiation underground and in the sky;
Animals and birds who live nearby are dying.

Oh, mercy, mercy me.
Ah things ain't what they used to be.
What about this overcrowded land?
How much more abuse from man can she stand?

Oh na, na,
My sweet Lord,
No, no, na, na, na,
My, my sweet Lord.

Merry Christmas, Darling

Words and Music by Richard Carpenter and Frank Pooler

recorded by The Carpenters

Greeting cards have all been sent,
The Christmas rush is through,
But I still have one wish to make,
A special one for you;
Merry Christmas darling,
We're apart that's true;
But I can dream and in my dreams,
I'm Christmasing with you.
Holidays are joyful,
There's always something new;
But every day's a holiday,
When I'm near to you.

Refrain:
The lights are on my tree,
I wish you could see,
I wish it every day.
The logs on the fire fill me with desire,
To see you and to say;
That I wish you a Merry Christmas,
Happy New Year too;
I've just one wish on this Christmas eve;
I wish I were with you.

Repeat Refrain

I wish I were with you.

Message in a Bottle
Written and Composed by Sting

recorded by The Police

Just a castaway,
An island lost at sea-o.
Anuzzer lonely day
No one here but me-o.
More loneliness than any man could bear.
Rescue me before I fall into despair-o.

Refrain:
I'll send an S.O.S. to the world.
I'll send an S.O.S. to the world.
I hope that someone gets my,
I hope that someone gets my,
I hope that someone gets my
Message in a bottle, yeah,
Message in a bottle, yeah.

A year has passed since I wrote my note,
But I should have known this right from the start.
Only hope can keep me together.
Love can mend your life, but love can break your heart.

Refrain

Walked out this morning,
I don't believe what I saw.
A hundred billion bottles washed up on the shore.
Seems like I'm not alone in being alone.
A hundred billion castaways looking for a home.

Refrain

I'm sending out an S.O.S.

Michelle
Words and Music by John Lennon and Paul McCartney

recorded by The Beatles

Michelle, ma belle,
These are words that go together well,
My Michelle.

Refrain:
Michelle, ma belle,
Sont les mots qui vont très bien ensemble,
Très bien ensemble.

I love you, I love you, I love you,
That's all I want to say.
Until I find a way,
I will say the only words I know that you'll understand.

Refrain

I need to, I need to, I need to,
I need to make you see,
Oh, what you mean to me.
Until I do I'm hoping you will know what I mean.
I love you.

I want you, I want you, I want you,
I think you know by now.
I'll get to you somehow.
Until I do I'm telling you so you'll understand.

Refrain

And I will say the only words I know that you'll understand;
My Michelle.

Midnight Sun

Words and Music by Lionel Hampton, Sonny Burke and Johnny Mercer

a standard recorded by Lionel Hampton and various other artists

Your lips were like a red and ruby ice,
Warmer than the summer night,
The clouds were like an alabaster palace
Rising to a snowy height.
Each star its own aurora borealis,
Suddenly you held me tight,
I could see the midnight sun.

I can't explain the silver rain that found me,
Or was that a moonlit veil?
The music of the universe around me,
Or was that a nightingale?
And then your arms miraculously found me,
Suddenly the sky turned pale,
I could see the midnight sun.

Was there such a night,
It's a thrill I still don't quite believe,
But after you were gone,
There was still some star-dust on my sleeve.

The flame of it may dwindle to an ember,
And the stars forget to shine,
And we may see the meadow in December,
Icy white and crystalline.
But, oh, my darling always I'll remember,
When your lips were close to mine,
And we saw the midnight sun.

Miss You

Words and Music by Mick Jagger and Keith Richards

recorded by The Rolling Stones

I've been holding out so long,
I've been sleeping all alone,
Lord I miss you.
I've been hanging on the phone,
I've been sleeping all alone,
I want to kiss you.

Hoo hoo hoo hoo…

Well, I've been haunted in my sleep,
You've been starring in my dreams,
Lord I miss you, child.
I've been waiting in the hall,
Been waiting on your call
When the phone rings.

Spoken:
It's just some friends of mine that say,
"Hey, what's the matter man?
We're gonna come around at twelve o'clock
With some Puerto Rican girls
That are just dyin' to meet you.
We're gonna bring a case of wine,
Hey, let's go mess and fool around,
You know we used to."

Sung:
Ha ha ha…

Everybody waits so long,
Oh! Baby, why you wait so long?
Won't you come on?
Come on!

Spoken:
I've been walking in Central Park,
Singing after dark,
People think I'm crazy.
I've been stumbling on my feet,
Shuffling thro' the street
Asking people,
"What's the matter with you, Jim boy?"
Sometimes what I want to say to myself,
Sometimes I say:

Sung:
Hoo hoo hoo hoo…

I guess I'm lying to myself,
It's just you and no one else,
Lord I won't miss you child.
You've just been blotting out my mind,
Fooling on my time,
No I won't miss you baby.
Lord I miss your touch.
Oh ooh.
Ha ha ha ha…

Missing You

Words and Music by John Waite, Charles Sanford and Mark Leonard

recorded by John Waite, Tina Turner, Brooks & Dunn

Missing you. Missing you.

Every time I think of you,
I always catch my breath.
And I'm still standing here,
And you're miles away,
And I'm wonderin' why you left.

And there's a storm that's ragin'
Through my frozen heart tonight.
I hear your name
In certain circles,
And it always makes me smile.
I spend my time
Thinkin' about you,
And it's almost drivin' me wild.
And there's a heart that's breakin'
Down this long distance line tonight.

I ain't missin' you at all
Since you've been gone away.
I ain't missin' you,
No matter what I might say.

There's a message in the wire,
And I'm sending you this signal tonight.
You don't know how desperate I've become,
And it looks like I'm losin' this fight.

In your world I have no meaning,
Though I'm trying hard to understand.
And it's my heart that's breakin'
Down this long distance line tonight.

I ain't missin' you at all
Since you've been gone away.
I ain't missin' you,
No matter what my friends say.

And there's a message that I'm sendin' out,
Like a telegraph to your soul.
And if I can't bridge this distance,
Stop this heartbreak overload.
And…

I ain't missin' you at all
Since you've been gone away.
I ain't missin' you,
No matter what my friends say.

Mississippi Queen
Words and Music by Leslie West, Felix Pappalardi,
Corky Laing and David Rea
Copyright © 1970 by BMG Songs, Inc.
Copyright Renewed

recorded by Mountain

Mississippi Queen,
If you know what I mean
Mississippi Queen,
She taught me everything.

Way down around Bicksburg,
Around Louisiana way,
Lives a Cajun lady
Called the Mississippi Queen.

Refrain:
You know she was a dancer,
She moved better on wine.
While the rest of them dudes was gettin' their kicks,
Buddy, beg your pardon, I was gettin' mine.

Mississippi Queen,
If you know what I mean.
Mississippi Queen,
She taught me everything.

This lady, she asked me,
If I would be her man.
You know that I told her
I'd do what I can
To keep her lookin' pretty,
Buy her dresses that shine.
While the rest of them dudes was makin' their bread,
Buddy, beg your pardon, I was losin' mine.

Refrain

Hey, Mississippi Queen.

Mister Sandman
Lyric and Music by Pat Ballard
© 1954 (Renewed) EDWIN H. MORRIS & COMPANY,
A Division of MPL Communications, Inc.

recorded by The Chordettes, Emmylou Harris

Boy:
Mister Sandman, bring me a dream,
Make her complexion like peaches and cream.
Give her two lips like roses in clover,
Then tell me that my lonesome nights are over.

Girl:
Mister Sandman, bring me a dream,
Make him the cutest that I've ever seen.
Give him the word that I'm not a rover,
Then tell me that my lonesome nights are over.

Refrain (both versions):
Sandman, I'm so alone;
Don't have nobody to call my own.
Please turn on your magic beam,
Mister Sandman, bring me a dream.

Mr. Wonderful

Words and Music by Jerry Bock, Larry Holofcener and George David Weiss

from the musical *Mr. Wonderful*
recorded by Sarah Vaughan, Peggy Lee and other artists

Why this feeling?
Why this glow?
Why the thrill when you say, "Hello!"?
It's a strange and tender magic you do.
Mr. Wonderful,
That's you!

Why this trembling when you speak?
Why this joy when you touch my cheek?
I must tell you what my heart knows is true:
Mr. Wonderful, that's you!

And why this longing to know your charms;
To spend forever here in your arms!
Oh! there's much more I could say,
But the words keep slipping away;
And I'm left with only one point of view:
Mr. Wonderful,
That's you!

One more thing, then I'm through;
Mr. Wonderful,
Mr. Wonderful,
Mr. Wonderful, I love you!

Misty

Words by Johnny Burke
Music by Erroll Garner

a standard recorded by Johnny Mathis and various other artists

Look at me,
I'm as helpless as a kitten up a tree,
And I feel like I'm clinging to a cloud,
I can't understand,
I get misty just holding your hand.

Walk my way,
And a thousand violins begin to play,
Or it might be the sound of your hello,
That music I hear,
I get misty, the moment you're near.

You can say that you're leading me on,
But it's just what I want you to do,
Don't you notice how hopelessly I'm lost,
That's why I'm following you.

On my own,
Would I wander through this wonderland alone,
Never knowing my right foot from my left,
My hat from my glove,
I'm too misty and too much in love.

Mona Lisa

Words and Music by Jay Livingston and Ray Evans

from the Paramount Picture *Captain Carey, U.S.A.*
a standard recorded by Nat "King" Cole and various other artists

In a villa in a little old Italian town
Lives a girl whose beauty shames the rose.
Many yearn to love her but their hopes all tumble down.
What does she want?
No one knows.

Refrain:
Mona Lisa, Mona Lisa men have named you.
You're so like the lady with the mystic smile.
Is it only 'cause you're lonely they have blamed you
For that Mona Lisa's strangeness in your smile?

Do you smile to tempt a lover, Mona Lisa,
Or is this your way to hide a broken heart?
Many dreams have been brought to your doorstep.
They just lie there, and they die there.
Are you warm, are you real, Mona Lisa,
Or just a cold and lonely, lovely work of art?

Refrain

Mood Indigo

Words and Music by Duke Ellington, Irving Mills and
Albany Bigard

featured in the musical revue *Sophisticated Ladies*
a standard recorded by Duke Ellington and various other
artists

You ain't been blue,
No, no, no.
You ain't been blue,
'Til you've had that Mood Indigo.
That feeling goes stealin' down to my shoes,
While I sit and sigh:
"Go 'long, blues."

Refrain:
Always get that mood indigo,
Since my baby said goodbye.
In the evenin' when lights are low,
I'm so lonesome I could cry,
'Cause there's nobody who cares about me,
I'm just a soul who's bluer than blue can be.
When I get that mood indigo,
I could lay me down and die.

Refrain

Moon River

Words by Johnny Mercer
Music by Henry Mancini

from the Paramount Picture *Breakfast at Tiffany's*
recorded by Andy Williams and various other artists

Moon River, wider than a mile;
I'm crossing you in style someday.
Old dream maker, you heart breaker,
Wherever you're goin', I'm goin' your way.

Two drifters, off to see the world.
There's such a lot of world to see.
We're after the same rainbow's end.
Waitin' 'round the bend,
My Huckleberry friend,
Moon River and me.

Moonlight Becomes You

Words by Johnny Burke
Music by James Van Heusen

from the Paramount Picture *Road to Morocco*
a standard recorded by Glenn Miller, Harry James,
Frank Sinatra and various other artists

Stand there just a moment, darling,
Let me catch my breath.
I've never seen a picture quite so lovely.
How did you ever learn to look so lovely?

Moonlight becomes you,
It goes with your hair,
You certainly know the right thing to wear.

Moonlight becomes you,
I'm thrilled at the sight.
And I could get so romantic tonight.

You're all dressed up to go dreaming,
Now don't tell me I'm wrong,
And what a night to go dreaming,
Mind if I tag along?

If I say I love you,
I want you to know
It's not just because there's moonlight,
Although moonlight becomes you.

Moonlight Cocktail

Lyric by Kim Gannon
Music by Lucky Roberts

from the film *A Night in Casablanca*
a standard recorded by Glenn Miller with Ray Eberle and
various other artists

Coupl'a jiggers of moonlight and add a star.
Pour in the blue of a June night and one guitar.
Mix in a coupl'a dreamers and there you are.
Lovers hail the moonlight cocktail.

Now add a coupl'a flowers, a drop of dew,
Stir for a coupl'a hours till dreams come true.
As to the number of kisses, it's up to you.
Moonlight cocktails need a few.

Cool it in the summer breeze,
Serve it in the starlight underneath the trees.
You'll discover tricks like these
Are sure to make your moonlight cocktail please.

Follow the simple directions and they will bring
Life of another complexion, where you'll be king.
You will awake in the morning and start to sing.
Moonlight cocktails are the thing.

More (Ti guardero' nel cuore)

Music by Nino Oliviero and Riz Ortolani
Italian Lyrics by Marcello Ciorciolini
English Lyrics by Norman Newell
Copyright © 1962 by C.A.M. S.r.l. - Rome (Italy), Via Cola di Rienzo, 152

from the film *Mondo Cane*
recorded by Kai Winding, Vic Dana and various
other artists

More than the greatest love the world has known;
This is the love I'll give to you alone.
More than the simple words I try to say;
I only live to love you more each day.

More than you'll ever know,
My arms long to hold you so,
My life will be in your keeping,
Walking, sleeping, laughing, weeping.

Longer than always is a long, long time,
But far beyond forever you'll be mine.
I know I never lived before,
And my heart is very sure,
No one else could love you more.

More Than Words

Words and Music by Nuno Bettencourt and Gary Cherone
Copyright © 1990 COLOR ME BLIND MUSIC
All Rights Administered by ALMO MUSIC CORP.

recorded by Extreme

Sayin', "I love you"
Is not the words I want to hear from you.
It's not that I want you not to say.
But if you only knew how easy it would be,
To show me how you feel,
More than words is all you have to do to make it real.
Then you wouldn't have to say that you love me,
'Cause I'd already know.

Refrain:
What would you do if my heart was torn in two?
More than words to show you feel
That your love for me is real.
What would you say if I took those words away?
Then you couldn't make things new
Just by sayin', "I love you."

La di da da di da…
More than words.

Now that I have tried to talk to you
And make you understand.
All you have to do is close your eyes
And just reach out your hands.
And touch me, hold me close, don't ever let me go.

More than words is all I ever needed you to show.
Then you wouldn't have to say
That you love me,
'Cause I'd already know.

Refrain

More than words.

More Than You Know

Words by William Rose and Edward Eliscu
Music by Vincent Youmans
Copyright © 1929 by Chappell & Co., WB Music Corp. and LSQ Music
Copyright Renewed
All Rights for LSQ Music Administered by The Songwriters Guild Of America

from the musical *Great Day!*
a standard recorded by Billie Holiday and various other
artists

Whether you are here or yonder,
Whether you are false or true,
Whether you remain or wander
I'm growing fonder of you.

Even though your friends forsake you,
Even though you don't succeed,
Wouldn't I be glad to take you,
Give you the break you need.

More than you know,
More than you know,
Man o' my heart, I love you so.
Lately I find you're on my mind,
More than you know.

Whether you're right,
Whether you're wrong,
Man o' my heart I'll string along.
You need me so
More than you'll ever know.

Loving you the way that I do
There's nothing I can do about it,
Loving may be all you can give
But honey, I can't live without it.

Oh, how I'd cry,
Oh, how I'd cry,
If you got tired and said, "Goodbye,"
More than I'd show
More than you'd ever know.

The Most Beautiful Girl in the World

Words by Lorenz Hart
Music by Richard Rodgers
Copyright © 1935 by Williamson Music and Lorenz Hart Publishing Co. in the United States
Copyright Renewed
All Rights Administered by Williamson Music

from the musical *Jumbo*

We used to spend the spring together
Before we learned to walk;
We used to laugh and sing together
Before we learned how to talk.
With no reason for the season,
Spring would end as it would start.
Now the season has a reason
And there's springtime in my heart.

Refrain:
The most beautiful girl in the world
Picks my ties out,
Eats my candy,
Drinks my brandy—
The most beautiful girl in the world.
The most beautiful girl in the world
Isn't Garbo, isn't Dietrich,
But the sweet trick
Who can make me believe it's a beautiful world.
Social, not a bit,
Natural kind of wit.
She'd shine anywhere,
And she hasn't got platinum hair.
The most beautiful house in the world
Has a mortgage—
What do I care?
It's goodbye care
When my slippers are next to the ones that belong
To the one and only beautiful girl in the world.

Movin' Out (Anthony's Song)

Words and Music by Billy Joel
© 1977, 1981 IMPULSIVE MUSIC

recorded by Billy Joel

Anthony works in the grocery store,
Savin' his pennies for someday.
Mama Leone left a note on the door,
She said, "Sonny move out to the country."
Ah, but working too hard can give you a heart attack
Ack ack ack ack ack
You ought to know by now.
Who needs a house out in Hackensack?
Is that all you get for money?

Refrain:
And it seems such a waste of time,
If that's what it's all about.
Mama, if that's movin' up then I'm
Movin' out.
Mm, I'm movin' out.
Mm, Oo Oo, Oh Huh, Mm Hm.

You should never argue with a crazy
Mi mi mi mi mi mind
You ought to know by now.
You can pay Uncle Sam with the overtime.
Is that all you get for your money?
And if that's what you have in mind
Then that's what you're all about.
Good luck movin' up 'cause I'm
Movin' out.
Mm I'm movin' out

Sergeant O'Leary is walkin' the beat,
At night he becomes a bartender.
He works at Mister Cacciatore's down on Sullivan Street
Across from the medical center.
And he's tradin' in his Chevy for a Cadillac
Ack ack ack ack ack.
You ought to know by now.
If he can't drive with a broken back,
At least he can polish the fenders.

Refrain

I'm movin' out.
I'm movin' out.

The Music of the Night

Music by Andrew Lloyd Webber
Lyrics by Charles Hart
Additional Lyrics by Richard Stilgoe
© Copyright 1986 The Really Useful Group Ltd.
All Rights for the United States and Canada Administered by
    Universal - PolyGram International Publishing, Inc.

from the musical *The Phantom of the Opera*

Night-time sharpens, heightens each sensation;
Darkness stirs and wakes imagination.
Silently the senses abandon their defenses.
Slowly, gently night unfurls its splendor;
Grasp it, sense it, tremulous and tender.
Turn your face away from the garish light of day,
Turn your thoughts away from cold unfeeling light
And listen to the music of the night.

Close your eyes and surrender to your darkest dreams!
Purge your thoughts of the life you knew before!
Close your eyes, let your spirit start to soar,
And you'll live as you've never lived before.

Softly, deftly, music shall caress you.
Hear it, feel it secretly possess you.
Open up your mind, let your fantasies unwind
In this darkness which you know you cannot fight,
The darkness of the music of the night.

Let your mind start a journey through a strange, new world;
Leave all thoughts of the world you knew before.
Let your soul take you where you long to be!
Only then can you belong to me.

Floating, falling, sweet intoxication.
Touch me, trust me, savour each sensation.
Let the dream begin, let your darker side give in
To the power of the music that I write,
The power of the music of the night.

You alone can make my song take flight,
Help me make the music of the night.

My All
Words by Mariah Carey
Music by Mariah Carey and Walter Afanasieff

recorded by Mariah Carey

I am thinking of you
In my sleepless solitude tonight.
If it's wrong to love you,
Then my heart just won't let me be right
'Cause I've drowned in you
And I won't pull through
Without you by my side.

Refrain:
I'd give my all to have
Just one more night with you.
I'd risk my life to feel
Your body next to mine,
'Cause I can't go on
Living in the memory of our song.
I'd give my all for your love tonight.

Baby, can you feel me
Imagining I'm looking in your eyes?
I can see you clearly,
Vividly emblazoned in my mind,
And yet you're so far,
Like a distant star
I'm wishing on tonight.

Refrain Twice

Give my all for your love tonight.

My Blue Heaven
Lyric by George Whiting
Music by Walter Donaldson

a standard recorded by Eddie Cantor, Gene Austin,
Fats Domino and various other artists
featured in the films *Never a Dull Moment, Moon Over
Las Vegas, My Blue Heaven, Love Me or Leave Me,* and
the television series *M*A*S*H*

Day is ending,
Birds are wending
Back to the shelter of
Each little nest they love.
Night shades falling,
Love birds calling,
What makes the world go 'round?
Nothing but love!

Refrain:
When whippoorwills call
And evening is nigh
I hurry to my blue heaven.
A turn to the right,
A little white light
Will lead you to my blue heaven.
You'll see a smiling face,
A fireplace,
A cozy room,
A little nest that's nestled,
Where the roses bloom.
Just Mollie and me
And baby makes three.
We're happy in my blue heaven.

Moonbeams creeping,
Flowers are sleeping
Under a star-lit way,
Waiting another day.
Time for resting,
Birds are nesting,
Resting their weary wings,
Tired from play.

Refrain

My Coloring Book
Words and Music by Fred Ebb and John Kander

recorded by Barbra Streisand

In case you fancy coloring books,
And lots of people do,
I've a new one for you.
A most unusual coloring book, the kind you never see.
Crayons ready? Very well. Begin to color me.

These are the eyes that watched him
As he walked away.
Color them grey.
This is the heart that thought he would always be true.
Color it blue.
These are the arms that held him and touched him,
Then lost him somehow.
Color them empty now.
These are the beads I wore
Until she came between,
Color them green.

This is the room I sleep in and walk in and weep in
And hide in that nobody sees,
Color it lonely, please.
This is the man, the one I depended upon.
Color him gone.

My Father's Eyes
Words and Music by Eric Clapton

recorded by Eric Clapton

Sailing down behind the sun,
Waiting for my prince to come.
Praying for the healing rain
To restore my soul again.

Just a toe rag on the run.
How did I get here?
What have I done?
When will all my hopes arise?
How will I know him
When I look in…

Refrain:
My father's eyes,
(Look into my father's eyes.)
My father's eyes.
When I look in my father's eyes.
(Look into my father's eyes.)
My father's eyes.

Then the light begins to shine
And I hear those ancient lullabies.
And as I watch this seedling grow,
Feel my heart start to overflow.

Where do I find the words to say?
How do I teach him?
What do we play?
Bit by bit I'd realize
That's when I need them
That's when I need them
That's when I need…

Refrain

Then the jagged edge appears
Through the distant clouds of tears.
And I'm like a bridge that was washed away.
My foundations were made of clay.

And as my soul slides down to die,
How could I lose him?
What did I try?
Bit by bit I'd realize
That he was here with me.
I looked into…

Refrain Twice

My Favorite Things
Lyrics by Oscar Hammerstein II
Music by Richard Rodgers

from the musical *The Sound of Music*
a standard recorded by various artists

Raindrops on roses and whiskers on kittens.
Bright copper kettles and warm woolen mittens.
Brown paper packages tied up with strings,
These are a few of my favorite things.

Cream-colored ponies and crisp apple strudels,
Doorbells and sleigh-bells and schnitzel with noodles,
Wild geese that fly with the moon on their wings,
These are a few of my favorite things.

Girls in white dresses with blue satin sashes,
Snowflakes that stay on my nose and eyelashes,
Silver white winters that melt into springs,
These are a few of my favorites things.

When the dog bites,
When the bees stings,
When I'm feeling sad,
I simply remember my favorite things
And then I don't feel so bad!

My Foolish Heart
Words by Ned Washington
Music by Victor Young

from the film *My Foolish Heart*
a standard recorded by Billy Eckstine and various other
artists

The night is like a lovely tune,
Beware my foolish heart!
How white the ever constant moon;
Take care my foolish heart!
There's a line between love and fascination
That's hard to see on an evening such as this,
For they both give the very same sensation
When you're lost in the magic of a kiss.

His {Her} lips are much too close to mine,
Beware my foolish heart;
But should our eager lips combine
Then let the fire start.
For this time it isn't fascination,
Or a dream that will fade and fall apart,
It's love this time, it's love, my foolish heart.

My Funny Valentine
Words by Lorenz Hart
Music by Richard Rodgers

from the musical *Babes in Arms*
a standard recorded by many various artists

Behold the way our fine-feathered friend
His virtue doth parade.
Though knowest not, my dim-witted friend,
The picture thou hast made.
Thy vacant brow and thy tousled hair
Conceal thy good intent.
Thou noble, upright, truthful, sincere,
And slightly dopey gent, you're...

My funny Valentine,
Sweet comic Valentine,
You make me smile with my heart.
Your looks are laughable,
Unphotographable,
Yet you're my favorite work of art.
Is your figure less than Greek?
Is your mouth a little weak?
When you open it to speak
Are you smart?
But don't change a hair for me,
Not if you care for me,
Stay, little Valentine, stay!
Each day is Valentine's Day.

My Girl
Words and Music by William "Smokey" Robinson and
Ronald White

recorded by The Temptations

I've got sunshine
On a cloudy day;
When it's cold outside,
I've got the month of May.

Refrain:
I guess you say,
What can make me fell this way?
My girl,
Talking 'bout my girl.

I've got so much honey, the bees envy me;
I've got a sweeter song than the birds in the tree.

Refrain

I don't need no money, fortune or fame.
I've got all the riches, baby,
One man can claim.

Refrain

I've got sunshine on a cloudy day
With my girl;
I've even got the month of May
With my girl.
Talking 'bout, talking 'bout, talking 'bout
My girl.
Woo! My girl.
That's all I can talk about is my girl.

My Guy
Words and Music by William "Smokey" Robinson

recorded by Mary Wells

Nothing you could say can tear me away from my guy.
Nothing you could do 'cause I'm stuck like glue to my guy.
I'm sticking to my guy like a stamp to a letter.
Like birds of a feather, we stick together.
I can tell you from the start
I can't be torn apart
From my guy.

Nothing you could do could make me untrue to my guy.
Nothing you could buy could make me tell a lie to my guy.
I gave my guy my word of honor.
To be faithful and I'm gonna.
You best be believing,
I won't be deceiving
My guy.

As a matter of opinion I think he's tops.
My opinion is he's the cream of the crop.
As a matter of taste to be exact,
He's my ideal as a matter of fact.

No muscle-bound man could take my hand from my guy.
No handsome face could ever take the place of my guy.
He may not be a movie star,
But when it comes to being happy, we are.
There's not a man today
Who could take me away
From my guy.

My Heart Belongs to Daddy

Words and Music by Cole Porter

from the musical *Leave It to Me!*

I used to fall
In love with all
Those boys who maul
Refined ladies.
But now I tell
Each young gazelle
To go to hell—
I mean, Hades.
For since I've come to care
For such a sweet millionaire.

Refrain 1:
While tearing off
A game of golf
I may make a play for the caddy.
But when I do,
I don't follow through
'Cause my heart belongs to Daddy.
If I invite
A boy, some night,
To dine on my fine finnan haddie,
I just adore
His asking for more,
But my heart belongs to Daddy.
Yes, my heart belongs to Daddy,
So I simply couldn't be bad.
Yes, my heart belongs to Daddy,
Da-da, da-da-da, da-da-da, dad!
So I want to warn you, laddie,
Tho' I know you're perfectly swell,
That my heart belongs to Daddy
'Cause my Daddy, he treats it so well.

Refrain 2:
Saint Patrick's Day,
Although I may
Be seen wearing green with a paddy,
I'm always sharp
When playing the harp,
'Cause my heart belongs to Daddy.
Though other dames
At football games
May long for a strong undergraddy,
I never dream
Of making the team
'Cause my heart belongs to Daddy.
Yes, my heart belongs to Daddy.
So I simply couldn't be bad.
Yes, my heart belongs to Daddy,
Da-da, da-da-da, da-da-da, dad!
So I want to warn you laddie,

Tho' I simply hate to be frank,
That I can't be mean to Daddy
'Cause my Da-da-da-daddy might spank.
In matters artistic
He's not modernistic
So Da-da-da-daddy might speak.

My Heart Stood Still

Words by Lorenz Hart
Music by Richard Rodgers

from the musical *A Connecticut Yankee*
a standard recorded by various artists

Note: These are the original show lyrics

Martin:
I laughed at sweethearts
I met at schools;
All indiscreet hearts
Seemed romantic fools.
A house in Iceland
Was my heart's domain.
I saw your eyes;
Now castles rise in Spain!

Refrain:
I took one look at you,
That's all I meant to do,
And then my heart stood still!
My feet could step and walk,
My lips could move and talk,
And yet my heart stood still!
Though not a single word was spoken,
I could tell you knew,
That unfelt clasp of hands
Told me so well you knew.
I never lived at all
Until the thrill
Of that moment when
My heart stood still.

Sandy:
Through all my schooldays
I hated boys;
Those April Fool days
Brought me love-less joys.
I read my Plato,
Love I thought a sin;
But since your kiss,
I'm reading Missus Glynn!

Refrain

My Heart Will Go On
(Love Theme from 'Titanic')

Music by James Horner
Lyric by Will Jennings

from the Paramount and Twentieth Century Fox Motion
Picture *Titanic*
recorded by Celine Dion

Every night in my dreams I see you, I feel you.
That is how I know you go on.
Far across the distance and spaces between us
You have come to show you go on.

Refrain:
Near, far, wherever you are,
I believe that the heart does go on.
Once more you open the door
And you're here in my heart,
And my heart will go on and on.

Love can touch us one time
And last for a lifetime,
And never let go till we're gone.
Love was when I loved you;
One true time I hold to.
In my life we'll always go on.

Refrain

You're here, there's nothing I fear
And I know that my heart will go on.
We'll stay forever this way.
You are safe in my heart,
And my heart will go on and on.

My Life

Words and Music by Billy Joel

recorded by Billy Joel

Got a call from an old friend, we used to be real close.
Said he couldn't go on the American way.
Closed the shop, sold the house,
Bought a ticket to the West Coast.
Now he gives them a stand up routine in L.A.

I don't need you to worry for me 'cause I'm alright.
I don't want you to tell me it's time to come home.
I don't care what you say anymore, this is my life.
Go ahead with your own life. Leave me alone.

Refrain:
I never said you had to offer me a second chance.
(I never said you had to)
I never said I was a victim of circumstance.
(I never said)
I still belong
(Still belong)
Don't get me wrong,
(Get me wrong)
You can speak your mind, but not on my time.

They will tell you you can't sleep alone in a strange place.
Then they'll tell you can't sleep with somebody else.
Ah, but sooner or later you sleep in your own space.
Either way it's okay to wake up with yourself.

I don't need you to worry for me 'cause I'm alright.
I don't want you to tell me it's time to come home.
I don't care what you say anymore, this is my life.
Go ahead with your own life. Leave me alone.

Refrain

I don't care what you say anymore this is my life.
Go ahead with your own life. Leave me alone.
(Keep it to yourself, it's my life.)
(Keep it to yourself, it's my life.)

My Love

Words and Music by McCartney

recorded by Paul McCartney

And when I go away
I know my heart can stay with my love.
It's understood
It's in the hands of my love,
And my love does it good,
Wo wo wo wo…
My love does it good.

And when the cupboard's bare,
I'll still find something there with my love.
It's understood
It's everywhere with my love,
And my love does it good,
Wo wo wo wo…
My love does it good.

Wo wo I love,
Oh wo, my love,
Only my love holds the other key to me,
Oh wo, my love,
Oh my love
Only my love does it good to me.
Wo wo wo wo…
My love does it good.

Don't ever ask me why
I never say goodbye to my love.
It's understood
It's everywhere with my love,
And my love does it good,
Wo wo wo wo…
My love does it good.

Wo wo, I love,
Oh wo, my love,
Only my love does it good to me.
Wo wo wo wo…

My Love Is Your Love
Words and Music by Wyclef Jean and Jerry Duplessis

recorded by Whitney Houston

Clap your hands ya'll, s'alright.

If tomorrow is judgement day
And I'm standing on the front line,
And the Lord asked me what I did with my life,
I will say I spent it with you.

Clap your hands ya'll, s'alright.
Clap your hands ya'll, s'alright.

If I wake up in World War Three,
I see destruction and poverty,
And I feel like I wanna go home,
It's okay if you're coming with me.

Clap your hands…
Three Times

Refrain:
'Cause your love is my love
And my love is your love.
It would take an eternity to break us,
And the chains of *Amistad* couldn't hold us.

Repeat Refrain

Clap your hands…
Three Times

If I lose my fame and fortune
And I'm homeless on the street,
And I'm sleeping in Grand Central Station,
It's okay if you're sleeping with me.

Twice:
Clap your hands…

As the years they pass us by,
We stay young through each other's eyes.
And no matter how old we get oh,
It's okay as long as I've got you, babe.

Twice:
Clap your hands…

If I should die this very day,
Don't cry 'cause on earth we wasn't meant to stay.
No, no, no, no.
And no matter what the people say,
I'll be waiting for you after judgment day.

Refrain Three Times

Repeat and Fade:
Clap your hands …

My Melancholy Baby
Words by George Norton
Music by Ernie Burnett

a standard recorded by Bing Crosby, Barbra Streisand and
many other various artists

Come sweetheart mine,
Don't sit and pine,
Tell me of the cares that make you feel so blue.
What have I done?
Answer me Hon',
Have I ever said an unkind word to you?
My love is true,
And just for you,
I'd do almost anything at any time.
Dear, when you sigh
Or when you cry,
Something seems to grip this very heart of mine.

Refrain:
Come to me my melancholy baby.
Cuddle up and don't be blue.
All your fears are foolish fancy, maybe,
You know dear that I'm in love with you.
Every cloud must have a silver lining.
Wait until the sun shines through.
Smile my honey dear,
While I kiss away each tear.
Or else I shall be melancholy too.

Birds in the trees,
Whispering breeze,
Should not fail to lull you into peaceful dreams.
So tell me why
Sadly you sigh
Sitting at the window where the pale moon beams,
You shouldn't grieve,
Try and believe,
Life is always sunshine when the heart beats true;
Be of good cheer,
Smile thro' your tears,
When you're sad it makes me feel the same as you.

Refrain

My Old Flame
Words and Music by Arthur Johnston and Sam Coslow

from the Paramount Picture *Belle of the Nineties*
a standard recorded by Duke Ellington, Mae West,
Billie Holiday, Spike Jones and various other artists

The music seemed to be so reminiscent;
I knew I'd heard it somewhere before.
I racked my recollections as I listened
When suddenly I remembered once more.

My old flame,
I can't even think of his name.
But it's funny now and then,
How my thoughts go flashing back again,
To my old flame.

My old flame,
My new lovers all seem so tame.
For I haven't met a gent
So magnificent or elegant
As my old flame.

I've met so many who had fascinatin' ways,
A fascinatin' gaze in their eyes;
Some who took me up to the skies.
But their attempts at love,
Were only imitations of

My old flame.
I can't even think of his name.
But I'll never be the same,
Until I discover what became of
My old flame.

My Prayer
Music by Georges Boulanger
Lyric and Musical Adaptation by Jimmy Kennedy

recorded by Ray Eberle with Glenn Miller, The Ink Spots
and The Platters

When the twilight is gone
And no song bird is singing;
When the twilight is gone
You come into my heart.
And here in my heart you will stay
While I pray.

My prayer is to linger with you,
At the end of the day,
In a dream that's divine.

My prayer is a rapture in blue,
With the world far away,
And your lips close to mine.

Tonight while our hearts are a-glow,
Oh! Tell me the words
That I'm longing to know.

My prayer and the answer you give,
May they still be the same,
For as long as we live;
That you'll always be there,
At the end of my prayer.

My Romance
Words by Lorenz Hart
Music by Richard Rodgers

from the musical *Jumbo*
a standard recorded by Morton Downey, Margaret Whiting,
Dave Brubeck, Doris Day and various other artists

I won't kiss your hand, madam,
Crazy for you though I am.
I'll never woo you on bended knee,
No, madam, not me.
We don't need that flowery fuss.
No sir, madam, not for us.

My romance
Doesn't have to have a moon in the sky.
My romance
Doesn't need a blue lagoon standing by.
No month of May,
No twinkling stars.
No hideaway,

No soft guitars.
My romance
Doesn't need a castle rising in Spain,
Nor a dance
To a constantly surprising refrain.
Wide awake,
I can make my most fantastic dreams come true.
My romance
Doesn't need a thing but you.

My Ship
Words by Ira Gershwin
Music by Kurt Weill

from the Musical Production *Lady in the Dark*

My ship has sails that are made of silk,
The decks are trimmed with gold.
And of jam and spice
There's a paradise
In the hold.

My ship's aglow with a million pearls
And rubies fill each bin.
The sun sits high
In a sapphire sky
When my ship comes in.

I can wait the years
'Til it appears
One fine day one spring,
But the pearls and such
They won't mean much
If there's missing just one thing.

I do not care if that day arrives,
That dream need never be,
If the ship I sing
Doesn't also bring
My own true love to me.

If the ship I sing
Doesn't also bring
My own true love to me.

(You Make Me Feel Like) A Natural Woman
Words and Music by Gerry Goffin, Carole King and Jerry Wexler

recorded by Aretha Franklin and Carole King

Lookin' out on the morning rain,
I used to feel uninspired.
And when I knew I'd have to face another day,
Lord, it made me feel so tired.
Before the day I met you,
Like was so unkind.
Your love was the key to my peace of mind,

Refrain 1:
'Cause you make me feel,
You make me feel,
You make me feel like a natural woman.
Oh, baby, what you've done to me!
(What you've done to me!)
You make me feel so good inside. (Good inside.)
And I just want to be (Want to be)
Close to you.
You make me feel so alive!

Refrain 2:
You make me feel,
You make me feel,
You make me feel like a natural, natural woman.

Repeat Refrain 2

When my soul was in the lost and found,
You came along to claim it.
I didn't know just what was wrong with me,
'Til your kiss helped me name it.
Now I'm no longer doubtful
Of what I'm living for,
'Cause if I make you happy
I don't need to do more,

Refrain 1

Refrain 2

A natural woman.

Nature Boy

Words and Music by Eden Ahbez

recorded by Nat "King" Cole

There was a boy,
A very strange, enchanted boy;
They say he wandered very far,
Very far over land and sea.
A little shy
And sad of eye,
But very wise was he.

And then one day,
One magic day, he passed my way
And as we spoke of many things,
Fools and kings,
This he said to me:
"The greatest thing
You'll ever learn
Is just to love and be loved in return."

The Nearness of You

Words by Ned Washington
Music by Hoagy Carmichael

from the Paramount Picture *Romance in the Dark*
a standard recorded by various artists

It's not the pale moon that excites me,
That thrills and delights me.
Oh no, it's just the nearness of you.

It isn't your sweet conversation
That brings this sensation,
Oh no, it's just the nearness of you.

When you're in my arms,
And I feel you so close to me,
All my wildest dreams come true.

I need no soft light to enchant me,
If only you'll grant me
The right
To hold you ever so tight,
And to feel in the night,
The nearness of you.

Never Been to Spain

Words and Music by Hoyt Axton

recorded by Three Dog Night

Well, I never been to Spain but I kinda like the music.
Say the ladies are insane there,
And they sure know how to use it.
They don't abuse it, never gonna lose it, I can't refuse it,
Mmm, mmm, mmm.

Well, I never been to England but I kinda like the Beatles.
Well, I headed for Las Vegas,
Only made it out to Needles.
Can you feel it?
Must be real, it feels so good, feels so good.

Refrain:
Well, I never been to heaven but I've been to Oklahoma.
Oh, they tell me I was born there,
But I really don't remember.
In Oklahoma not Arizona, what does it matter?
What does it matter?

Well, never been to Spain but I kinda like the music.
Say the ladies are insane there
And they sure know how to use it.
They don't abuse it, never gonna lose it, I can't refuse it.

Refrain

New Kid in Town

Words and Music by John David Souther, Don Henley and
Glenn Frey

recorded by The Eagles

There's talk on the street; it sounds so familiar.
Great expectations, everybody's watching you.
People you meet, they all seem to know you.
Even your old friends treat you like you're something new.
Johnny-come-lately, the new kid in town.
Everybody loves you, so don't let them down.

You look in her eyes; the music begins to play.
Hopeless romantics, here we go again.
But after a while you're looking the other way.
It's those restless hearts that never mend.
Johnny-come-lately, the new kid in town.
Will she still love you when you're not around?

There's so many things you should have told her,
But night after night you're willing to hold her,
Just hold her.
Tears on your shoulder.

There's talk on the street; it's there to remind you
That it doesn't really matter which side you're on.

You're walking away and they're talking behind you.
They will never forget you till somebody new comes along.

Where you been lately?
There's a new kid in town.
Everybody loves him, don't they?
No he's holding her, and you're still around.
Oh, my, my.

There's a new kid in town,
Just another new kid in town.
Ooh, hoo.
Everybody's talking 'bout the new kid in town,
Ooh, hoo.
Everybody's walking like the new kid in town.
There's a new kid in town.
I don't want to hear it. There's a new kid in town.
I don't want to hear it. There's a new kid in town.

New York State of Mind
Words and Music by Billy Joel
© 1975, 1978 JOEL SONGS

recorded by Billy Joel

Some folks like to get away,
Take a holiday
From the neighborhood,
Hop a flight to Miami Beach or to Hollywood.
But I'm takin' a Greyhound on the Hudson River line.
I'm in a New York state of mind.

I've seen all the movie stars
In their fancy cars
And their limousines,
Been high in the Rockies under the evergreens.
But I know what I'm needin',
And I don't want to waste more time.
I'm in a New York state of mind.

Refrain:
It was so easy livin' day by day,
Out of touch with the rhythm and blues.
And now I need a little give and take.
The New York Times and the *Daily News.*

Comes down to reality,
And it's fine with me 'cause I've let it slide.
Don't care if it's Chinatown or on Riverside.
I don't have any reasons.
I've left them all behind.
I'm in a New York state of mind.

Refrain

Repeat Verse 3

I don't have any reasons.
I've left them all behind.
I'm in a New York state of mind.

The Next Time I Fall
Words and Music by Paul Gordon and Bobby Caldwell
© 1986 EMI BLACKWOOD MUSIC INC., SIN-DROME MUSIC, CHAPPELL & CO.
  and FRENCH SURF MUSIC
All Rights for SIN-DROME MUSIC Controlled and Administered by
  EMI BLACKWOOD MUSIC INC.
All Rights for FRENCH SURF MUSIC Controlled and Administered by CHAPPELL & CO.

recorded by Peter Cetera with Amy Grant

Love, like a road that never ends.
How it leads me back again
To heartache,
I'll never understand.
Darling, I put my heart upon the shelf
'Til the moment was right. And I tell myself

Refrain:
Next time I fall in love
I'll know better what to do.
Next time I fall in love,
Ooh, Ooh, Ooh.
The next time I fall in love,
The next time I fall in love
It will be with you.

Oh, now, as I look into your eyes,
Well, I wonder if it's wise
To hold you like I've wanted to before.

Tonight, ooh, I was thinking that you might
Be the one who breathes life in this heart of mine.

Refrain

(It will be with you.)
Next time I'm gonna follow through.
And if it drives me crazy,
I will know better why
The next time I try.

Refrain Twice

Night Fever
Words and Music by Barry Gibb, Maurice Gibb and
Robin Gibb
Copyright © 1977 by Gibb Brothers Music
All Rights Administered by Careers-BMG Music Publishing, Inc.

from the film *Saturday Night Fever*
recorded by The Bee Gees

Listen to the ground;
There is movement all around.
There is something goin' down,
And I can feel it.
On the waves of the air,
There is dancin' out there.
If it's somethin' we can share,
We can steal it.

Refrain:
And that sweet city woman,
She moves through the light,
Controlling my mind and my soul.
When you reach out for me, yeah,
And the feelin' is bright,
Then I get night fever, night fever.
We know how to do it.
Gimme that night fever, night fever,
We know how to show it.
Here I am,
Prayin' for this moment to last,
Livin' on the music so fine,
Borne on the wind,
Makin' it mine.
Night fever, night fever.
We know how to do it.
Gimme that night fever, night fever.
We know how to show it.

In the heat of our love,
Don't need no help for us to make it.
Gimme just enough to take us to the mornin'.
I got the fire in my mind.
I got higher in my walkin'.
And I'm glowin' in the dark;
I give you warnin'.

Repeat Refrain

Night fever, night fever.
We know how to do it.
Gimme that night fever, night fever,
We know how to show it...

A Nightingale Sang in Berkeley Square
Lyric by Eric Maschwitz
Music by Manning Sherwin
Copyright © 1940 The Peter Maurice Music Co., Ltd., London, England
Copyright Renewed and Assigned to Shapiro, Bernstein & Co., Inc.,
    New York for U.S.A. and Canada

a standard recorded by various artists

Note: Berkeley is pronounced Barkly

That certain night, the night we met,
There was magic abroad in the air.
There were angels dining at the Ritz,
And a nightingale sang in Berkeley Square.

I may be right, I may be wrong,
But I'm perfectly willing to swear
That when you turned and smiled at me
A nightingale sang in Berkeley Square.

The moon that lingered over London town,
Poor puzzled moon, he wore a frown.
How could he know we two were so in love?
The whole darn world seemed upside down.

The streets of town were paved with stars
It was such a romantic affair.
And as we kissed and said "goodnight,"
A nightingale sang in Berkeley Square.

How strange it was, how sweet and strange,
There was never a dream to compare
With that hazy, crazy night we met,
When a nightingale sang in Berkeley Square.

This heart of mine beats loud and fast,
Like a merry-go-round in a fair,
For we were dancing cheek to cheek
And a nightingale sang in Berkeley Square.

When dawn came stealing up all gold and blue
To interrupt our rendezvous,
I still remember how you smiled and said,
"Was that a dream or was it true?"

Our homeward step was just as light
As the tap-dancing feet of Astaire
And like an echo far away,
A nightingale sang in Berkeley Square.

I know 'cause I was there,
That night in Berkeley Square.

Nights in White Satin
Words and Music by Justin Hayward
© Copyright 1967 (Renewed), 1968 (Renewed) and 1970 (Renewed)
    Tyler Music Ltd., London, England
TRO - Essex Music, Inc., New York, controls all publication rights for the U.S.A. and Canada

recorded by The Moody Blues

Nights in white satin,
Never reaching the end,
Letters I've written,
Never meaning to send.

Beauty I've always missed
With these before,
Just what the truth is
I can't say anymore.

'Cause I love you.
Yes, I love you.
Oh, how I love you.

Gazing at people,
Some hand in hand,
Jut what I'm going through,
They can't understand.

Some try to tell me
Thoughts they cannot defend,
Just what you want to be
You'll be in the end.

And I love you.
Yes, I love you.
Oh, how I love you.

No More "I Love You's"

Words and Music by David Freeman and Joseph Hughes

recorded by Annie Lennox

Do bi do bi do do do oh,…

I used to be lunatic from the gracious days.
I used to be woebegone
And so restless nights.
My aching heart would bleed for you to see.
Oh but now
I don't find myself bouncing home,
Whistling buttonhole tunes to make me cry,

Refrain:
No more "I love you's"
A language is leaving me.
No more "I love you's"
Changes are shifting outside the words.
(The lover speaks about the monsters.)

Do bi do bi…

I used to have demons in my room at night
Desire, despair, desire, so many monsters.
Oh but now
I don't find myself bouncing home
Whistling buttonhole tunes to make me cry.

No more "I love you's"
A language is leaving me.
No more "I love you's"
A language is leaving me in silence.
No more "I love you's"
Changes are shifting outside the words.

No more "I love you's"
A language is leaving me.
No more "I love you's."
Changes are shifting outside the words,
(Do bi do bi do do do oh)
Outside the words.
(Do bi do bi do do do oh.)

No Particular Place to Go

Words and Music by Chuck Berry

recorded by Chuck Berry

Riding along in my automobile,
My baby beside me at the wheel.
I stole a kiss at the turn of a mile,
My curiosity running wild.
Cruising and playing the radio,
With no particular place to go.

Riding along in my automobile,
I was anxious to tell her the way I feel.
So I told her softy and sincere,
And she leaned and whispered in my ear.
Cuddling more and driving slow,
With no particular place to go.

No particular place to go,
So we parked way out on the cocamo.
The night was young and the moon was gold,
So we both decided to take a stroll.
Can you imagine the way I felt?
I couldn't unfasten her seat belt.

Riding along in my calaboose,
Still trying to get her belt unloose.
All the way home I held a grudge,
For the safety belt that wouldn't budge.
Cruising and playing the radio,
With no particular place to go.

Nobody Loves Me Like You Do

Words by Pamela Phillips
Music by James P. Dunne

recorded by Anne Murray with Dave Loggins

Female:
Like a candle burning bright,
Love is glowing in your eyes.
A flame to light our way,
That burns brighter every day;
Now I have you;
Nobody loves me like you do.

Male:
Like a leaf upon the wind,
I could find no place to land.
I dreamed the hours away,
And wondered every day,
Do dreams come true?
Nobody loves me like you do.

Refrain
Both:
What if I never met you?
Where would I be right now?

Funny how life just falls in place somehow.
Male: You touched my heart in places
Female: That I never even knew.
Both: Nobody loves me like you do.

Male: I was words without a tune.
Female: I was a song still unsung.
Male: A poem with no rhyme,
Female: A dancer out of time.
Both:
But now there's you.
Nobody loves me like you do.

Refrain

Nobody loves me,
Nobody love me like you do.
Nobody loves me like you do.

Norwegian Wood
(This Bird Has Flown)
Words and Music by John Lennon and Paul McCartney

recorded by The Beatles

Refrain:
I once had a girl,
Or should I say
She once had me;
She showed me her room,
Isn't it good
Norwegian wood.

She asked me to stay and she told me to sit anywhere.
So I looked around and I noticed there wasn't a chair.

I sat on a rug
Biding my time,
Drinking her wine.
We talked until two
And then she said,
"It's time for bed."

Refrain

She told me she worked in the morning and started to laugh.
I told her I didn't and crawled off to sleep in the bath.

And when I awoke
I was alone,
This bird had flown.
So I lit a fire,
Isn't it good
Norwegian wood.

Nothing from Nothing
Words and Music by Billy Preston and Bruce Fisher

recorded by Billy Preston

Refrain:
Nothing from nothing leaves nothing,
You gotta have something if you wanna be with me.
Nothing from nothing leaves nothing,
You gotta have something if you wanna be with me.

I'm not tryin' to be your hero,
'Cause that zero is too cold for me.
I'm not tryin' to be your highness,
'Cause that minus is too low to see.

Nothing from nothing leaves nothing,
And I'm not stuffin', believe you me.
Don't you remember I told ya,
I'm a soldier in the war on poverty.

Refrain

Nowhere Man
Words and Music by John Lennon and Paul McCartney

recorded by The Beatles

He's a real nowhere man,
Sitting in his nowhere land,
Making all his nowhere plans for nobody.

Doesn't have a point of view,
Knows not where he's going to,
Isn't he a bit like you and me?

Nowhere man, please listen;
You don't know what you're missing.
Nowhere man,
The world is at your command.

He's as blind as he can be,
Just sees what he wants to see,
Nowhere man can you see me at all?

Nowhere man, don't worry,
Take you're time, don't hurry.
Leave it all
Till somebody else lends you a hand.

Doesn't have a point of view,
Knows not where he's going to.
Isn't he a bit like you and me?

Nowhere man please listen;
You don't know what you're missing,
Nowhere man,
The world is at your command.

He's a real nowhere man,
Sitting in his nowhere land,
Making all his nowhere plans for nobody,
Making all his nowhere plans for nobody,
Making all his nowhere plans for nobody.

Oh, Pretty Woman

Words and Music by Roy Orbison and Bill Dees

recorded by Roy Orbison, Van Halen

Pretty woman,
Walking down the street,
Pretty woman,
The kind I like to meet,
Pretty woman.
I don't believe you, you're not the truth.
No one could look as good as you.

Pretty woman,
Won't you pardon me,
Pretty woman,
I couldn't help but see,
Pretty woman,
That you look lovely as can be.
Are you lonely just like me?

Pretty woman, stop awhile,
Pretty woman, talk awhile,
Pretty woman, give your smile to me.
Pretty woman, yeah, yeah, yeah.

Pretty woman, look my way,
Pretty woman, say you'll stay with me.
'Cause I need you, I'll treat you right.
Come with me, baby.
Be mine tonight.

Pretty woman,
Don't walk on by,
Pretty woman,
Don't make me cry,
Pretty woman, don't walk away.
Hey, O.K.
If that's the way it must be, O.K.

I guess I'll go on home, it's late.
There'll be tomorrow night, but wait!
What do I see?
Is she walking back to me?
Yeah, she's walking back to me!
Oh, pretty woman.

Oh, What a Beautiful Mornin'

Lyrics by Oscar Hammerstein II
Music by Richard Rodgers

from the musical *Oklahoma!*

There's a bright golden haze on the meadow,
There's a bright golden haze on the meadow.
The corn is as high as an elephant's eye,
An' it looks like it's climbin' clear up to the sky.

Refrain:
Oh, what a beautiful mornin',
Oh, what a beautiful day.
I got a beautiful feelin'
Everything's goin' my way.

All the cattle are standin' like statues,
All the cattle are standin' like statues.
They don't turn their heads as they see me ride by,
But a little brown maverick is winkin' her eye.

Refrain

All the sounds of the earth are like music,
All the sounds of the earth are like music.
The breeze is so busy it don't miss a tree,
And a ol' weepin' willer is laughin' at me.

Refrain

Oh what a beautiful day!

On a Clear Day
(You Can See Forever)

Words by Alan Jay Lerner
Music by Burton Lane

from the musical *On a Clear Day You Can See Forever*
recorded by Barbra Streisand and other artists

On a clear day,
Rise and look around you,
And you'll see who you are.
On a clear day,
How it will astound you,
That the glow of your being
Outshines every star.

You feel part of
Every mountain, sea and shore.
You can hear,
From far and near,
A world you've never heard before.
And on a clear day,
On that clear day,
You can see forever
And ever and ever and evermore!

On a Slow Boat to China

By Frank Loesser

a standard recorded by Kay Kyser, Freddy Martin,
Art Lund, Benny Goodman and various other artists

I'd love to get you
On a slow boat to China,
All to myself, alone.
Get you and keep you
In my arms evermore,
Leave all your lovers
Weeping on the far away shore.

Out on the briny
With a moon big and shiny,
Melting your heart of stone.
I'd love to get you
On a slow boat to China,
All to myself alone.

There's no verse to this song
'Cause I don't want to wait a moment too long,
To say that…

Repeat Verses

On Broadway

Words and Music by Barry Mann, Cynthia Weil,
Mike Stoller and Jerry Leiber

recorded by The Drifters, George Benson
featured in the films *All That Jazz* and *A Chorus Line*

They say the neon lights are bright
On Broadway;
They say there's always magic in the air;
But when you're walkin' down the street,
And you ain't had enough to eat,
The glitter rubs right off and you're nowhere.

They say the women treat you fine
On Broadway;
But lookin' at them just gives me the blues;
'Cause how ya gonna make some time,
When all you got is one thin dime,
And one thin dime won't even shine your shoes.

They say that I won't last too long
On Broadway;
I'll catch a Greyhound bus for home, they say;
But they're dead wrong, I know they are.
'Cause I can play this here guitar,
And I won't quit till I'm a star on Broadway.

On My Own

Music by Claude-Michel Schönberg
Lyrics by Alain Boublil, Herbert Kretzmer, John Caird,
Trevor Nunn and Jean-Marc Natel

from the musical *Les Misérables*

On my own, pretending he's beside me.
All alone, I walk with him 'til morning.
Without him, I feel his arms around me.
And when I lose my way,
I close my eyes and he has found me.

In the rain, the pavement shines like silver.
All the lights are misty in the river.
In the darkness the trees are full of starlight.
And all I see is him and me forever and forever.

And I know it's only in my mind
That I'm talking to myself and not to him.
And although I know that he is blind,
Still I say there's a way for us.

I love him, but when the night is over,
He is gone, the river's just a river.
Without him the world around me changes.
The trees are bare
And everywhere the streets are full of strangers.

I love him but every day I'm learning,
All my life I've only been pretending.
Without me his world will go on turning.
The world is full of happiness that I have never known.

I love him,
I love him,
I love him,
But only on my own.

On the Street Where You Live

Words by Alan Jay Lerner
Music by Frederick Loewe

from the musical *My Fair Lady*

I have often walked
Down this street before
But the pavement always stayed beneath my feet before.
All at once am I,
Several stories high,
Knowing I'm on the street where you live.

Are there lilac trees
In the heart of town?
Can you hear a lark in any other part of town?
Does enchantment pour
Out of every door?
No, it's just on the street where you live.

And oh, the towering feeling,
Just to know somehow you are near!
The overpowering feeling
That any second you may suddenly appear!

People stop and stare,
They don't bother me;
For there's nowhere else on earth that I would rather be.

Let the time go by,
I won't care if I
Can be here on the street where you live.

On the Sunny Side of the Street

Lyric by Dorothy Fields
Music by Jimmy McHugh

a standard featured in various musicals and films
recorded by various artists

Grab your coat and get your hat,
Leave your worries on the doorstep
Just direct your feet,
To the sunny side of the street.

Can't you hear the pitter-pat?
And that happy tune is your step.
Life can be so sweet,
On the sunny side of the street.

I used to walk in the shade
With those blues on parade,
But I'm not afraid
This rover
Crossed over.
If I never had a cent,
I'd be rich as Rockefeller.
Gold dust at my feet
On the sunny side of the street.

On the Wings of Love

Words and Music by Jeffrey Osborne and Peter Schless

recorded by Jeffrey Osborne

Just smile for me and let the day begin.
You are the sunshine that lights my heart within.
And I'm sure that you're an angel in disguise.
Come take my hand and together we will ride.

Refrain:
On the wings of love, up and above the clouds;
The only way to fly is on the wings of love.
On the wings of love,
Only the two of us together flying high.

You look at me and I begin to melt,
Just like the snow, when a ray of sun is felt.
And I'm crazy 'bout you, baby, can't you see?
I'd be so delighted if you would come with me.

Refrain

Yes, you belong to me, and I'm yours exclusively.
And right now we live and breathe together.
Inseparable it seems, we're flowing like a stream running free.
Traveling on the wings of love.

Refrain

Together flying high.

Refrain

Flying high upon the wings of love, of love.

On Top of Spaghetti

Words and Music by Tom Glazer

recorded by Tom Glazer

On top of spaghetti all covered with cheese,
I lost my poor meatball when somebody sneezed.
It rolled off the table and onto the floor,
And then my poor meatball rolled out of the door.

It rolled in the garden and under a bush,
And then my poor meatball was nothing but mush.
The mush was as tasty as tasty could be,
And early next summer, it grew into a tree.

The tree was all covered with beautiful moss;
It grew lovely meatballs and tomato sauce.
So if you eat spaghetti all covered with cheese,
Hold onto your meatballs and don't ever sneeze.

Spoken:
A-choo!

Once in a Lifetime

Words and Music by Leslie Bricusse and Anthony Newley

from the musical production
Stop the World—I Want to Get Off

Just once in a lifetime.
A man knows a moment
One wonderful moment
When fate takes his hand.
And this is my moment
My once in a lifetime
When I can explore
A new and exciting land.

For once in a lifetime
I feel like a giant.
I soar like an eagle
As tho' I had wings;
For this is my moment,
My destiny calls me,
And tho' it may be just once in a lifetime
I'm going to do great things.

One

Music by Marvin Hamlisch
Lyric by Edward Kleban

from the musical *A Chorus Line*

One
Singular sensation
Every step that she takes.
One
Thrilling combination
Every move that she makes.
One smile and suddenly nobody else will do.
You know you'll never be lonely with you-know-who.

One
Moment in her presence
And you can forget the rest.
For the girl is second best to none, son.
Ooh! Sigh!
Giver her your attention,
Do I really have to mention
She's the one?

One Fine Day

Words and Music by Gerry Goffin and Carole King

recorded by The Chiffons, Carole King

One fine day you'll look at me,
And you will know our love was meant to be.
One fine day
You're gonna want me for your girl.

The arms I long for
Will open wide,
And you'll be proud
To have me walking by your side.
One fine day
You're gonna want me for your girl.

Though I know you're the kind of boy
Who only wants to run around.
I'll keep waiting and someday, darling,
You'll come to me when you want to settle down, oh.

One fine day
We'll meet once more,
And then you'll want the love you threw away before.
One fine day,
You're gonna want me for your girl.

One fine day,
Oh, oh,
One fine day,
You're gonna want me for your girl.
Shoo-be-do-be-do-be-do-be-do wah...

One for My Baby
(And One More for the Road)

Lyric by Johnny Mercer
Music by Harold Arlen

from the film *The Sky's the Limit*
a standard recorded by Fred Astaire, Frank Sinatra and
various other artists

It's quarter to three,
There's no one in the place except you and me,
So, set 'em up, Joe
I've got a little story you ought to know.
We're drinking, my friend,
To the end of a brief episode,
Make it one for my baby and one more for the road.

I got the routine,
So drop another nickel in the machine,
I'm feelin' so bad,
I wish you'd make the music dreamy and sad,
Could tell you a lot,
But you've got to be true to your code,
Make it one for my baby and one more for the road.

You'd never know it,
But buddy, I'm kind of a poet
And I've got things to say,
And when I'm gloomy,
You simply listen to me,
Until it's talked away,
Well, that's how it goes
And Joe, I know you're getting anxious to close,
So, thanks for the cheer,
I hope you didn't mind my bending your ear,
This torch that I've found
Must be drowned,
Or soon might explode.
Make it one for my baby and one more for the road,
That long, long road.

One Less Bell to Answer

Lyric by Hal David
Music by Burt Bacharach
Copyright © 1967 (Renewed) Casa David and New Hidden Valley Music

recorded by The 5th Dimension

One less bell to answer.
One less egg to fry.
One less man to pick up after.
I should be happy, but all I do is cry.

Group:
Cry, cry,
No more laughter.

Solo:
I should be happy.

Group:
Oh, why did he go?

Solo:
Oh, I only know that since he left
My life's so empty.
Though I try to forget,
It just can't be done.
Each time the doorbell rings
I still run.

I don't know how in the world
To stop thinking of him
'Cause I still love him so.
I end each day the way I start out,
Cryin' my heart out.

One less bell to answer.
One less egg to fry.
One less man to pick up after.
No more laughter,
No more love
Since he went away.

Group:
Ah, ah, ah...

One More Night

Words and Music by Phil Collins

recorded by Phil Collins

I've been trying for so long
To let you know,
Let you know how I feel,
And if I stumble, if I fall
Just help me back,
So I can make you see.

Please give me one more night,
Give me one more night.
One more night,
'Cause I can't wait forever.
Give me just one more night,
Oh, just one more night,
Oh, one more night,
'Cause I can't wait forever.

I've been sitting here so long
Wasting time,
Just staring at the phone,
And I was wondering should I call you
Then I thought,
Maybe you're not alone.

Please give me one more night,
Give me just one more night,
One more night.
'Cause I can't wait forever.
Please give me one more night,
Oh, just one more night,
Oh, one more night,
'Cause I can't wait forever.

Give me one more night,
Give me just one more night,
Just one more night
'Cause I can't wait forever.

Like a river to the sea,
I will always be with you,
And if you sail away
I will follow you.
Give me one more night,
Give me just one more night,
Oh, one more night
'Cause I can't wait forever.

I know there'll never be a time
You'll ever feel the same,
And I know it's only right.
But if you change your mind,
You know that I'll be here,
And maybe we both can learn.

Give me just one more night,
Give me just one more night.
One more night,
'Cause I can't wait forever.
Give me just one more night,
Give me just one more night,
Oh, one more night,
'Cause I can't wait forever.

Ooh, ooh, ooh…

One Sweet Day

Words and Music by Mariah Carey, Walter Afanasieff,
Shawn Stockman, Michael McCary, Nathan Morris and
Wanya Morris

recorded by Mariah Carey & Boyz II Men

Sorry I never told you
All I wanted to say.
And now it's too late to hold you,
'Cause you've flown away,
So far away.

Never had I imagined
Living without your smile.
Feeling and knowing you hear me,
It keeps me alive,
Alive.

Refrain:
And I know you're shining down on me from heaven,
Like so many friends we've lost along the way.
And I know eventually we'll be together
One sweet day.

Darling, I never showed you,
Assumed you'd always be there.
I, I took your presence for granted,
But I always cared,
And I miss the love we shared.

Refrain

The One That You Love

Words and Music by Graham Russell

recorded by Air Supply

Now the night has gone;
Now the night has gone away;
Doesn't seem that long;
We hardly had two words to say.
Hold me in your arms for just another day,
I promise this one will go slow;
Oh, we have the right you know;
We have the right you know.

Don't say the morning's come;
Don't say the morning's come so soon.
Must we end this way,
When so much here is hard to lose?
Love is everywhere;
I know it is;
Such moments as this are too few;
Oh, it's all up to you;
It's all up to you.

Refrain:
Here I am,
The one that you love,
Asking for another day;
Understand, the one that you love,
Loves you in so many ways.

Tell me we can stay.
Tell me we can stay, oh please.
They are the words to say,
The only words I can believe.
Hold me in your arms for just another day,
I promise this one will go slow;
Oh, we have the right you know;
We have the right you know.

Refrain Twice

Repeat and Fade:
The night has gone,
A part of yesterday;
I don't know what to say;
I don't know what to say.
Here I am,
The one that you love,
Asking for another day;
Understand, the one that you love,
Loves you in so many ways.

One Toke Over the Line

Words and Music by Michael Brewer and
Thomas E. Shipley

recorded by Brewer & Shipley

Refrain:
One toke over the line, Sweet Jesus,
One toke over the line.
Sittin' downtown in a railway station,
One toke over the line.
Waitin' for the train that goes home, sweet Mary,
Hopin' that the train is on time.
Sittin' downtown in a railway station,
One toke over the line.

Who do you love?
I hope it's me.
I been changin'
As you can plainly see.
I felt the joy and I learned about the pain
That my mama said,
If I should choose to make a part of me,
Would surely strike me dead.
And now I'm…

Refrain

I sailed away
A country mile.
But now I'm returnin',
Showin' off my smile.
I met all the girls and I loved myself a few,
But to my surprise
Like everything else that I've been through,
It opened up my eyes.
And now I'm…

Refrain

I was born to give and take,
But as I keep on growin',
I'm gonna make some mistakes.
Sun is gonna set and the bird is gonna wing,
They do not lie.
My last wish will be just one thing;
I'm smilin' when I die.

Refrain

Only the Good Die Young

Words and Music by Billy Joel

recorded by Billy Joel

Come out, Virginia, don't let me wait.
You Catholic girls start much too late,
Ah, but sooner or later it comes down fate.
I might as well be the one.

Well they showed you a statue and told you to pray.
They built you a temple and locked you away,
Ah, but they never told the price that you pay,
The things that you might have done,

For only the good die young,
That's what I said.
Only the good die young,
Only the good die young.

You might have heard I run with a dangerous crowd.
We ain't too pretty, we ain't too proud.
We might be laughing a bit too loud,
But that never hurt no one.

So come on Virginia, show me a sign,
Send up a signal, I'll throw you a line.
That stained glass curtain you're hiding behind
Never lets in the sun.

Darlin', only the good die young, woah,
Only the good die young.
Only the good die young.

You got a nice white dress and a party on your confirmation.
You've got a brand new soul,
And a cross of gold.
It's a pity they didn't give you quite enough information.
You didn't count on me
When you were counting on your rosary.
Oh, oh, oh.

And they say there's a heaven for those who will wait.
Some say it's better, but I say it ain't.
I'd rather laugh with the sinners than cry with the saints;
The sinners are much more fun.

You know that only the good die young,
That's what I say.
Only the good die young,
Only the good die young.

Said your mother told you
All I could give was a reputation.
She never cared for me,
But did she ever say a prayer for me?

Repeat from Top and Fade

Only You (And You Alone)

Words and Music by Buck Ram and Ande Rand

recorded by The Platters, The Hilltoppers and
Franck Pourcel's French Fiddles

Only you
Can make this world seem right,
Only you
Can make the darkness bright.
Only you and you alone
Can thrill me like you do,
And fill my heart with love
For only you.

Only you
Can make this change in me
For it's true,
You are my destiny.
When you hold my hand,
I understand
The magic that you do.
You're my dream come true,
My one and only you.

Operator
(That's Not the Way It Feels)

Words and Music by Jim Croce

recorded by Jim Croce

Operator,
Could you help me place this call?
You see, the number on the match book is old and faded.
She's living in L.A.
With my best old ex-friend, Ray,
A guy she said she knew well and sometimes hated.

Refrain:
Isn't that the way they say it goes?
But let's forget all that,
And give me the number, if you can find it,
So I can call just to tell them I'm fine and to show
I've overcome the blow,
I've learned to take it well.
I only wish my words could just convince myself
That it wasn't real,
But that's not the way it feels.

Operator,
Could you help me place this call,
'Cause I can't read the number that you just gave me.
There's something in my eyes;
You know it happens every time
I think about the love that I thought would save me.

Refrain

Operator,
Let's forget about this call;
There's no one there I really wanted to talk to.
Thank you for your time
'Cause you've been so much more than kind,
And you can keep the dime.

Refrain

Our House

Words and Music by Graham Nash

recorded by Crosby, Stills, Nash & Young

I'll light the fire;
You place the flowers in the vase
That you bought today.
Staring at the fire
For hours and hours
While I listen to you play your love songs
All night long for me,
Only for me.

Come to me now
And rest your head for just five minutes;
Everything is done.

Such a cozy room.
The windows are illuminated
By the evening sunshine through them:
Fiery gems for you,
Only for you.

Refrain:
Our house
Is a very, very, very fine house,
With two cats in the yard.
Life used to be so hard;
Now everything is easy 'cause of you.
And, ah.

La la la…

Refrain

And, ah,
I'll light the fire,
While you place the flowers in the vase
That you bought today.

Our Love

Words and Music by Al Jarreau, Jay Graydon and
Tom Canning

recorded by Natalie Cole

There's a land where lovers dream,
Where poets dwell:
We can sail tomorrow.
There is always room for one who wishes well.
There are doubters who
Will be welcome, too.
When you can't afford the fare,
There's a wish to borrow.

Refrain:
Our love,
We must never doubt it.
Our love, when you think about it,
Love like ours will live a thousand years.

Yes, I know you've heard the story without end,
And you're uninspired.
Still, a walk without a wish cannot begin.
If you wish at all, we can conquer all;
Learn to walk and run again
As we chase Goliath.

Refrain

Repeat Verse 1 and Fade

Out of My Dreams

Lyrics by Oscar Hammerstein II
Music by Richard Rodgers

from the musical *Oklahoma!*

Refrain:
Out of my dreams and into your arms I long to fly.
I will come as evening comes to woo a waiting sky.
Out of my dreams and into the hush of falling shadows,
When the mist is low and stars are breaking through,
Then out of my dreams I'll go
Into a dream with you.

Won't have to make up any more stories, you'll be there!
Think of the bright midsummer night glories we can share.
Won't have to go on kissing a daydream, I'll have you.
You'll be real, real as the white moon lighting the blue.

Refrain

Out of Nowhere

Words by Edward Heyman
Music by Johnny Green

from the Paramount Picture *Dude Ranch*
featured in the film *The Joker Is Wild*
recorded by Guy Lombardo, Frank Sinatra, Lena Horne,
Artie Shaw and various other artists

You came to me from out of nowhere,
You took my heart and found it free.
Wonderful dreams, wonderful schemes from nowhere;
Make every hour sweet as a flower for me.

If you should go back to your nowhere,
Leaving me with a memory.
I'll always wait for your return out of nowhere;
Hoping that you'll bring your love to me.

Refrain:
When I least expected
Kindly fate directed
You to make each dream of mine come true.
And if it's clear or raining
There is no explaining
Things just happen and so did you.

Repeat Verses

Owner of a Lonely Heart

Words and Music by Trevor Horn, Jon Anderson,
Trevor Rabin and Chris Squire

recorded by Yes

Move yourself.
You always live your life
Never thinking of the future.
Prove yourself.
You are the move you make.
Take your chances, win or loser.
See yourself.
You are the steps you take.
You and you, and that's the only way.
Shake, shake yourself.
You've ev'ry move you make.
So the story goes.

Refrain:
Owner of a lonely heart.
Owner of a lonely heart.
(Much better than a)
Owner of a broken heart.
Owner of a lonely heart.

Say you don't want to change it.
You've been hurt so before.
Watch it now,
The eagle in the sky,
How he dancin' one and only.
You lose yourself.
No, not for pity's sake.
There's no real reason to be lonely.
Be yourself.
Give your free will a chance.
You've got to want to succeed.

Refrain

After my own indecision,
They confused me so.
My love said never question your will at all.
In the end you've got to go.
Look before you leap
And don't you hesitate at all. No, no.

Refrain Twice

Sooner or later each conclusion
Will decide the lonely heart.
(Owner of a lonely heart.)
It will excite it,
Will delight it,
Will give a better start.
(Owner of a lonely heart.)
Don't deceive your free will at all.

Twice:
Don't deceive your free will at all.
Don't deceive your free will at all.
Just receive it.
Just receive it.

Papa Was a Rollin' Stone
Words and Music by Norman Whitfield and Barrett Strong
© 1972 (Renewed 2000) STONE DIAMOND MUSIC CORP.
All Rights Controlled and Administered by EMI BLACKWOOD MUSIC INC.

recorded by The Temptations

It was the third of September;
That day I'll always remember,
'Cause that was the day that my daddy died.
I never got the chance to see him;
Never heard nothin' but bad things about him.
Mama I'm depending on you to tell me the truth.

Spoken:
Mama just looked at him and said, "Son,

Refrain, Sung:
Papa was a rollin' stone.
Wherever he laid his hat was his home.
And when he died,
All he left us was alone."

Hey, Mama, I heard Papa call himself a jack of all trades.
Tell me, is that what sent Papa to an early grave?
Folks say Papa would beg, borrow or steal to pay his bills.
Hey, Mama, folks say Papa was never much on thinkin';
Spent most of his time chasin' women and drinkin'!
Mama, I'm depending on you
To tell me the truth.

Spoken:
Mama just hung her head and said, "Son…

Refrain

Paperback Writer
Words and Music by John Lennon and Paul McCartney
Copyright © 1966 Sony/ATV Songs LLC
Copyright Renewed
All Rights Administered by Sony/ATV Music Publishing, 8 Music Square West,
   Nashville, TN 37203

recorded by The Beatles

Paperback writer, paperback writer.
Dear Sir or Madam, will you read my book?
It took me years to write, will you take a look?
It's based on a novel by a man named Lear,
And I need a job.
So I want to be a paperback writer.
Paperback writer.

It's the dirty story of a dirty man,
And his clinging wife doesn't understand.
His son is working for the *Daily Mail;*
It's a steady job,
But he wants to be a paperback writer.
Paperback writer.

It's a thousand pages, give or a take a few;
I'll be writing more in a week or two,
I can make it longer if you like the style,
I can change it 'round,
And I want to be a paperback writer,
Paperback writer.

If you really like it you can have the rights,
It could make a million for you overnight.
If you must return it you can send it here,
But I need a break,
And I want to be a paperback writer.
Paperback writer.

Part of the Plan
Words and Music by Dan Fogelberg

recorded by Dan Fogelberg

I have these moments all steady and strong;
I'm feeling so holy and humble.
The next thing I know I'm all worried and weak,
And I feel myself starting to crumble.

The meanings get lost
And the teachings get tossed
And you don't know what you're goin' to do next.
You wait for the sun
But it never quite comes;
Some kind of message comes through to you,
Some kind of message comes through,
And it says to you:

Refrain:
"Love when you can,
Cry when you have to;
Be who you must,
That's a part of the plan.
Await your arrival with simple survival
And one day we'll all understand,
One day we'll all understand,
One day we'll all understand."

I had a woman who gave me her soul,
But I wasn't ready to take it.
Her heart was so fragile and heavy to hold
And I was afraid I might break it.

Your conscience awakes
And you see your mistakes
And you wish someone would buy your confessions.
The days miss their mark
And the night gets so dark
And some kind of message comes through to you,
Some kind of message shoots through,
And it says to you:

Refrain

There is no Eden or heavenly gates,
That you're gonna make it to one day.
But all of the answers you seek can be found
In the dreams that you dream on the way.

The Party's Over
Words by Betty Comden and Adolph Green
Music by Jule Styne

from the musical *Bells Are Ringing*

The party's over,
It's time to call it a day.
They've burst your pretty balloon
And taken the moon away.
It's time to wind up
The masquerade.
Just make your mind up
The piper must be paid.

The party's over,
The candles flicker and dim.
You danced and dreamed through the night,
It seemed to be right,
Just being with him.
Now you must wake up,
All dreams must end.
Take off your make-up,
The party's over,
It's all over,
My friend.

Passion
Words and Music by Rod Stewart, Phil Chen,
Gary Grainger, Kevin Savigar and Jim Cregan

recorded by Rod Stewart

Somebody somewhere,
In the heat of the night,
Looking pretty dangerous,
Running out of patience.

Tonight in the city
You won't find any pity.
Hearts are being twisted,
Another lover cheated, cheated.

In the bars and cafés, passion,
In the streets and the alleys, passion,
A lot of pretending, passion,
Everybody searching, passion.

Refrain:
Once in love you're never out of danger,
One hot night spent with a stranger.
All you wanted was somebody to hold on to, yeah.
Passion, passion.

New York, Moscow, passion,
Hong Kong, Tokyo, passion.
Paris and Bangkok, passion,
A lotta people ain't got, passion.

Refrain

Hear on the radio, passion,
Read it in the paper, passion,
Hear it in the churches, passion,
See it in the school yards, passion.

Refrain

Alone in your bed at night, passion,
It's half past midnight, passion,
As you turn out you sidelight, passion,
Something ain't right, passion.

Refrain

There's no passion,
There's no passion…

Peggy Sue
Words and Music by Jerry Allison, Norman Petty and
Buddy Holly
© 1957 (Renewed) MPL COMMUNICATIONS, INC. and WREN MUSIC CO.

recorded by Buddy Holly

If you knew Peggy Sue,
Then you'd know why I feel blue
About Peggy,
'Bout my Peggy Sue
Oh, well, I love you, gal,
Yes, I love you, Peggy Sue.

Peggy Sue, Peggy Sue,
Oh, how my heart yearns for you,
Oh, Pa-heggy,
My Pa-heggy Sue.
Oh, well, I love you, gal,
Yes, I love you, Peggy Sue.

Peggy Sue, Peggy Sue,
Pretty, pretty, pretty, pretty Peggy Sue,
Oh, my Peggy
My Peggy Sue
Oh, well, I love you gal,
And I need you, Peggy Sue.

I love you, Peggy Sue,
With a love so rare and true,
Oh, Peggy,
My Peggy Sue
Oh, well, I love you, gal
Yes, I want you,
Peggy Sue.

Pennies from Heaven
Words by John Burke
Music by Arthur Johnston
Copyright © 1936 by Chappell & Co.
Copyright Renewed

from the film *Pennies from Heaven*
recorded by Bing Crosby and various other artists

Every time it rains, it rains pennies from heaven.
Don't you know each cloud contains pennies from heaven.
You'll find your fortune falling all over town.
Be sure that your umbrella is upside down.

Trade them for a package of sunshine flowers.
If you want the things you love, you must have showers.
So when you hear it thunder don't get under a tree,
There'll be pennies from heaven for you and me.

Penny Lane
Words and Music by John Lennon and Paul McCartney
Copyright © 1967 Sony/ATV Songs LLC
Copyright Renewed
All Rights Administered by Sony/ATV Music Publishing, 8 Music Square West,
    Nashville, TN 37203

recorded by The Beatles

In Penny Lane there is a barber showing photographs
Of every head he's had the pleasure to know.
And all the people that come and go,
Stop and say, "Hello."

On the corner is a banker with a motorcar,
The little children laugh at him behind his back,
And the banker never wears a mac
In the pouring rain—very strange!

Penny Lane in is in my ears and in my eyes,
There beneath the blue suburban skies,
I sit and meanwhile back…

In Penny Lane there is a fireman with an hourglass,
And in his pocket is a portrait of the Queen,
He likes to keep his fire engine clean,
It's a clean machine!

Penny Lane is in my ears and in my eyes,
Full of fish and finger pies,
In summer meanwhile back…

Behind the shelter in the middle of the roundabout,
The pretty nurse is selling poppies from a tray,
And though she feels as if she's in a play,
She is anyway.

In Penny Lane the barber shaves another customer,
We see the banker sitting waiting for a trim,
And then the fireman rushes in
From the pouring rain—very strange!

Penny Lane is in my ears and in my eyes,
There beneath the blue suburban skies,
I sit and meanwhile…

Penny Lane is in my ears and in my eyes,
There beneath the blue suburban skies,
Penny Lane.

Penthouse Serenade
Words and Music by Will Jason and Val Burton

a standard recorded by various artists

Picture a penthouse way up in the sky,
With hinges on chimneys for stars to go by;
A sweet slice of heaven for just you and I
When we're alone.

From all of society we'll stay aloof,
And love in propriety there on the roof,
Two heavenly hermits we will be in truth,
When we're alone.

We'll see life's mad pattern,
As we view old Manhattan.
Then we can thank our lucky stars,
That we're living as we are.

In our little penthouse we'll always contrive,
To keep love and romance forever alive,
In view of the Hudson just over the Drive,
When we're alone.

People
Words by Bob Merrill
Music by Jule Styne

from the musical *Funny Girl*
recorded by Barbra Streisand

We travel single, O,
Maybe we're lucky,
But I don't know.
With them, just let one kid fall down
And seven mothers faint.
I guess we're both happy,
But maybe we ain't.

People, people who need people
Are the luckiest people in the world.
We're children, needing other children,
And yet letting our grown-up pride
Hide all the need inside,
Acting more like children, than children.

Lovers are very special people,
They're the luckiest people in the world.
With one person, one very special person,
A feeling deep in your soul says:
You were half now you're whole.
No more hunger and thirst, but first,
Be a person who needs people.
People who need people
Are the luckiest people in the world.

People of the South Wind
Words and Music by Kerry Livgren

recorded by Kansas

There are some who can still remember
All the things that we used to do.
But the days of our youth were numbered,
And the ones who survive it are few.

Oh, I can still see their smiling faces
When the times were so good.
All in the old familiar places.
I'd go back, if I could,

To the people of the south wind,
To the people of the southern wind,
To the people of the south wind,
To the people of the southern wind.

Well it's a hard thing to face the music,
But it's something everybody has got to do.
So I hope that I can always remember
All the crazy times we had to go through.

Now it's a dream that is slowly fading.
Oh, I don't want to go.
All of the memories are evading.
And I want you to know,

It's the people of the south wind,
It's the people of the southern wind,
With the people of the south wind,
With the people of the southern wind.

Now we've traveled all across the oceans,
And we've seen what there is to see.
But I guess it's not the proper solution,
'Cause it's all about the same to me.

Now I look back and it makes me wonder
Why we just couldn't see.
All of the battles we fought and won there.
Oh, I wish that I could be,

With the people of the south wind,
With the people of the southern wind,
With the people of the south wind,
With the people of the southern wind…

Repeat and Fade

People Will Say We're in Love

Lyrics by Oscar Hammerstein II
Music by Richard Rodgers

from the musical *Oklahoma!*

Verse (Girl):
Why do they think up stories that link my name with yours?
Why do the neighbors chatter all day, behind their doors?
I know a way to prove what they say is quite untrue.
Here is the gist, a practical list of "don'ts" for you.

Refrain:
Don't throw bouquets at me,
Don't please my folks too much,
Don't laugh at my jokes too much—
People will say we're in love!

Don't sigh and gaze at me,
Your sighs are so like mine,
You eyes mustn't glow like mine—
People will say we're in love!

Don't start collecting things
Give me my rose and glove;
Sweetheart, they're suspecting things—
People will say we're in love!

Verse 2 (Boy):
Some people claim that you are to blame as much as I.
Why do you take the trouble to bake my fav'rite pie?
Grantin' your wish, I carved our initials on the tree!
Jist keep a slice of all the advice you give so free.

Refrain 2:
Don't praise my charm too much,
Don't look so vain with me,
Don't stand in the rain with me—
People will say we're in love!

Don't take my arm too much,
Don't keep your hand in mine.
You hand looks so grand in mine,
People will say we're in love!

Don't dance all night with me,
Till the stars fade from above.
They'll see it's all right with me,
People will say we're in love!

(You've Got) Personality

Words and Music by Lloyd Price and Harold Logan

recorded by Lloyd Price

Over and over, I tried to prove my love to you.
Over and over, what more can I do?
Over and over, my friends say I'm a fool.
But over and over, I'll be a fool for you.

Refrain:
'Cause you've got personality,
Walk, personality, talk, personality,
Smile, personality, charm personality,
Love personality,
And you've got a great big heart.
So, over and over, oh, I'll be a fool for you.
Now, over and over, what more can I do?

Over and over, I said that I loved you.
Over and over, honey, now it's the truth.
Over and over, they still say I'm a fool.
But over and over, I'll be a fool for you.

Refrain

Philadelphia Freedom

Words and Music by Elton John and Bernie Taupin

recorded by Elton John

I used to be a rolling stone, you know
If the cause was right.
I'd leave
To find the answer on the road.
I used to be a heart beating for someone.
But the times have changed,
The less I say the more my work gets done.

Refrain:
'Cause I live and breathe this Philadelphia freedom.
From the day that I was born I waved the flag.
Philadelphia freedom took me knee-high to a man, yeah!
Gave me peace of mind my daddy never had.
Oh, Philadelphia freedom
Shine on me,
I love it.
Shine the light
Through the eyes of the one left behind.
Shine the light, shine the light.
Shine the light. Won't you shine the light?
Philadelphia freedom,
I love-ove-ove you,
Yes I do.

If you choose to, you can live your life alone.
Some people choose the city,
Some others choose the good old family home.
I like living easy without family ties,
'Til the whippoorwill of freedom zapped me
Right between the eyes.

Refrain

Don't you know I love you?
Don't you know I love you?
Yes I do.
(Philadelphia freedom)
Don't you know that I love you?

Repeat and Fade

Piano Man
Words and Music by Billy Joel
© 1973, 1974 JOEL SONGS

recorded by Billy Joel

It's nine o'clock on a Saturday,
The regular crowd shuffles in.
There's an old man sitting next to me
Makin' to his tonic and gin.
He says "Son, can you play me a memory?
I'm not really sure how it goes,
But its sad and it's sweet
And I knew it complete
When I wore a younger man's clothes."
Da da da da da da da...

Refrain:
Sing us a song, you're the piano man.
Sing us a song tonight.
Well, we're all in the mood for a melody,
And you've got us feelin' alright.

Now John at the bar is a friend of mine.
He gets me my drinks for free.
And he's quick with a joke or to light up your smoke,
But there's someplace that he'd rather be.
He says, "Bill, I believe this is killing me,"
As a smile ran away from his face.
"Well, I'm sure that I could be a movie star,
If I could get out of this place."
Da da da da da da da...

Refrain

Now Paul is a real estate novelist,
Who never had time for a wife,
And he's talkin' with Davy who's still in the Navy,
And probably will be for life.
And the waitress is practicing politics,
As the businessmen slowly get stoned.
Yes, they're sharing a drink they call loneliness,
But it's better than drinking alone.
Da da da da da da da...

Refrain

It's a pretty good crowd for a Saturday,
And the manager gives me a smile,
'Cause he knows that it's me they've been coming to see,
To forget about life for a while.
And the piano sounds like a carnival,
And the microphone smells like a beer.
And they sit at the bar and put bread in my jar
And say, "Man what are you doin' here?"

Refrain

Pick Yourself Up
Words by Dorothy Fields
Music by Jerome Kern
Copyright © 1936 by Aldi Music and Universal - PolyGram International Publishing, Inc.
Copyright Renewed
All Rights for Aldi Music Administered by The Songwriters Guild Of America

from the film *Swing Time*

Nothing's impossible I have found.
For when my chin is on the ground,
I pick myself up,
Dust myself off,
Start all over again.

Don't lose your confidence if you slip,
Be grateful for a pleasant trip,
And pick yourself up,
Dust yourself off,
Start all over again.

Work like a soul inspired
'Til the battle of the day is won.
You may be sick and tired,
But you'll be a man, my son!

Will you remember the famous men,
Who had to fall to rise again?
So take a deep breath,
Pick yourself up,
Dust yourself off,
Start all over again.

Picnic
Words by Steve Allen
Music by George W. Duning
Copyright © 1955, 1956 Shapiro, Bernstein & Co., Inc. - Film Division, New York
Copyright Renewed 1983, 1984, Assigned to Meadowlane Music, Inc. and Shapiro,
   Bernstein & Co., Inc. - Film Division, New York

from the Columbia Technicolor Picture *Picnic*

On a picnic morning,
Without a warning,
I looked at you,
And somehow I knew.

On a day for singing,
My heart went winging,
A picnic grove was our rendezvous.
You and I in the sunshine,
We strolled the fields and farms,
At the last light of evening.
I held you in my arms.

Now when days grow stormy
And lonely for me,
I just recall picnic time with you.

Repeat Last Three Lines

Piece of My Heart
Words and Music by Bert Berns and Jerry Ragovoy

recorded by Janis Joplin with Big Brother & The Holding
Company

Didn't I make you feel
Like you were the only man?
Didn't I give you everything that a woman possibly can?
But with all the love I give you,
It's never enough,
But I'm gonna show you, baby,
That a woman can be tough.

Refrain:
So go on, go on, go on, go on,
Take it!
Take another piece of my heart now, baby.
Break it!
Break another little piece of my heart now, baby.
Have a!
Have another little piece of my heart now, baby.
You know you got it if it makes you feel good.

You're out in the street lookin' good,
And you know deep down in your heart that ain't right.
And oh, you never, never hear me when I cry at night.
Whoa-oh-oh.
I tell myself that I can't stand the pain,
But when you hold me in your arms I say it again.

Refrain

Please Mr. Postman
Words and Music by Robert Bateman, Georgia Dobbins,
William Garrett, Freddie Gorman and Brian Holland

recorded by The Marvelettes and The Carpenters

Oh yes, wait a minute, Mister Postman.
Wait, Mister Postman.

Refrain:
Mister Postman look and see,
Is there a letter in your bag for me?
I've been waiting a long, long time,
Since I heard from that girl (boy) of mine.

There must be some word today,
From my girlfriend (boyfriend) so far away.
Please, Mister Postman look and see,
If there's a letter, a letter for me?
I've been standing here waiting, Mister Postman,
So patiently, for just a card or just a letter,
Saying that she's (he's) returning home to me.

Refrain

So many days you've passed me by,
See the tears standing in my eyes,
You didn't stop to make me feel better
By leaving me a card or a letter,
Mister Postman,
Mister Postman, look and see,
Is there a letter in your bag for me?
I've been waiting for such a long time
Since I heard from that girlfriend (boyfriend) of mine.

You gotta wait a minute, wait a minute, oh yeah.
Wait a minute, wait a minute, oh yeah.
You gotta wait a minute, wait a minute, oh yeah.
Check it and see
One more time for me.

You gotta wait a minute, wait a minute, oh yeah.
Mister Postman, oh yeah.
Deliver the letter,
The sooner the better.

Repeat and Fade:
You gotta wait a minute, wait a minute, oh yeah.
Wait a minute, wait a minute, oh yeah.
You gotta wait a minute, wait a minute, oh yeah.

Point of Know Return

Words and Music by Steve Walsh, Phil Ehart and
Robert Steinhardt

recorded by Kansas

I heard the men saying something.
The captains tell
They pay you well.
And they say they need sailing men
To show the way
And leave today.
Was it you that said,
"How long? How long?"

They say the sea turns so dark that
You know it's time
You see the sign.
They say the point demons guard
Is an ocean grave
For all the brave.
Was it you that said,
"How long? How long?"

"How long to the point of know return?"

Your father, he said he needs you.
Your mother, she said she loves you.
Your brothers, they echo the words
"How far to the point of know return,
To the point of know return?
Well, how long?
How long?"

Today I found a message floating
In the sea
From you to me.
You wrote that when you could see it,
You cried with fear
The point was near.
Was it you that said,
"How long? How long?"

"How long to the point of know return, know return?
How long?"

The Power of Love

Words by Mary Susan Applegate and Jennifer Rush
Music by Candy Derouge and Gunther Mende

recorded by Celine Dion

The whispers in the morning,
Of lovers sleeping tight,
Are rolling by like thunder now,
As I look into your eyes.

I hold on to your body,
And feel each move you make.
Your voice is warm and tender,
A love that I could not forsake.

Refrain:
'Cause I'm your lady
And you are my man.
Whenever you reach for me,
I'll do all that I can.

Even though there may be times
It seems I'm far away,
Never wonder where I am
'Cause I am always by your side.

Refrain

We're heading for something,
Somewhere I've never been.
Sometimes I am frightened
But I'm ready to learn
'Bout the power of love.

The sound of your heart beating
Made it clear and suddenly.
The feeling that I can't go on
Is light years away.

Refrain

We're heading for something,
Somewhere I've never been.
Sometimes I'm frightened
But I'm ready to learn
'Bout the power of love.
The power of love.

Power to the People

Words and Music by John Lennon

recorded by John Lennon & Yoko Ono with The Plastic
Ono Band

Power to the people. Power to the people.
Power to the people. Power to the people.

Refrain:
Power to the people. Power to the people.
Power to the people. Power to the people right on.

You say you want a revolution,
We'd better get on it right away.
Well let's get on you feet,
End of the street
Singing:

Refrain

A million workers workin' for nothing,
You better give them what they really own.
We gotta put you down
When we come into town,
Singing:

Refrain

I gonna ask you comrades and brothers,
How do you treat your old woman back home?
She's gotta be herself
So she can give us help,
Singing:

Refrain Twice

Precious and Few
Words and Music by Walter D. Nims

recorded by Climax

Precious and few are the moments we two can share;
Quiet and blue like the sky I'm hung over you.
And if I can't find my way back home
It just wouldn't be fair
'Cause precious and few
Are the moments we two can share.

Baby, it's you on my mind, your love is so rare
Being with you is a feeling I just can't compare.
And if I can't hold you in my arms
It just wouldn't be fair,
'Cause precious and few
Are the moments we two can share.

Puff the Magic Dragon
Words and Music by Lenny Lipton and Peter Yarrow

recorded by Peter, Paul & Mary

Puff, the magic dragon, lived by the sea
And frolicked in the autumn mist in a land called Honahlee.
Little Jackie Paper loved that rascal Puff,
And brought him strings and sealing wax and other fancy stuff.

Refrain:
Oh! Puff, the magic dragon, lived by the sea,
And frolicked in the autumn mist in a land called Honahlee.
Puff, the magic dragon, lived by the sea,
And frolicked in the autumn mist in a land called Honahlee.

Together they would travel on a boat with billowed sail;
Jackie kept a lookout perched on Puff's gigantic tail.
Noble kings and princes would bow whene'er they came,
Pirate ships would lower their flag when Puff roared out
his name.

Refrain

A dragon lives forever, but not so little boys,
Painted wings and giant rings make way for other toys.
One grey night it happened, Jackie Paper came no more,
And Puff, that magic dragon, he ceased his fearless roar.

Refrain

His head was bent in sorrow, green scales fell like rain;
Puff no longer went to play along the cherry lane.
Without his life-long friend, Puff could not be brave,
So Puff, that mighty dragon, sadly slipped into his cave.

Refrain

Puttin' On the Ritz
Words and Music by Irving Berlin

from the Motion Picture *Puttin' On the Ritz*
a standard recorded by various artists

Have you seen the well-to-do
Up and down Park Avenue,
On that famous thoroughfare
With their noses in the air.
High hats and Arrow collars,
White spats and lots of dollars,
Spending ev'ry dime
For a wonderful time.

If you're blue and you don't know where to go to,
Why don't you go where fashion sits,
Puttin' on the Ritz.

Different types who wear a day coat,
Pants with stripes and cut-away coat, perfect fits,
Puttin' on the Ritz.

Strolling up the avenue so happy.
All dressed up just like the English chappie,
Very snappy.
Come let's mix where Rockefellers walk
With sticks or "um-ber-el-las" in their mitts,
Puttin' on the Ritz.

The Rainbow Connection

Words and Music by Paul Williams and Kenneth L. Ascher

from the film *The Muppet Movie*

Why are there so many songs about rainbows,
And what's on the other side?
Rainbows are visions, but only illusions,
And rainbows have nothing to hide.
So we've been told, and some choose not to believe it;
I know they're wrong; wait and see
Someday we'll find it,
The rainbow connection;
The lovers, the dreamers, and me.

Who said that every wish would be heard and answered
When wished on the morning star?
Somebody thought of that, and someone believed it;
Look what it's done so far.
What's so amazing that keeps us star-gazing
And what do we think we might we might see?
Someday we'll find it,
The rainbow connection;
The lovers, the dreamers, and me.

All of us under its spell;
We know that it's probably magic.
Have you been half asleep and have you heard voices?
I've heard them calling my name.

Is this the sweet sound that calls the young sailors?
The voice might be one and the same.
I've heard it too many times to ignore it.
It's something that I'm supposed to be.
Someday we'll find it,
The rainbow connection;
The lovers, the dreamers, and me.

Raindrops Keep Fallin' on My Head

Lyric by Hal David
Music by Burt Bacharach

from the film *Butch Cassidy and the Sundance Kid*
recorded by B.J. Thomas

Raindrops keep fallin' on my head,
And just like the guy whose feet are too big for his bed,
Nothin' seems to fit.
Those raindrops are fallin' on my head.
They keep fallin'.

So I just did me some talkin' to the sun.
And I said I didn't like the way he got things done.
Sleepin' on the job.
Those, raindrops are fallin' on my head.
They keep fallin'.

But there's one thing
I know
The blues they send to meet me
Won't defeat me.
It won't be long
Till happiness steps up to greet me.

Raindrops keep fallin' on my head,
But that doesn't mean my eyes will soon be turnin' red.
Cryin's not for me
'Cause I'm never gonna stop the rain by complainin'.
Because I'm free
Nothin's worryin' me.

Rainy Days and Mondays

Lyrics by Paul Williams
Music by Roger Nichols

recorded by The Carpenters

Talkin' to myself and feelin' old,
Sometimes I'd like to quit.
Nothing ever seems to fit.
Hangin' around, nothing to do but frown;
Rainy days and Mondays always get me down.

What I've got they used to call the blues,
Nothing is really wrong,
Feelin' like I don't belong.
Walkin' around, some kind of lonely clown;
Rainy days and Mondays always get me down.

Refrain:
Funny but it seems I always wind up here with you,
Nice to know somebody loves me.
Funny but it seems that it's the only thing to do,
Run and find the one who loves me.

What I feel has come and gone before,
No need to talk it out,
We know what it's all about.
Hangin' around, nothing to do but frown;
Rainy days and Mondays always get me down.

Refrain

What I feel has come and gone before,
No need to talk it out,
We know what it's all about.
Hangin' around, nothing to do but frown;
Rainy days and Mondays always get me down.
Hangin' around, nothing to do but frown;
Rainy days and Mondays always get me down.
Rainy days and Mondays always get me down.

Reach Out and Touch
(Somebody's Hand)

Words and Music by Nickolas Ashford and
Valerie Simpson

recorded by Diana Ross

Refrain:
Reach out and touch somebody's hand,
Make this world a better place if you can.
Reach out and touch somebody's hand,
Make this world a better place if you can.
(Just try)

Take a little time out of your busy day,
To give encouragement to someone who's lost the way.
Or would I be talking to a stone
If I asked you to share a problem that's not your own.
We can change things if we start giving.

Refrain

If you see an old friend on the street
And he's down, remember, his shoes could fit your feet.
Just try a little kindness and you'll see
It's something that comes very naturally.
We can change things if we start giving.

Why don't you
Reach out and touch somebody's hand.

Real World

Written by Rob Thomas

recorded by Matchbox 20

Well, I wonder what it's like to be the rainmaker.
I wonder what it's like to know that I made the rain.
I'd store it in boxes with little yellow tags on every one.
And you can come and see them when I'm done,
When I'm done.

I wonder what it's like to be a super hero.
I wonder where I'd go if I could fly around downtown, yeah.
From some other planet I get this funky high on yellow sun.
And boy, I bet my friends would all be stunned.
Yeah.

Refrain:
Straight up, what did you hope to learn about here?
If I were someone else would this all fall apart?
Strange, where were you when we started this gig?
I wish the real world would just stop hasslin' me
And you, to you, yeah me.

Well I wonder what it's like to be the head honcho.
I wonder what I'd do if they all did just what they said.
Well, I'd shout out an order,
I think we're out of this, man, get me some.
Boy, don't make me wanna change my tone, my tone.

Refrain

Please don't change, please don't break.
Well, the only thing that seems to work at all is you.
Please don't change at all from me, to you,
And you, to me, yeah, yeah.

Refrain

I wish the real world would just stop hasslin' me.
I wish the real world would just stop hasslin' me,
And you, and me.

Reflection

Music by Matthew Wilder
Lyrics by David Zippel

from Walt Disney Pictures' *Mulan*
recorded by Christina Aguilera

Look at me,
You may think you see who I really am,
But you'll never know me.
Every day it's as if I play a part.

Now I see if I wear a mask I can fool the world,
But I cannot fool my heart.
Who is that girl I see staring straight back at me?
When will my reflection show who I am am inside?
I am now in a world where I have to hide my heart
And what I believe in.

But somehow I will show the world
What's inside my heart and be loved for who I am.
Who is that girl I see staring straight back at me?
Why is my reflection someone I don't know?
Must I pretend that I'm someone else for all time?
When will my reflection show who I am?
Inside, there's a heart that must be free to fly,
That burns with a need to know the reason why.

Why must we all conceal what we think, how we feel?
Must there be a secret me I'm forced to hide?
I won't pretend that I'm someone else for all time.
When will my reflection show who I am inside?
When will my reflection show who I am inside?

Remember Me This Way

Music by David Foster
Lyrics by Linda Thompson

from the Universal Motion Picture *Casper*
recorded by Jordan Hill

Every now and then
We find a special friend
Who never lets us down,
Who understands it all,
Reaches out each time you fall.
You're the best friend that I've found.

I know you can't stay,
But part of you will never, ever go away;
Your heart will stay.

Refrain:
I'll make a wish for you and hope it will come true:
That life will just be kind to such a gentle mind.
If you lose your way, think back on yesterday.
Remember me this way.
Remember me this way.

I don't need eyes to see
The love you bring to me,
No matter where I go.

And I know that you'll be there,
Forevermore a part of me;
You're everywhere.
I'll always care.

Refrain

And I'll be right behind your shoulder watching you.
I'll be standing by your side in all you do.
And I won't ever leave,
As long as you believe.
You just believe.

Refrain

This way.

Respect

Words and Music by Otis Redding

recorded by Aretha Franklin

What you want, baby I got.
What you need, you know I got it.
All I'm asking is for a little respect, when you come home.
Baby, when you come home, respect.

I ain't gonna do you wrong while you gone.
I ain't gonna do you wrong 'cause I don't wanna.
All I'm asking is for a little respect, when you come home.
Baby, when you come home, respect.

I'm out to give you all my money.
But all I'm askin' in return, honey,
Is to give me my proper respect when you get home.
Yeah, baby, when you get home.

Ooh, your kisses, sweeter than honey.
But guess what, so here's my money.
All I want you to do for me is give me some here,
When you get home. Yeah, baby, when you get home.

R-E-S-P-E-C-T, find out what it means to me,
R-E-S-P-E-C-T, take out T-C-P.

Repeat and Fade:
A little respect.

Respect Yourself

Words and Music by Mack Rice and Luther Ingram

recorded by The Staple Singers

If you disrespect everybody that you run into,
How in the world do you think
Everybody s'posed to respect you?
If you don't give a heck
About the man with the Bible in his hand,
Just get out of the way and let the gentleman do his thing.
You the kind of gentleman want everything your way.
Take the sheet off your face, boy, it's a brand new day.
Respect yourself.

Refrain:
Respect yourself.
'Cause if you don't respect yourself
Ain't nobody gonna give a good,
Good hoot-e-nanny, boy!
Respect yourself, respect yourself.

If you're walking around thinking that the world
Owes you something 'cause you're here,
You're going out the world backward like you did
When you first came 'ere.
Keep talking about the president won't stop air pollution.
Put you hand over your mouth when you cough;
That'll help the solution.
You cuss around women folk, don't even know their name,
Then you're dumb enough to think it makes you a big ole man.

Refrain

Return to Sender

Words and Music by Otis Blackwell and Winfield Scott

from the film *Girls! Girls! Girls!*
recorded by Elvis Presley

I gave a letter to the postman; He put it in his sack.
Bright and early next morning he brought my letter back.

Refrain:
She wrote up on it:
Return to sender, address unknown.
No such number, no such zone.

We had a quarrel, a lover's spat.
I write to say I'm sorry but my letter keeps coming back.

So then I dropped it in the mailbox
And sent it Special D.
Bright and early next morning, it came right back to me.

Refrain

This time I'm gonna take it myself and put it right in her hand.
And if it comes back the very next day,
Then I'll understand the writing on it.

Twice:
Return to sender, address unknown.
No such number no such zone.

Revolution

Words and Music by John Lennon and Paul McCartney

recorded by The Beatles

You say you want a revolution
Well, you know
We all want to change the world
You tell me that it's evolution
Well, you know
We all want to change the world
But when you talk about destruction
Don't you know that you can count me out
Don't you know it's going to be alright
Alright, alright

You say you want a real solution
Well, you know
We'd all love to see the plan
You ask me for a contribution
Well, you know
We're doing what we can
But if you want money for people with minds that hate
All I can tell you is brother you have to wait
Don't you know it's going to be alright
Alright, alright

You say you'll change the Constitution
Well, you know
We all want to change your head
You tell me it's the institution
Well, you know
You better free your mind instead
But if you carrying pictures of Chairman Mao
You ain't going to make it with me anyhow
Don't you know it's going to be alright
Alright, alright
Alright, alright…

Rhiannon

Words and Music by Stevie Nicks

recorded by Stevie Nicks

Rhiannon rings like a bell thru the night,
And wouldn't you love to love her?
Takes to the sky like a bird in flight
And who will be her lover?

Refrain:
All your life you've never seen a woman
Taken by the wind.
Would you stay if she promised you heaven?
Will you ever win?
Will you ever win?

She is like a cat in the dark,
And then she is the darkness.
She rules her life like a fine skylark,
And when the sky is starless.

Refrain

Rhiannon.
Rhiannon.

Repeat and Fade:
Dreams unwind; love's a state of mind.

Rhythm of the Night

Words and Music by Diane Warren

recorded by DeBarge

When it feels like the world is on your shoulders,
And all of the madness has got you goin' crazy,
It's time to get out.
Step out into the street where all of the action
Is right there at your feet.

Well, I know a place where we can dance the whole
   night away,
Underneath electric stars.
Just come with me and we can shake your blues
   right away.
You'll be doing fine once the music starts, oh.

Refrain:
Feel the beat of the rhythm of the night,
Dance until the morning light.
Forget about the worries on your mind,
You can leave them all behind.
Feel the beat of the rhythm of the night,
Oh the rhythm of the night,
Oh, yeah.

Look out on the street now; the party's just beginning,
The music's playing; a celebration's starting.
Under the street lights the scene is being set.
A night for romance, a night you won't forget.
So come join in the fun,
This ain't no time to be staying home,
Ooh, there's too much going on.
Tonight is gonna be a night like you've never known.
We're gonna have a good time the whole night long, oh.

Refrain

So come join in the fun,
This ain't no time to be staying home,
Ooh, there's too much going on.
Tonight is gonna be a night like you've never known.
We're gonna have a good time the whole night long, oh.

Repeat and Fade:
Feel the beat of the rhythm of the night,
Dance until the morning light.
Forget about the worries on your mind,
You can leave them all behind.

Ribbon in the Sky
Words and Music by Stevie Wonder
© 1982 JOBETE MUSIC CO., INC. and BLACK BULL MUSIC
   c/o EMI APRIL MUSIC INC.

recorded by Stevie Wonder

Oh, so long for this night I prayed
That a star would guide you my way
To share with me this special day
Where a ribbon's in the sky for our love.

If allowed, may I touch your hand
And if please may I once again,
So that you too will understand
There's a ribbon in the sky for our love.

Doo doo doo…

This is not a coincidence,
And far more than a lucky chance,
But what is that was always meant
Is our ribbon in the sky for our love, love.

We can't lose with God on our side.
We'll find strength in each tear we cry.
From now on it will be you and I
And our ribbon in the sky,
Ribbon in the sky
A ribbon in the sky for our love.

Ooh, ooh…

There's a ribbon in the sky for our love.

Ridin' the Storm Out
Words and Music by Gary Richrath
© 1973 EMI SOSAHA MUSIC INC. and JONATHAN THREE MUSIC

recorded by REO Speedwagon

Ridin' the storm out,
Waitin' for the thaw out
On a full moon night in the Rocky Mountain winter.
Wine bottle's low
Watching for the snow
And thinkin' about what I've been missin' in the city.

Refrain:
And I'm not missin' a thing,
Watching the full moon crossin' the range.
Ridin' the storm out. Ridin' the storm out.
Ridin' the storm out. Ridin' the storm out.

Lady beside me,
Well, she's there to guide me.
She says that alone we've finally found our home.
Well, the wind outside is frightenin',
But it's kinder than lightnin' life in the city.
A hard life to live, but it gives back what you give.

Refrain

Whoa, yes, I am.

Repeat Verse 1

Refrain

Oh no. Oh no. Oh, oh, oh, oh.

Ring of Fire

Words and Music by Merle Kilgore and June Carter

recorded by Johnny Cash

Love is a burning thing
And it makes its fiery ring
Bound by wild desires,
I fell into a ring of fire.

Refrain:
I fell into a burning ring of fire
I went down, down, down
And the flames went higher.
And it burns, burns, burns,
The ring of fire,
The ring of fire.

The taste of love is sweet
When hearts like ours beat.
I fell for you like a child,
Oh, but the fire went wild.

Refrain

Repeat and Fade:
And it burns, burns, burns,
The ring of fire,
The ring of fire.

The River of Dreams

Words and Music by Billy Joel

recorded by Billy Joel

In the middle of the night
I go walking in my sleep,
From the mountains of faith
To a river so deep.
I must be looking for something,
Something sacred I lost.
But the river is wide
And it's too hard to cross.
And even though I know the river is wide
I walk down every evening and stand on the shore,
And try to cross to the opposite side
So I can finally find what I've been looking for.

In the middle of the night
I go walking in my sleep,
Through the valley of fear
To a river so deep.
And I've been searching for something,
Taken out of my soul,
Something I would never lose
Something somebody stole.
I don't know why I go walking at night,
I'm tired and I don't want to walk anymore.
I hope it doesn't take the rest of my life
Until I find out what it is I've been looking for.

In the middle of the night,
I go walking in my sleep,
Through the jungle of doubt
To a river so deep.
I know I'm searching for something,
Something so undefined
That it can only be seen
By the eyes of the blind,
In the middle of the night.

I'm not sure about a life after this,
God knows I've never been a spiritual man,
Baptized by the fire,
I wade into the river that runs
To the promised land.

In the middle of the night,
I go walking in my sleep,
Through the desert of truth
To the river so deep.
We all end in the ocean
We all start in the stream.
We're all carried along
By the river of dreams,

In the middle of the night.
I go walking in the,
In the middle of the
I go walking in the,
In the middle of the…

Rock Around the Clock

Words and Music by Max C. Freedman and
Jimmy DeKnight

recorded by Bill Haley and His Comets
featured in the film *The Blackboard Jungle*

One, two, three o'clock, four o'clock rock
Five, six, seven o'clock, eight o'clock rock
Nine, ten, eleven o'clock, twelve o'clock rock
We're gonna rock around the clock tonight

Put your glad rags on and join me, Hon
We'll have some fun when the clock strikes one.

Refrain:
We're gonna rock around the clock tonight
We're gonna rock, rock, rock, 'til broad daylight
We're gonna rock, gonna rock around the clock tonight

When the clock strikes two, and three and four
If the band slows down we'll yell for more

Refrain

284

When the chimes ring five and six and seven
We'll be rockin' up in seventh heav'n

Refrain

When it's eight nine, ten, eleven, too
I'll be goin' strong and so will you

Refrain

When the clock strike twelve, we'll cool off, then
Start a rockin' 'round the clock again

Refrain

Rockin' into the Night
Words and Music by Frank Sullivan, Jim Peterik and
Robert Gary Smith

recorded by .38 Special

Cruisin' down the motorway, got my girl by my side.
We're both a little anxious, oo, we got love on our mind.

Waiting, anticipating, for the fireworks in the night.
Well, I swear we were doin' eighty
When we saw those motel lights.
And we were rockin' into the night,
Rockin' into the night, yeah…
Out on the back street, taking love where I can,
I found a sweet Madonna, oo, with a Bible in her hand.
She's waiting, anticipating,
Well, for someone to save her soul.
Well, I ain't no new messiah,
But I'm close enough for rock and roll.

And we were rockin' into the night,
Rockin' into the night.
Rockin' into the night.

And she's pullin' in yes, she's pullin' in.

Waiting, anticipating for the fireworks in the night.
Well, I swear we were doin' eighty
When we saw those motel lights.
We were rockin', rockin' into the night,
Ooo, Yeah…
We were rockin', rockin' into the night,
Ooo, Yeah…
Rockin' into the night, rockin' into the night,
Hoo, rockin'!

Rocky Mountain High
Words by John Denver
Music by John Denver and Mike Taylor

recorded by John Denver

He was born in the summer of his twenty-seventh year,
Comin' home to a place he'd never been before.
He left yesterday behind him,
You might say he was born again,
You might say he found a key for every door.

When he first came to the mountains his life was far away,
On the road and hangin' by a song.
But the string's already broken and doesn't really care,
It keeps changin' fast and it don't last for long.

But the Colorado Rocky Mountain high
I've seen it rainin' fire in the sky.
The shadow from the starlight
Is softer than a lullaby.
Rocky Mountain high,
Rocky Mountain high.

He climbed cathedral mountains,
He saw silver clouds below,
He saw everything as far as you can see.
And they say that he got crazy once
And tried to touch the sun,
And he lost a friend but kept a memory.

Now he walks in quiet solitude, the forests and the streams
Seeking grace in every step he takes.
His sight has turned inside himself to try and understand
The serenity of a clear blue mountain lake.

And the Colorado Rocky Mountain high,
I've seen it rainin' fire in the sky.
Talk to God and listen to the casual reply.
Rocky Mountain high.

Now his life is full of wonder
But his heart still knows some fear
Of a simple thing he cannot comprehend.
Why they try to tear the mountains down
To bring in a couple more
More people, more scars upon the land.

And the Colorado Rocky Mountain high,
I've seen it rainin' fire in the sky.
I know he'd be a poorer man if he never saw an eagle fly.
Rocky Mountain high

It's a Colorado Rocky mountain high,
I've seen it rainin' fire in the sky.
Friends around the campfire
And everybody's high.
Rocky Mountain high…

Rocky Raccoon

Words and Music by John Lennon and Paul McCartney

recorded by The Beatles

Now somewhere in the black mountain hills of Dakota
There lives a young boy named Rocky Raccoon.
And one day his woman ran off with another guy,
Hit young Rocky in the eye. Rocky didn't like that.
He said "I'm gonna get that boy."
So one day he walked into town:

Booked himself a room
In the local saloon.
Rocky Raccoon
Checked into his room,
Only to find Gideon's Bible.
Rocky had come,
Equipped with a gun,
To shoot off the legs of his rival.

His rival it seems
Had broken his dreams,
By stealing the girl of his fancy.
Her name was Magill,
And she called herself Loll,
But everyone knew her as Nancy.

Now she and her man,
Who called himself Dan,
Were in the next room at the hoe down.
Rocky burst in,
And grinning a grin,
He said, "Danny boy, this is a showdown."

But Daniel was hot,
He drew first and shot,
And Rocky collapsed in a corner.
Now the doctor cam in,
Stinking of gin,
And proceeded to lie on the table.

He said Rocky you met your match,
And Rocky said, "Doc, it's only a scratch,
And I'll be better.
I'll be better Doc as soon as I'm able."

Now Rocky Raccoon,
He fell back in his room,
Only to find Gideon's Bible.
Gideon checked out,
And he left it no doubt,
To help with good Rocky's revival.

Route 66

By Bobby Troup

recorded by The King Cole Trio, Bing Crosby, Manhattan
Transfer and other artists

If you ever plan to motor west
Travel my way, take the highway that's the best.
Get your kicks on Route Sixty-Six!

It winds from Chicago to L.A.
More than two thousand miles all the way.
Get your kicks on Route Sixty-Six!

Now you go through Saint Looey,
Joplin, Missouri
And Oklahoma City is mighty pretty. You'll see
Amarillo, Gallup, New Mexico;
Flagstaff, Arizona;
Don't forget Winona,
Kingman, Barstow, San Bernadino.

Won't you get hip to this timely tip:
When you make that California trip
Get your kicks on Route Sixty-Six!

Roxanne

Written and Composed by Sting

recorded by The Police

Roxanne, you don't have to put on the red light.
Those days are over;
You don't have to sell your body to the night.
Roxanne, you don't have to wear that dress tonight,
Walk the streets for money;
You don't care if it's wrong or if it's right.

Refrain:
Roxanne, you don't have to put on the red light.
Roxanne, you don't have to put on the red light.
Roxanne, (Put on the red light.)

I loved you since I knew ya.
I wouldn't talk down to ya.
I have to tell you just how I feel:
I won't share you with another boy.
I know my mind is made up,
So, put away your makeup.
Told you once I won't tell you again,
It's a crime by the way…

Refrain

The Saga of Jenny

Words by Ira Gershwin
Music by Kurt Weill

from the musical *Lady in the Dark*
featured in the film *Star!*

There once was a girl named Jenny,
Whose virtues were varied and many,
Excepting that she was inclined
Always to make up her mind,
And Jenny points a moral
With which you cannot quarrel,
As you will find.

Jenny made her mind up when she was three,
She, herself, was going to trim the Christmas tree;
Christmas Eve she lit the candles, tossed the tapers away.
Little Jenny was an orphan on Christmas Day.

Poor Jenny! Bright as a penny!
Her equal would be hard to find.
She lost one dad and mother,
A sister and a brother,
But she would make up her mind.

Jenny made her mind up when she was twelve,
That into foreign languages she would delve,
But at seventeen to Vassar it was quite a blow
That in twenty-seven languages she couldn't say no.

Poor Jenny! Bright as a penny!
Her equal would be hard to find.
To Jenny I'm beholden,
Her heart was big and golden,
But she would make up her mind.

Jenny made her mind up at twenty-two,
To get herself a husband was the thing to do,
She got herself all dolled up in her satins and furs,
And she got herself a husband, but he wasn't hers.

Poor Jenny! Bright as a penny!
Her equal would be hard to find.
Deserved a bed of roses,
But history discloses,
That she would make up her mind.

Jenny made her mind up at thirty-nine,
She would take a trip to the Argentine.
She was only on vacation, but the Latins agree,
Jenny was the one who started the Good Neighbor Policy.

Poor Jenny! Bright as a penny!
Her equal would be hard to find.
Oh, passion doesn't vanish,
In Portugese or Spanish,
But she would make up her mind.

Jenny made her mind up at fifty-one,
She would write her memoirs before she was done,
The very day her book was published history relates
There were wives who shot their husbands
In some thirty-three states.

Poor Jenny! Bright as a penny!
Her equal would be hard to find.
She could give cards and spadies,
To many other ladies,
But she would make up her mind.

Jenny made her mind up at seventy-five,
She would live to be the oldest woman alive,
But gin and rum and destiny play funny tricks
And poor Jenny kicked the bucket at seventy-six.

Jenny points a moral,
With which you cannot quarrel,
Makes a lot of common sense.
Jenny and her saga,
Prove that you are gaga,
If you don't keep sitting on the fence.

Jenny and her story point the way to glory,
To all men and woman kind.
Anyone with a vision, comes to this decision,
Don't make up, you shouldn't make up,
You mustn't make up, oh never make up
Anyone with a vision, comes to this decision,
Don't make up your mind!

Sailing

Words and Music by Christopher Cross

recorded by Christopher Cross

Well, it's not far down to paradise,
At least it's not for me.
And if the wind is right you can sail away
And find tranquility.
Oh, the canvas can do miracles,
Just you wait and see.
Believe me.

It's not far to never-never-land,
No reason to pretend.
And if the wind is right you can find the joy
Of innocence again.
Oh, the canvas can do miracles,
Just you wait and see.
Believe me.

Refrain:
Sailing,
Takes me away,
To where I've always heard it could be.
Just a dream and the wind to carry me,
And soon I will be free.

Fantasy,
It gets the best of me
When I'm sailing.

All caught up in the reverie,
Every word is a symphony.
Won't you believe me?

Refrain

Well, it's not far back to reality,
At least it's not for me.
And if the wind is right you can sail away,
And find serenity.
Oh, the canvas can do miracles,
Just you wait and see.
Believe me.

Refrain

Sam, You Made the Pants Too Long

Words by Fred Whitehouse and Milton Berle

recorded by Joe E. Lewis, Vaughn Monroe,
Barbra Streisand

Trousers grading, slowly dragging through the street.
Yes! I'm walking, but I'm walking without feet.
I'm not finding fault at all,
You're too big and I'm too small.
But Sam, you promised me both ends would meet.

You made the coat and vest fit the best,
You made the lining nice and strong.
But Sam, you made the pants too long.

You made the peak lapel look so swell,
So who am I to say you're wrong.
But Sam, you made the pants too long.

They got a belt and they got suspenders,
So what can they lose?
But what good are belts and what good suspenders
When the pants are hanging over the shoes?

You feel a winter breeze up and down the knees
The belt is where the tie belongs
'Cause Sam, Sam, Sam, you made the pants too long.

Satin Doll

Words by Johnny Mercer and Billy Strayhorn
Music by Duke Ellington

a standard recorded by Duke Ellington and various artists

Cigarette holder
Which wigs me
Over her shoulder,
She digs me
Out cattin' that satin doll.

Baby shall we go
Out skippin'
Careful amigo,
You're flippin'
Speaks Latin that satin doll.

She's nobody's fool,
So I'm playing it cool as can be,
I'll give it a whirl,
But I ain't for no girl catching me.

Spoken:
Switch-E-Rooney

Sung:
Telephone numbers well you know,
Doing my rhumbas with uno,
And that 'n' my satin doll.

Save the Best for Last

Words and Music by Phil Galdston, Jon Lind and
Wendy Waldman

recorded by Vanessa Williams

Sometimes the snow comes down in June.
Sometimes the sun goes 'round the moon.
I see the passion in your eyes.
Sometimes it's all a big surprise.

'Cause there was a time when all I did
Was wish you'd tell me this was love.
It's not the way I hoped or how I planned,
But somehow it's enough.

And now we're standing face to face
Isn't this world a crazy place?
Just when I thought our chance had passed,
You go and save the best for last.

All of the nights you came to me
When some silly girl had set you free.
You wondered how you'd make it through.
I wondered what was wrong with you.

'Cause how could you give your love
To someone else and share your dreams with me?
Sometimes the very thing you're looking for
Is the one thing you can't see.

But now we're standing face to face,
Isn't this world a crazy place?
Just when I thought our chance had passed
You go and save the best for last.

Sometimes the very thing you're looking for
Is the one thing you can't see.

Sometimes the snow comes down in June.
Sometimes the sun goes 'round the moon.
Just when I thought a chance had passed,
You go and save the best for last.
You went and saved the best for last.

Saving All My Love for You
Words by Gerry Goffin
Music by Michael Masser

recorded by Whitney Houston

A few stolen moments is all that we share.
You've got your family and they need you there.
Though I try to resist,
Being last on you list,
But no other man's gonna do,
So I'm saving all my love for you.

It's not very easy living all alone.
My friends try and tell me find a man of my own.
But each time I try,
I just break down and cry.
'Cause I'd rather be home feelin' blue,
So I'm saving all my love for you.

You used to tell me we'd run away together;
Love gives you the right to be free.
You said: "Be patient. Just wait a little longer,"
But that's just an old fantasy.
I've got to get ready, just a few minutes more.
Gonna get that old feelin' when you walk through that door.
'Cause tonight is the night for feeling all right.
We'll be making love the whole night through,
So I'm saving my love,
Yes I'm saving my love,
Yes I'm saving all my love for you.

No other woman is gonna love you more.
'Cause tonight is the night that I'm feeling all right.
We'll be making love the whole night through;
So I'm saving all my love,
Yes, I'm saving all my loving,
Yes I'm saving all my love for you.
For you.

Scotch and Soda
Words and Music by Dave Guard

recorded by The Kingston Trio, Mac Wiseman, Ray Price

Scotch and soda, mud in your eye,
Baby, do I feel high, oh me, oh my,
Do I feel high.
Dry martini, jigger of gin,
Oh, what a spell you've got me in, oh, my,
Do I feel high.

People won't believe me,
They'll think that I'm jesting.
But I could feel the way I feel,
And still be on the wagon.
All I need is one of your smiles,
Sunshine of your eyes, or me, oh my,
Do I feel higher than a kite can fly!
Give me lovin', baby, I feel high.

Sea of Love
Words and Music by George Khoury and Philip Baptiste

recorded by Phil Phillips & The Twilights, Del Shannon,
The Honeydrippers
featured in the film *Sea of Love*

Do you remember when we met,
That's the day I knew you were my pet.
I want to tell you
Just how much I love you.

Come with me my love
To the sea, the sea of love.
I want to tell you
Just how much I love you.

Come with me
To the sea
Of love.

Repeat Verse 1

Come with me
To the sea
Of love.

Come with me
My love
To the sea,
The sea of love.

I want to tell you
Just how much I love you.
I want to tell you,
Oh, how much
I love you.

Seasons of Love

Words and Music by Jonathan Larson

from the musical *Rent*

Five hundred twenty-five thousand six hundred minutes,
Five hundred twenty-five thousand moments so dear.
Five hundred twenty-five thousand six hundred minutes.
How do measure,
Measure a year?

In daylights, in sunsets,
In midnights, in cups of coffee,
In inches, in miles, in laughter, in strife,
In five hundred twenty-five thousand six hundred minutes.
How do you measure a year in the life.

How about love?
How about love?
How about love?
Measure in love.
Seasons of love,
Seasons of love.

Five hundred twenty-five thousand six hundred minutes,
Five hundred twenty-five thousand journeys to plan.
Five hundred twenty-five thousand six hundred minutes.
How do you measure the life of a woman or a man?

In truth that she learned,
Or in times that he cried,
In bridges he burned,
Or the way that she died.
It's time now to sing out,
Though the story never ends.
Let's celebrate, remember,
A year in the life of friends.

Remember the love,
Remember the love,
Remember the love,
Measure in love,
Seasons of love,
Seasons of love.

Second Hand Rose

Words by Grant Clarke
Music by James F. Hanley

from the musical *Ziegfeld Follies of 1921*
recorded by Fanny Brice, Barbra Streisand
featured in the film *Funny Girl*

Verse:
Father has a business,
Strictly second hand,
Everything from toothpicks
To a baby grand.
Stuff in our apartment
Came from father's store.
Even clothes I'm wearing,
Someone wore before.
It's no wonder
That I feel abused.
I never get a thing
That ain't been used.

I'm wearing second hand hats, second hand clothes,
That's why they call me second hand Rose.
Even our piano in the parlor,
Father bought for ten cents on the dollar.
Second hand pearls,
I'm wearing second hand curls.
I never get a single thing that's new.
Even Jake the plumber, he's the man I adore,
Had the nerve to tell me he's been married before.
Everyone knows that I'm just second hand Rose,
From Second Avenue.

I'm wearing second hand shoes, second hand hose,
All the girls hand me their second hand beaux.
Even my pajamas when I don 'em
Have somebody else's initials on 'em.
Second hand rings, I'm sick of second hand things.
I never get what other girlies do.
Once while strolling through the Ritz
A girl got my goat,
She nudged her friend and said,
"Ooh look, here's my old fur coat."
Everyone knows that I'm just Second Hand Rose,
From Second Avenue.

Semi-Charmed Life

Words and Music by Stephan Jenkins

recorded by Third Eye Blind

I'm packed and I'm holding.
I'm smiling, she's living, she's golden, she lives for me.
Says she lives for me.
Ovation, her own motivation.
She comes 'round and she goes down on me.
And I make her smile like a drug for you.
Do ever what you want to do.

Coming over you.
Keep on smiling what we go through.
One stop to the rhythm that divides you.
And I speak to you like the chorus to the verse.
Chop another line like a coda with a curse.
Come on like a freak show takes the stage.
We give them the games we play.
She said "I want something else
To get me through this semi-charmed life."
Baby, baby, I want something else.
I'm not listening when you say goodbye."

Do, do, do…
The sky, it was gold, it was rose.
I was taking sips of it through my nose.
And I wish I could get back there,
Someplace back there.
Smiling in the pictures you would take.
Doing crystal meth will lift you up until you break.
It won't stop. I won't come down,
I keep stock with a tick-tock rhythm.
A bump for the drop and then I bumped up,
I took the hit I was given then I bumped again,
Then I bumped again.
You said, "How do I get back there
To the place where I fell asleep inside you?"
How do I get myself back to the place where you said,
"I want something else
To get me through this semi-charmed life."
Baby, baby, I want something else.
I'm not listening when you say goodbye.

I believe in the sand beneath my toes.
The beach gives a feeling, an earthy feeling
I believe in the faith that grows.
And the four right chords and make me cry.
When I'm with you I feel like I could die
And that would be all right, all right.
And when the plane came in she said she was crashing.
The velvet, it rips.
In the city we tripped on the urge to feel alive.
But now I'm struggling to survive.
Those days you were wearing that velvet dress.
You're the priestess, I must confess.
Those little red panties, they pass the test.
Slide up around the belly, face down on the mattress.
One. And you hold me and we are broken.
Still, it's all that I want to do, just a little now.
Feel myself, head made of the ground.
I'm scared, I'm not coming down, no, no.
And I won't run for my life.
She's got her jaws just locked now in her smile
But nothing is right, all right.
And I want something else
To get me through this semi-charmed life.
Baby, I want something else,
Not listening when you say goodbye, goodbye.

The sky, it was gold, it was rose.
I was taking sips of it through my nose.
And I wish I could get back there,
Someplace back there in the place we used to stay.

Sentimental Journey
Words and Music by Bud Green, Les Brown and
Ben Homer

a standard recorded by Doris Day with Les Brown, Ella
Fitzgerald, The Ames Brothers and various other artists

Verse:
Every rolling stone gets to feel alone
When home, sweet home is far away.
I'm a rolling stone who's been so alone
Until today.

Refrain:
Gonna take a sentimental journey,
Gonna set my heart at ease,
Gonna make a sentimental journey
To renew old memories.

Got my bag, I got my reservation,
Spent each dime I could afford.
Like a child in wild anticipation,
Long to hear that "All aboard."

Seven,
That's the time we leave, at seven.
I'll be waitin' up for heaven,
Countin' every mile of railroad track
That takes me back.

Never thought my heart could be so "yearny."
Why did I decide to roam?
Gotta take this sentimental journey,
Sentimental journey, sentimental journey home.

Separate Lives
Words and Music by Stephen Bishop

Love Theme from *White Nights*
recorded by Phil Collins & Marilyn Martin

You called me from the room in your hotel
All full of romance for someone you had met,
And telling me how sorry you were,
Leaving so soon,
And that you miss me sometimes
When you're alone in your room.
Do I feel lonely too?

You have no right to ask me how I feel.
You have no right to speak to me so kind.
I can't go on holding onto ties
Now that we're living
Sep'rate lives.

Well, I held on to let you go.
And if you lost your love for me,
You never let it show.
There was no way to compromise.
So now we're livin'
Separate lives.

Oh, it's so typical;
Love leads to isolation.
So you build that wall,
So you build that wall
And make it stronger.

You have no right to ask me how I feel.
You have no right to speak to me so kind.
Someday I might find myself looking in your eyes.
But for now we'll go on living separate lives.
Yes, for now we'll go on
Living separate lives.

September Song
Words by Maxwell Anderson
Music by Kurt Weill

from the Musical Play *Knickerbocker Holiday*
a standard recorded by Frank Sinatra, Stan Kenton and
various other artists

Male:
When I was a young man courting the girls,
I played me a waiting game;
If a maid refused me with tossing curls,
I let the old earth take a couple of whirls,
While I plied her with tears in lieu of pearls
And as time came around she came my way,
As time came around she came.

Refrain:
Oh, it's a long, long while
From May to December,
But the days grow short
When you reach September.
When the autumn weather
Turns the leaves to flame,
One hasn't got time for the waiting game.
Oh, the days dwindle down
To a precious few,
September, November!
And these precious days
I'll spend with you,
These precious days
I'll spend with you.

Female:
When you meet with the young men early in spring,
They court you in song and rhyme,
They woo you with words and clover ring,
But if you examine the goods they bring,
They have little to offer but the songs they sing
And a plentiful waste of time of day,
A plentiful waste of time.

Refrain

Sgt. Pepper's Lonely Hearts Club Band
Words and Music by John Lennon and Paul McCartney

recorded by The Beatles

It was twenty years ago today
That Sgt. Pepper taught the band to play.
They've been going in and out of style
But they're guaranteed to raise a smile.
So may I introduce to you
The act you've known for all these years,
Sgt. Pepper's Lonely Hearts Club Band.

We're Sgt. Pepper's Lonely Hearts Club Band,
We hope you will enjoy the show.
We're Sgt. Pepper's Lonely Hearts Club Band,
Sit back and let the evening go.
Sgt. Pepper's lonely
Sgt. Pepper's lonely
Sgt. Pepper's Lonely Hearts Club Band.

It's wonderful to be here,
It's certainly a thrill.
You're such a lovely audience
We'd like to take you home with us,
We'd love to take you home.

I don't really want to stop the show
But I thought you might like to know
That the singer's going to sing a song
And he wants you all to sing along.
So may I introduce to you
The one and only Billy Shears
And Sgt. Pepper's Lonely Hearts Club Band.

Shall We Dance?

Lyrics by Oscar Hammerstein II
Music by Richard Rodgers

from the musical *The King and I*

We've just been introduced,
I do not know you well,
But when the music started,
Something drew me to your side.
So many men and girls are in each other's arms—
It made me think we might be
Similarly occupied.

Refrain:
Shall we dance?
On a bright cloud of music shall we fly?
Shall we dance?
Shall we then say "Good night" and mean "Good bye"?
Or, perchance,
When the last little star has left the sky,
Shall we still be together
With our arms around each other
And shall you be my new romance?
On the clear understanding
That this kind of thing can happen,
Shall we dance?
Shall we dance?
Shall we dance?

Shattered

Words and Music by Mick Jagger and Keith Richards

recorded by The Rolling Stones

Uh huh. Shattered. Uh huh. Shattered.

Spoken:
Love and hope and sex and dreams
Are still survivin' on the streets.
Look at me!
I'm in tatters.
I been shattered.

Sung:
Shattered.

Spoken:
Friends are so alarming and my lover's never charming.
Life's just a cocktail party on the street.
Big Apple people dressed in plastic bags directing traffic.
Some kind-a fashion.

Sung:
Shattered.

Spoken:
Laughter, joy and loneliness
And sex, and sex, and sex, and sex and
Look at me!
I'm in tatters.
I'm a-shattered.

Sung:
Shattered.

Spoken:
All this chitter chatter, chitter chatter,
Chitter chatter, 'bout shmatter, shmatter, shmatter.
I can't give it away on Seventh Avenue.
This town's been wearin' tatters. Uh huh.

Sung:
Sah-doo-bee. Shattered.

Spoken:
Work and work for love and sex.
Ain't you hungry for success?
Success, success, success!
Does it matter? I'm shattered.
Does it matter?
Pride and joy and greed and sex,
That's what makes our town the best.
Pride and joy and dirty dreams
Are still survivin' on the streets and look at me!
I'm in tatters. Yeah! I been battered.
What does it matter? What does it matter?
Uh huh, does it matter?

Uh huh, I'm a-shattered.
Mm. I'm shattered.

Sung:
Sha-doo-bee.

Spoken:
Shattered.
Don't you know the crime rate's goin'
Up, up, up, up, up?
To live in this town you must be
Tough, tough, tough, tough, tough, tough, tough.
My brain's been battered,
Splattered all over Manhattan.
Uh huh. What say?

Sung:
Sha-doo-bee. Shattered. Sha-doo-bee.
Shattered Sha-doo-bee.
Uh huh. This town's full of money grabbers.
Go ahead! Bite the Big Apple.
Don't mind the maggots!

Uh huh. Shattered. Sah-doo-bee.
My brain's been battered!
My family came around 'n' flatter, flatter,
Flatter, flatter, flatter, flatter, flatter.
Pile it up! Pile it up!
Pile it high on the platter.

She

Lyric by Herbert Kretzmer
Music by Charles Aznavour

recorded by Charles Aznavour
featured in the film *Notting Hill*

She may be the face I can't forget
A trace of pleasure or regret,
May be my treasure or the price I have to pay.
She may be the song that summer sings,
May be the chill that autumn brings,
May be a hundred different things
Within the measure of a day.

She may be the beauty or the beast,
May be the famine or the feast,
May turn each day into a heaven or hell.
She may be the mirror of my dream,
A smile reflected in a stream,
She may not be what she may seem inside her shell.

She who always seems so happy in a crowd,
Who's eyes can be so private and so proud,
No one's allowed to see them when they cry.
She may be the love that cannot hope to last,
May come to me from shadows of the past
That I'll remember 'til the day I die.

She may be the reason I survive,
The why and wherefore I'm alive,
The one I'll care for through the rough and ready years.
Me, I'll take her laughter and her tears
And make them all my souvenirs,
For where she goes I've got to be,
The meaning of my life is she, she, she.

She Came in Through the Bathroom Window

Words and Music by John Lennon and Paul McCartney

recorded by The Beatles

She came in through the bathroom window,
Protected by a silver spoon,
But now she sucks her thumb and wonders,
By the banks of her own lagoon.

Didn't anybody tell her?
Didn't anybody see?
Sundays on the phone to Monday,
Tuesdays on the phone to me.

She said she'd always been a dancer.
She worked at fifteen clubs a day.
And though she thought I knew the answer,
Well I knew I could not say.

And so I quit the police department,
And got myself a steady job.
And though she tried her best to help me,
She could steal but she could not rob.

Didn't anybody tell her?
Didn't anybody see?
Sundays on the phone to Monday,
Tuesdays on the phone to me.

She (He) Touched Me

Lyric by Ira Levin
Music by Milton Schafer

from the musical *Drat! The Cat!*
recorded by Barbra Streisand

Note: Though the original lyric was "She Touched Me,"
the song has become best known as "He Touched Me" due
to Barbra Streisand's recording

She (He) touched me,
She (He) put her hand near mine and then
She (He) touched me.
I felt a sudden tingle when she touched me,
A sparkle, a glow!

She (He) knew it,
It wasn't accidental,
No, she (he) knew it.
She (He) smiled and seemed to tell me so all through it,
She (He) knew it, I know.

She's (He's) real and world is alive and shining.
I feel such a wonderful drive toward valentining..
She (He) touched me, I simply have to face the fact,
She (He) touched me.
Control myself and try to act as if I remember my name.
But she (he) touched me,
She (He) touched me,
And suddenly nothing is the same.

She's Always a Woman

Words and Music by Billy Joel
© 1977, 1978 IMPULSIVE MUSIC

recorded by Billy Joel

She can kill with a smile.
She can wound with her eyes.
She can ruin your faith
With her casual lies.
And she only reveals
What she wants you to see.
She hides like a child,
But she's always a woman to me.

She can lead you to love,
She can take you or leave you.
She can ask for the truth,
But she'll never believe you,
And she'll take what you give her
As long as it's free,
Yeah, she steals like a thief,
But she's always a woman to me.

Refrain:
Oh, she takes care of herself,
She can wait if she wants,
She's ahead of her time.
Oh, and she never gives out
And she never gives in,
She just changes her mind.

And she'll promise you more
Than the garden of Eden.
Then she'll carelessly cut you
And laugh while you're bleedin'.
But she brings out the best
And the worst you can be,
Blame it all on yourself
'Cause she's always a woman to me.

Refrain

She is frequently kind
And she's suddenly cruel.
She can do as she pleases,
She's nobody's fool.
But she can't be convicted,
She's earned her degree.
And the most she will do
Is throw shadows at you,
But she's always a woman to me.

She's Gone

Words and Music by Daryl Hall and John Oates
Copyright © 1973, 1974 by Unichappell Music Inc.

recorded by Hall & Oates

Everybody's high on consolation,
Everybody's tryin' to tell me what is right for me, yeah.
I need a drink and a quick decision,
Now it's up to me, oo, what will it be?

Get up in the morning and look in the mirror,
I'm worn as her toothbrush hangin' in the stand, yeah.
My face ain't lookin' any younger.
Now I can see love's taken her toll on me.

Refrain:
She's gone, oh, I, oh, I,
I better learn how to face it.
She's gone, she's gone, oh, I, oh, I
I'd pay the devil to replace her.
She gone, and she's gone, oh I, what went wrong?

Think I'll spend eternity in the city;
Let the carbon and monoxide choke my thoughts away, yeah.
Pretty bodies help dissolve the memories,
They can never be what she was to me.

Refrain Twice

She's Gonna Make It

Words and Music by Kent Blazy, Kim Williams and
Garth Brooks
Copyright © 1994, 1997 by Careers-BMG Music Publishing, Inc., A Hard Day's Write Music,
    Sony/ATV Tunes LLC, Kim Williams Music, Major Bob Music, Inc. and No Fences Music
All Rights for A Hard Day's Write Music Administered by Careers-BMG Music Publishing, Inc.
All Rights for Sony/ATV Tunes LLC and Kim Williams Music Administered by
    Sony/ATV Music Publishing, 8 Music Square West, Nashville, TN 37203

recorded by Garth Brooks

He followed her to work this morning.
He'd never seen that dress before.
And she seemed to sail right though those dark clouds
  forming,
That he knows he's headed for.
After seven years of marriage, he wanted out.
Now after seven months of freedom it's clear
That there's no doubt,
She's gonna make it and he never will.

He's at the foot of the mountain, she's over that hill.
He's sinkin' at sea, and her sails are filled.
She's gonna make and he never will.
And you know it's not like she's forgot about him.
She's just dealing with the pain.
And the fact that she survived so well without him
You know it's driving him insane.
And the crazy thing about it is she'd take him back,
But the fool in him that walked out
Is the fool that just won't ask.

She's gonna make it and he never will.
He's at the foot of the mountain, she's over that hill.
He's sinking at sea and her sails are filled.
She's gonna make it and he never will.
Lord, she's gonna make it, he never will.

She's Got a Way
Words and Music by Billy Joel
© 1971 (Renewed 1999) IMPULSIVE MUSIC

recorded by Billy Joel

She's got a way about her.
I don't know what it is,
But I know that I can't live without her.
She's got a way of pleasin'.
I don't know what it is,
But there doesn't have to be a reason anywhere.

She's got a smile that heals me.
I don't know what it is,
But I have to laugh when she reveals me.
She's got a way of talkin'.
I don't know what it is,
But it lifts me up when we are walkin' anywhere.

She comes to me when I'm feelin' down,
Inspires me without a sound.
She touches me and I get turned around.
She's got a way of showin' how I make her feel,
And I find the strength to keep on goin'.

She's got a light around her,
And everywhere she goes,
A million dreams of love surround her everywhere.
She comes to me when I'm feelin' down,
Inspires me without a sound.
She touches me, I get turned around.
Oh, oh, oh.

She's got a smile that heals me.
I don't know why it is,
But I have to laugh when she reveals me.
She's got a way about her.
I don't know what it is,
But I know that I can't live without her anyway.

She's So Cold
Words and Music by Mick Jagger and Keith Richards
© 1980 EMI MUSIC PUBLISHING LTD.
All Rights for the U.S. and Canada Controlled and
    Administered by COLGEMS-EMI MUSIC INC.

recorded by The Rolling Stones

I'm so hot for her, I'm so hot for her,
I'm so hot for her and she's so cold.
I'm so hot for her, I'm so hot for her,
I'm so hot for her and she's so cold.
I'm a burning bush, I'm the burning fire,

I'm the bleeding volcano.
I'm so hot for her, I'm so hot for her,
I'm so hot for her and she's so cold.

Yes, I've tried rewiring her, tried refiring her,
I think her engine is permanently stalled.
She's so cold, she's so cold,
She's so cold, cold, cold,
Like a tomb of stone.
She's so cold, she's so cold,
She's so cold, cold, cold,
Like an ice cream cone.
She's so cold, she's so cold,
When I touched her my hand just froze.

I'm so hot for her, I'm so hot for her,
I'm so hot for her, she's so cold.
Put your hand on the heat, put your hand on the heat,
I'm coming on baby let's go, go.
She's so cold, she's so cold, cold, she's so c,c,c,c,cold,
But she's beautiful.

She's so cold.
She's so cold, she's so cold,
I think she was born in an arctic zone.
She's so cold, she's so cold, cold, cold.
When I touched her, my hand just froze.
She's so cold, she's so god-damn cold,
She's so cold, cold, cold,
She's so cold.

Who will believe you were a beauty indeed,
When the days get shorter and the nights get long?
Light fades and the rain comes;
Nobody will know
When you're old, when your old,
Nobody will know that you was a beauty,
A sweet, sweet, beauty, a sweet, sweet beauty,
But stone, stone cold.
You're so cold, You're so cold, cold, cold.
You're so cold, you're so cold.
I'm so hot for you, I'm so hot for you,
I'm so hot for you and you're so cold.

Repeat and Fade:
I'm a burning bush, I'm the burning fire,
I'm the bleeding volcano.

Side by Side
Words and Music by Harry Woods
Copyright © 1927 Shapiro, Bernstein & Co., Inc., New York
Copyright Renewed

a standard recorded by Kay Starr and various other artists

Oh! We ain't got a barrel of money,
Maybe we're ragged and funny,
But we'll travel along,
Singin' a song,
Side by side.

Don't know what's comin' tomorrow,
Maybe it's trouble and sorrow,
But we'll travel the road,
Sharin' the load,
Side by side.

Through all kinds of weather,
What if the sky should fall,
Just as long as we're together,
It doesn't matter at all.

When they've all had their quarrels and parted,
We'll be the same as we started,
Just travelin' along,
Singin' a song,
Side by side.

The Sign
Words and Music by buddha, joker, jenny and linn
Copyright © 1993 by Megasong Publishing APS
All Rights for the U.S. Administered by Careers-BMG Music Publishing, Inc.

recorded by Ace of Base

I got a new life.
You'd hardly recognize me.
I'm so glad.
How could a person like me check on you?
Why do I bother when you're not the one for me?

Is enough enough?
I saw the sign and opened my eyes.
I saw the sign.
Life is demanding without understanding.
I saw the sign and it opened my eyes.
I saw the sign.
No one's gonna drag you up
To get into the light where you belong
(But where do you belong?)

I saw the sign and it opened up my mind.
And I am happy now livin' without you.
I loved you, oh, oh, oh.
I saw the sign and it opened up my eyes
I saw the sign.

No one's gonna drag you up
Into the light where you belong.
(I saw the sign. I saw the sign.)
I saw the sign.
(I saw the sign. I saw the sign.
I saw the sign. I saw the sign.)
I saw the sign and it opened up my eyes.
I saw the sign.

Silhouettes
Words and Music by Frank C. Slay Jr. and Bob Crewe
Copyright © 1957 (Renewed) by Regent Music Corporation (BMI)

recorded by The Rays, The Diamonds,
Steve Gibson & The Redcaps, Herman's Hermits

Took a walk and passed your house late last night,
All the shades were pulled and drawn 'way down tight;
From within a dim light cast
Two silhouettes on the shade,
Oh, what a lovely couple they made.

Put his arms around your waist, held you tight,
Kisses I could almost taste in the night,
Wondered why I'm not the guy
Who's silhouette's on the shade
I couldn't hide the tears in my eyes.

Lost control, and rang your bell, I was sore,
"Let me in or else I'll beat down your door."
When two strangers, who had been
Two silhouettes on the shade
Said to my shock, "You're on the wrong block."

Rushed down to your house with wings on my feet,
Loved you like I've never loved you my sweet,
Vowed that you and I would be
Two silhouettes on the shade
All of our days,
Two silhouettes on the shade.

Silver Threads and Golden Needles
Words and Music by Dick Reynolds and Jack Rhodes
© 1956 (Renewed 1984) BEECHWOOD MUSIC CORP., FORT KNOX MUSIC, INC.
and TRIO MUSIC COMPANY, INC. for the U.S.A.
All Rights for the world excluding U.S.A. Controlled and
Administered by BEECHWOOD MUSIC CORP.

recorded by The Springfields, Linda Ronstadt, Jody Miller,
The Cowsills

I don't want your lonely mansion,
With a tear in every room.
All I want's the love you promised
Beneath the hallowed moon.

But you think I should be happy,
With your money and your name,
And hide myself in sorrow
While you play your cheatin' game.

Refrain:
Silver threads and golden needles
Cannot mend this heart of mine,
And I dare not drown my sorrow
In the warm glow of your wine.

But you think I should be happy,
With your money and your name
And hide myself in sorrow
While you play your cheatin' game.

Refrain

You can't buy my love with money.
For I never was that kind,
Silver threads and golden needles
Cannot mend this heart of mine.

Since I Don't Have You

Words and Music by James Beaumont, Janet Vogel,
Joseph Verscharen, Walter Lester, Lennie Martin,
Joseph Rock and John Taylor
Copyright © 1959 by Bonnyview Music Corp.
Copyright Renewed
All Rights Administered by Southern Music Pub. Co. Inc.

recorded by The Skyliners, Chuck Jackson, Eddie Holman,
Art Garfunkel, Don McLean

I don't have plans and schemes
And I don't have daydreams.
I don't have anything
Since I don't have you.

I don't have fond desires
And I don't have happy hours.
I don't have anything
Since I don't have you.

I don't have happiness
And I guess I never will ever again.
When you walked out on me
In walked misery,
And he's been here since then.

Now I don't have much to share,
And I don't have one to care.
I don't have anything
Since I don't have you you you you
You you you you
You you you you
You.

Sincerely

Words and Music by Alan Freed and Harvey Fuqua
Copyright © 1954 ALAN FREED MUSIC and LIASON II PUBLISHING, INC.
Copyright Renewed

recorded by The McGuire Sisters

Sincerely, oh, yes, sincerely,
'Cause I love you so dearly.
Please say you'll be mine.
Sincerely, oh, you know how I love you.
I'll do anything for you;
Please say you'll be mine.

Oh, Lord, won't you tell me why I love that fella [girl] so?
He [she] doesn't want me.
Oh, I'll never, never, never, never let him [her] go.
Sincerely, oh, you know how I love you!
I'll do anything for you.
Please say you'll be mine.

Sing for Your Supper

Words by Lorenz Hart
Music by Richard Rodgers
Copyright © 1938 by Williamson Music and The Estate Of Lorenz Hart in the United States
Copyright Renewed
All Rights on behalf of The Estate Of Lorenz Hart Administered by WB Music Corp.

from the musical *The Boys from Syracuse*

Hawks and crows do lots of things,
But the canary only sings.
She is a courtesan on wings—
So I've heard.
Eagles and storks are twice as strong.
All the canary knows is a song.
But the canary gets along—
Gilded bird!

Sing for your supper,
And you'll get breakfast.
Songbirds always eat
If their song is sweet to hear.
Sing for your luncheon,
And you'll get dinner.
Dine with wine of choice,
If romance is in your voice.
I heard from a wise canary
Trilling makes a fellow willing,
So, little swallow, swallow now.
Now is the time to
Sing for your supper,
And you'll get breakfast.
Songbirds are not dumb,
They don't buy a crumb
Of bread,
It's said.
So sing and you'll be fed.

Singing the Blues

Words and Music by Melvin Endsley

recorded by Marty Robbins, Guy Mitchell

Well I never felt more like singing the blues
'Cause I never thought that I'd ever lose your love, dear,
Why'd you do me this way?

Well, I never felt more like crying all night
'Cause everything's wrong and nothing's right
Without you.
You got me singing the blues.

The moon and stars no longer shine,
The dream is gone I thought was mine.
There's nothing left for me to do
But cry over you.

Well, I never felt more like running away
But why should I go
'Cause I couldn't stay without you.
You got me singing the blues.

Sir Duke

Words and Music by Stevie Wonder

recorded by Stevie Wonder

Music is a world within itself
With a language we all understand,
With an equal opportunity
For all to sing, dance and clap their hands.
But just because a record has a groove,
Don't make it in the groove,
But you can tell right away at letter A
When the people start to move.

Refrain:
They {you} can feel it all over.
They {you} can feel it all over, people.
They {you} can feel it all over.
They {you} can feel it all over, people go!

Music knows it is and always will be
One of the things that life just won't quit.
But here are some of music's pioneers,
That time will not allow us to forget now.
For there's Basie, Miller, Satchmo
And the king of all, Sir Duke,
With a voice like Ella's ringin' out
There's no way the band can lose.

Refrain

Sit Down You're Rockin' the Boat

By Frank Loesser

from the musical *Guys and Dolls*

I dreamed last night I got on the boat to heaven
And by some chance I had brought my dice along.
And there I stood and I hollered, "Someone fade me,"
But the passengers they knew right from wrong.

For the people all said, "Sit down,
Sit down, you're rockin' the boat;
And the devil will drag you under
By the sharp lapel of your checkered coat;
Sit down, sit down, sit down, sit down,
Sit down, you're rockin' the boat.

I sailed away on that little boat to heaven
And by some chance found a bottle in my fist.
And there I stood nicely passin' out the whiskey,
But the passengers were bound to resist.

For all the people said, "Beware,
Beware you'll scuttle the ship;
And the devil will drag you under
By the fancy tie 'round your wicked throat;
Sit down, sit down, sit down, sit down,
Sit down, you're rockin' the boat.

And as I laughed at those passengers to heaven
A great big wave came and washed me overboard.
And as I sank, and I hollered, "Someone save me,"
That's the moment I woke up, thank the Lord.

And I said to myself, "Sit down,
Sit down, you're rockin' the boat."
Said to myself, "Sit down, you're rockin' the boat."
And the devil will drag you under
With a soul so heavy you'd never float;
Sit down, sit down, sit down, sit down,
Sit down, you're rockin' the boat.

Sixteen Tons

Words and Music by Merle Travis

recorded by Tennessee Ernie Ford

Some people say a man is made out of mud
A poor man's made out of muscle and blood,
Muscle and blood and skin and bones,
A mind that's weak and back that's strong.

Refrain:
You load sixteen tons. What do you get?
Another day older and deeper in debt.
Saint Peter, don't you call me 'cause I can't go
I owe my soul to the company store.

I was born one mornin' when the sun didn't shine
I picked up my shovel and I walked to the mine,
I loaded sixteen tons of number nine coal.
And the straw boss said, "Well-a bless my soul."

Refrain

I was born one mornin', it was drizzling rain
Fightin' and trouble are my middle name.
I was raised in a cane brake by an ole mama lion.
Cain't no hightoned woman make me walk the line.

Refrain

If you see me comin' better step aside
A lotta men didn't a lotta men died.
One first of iron the other of steel.
If the right one don't-a get you, then the left one will.

Refrain

Skylark
Words by Johnny Mercer
Music by Hoagy Carmichael

a standard recorded by Ray Eberle with Glenn Miller,
Dinah Shore, Bing Crosby and various artists

Skylark,
Have you anything to say to me?
Won't you tell me where my love can be?
Is there a meadow in the mist,
Where someone's waiting to be kissed?

Skylark,
Have you seen a valley green with spring?
Where my heart can go a journeying?
Over the shadows the rain,
To a blossom covered lane?

And in your lonely flight,
Haven't you heard the music in the night?
Wonderful music, faint as a "will-o' the wisp,"
Crazy as a loon,
Sad as a gypsy serenading the moon.

Skylark,
I don't know if I can find these things.
But my heart is riding on your wings,
So, if you see them anywhere
Won't you lead me there?

A Sleepin' Bee
Lyric by Truman Capote and Harold Arlen
Music by Harold Arlen

from the musical *House of Flowers*
recorded by Barbra Streisand and various other artists

When you're in love and you are wonderin',
If he really is the one.
There's an ancient sign sure to tell you
If your search is over and done.
Catch a bee and if he don't sting you,
You're in a spell that's just begun.
It's a guarantee 'till the end of time
Your true love you have won, have won.

When a bee lies sleepin'
In the the palm of your hand,
You're bewitched and deep in
Love's long looked after land.

Where you'll see a sun-up sky
With a mornin' new,
And where the days go laughin' by
As love comes a-callin' on you.

Sleep on, bee, don't waken,
Can't believe what just passed.
He's mine for the takin',
I'm so happy at last.

Maybe I dreams, but he seems
Sweet golden as a crown,
A sleepin' bee done told me,
I'll walks with feet off the groun'
When my one true love I has foun'.

Repeat Entire Song

Small World
Words by Stephen Sondheim
Music by Jule Styne

from the musical *Gypsy*

Funny, you're a stranger who's come here,
Come from another town.
Funny, I'm a stranger myself here.
Small world, isn't it?

Funny, you're a girl who goes traveling,
Rather than settling down.
Funny, 'cause I'd love to go traveling.
Small world, isn't it?

We have so much in common,
It's a phenomenon.
We could pool our resources
By joining forces from now on.

Lucky, you're a girl who likes children,
That's an important sign.
Lucky, 'cause I'd love to have children.
Small world, isn't it? Funny, isn't it?
Small and funny and fine.

Smoke on the Water
Words and Music by Ritchie Blackmore, Ian Gillan,
Roger Glover, Jon Lord and Ian Paice

recorded by Deep Purple

We all came to Montreux
On the Lake Geneva shoreline
To make records with the mobile,
We didn't have much time.
But Frank Zappa and the Mothers
Were at the best place around.
But some stupid with a flare gun
Burned the place to the ground.

Refrain:
Smoke on the water, a fire in the sky.
Smoke on the water.

They burned down the gambling house,
It died with an awful sound.
A funky Claude was running in and out,
Pulling kids on the ground.
When it all was over,
We had to find another place.
But Swiss time was running out,
It seemed that we would lose the race.

Refrain

We ended up at the Grand Hotel,
It was empty, cold and bare.
But with the Rollin Truck Stones thing just outside,
Making our music there.
With a few red lights, a few old beds,
We made a place to sweat.
No matter what we got out of this,
I know we'll never forget.

Refrain

So Far Away
Words and Music by Carole King

recorded by Carole King

So far away!
Doesn't anybody stay in one place anymore?
It would be so fine to see your face at my door.
Doesn't help to know that you're just time away.
Long ago, I reached for you and there you stood.
Holding you again could only do me good.
How I wish I could, but you're so far away!

One more song about movin' along the highway.
Can't say much of anything that's new.
If I could only work this life out my way,
I'd rather spend it bein' close to you.
But you're so…

Repeat Verse 1

Yeah, you're so far away!
Travelin' around sure gets me down and lonely.
Nothin' else to do but close my mind.
I sure hope the road don't come to own me.
There's so many dreams I've yet to find.
But you're so far away!

Repeat Verses 1 and 2 and Fade

Solitude
Words and Music by Duke Ellington, Eddie De Lange and
Irving Mills

a standard recorded by Duke Ellington and various
other artists
featured in the musical revue *Sophisticated Ladies*

In my solitude you haunt me
With reveries of days gone by.
In my solitude you taunt me
With memories that never die.
I sit in my chair,
Filled with despair,
Nobody could be so sad.
With gloom everywhere
I sit and stare,
I know that I'll soon go mad.
In my solitude,
I'm praying
Dear Lord above,
Send back my love.

Some Enchanted Evening

Lyrics by Oscar Hammerstein II
Music by Richard Rodgers

from the musical *South Pacific*

Some enchanted evening
You may see a stranger,
You may see a stranger
Across a crowded room.
And somehow you know,
You know even then,
That somewhere you'll see her again and again.

Some enchanted evening
Someone may be laughing,
You may hear her laughing
Across a crowded room—
And night after night,
As strange as it seems,
The sound of her laughter will sing in your dreams.

Who can explain it?
Who can tell you why?
Fools give you reasons—
Wise men never try.

Some enchanted evening
When you find your true love,
When you hear her call you
Across a crowded room,
Then fly to her side
And make her your own,
Or all through your life
You may dream all alone.
Once you have found her,
Never let her go.
Once you have found her,
Never let her go.

(She's) Some Kind of Wonderful

Words and Music by John Ellison

recorded by Grand Funk Railroad

I don't need a whole lot's of money.
I don't need a big fine car.
I got everything that a man could want.
I got more then I could ask for.
I, I don't have to run around.
I don't have to stay out all night.
'Cause I got me a sweet, sweet lovin' woman
And she knows just how to treat me right.

Refrain:
Well, my baby, she's alright.
She's clean out of sight.
Don't you know that she's,
She's some kind of wonderful.
She's some kind of wonderful.
Yeah, she is, she's some kind of wonderful.
Yeah, yeah, yeah, yeah.

When I hold her in my arms,
You know she sets my soul on fire.
Ooh, when my baby kisses me
My heart becomes filled with desire.
When she wraps her lovin' arms around me
It about drives me out of my mind.
Yeah, when my baby kisses me
Chills run up and down my spine.

Refrain

Now is there anybody
Got a sweet little woman like mine?
There's got to be somebody
Got a sweet little woman like mine.
Yeah. Now can I witness?
Can I get a witness?
Well, can I get a witness?
Can I get a witness?
Can I get a witness?
Can I get a witness?
I'm talkin', talkin' 'bout my baby.

Repeat and Fade:
She's some kind of wonderful.
Talkin' 'bout my baby.
She's some kind of wonderful.

Somebody Loves Me

Words by B.G. DeSylva and Ballard MacDonald
Music by George Gershwin
French Version by Emelia Renaud

from the musical revue *George White's Scandals of 1924*
a standard recorded by Peggy Lee, Ella Fitzgerald and
various other artists

When this old world began
It was heaven's plan.
There should be a girl for every single man.
To my great regret
Someone has upset,
Heaven's pretty program for we've never met.
I'm clutching at straws,
Just because
I may meet her yet.

Refrain:
Somebody loves me
I wonder who,
I wonder who she can be.
Somebody loves me
I wish I knew,
Who can she be worries me.
For every girl who passes me I shout, Hey! maybe
You were meant to be my loving baby.
Somebody loves me
I wonder who,
Maybe it's you.

Repeat Refrain

Someday

Music by Alan Menken
Lyrics by Stephen Schwartz

from Walt Disney's *The Hunchback of Notre Dame*
recorded by All-4-One

Someday when we are wiser,
When the world's older,
When we have learned,
I pray someday we may yet live
To live and let live.

Someday life will be fairer,
Need will be rarer,
And greed will not pay.
Godspeed this millennium on its way,
Let it come someday.

Someday our fight will be won then,
We'll stand in the sun then
That bright afternoon.
Till then on days when the sun is gone,
We'll hang on and we'll wish upon the moon.

There are some days dark and bitter,
Seems we haven't got a prayer,
But a prayer for someday better
Is the one thing we all share.

Someday when we are wiser,
When the world's older,
When we have learned,
I pray someday we may yet live
To live and let live.

Someday life will be fairer,
Need will be rarer,
Greed will not pay.
Godspeed this millennium on its way,
Let it come, wish upon the moon.
One day, someday soon.
One day, someday soon.

Someone Like You

Words by Leslie Bricusse
Music by Frank Wildhorn

from the musical *Jekyll & Hyde*

I peered through the windows, watched life go by
Dreamed of tomorrow, but stayed inside.
The past was holding me, keeping life at bay.
I wandered, lost in yesterday,
Wanting to fly, but scared to try.

Then someone like you found someone like me.
And suddenly nothing is the same.
My heart's taken wing, I feel so alive,
'Cause someone like you found me.

It's like you took my dreams, made each one real,
You reached inside of me and made me feel.
And now I see a world I've never seen before.
Your love has opened every door;
You've set me free, now I can soar.

For someone like you found someone like me.
You touched my heart, nothing is the same.
There's a new way to live, a new way to love,
'Cause someone like you found me.

Oh, someone like you found someone like me.
And suddenly nothing will ever be the same.
My heart's taken wing, and I feel so alive,
'Cause someone like you loves me,
Loves me.

Someone Saved My Life Tonight

Words and Music by Elton John and Bernie Taupin

recorded by Elton John

When I think of those east end lights,
Muggy nights,
The curtains drawn
In the little downstairs
Prima donna, lord, you really should have been there.
Sitting like a princess perched in her electric chair.
And it's one more beer
And I don't hear you anymore.
We've all gone crazy lately,
My friends out there rollin' the basement floor.

Refrain:
And someone saved my life tonight,
Sugar bear.
You almost had your hooks in me
Didn't you dear?
You nearly had me roped and tied,
Altar bound, hypnotized,
Sweet freedom whispered in my ear.
You're a butterfly,
And butterflies are free to fly,
Fly away high away bye bye.

I never realized the passing hours
Of evening showers,
A slip noose hanging in my darkest dreams.
I'm strangled by your haunted social scene
Just a pawn out-played by a dominating queen.
It's four-o'clock in the morning
Damn it!
Listen to me good.
I'm sleeping with myself tonight,
Saved in time, thank God my music's still alive

Refrain

And I would have walked head on
Into the deep end of a river,
Clinging to your stocks and bonds,
Paying your H. P. demands forever.
They're coming in the morning with a truck
To take me home.
Someone saved my life tonight,
Someone saved my life tonight,
Someone saved my life tonight,
Someone saved my life tonight,
Someone saved my life tonight,
So save your strength
And run the field you play alone.

Refrain

Someone saved my life tonight,
Someone saved my life tonight.

Something About the Way You Look Tonight
Words and Music by Elton John and Bernie Taupin

recorded by Elton John

There was a time I was everything and nothing all in one.
When you found me, I was feeling like a cloud across the sun.

Well, I need to tell you how you light up every second
 of the day,
But in the moonlight, you just shine like a beacon of the bay.

Refrain:
I can't explain,
But there's something about the way you look tonight,
Takes my breath away.
It's that feeling I get about you deep inside.
And I can't describe,
But there's something about the way you look tonight,
Takes my breath away.
The way you look tonight.

With that smile you pull the deepest secrets from my heart.
In all honesty, I'm speechless and I don't know where to
start.

Refrain

The way you look tonight…

Something to Talk About (Let's Give Them Something to Talk About)
Words and Music by Shirley Eikhard

recorded by Bonnie Raitt
featured in the film *Something to Talk About*

People are talking,
Talking about people.
I hear them whisper,
"You won't believe it."
They think we're lovers
Kept undercover.
I just ignore it.
They keep saying we
Laugh just a little too loud,
Stand just a little too close,
We stare just a little too long.
Maybe they're seeing something we don't, darling.

Let's give them something to talk about.
Let's give them something to talk about.
I wanna give them something to talk about.
I want your love.

I feel so foolish.
I never noticed that,
Baby, you're acting so nervous
Like you're falling.
It took a rumor
To make me wonder.
Now I'm convinced that
You're going under, now.
Thinking about you every day,
Dreaming about you every night,
Hoping that you feel the same way.
Now that we know it, let's really show it, baby.

Come on, give them something to talk about.
A little mystery to figure out.
I wanna give them something to talk about,
Talk about love.

Give a little something to talk about
I got some mystery, why don't you just figure out.
Give them something to talk about.
How about love?
Listen up, baby.
A little mystery won't hurt.
Give them something to talk about.
How about love?

Something Wonderful

Lyrics by Oscar Hammerstein II
Music by Richard Rodgers

from the musical *The King and I*

This is a man who thinks with his heart,
His heart is not always wise.
This is a man who stumbles and falls,
But this is a man who tries.
This is a man you'll forgive and forgive,
And help and protect, as long as you live…

He will not always say
What you would have him say,
But now and then he'll say
Something wonderful.

The thoughtless things he'll do
Will hurt and worry you,
But now and then he'll do
Something wonderful.

He has a thousand dreams
That won't come true.
You know that he believes in them
And that's enough for you.
You'll always go along,
Defend him when he's wrong
And tell him, when he's strong
He is wonderful.
He'll always need your love—
And so he'll get your love—
A man who needs your love
Can be wonderful!

Sometimes When We Touch

Words by Dan Hill
Music by Barry Mann

recorded by Dan Hill

You ask me if I love you,
And I choke on my reply.
I'd rather hurt you honestly
Than mislead you with a lie.
And who am I to judge you
On what you say or do?
I'm only just beginning
To see the real you.

Refrain:
And sometimes when we touch,
The honesty's too much,
And I have to close my eyes and hide.
I wanna hold you till I die,
Till we both break down and cry,
I wanna hold you
Till the fear in me subsides.

Romance and all its strategy
Leaves me battling with my pride
But through the insecurity
Some tenderness survives.
I'm just another writer
Still trapped within my truths;
A hesitant prize-fighter
Still trapped within my youth.

At times I'd like to break you
And drive you to your knees.
At times I'd like to break through
And hold you endlessly.

At times I understand you,
And I know how hard you've tried,
I've watched while love commands you,
And I've watched love pass you by.
At times I think we're drifters,
Still searching for a friend,
A brother or a sister.
But then the passion flares again.

Refrain

Somewhere in the Night

Words and Music by Will Jennings and Richard Kerr

recorded by Barry Manilow

Time, you found time enough to love,
And I found love enough to hold you.
So tonight I'll stir the fire you feel inside
Until the flames of love enfold you.
Layin' beside you, lost in the feeling,
So glad you opened my door.
Come with me, somewhere in the night we will know
Everything lovers can know.
You're my song, music too magic to end,
I'll play you over and over again.
Lovin' so warm, movin' so right,
Closin' our eyes, and feelin' the light,
We'll just go on burnin' bright,
Somewhere in the night.

You'll sleep when the mornin' comes.
And I'll lie and watch you sleepin'.
And you'll smile when you dream about the night,
Like it's a secret you've been keepin'.
Layin' beside you, lost in the feeling,
So glad you opened my door.
You're my song, music too magic to end,
I'll play you over and over again.
Lovin' so warm, movin' so right,
Closin' our eyes and feelin' the light.
We'll just go on burnin' bright,
Somewhere in the night.
We'll just go on burnin' bright,
Somewhere in the night.

Sooner or Later
(I Always Get My Man)

Words and Music by Stephen Sondheim

from the film *Dick Tracy*

Sooner or later you're gonna be mine.
Sooner or later you're gonna be fine.
Baby, it's time that you faced it,
I always get my man.

Sooner or later you're gonna decide.
Sooner or later there's nowhere to hide.
Baby, it's time, so why waste it in chatter?
Let's settle the matter.
Baby, you're mine on a platter,
I always get my man.

But if you insist, babe,
The challenge delights me.
The more you resist, babe,
The more it excites me.
And no one I've kissed, babe,
Ever fights me again.
If you're on my list,
It's just a question of when.
When I get a yen,
Then baby, Amen.
I'm counting to ten,
And then

I'm gonna love you like nothing you've known.
I'm gonna love you, and you all alone.
Sooner is better than later but lover,
I'll hover,
I'll plan.
This time I'm not only getting,
I'm holding my man.

Sophisticated Lady

Words and Music by Duke Ellington, Irving Mills and
Mitchell Parish

a standard recorded by Duke Ellington, Art Tatum,
Stan Kenton and various other artists
featured in the musical revue *Sophisticated Ladies*

They say into your early life romance came
And this heart of yours burned a flame,
A flame that flickered one day
And died away.
Then, with disillusion deep in your eyes
You learned that fools in love soon grow wise.

The years have changed you, somehow
I see you now…
Smoking, drinking,
Never thinking of tomorrow,
Nonchalant.
Diamonds shining,
Dancing, dining
With some man in a restaurant.
Is that all you really want?
No, sophisticated lady,
I know
You miss the love you lost long ago,
And when nobody is nigh
You cry.

Sorry Seems to Be the Hardest Word

Words and Music by Elton John and Bernie Taupin

recorded by Elton John

What have I got to do to make you love me?
What have I got to do to make you care?
What do I do when lightning strikes me
And I wake to find that you're not there?
What do I do to make you want me?
What have I gotta do to be heard?
What do I say when it's all over?
Sorry seems to be the hardest word.

Refrain:
It's sad, (It's so sad.)
It's so sad.
It's a sad, sad situation,
And it's getting more and more absurd.
It's sad, (It's so sad.)
It's so sad.
Why can't we talk it over?
Always seems to me
That sorry seems to be the hardest word.

What do I do to make you love me?
What have I gotta do to be heard?
What do I do when lightning strikes me?
What have I got to do,
What have I got to do?
Sorry seems to be the hardest word.

(You're My) Soul and Inspiration

Words and Music by Barry Mann and Cynthia Weil

recorded by The Righteous Brothers

Girl, I can't let you do this,
Let you walk away.
Girl, how can I live through this,
When you're all I wake for each say?
Baby:

Refrain:
You're my soul and my life's inspiration,
You're all I've got to get me by.
You're my soul and my life's inspiration.
Without you baby what good am I?

I never had much goin',
But at least I had you.
How can you walk out knowin'
I ain't got nothin' left if you do?

Refrain

What good am I?

Spoken:
Baby, I can't make it without you,
And I'm, I'm tellin' you honey that
You're my reason for laughin' and for cryin',
For livin' and for dyin'.

Sung:
Baby, I can't make it without you.
Please, I'm beggin' you baby,
If you go it'll kill me.
I swear it, I can't live without you.

Refrain

What good am I?

Repeat and Fade:
You're my soul and my heart's inspiration.
You're all I need to get me by.

The Sound of Music

Lyrics by Oscar Hammerstein II
Music by Richard Rodgers

from the musical *The Sound of Music*

My day in the hills has come to an end, I know.
A star has come out to tell me it's time to go,
But deep in the dark-green shadows
Are voices that urge me to stay.
So I pause and I wait and I listen
For one more sound,
For one more lovely thing
That the hills might say…

The hills are alive
With the sound of music,
With songs they have sung
For a thousand years.
The hills fill my heart
With the sound of music—
My heart wants to sing
Every song it hears.

My heart wants to beat
Like the wings of the birds that rise
From the lake to the trees.
My heart wants to sigh like a chime that flies
From a church on a breeze,
To laugh like a brook when it trips and falls
Over stones in its way,
To sing through the night
Like a lark that is learning to pray—

I go to the hills when my heart is lonely,
I know I will hear what I've heard before.
My heart will be blessed with the sound of music
And I'll sing once more.

Southern Cross

Words and Music by Stephen Stills, Richard Curtis and Michael Curtis

recorded by Crosby, Stills & Nash

Got out of town on a boat
Gon' to southern islands.
Sailing a reach before a following sea.
She was making for the trades
On the outside
And the downhill run to Papeete.

Off the wind on this heading,
Lie the Marquesas.
We got eighty feet of waterline,
Nicely makin' way.
In a noisy bar in Avalon,
I tried to call you.
But on the midnight watch I realized
Why twice you ran away.

Refrain:
Think about how many times I have fallen.
Spirits are usin' me; larger voices callin'.
What heaven brought you and me
Cannot be forgotten.
I have been around the world,
Lookin' for that woman-girl
Who knows love can endure.
And you know it will.

When you see the Southern Cross
For the first time,
You understand now why you came this way.
'Cause the truth you might be runnin' from is so small.
But it's big as the promise,
The promise of a comin' day.

So I'm sailing tomorrow.
My dreams are a-dying.
And my love is an anchor tied to you,
Tied with a silver chain.
I have my ship,
And all her flags are a-flying.
She is all that I have left,
And music is her name.

Refrain

So we cheated and we lied and we tested.
And we never failed to fail.
It was the easiest thing to do.
You will survive being bested.
Somebody fine will come along,
Make me forget about loving you
In the Southern Cross.

Space Oddity

Words and Music by David Bowie

recorded by David Bowie

Ground Control to Major Tom.
Ground Control to Major Tom.
Take your protein pills and put your helmet on.
Ground Control to Major Tom.
(*Spoken:* Ten, nine, eight, seven, six,)
commencing countdown, engines on.
(five, four, three, two, one, liftoff.)
Checking ignition and may God's love be with you.

This is Ground Control to Major Tom,
You've really made the grade.
And the papers want to know whose shirts you wear.
Now it's time to leave the capsule if you dare.

This is Major Tom to Ground Control,
I'm stepping through the door.
And I'm floating in a most peculiar way.
And the stars look very different today.

For here am I sitting in a tin can,
Far above the world.
Planet Earth is blue, and there's nothing I can do.

Though I'm past one hundred thousand miles,
I'm feeling very still.
And I think my spaceship knows which way to go.
Tell my wife I love her very much. She knows.

Ground Control to Major Tom,
You circuit's dead, there's something wrong.
Can you hear me Major Tom?
Can you hear me Major Tom?
Can you hear me Major Tom?
Can you…

Here am I floating 'round my tin can,
Far above the world.
Planet Earth is blue, and there's nothing I can do.

Speak Low

Words by Ogden Nash
Music by Kurt Weill

from the Musical Production *One Touch of Venus*

Speak low when you speak, love,
Our summer day withers away too soon, too soon.
Speak low when you speak, love,
Our moment is swift, like ships adrift,
We're swept adrift, too soon.

Speak low darling, speak low
Love is a spark lost in the dark too soon, too soon.
I feel wherever I go
That tomorrow is near,
Tomorrow is here and always too soon.

Time is so old and love is so brief,
Love is pure gold and time a thief.
We're late darling, we're late
The curtain descends,
Everything ends too soon, too soon,
I wait darling, I wait.
Will you speak low to me,
Speak love to me and soon.

Speak Softly, Love (Love Theme)
Words by Larry Kusik
Music by Nino Rota
Copyright © 1972 (Renewed 2000) by Famous Music Corporation

from the Paramount Picture *The Godfather*
recorded by Andy Williams

Speak softly, love, and hold me warm against your heart.
I feel your words, the tender, trembling moments start.
We're in a world our very own,
Sharing a love that only few have ever known.
Wine colored days warmed by the sun,
Deep velvet nights when we are one.

Speak softly, love, so no one hears us but the sky.
The vows of love we make will live until we die.
My life is yours, and all because
You came into my world with love so softly, love.

Repeat Song

Spinning Wheel
Words and Music by David Clayton Thomas
© 1968 (Renewed 1996) EMI BLACKWOOD MUSIC INC. and BAY MUSIC LTD.
All Rights Controlled and Administered by EMI BLACKWOOD MUSIC INC.

recorded by Blood, Sweat & Tears

What goes up
Must come down,
Spinning wheel
Got to go 'round.
Talkin' 'bout your troubles, it's a crying shame'
Ride a painted pony let the spinning wheel spin.
You got no money,
You got no home,
Spinning wheel
All alone.

Talkin' 'bout your troubles and you, you never learn,
Ride a painted pony, let the spinning wheel turn.
Did you find your directing sign
On the straight and narrow highway?
Would you mind a reflecting sign?
Just let it shine within your mind,

And show you the colors that are real.

Someone's waiting
Just for you,
Spinning wheel
Spinning true.
Drop all your troubles by the riverside,
Ride a painted pony, let the spinning wheel fly.

Splish Splash
Words and Music by Bobby Darin and Murray Kaufman
Copyright © 1958 by Unart Music Corporation
Copyright Renewed and Assigned to Alley Music Corp., Trio Music Company, Inc.
   and Unart Music Corporation
All Rights on behalf of Unart Music Corporation Assigned to EMI Catalogue Partnership
   and Controlled and Administered by EMI Unart Catalog Inc.

recorded by Bobby Darin

Splish Splash, I was taking a bath
Long about a Saturday night.
Rub-a-dub, just relaxing in the tub
Thinking everything was alright.
Well, I stepped out the tub, put my feet on the floor,
I wrapped the towel around me
And I opened the door, and then
Splish, Splash! I jumped back in the bath.
Well, how was I to know there was a party going on?

They was a-splishin' and a-splashin',
Reelin' with the feelin',
movin' and a-groovin',
Rockin' and a-rollin', yeah!

Bing bang, I saw the whole gang
Dancing on my living room rug, yeah!
Flip flop, they was doing the bop.
All the teens had the dancing bug.
There was lollipop with-a Peggy Sue
Good Golly, Miss Molly was-a even there, too!
Ah, well-a, splish splash, I forgot about the bath.
I went and put my dancing shoes on, yeah.

I was a-rollin' and a-strollin',
Reeling with the feelin',
Moving and a-groovin',
Splishin' and a-splashin', yeah!

Yes, I was a-splishin' and a-splashin',
I was a-rollin' and a-strollin',
Yeah, I was a-movin' and a-groovin',
We was a-reeling with the feeling,
We was a-rollin' and a-strollin',
Movin' with the groovin',
Splish splash, yeah!

Splishin' and a-splashin',
I was a-splishin' and a-splashin',
I was a-movin' and a-groovin',
Yeah, I was a-splishin' and a-splashin'.

Spring Will Be a Little Late This Year

By Frank Loesser
© 1943 (Renewed) FRANK MUSIC CORP.

from the Motion Picture *Christmas Holiday*
a standard recorded by various artists

January and February
Were never so empty and gray
Tragically I feel like crying
"Without you, my darling, I'm dying,"
But let's rather put it this way.

Spring will be a little late this year,
A little late arriving in my lonely world over here
For you have left me, and where is our April of old?
You have left me, and winter continues cold, as if to say

Spring will be a little slow to start,
A little slow reviving that music it made in my heart.
Yes, time heals all things, so I needn't cling to this fear,
It's merely that spring will be a little late this year.

Stand Back

Words and Music by Stevie Nicks
Copyright © 1983 Welsh Witch Music and Controversy Music
All Rights on behalf of Welsh Witch Music Administered by Sony/ATV Music Publishing,
  8 Music Square West, Nashville, TN 37203
All Rights on behalf of Controversy Music Administered by WB Music Corp.

recorded by Stevie Nicks

No one looked as I walked by.
Just an invitation would have been just fine.
Said no to him again and again.
First he took my heart, then he ran.

No one knows how I feel,
What I say unless you read between the lines.
One man walked away from me.
First he took my hand.
Take me home.

Refrain:
In the middle of my room I did not hear from you.
It's alright, it's alright,
To be standing in a line (Standing in a line,)
To be standing in a line.
I would cry.
Well I need a little sympathy.

Do not turn away my friend.
Like a willow, I can bend
No man calls my name.
No man came.
So I walked on down away from you.
Maybe your attention was more than you could do.
One man did not call.
He asked for my love
And that was all.

Refrain

Well I need a little sympathy.

Stand By Me

Words and Music by Ben E. King, Jerry Leiber and
Mike Stoller
© 1961 (Renewed) JERRY LEIBER MUSIC, MIKE STOLLER MUSIC
  and MIKE & JERRY MUSIC LLC

recorded by Ben E. King
featured in the film *Stand by Me*

When the night has come and the land is dark
And the moon is the only light we'll see.
No I won't be afraid, no I won't be afraid
Just as long as you stand,
Stand by me.

Refrain:
So darling, darling,
Stand by me,
Oh, stand by me,
Oh, stand,
Stand by me,
Stand by me.

If the sea that we look upon should tumble and fall
Or the mountain crumble in the sea.
I won't cry, no I won't shed a tear
Just as long as you stand
Stand by me.

Refrain

Whenever you're in trouble won't you stand by me
Oh, stand by me,
Oh, stand by me,
Stand by me.

Refrain

Star Dust

Words by Mitchell Parish
Music by Hoagy Carmichael
Copyright © 1928 by Hoagy Publishing Company and EMI Mills Music, Inc.
Copyright Renewed
All Rights for Hoagy Publishing Company Administered by PSO Limited
All Rights outside the USA Controlled by EMI Mills Music, Inc. (Publishing)
  and Warner Bros. Publications U.S. Inc. (Print)

a standard recorded by Isham Jones, Bing Crosby,
Louis Armstrong, Artie Shaw and many various artists

…And now the purple dusk of twilight time
Steals across the meadows of my heart.
High up in the sky the little stars climb,
Always reminding me that we're apart.
You wandered down the lane and far away,
Leaving me a song that will not die.
Love is now the star dust of yesterday,
The music of the years gone my.

Refrain:
Sometimes I wonder why I spend the lonely night
Dreaming of a song.
The melody haunts my reverie

And I am once again with you,
Then our love was new,
And each kiss an inspiration.
But that was long ago:
Now my consolation is in the star dust of a song.

Beside a garden wall, when stars are bright,
You are in my arms.
The nightingale
Tells his fairy tale
Of paradise, where roses grew.
Tho' I dream in vain,
In my heart it will remain;
My star dust melody
The memory of love's refrain.

The Star Spangled Banner

Words by Francis Scott Key
Music by John Stafford Smith

national anthem of The United States of America

Oh say, can you see, by the dawn's early light,
What so proudly we hailed at the twilight's last gleaming?
Whose broad stripes and bright stars, thro' the perilous fight,
O'er the ramparts we watched were go gallantly streaming?
And the rockets red glare, the bombs bursting in air
Gave proof through the night that our flag was still there.
O say, does that star-spangled banner yet wave
O'er the land of the free and the home of the brave?

On the shore dimly seen thro' the mists of the deep,
Where the foe's haughty host in dread silence reposes,
What is that which the breeze, o'er the towering steep,
As it fittingly blows, half conceals, half discloses?
Now it catches the gleam of the morning's first beam,
In full glory reflected now shines in the stream.
'Tis the star-spangled banner o long may it wave
O'er the land of the free and the home of the brave.

And there is the band who so vauntingly swore,
'Mid the havoc of war and the battle's confusion,
A home and a country they'd leave us no more?
Their blood has washed out their foul footstep's pollution.
No refuge could save the hireling and slave
From the terror of fight or the gloom of the grave;
And the star-spangled banner in triumph doth wave
O'er the land of the free and the home of the brave.

O thus be it ever, when free men shall stand
Between their loved homes and the war's desolation;
Blest with victory and peace, may the heaven-rescued land
Praise the Power that hath made and preserved us a nation!
Then conquer we must, when our cause it is just,
And this be our honor motto, "In God is our trust!"
And the star-spangled banner in triumph shall wave
O'er the land of the free and the home of the brave.

Start Me Up

Words and Music by Mick Jagger and Keith Richards

recorded by The Rolling Stones

If you start me up, if you start me up,
I'll never stop.
You can start me up, you can start me up,
I'll never stop.
I've been running hot;
You got me just about to blow my top.

You can start me up. you can start me up,
I never stop, never stop, never stop, never stop.
You make a grown man cry.
You make a grown man cry.
You make a grown man cry.
Spread out the oil, the gasoline.
I walk smooth, ride in a mean, mean machine.
Start it up.

You can start me up, kick on the starter,
Give it all you've got.
I can't compete with riders in the other heats.
You can rough it up, if you like it
You can slide it up, slide it up, slide it up, slide it up.
Don't make a grown man cry.
My eyes dilate, my lips go green,
My hands are greasy, she's a mean, mean machine.
Start it up.

Start me up,
Ah, you've got to, you've got to,
Never, never, never stop.
You make a grown man cry.
You make a grown man cry.
You make a grown man cry.
Ride like the wind, at double speed.
I'll take you places that you've never, never seen.
If you start it up,
Love the day when we will never stop,
Never stop, never, never, never stop.

Statesboro Blues

Words and Music by Willy McTell

recorded by The Allman Brothers Band and other artists

Wake up, mama, turn your lamp down low.
Wake up, mama, turn your lamp down low.
Ya got no nerve, baby
To turn Uncle John from your door.

I woke up this mornin', and I had them Statesboro blues.
I woke up this mornin', and I had them Statesboro blues.
Well, I looked over in the corner, baby,
Your grandpa seem to have them too.

Well my mama died and left me, my papa died and left me.
I ain't good lookin', baby, but I'm someone sweet and kind.
I'm goin' to the country, baby,
Do you wanna go?

Spoken:
If you can't make it, baby,

Sung:
Your sister Lucille said she wanna go.

Spoken:
Well I sho' nuff tell ya…

Sung:
I love that woman better than any woman I've ever seen.
Well, I love that woman better that any woman I've ever seen.
Well, she treat me like a king, yeah, yeah, yeah.
I treat her like a doggone queen.

Refrain

Life goin' nowhere.
Somebody help me.
Somebody help me, yeah.
Life goin' nowhere.
Somebody help me, yeah.
Stayin' alive.

Repeat Verse 1

Refrain

Life goin' nowhere.
Somebody help me.
Somebody help me, yeah.
Life goin' nowhere.
Somebody help me, yeah.
I'm stayin' alive.

Stayin' Alive
Words and Music by Barry Gibb, Maurice Gibb and
Robin Gibb

from the film *Saturday Night Fever*
recorded by The Bee Gees

Well, you can tell by the way I use my walk,
I'm a woman's man; no time to talk.
Music loud and women warm,
I've been kicked around since I was born
And now it's all right.
It's O.K
And you may look the other way.
We can try
To understand
The New York Times' effect on man.

Refrain:
Whether you're a brother of whether you're a mother,
You're stayin' alive, stayin' alive.
Feel the city breakin' and everybody shakin',
And we're stayin' alive, stayin' alive.
Ah, ha, ha, ha, stayin' alive, stain' alive,
Ah, ha, ha, ha, stayin' alive.

Well now, I get low and I get high,
And if I can't get either, I really try.
Got the wings of heaven on my shoes.
I'm a dancin' man and I just can't lose.
You know it's all right.
It's O.K.
I'll live to see another day.
We can try
To understand
The *New York Times'* effect on man.

Stella by Starlight
Words by Ned Washington
Music by Victor Young

from the Paramount Picture *The Uninvited*
a standard recorded by Harry James, Frank Sinatra,
Buddy Greco, Charlie Parker and various other artists

The song a robin sings
Through years of endless springs.
The murmur of a brook at eventide
That ripples by a nook where two lovers hide.
A great symphonic theme,
That's Stella by starlight and not a dream.
My heart and I agree
She's everything on earth to me.

Steppin' Out with My Baby
Words and Music by Irving Berlin

from the Motion Picture Irving Berlin's *Easter Parade*
recorded by Tony Bennett and other artists

If I seem to scintillate
It's because I've got a date,
A date with a package of
The good things that come with love.
You don't have to ask me,
I won't waste you're time.
But if you should ask me
Why I feel sublime,

Refrain:
I'm steppin' out with my baby.
Can't go wrong 'cause I'm right.
It's for sure not for maybe,
That I'm all dressed up tonight.
Steppin' out with my honey,
Can't be bad to feel so good.
Never felt quite so sunny.
And I keep on knockin' wood,
There'll be smooth sailin' 'cause I'm trimmin' my sails.
In my top hat and my white tie and my tails.

Steppin' out with my baby,
Can't go wrong 'cause I'm in right.
Ask me when will the day be
The big day may be tonight.

Stop! In the Name of Love

Words and Music by Lamont Dozier, Brian Holland and
Edward Holland

recorded by The Supremes

Stop! In the name of love
Before you break my heart.
Baby, baby, I'm aware of where you go
Each time you leave my door.
I watch you walk down the street,
Knowing your other love you meet.
But this time before you run to her
Leaving me alone to cry:

Haven't I been good to you?
Haven't I been sweet to you?
Stop! In the name of love
Before you break my heart,
Stop! In the name of love
Before you break my heart.
Think it over,
Think it over.

I've known of your,
Your secluded nights,
I've even seen her maybe once or twice.
But is her sweet expression
Worth more than my love and affection?
This time before you leave my arms
And rush off to her charms:

Haven't I been good to you?
Haven't I been sweet to you?
Stop! In the name of love
Before you break my heart,
Stop! In the name of love
Before you break my heart.
Think it over,
Think it over.

I've tried so hard,
Hard to be patient
Hoping that you'd stop this infatuation.
But each time you are together
I'm so afraid I'm losing you forever.

Stop! In the name of love
Before you break my heart,
Stop! In the name of love
Before you break my heart.

Repeat

Stormy Weather
(Keeps Rainin' All the Time)

Lyric by Ted Koehler
Music by Harold Arlen

from the Cotton Club revues
a standard recorded by Ethel Waters, Lena Horne,
Judy Garland and various other artists
featured in the film *Stormy Weather*

Don't know why
There's no sun up in the sky,
Stormy weather,
Since my man and I ain't together,
Keeps rainin' all the time.
Life is bare,
Gloom and misery everywhere,
Stormy weather,
Just can't get my poor self together.

I'm weary all the time, the time,
So weary all the time.
When he went away then walked in and met me.
If he stays away old rockin' chair will get me.
All I do is pray the Lord above will let me
Walk in the sun once more.

Refrain:
Can't go on,
Everything I had is gone,
Stormy weather,
Since my man and I ain't together,
Keeps rainin' all the time,
Keeps rainin' all the time.

I walk around, heavy hearted and sad.
Night comes around and I'm still feelin' bad.
Rain pouring' down, blindin' every hope I had.
This pitterin' patterin' beatin' an' splatterin' drives me mad.
Love, love, love, love,
This misery is just too much for me.

Refrain

Story of My Father
Words and Music by Abbey Lincoln

recorded by Abbey Lincoln and other artists

Do we kill ourselves on purpose?
Is destruction all our own?
Are we dying for a reason?
Is our leaving on our own?

Are the people suicidal?
Did we come this far to die?
Of ourselves are we to perish
For this useless, worthless lie?

My father had a kingdom,
My father wore a crown.
They said he was an awful man,
He tried to live it down.

My father built his houses,
And he kept his folks inside,
His images were stolen,
And his beauty was denied.

My brothers are unhappy,
My sisters they are too,
My mother prays for glory,
And my father stands accused.

My father, yes my father,
A brave and skillful man,
He fed and served his people,
With the magic of his hand.

My father, yes my father,
His soul was sorely tried,
'Cause his images were stolen,
And his beauty was denied.

Sometimes the river's calling,
Sometimes the shadow's fall,
That's when he's like a mountain,
Rising master over all.

The story of my father,
Is the one I tell and give,
It's the power and the glory,
Of the life I make and live.

My father has a kingdom,
My father wears a crown,
And he lives within the people,
In the lives he handed down.

My father has a kingdom,
My father wears a crown,
And through the spirit of my mother,
Lord, the crown was handed down.

Straight from the Heart
Words and Music by Dickey Betts and Johnny Cobb

recorded by The Allman Brothers Band

You've heard every line before.
My life's a revolving door
With no way out and no way in.
You know just what's on my mind.
Could you take a chance one more time?
Maybe we could start all over again.
Straight from the heart.
Baby, my love.

Refrain:
Your eyes can't tell a lie.
I can see what you're feelin' inside.
Don't give up before we start,
'Cause this time love is straight from the heart,
Straight from the heart.

I know what they're telling you.
I wish I could say that it's not true.
Love is so hard to find,
I wish I could say that it's not true.
Love is so hard to find,
But I never took the time.
I never let you in.
Please, let me try again.
Straight from the heart.

Refrain

I thought I knew about love,
But I didn't know at all.
Didn't take the tine to see
Until I started to fall
Straight from the heart.
Straight from the heart.

Strange Brew
Words and Music by Eric Clapton, Felix Pappalardi and
Gail Collins

recorded by Cream

Strange brew, killing what's inside of you.

She's a witch of trouble in electric blue.
In her own mad mind she's in love with you, with you.
Now what you gonna do?
Strange brew, killing what's inside of you.

She's some kind of demon dusting in the flue,
If you don't watch out, it'll stick to you, to you.
What kind of fool are you?
Strange brew, killing what's inside of you.

On a boat in the middle of a raging sea,
She would make a scene for it all to be ignored.
And wouldn't you be bored?
Strange brew, killing what's inside of you.

Strange Fruit
Words and Music by Lewis Allan

recorded by Billie Holiday
featured in the film *Lady Sings the Blues*

Southern trees bear a strange fruit,
Blood on the leaves and blood at the root,
Black body swinging in the Southern breeze,
Strange fruit hanging from the poplar trees.

Pastoral scene of the gallant south,
The bulging eyes and the twisted mouth,
Scent of magnolia sweet and fresh,
And the sudden smell of burning flesh!

Here is a fruit for the crows to pluck,
For the rain to gather, for the wind to suck,
For the sun to rot, for a tree to drop,
Here is a grange and bitter crop.

Strawberry Fields Forever
Words and Music by John Lennon and Paul McCartney

recorded by The Beatles

Refrain:
Let me take you down,
'Cause I'm going to Strawberry Fields.
Nothing is real,
And nothing to get hung about,
Strawberry Fields forever.

Living is easy with eyes closed,
Misunderstanding all you see.
It's getting hard to be someone,
But it all works out,
It doesn't matter much to me.

No one I think is in my tree,
I mean it must be high or low.
That is, you know you can't tune in,
But it's alright,
That is I think it's not too bad.

Refrain

Always, no sometimes, think it's me,
But you know when it's a dream.
I think I know I mean a "Yes",
But it's all wrong,
That is I think I disagree.

Refrain

Strawberry Fields forever

Summer in the City
Words and Music by John Sebastian, Steve Boone and
Mark Sebastian

recorded by The Lovin' Spoonful

Hot town, summer in the city,
Back o' my neck getting dirty and gritty.
Been down, isn't it a pity;
Doesn't seem to be a shadow in the city.
All around people lookin' half dead,
Walkin' on the sidewalk hotter than a match, yeah,

Refrain:
But at night it's a different world;
Go out and find a girl.
Come on, come on, and dance all night,
Despite the heat it'll be alright.
And babe, don't you know it's a pity,
The days can't be like the nights
In the summer in the city,
In the summer in the city,.

Cool town, evenin' in the city,
Dressed up so fine and-a lookin' so pretty.
Cool cat, lookin' for a kitty;
Gonna look in every corner of the city.
'Til I'm wheezin' like a bus stop.
Runnin' up the stairs gonna meet you on the roof-top.

Refrain

Repeat Entire Song

Summer Nights

Lyric and Music by Warren Casey and Jim Jacobs

from the musical *Grease*
recorded by John Travolta & Olivia Newton-John

Boy: Summer lovin' had me blast.
Girl: Summer lovin' happened so fast.
Boy: Met a girl crazy for me.
Girl: Met a boy, cute as can be.

Summer days drifting away
To, uh, oh, those summer nights.

Well-a, well-a, well-a
Tell me more. Tell me more.
Did you get very far?
Tell me more. Tell me more.
Like, does he have a car?

Boy: She swam by me. She got a cramp.
Girl: He ran by me, got my suit damp.
Boy: Saved her life, she nearly drowned.
Girl: He showed of, splashing around.

Summer sun, something's begun
But, uh, oh, those summer nights.

Well-a, well-a, well-a uh.
Tell me more. Tell me more.
Was it love at first sight?
Tell me more. Tell me more.
Did she put up a fight?

Boy: Took her bowling in the arcade.
Girl: We went strolling; drank lemonade.
Boy: We made out under the dock.
Girl: We stayed out till ten o'clock.

Summer fling don't mean a thing
But uh, oh, those summer nights.

Tell me more, tell me more.
But you don't got to brag.
Tell me more, tell me more.
'Cause he sounds like a drag.
Shu-da bop bop. Shu-da bop bop.
Shu-da bop bop. Shu-da bop bop.

Girl: He got friendly, holding my hand.
Boy: She got friendly, down in the sand.
Girl: He was sweet; just turned eighteen.
Boy: She was good. You know what I mean.

Summer heat; boy and girl meet.
But, uh, oh those summer nights.

Tell me more. Tell me more.
How much dough did he spend?
Tell me more. Tell me more.
Could she get me a friend?

Girl: It turned colder; that's where it ends.
Boy: So I told her we'd still be friends.
Girl: Then we made our true love vow.
Boy: Wonder what she's doin' now.

Summer dreams
Ripped at the seams
But, oh, those summer nights.
Tell me more.
Tell me more.

Sunshine of Your Love

Words and Music by Jack Bruce, Pete Brown and
Eric Clapton

recorded by Cream

It's getting near dawn when lights close their tired eyes.
I'll soon be with you, my love,
To give you my dawn surprise,
I'll be with you darling, soon.
I'll be with you when the stars start falling.

Refrain:
I've been waiting so long to be where I'm going
In the sunshine of your love.

I'm with you my love; the light shining through on you.
Yes, I'm with you, my love.
It's the morning and just we two.
I'll stay with you darling, now,
I'll stay with you till my seeds are dried up.

I've been waiting so long,
I've been waiting so long,
I've been waiting so long to be where I'm going
In the sunshine of your love.

Sunshine on My Shoulders

Words by John Denver
Music by John Denver, Mike Taylor and Dick Kniss

recorded by John Denver

Refrain:
Sunshine on my shoulders makes me happy,
Sunshine in my eyes can make me cry.
Sunshine on the water looks so lovely,
Sunshine almost always makes me high.

If I had a day that I could give you,
I'd give to you a day just like today.
If I had a song that I could sing for you,
I'd sing a song to make you feel this way.

Refrain

If I had a tale that I could tell you,
I'd tell a tale sure to make you smile.
If I had a wish that I could wish for you,
I'd make a wish for sunshine all the while.

Refrain

Sunshine almost always makes me high...

Sunshine Superman
Words and Music by Donovan Leitch

recorded by Donovan

Sunshine came softly through my
Window today.
Could've tripped out easily
But I've a-changed my ways.
It'll take time, I know it,
But in a while,
You're gonna be mine, I know it,
We'll do it in style.

'Cause I made my mind up,
You're going to be mine!
I'll tell you right now,
Any trick in the book now baby,
A-that I can find.

Refrain:
'Cause I made my mind up,
You're going to be mine.
I'll tell you right now,
Any trick in the book, now, baby,
A-that I can find.

Everybody's hustlin' just to
Have a little scene.
When I say we'll be cool I think that
You know what I mean.
We stood on the beach at sunset,
Do you remember when?
I know a beach where baby,
A-it never ends.

When you've made your mind up,
Forever to be mine.
I'll tell you right now,
I'll pick up your hand and slowly,
Blow your little mind.

Refrain

Superman or Green Lantern ain't got
Nothin' on me.
I can make like a turtle and dive
For pearls in the sea.
A you-you-you can just sit there a-thinkin'
On your velvet throne,
'Bout all the rainbows you can
Have for your own.

When you've made your mind up,
forever to be mine.

I'll pick up your hand and slowly
Blow your little mind,
When you've made your mind up
Forever to me mine.

Supper Time
Words and Music by Irving Berlin

from the Stage Production *As Thousands Cheer*
recorded by Ethel Waters and various other artists

Supper time,
I should set the table 'cause it's supper time.
Somehow I'm not able 'cause that man o'mine
Ain't comin' home no more.

Supper time,
Kids will soon be yellin' for their supper time.
How'll I keep from tellin' that that man o'mine
Ain't comin' home no more.

How'll I keep explainin'
When they ask me where he's gone?
How'll I keep from cryin' when I bring their supper on?
How can I remind them to pray at their humble board?
How can I be thankful when they start to thank the
 Lord, Lord.

Supper time,
I should set the table 'cause it's supper time.
Somehow I'm not able 'cause that man o'mine
Ain't comin' home no more.
Ain't comin' home no more.

Surfin' U.S.A.

Words and Music by Chuck Berry

recorded by The Beach Boys

If everybody had an ocean across the U.S.A.
Then everybody'd be surfin', like California.
You'd see them wearin' their baggies
Huarachi sandals too.
A bushy, bushy blond hairdo,
Surfin' U.S.A.

You'll catch 'em surfin' at Del Mar, Ventura County Line,
Santa Cruz and Tressels, Australia's Narabine,
All over Manhattan and down Doheny way.
Everybody's gone surfin', surfin' U.S.A.

Will all be plannin' out a route
We're gonna take real soon,
We're waxing down our surf boards,
We can't wait for June.
We'll all be gone for the summer,
We're on safari to stay.
Tell the teacher we're surfin',
Surfin' U.S.A.

At Haggarty's and Swami's, Pacific Palisades,
San Onofre and Sunset Redondo Beach, L.A.
All over La Jolla, and at Waiamea Bay.
Everybody's gone surfin',
Surfin' U.S.A.

The Surrey with the Fringe on Top

Lyrics by Oscar Hammerstein II
Music by Richard Rodgers

from the musical *Oklahoma!*
a standard recorded by various jazz artists

When I take you out tonight with me,
Honey, here's the way it's goin' to be:
You will set behind a team of snow-white horses
In the slickest gig you ever see!

Chicks and ducks and geese better scurry
When I take you out in the surrey,
When I take you out in the surrey with the fringe on top.
Watch that fringe and see how it flutters
When I drive them high-steppin' strutters
Nosey-pokes'll peek through their shutters
And their eyes will pop!
The wheels are yeller, the upholstery's brown,
The dashboard's genuine leather,

With isinglass curtains you can roll right down
In case there's a change in the weather;
Two bright side lights winkin' and blinkin',
Aint no finer rig, I'm a-thinkin';
You c'n keep yer rig if you're thinkin' 'at I'd keer to swap
Fer that shiny little surrey with the fringe on the top.

Would y' say the fringe was made of silk?
Wouldn't have no other kind but silk.
Has it really got a team of snow-white horses?
One's like snow—the other's more like milk.

All the world'll fly in a flurry
When I take you out in the surrey,
When I take you out in the surrey with the fringe on top.
When we hit the road, hell for leather,
Cats and dogs'll dance in the heather,
Birds and frogs'll sing altogether,
And the toads will hop!
The wind'll whistle as we rattle along,
The cows'll moo in the clover,
The river will ripple out a whispered song,
And whisper it over and over:
Don't you wisht y'd go on forever?
Don't you wisht y'd go on forever?
Don't you wisht y'd go on ferever and ud never stop
In that shiny little surrey with the fringe on the top?

I can see the stars gittin' blurry
When we ride back home in the surrey,
Drivin' slowly home in the surrey with the fringe on top.
I can feel the day gittin' older,
Feel a sleepy head near my shoulder,
Noddin', droopin' close to my shoulder till it falls, kerplop!
The sun is swimmin' on the rim of a hill,
The moon is takin' a header,
And jist as I'm thinkin' all the earth is still,
A lark'll wake up in the medder…
Hush! You bird, my baby's a-sleepin'—
Maybe got a dream worth a-keepin'.
Whoa! You team, and jist keep a-creepin' at a slow clip-clop;
Don't you hurry with the surrey with the fringe on the top.

Sussudio

Words and Music by Phil Collins

recorded by Phil Collins

There's a girl that's been on my mind
All the time,
Su Sussudio, oh, oh.
Now she don't even know my name,
But I think she likes me just the same,
Su Sussudio, oh, oh.
Ah, if she called me I'd be there.
I'd come running anywhere.

She's all I need, all my life.
I feel so good
If I just say the word,
Su Sussudio.
Just say the word, oh, Sussudio.

Now I know that I'm too young,
My life has just begun,
Su Sussudio, oh, oh.
Ooh, give me a chance,
Give me a sign,
I'll show her anytime,
Su Sussudio, oh, oh.
Ah, I've got to have her,
Have her now.
I've got to get closer but I don't know how.
She makes me nervous and makes me scared,
But I'll feel so good…

Refrain

I'll just say the word,
Su Sussudio.
Just say the word, oh, Sussudio.

Just say the word.
Ooh, just, just, just say the word.
Just say the word.
Su Su Sussudio.
Su Sussudio.
Su Sussudio.
Su Sussudio, sudio, Su Sussudio
Just say the word.
Su Sussudio.
Say the word…

Sweet Baby James
Words and Music by James Taylor
© 1970 (Renewed 1998) EMI BLACKWOOD MUSIC INC.
  and COUNTRY ROAD MUSIC INC.
All Rights Controlled and Administered by EMI BLACKWOOD MUSIC INC.

recorded by James Taylor

There is a young cowboy, he lives on the range,
His horse and his cattle are his only companions.
He works in the saddle and sleeps in the canyons,
Waiting for summer, his pastures to change.
And as the moon rises he sits by his fire,
Thinking about women and glasses of beer,
And closing his eyes as the doggies retire.
He sings out a song which is soft but it's clear,
As if maybe someone could hear.
He says

Refrain:
Goodnight you moonlight ladies,
Rockabye Sweet Baby James.
Deep greens and blues are the colors I choose,
Won't you let me go down in my dreams,
And rockabye Sweet Baby James.

The first of December was covered with snow
So was the turnpike from Stockbridge to Boston
The Berkshires seemed dream-like on account of that
  frosting
With ten miles behind me and ten thousand more to go.

There's a song that they sing when they take to the highway,
A song that they sing when they take to the sea,
A song that they sing of their home in the sky,
Maybe you can believe it if it helps you to sleep,
But singing works just fine for me.

Refrain

Sweet Dreams (Are Made of This)
Words and Music by David A. Stewart and Annie Lennox
Copyright © 1983 by BMG Music Publishing Limited
All Rights for the U.S. Administered by BMG Songs, Inc.

recorded by The Eurythmics

Refrain:
Sweet dreams are made of this,
Who am I to disagree?
I travel the world
And the seven seas,
Everybody's looking for something.

Some of them want to use you,
Some of them want to get used by you,
Some of them want to abuse you,
Some of them want to be abused.

Refrain

Hold your head up,
Keep your head up, movin' on.
Hold your head up, movin' on.
Keep your head up, movin' on.
Keep your head up, movin' on.
Hold your head up, movin' on.
Keep your head up, movin' on.
Hold your head up, movin' on,
Keep your head up…

Sweet Emotion

Words and Music by Steven Tyler and Tom Hamilton

recorded by Aerosmith

Sweet emotion. Sweet emotion.
You talk about things and nobody cares.
You wearin' out things that nobody wears.
You're callin' my name but I gotta make clear,
I can't say, baby, where I'll be in a year.
Some sweet talkin' mama with a face like a gent
Said my get up and go must have got and went.
Well I got good news, she's a real good liar
'Cause my back stage boogie set yo' pants on fire.

Sweet emotion, sweet emotion.
I pulled into town in a police car;
Your daddy said I took you just a little too far.
You're tellin' her things but your girlfriend lied;
You can't catch me 'cause the rabbit done died.
Stand in front just a-shakin' your ass;
I'll take you backstage, you can drink from my glass.
I'm talking 'bout somethin' you can sure understand,
'Cause a month on the road
And I'll be eatin' from your hand.

Repeat and Fade:
Sweet emotion, Sweet emotion.

The Sweetest Days

Words and Music by Jon Lind, Wendy Waldman
and Phil Galdston

recorded by Vanessa Williams

You and I in this moment,
Holding the night so close,
Hanging on, still unbroken
While outside the thunder rolls.
Listen now, you can hear my heart beat
Warm against life's bitter cold.
These are the days,
The sweetest days we'll know.

There are times that scare me.
We'll rattle the house like the wind,
Both of us so unbending.
We battle the fear within.
All the while life is rushing by us.
Hold it now and don't let go.
These are the days,
The sweetest days we'll know.

So, we'll whisper a dream here in the darkness,
Watching the stars till their gone.
And when even the memories have all faded away,
These days gone on and on.
Listen, you can hear my heart beat.
Hold me now and don't let go.
(These are the days)
Every day is the sweetest day we'll know.
(These are the days)
The sweetest days we'll ever know.

The Sweetest Sounds

Lyrics and Music by Richard Rodgers

from the musical *No Strings*

What do I really hear?
What is in the ear of my mind?
Which sounds are true and clear,
And which will never be defined?

The sweetest sounds I'll ever hear
Are still inside my head.
The kindest words I'll ever know
Are waiting to be said.
The most entrancing sight of all
Is yet for me to see.
And the dearest love in all the world
Is waiting somewhere for me.
Is waiting somewhere,
Somewhere for me.

Take Me Home, Country Roads

Words and Music by John Denver, Bill Danoff and Taffy Nivert

recorded by John Denver

Almost heaven, West Virginia,
Blue Ridge Mountains, Shenandoah River.
Life is old there, older than the trees,
Younger than the mountains growin' like a breeze.

Refrain:
Country roads, take me home
To the place I belong:
West Virginia, mountain momma,
Take me home, country roads.

All memories gather 'round her,
Miner's lady, stranger to blue water.
Dark and dusty, painted on the sky,
Misty taste of moonshine, teardrop in my eye.

Refrain

I hear her voice, in the mornin' hour she calls me,
The radio reminds me of my home far away,
And drivin' down the road I get a feelin'
That I should have been home yesterday,
Yesterday.

Refrain

Country roads, take me home.

Take the "A" Train

Words and Music by Billy Strayhorn

a standard recorded by Duke Ellington and other artists

You must take the "A" train
To go to Sugar Hill way up in Harlem.
If you miss the "A" train,
You'll find you've missed the quickest way to Harlem.

Hurry, get on now it's coming.
Listen to those rails a-thrumming.
All 'board!
Get on the "A" train,
Soon you will be on Sugar Hill in Harlem.

Takin' Care of Business

Words and Music by Randy Bachman

recorded by Bachman-Turner Overdrive

They get up every mornin'
From the 'larm clock's warnin',
Take the eight-fifteen into the city.
There's a whistle up above and
People pushin', people shovin'
And the girls who try to look pretty.
And if your train's on time,
You can get to work by nine,
And start your slavin' job to get your pay.
If you ever get annoyed,
Look at me, I'm self-employed,
I love to work at nothin' all day.

Refrain:
And I've been takin' care of business,
Every day.
Takin' care of business,
Every way.
I've been takin' care of business
It's all mine,
Takin' care of business and workin' over-time,
Work out.

There's work easy as fishin',
You could be a musician
If you can make sounds loud or mellow.
Get a second-hand guitar,
Chances are you'll go far
If you get in with the right bunch of fellows.
People see you havin' fun,
Just a lyin' in the sun,
Tell them that you like it this way.
It's the work that we avoid
And we're all self-employed,
We love to work at nothin' all day.

Refrain

Tangerine

Words by Johnny Mercer
Music by Victor Schertzinger

from the Paramount Picture *The Fleet's In*
recorded by Bob Eberly & Helen O'Connell with Jimmy Dorsey, and various other artists

South American stories
Tell of a girl who is quite a dream,
The beauty of her race.
Though you'll doubt all the stories
And think the tales just a bit extreme,
Wait till you see her face.

Tangerine, she is all they claim
With her eyes of night and lips as bright as flame.
Tangerine, when she dances by
Senoritas stare and caballeros sigh.

And I've seen toasts to Tangerine
Raised in bar across the Argentine.
Yes, she has them all on the run,
But her heart belongs to just one.
Her heart belongs to Tangerine.

Tapestry
Words and Music by Carole King
© 1971 (Renewed 1999) COLGEMS-EMI MUSIC INC.

recorded by Carole King

My life has been a tapestry of rich and royal hue,
An everlasting vision of the ever-changing view.
A wondrous woven magic in bits of blue and gold
A tapestry to feel and see, impossible to hold.

Once, amid the soft, silver sadness in the sky,
There came a man of fortune, a drifter passing by.
He wore a torn and tattered cloth around his leathered hide,
And a coat of many colors, yellow, green on either side.

He moved with some uncertainty, as if he didn't know
Just what he was there for, or where he ought to go.
Once he reached for something golden, hanging from a tree,
And his hand came down empty.

Soon within my tapestry, along the rutted road,
He sat down on a river rock and turned into a toad.
It seemed that he had fallen into someone's wicked spell,
And I wept to see him suffer, though I didn't know him well.

As I watched in sorrow, there suddenly appeared
A figure, gray and ghostly, beneath a flowing beard.
In times of deepest darkness, I've seen him dressed in black.
Now my tapestry's unraveling; he's come to take me back.
He's come to take me back.

Teach Your Children
Words and Music by Graham Nash
Copyright © 1970 Nash Notes
Copyright Renewed
All Rights Administered by Sony/ATV Music Publishing, 8 Music Square West,
    Nashville, TN 37203

recorded by Crosby, Stills, Nash & Young

You who are on the road
Must have a code
That you can live by,
And so
Become yourself,
Because the past
Is just a goodbye.

Teach your children well;
Their father's hell
Did slowly go by.
And feed
Them on your dreams,
The one they pick,
The one you'll know by.

Refrain:
Don't you ever ask them why;
If they told you, you would cry,
So just look at them and sigh
And know they love you.

(Can you hear and do you care?
Do you see,
You must be free,
To teach your children?
You'll believe they'll make a world
That we can live in.)

Teach your parents well;
Their children's hell
Will slowly go by.
And feed them on your dreams,
The one they pick,
The one you'll know by.

Refrain

The Tears of a Clown
Words and Music by Stevie Wonder, William "Smokey"
Robinson and Henry Cosby
© 1967 (Renewed 1995) JOBETE MUSIC CO., INC. and BLACK BULL MUSIC
    c/o EMI APRIL MUSIC INC.

recorded by The Miracles

Now if there's a smile upon my face
It's only there trying to fool the public;
But when it comes down to fool you,
Now honey that's quite a different subject.
Don't let my glad expression
Give you the wrong impression;
Really I'm sad,
Oh, sadder than sad,
You're gone and I'm hurt so bad,
Like a clown, I pretend to be glad.

Refrain:
Now there's some sad things known to man
But ain't too much sadder than
The tears of a clown,
When there's no one around.

Oh yeah, baby,
Now if I appear to be carefree,
It's only to camouflage my sadness;
In order to shield my pride
I try to cover this hurt with a show of gladness.
But don't let my show convince you
That I've been happy since you decided to go,
I need you so, I'm hurt and I want you to know,
But for others I put on a show.

Just like Pagliacci did,
I try to keep my sadness hid,
Smiling in the public eye
But in my lonely room I cry
The tears of clown.

Oh, yeah baby!
Now, if there's a smile on my face
Don't let my glad expression
Give you the wrong impression.
Don't let this smile I wear
Make you think that I don't care.

Tell Me on a Sunday

Music by Andrew Lloyd Webber
Lyrics by Don Black

from the musical *Song and Dance*

Don't write a letter when you want to leave.
Don't call me at 3 A.M. from a friend's apartment.
I'd like to choose
How I hear the news.
Take me to a park that's covered with trees.
Tell me on a Sunday, please.

Let me down easy, no big song and dance.
No long faces, no long looks, no deep conversation.
I know the way
We should spend the day.
Take me to a zoo that's got chimpanzees.
Tell me on a Sunday, please.

Don't want to know who's to blame,
It won't help knowing.
Don't want to fight
Day and night,
Bad enough you're going.

Don't leave me in silence with no words at all.
Don't get drunk and slam the door,
That's no way to end this.
I know how I want to say goodbye.
Find a circus ring with a flying trapeze.
Tell me on a Sunday, please.

I don't want to fight day and night,
Bad enough you're going.

Don't leave in silence with no words at all.
Don't get drunk and slam the door,
That's no way to end this.
I know how I want you to say goodbye.
Don't run off in the pouring rain.
Don't call me as they call your plane.
Take the hurt out of all the pain.
Take me to a park that's covered with trees.
Tell me on a Sunday, please.

Ten Cents a Dance

Words by Lorenz Hart
Music by Richard Rodgers

from the musical *Simple Simon*
featured in the film *Love Me or Leave Me*
recorded by Ruth Etting, Doris Day and other artists

I work at the Palace Ballroom,
But gee, that place is cheap;
When I get back to my chilly hall room
I'm much too tired to sleep.
I'm one of those lady teachers,
A beautiful hostess, you know,
One that the palace features
At exactly a dime a throw.

Refrain:
Ten cents a dance;
That's what they pay me.
Gosh, how they weigh me down!
Ten cents a dance,
Pansies and rough guys,
Tough guys who tear my gown!
Seven to midnight, I hear drums,
Loudly the saxophone blows,
Trumpets are tearing my eardrums.
Customers crush my toes.
Sometimes I think I've found my hero
But it's a queer romance
All that you need is a ticket;
Come on, big boy, ten cents a dance!

Fighters and sailors and bowlegged tailors
Can pay for their tickets and rent me!
Butchers and barbers and rats from the harbors
Are sweethearts my good luck has sent me.
Though I've a chorus of elderly beaux
Stockings are porous with holes at the toes.
I'm here till closing time
Dance and be merry, it's only a dime.

Sometimes I think I've found my hero
But it's a queer romance,
All that you need is a ticket!
Come on, big boy, ten cents a dance!

Tennessee Waltz

Words and Music by Redd Stewart and Pee Wee King

recorded by Patti Page

I was waltzing with my darlin'
To the Tennessee waltz,
When an old friend I happened to see.

Introduced him to my loved one
And while they were waltzing,
My friend stole my sweetheart from me.

I remember the night and the Tennessee Waltz.
Now I know just how much I have lost.
Yes, I lost my little darlin' the night they were playing
The beautiful Tennessee Waltz.

Thank God I Found You

Words and Music by Mariah Carey, James Harris III and
Terry Lewis

recorded by Mariah Carey featuring Joe & 98 Degrees

Female:
I would give up everything
Before I would separate myself from you.
After so much suffering
I finally found unvarnished truth.
I was all by myself for the longest time,
So cold inside,
And the hurt from the heartache would not subside;
I felt like dying,
Until you saved my life.

Refrain, Background:
Thank God I found you.
I was lost without you.
My every wish and every dream
Somehow became reality
When you brought the sunlight,
Completed my whole life.
I'm overwhelmed with gratitude
'Cause baby, I'm so thankful I found you.

Male:
And I will give you everything;
There's nothing in this world I wouldn't do
To ensure your happiness.
I'll cherish every part of you
'Cause without you beside me I can't survive;
Don't want to try.
If you're keeping me warm each and every night,
I'll be all right,
'Cause I need you in my life.

Refrain

Female:
I was so desolate before you came to me.

Background:
Looking back…looking back.

Male:
I guess.

Both:
It shows that we were destined
To shine after the rain
To appreciate the gift of what we have.

Refrain Twice

Female:
I'm overwhelmed with gratitude;
My baby, I'm so thankful I found you.

Male:
Yeah.

Thanks for the Memory

Words and Music by Leo Robin and Ralph Rainger

from the Paramount Picture *Big Broadcast of 1938*
a standard recorded by Bob Hope & Shirley Ross and
other artists

Thanks for the memory
Of candlelight and wine,
Castles on the Rhine,
The Parthenon and moments on the Hudson River Line.
How lovely it was!

Thanks for the memory
Of rainy afternoons,
Swingy Harlem tunes
And motor trips and burning lips and burning toast and prunes.
How lovely it was!

Many's the time that we feasted
And many's the time that we fasted.
Oh, well, it was swell while it lasted;
We did have fun and no harm done.

And thanks for the memory
Of sunburns at the shore,
Nights in Singapore.
You might have been a headache
But you never were a bore,
So thank you so much.

Thanks for the memory
Of sentimental verse,
Nothing in my purse,
And chuckles when the preacher said
"For better of for worse."
How lovely it was!

Thanks for the memory
Of lingerie with lace,
Pilsner by the case
And how I jumped
The day you trumped
My one and only ace.
How lovely it was!

We said goodbye with a highball;
Then I got as "high" as a steeple.
But we were intelligent people;
No tears, no fuss,
Hurray for us.

So thanks for the memory
And strictly *entre nous,*
Darling, how are you?
And how are all the little dreams
That never did come true?
Awfully glad I met you,
Cheerio and toodle-oo
And thank you so much!

That Old Black Magic
Words by Johnny Mercer
Music by Harold Arlen

from the Paramount Picture *Star Spangled Rhythm*
a standard recorded by Glenn Miller, Frank Sinatra,
Louis Prima and other artists
featured in the films *Here Come the Waves, When You're
Smiling, Meet Danny Wilson, Senior Prom, Bustop*

That old black magic has me in its spell.
That old black magic that you weave so well.
Those icy fingers up and down my spine.
The same old witchcraft when your eyes meet mine.
The same old tingle that I feel inside
And then that elevator starts its ride
And down and down I go,
'Round and 'round I go
Like a leaf that's caught in the tide.

I should stay away but what can I do
I hear your name and I'm aflame,
Aflame with such a burning desire
That only your kiss can put out the fire.
For you're the lover I have waited for.
The mate that fate had me created for
And every time your lips meet mine
Darling down and down I go,
'Round and 'round I go in a spin,
Loving the spin I'm in
Under that old black magic called love!

That'll Be the Day
Words and Music by Jerry Allison, Norman Petty and
Buddy Holly

recorded by Buddy Holly & The Crickets

Well, you give me all your lovin'
And your turtle-dovin',
All your hugs an' your money too;
Well, you know you love me, baby,
Until you tell me, maybe, that someday, well,
I'll be through! Well,

Refrain:
That'll be the day,
When you say goodbye,
Yes, that'll be the day,
When you make me cry,
Ah you say you're gonna leave,
You know it's a lie,
'Cause that'll be the day when I die.

Well, when Cupid shot his dart,
He shot it at your heart,
So if we ever part and I leave you,
You say you told me an' you
Told me boldly, that some way, well,
I'll be through. Well,

Refrain

That's All Right
Words and Music by Arthur Crudup

recorded by Big Boy Crudup, Elvis Presley, Marty Robbins

Well, that's all right, Mama,
That's all right for you,
That's all right, Mama,
Just any way you do.
Now that's all right.

Refrain:
That's all right.
That's all right,
That's all right now Mama,
Any way you do.

Well, mama she done told me.
Papa done told me too;
"Son that gal you're foolin' with,
She just ain't no good for you."
But…

Refrain

I'm leavin' town now baby,
I'm leavin' town for sure.
Well, then you won't ah be bothered with me
Hangin' round your door,
But…

Refrain

Ah, da, da, dee…
I need you're lovin'.

Refrain

That's Amoré (That's Love)
Words by Jack Brooks
Music by Harry Warren

from the Paramount Picture *The Caddy*
recorded by Dean Martin

In Napoli, where love is king,
When boy meets girl, here's what they sing:

When the moon hits your eye
Like a big pizza pie,
That's amoré.
When the world seems to shine
Like you've had too much wine,
That's amoré.
Bells will ring, ting-a-ling-a-ling,
Ting-a-ling-a-ling, and you sing,
"Veeta bella."
Hearts will play, tippy-tippy-tay,
Tippy-tippy-tay like a gay tarantella.
(Lucky fella)

When the stars make you drool
Just like pasta fazool,
That's amoré.
When you dance down the street
With a cloud at you feet,
You're in love.
When you walk in a dream
But you know you're not dreaming,
Signoré.
Scuza me, but you see,
Back in old Napoli,
That's amoré.

That's Entertainment
Words by Howard Dietz
Music by Arthur Schwartz

from the film *The Band Wagon*

The clown with his pants falling down,
Or the dance that's a dream of romance,
Or the scene where the villain is mean;
That's entertainment!

The lights on the lady in tights,
Or the bride with a guy on the side,
Or the ball where she gives him her all,
That's entertainment!

The plot can be hot, simply teeming with sex,
A gay divorcee who is after her "ex."
It can be Oedipus Rex
Where a chap kills his father,
And causes a lot of bother.

The clerk who is thrown out of work by the boss
Who is thrown for a loss by the skirt
Who is doing him dirt;
The world is a stage,
The stage is a world of entertainment!

That's What Love Is All About
Words and Music by Michael Bolton and Eric Kaz

recorded by Michael Bolton

There was a time,
We thought our dream was over,
When you and I had surely reached the end.
Still, here we are.
The flame is strong as ever.
All because we both kept holding on.
We know we can weather any storm.

Refrain:
Baby that's what love is all about,
Two hearts that found a way somehow
To keep the fire burning.
It's something we could never live without.
If it takes forever, we can work it out
Beyond a shadow of a doubt.
Baby, that's what love is all about.

As the time goes by,
We learned to rediscover
The reason why this dream of ours survives.
Through thick and thin,
We're destined for each other,
Knowing we can reach the other side,
Far beyond the mountains of our pride.

Refrain

Oh, ridin' the good times is easy.
The hard times can tear you apart.
There'll be times in your heart
When the feelin' is gone,
But ya keep on believing
And ya' keep holdin' on.

Refrain

There Is Nothin' Like a Dame
Lyrics by Oscar Hammerstein II
Music by Richard Rodgers

from the musical *South Pacific*

We got sunlight on the sand,
We got moonlight on the sea,
We got mangoes and bananas
You can pick right off a tree,
We got volleyball and ping-pong
And a lot of dandy games—
What ain't we got?
We ain't got dames.

We get packages from home,
We get movies, we get shows,
We get speeches from our skipper
And advice from Tokyo Rose,
We get letters doused with perfume,
We get dizzy from the smell!
What don't we get?
You know darn well!

We have nothin' to put on a clean white suit for.
What we need is what there ain't no substitute for.

Refrain:
There is nothin' like a dame,
Nothin' in the world,
There is nothin' you can name
That is anythin' like a dame!

We feel restless, we feel blue,
We feel lonely and, in brief
We feel ev'ry kind of feeling
But the feeling of relief.
We feel hungry as the wolf felt
When he met Red Riding Hood.
What don't we feel?
We don't feel good!

Lot of things in life are beautiful,
But brother,
There is one particular thing that is nothin' whatsoever
In any way, shape or form like any other.

Refrain

There are no books like a dame,
A nothin' looks like a dame.
There are no drinks like a dame,
And nothin' thinks like a dame,
And nothin' acts like a dame,
Or attracts like a dame.
There ain't a thing that's wrong with any man here
That can't be cured by puttin' him near
A girly, womanly, female, feminine dame!

There'll Be Some Changes Made
Words by Billy Higgins
Music by W. Benton Overstreet

a standard recorded by Ethel Waters, Bunny Berigan,
Sophie Tucker, Gene Krupa and various other artists

They say don't change the old for the new,
But I've found out this never will do
When you grow old you don't last long
You're here today and then tomorrow you're gone,
I loved a man (gal) for many years gone by,
I thought his (her) love for me would never die,
He (She) made some changes that would never do
From now on I'm goin' to make some changes too.

Refrain:
For there's a change in the weather
There's a change in the sea
So from now on there'll be a change in me.
My walk will be different, my talk and my name
Nothin' about me is goin' to be the same.
I'm goin' to change my way of livin' if that ain't enough,
Then I'll change the way that I strut my stuff,
'Cause nobody wants you when you're old and gray.
There'll be some changes made.

They say the old-time things are the best,
That may be very good for all the rest.
But I'm goin' to let the old things be
'Cause they are certainly not suited for me.
There was a time when I thought that way,
That's why I'm all alone here today.
Since every one of these days seeks something new,
From now on I'm goin' to seek some new things too.

For there's a change in the fashions,
Ask the feminine folks.
Even Jack Benny has been changing some jokes.
I must make some changes from old to the new.
I must do things just the same as others do.
I'm goin' to change my long, tall Mamma (Daddy)
For a little, short fat,
Goin' to change the number where I live at.
I must have some lovin' or I'll fade away,
There'll be some changes made.

There's a Kind of Hush
(All Over the World)
Words and Music by Les Reed and Geoff Stephens
© 1966, 1967 (Renewed 1994, 1995) DONNA MUSIC, LTD.
All Rights for the U.S. and Canada Controlled and
   Administered by GLENWOOD MUSIC CORP.

recorded by Herman's Hermits

There's a kind of hush,
All over the world tonight,
All over the world,
You can hear the sounds
Of lovers in love.
You know what I mean.
Just the two of us
And nobody else in sight,
There's nobody else
And I'm feeling good,
Just holding you tight.

So listen very carefully
Closer now and you will see what I mean
It isn't a dream.
The only sound that you will hear
Is when I whisper in your ear,
I love you,
Forever and ever.

There's a kind of hush,
All over the world tonight.
All over the world,
You can hear the sounds
Of lovers in love.

Repeat Song

There's a Small Hotel
Words by Lorenz Hart
Music by Richard Rodgers
Copyright © 1936 by Williamson Music and The Estate Of Lorenz Hart in the United States
Copyright Renewed
All Rights on behalf of The Estate Of Lorenz Hart Administered by WB Music Corp.

from the musical *On Your Toes*

Frankie:
I'd like to get away, Junior,
Somewhere alone with you.
It could be oh, so gay, Junior!
You need a laugh or two.

Junior:
A certain place I know, Frankie,
Where funny people can have fun.
That's where we two will go, darling,
Before you can count up
One, two, three
For…

Refrain:
There's a small hotel
With a wishing well;
I wish that we were there
Together.
There's a bridal suite;
One room bright and neat,
Complete for us to share
Together.

Looking through the window
You can see a distant steeple;
Not a sign of people,
Who wants people?
When the steeple bell says,
"Goodnight, sleep well,"
We'll thank the small hotel
Together.

Refrain

Looking through the window
You can see a distant steeple;
Not a sign of people,
Who wants people?
When the steeple bell says,
"Goodnight, sleep well,"
We'll thank the small hotel.
We'll creep into our little shell
And we will thank the small hotel
Together.

There's No Business
Like Show Business

Words and Music by Irving Berlin
© Copyright 1946 by Irving Berlin
Copyright Renewed

from the Stage Production *Annie Get Your Gun*
featured in the film *There's No Business Like Show Business*

The butcher, the baker, the grocer, the clerk
Are secretly unhappy men because
The butcher, the baker, the grocer, the clerk
Get paid for what they do but no applause.
They'd gladly bid their dreary jobs goodbye,
For anything theatrical and why.

There's no business like show business
Like no business I know.
Everything about it is appealing.
Everything the traffic will allow.
Nowhere could you get that happy feeling
When you are stealing
That extra bow.

There's no people like show people.
They smile when they are low.
Even with a turkey that you know will fold,
You may be stranded out in the cold.
Still you wouldn't change it for a sack of gold.
Let's go on with the show.

The costumes, the scenery, the make-up, the props,
The audience that lifts you up when you're down,
The headaches, the heartaches, the backaches, the flops
The sheriff who escorts you out of town.
The opening when your heart beats like a drum,
The closing when the customers won't come.

There's no business like show business
Like no business I know.
You get word before the show has started
That you favorite uncle died at dawn.
Top of that your Pa and Ma have parted,
You're broken-hearted but you go on.

There's no people like show people.
They don't run out of dough.
Angels come from everywhere with lots of jack.
And when you lose it, there's no attack.
Where could you get money that don't give back.
Let's go on with the show.

The cowboys, the tumblers, the wrestlers, the clowns,
The roustabouts who move the show at dawn,
The music, the spotlights, the people, the towns,
Your baggage with the labels pasted on.
The sawdust and the horses and the smell,
The towel you've taken from the last hotel.

There's no business like show business
Like no business I know.
Traveling thru the country will be thrilling.
Standing out in front on opening nights.
Smiling as you watch the theatre filling,
And there's your billing out there in lights.

There's no people like show people.
They smile when they are low.
Yesterday they told you you would not go far.
That night you open and there you are.
Next day on your dressing room they've hung a star.
Let's go on with the show.

These Are the Best Times

Words and Music by Shane Tatum
© 1973 Wonderland Music Company, Inc.

from Walt Disney Productions' *Superdad*

These are the best times,
The moments we can't let slip away.
Life's little game we play,
Living from day to day.

But once in a lifetime,
A minute like this is our to share.
Remember these moments well,
For moments like these are rare…

As dreams and golden rainbows,
Soft as night when summer wind blows by
Together we laugh and cry,
Together we'll learn to fly.

Come take my hand,
Together we'll cross the timeless sands,
Chasing the endless sun
Living our lives as one.

They Say It's Wonderful

Words and Music by Irving Berlin
© Copyright 1946 by Irving Berlin
Copyright Renewed

from the Stage Production *Annie Get Your Gun*

Annie:
Rumors fly and you can't tell where they start,
'Specially when it concerns a person's heart.
I've heard tales that could set my heart a-glow.
Wish I knew if the things I hear are so.

They say that falling in love is wonderful,
It's wonderful so they say.
And with a moon up above,
It's wonderful,
It's wonderful so they tell me.

I can't recall who said it,
I know I never read it.
I only know they tell me that love is grand,
And the thing that's known as romance is wonderful,
Wonderful in every way,
So they say.

Frank:
Rumors fly and you often leave a doubt,
But you've come to the right place to find out.
Everything that you've heard is really so.
I've been there once or twice and I should know.

You'll find that falling in love is wonderful,
It's wonderful.

Annie:
So you say.

Frank:
And with a moon up above,
It's wonderful, it's wonderful.

Annie:
So you tell me.

Frank:
To leave your house some morning,
And without any warning,
You're stopping people
Shouting that love is grand.
And to hold a man in your arms is wonderful,
Wonderful in every way,

Annie:
So you say.

This Can't Be Love
Words by Lorenz Hart
Music by Richard Rodgers
Copyright © 1938 by Williamson Music and The Estate Of Lorenz Hart in the United States
Copyright Renewed
All Rights on behalf of The Estate Of Lorenz Hart Administered by WB Music Corp.

from the musical *The Boys from Syracuse*
a standard recorded by various artists

In Verona, my late cousin Romeo
Was three times as stupid as my Dromio.
For he fell in love
And then he died of it.
Poor half-wit!

Refrain:
This can't be love
Because I feel so well;
No sobs, no sorrows, no sighs.
This can't be love,
I get no dizzy spell,
My head is not in the skies.
My heart does not stand still;
Just hear it beat!

This is too sweet
To be love.
This can't be love
Because I feel so well,
But still I love to look in your eyes.

Though your cousin loved my cousin Juliet,
Loved her with a passion much more truly yet,
Some poor playwright
Wrote their drama just for fun.
It won't run!

Refrain

This Guy's in Love with You
Lyric by Hal David
Music by Burt Bacharach
Copyright © 1968 (Renewed) Casa David and New Hidden Valley Music

recorded by Herb Alpert, Dionne Warwick

You see this guy,
This guy's in love with you.
Yes, I'm in love.
Who looks at you the way I do?
When you smile,
I can tell we know each other very well.
How can I show you
I'm glad I got to know you.
'Cause

I've heard some talk.
They say you think I'm fine.
This guy's in love,
And what I'd do to make you mine.
The me now, is it so?
Don't let me be the last to know.
My hands are shaking.
Don't let my heart keep breaking
'Cause

I need your love,
I want your love.
Say you're in love,
In love with this guy.
If not, I'll just die.

This Is the Moment

Words by Leslie Bricusse
Music by Frank Wildhorn

from the musical *Jekyll & Hyde*

This is the moment, this is the day,
When I send all my doubts and demons on their way.
Every endeavor I have made ever come in into play,
Is here and now today.

This is the moment, this is the time
When the momentum and the moment are in rhyme.
Give me this moment, this precious chance.
I'll gather up my past and make some sense at last.

This is the moment when all I've done,
All of the dreaming, scheming and screaming become one!
This is the day, see it sparkle and shine,
When all I've lived for becomes mine!

For all these years I've faced the world alone,
And now the time has come
To prove to them I made it on my own.

This is the moment, my final test.
Destiny beckoned, I never reckoned second best.
I won't look down, I must not fall.
This is the moment, the sweetest moment of them all!

This is the moment. Damn all the odds.
This day or never, I'll sit forever with the gods!
When I look back, I will always recall,
Moment for moment, this was the moment,
The greatest moment of all.

This Land Is Your Land

Words and Music by Woody Guthrie

recorded by Woodie Guthrie

This land is your land, this land is my land,
From California to the New York island,
From the redwood forest to the Gulf Stream waters;
This land was made for you and me.

As I was walking that ribbon of highway,
I saw above me the endless skyway;
I saw below me that golden valley;
This land was made for you and me.

I've roamed and rambled and I followed my footsteps,
To the sparkling sand of diamond desserts;
And all around me a voice was sounding;
This land was made for you and me.

When the sun came shining, and I was strolling,
And the wheat fields waving and the dust clouds rolling,
As the fog was lifting a voice was chanting:
This land was made for you and me.

As I went walking, I saw a sign there,
And on the sign it said "No trespassing."
But on the other side it didn't say nothing,
That side was made for you and me.

In the shadow of the steeple, I saw my people,
By the relief office I seen my people;
As they stood there hungry, I stood there asking,
Is this land made for you and me?

Nobody living can ever stop me,
As I go walking that freedom highway;
Nobody living can ever make me turn back.
This land was made for you and me.

This Masquerade

Words and Music by Leon Russell

recorded by George Benson

Are we really happy here with this lonely game we play,
Looking for words to say?
Searching but not finding understanding in any way,
We're lost in a masquerade.

Both afraid to say we're just to far away
From being close together from the start.
We tried to talk it over, but the words got in the way.
We're lost inside this lonely game we play.

Thoughts of leaving disappear everytime I see your eyes.
No matter how hard I try
To understand the reasons that we carry on this way,
We're lost in this masquerade.

This Nearly Was Mine

Lyrics by Oscar Hammerstein II
Music by Richard Rodgers

from the musical *South Pacific*

One dream in my heart,
One love to be living for,
One love to be living for,
This nearly was mine.

One girl for my dream,
One partner in paradise,
This promise of paradise,
This nearly was mine.

Close to my heart she came,
Only to fly away,
Only to fly as day flies from moonlight.

Now, now I'm alone
Still dreaming of paradise,
Still saying that paradise
Once nearly was mine.

So clear and deep are my fancies
Of things I wish were true,
I'll keep remembering evenings
I wish I'd spent with you.

I'll keep remembering kisses
From lips I'll never own,
And all the lovely adventures
That we have never known.

Now, now I'm alone
Still dreaming of paradise,
Still saying that paradise
Once nearly was mine.

This Will Be
(An Everlasting Love)
Words and Music by Marvin Yancy and Chuck Jackson

recorded by Natalie Cole

This will be an everlasting love,
This will be the one I've waited for.
This will be the first time anyone has loved me, oh!

I'm so glad he found me in time,
I'm so glad that he rectified my mind.
This will be an everlasting love for me, oh!

Loving you is some kind of wonderful,
Because you've shown me just how much you care.
You've given me the thrill of a lifetime
And made me believe you've got more thrills to spare, oh!
This will be an everlasting love,
Oh, yes it will, now.

You've brought a lot of sunshine into my life,
You've filled me with happiness I never knew.
You gave me more joy than I ever dreamed of
And no one, no one can take the place of you.

This will be, you and me,
Yessiree, eternally
Hugging and squeezing and kissing and pleasing
Together forever through rain or whatever.

This will be you and me.
So long as I'm living my love I'll be giving to you.
I'll be serving 'cause you're so deserving.

Those Were the Days
Words and Music by Gene Raskin

recorded by Mary Hopkin

Once upon a time there was a tavern
Where we used to raise a glass or two.
Remember how we laughed away the hours,
And dreamed of all the great things we would do.

Refrain:
Those were the days my friend.
We thought they'd never end,
We'd sing and dance
Forever and a day;
We'd live the life we choose,
We'd fight and never lose,
For we were young and sure to have our way.
La la la la, la la
La la la la, la la
Those were the days,
Oh yes, those were the days.

Then the busy years went rushing by us.
We lost our starry notions on the way.
If by chance I'd see you in the tavern,
We'd smile at one another and we'd say—

Refrain

Just tonight I stood before the tavern.
Nothing seemed the way it used to be.
In the glass I saw a strange reflection,
Was that lonely fellow really me?

Refrain

Through the door there came familiar laughter.
I saw your face and heard you call my name.
Oh my friends we're older but no wiser,
For in our hearts the dreams are still the same.

Refrain

Thou Swell

Words by Lorenz Hart
Music by Richard Rodgers

from the musical *A Connecticut Yankee*

Babe, we are well met,
As in a spell met;
I lift my helmet,
Sandy,
You're just dandy.
For just this here lad.
You're such a fistful,
My eyes are mistful;
Are you too wistful
To care?
Do say you care
To say, "Come near lad."
You are so graceful;
Have you wings?
You have a face full
Of nice things;
You have no speaking voice, dear,
With every word it sings.

Refrain:
Thou swell!
Thou witty!
Thou sweet!
Thou grand!
Wouldst kiss me pretty?
Wouldst hold my hand?
Both thine eyes are cute too;
What they do to me.
Hear me holler
I choose a
Sweet lollapalooza
In thee.

I'd feel so rich in
A hut for two
Two rooms and kitchen
I'm sure would do;
Give me just a plot of,
Not a lot of land
And,
Thou swell!
Thou witty!
Thou grand!

Thy words are queer, Sir,
Unto mine ear, Sir,
Yet thou'rt a dear, Sir,
To me.
Thou could'st woo me.
Now could'st thou try, knight.
I'd murmur "Swell" too,
And like it well too.
More thou wilt tell to
Sandy.
Thou art dandy;

Now art thou my knight.
Thine arms are martial,
Thou hast grace.
My cheek is partial
To they face.
And if thy lips grow weary,
Mine are their resting place.

Refrain

3 AM

Lyrics by Rob Thomas
Music by Rob Thomas, Brian Yale, John Leslie Goff and
John Joseph Stanley

recorded by Matchbox 20

She says it's cold outside
And she hands me my rain coat.
She's always worried about things like that.
Well, she said it's all gonna end
And it might as well be my fault.

Refrain:
And she only sleeps when it's rainin'.
And she screams, and her voice is strainin'.
She says, "Baby, it's three a.m., I must be lonely."
When she says, "Baby,"
Well, I can't help but be scared of it all sometimes.
And the rain's gonna wash away, I believe it.

Well she's gotta little bit of somethin',
God, it's better than nothin'.
And in her color portrait world
She believes that she's got it all.
She swears the moon don't hang
Quite as high as it used to.

Refrain

Well, she believes that life isn't made up
Of all that she used to.
And the clock on the wall
Has been stuck at three for days and days.
She thinks that happiness is a mat
That sits on her door way.

But outside it stopped rainin'.
Yeah, but she says, "Baby, well it's three a.m., I must be lonely."
When she says, "Baby,"
Well, I can't help but be scared of it all sometimes.
And the rain's gonna wash away, I believe this.
"Well, it's three a.m., I must be lonely."
Well, I must feel lonely.
When she says, "Baby,"
Well, I can't help but be scared of it all sometimes.

Three Coins in the Fountain

Words by Sammy Cahn
Music by Jule Styne

from the film *Three Coins in the Fountain*
recorded by Frank Sinatra

Three coins in the fountain,
Each one seeking happiness,
Thrown by three hopeful lovers,
Which one will the fountain bless?

Three coins in the fountain,
Each heart longing for its home,
There they lie in the fountain
Somewhere in the heart of Rome.

Which one will the fountain bless?
Which one will the fountain bless?
Three coins in the fountain,
Through the ripples they shine
Just one wish will be granted
One heart will wear a valentine.
Make it mine!
Make it mine!
Make it mine!

Three Times a Lady

Words and Music by Lionel Richie

recorded by The Commodores

Thanks for the times that you've given me,
The memories are all in my mind.
And now that we've come to the end of our rainbow,
There's something I must say out loud:

Refrain:
You're once, twice, three times a lady,
And I love you,
Yes, your once, twice, three times a lady,
And I love you,
I love you.

When we are together, the moments I cherish,
With every beat of my heart,
To touch you, to hold you, to feel you, to need you,
There's nothing to keep us apart.

Refrain

Through the Years

Words and Music by Steve Dorff and Marty Panzer

recorded by Kenny Rogers

I can't remember when you weren't there,
When I didn't care for anyone but you,
I swear we've been through everything there is,
Can't imagine anything we've missed.
Can't imagine anything the two of us can't do.

Through the years
You've never let me down,
You've turned my life around.
The sweetest days I've found
I've found with you.

Through the years,
I've never been afraid,
I've loved the life we've made,
And I'm so glad I've stayed
Right here with you
Through the years.

I can't remember what I used to do,
Who I trusted
Who I listened to before.
I swear you've taught me everything I know,
Can't imagine needing someone so.

Through the years,
I've never been afraid,
I've loved the life we've made,
And I'm so glad I've stayed
Right here with you
Through the years.

Ticket to Ride

Words and Music by John Lennon and Paul McCartney

recorded by The Beatles

I think I'm gonna be sad,
I think it's today, yeah.
The girl that's driving me mad,
Is going away.

Refrain
She's got a ticket to ride.
She's got a ticket to ri-hi-hide.
She's got a ticket to ride.
But she don't care.

She said that living with me,
Is bringing her down, yeah.
For she would never be free,
When I was around.

Refrain

I don't know why she's riding so high.
She ought to think twice,
She ought to do right by me.
Before she gets to saying goodbye,
She ought to think twice,
She ought to do right by me.

I think I'm gonna be sad,
I think it's today, yeah.
The girl that's driving me mad,
Is going away.

Refrain

I don't know why she's riding so high,
She ought to think twice,
She ought to do right by me.
Before she gets to saying goodbye,
She ought to think twice,
She ought to do right by me.

She said that living with me,
Is bringing her down, yeah.
For she would never be free,
When I was around.

Refrain

My baby don't care!

Till There Was You
By Meredith Willson

from Meredith Willson's *The Music Man*
recorded by The Beatles

There were bells
On the hill,
But I never heard them ringing.
No, I never heard them at all
Till there was you.

There were birds
In the sky
But I never heard them singing,
No, I never saw them at all,
Till there was you.

And there was music
And there were wonderful roses,
They tell me
In sweet fragrant meadows of dawn,
And dew.

There was love
All around,
But I never heard it singing,
No, I never heard it at all
Till I there was you.

Time After Time
Words and Music by Cyndi Lauper and Rob Hyman

recorded by Cyndi Lauper, Inoj

Lyin' in my bed I hear the clock tick and think of you,
Caught up in circles confusion is nothing new.
Flash back
Warm nights,
Almost left behind.
Suitcase of memories
Time after time.

Sometimes you picture me
I'm walking too far ahead.
You're calling to me,
Can't hear what you've said.
Then you say go slow,
I fall behind.
The second hand unwinds.

Refrain:
If you're lost you can look
And you will find me
Time after time.
If you fall I will catch you
I'll be waiting
Time after time.

Repeat Refrain

After my picture fades
And darkness returned to gray.
Watching through windows,
You're wondering if I'm O.K.
Secrets stolen
From deep inside.
The drum beats out of time.

Refrain

Time after time.

A Time for Us (Love Theme)
Words by Larry Kusik and Eddie Snyder
Music by Nino Rota

from the Paramount Picture *Romeo and Juliet*
recorded by Andy Williams

A time for us, someday there'll be,
When chains are torn by courage born
Of a love that's free.
A time when dreams, so long denied
Can flourish, as we unveil the love we now must hide.

A time for us at last to see,
A life worthwhile for you and me.
And with our love through tears and thorns,
We will endure as we pass surely through every storm.
A time for us someday there'll be,
A new world, a world of shining hope for you and me.

Time in a Bottle
Words and Music by Jim Croce

recorded by Jim Croce

If I could save time in a bottle,
The first thing that I'd like to do,
Is to save every day 'til eternity passes away,
Just to spend them with you.

If I could make days last forever,
If words could make wishes come true,
I'd save every day like a treasure and then
I would spend them with you.

Refrain:
But there never seems to be enough time
To do the things you want to do
Once you find them.
I've looked round enough to know
That you're the one I want to go through time with.

If I had a box just for wishes,
And dreams that had never come true,
The box would be empty,
Except for the memory
Of how they were answered by you.

Refrain

To Be with You
Words and Music by Eric Martin and David Grahame

recorded by Mr. Big

Hold on, little girl,
Show me what he's done to you.
Stand up, little girl,
A broken heart can't be that bad.
When it's through, it's through.
Fate will twist the both of you.
So come on, baby, come on over,
Let me be the one to show you.

Refrain:
I'm the one who wants to be with you.
Deep inside I hope you feel it too.
(Feel it too.)
Waited on a line of greens and blues,
Just to be the next to be with you.

Build up your confidence,
So you can be on top for once.
Wake up, who cares about
Little boys that talk too much.
I seen it all go down.
Your game of love was all rained out.
So come on, baby, come on over,
Let me be the one to hold you.

Refrain

Why be alone, when we can be together, baby?
You can make my life worthwhile.
I can make you start to smile.

When it's through, it's through.
Fate will twist the both of you.
So come on, baby, come on over,
Let me be the one to show you.

Refrain

Just to be the next to be with you.

To Love You More
Words and Music by David Foster and Junior Miles

recorded by Celine Dion

Take me back into the arms I love.
Need me like you did before.
Touch me once again
And remember when
There was no one that you wanted more.

Don't go, you know you'll break my heart.
She won't love you like I will.
I'm just the one who'll stay,
When she walks away,
And you know I'll be standing here still.

Refrain:
I'll be waiting for you,
Here inside my heart.
I'm the one who wants to love you more.
You will see I can give you
Everything you need.
Let me be the one to love you more.

See me as if you never know.
Hold me so you can't let go.
Just believe in me.
I will make you see
All the things that your heart needs to know.

Refrain

And some way, all the love that we had can be saved.
Whatever it takes, we'll find a way.
I will make you see
All the things that your heart needs to know.

I'll be waiting for you,
Here inside my heart.
I'm the one who wants to love you more.
Can't you see I can give you
Everything you need.
Let me be the one to love you more.

Tom Dooley

Words and Music Collected, Adapted and Arranged by
Frank Warner, John A. Lomax and Alan Lomax
From the singing of Frank Proffitt

recorded by The Kingston Trio

Refrain:
Hang down you head, Tom Dooley,
Hang down you head and cry,
Hand down your head, Tom Dooley,
Poor boy, you're bound to die.

I met her on the mountain,
And there I took her life,
I met her on the mountain
And stabbed her with my knife.

Refrain

This time tomorrow,
Reckon where I'll be?
If it had'n-a been for Grayson
I'd-a been in Tennessee.

Refrain

This time tomorrow,
Reckon where I'll be?
In some lonesome valley
A-hangin' on a white oak tree.

Refrain

Tonight I Celebrate My Love

Words and Music by Michael Masser and Gerry Goffin

recorded by Peabo Bryson & Roberta Flack

Tonight I celebrate my love for you;
It seems that natural thing to do.
Tonight no one's gonna find us,
We'll have the world behind us,
When I make love to you.

Tonight I celebrate my love for you;
And hope that deep inside you feel it too.
Tonight our spirits will be climbing
To a sky lit up with diamonds
When I make love to you
Tonight.

Refrain:
Tonight I celebrate my love for you
And the midnight sun
Is gonna come shining through.
Tonight there'll be no distance between us.
What I want most to do
Is to get close to you tonight.

Tonight I celebrate my love for you.
And soon this old world will seem brand new.
Tonight we will both discover
How friends turn into lovers,
When I make love to you.

Refrain

Tonight's the Night
(Gonna Be Alright)

Words and Music by Rod Stewart

recorded by Rod Stewart

Stay away from my window;
Stay away from my back door, too.
Disconnect the telephone line;
Relax, baby, and draw the blind.

Kick off your shoes and sit right down
And loosen up that pretty French gown.
Let me pour you a good long drink;
Ooh, baby, don't you hesitate.

Refrain:
'Cause
Tonight's the night;
It's gonna be alright.
'Cause I love you, girl;
Ain't nobody gonna stop us now.

Come on angel, my heart's on fire;
Don't deny your man's desire.
You'd be a fool to stop this tide;
Spread your wings and let me come inside.

Refrain

Don't say a word, my virgin child;
Just let your inhibitions run wild.
The secret is about to unfold
Upstairs before the night's too old.

Refrain

Too Late Now

Words by Alan Jay Lerner
Music by Burton Lane

from the film *Royal Wedding*

Too late now to forget your smile;
The way we cling when we've danced awhile;
Too late now to forget and go on to someone new.

Too late now to forget your voice;
The way one word makes my heart rejoice;
Too late now to imagine myself away from you.

All the things we've done together
I relive when we're apart.
All the tender fun together
Stays on my heart.
How could I ever close the door,
And be the same as I was before?
Darling, no, no, I can't anymore;
It's too late now.

Top Hat, White Tie and Tails

Words and Music by Irving Berlin

from the RKO Radio Motion Picture *Top Hat*

I just got an invitation through the mails.
"Your presence is requested this evening, it's formal."
A top hat, a white tie and tails.

Nothing now could take the wind out of my sails,
Because I'm invited to step out this evening
With top hat and white tie and tails.

I'm puttin' on my top hat,
Tyin' up my white tie,
Brushin' off my tails.

I'm dudin' up my shirt front,
Puttin' in the shirt studs,
Polishin' my nails.

I'm steppin' out, my dear,
To breathe an atmosphere
That simply reeks with class.

And I trust that you'll excuse
My dust as I step on the gas.
For I'll be there,
Puttin' down my top hat,
Mussin' up my white tie,
Dancin' in my tails.

Top of the World

Words and Music by John Bettis and Richard Carpenter

recorded by The Carpenters

Such a feelin's comin' over me,
There is wonder in most everything I see,
Not a cloud in the sky got the sun in my eyes,
And I won't be surprised if it's a dream.
Everything I want the world to be,
Is now coming true especially for me,
And the reason is clear,
It's because you are here,
You're the nearest thing to heaven that I've seen.

Refrain:
I'm on the top of the world
Lookin' down on creation
And the only explanation I can find,
Is the love that I've found,
Ever since you've been around,
Your love's put me at the top of the world.

Something in the wind has learned my name,
And it's tellin' me that things are not the same,
In the leaves on the trees and touch of the breeze,
There's a pleasin' sense of happiness for me.
There is only one wish on my mind,
When this day is through I hope that I will find,
That tomorrow will be just the same for you and me,
All I need will be mine if you are here.

Refrain

Torn
Words and Music by Phil Thornalley, Scott Cutler and Anne Previn

recorded by Natalie Imbruglia

I thought I saw a man brought to life.
He was warm, he came around
Like he was dignified.
He showed me what it was to cry.
Well, you couldn't be that man I adored.
You don't seem to know or seem to care
What your heart is for.
Well, I don't know him anymore.
There's nothing where he used to lie.
My conversation has run dry.
That's what's going on.
Nothing's fine,

Refrain:
I'm torn.
I'm all out of faith,
This is how I feel.
I'm cold and I am shamed
Lying naked on the floor.
Illusion never changed into something real.
I'm wide awake
And I can see the perfect sky is torn.
You're a little late.
I'm already torn.

So, I guess the fortune teller's right.
I should've seen just what was there
And not some holy light.
But you crawled beneath my veins, and now
I don't care,
I have no luck.
I don't miss it all that much.
There's just so many things
That I can't touch.

Refrain

Torn.
Ooh, ooh.
There's nothing where he used to lie.
My inspiration has run dry.
That's what's going on.
Nothing's right,

Refrain

I'm all out of faith,
This is how I feel.
I'm cold and I'm bound and broken on the floor.
You're a little late.
I'm already torn.
Torn.

Total Eclipse of the Heart
Words and Music by Jim Steinman

recorded by Bonnie Tyler, Nicki French

Turn around,
Every now and then I get a little bit lonely
And you're never coming around.
Turn around.
Every now and then I get a little bit tired
Of listening to the sound of my tears,
Turn around.
Every now and then I get a little but nervous
That the rest of all the years have gone by.
Turn around.
Every now and then I get a little bit terrified
And then I see the look in your eyes.
Turn around,
Bright eyes.
Every now and then I fall apart.

Turn around,
Every now and then I get a little bit restless
And I dream of something wild.
Turn around.
Every now and then I get a little bit tired
Of listening to the sound of my tears,
Turn around.
Every now and then I get a little bit angry
And I know I've got to get out and cry.
Turn around.
Every now and then I get a little bit terrified
But then I see the look in your eyes.
Turn around,
Bright eyes.
Every now and then I fall apart,
Bright eyes
Every now and then I fall apart.

And I need you now tonight
And I need you more than ever.
And if you only hold me tight,
We'll be holding on forever.
And we'll only be making it right
'Cause we'll never be wrong.
Together we can take it to the end of the line.
Your love is like a shadow on me all of the time.
I don't know what to do
And I'm always in the dark,
We're living in a powder keg
And giving off sparks.

I really need you tonight.
Forever's gonna start tonight.
Forever's gonna start tonight.

Once upon a time
I was falling in love,
But now I'm only falling apart.

There's nothing I can do,
A total eclipse of the heart.
Once upon a time there was light in my life,
But there's only love in the dark.
Nothing I can say,
A total eclipse of the heart.

Turn around
Every now and then
I know you'll never be
The boy you always wanted to be.
Turn around.
But every now and then
I know you'll always be
The only boy who wanted me the way that I am.
Turn around.
Every now and then
I know there's no one in the universe
As magical and wondrous as you.
Turn around.
Every now and then
I know there's nothing any better
There's nothing that I just wouldn't do.

Touch a Hand, Make a Friend
Words and Music by Carl Hampton, Homer Banks and
Raymond Jackson
Copyright © 1973 IRVING MUSIC, INC.
Copyright Renewed

recorded by The Staple Singers

Can't you feel it in your bones, y'all?
A change is coming on.
From every walk of life,
People are seeing the light.
Can't you feel it in your hearts now?
A new thing is takin' shape;
Reach out, touch a hand, y'all.

Make a friend if you can.
Hey, what about you my friend?
Ain't time you come on in?
Live the united way.
Why don't you join us today?

It's being reflected,
In the attitudes of others just like you.
Reach out touch a hand, y'all.
Make a friend if you can.
Every day people are waking up
To the new one another;
We're on our way,
Making the world a better place.

Three Times:
Reach out, touch a hand.
Make a friend if you can.
Reach out, touch a hand,
Make a friend if you can.

True Love
Words and Music by Cole Porter
Copyright © 1955, 1956 by Chappell & Co.
Copyrights Renewed, Assigned to Robert H. Montgomery, Trustee of the Cole Porter Musical and
   Literary Property Trusts
Chappell & Co. owner of publication and allied rights throughout the world

from the film *High Society*

Sun-tanned, wind-blown
Honeymooners at last alone,
Feeling far above par,
Oh, how lucky we are
While

I give to you and you give to me
True love, true love.
So, on and on it will always be
True love, true love.
For you and I
Have a guardian angel on high
With nothing to do
But to give to you and to give to me
Love, forever true.

Truly, Madly, Deeply
Words and Music by Daniel Jones and Darren Hayes
© 1996 ROUGH CUT MUSIC PTY LTD and
EMI MUSIC PUBLISHING AUSTRALIA PTY. LTD.
All Rights Controlled and Administered by EMI BLACKWOOD MUSIC INC.

recorded by Savage Garden

I'll be your dream, I'll be your wish,
I'll be your fantasy.
I'll be your hope,
I'll be your love
Be everything that you need.
I'll love you more with every breath,
Truly, madly, deeply do.

I will be strong, I will be faithful,
'Cause I'm counting on a new beginning.
A reason for living,
A deeper meaning, yeah.

Refrain:
I want to stand with you on a mountain,
I want to bathe with you in the sea.
I want to lay like this forever,
Until the sky falls down on me.

And then the stars are shining brightly
In the velvet sky,
I'll make a wish and send it to heaven,
Then make you want to cry
The tears of joy
For all the pleasure in the certainty,
That we're surrounded by the comfort
And protection of the highest powers,
In lonely hours,
The tears devour you.

Refrain

Oh, can you see it baby?
You don't have to close your eyes
'Cause it's standing right beside you, ooh.
All that you need will surely come.

Repeat Verse 1

Refrain

Try to Remember
Words by Tom Jones
Music by Harvey Schmidt
Copyright © 1960 by Tom Jones and Harvey Schmidt
Copyright Renewed
Chappell & Co. owner of publication and allied rights throughout the world

from the musical *The Fantasticks*

Try to remember the kind of September
When life was slow and oh, so mellow.
Try to remember the kind of September
When grass was green and grain was yellow.
Try to remember the kind of September
When you were a tender and callow fellow.
Try to remember and if you remember
Then follow.

Echo:
Follow, follow, follow, follow,
Follow, follow, follow, follow.

Try to remember when life was so tender
That no one wept except the willow.
Try to remember when life was so tender
That dreams were kept beside your pillow.

Try to remember when life was so tender
That love was an ember about to billow.
Try to remember and if you remember
Then follow.

Echo

Deep in December it's nice to remember
Although you know the snow will follow.
Deep in December it's nice to remember
Without a hurt the heart is hollow.
Deep in December, it's nice to remember
The fire of September that made us mellow.
Deep in December our hearts should remember
And follow.

Echo

Tubthumping
Words and Music by Nigel Hunter, Bruce Duncan,
Alice Nutter, Louise Watts, Paul Greco, Darren Hamer,
Allen Whalley and Judith Abbott
© 1997 EMI MUSIC PUBLISHING GERMANY GMBH
All Rights in the United States and Canada Controlled and Administered by
EMI BLACKWOOD MUSIC INC.

recorded by Chumbawamba

We'll be singing,
When we're winning.
We'll be singing,
When we're winning.

Refrain:
I get knocked down, but I get up again.
You're never gonna keep me down.
I get knocked down,
But I get up again.
You're never gonna keep me down.
I get knocked down,
But I get up again.
You're never gonna keep me down.
I get knocked down,
But I get up again.
You're never gonna keep me down.

Verse:
Pissing the night away.
Pissing the night away.

Spoken:
He drinks a whiskey drink,
He drinks a vodka drink,
He drinks a lager drink,
He drinks a cider drink.
He sings the songs that remind him of the good times.
He sings the songs that remind him of the better times.

Oh Danny boy, Danny boy, Danny boy.

Refrain

Repeat Verse

Don't cry for me next door neighbor.

Refrain

Twice:
I get knocked down,
But I get up again.
You're never gonna keep me down.
I get knocked down,
But I get up again.
You're never gonna keep me down.

Tumbling Dice
Words and Music by Mick Jagger and Keith Richards
© 1972 (Renewed 2000) EMI MUSIC PUBLISHING LTD.
All Rights for the U.S. and Canada Controlled and Administered by COLGEMS-EMI MUSIC INC.

recorded by The Rolling Stones

Women think I'm tasty
But they're always trying to waste me
And make me burn the candle right down,
But baby, baby, I don't need no jewels in my crown.

'Cause all you women
Is low down gamblers,
Cheatin' like I don't know how,
But baby, baby, there's fever in the funk house now.

This low down bitchin' got my poor feet a-itchin',
You know, you know the deuce is still wild.
Baby, baby I can't stay, you got to roll me
And call me the tumblin' dice.

Always in a hurry,
I never stop to worry,
Don't you see the time flashin' by.
Honey, got no money,
I'm all sixes and sevens and nines.

Say now, baby, I'm the rank outsider,
You can be my partner in crime.
But baby, I can't stay,
You got to roll me and call me tumblin' dice.

Twice:
Oh, my, me, me, I'm the lone crap shooter,
Playin' the field every night.
Baby, can't stay, you got to roll me
And call me tumblin' dice.
Got to roll me
And call me the tumblin' dice.

Turn! Turn! Turn!
(To Everything There Is a Season)
Words from the Book of Ecclesiastes
Adaptation and Music by Pete Seeger
TRO - © Copyright 1962 (Renewed) Melody Trails, Inc., New York, NY

recorded by The Byrds

To everything (turn, turn, turn)
There is a season (turn, turn, turn)
And a time for every purpose under heaven.
A time to be born, a time to die
A time to plant, a time to reap;
A time to kill, a time to heal;
A time to laugh, a time to weep.

To everything (turn, turn, turn)
There is a season (turn, turn, turn)
And a time for every purpose under heaven.

A time to build up,
A time to break down;
A time to dance, a time to mourn;
A time to cast away stones,
A time to gather stones together.

To everything (turn, turn, turn)
There is a season (turn, turn, turn)
And a time for every purpose under heaven.

A time of love, a time of hate;
A time of war, a time of peace;
A time you may embrace,
A time to refrain from embracing.

To everything (turn, turn, turn)
There is a season (turn, turn, turn)
And a time for every purpose under heaven.

Tuxedo Junction
Words by Buddy Feyne
Music by Erskine Hawkins, William Johnson and
Julian Dash
Copyright © 1939, 1940 (Renewed) by Music Sales Corporation (ASCAP) and Rytvoc, Inc.

a standard recorded by Erskine Hawkins, Glenn Miller,
Manhattan Transfer and various other artists

Feelin' low!
Rockin' slow!
Want to go
Right back where I belong.

Way down South
In Birmingham,
I mean South
In Alabam's
And old place
Where people go to dance the night away.

They all drive
Or walk for miles
To get jive
That Southern style,
Slow jive
That makes you want to dance 'til break of day.

It's a junction
Where the town folks meet.
At each function,
In their tux they greet you.
Come on down,
Forget you care.
Come on down
You'll find me there.
So long town!
I'm headin' for Tuxedo Junction now.

Repeat From Verse 1

Twilight Time

Lyric by Buck Ram
Music by Morty Nevins and Al Nevins

recorded by The Platters

Heavenly shades of night are falling,
It's twilight time.
Out of the mist your voice is calling,
It's twilight time.
When purple colored curtains mark the end of day,
I hear you, my dear, at twilight time.

Deepening shadows gather splendor,
As day is done.
Fingers of night will soon surrender
The setting sun.
I count the moments, darling till you're here with me.
Together, at last at twilight time.

Here in the afterglow of day
We keep our rendezvous beneath the blue.
Here in the sweet and same old way
I fall in love again as I did then.

Deep in the dark your kiss will thrill me
Like days of old.
Lighting the spark of love that fills me
With dreams untold.
Each day I pray for evening just to be with you,
Together at last at twilight time.

Twist and Shout

Words and Music by Bert Russell and Phil Medley

recorded by The Isley Brothers, The Beatles

Refrain:
Well, shake it up, baby, now.
(Shake it up, baby.)
Twist and shout.
(Twist and shout.)
Come on, come on, come on, come on, baby, now
(Come on baby.)
Come on and work it on out.
(Work it on out, oo.)

Well work it on out, honey.
You know you look so good.
(Look so good.)
You know you got me goin' now,
(Got me goin')
Just like I knew you would.
(Like I knew you would, oo.)

Verse:
You know you're a twisty little girl.
(Twisty little girl.)
You know you twist so fine.
(Twist so fine.)
Come on, and twist a little closer now.
(Twist a little closer.)
And let me know that you're mine.
Let me know you're mine.

Refrain

Repeat Verse

Refrain

Well shake it, shake it, baby, now.
(Shake it up, baby.)
Well, shake it, shake it, shake it, baby, now.
(Shake it up, baby.)
Well, shake it, shake it, shake it, baby, now.
(Shake it up, baby.)

Two of Us

Words and Music by John Lennon and Paul McCartney

recorded by The Beatles

Two of us riding nowhere
Spending someone's hard-earned pay.
You and me Sunday driving
Not arriving on our way back home.

Refrain:
We're on our way home,
We're on our way home,
We're going home.

You and I have memories,
Longer than the road that stretches out ahead,
Two of us sending postcards,
Writing letters on my wall,
You and me burning matches,
Lifting latches on our way back home.

Refrain

Two of us wearing raincoats
Standing solo in the sun.
You and me chasing paper
Getting nowhere on our way back home.

We're on our way home.
We're on our way home.
We're on our way home.

Two Out of Three Ain't Bad

Words and Music by Jim Steinman

recorded by Meat Loaf

Baby, we can talk all night,
But that ain't getting us nowhere.
I've told you everything I possibly can,
There's nothing left inside of here.
And maybe you cry all night,
But that'll never change the way I feel.
The snow is really piling up outside,
And I wish you wouldn't make me leave here.

I poured it on and I poured it out,
I tried to show you just how much I care.
I'm tired of words and I'm too hoarse to shout,
But you've been cold to me so long,
I'm crying icicles instead of tears.

And all I can do is keep on telling you,
I want you,
I need you,
But there ain't no way I'm ever gonna love you,
Now, don't be sad,
(Don't be sad)
'Cause two out of three ain't bad.
Now don't be sad,
'Cause two out of three ain't bad.

You'll never find your gold on a sandy beach.
You'll never drill for oil on a city street.
I know you're looking for a ruby in a mountain of rocks,
But there ain't no Coupe de Ville
Hiding at the bottom of a Cracker Jack box.

I can't lie,
I can't tell you that I'm something I'm not,
No matter how I try.
I'll never be able to give you
Something that I just haven't got.
There's only one girl that I will ever love,
And that was so many years ago.
And though I know I'll never get her out of my heart,
She never loved me back,
Ooh, I know.

I remember how she left me on a stormy night,
She kissed me and got out of our bed.
And though I pleaded,
And I begged her not to walk out that door,
She packed her bags and turned right away.
And she kept on telling me,
She kept on telling me,
She kept on telling me,

Twice:
"I want you, I need you,
But there ain't no way I'm ever gonna love you,
Now don't be sad,
(Don't be sad)
'Cause two out of three ain't bad

Now don't be sad,
'Cause two out of three ain't bad.
Baby, we can talk all night,
But that ain't getting us nowhere.

Unchained Melody

Lyric by Hy Zaret
Music by Alex North
© 1955 (Renewed) FRANK MUSIC CORP.

from the film *Unchained*
recorded by Les Baxter, Al Hibbler, Roy Hamilton,
The Righetous Brothers
featured in the film *Ghost*

Oh, my love, my darling,
I've hungered for your touch,
A long, lonely time.
Time goes by so slowly
And time can do so much,
Are you still mine?
I need your love, I need your love,
God speed your love to me!

Lonely rivers flow to the sea,
To the sea,
To the open arms
Of the sea.

Lonely rivers sigh,
"Wait for me,
Wait for me!"
I'll be coming home,
Wait for me.

Repeat Verse 1

Under the Boardwalk

Words and Music by Artie Resnick and Kenny Young
Copyright © 1964 by Alley Music Corp. and Trio Music Company, Inc.
Copyright Renewed

recorded by The Drifters

Oh, when the sun beats down
And burns the tar up on the roof,
And your shoes get so hot
Your wish your tired feet were fireproof;
Under the boardwalk,
Down by the sea, yeah,
On a blanket with my baby's where I'll be.

Refrain:
(Under the boardwalk.)
Out of the sun,
(Under the boardwalk.)
We'll be havin' some fun.
(Under the boardwalk.)
People walkin' above
(Under the boardwalk.)
We'll be fallin' in love
Under the boardwalk, boardwalk.

From the park you hear
The happy sound of a carousel.
You can almost taste the hot dogs
And French fries they sell.
Under the boardwalk,
Down by the sea, yeah,
On a blanket with my baby's where I'll be.

Refrain

Under the boardwalk,
Down by the sea, yeah,
On a blanket with my baby's where I'll be.

Refrain

Unexpected Song

Music by Andrew Lloyd Webber
Lyrics by Don Black
© Copyright 1982 The Really Useful Group Ltd. and Dick James Music Ltd.
All Rights for the United States and Canada Administered by Universal - PolyGram International
   Publishing, Inc. and Universal - Songs Of PolyGram International, Inc.

from the musical *Song and Dance*

I have never felt like this,
For once I'm lost for words,
Your smile has really thrown me.
This is not like me at all,
I never thought I'd know
The kind of love you've shown me.

Refrain:
Now no matter where I am,
No matter what I do,
I see your face appearing
Like an unexpected song,
An unexpected song
That only we are hearing.

I don't know what's going on,
Can't work it out at all.
Whatever made you choose me?
I just can't believe my eyes,
You look at me as though
You couldn't bear to lose me.

Refrain

I have never felt like this.
For once I'm lost for words,
Your smile has really thrown me.
This is not like me at all,
I never thought I'd know
The kind of love you've shown me.

Now no matter where I am,
No matter what I do,
I see your appearing
Like an unexpected song,
An unexpected song
That only we are hearing.
Like an unexpected song,
An unexpected song
That only we are hearing.

Until It's Time for You to Go

Words and Music by Buffy Sainte-Marie
Copyright © 1965, 1967 by Gypsy Boy Music, Inc.
Copyright Renewed

recorded by Buffy Sainte-Marie, Elvis Presley

I'm not a dream, I'm not an angel, I'm a man;
You're not a queen you're a woman take my hand.
We'll make a space in the lives that we planned.
And here we'll stay until it's time for you to go.

Refrain:
Yes we're different, worlds apart, we're not the same.
We laughed and played at the start like in a game.
You could have stayed outside my heart but in you came.
And here you'll stay until it's time for you to go.
Don't ask why.
Don't ask how.
Don't ask forever.
Love me now!

This love of mine had no beginning, has no end;
I was an oak now I'm a willow now I can bend.
And tho' I'll never in my life see you again.
Still I'll stay until it's time for you to go.

Up Where We Belong

Words by Will Jennings
Music by Buffy Sainte-Marie and Jack Nitzsche
Copyright © 1982 by Famous Music Corporation and Ensign Music Corporation

from the film *Up Where We Belong*
from the film *An Officer and a Gentleman*
recorded by Joe Cocker & Jennifer Warnes

Who knows what tomorrow brings;
In a world, few hearts survive.
All I know is the way I feel.
When it's real,
I keep it alive.
The road is long.
There are mountains in our way,
But we climb a step every day.

Refrain:
Love lift us up where we belong,
Where the eagle cry
On a mountain high.
Love lift us up where we belong,
Far from the world we know;
Up where the clear winds blow.

Some hang on to "used to be,"
Live their lives looking behind.
All we have is here and now;
All our life, out there to find.
The road is long.
There are mountains in our way,
But we climb them a step every day.

Refrain

Time goes by, no time to cry,
Life's you and I,
Alive,
Today.

Refrain

Valentine

Words and Music by Jack Kugell and Jim Brickman
© 1996 EMI APRIL MUSIC INC., DOXIE MUSIC, MULTISONGS, INC. and
    BRICKMAN ARRANGEMENT
All Rights for DOXIE MUSIC Controlled and Administered by EMI APRIL MUSIC INC.
All Rights for BRICKMAN ARRANGEMENT Administered by MULTISONGS, INC.

recorded by Jim Brickman with Martina McBride

If there were no words,
No way to speak,
I would still hear you.
If there were no tears,
No way to feel inside,
I'd still feel for you.

Refrain:
And even if the sun refused to shine,
Even if romance ran out of rhyme,
You would sill have my heart
Until the end of time.
You're all I need my love,
My valentine.

All of my life,
I have been waiting for all you give to me.
You've opened my eyes and shown me
How to love unselfishly.
I've dreamed of this a thousand times before,
But in my dreams I couldn't love you more.
I will give you my heart until the end of time.
'Cause all I need is you,
My valentine.

Refrain

My valentine.

The Very Thought of You
Words and Music by Ray Noble

a standard recorded by Ray Noble, Benny Carter,
Billie Holiday and various other artists

The very thought of you,
And I forget to do
The little ordinary things
That everyone ought to do.

I'm living in a kind of daydream,
I'm happy as a king,
And foolish though it may seem,
To me that's everything.

The mere idea of you,
The longing here for you,
You'll never know how slow
The moments go
'Til I'm near to you.

I see your face in every flower;
Your eyes in stars above.
It's just the thought of you,
The very thought of you, my love.

Victim of Love
Words and Music by John David Souther, Don Henley,
Glenn Frey and Don Felder

recorded by The Eagles

What kind of love have you got?
You should be home, but you're not.
A room full of noise and dangerous boys,
Still make you thirsty and hot.
I heard about you and that man.
There's just one thing I don't understand.
You say he's a liar,
And he put out your fire.
How come you still got his gun in your hand?

Victim of love, I see a broken heart.
You got your stories to tell.
Victim of love, it's such an easy part.
And you know how to play it so well.

Some people never come clean.
I think you know what I mean.
You're walkin' the wire,
Pain and desire,
Lookin' for love in between.
Tell me your secrets; I'll tell you mine.
This ain't no time to be cool.
And tell all your girlfriends,
Your "been around the world" friends
That talk is for losers and fools.

Victim of love, I see a broken heart.
I could be wrong, but I'm not.
Victim of love we're not so far apart,
Show me, what kind of love have you got?

Victim of love, you're just a victim of love.
I could be wrong, but I'm not.
Victim of love now you're a victim of love.
What kind of love have you got?
What kind of love have you got?
What kind of love have you got?

Vienna
Words and Music by Billy Joel

recorded by Billy Joel

Slow down you crazy child,
You're so ambitious for a juvenile.
But then if your so smart,
Tell me why you are still so afraid?

Where's the fire, what's the hurry about?
You better cool it off before you burn it out.
You got so much to do and only so many hours in a day.
But you know that when the truth is told,
That you can get what you want or you can just get old.
You're gonna kick off before you even get half-way through.
When will you realize,
Vienna waits for you.

Slow down you're doin' fine.
You can't be everything before your time.
Although it's so romantic on the borderline tonight,
Tonight.

Too bad, but it's the life you lead,
You're so ahead of yourself that you forgot what you need.
Though you can see when you're wrong
You know you can't always see when you're right.
You're right.
You got your passion
You got your pride.
But don't you know that only fools are satisfied?
Dream on but don't imagine they'll all come true.
When will you realize, Vienna waits for you.

Slow down you crazy child.
Take the phone off the hook and disappear for a while.
It's alright you can afford to lose a day or two.
When will you realize Vienna waits for you.

And you know that when the truth is told,
That you can get what you want or you can just get old.
You're gonna kick off before you even get halfway through.
Why don't you realize, Vienna waits for you.
When will you realize, Vienna waits for you.

Wait Till You See Her

Words by Lorenz Hart
Music by Richard Rodgers

from the musical *By Jupiter*

My friends who knew me
Never would know me,
They'd look right through me,
Above and below me
And ask, "Who's that man?
Who is that man?
That's not my lighthearted friend!"
Meeting one girl
Was the start of the end.
Love is a simple emotion
A friend should comprehend.

Refrain:
Wait till you see her,
See how she looks.
Wait till you hear her laugh.
Painters of paintings,
Writers of books,
Never could tell the half.
Wait till you feel
The warmth of her glance,
Pensive and sweet and wise.
All of it lovely,
All of it thrilling,
I'll never be willing to free her.
When you see her
You won't believe your eyes.

Waiting on a Friend

Words and Music by Mick Jagger and Keith Richards

recorded by The Rolling Stones

Watching girls go passing by,
It ain't the latest thing,
I'm just standing in a doorway.
I'm just trying to make some sense.

Out of these girls passing by,
The tales they tell of men.
I'm not waiting on a lady.
I'm just waiting on a friend.

I'm just waiting on a friend,
Just waiting on a friend.
I'm just waiting on a friend,
Just waiting on a friend.

A smile relieves a heart that grieves,
Remember what I said.
I'm not waiting on a lady.
I'm just waiting on a friend.

Don't need a whore, don't need no booze,
Don't need a virgin priest.
But I need someone I can cry to.
I need someone to protect.

I'm just waiting on a friend,
Just waiting on a friend.
I'm just waiting on a friend,
Just waiting on a friend.

Wake Up Little Susie

Words and Music by Boudleaux Bryant and Felice Bryant

recorded by The Everly Brothers

Wake up, little Susie, wake up.
Wake up, little Susie, wake up.

We've both been sound asleep,
Wake up, little Susie and weep.
The movie's over it's four o'clock
And we're in trouble deep.

Refrain:
Wake up, little Susie, wake up little Susie,
Well, what are we gonna tell your Mama?
What are we gonna tell your Pa?
What are we gonna tell our friends when they say,
"Ooh la la"
Wake up, little Susie, wake up, little Susie.

Well, we told your Mama that we'd be in by ten.
Well, Susie baby, looks like we goofed again
Wake up, little Susie, wake up, little Susie
We've gotta go home.

The movie wasn't so hot,
It didn't have much of a plot.
We fell asleep, and our goose is cooked,
Our reputation is shot.

Refrain

Walk Like an Egyptian

Words and Music by Liam Sternberg

recorded by The Bangles

All the old paintings on the tomb,
They do the sand dance, don't you know.
If they move too quick, (Oh, way, oh).
They're falling down like a domino.
All the bazaar men by the Nile,
They got the money on a bet.
Gold crocodiles, (Oh, way, oh)
They snap their teeth on your cigarette.
Foreign types with the hookah pipes say,
"Way, oh, way, oh, way, oh, way, oh."
Walk like an Egyptian.

The blonde waitresses take their trays.
They spin around and they cross the floor.
They've got the moves. (Oh, way, oh).
You drop your drink, then they bring you more.
All the school kids so sick of books,
They like the punk and the metal band.
Then the buzzer rings, (Oh, way, oh)
They're walkin' like an Egyptian.
All the kids in the marketplace say,
(Way, oh, way, oh, way, oh, way, oh).
Walk like an Egyptian.

Slide your feet up the street, bend your back,
Shift your arm, then you pull it back.
Life's hard, you know, (Oh, way, oh)
So strike a pose on a Cadillac.

If you wanna find all the cops
They're hanging out in the donut shops.
They sing and dance, (Oh, way, oh)
They spin the club, cruise down the block.
All the Japanese with their yen,
The party boys call the Kremlin.
And the Chinese know, (Oh, way, oh)
They walk the line like Egyptians.
All the cops in the donut shop say,
(Way, oh, way, oh, way, oh, way, oh).
Walk like an Egyptian.
Walk like an Egyptian.

Walk Right In

Words and Music by Gus Cannon and H. Woods

recorded by The Rooftop Singers

Walk right in,
Set right down,
Daddy, let your mind roll on.
Walk right in,
Set right down,
Daddy, let your mind roll on.

Refrain:
Everybody's talkin' 'bout a new way o' walkin',
Do you wanna lose your mind?

Walk right in,
Set right down,
Daddy, let your mind roll on.

Walk right in,
Set right down,
Baby, let your hair hang down.
Walk right in,
Set right down,
Baby, let your hair hang down.

Refrain

Walk right in,
Set right down,
Baby, let your hair hang down.

Walk This Way

Words and Music by Steven Tyler and Joe Perry

recorded by Aerosmith, Run D.M.C.

Back stroke lover always hidin' 'neath the covers
Till I talked to your daddy, he say.
He said, "You ain't seen nothin'
Till you're down on a muffin,
Then you're sure to be a changin' your ways."
I meet a cheerleader, was a real young bleeder, oh,
The times I could reminisce;
'Cause the best things of lovin'
With her sister and her cousin
Only started with a little kiss.
Spoken:
Like this.

See-saw swinger with the boys in the school
And your feet flyin' up in the air,
Singin' "Hey, diddle, diddle,"
With your kitty in the middle of the swing
Like you didn't care.
So I took a big glance
At the high school dance
With a missy who was ready to play.
Was it me she was foolin'
'Cause she knew what she was doin',
When I knowed love was here to stay,
Spoken:
When she told me to,
Sung:
Walk this way, talk this way.

School girl sweeties with a classy, kind-a sassy
Little skirts climbin' up to their knees;
There was three young ladies in the school gym locker
When I noticed they was lookin' at me.
I was a high school loser,
Never made it with a lady
Till the boys told me somethin' I missed.
Then my next door neighbor with a daughter had a favor,
So I gave her just a little kiss
Spoken:
Like this.

See-saw swinger with the boys in the school
And your feet flyin' up in the air,
Singin' "Hey, diddle, diddle,"
With your kitty in the middle of the swing
Like you didn't care.
So I took a big glance
At the high school dance
With a missy who was ready to play.
Was it me she was foolin'
'Cause she knew what she was doin'
When she taught me how to
Walk this way.
Spoken:
When she told me to,
Sung:
Walk this way, talk this way,
Spoken:
And just gimme a kiss, like this.

Walking the Floor Over You
Words and Music by Ernest Tubb
Copyright © 1941 by Unichappell Music Inc. and Elvis Presley Music
Copyright Renewed

recorded by Ernest Tubb

You left me and you went away.
You said that you'd be back in just a day.
You've broken your promise and you left me here alone,
I don't know why you did,
Dear but I know that you're gone.

Refrain:
I'm walking the floor over you.
I can't sleep a wink that is true.
I'm hoping and I'm praying as my heart breaks right in two.
Walking the floor over you.

Darling, you know I love you well,
Love you more than I can ever tell.
I thought that you wanted me and always would be mine,
But you went and left me here with troubles on my mind.

Refrain

Now, someday you may be lonesome too,
Walking the floor is good for you.
Just keep right on walking and it won't hurt you to cry,
Remember that I love you and I will the day I die.

Refrain

Waltz for Debby
Lyric by Gene Lees
Music by Bill Evans
TRO–© Copyright 1964 (Renewed), 1965 (Renewed), 1966 (Renewed) Folkways Music
  Publishers, Inc., New York, NY

recorded by Bill Evans

In her own sweet world,
Populated by dolls and clowns and a prince
And a big purple bear,
Lives my favorite girl.
Unaware of the worried frowns
That we weary grownups all wear.
In the sun, she dances to silent music,
Songs that are spun of gold somewhere in her little head.

One day all too soon,
She'll grow up and she'll leave her dolls
And her prince and her silly old bear.
When she goes they will cry
As they whisper goodbye.
They will miss her, I fear,
But then, so will I.

War
Words and Music by Norman Whitfield and Barrett Strong
© 1970 (Renewed 1998) JOBETE MUSIC CO., INC.
All Rights Controlled and Administered by EMI BLACKWOOD MUSIC INC. on behalf of
  STONE AGATE MUSIC (A Division of JOBETE MUSIC CO., INC.)

recorded by Edwin Starr, Bruce Springsteen

War, uh! What is it good for?
Absolutely nothing.
War, uh! What is it good for?
Absolutely nothing.
Say it again.
War, uh! What is it good for?
Absolutely nothing.

War, I despise
'Cause it means destruction of innocent lives.
War means tears in thousands of mother's eyes
When their sons go out to fight and lose their lives.
I said:

War, uh! What is it good for?
Absolutely nothing;
Say it again;
War, uh! What is it good for?
Absolutely nothing.

War, it's nothing but a heartbreaker;
War, friend only to the undertaker.
War is an enemy to all mankind.
The thought of war blows my mind.
War has caused unrest within the younger generation;
Induction then destruction, who wants to die? Ah,
War, uh um;
What is it good for,
You tell me nothing, um!

War, uh! What is it good for?
Absolutely nothing.
Good God, war, it's nothing but a heartbreaker;
War, friend only to the undertaker.

Wars have shattered many a young man's dreams;
Made him disabled, bitter and mean.
Life is much too short and precious
To spend fighting wars each day.
War can't give life, it can only take it away, ah
War, uh um! What is it good for?
Absolutely nothing, um.
War, good God Almighty,
Listen, what is it good for?
Absolutely nothing, yeah.
War, it's nothing but a heartbreaker;
War, friend only to the undertaker.
Peace, love and understanding,
Tell me is there no place for them today?
They say we must fight to keep our freedom,
But Lord knows it's gotta be a better way.
I say war, uh um, yeah, yeah.
What is it good for?
Absolutely nothing;
Say it again;
War, yeah yea, yea, yea, yea,
What is it good for?
Absolutely nothing;
Say it again;
War, nothing but a heartbreaker;
What is it good for? …
Friend only to the undertaker…

Waterfalls

Words and Music by Marqueze Etheridge, Lisa Nicole
Lopes, Rico R. Wade, Pat Brown and Ramon Murray

recorded by TLC

A lonely mother gazing out of her window
Staring at a son she just can't touch.
If at any time he's in a jam she'll be by his side,
But he doesn't realize he hurts her so much.
But all the praying just ain't helping at all,
'Cause he can't seem to keep his self out of trouble.
So, he goes out and he makes his money
The best way he knows how,
Another body laying cold in the gutter.
Listen to me.

Refrain:
Don't go chasing waterfalls.
Please stick to the rivers and the lakes that you're used to.
I know that you're gonna have it your way or nothing at all,
But I think you're moving too fast.

Little precious has a natural obsession
For temptation, but he just can't see.
She gives him loving that his body can't handle,
But all he can say is, "Baby, it's so good to me."
One day he goes and takes a glimpse in the mirror,
But he doesn't recognize his won face.
His health is fading and doesn't know why.
Three letters took him to his final resting place.
Y'all don't hear me.

Refrain

Rap:
I seen a rainbow yesterday
But too many storms have come and gone
Leavin' a trace of not one God-given ray
Is it because my life is ten shades of gray
I pray all ten fade away.
Seldom praise Him for the sunny days
And like His promises true
Only my faith can undo
The many chances I blew.
To bring my life to a new
Clear blue and unconditional skies
Have dried the tears from my cycs.
No more lonely cries
My only bleedin' hope
Is for the folk who can't cope
Wit such an endurin' pain
That it keeps 'em in the pourin' rain.
Who's to blame
For tootin' caine in your own vein.
What a shame
You shoot and aim for someone else's brain.
You claim the insane
Name this day in time
For fallin' prey to crime.
I say the system got you victim to your own mind.
Dreams are hopeless aspirations
In hopes of comin' true.
Believe in yourself.
The rest is up to me and you.

Refrain, Sung

'Way Down Yonder in New Orleans

Words and Music by Henry Creamer and J. Turner Layton

introduced in the musical revue *Spice of 1922*
a standard recorded by Blossom Seeley, Bob Haymes,
Freddy Cannon and various other artists

'Way down yonder in New Orleans
In the land of dreamy scenes
There's a garden of Eden
That's what I mean.
Creole babies with flashing eyes
Softly whisper tender sighs,

"Stop!
Oh! Won't you give your lady fair
A little smile?"
Stop!
You bet your life you'll linger there
A little while.

Refrain:
There is heaven right here on earth
With those beautiful queens
'Way down yonder in New Orleans.

Repeat Verses

They've got angels right here on earth
Wearing little blue jeans
'Way down yonder in New Orleans.

The Way We Were
Words by Alan and Marilyn Bergman
Music by Marvin Hamlisch

from the film *The Way We Were*
recorded by Barbra Streisand

Memories
Light the corners of my mind.
Misty water-color memories
Of the way we were.

Scattered pictures
Of the smiles we left behind,
Smiles we gave to one another
For the way we were.

Can it be that it was all so simple then,
Or has time rewritten every line?
If we had the chance to do it all again,
Tell me would we? Could we?

Memories
May be beautiful, and yet,
What's too painful to remember
We simply choose to forget.

So it's the laughter
We will remember,
Whenever we remember
The way we were,
The way we were.

The Way You Look Tonight
Words by Dorothy Fields
Music by Jerome Kern

from the film *Swing Time*
a standard recorded by many various artists
featured in the film *My Best Friend's Wedding*

Someday
When I'm awfully low,
When the world is cold,
I will feel a glow just thinking of you
And the way you look tonight.

Oh, but you're lovely,
With your smile so warm,
And your cheek so soft,
There is nothing for me but to love you,
Just the way you look tonight.

With each word your tenderness grows,
Tearing my fear apart,
And that laugh that wrinkles your nose
Touches my foolish heart.

Lovely,
Never, never change,
Keep that breathless charm,
Won't you please arrange it,
'Cause I love you,
Just the way you look tonight,
Just the way you look tonight.

We Built This City
Words and Music by Bernie Taupin, Martin Page,
Dennis Lambert and Peter Wolf

recorded by Starship

We built this city,
We built this city on rock and roll.
Built this city,
We built this city on rock and roll.

Say you don't know me or recognize my face.
Say you don't care who goes to that kind of place.
Knee-deep in the hoopla, sinking in your fight,
Too many runaways eating up the night.

Refrain:
Marconi plays the mamba,
Listen to the radio.
Don't you remember?
We built this city,
We built this city on rock and roll.

We built this city,
We built this city on rock and roll.
Built this city,
We built this city on rock and roll.

Someone always playing corporation games.
Who cares? They're always changing corporation names.
We just want to dance here, someone stole the stage.
The call us irresponsible, write us off the page.

Refrain

Who counts the money underneath the bar?
Who rides the wrecking ball in two rock guitars?
Don't tell us you need us, 'cause we're the ship of fools,
Looking for America calling through your schools.

Refrain

It's just another Sunday in a tired old street.
Police have got the choke-hold,
Oh, oh, oh, but we just lost the beat.

Refrain

We built, we built this city, now.
We built, we built this city.

We Can Work It Out
Words and Music by John Lennon and Paul McCartney

recorded by The Beatles, Stevie Wonder

Try to see it my way
Do I have to keep on talking till I can't go on?
While you see it your way
Run a risk of knowing that our love may soon be gone.
We can work it out.
We can work it out.

Think of what I'm saying
You can get it wrong and still you think that it's alright.
Think of what I'm saying
We can work it out and get it straight or say good-night.
We can work it out.
We can work it out.

Refrain:
Life is very short and there's no time
For fussing and fighting my friend.
I have always thought that it's a crime
So I will ask you once again.

Try to see it my way
Only time will tell if I am right or I am wrong.
While you see it your way
There's a chance that we might fall apart before too long.
We can work it out.
We can work it out.

Try to see it my way
Only time will tell if I am right or I am wrong.
While you see it your way
There's a chance that we might fall apart before too long.
We can work it out.
We can work it out.

We Didn't Start the Fire
Words and Music by Billy Joel

recorded by Billy Joel

Harry Truman, Doris Day, Red China, Johnnie Ray,
South Pacific, Walter Winchell, Joe DiMaggio.
Joe McCarthy, Richard Nixon, Studebaker, television,
North Korea, South Korea, Marilyn Monroe.

Rosenbergs, H-Bomb, Sugar Ray, Panmunjom,
Brando, *The King and I*, and *The Catcher in the Rye,*
Eisenhower, vaccine, England's got a new queen.
Marciano, Liberace, Santayana goodbye.

We didn't start the fire.
It was always burning
Since the world's been turning.
We didn't start the fire.
No, we didn't light it, but we tried to fight it.

Joseph Stalin, Mallenkov, Nasser and Prokofiev,
Rockefeller, Campanella, Communist Bloc.
Roy Cohn, Juan Perón, Toscanini, Dacron.
Dien Bien Phu falls, "Rock Around the Clock."
Einstein, James Dean, Brooklyn's got a winning team,
Davy Crockett, Peter Pan, Elvis Presley, Disneyland.
Bardot, Budapest, Alabama, Kruschev,
Princess Grace, *Peyton Place*,
Trouble in the Suez.

Refrain:
We didn't start the fire.
It was always burning
Since the world's been turning.
We didn't start the fire.
No we didn't light it,
But we tried to fight it.

Little Rock, Pasternak, Mickey Mantle, Kerouac,
Sputnik, Chou En-Lai, *Bridge on the River Kwai,*
Lebanon, Charles de Gaulle, California baseball,
Stark-weather homicide, Children of Thalidomide.

Oh, Buddy Holly, Ben Hur, space monkey, Mafia,
Hula-Hoops, Castro, Edsel is a no go.
U-2, Syng-man Rhee, payola and Kennedy.
Chubby Checker, *Psycho*, Belgians in the Congo.

Refrain

Hemingway, Eichmann, *Stranger in a Strange Land*,
Dylan, Berlin, Bay of Pigs invasion.
Lawrence of Arabia, British Beatlemania.
Ole Miss, John Glenn, Liston beats Patterson.
Pope Paul, Malcolm X,
British politician sex,
J.F.K. blown away
What else do I have to say?

Refrain

Birth control, Ho Chi Minh, Richard Nixon back again.
Moonshot, Woodstock, Watergate, punk rock.
Begin, Reagan, Palestine, terror on the airline.
Ayatollahs in Iran, Russians in Afghanistan.
"Wheel of Fortune," Sally Ride, heavy metal, suicide,
Foreign debts, homeless vets, AIDS, crack, Bernie Goetz.
Hypodermics on the shores,
China's under martial law.
Rock and roller cola wars,
I can't take it anymore,

We didn't start the fire.
It was always burning,
Since the world's been turning.
We didn't start the fire.
But when we are gone
Will it still burn on,
And on, and on, and on, and on,
And on, and on, and on, and on.

We didn't start the fire.
It was always burning
Since the world's been turning.
We didn't start the fire.
No, we didn't light it, but we tried to fight it.

We Go Together
Lyric and Music by Warren Casey and Jim Jacobs
© 1971, 1972 WARREN CASEY and JIM JACOBS
Copyright Renewed

from the musical *Grease*

We go together,
Like ra-ma la-ma la-ma ka ding-a da ding-dong.
Remembered forever
As shoo-bop-sha-wad-da wad-da yip-pi-ty boom-de-boom.
Chang chang ah chan-it-ty chang-shoo bop.
That's the way it should be, wha oooh, yeah!.
We're one of a kind
Like dip da dip da dip doo wop-a doo-bee doo,
Our names are signed
Boogedy boogedy boogedy boogedy shooby doo wop
  she bop.
Chang chang ah changitty chang-shoo bop,
We'll always bee-ee like one.
Wa wa wa waaah.

When we go out at night, and stars are shining bright
Up in the skies above.
Or at the high school dance, where you can find romance,
Maybe it might be love.

We're for each other
Like-a wop ba-ba lu-mop and wop bam boom.
Just like my brother
Is sha-na-na-na-na-na yip-pi-ty dip-de doom
Chang chang ah changitty-chang–shoo bop,
We'll always be together, together.

We Gotta Get Out of This Place
Words and Music by Barry Mann and Cynthia Weil
© 1965 (Renewed 1993) SCREEN GEMS-EMI MUSIC INC.

recorded by The Animals

In this dirty old part of the city
Where the sun refuse to shine,
People tell me there ain't no use in tryin'.
My little girl, you're so young and pretty.
And one thing I know is true:
You'll be dead before your time is through.
See my daddy in bed. He's dyin'.
You know, his hair is turning grey.
He's been working and slaving his life away.

Gotta work.
Work.
We gotta work.
Work, work, work, work.

We gotta get out of this place
If it's the last thing we ever do.
We gotta get out of this place.
Girl, there's a better life for me and you.

We Just Disagree
Words and Music by Jim Krueger
© 1976, 1977 EMI BLACKWOOD MUSIC INC. and BRUISER MUSIC
All Rights Controlled and Administered by EMI BLACKWOOD MUSIC INC.

recorded by Dave Mason, Billy Dean

Been away.
Haven't seen you in a while.
How've you been?
Have you changed your style?
And do you think that we're grown up different?
It don't seem the same.
Seems you've lost your feel for me.

Refrain:
So let's leave it alone
'Cause we can't see eye to eye.
There ain't no good guy.
There ain't no bad guy.
There's only you and me, and we just disagree.

Ooh. Oh, oh.
I'm going back to a place that's far away.
How 'bout you?
Have you got a place to stay?
Why should I care when I'm just tryin' to get along?
We were friends.
But now it's the end of our love song.

Refrain Twice

We Will Rock You
Words and Music by Brian May
© 1977 QUEEN MUSIC LTD.
All Rights Controlled and Administered by BEECHWOOD MUSIC CORP.

recorded by Queen

Buddy you're a boy
Make a big noise
Playin' in the street
Gonna be a big man someday.
You got mud on yo' face
You big disgrace
Kickin' your can all over the place.
Singin' we will, we will rock you.
We will, we will rock you.

Buddy you're a young man,
Hard man
Shootin' in the street
Gonna take on the world some day.
You got mud on yo' face
You big disgrace
Wavin' your banner all over the place.
Singin' we will, will rock you.
We will, we will rock you.

Buddy you're an old man,
Poor man
Pleadin' with your eyes
Gonna make you some peace someday.
You got mud on yo' face
You big disgrace
Somebody better put you back into your place
Singin' we will, we will rock you,
We will, we will rock you.
We will, we will rock you.

We're in This Love Together
Words and Music by Keith Stegall and Roger Murrah
© 1980 EMI BLACKWOOD MUSIC INC. and CAREERS-BMG MUSIC PUBLISHING, INC.

recorded by Al Jarreau

It's a diamond ring, it's a precious thing,
And we never want to lose it.
It's like a favorite song that we love to sing,
Every time we hear the music.

Refrain:
And we're in this love together;
We got the kind that'll last forever.
We're in this love together;
And like berries on the vine
It gets sweeter all the time.

It's like a rainy night and candle light,
And ooh, it's so romantic.
We got the whole thing working out so right,
And it's just the way we planned it.

Refrain

We're in this love together:
We got the kind that'll last forever.
We're in this love together;
We got the kind that'll last forever and evermore.

We've Only Just Begun
Words and Music by Roger Nichols and Paul Williams
Copyright © 1970 IRVING MUSIC, INC.
Copyright Renewed

recorded by The Carpenters

We've only just begun to live,
White lace and promises,
A kiss for luck and we're on our way.

Before the rising sun we fly,
So many roads to choose,
We start out walking and learn to run.

Refrain:
And yes, we've just begun.
Sharing horizons that are new to us,
Watching the signs along the way.
Talking it over just the two of us,
Working together day to day, together.

And when the evening comes we smile,
So much of life ahead,
We'll find a place where there's room to grow.

Refrain

And when the evening comes we smile,
So much of life ahead,
We'll find a place where there's room to grow.

And yes, we've just begun.

Wedding Bell Blues
Words and Music by Laura Nyro
© 1966 (Renewed 1994), 1976 EMI BLACKWOOD MUSIC INC.

recorded by The 5th Dimension

Bill, I love you so,
I always will.
I look at you and you see the passion eyes of May.
Oh, but am I ever gonna see my wedding day?
Oh, I was on your side, Bill
When you were losin'
I'd never scheme or lie;
Bill, there's foolin'.
But kisses and love won't carry me
Till you marry me.

Bill, I love you so,
I always will.
And in your voice
I hear a choir of carousels.
Oh, but am I ever gonna hear my wedding bells.
I was the one came runnin'
When you were lonely.
I haven't lived one day,
Not lovin' you only.
But kisses and love won't carry me
Till you marry me.

Bill, I love you so, I always will.
And though devotion rules my heart,
I take no bows.
Oh but Bill, you know I wanna take my wedding vows.
Come on Bill,
So come on, Bill.
I got the wedding bell blues!

Bill! I love you so,
I always will,
I got the wedding bell blues.

What a Diff'rence a Day Made
English Words by Stanley Adams
Music and Spanish Words by Maria Grever
Copyright © 1934 by Edward B. Marks Music Company
Copyright Renewed and Assigned to Stanley Adams Music, Inc. and Zomba Golden Sands Inc.
All Rights for Stanley Adams Music, Inc. Administered by The Songwriters Guild Of America

a standard recorded by Benny Carter, Charlie Barnet,
Dinah Washington and various other artists

What a diff'rence a day made,
Twenty four little hours,
Brought the sun and the flowers,
Where there used to be rain.

My yesterday was blue dear,
Today I'm part of you dear,
My lonely nights are thru dear,
Since you said you were mine,

What a diff'rence a day makes,
There's a rainbow before me,
Skies above can't be stormy
Since that moment of bliss;

That thrilling kiss.
It's heaven when you
Find romance on your menu.
What a diff'rence a day made.
And the diff'rence is you.

What a Wonderful World
Words and Music by George David Weiss and Bob Thiele
Copyright © 1967 by Range Road Music Inc., Quartet Music, Inc. and Abilene Music, Inc.
Copyright Renewed

recorded by Louis Armstrong
featured in the film *Good Morning Vietnam*

I see trees of green, red roses too,
I see them bloom for me and you,
And I think to myself
What a wonderful world.

I see skies of blue and clouds of white,
The bright blessed day, the dark sacred night,
And I think to myself
What a wonderful world.

The colors of the rainbow, so pretty in the sky
Are also on the faces of people goin' by.
I see friends shakin' hands, sayin', "How do you do?"
They're really sayin', "I love you."

I hear babies cry, I watch them grow.
They'll learn much more than I'll ever know.
And I think to myself,
What a wonderful world.
Yes, I think to myself
What a wonderful world.

What I Did for Love

Music by Marvin Hamlisch
Lyric by Edward Kleban

from the musical *A Chorus Line*

Kiss today goodbye,
The sweetness and the sorrow.
We did what we had to do,
And I can't regret
What I did for love,
What I did for love.

Look, my eyes are dry,
The gift was ours to borrow.
It's as if we always knew,
But I won't forget
What I did for love,
What I did for love.

Gone, love is never gone,
As we travel on,
Love's what we'll remember.

Kiss today goodbye
And point me toward tomorrow.
Wish me luck, the same to you.
Won't forget, can't regret
What I did for love.

What Kind of Fool Am I?

Words and Music by Leslie Bricusse and Anthony Newley

from the Musical Production
Stop the World—I Want to Get Off

Refrain:
What kind of fool am I?
Who never fell in love,
It seems that I'm the only one
That I have been thinking of.
What kind of man is this?
An empty shell,
A lovely cell in which
An empty heart must dwell.

What kind of lips are these
That lied with every kiss?
That whispered empty words of love
That left me alone like this?
Why can't I fall in love
Like any other man
And maybe then I'll know
What kind of fool I am.

What kind of clown am I?
What do I know of life?
Why can't I cast away the mask
Of play and live my life?
Why can't I fall in love
'Til I don't give a damn
And maybe then I'll know
What kind of fool I am.

What Now My Love

(Original French Title: "Et Maintenant")
Original French Lyric by Pierre Delanoe
Music by Gilbert Becaud
English Adaptation by Carl Sigman

recorded by Gilbert Becaud, Herb Alpert & The Tijuana Brass, Sonny & Cher

What now my love, now that you left me,
How can I live through another day.
Watching my dreams turning to ashes,
And my hopes into bits of clay.
Once I could see, once I could feel,
Now I am numb, I've become unreal.
I walk the night without a goal,
Stripped of my heart, my soul.

What now my love, now that it's over,
I feel the world closing in on me.
Here come the stars tumbling around me,
There's the sky, where the sea should be.
What now my love, now that you're gone,
I'd be a fool to go on and on,
No one would care, no one would cry,
If I should live or die.

What now my love, now there is nothing,
Only my last goodbye.

What the World Needs Now Is Love

Lyric by Hal David
Music by Burt Bacharach

recorded by Jackie DeShannon

Refrain:
What the world needs now is love, sweet love,
It's the only thing that there's just too little of.
What the world needs now is love, sweet love,
No, not just for some, but for everyone.

Lord, we don't need another mountain,
There are mountains and hillsides enough to climb;
There are oceans and rivers enough to cross,
Enough to last, till the end of time.

Refrain

Lord, we don't need another meadow,
There are cornfields and wheat fields enough to grow;
There are sunbeams and moonbeams enough to shine,
Oh, listen, Lord, if you want to know.

Refrain

No not just for some,
Oh, but just for everyone.

What'll I Do?
Words and Music by Irving Berlin

from the *Music Box Revue of 1924*
a standard recorded by Nat "King" Cole, Frank Sinatra,
Linda Ronstadt and various other artists

Gone is the romance that was so divine.
'Tis broken and cannot be mended.
You must go your way and I must go mine.
But now that our love dreams have ended,

Refrain:
What'll I do when you are far away,
And I am blue, what'll I do?
What'll I do when I am wondering who
Is kissing you, what'll I do?
What'll I do with just a photograph
To tell my troubles to?
When I'm alone with only dreams of you,
That won't come true, what'll I do?

Do you remember a night filled with bliss?
The moonlight was softly descending.
Your lips and my lips were tied with a kiss.
A kiss with an unhappy ending.

Repeat Refrain

What's Going On
Words and Music by Marvin Gaye, Al Cleveland and
Renaldo Benson

recorded by Marvin Gaye, Cyndi Lauper

Mother, mother there's too many of you crying.
Brother, brother, brother, there's far too many of you dying.
You know we've got to find a way
To bring some lovin' here today, yeah!

Refrain:
Picket lines and picket signs,
Don't punish me with brutality;
Talk to me so you can see;
Oh, what's going on.
What's going on yeah, what's going on,
Oh, what's going on.
Ah, ah, ah, ah..
I-yi-yi…
Ya, ya, ya.
I yi, yi…
Ya, ya, ya…

Scat Section

Father, father we don't need to escalate you see,
War is not the answer for only love can conquer hate
You know we've got to find a way
To bring some lovin' here today.

Refrain

Father, father everybody thinks we're wrong
Oh, but who are they to judge us,
Simple because our hair is long?
Oh you know we've got to find a way
To bring some understanding here today.

Refrain

What's New?
Words by Johnny Burke
Music by Bob Haggart

a standard recorded by Bob Crosby, Benny Goodman, Bing
Crosby, Stan Getz, Linda Ronstadt and various other artists

What's new?
How is the world treating you?
You haven't changed a bit;
Lovely as ever, I must admit.
What's new?
How did that romance come through?
We haven't met since then,
Gee, but it's nice to see you again.

What's new?
Probably I'm boring you,
But seeing you is grand,
And you were sweet to offer your hand.
I understand, adieu!
Pardon my asking what's new.
Of course you couldn't know,
I haven't changed,
I still love you so.

Whatever Gets You Through the Night

Words and Music by John Lennon
© 1974 LENONO.MUSIC
All Rights Controlled and Administered by EMI BLACKWOOD MUSIC INC.

recorded by John Lennon & The Plastic Ono Nuclear Band

Whatever gets you through the night 'sal right, 'sal right.
It's your money or your life, 'sal right, 'sal right.
Don't need a sword to cut thru' flowers, oh no, oh no.
Whatever gets you through your life 'sal right, 'sal right.
Do it wrong or do it right 'sal right, 'sal right.
Don't need a watch to waste you time, oh no, oh no.

Refrain:
Hold me darlin', come on listen to me.
I won't do you no harm.
Trust me darlin', come on listen to me,
Come one listen to me,
Come on listen, listen.

Whatever gets you to the light, 'sal right, 'sal right.
Out the blue or out of sight, 'sal right, 'sal right.
Don't need a gun to blow your mind, oh no, oh no.

Refrain

Repeat Refrain and Fade

When I Fall in Love

Words by Edward Heyman
Music by Victor Young
Copyright © 1952 by Chappell & Co. and Intersong U.S.A., Inc.
Copyright Renewed

from the film *One Minute to Zero*
recorded by Nat "King" Cole, Doris Day, The Lettermen,
Celine Dion & Clive Griffin
featured in the film *Sleepless in Seattle*

When I fall in love
It will be forever,
Or I'll never fall in love.

In a restless world like this is,
Love is ended before it's begun,
And too many moonlight kisses
Seem to cool in the warmth of the sun.

When I give my heart
It will be completely,
Or I'll never give my heart.

And the moment I can feel
That you feel that way too
Is when I fall in love with you.

When I'm Sixty-Four

Words and Music by John Lennon and Paul McCartney
Copyright © 1967 Sony/ATV Songs LLC
Copyright Renewed
All Rights Administered by Sony/ATV Music Publishing, 8 Music Square West,
  Nashville, TN 37203

recorded by The Beatles

When I get older,
Losing my hair,
Many years from now,
Will you still be sending me a valentine,
Birthday greetings and a bottle of wine?

If I'd been out till quarter to three,
Would you lock the door?
Will you still need me,
Will you still feed me,
When I'm sixty-four?

You'll be older too,
And if you say the word,
I could stay with you.

I could be handy,
Mending a fuse,
When your lights have gone.
You can knit a sweater by the fireside;
Sunday morning go for a ride.

Doing the garden,
Digging the weeds,
Who could ask for more?
Will you still need me,
Will you still feed me,
When I'm sixty-four?

Every summer we can rent a cottage,
In the Isle of Wight if it's not too dear.
We shall scrimp and save.
Grandchildren on your knee,
Vera, Chuck and Dave.

Send me a postcard,
Drop me a line,
Stating point of view.
Indicate precisely what you mean to say,
Yours sincerely, wasting away.

Give me your answer,
Fill in a form;
Mine for evermore.
Will you still need me,
Will you still feed me,
When I'm sixty-four?

When Irish Eyes Are Smiling

Words by Chauncey Olcott and George Graff, Jr.
Music by Ernest R. Ball

a singalong standard

When Irish eyes are smiling,
Sure, it's like a morn in spring.
In the lilt of Irish laughter
You can hear the angels sing.

When Irish hearts are happy,
All the world seems bright and gay.
And when Irish eyes are smiling,
Sure they steal your heart away.

When She Loved Me

Music and Lyrics by Randy Newman

from Walt Disney Pictures' *Toy Story 2* – A Pixar Film
recorded by Sarah McLachlan

When somebody loved me, everything was beautiful.
Every hour we spent together lives within my heart.
And when she was sad, I was there to dry her tears;
And when she was happy, so was I, when she loved me.

Through the summer and the fall,
We had each other that was all.
Just she and I together, like it was meant to be.
And when she was lonely, I was there to comfort her,
And I knew that she loved me.

So the years went by; I stayed the same.
But she began to drift away; I was left alone.
Still I waited for the day when she'd say,
"I will always love you."

Lonely and forgotten, never thought she'd look my way,
And she smiled at me and held me just like she used to,
Like she loved me when she loved me.
When somebody loved me, everything was beautiful.
Every hour we spent together lives within my heart,
When she loved me.

When Sunny Gets Blue

Lyric by Jack Segal
Music by Marvin Fisher

a standard recorded by Johnny Mathis and various
other artists

When Sunny gets blue
Her eyes get gray and cloudy.
Then the rain begins to fall.
Pitter patter, pitter patter,
Love is gone so what can matter?
No sweet lover man comes to call.

When Sunny gets blue,
She breathes a sigh of sadness,
Like the wind that stirs the trees.
Wind that sets the leaves to swayin',
Like some violins are playin'
Weird and haunting melodies.

People used to love
To hear her laugh, see her smile.
That's how she got her name.
Since that sad affair,
She's lost her smile,
Changed her style.
Somehow she's not the same.

But memories will fade,
And pretty dreams will rise up
Where her other dream fell through.
Hurry new love, hurry here
To kiss away each lonely tear,
And hold her near when Sunny gets blue.
Hold her near when Sunny gets blue.

When You Believe
(From The Prince Of Egypt)

Words and Music Composed by Stephen Schwartz
with Additional Music by Babyface

from the film *The Prince of Egypt*
recorded by Whitney Houston & Mariah Carey

Many nights we prayed,
With no proof anyone could hear.
In our hearts a hopeful song we barely understood.
Now we are not afraid,
Although we know there's much to fear.
We were moving mountains long before we knew we could.

Refrain:
There can be miracles,
When you believe.
Though hope is frail,
It's hard to kill.

Who knows what miracles you can achieve?
When you believe, somehow you will.
You will when you believe.

In this time of fear,
When prayer so often proves in vain,
Hope seems like the summer birds,
Too swiftly flown away.
Yet now I'm standing here,
My heart so full I can't explain,
Seeking faith and speaking words
I never thought I'd say:

There can be miracles,
When you believe.
Though hope is frail,
It's hard to kill.
Who knows what miracles you can achieve?
When you believe,
Somehow you will.
You will when you believe.

They don't always happen when you ask.
And it's easy to give in to your fear.
But when you're blinded by your pain,
Can't see your way clear through the rain,
A small but still resilient voice
Says help is very near.

Refrain

You will when you,
You will when you believe,
Just believe,
Just believe.
You will when you believe.

When You Say Nothing at All
Words and Music by Paul Overstreet and Don Schlitz

recorded by Keith Whitley, Alison Krauss & Union Station
featured in the film *Notting Hill*

It's amazing how you can speak right to my heart.
Without saying a word you can light up the dark.
Try as I may I could never explain
What I hear when you don't say a thing.

Refrain:
The smile on your face lets me know that you need me.
There's truth in your eyes saying you'll never leave me.
A touch of your hand says you'll catch me if ever I fall.
Now you say it's best when you say nothing at all.

All day long I can hear people talking out loud,
But when you hold me near you drown out the crowd.
Old Mister Webster could never define
What's being said between your heart and mine.

Refrain

Where Do I Begin (Love Theme)
Words by Carl Sigman
Music by Francis Lai

from the Paramount Picture *Love Story*
recorded by Andy Williams, Henry Mancini, Francis Lai

Where do I begin,
To tell the story of how great a love can be,
The sweet love story that is older than the sea,
The simple truth about the love she brings to me?
Where do I start?

With her first hello,
She gave a meaning to this empty world of mine;
There'll never be another love, another time;
She came into my life and made the living fine.
She fills my heart.

She fills my heart
With very special things,
With angel songs,
With wild imaginings,
She fills my soul
With so much love
That anywhere I go
I'm never lonely.
With her long,
Who could be lonely?
I reach for her hand,
It's always there.

How long does it last?
Can love be measured by the hours in a day?
I have no answers now, but this much I can say:
I know I'll need her 'til the stars all burn away
And she'll be there.

Where Do You Go

Words and Music by G. Mart, Peter Bischof-Fallenstein and James Walls

recorded by No Mercy

Refrain:
Where do you go, my lovely?
Where do you go?
I wanna know, my lovely.
I wanna know; where do you go?
Oh, ay oh.
I wanna know. Oh, ay, oh.
Where do you go?
Oh, oh oh, ay…
I wanna know.

You leave without a word,
No message, no number,
And now my head is pounding like roaring thunder.
You left me with a heartache deep inside,..
Girl, you should see me cry all night and I wonder.
Everybody says,
"What a shame! What is wrong?"
They don't like the game you play.
Heard you're hanging 'round every night until dawn.
Been waiting for you night and day.

Refrain

You gotta break the silence;
Don't keep me waiting.
Despite the river flowing to the sea,
You're running back to me.
Come hear what I'm saying.
Where do you go, my lovely.

Where do you go, oh, oh, ay oh…

Na na na dee dah…

Where do you, where do you go?
Where do you, where do you go?
Say it's with me.

Come back and dry the tears I cry for you, baby.
You gotta stop this heartache deep inside.
You've gotta help me make it through the night safely.
Come back and save me.
Where do you go, my lovely?

Refrain

Na na na…

Where Have All the Cowboys Gone?

Words and Music by Paula Cole

recorded by Mary Chapin Carpenter

Doo dit, doo doo dit…

Oh, you get me ready in your fifty-six Chevy.
Why don't we go sit down in the shade?
Take shelter on my front porch,
The dandelion sun's scorchin'.
Like a glass of cold lemonade?
I will do the laundry if you pay all the bills.

Refrain:
Where is my John Wayne?
Where is my prairie sun?
Where is my happy ending?
Where have all the cowboys gone?

Why don't you stay the evening,
Kick back and watch the T.V.,
And I'll fix a little something to eat.
Oh, I know you're back hurts from workin' on the tractor.
How do you take your coffee, my sweet?
I will raise the children if you pay all the bills.

Refrain

I am wearing my new dress tonight,
But you don't even notice me.
Say our goodbyes. Say our goodbyes,
Say our goodbyes.

Spoken:
We finally sold the Chevy when we had another baby
And you took that job in Tennessee.
You made friends at the farm
And you join 'em at the bar almost every single day
  of the week.
I will wash the dishes while you go have a beer.

Refrain

Repeat ad lib:
Where is my Marlboro man?
Where is his shiny gun?
Where is my lonely ranger?
Where have all the cowboys gone?

Where Have All the Flowers Gone?

Words and Music by Pete Seeger

recorded by The Kingston Trio

Where have all the flowers gone?
Long time passing.
Where have all the flowers gone?
Long time ago.
Where have all the flowers gone?
The girls picked them every one .

Refrain:
Oh, when will they ever learn?
Oh, when will they ever learn?

Where have all the young girls gone?
Long time passing.
Where have all the young girls gone?
They've taken husbands every one.

Refrain

Where have all the young men gone?
Long time passing.
Where have all the young men gone?
Long time ago.
Where have all the young men gone?
They're all in uniform.

Refrain

Where have all the soldiers gone?
Long time passing.
Where have all the soldiers gone?
Long time ago.
Where have all the soldiers gone?
They're gone to graveyards, every one.

Refrain

Where have all the graveyards gone?
Long time passing.
Where have all the graveyards gone?
Long time ago.
Where have all the graveyards gone?
They're covered with flowers, every one.

Refrain

Repeat Verse One and Refrain

Where Is Love?

Words and Music by Lionel Bart

from the Columbia Pictures – Romulus Motion Picture
Production of Lionel Bart's *Oliver!* (originally a stage musical)

Where is love?
Does it fall from skies above?
Is it underneath the willow tree
That I've been dreaming of?

Where is she
Who I close my eyes to see?
Will I ever know the sweet "hello"
That's meant for only me?

Who can say where she may hide?
Must I travel far and wide
Till I am beside the someone who
I can mean something to?
Where, where is love?

Every night I kneel and pray,
Let tomorrow be the day
When I see the face of someone who
I can mean something to?
Where, where is love?

Where or When

Words by Lorenz Hart
Music by Richard Rodgers

from the musical *Babes in Arms*
a standard recorded by various artists

When you're awake, the things you think
Come from the dreams you dream.
Thought has wings, and lots of things
Are seldom what they seem.
Sometimes you think you've lived before
All that you live today.
Things you do come back to you,
As though they knew the way.
Oh, the tricks the mind can play!

Refrain:
It seems we stood and talked like this before,
We looked at each other in the same way then,
But I can't remember where or when.
The clothes you're wearing are the clothes you wore,
The smile you are smiling you were smiling then.
But I can't remember where or when.
Some things that happen, for the first time
Seem to be happening again.
And so it seems that we have met before,
And laughed before, and loved before.
But who knows where or when!

Where the Boys Are

Words and Music by Howard Greenfield and Neil Sedaka

from the film *Where the Boys Are*
recorded by Connie Francis

Where the boys are
Someone waits for me:
A smiling face, a warm embrace,
Two arms to hold me tenderly.

Where the boys are
My true love will be.
He's walking down some street in town
And I know he's looking there for me.

In the crowd of a million people,
I'll find my valentine,
Then I'll climb to the highest steeple
And tell the world he's mine.

Till he holds me
I will wait impatiently,
Where the boys are,
Where the boys are,
Where the boys are,
Someone waits for me.

While We're Young

Words by Bill Engvick
Music by Morty Palitz and Alec Wilder

We must fulfill this golden time,
When hearts awake so shyly, softly.
Songs were made to sing while we're young.
Every day is spring while we're young.
None can refuse, time flies so fast,
Too dear to lose and too sweet to last.
Though it may be just for today,
Share our love we must, while we may.
So blue the skies,
All sweet surprise,
Shines before our eyes while we're young.

Repeat Song

Whistle Down the Wind

Music by Andrew Lloyd Webber
Lyrics by Jim Steinman

from the musical *Whistle Down the Wind*

Whistle down the wind,
Let your voices carry.
Drown out all the rain.
Light a patch of darkness,
Treacherous and scary
Howl at the stars,
Whisper when you're sleeping,
I'll be there to hold you
I'll be there to stop the chills
And all the weeping.
Make it clear and strong
So the whole night long
Every signal that you send
Until the very end
I will not abandon
You my precious friend.
So try and stem the tide
Then you'll raise a banner
Send a flare up in the sky.
Try to burn a torch
And try to build a bonfire
Every signal that you send
Until the very end, I'm there.
So whistle down the wind
For I have always been right here.

Make it clear and strong
So the whole night long
Every signal that you
Send until the very end
I will not abandon
You my precious friend
So try and stem the tide
Then you'll raise a banner
Send a flare up in the sky
Try to burn a torch
And try to build a bonfire
Every signal that you send
Until the very end, I'm there.

So whistle down the wind
For I have always been right here.

(There'll Be Bluebirds Over) The White Cliffs of Dover

Words by Nat Burton
Music by Walter Kent

recorded by Kay Kyser, Ray Eberle with Glenn Miller,
Kate Smith, Sammy Kaye, Bob Eberly with Jimmy Dorsey

There'll be bluebirds over
The white cliffs of Dover
Tomorrow, just you wait and see.

There'll be love and laughter
And peace ever after,
Tomorrow, when the whole world is free.

The shepherd will tend his sheep
The valley will bloom again
And Jimmy will go to sleep
In his own little room again.

There'll be bluebirds over
The white cliffs of Dover
Tomorrow, just you wait and see.

White Room

Words and Music by Jack Bruce and Pete Brown

recorded by Cream

In a white room with black curtains, near the station.
Black roof country, no gold pavements, tired starlings.
Silver horses, run down moonbeams in your dark eyes.
Dawn light smiles on your leaving my contentment.
I'll wait in this place where the sun never shines,
Wait in this place where the shadows run from themselves.

You said no strings could secure at the station.
Platform ticket, restless diesels, goodbye windows.
I walked into such a sad time at the station.
As I walked out, felt my own need just beginning.
I'll wait in this queue when the trains come back,
Lie with you where the shadows run from themselves.

At the party she was kindness in the hard crowd.
Consolation from the old wound now forgotten.
Yellow tigers crouched in jungles in her darks eyes.
She's just dressing goodbye windows, tired starlings.
I'll sleep in this place with the lonely crowd,
Lie in the dark where the shadows run from themselves.

A Whiter Shade of Pale

Words and Music by Keith Reid and Gary Brooker

recorded by Procol Harum

We skipped the light fandago,
Turned cartwheels 'cross the floor;
I was feeling kind of seasick,
The crowd called out for more.
The room was humming harder
As the ceiling flew away.
When we called for another drink
The waiter brought a tray.

Refrain:
And so it was that later
As the miller told his tale,
That her face, at first just ghostly,
Turned a whiter shade of pale.

She said, "I'm home on shore leave,"
Through in truth we were at sea;
So I took her by the looking glass
And forced her to agree.
Saying, "You must be the mermaid
Who took Neptune for a ride,"
But she smiled at me so sadly
That my anger straightaway died.

Refrain

She said, "There is no reason,
And the truth is plain to see,"
But I wandered through my playing cards
And would not let her be
One of sixteen vestal virgins
Who were leaving for the coast.
And although my eyes were open
They might just as well been closed.

Refrain

Who Can I Turn To
(When Nobody Needs Me)

Words and Music by Leslie Bricusse and Anthony Newley

from the musical
The Roar of the Greasepaint—The Smell of the Crowd
recorded by Anthony Newley, Tony Bennett

Who can I turn to
When nobody needs me?
My heart wants to know
And so I must go
Where destiny leads me.
With no star to guide me,
And no one beside me,
I'll go on my way,
And after the day,
The darkness will hide me.

And maybe tomorrow
I'll find what I'm after
I'll throw off my sorrow,
Beg steal or borrow
My share of laughter,
With you I could learn to,
With you on a new day,
But who can I turn to
If you turn away?

A Whole New World

Music by Alan Menken
Lyrics by Tim Rice

from Walt Disney's *Aladdin*
recorded by Peabo Bryson & Regina Belle

I can show you the world,
Shining, shimmering, splendid.
Tell me princess, now when
Did you last let your heart decide?

I can open your eyes
Take you wonder by wonder
Over, sideways and under
On a magic carpet ride.

A whole new world
A new fantastic point of view.
No-one to tell us no
Or where to go
Or say we're only dreaming.

A whole new world
A dazzling place I never knew.
But when I'm way up here
It's crystal clear
That now I'm in a whole new world with you.

Unbelievable sights
Indescribable feeling.
Soaring, tumbling, free-wheeling
Through an endless diamond sky.

A whole new world
A hundred thousand things to begin.
I'm like a shooting star
I've come so far
I can't go back
I'm in a whole new world.

With new horizons to pursue.
I'll chase them anywhere.
There's time to spare.
Let me share
This whole new world with you.

A whole new world,
That's where we'll be.
A thrilling chase,
A wond'rous place
For you and me.

Why

Words and Music by Annie Lennox

recorded by Annie Lennox

Why? Why?

How many times do I have to try to tell you
That I'm sorry for the things I've done? Ooh.
But when I start to try to tell you,
That's when you have to tell me,
Hey, this kind of trouble's only just begun. Yeah.
I tell myself too many times,
Why don't you ever learn to keep your big mouth shut?
That's why it hurts so bad to hear the words,
That keep on falling from your mouth,
Falling from your mouth,
Falling from your mouth.
Tell me why? Why?

I may be mad, I may be blind.
Or maybe viciously unkind.
But I can still read what you're thinking. Oo.
But I've heard it said too many times
That you'd be better off.
Besides, why can't you see this boat is sinking?
This boat is sinking.
Let's go down to the water's edge
And we can cast away those doubts.
Some things are better left unsaid,
But they still turn me inside out,
Turning inside out,
Turning inside out.
Tell me why? Why?

This is the fall guy in every bed.
These are the words I never said.
This is the path I'll never tread
These are the dreams I'll dream instead.
This is the joy that's seldom spread.
These are the tears, the tears we shed.
This is the fear. This is the dread.
These are the contents of my head.
These are the years that we've spent
This is what we represent.
This is how I feel.
Do you know how I feel?
'Cause if you think you know…
I don't think you know what I feel.

Spoken:
I don't think you know what I feel.
You don't know what I feel.

Why Did I Choose You?
Lyric by Herbert Martin
Music by Michael Leonard

from the musical *The Yearling*
recorded by Barbra Streisand

Why did I choose you?
What did I see in you?
I saw the heart you hide so well;
I saw a quiet man who had a gentle way,
A way that caught me in its glowing spell.

Why did I want you?
What could you offer me?
A love to last a lifetime through.
And when I lost my heart so many years ago,
I lost it lovingly and willingly to you.
If I had to choose again, I would still choose you.

Will It Go Round in Circles
Words and Music by Billy Preston and Bruce Fisher

recorded by Billy Preston

I've got a song I ain't got no melody,
How'm I gonna sing it to my friends?
I've got a song I ain't got no melody,
How'm I gonna sing it to my friends?

Refrain:
Will it go 'round in circles?
Will it fly high like a bird up in the sky?
Will it go 'round in circles?
Will it fly high like a bird up in the sky?

Refrain

I've got a lil' story ain't got no moral,
Let the bad guy win every once in a while.
I've got a story ain't got no moral,
Let the bad guy win every once in a while.

Refrain

I've got a lil' dance ain't got no steps,
I'm gonna let the music move me around.
I've got a dance I ain't got no steps,
I'm gonna let the music move me around.

Repeat Verse One

Repeat Refrain and Fade

Will You Love Me Tomorrow (Will You Still Love Me Tomorrow)
Words and Music by Gerry Goffin and Carole King

recorded by The Shirelles, Carole King

Tonight you're mine completely.
You give your love so sweetly.
Tonight the light of love is in your eyes,
But will you love me tomorrow?

Is this a lasting treasure
Or just a moment's pleasure?
Can I believe the magic of your sighs?
Will you still love me tomorrow?

Tonight with words unspoken,
You say that I'm the only one.
But will my heart be broken
When the night meets the morning sun?

I'd like to know that your love
Is love that I can be sure of.
So tell me now, and I won't ask again.
Will you still love me tomorrow?
Will you still love me tomorrow?

Winchester Cathedral
Words and Music by Geoff Stephens

recorded by The New Vaudeville Band

Winchester Cathedral
You're bringing me down.
You stood and watched as
My baby left town.

You could have done something
But you didn't try.
You didn't do nothing
You let her walk by.

Now everyone knows
Just how much I needed that girl.
She wouldn't have gone far away
If only you'd started ringing your bell.

Repeat Verse One

A Wink and a Smile
Music by Marc Shaiman
Lyrics by Ramsey McLean

featured in the TriStar Motion Picture *Sleepless in Seattle*
recorded by Harry Connick, Jr.

I remember the days of just keeping time,
Of hanging around in sleepy towns forever;
Back roads empty for miles.
Well, you can't have a dream and cut it to fit,
But when I saw you,
I knew we'd go together like a wink and a smile.

Leave your old jalopy by the railroad track.
We'll get a hip double dip tip-toppy two seat Cadillac.
So you can rev her up; and don't go slow,
It's only green lights and "All rights."
Lets go together with a wink and a smile.

Give me a wink and a smile.

We'd go together like a wink and a smile.
Now my heart hears music; such a simple song.
Sing it again; the notes never end.
This is where I belong.

Just the sound of your voice, the light in your eyes,
We're so far away from yesterday, together,
With a wink and a smile.
We go together like a wink and a smile.

Witchcraft
Lyric by Carolyn Leigh
Music by Cy Coleman

recorded by Frank Sinatra

Shades of old Lucretia Borgia!
There's a devil in you tonight
'N' although my heart adores ya
My head says it ain't right,
Right to let you make advances, oh no!
Under normal circumstances, I'd go but oh!

Those fingers in my hair,
That sly, come hither stare
That strips my conscience bare,
It's witchcraft.

And I've got no defense for it,
The heat is too intense for it,
What good would common sense for it do?
'Cause it's witchcraft!
Wicked witchcraft.
And although I know it's strictly taboo.
When you arouse the need in me,
My heart says, "Yes, indeed" in me.
"Proceed with what you're leadin' me to!"
It's such an ancient pitch
But one I wouldn't switch
'Cause there's no nicer witch than you!

With a Little Help from My Friends
Words and Music by John Lennon and Paul McCartney

recorded by The Beatles

What would you do if sang out of tune,
Would you stand up and walk out on me?
Lend me your ears and I'll play you a song,
And I'll try not to sing out of key.

Oh, I get by with a little help from my friends.
I get high with a little help from my friends.
I'm gonna try with a little help from my friends.

What do I do when my love is away?
(Does it worry you to be alone.)
How do I feel by the end of the day?
(Are you sad because you're on your own.)

No, I get by with a little help from my friends.
I get high with a little help from my friends.
I'm gonna try with a little help from my friends.

Do you need anybody?
I need somebody to love.
Could it be anybody?
I want somebody to love.

Would you believe in a love at first sight?
Yes I'm certain that it happens all the time.
What do you see when you turn out the light?
I can't tell you but I know it's mine.

Oh I get by with a little help from my friends.
I get high with a little help from my friends.
I'm gonna try with a little help from my friends.

Do you need anybody?
I just need someone to love.
Could it be anybody?
I want somebody to love.

Oh I get by with a little help from my friends.
I get high with a little help from my friends.
I'm gonna try with a little help from my friends.
Yes, I get by with a little help from my friends.

With a Song in My Heart
Words by Lorenz Hart
Music by Richard Rodgers

from the musical *Spring Is Here*
a standard recorded by various artists

Though I know that we meet every night
And we couldn't have changed since the last time,
To my joy and delight,
It's a new kind of love at first sight.
Though it's you and it's I all the time,
Every meeting's a marvelous pastime.
You're increasingly sweet,
So whenever we happen to meet
I greet you…

Refrain:
With a song in my heart
I behold your adorable face.
Just a song at the start,
But it soon is a hymn to your grace.
When the music swells
I'm touching your hand;
It tells that you're standing near, and…
At the sound of your voice
Heaven opens its portals to me.
Can I help but rejoice
That a song such as ours came to be?
But I always knew
I would live life through,
With a song in my heart for you.

Oh, the moon's not a moon for a night
And these stars will not twinkle and fade out,
And the words in my ears
Will resound for the rest of my years.
In the morning I'll find with delight
Not a note of music is played out.
It will be just as sweet,
And an air that I'll live to repeat,
I greet you…

Refrain

With One Look
Music by Andrew Lloyd Webber
Lyrics by Don Black and Christopher Hampton,
with contributions by Amy Powers

from the musical *Sunset Boulevard*

With one look I can break your heart,
With one look I play every part.
I can make your sad heart sing,
With one look you'll know all you need to know.

With one smile I'm the girl next door
Or the love that you've hungered for.
When I speak it's with my soul
I can play any role.

No words can tell the stories my eyes tell,
Watch me when I frown, you can't write that down.
You know I'm right, it's there in black and white,
When I look your way you'll hear what I say.

Yes, with one look I put words to shame,
Just one look sets the screen aflame.
Silent music starts to play,
One tear in my eye makes the whole world cry.

With one look they'll forgive the past,
They'll rejoice I've returned at last
To my people in the dark,
Still out there in the dark.

Silent music starts to play.
With one look you'll know all you need to know.
With one look I'll ignite a blaze,
I'll return to my glory days.

They'll say Norma's back at last.
This time I'm staying for good,
I'll be back where I was born to be,
With one look I'll be me.

Woman from Tokyo

Words and Music by Ritchie Blackmore, Ian Gillan,
Roger Glover, Jon Lord and Ian Paice

recorded by Deep Purple

Fly into the risin' sun.
Faces smilin' every one. Yeah!
She is a whole new tradition. Ow!
I feel it in my heart!

Refrain:
My woman from Tokyo.
She makes me see.
My woman from Tokyo.
She's so good to me.

Talk about her like a queen,
Dancing in an eastern dream.
Yeah, she makes me feel like a river, ow!
That carries me away.

Refrain

Risin' from the neon gloom,
Shinin' like a crazy moon.
Yeah, she tuns me on like a fire.
Ow! I get high!

Refrain

When I'm at home an' I, I just don't belong.

So far away from the garden we love.
She is what moves in the soul of a dove.
Soon I shall see just how black was my night,
When we're alone in her city of light.
Oooo…

Refrain

Woman in Love

Words and Music by Barry Gibb and Robin Gibb

recorded by Barbra Streisand

Love is a moment in space,
When the dream is gone
It's a lonelier place.
I kiss the morning goodbye.
But down inside
You know we never know why.
The road is narrow and long
When eyes meet eyes
And the feeling is strong.
I turn away from the wall.
I stumble and fall,
But I give you it all.

Refrain:
I am a woman in love
And I'd do anything
To get you into my world
And hold you within.
It's a right I defend
Over and over again.

With you eternally mine,
In love there is
No measure of time.
We planned it all at the start,
That you and I
Live in each other's hearts.
We may be oceans away
You feel my love
I hear what you say.
The truth is ever a lie.
I stumble and fall,
But I give you it all.

Refrain

I am a woman in love
And I'm talkin' to you.
I know how you feel,
What a woman can do.
It's a right I defend
Over and over again

Refrain

A Wonderful Day Like Today

Words and Music by Leslie Bricusse and Anthony Newley

from the musical
The Roar of the Greasepaint—The Smell of the Crowd

On a wonderful day like today
I defy any cloud to appear in the sky.
Dare any raindrop to plop in my eye
On a wonderful day like today.

On a wonderful morning like this
When the sun is as big as a yellow balloon
Even the sparrows are singing in tune
On a wonderful morning like this.

On a morning like this
I could kiss everybody
I'm so full of love and good will.
Let me say furthermore
I'd adore everybody
To come and dine.
The pleasure's mine.
And I will pay the bill.

May I take this occasion to say
That the whole human race should go down on its knees,
Show that we're grateful for mornings like these.
For the world's in a wonderful way
On a wonderful day like today.

Wonderful Tonight
Words and Music by Eric Clapton

recorded by Eric Clapton

It's late in the evening; she's wondering what clothes to wear.
She puts on her makeup and brushes her long blonde hair.
And then she asks me, "Do I look all right?"
And I say, "Yes, you look wonderful tonight."

We go to a party, and everyone turns to see
This beautiful lady is walking around with me.
And then she asks me, "Do you feel all right?"
And I say, "Yes, I feel wonderful tonight."

I feel wonderful because I see the love light in your eyes.
Then the wonder of it all is that you just don't realize
How much I love you.

It's time to go home now, and I've got an aching head.
So I give her the car keys, and she helps me to bed.
And then I tell her, as I turn out the light, I say,
"My darling, you are wonderful tonight.
Oh, my darling, you are wonderful tonight."

Wonderwall
Words and Music by Noel Gallagher

recorded by Oasis

Today is gonna be the day
That they're gonna throw it back to you.
By now you should have somehow realized
What you gotta do.
I don't believe that anybody feels
The way I do about you now.

Backbeat, the word is on the street
That the fire in your heart is out.
I'm sure you've heard it all before,
But you never really had a doubt.
I don't believe that anybody feels
The way I do about you now.

And all the roads we have to walk are winding,
And all the lights that lead us there are blinding.
There are many things that I would like to say to you,
But I don't know how.
Because maybe you're gonna be the one that saves me.
And after all you're my wonderwall.

Today was gonna be the day,
But they'll never throw it back to you.
By now you should have somehow realized
What you're not to do.
I don't believe that anybody feels
The way I do about you now.
And all the roads that lead you there were winding,
And all the lights that light the way are blinding.
There are many things that I would like to say to you,
But I don't know how.

Three Times:
I said maybe you're gonna be the one that saves me.
And after all you're my wonderwall.

I said maybe (I said maybe).
You're gonna be the one that saves me.
(Saves me.)
You're gonna be the one that saves me.

Written in the Stars
Music by Elton John
Lyrics by Tim Rice

from Walt Disney Theatrical Production *Aïda*
recorded by Elton John & LeAnn Rimes

Male:
I am here to tell you we can never meet again.
Simple really, isn't it?
A word or two and then a lifetime of not knowing
Where or why or when.
You think of me or speak of me
Or wonder what befell
The someone you once loved
So long ago so well.

Female:
Never wonder what I'll feel as living shuffles by.
You don't have to ask me and I need not reply.
Every moment of my life from now until I die
I will think or dream of you and fail to understand
How a perfect love can be confounded out of hand.

Both:
Is it written in the stars?
Are we paying for some crime?
Is that all that we are good for,
Just a stretch of mortal time?
Is this God's experiment in which we have no say?
In which we're given paradise, but only for a day.

Male:
Nothing can be altered. Oh, there is nothing to decide.
No escape, no change of heart nor any place to hide.

Female:
You are all I'll ever want but this I am denied.
Sometimes in my darkest thoughts
I wish I never learned what it is
To be in love and have that love returned.

Both:
Is it written in the stars?
Are we paying for some crime?
Is that all that we are good for,
Just a stretch of mortal time?
Is this God's experiment in which we have no say?
In which we're given paradise, but only for a day.
Is it written in the stars?
Are we paying for some crime?
Is that all that we are good for,
Just a stretch of mortal time?

Male:
In which we have no say?

Female:
In which we're given paradise only

Both:
For a day.

Yellow Submarine
Words and Music by John Lennon and Paul McCartney

from the film *Yellow Submarine*
recorded by The Beatles

In the town where I was born,
Lived a man who sailed the sea.
And he told us of his life,
In the land of submarines.
So we sailed up to the sun,
Till we found the sea of green.
And we lived beneath the waves
In our yellow submarine.

Refrain:
We all live in a yellow submarine,
Yellow submarine, yellow submarine.
We all live in a yellow submarine,
Yellow submarine, yellow submarine.

And our friends are all on board,
Many more of them live next door.
And the band begins to play:
(Instrumental)

Refrain

As we live a life of ease,
Every one of us has all we need.
Sky of blue and sea of green
In our yellow submarine.

Yesterday
Words and Music by John Lennon and Paul McCartney

recorded by The Beatles

Yesterday, all my troubles seemed so far away,
Now it looks as though they're here to stay,
Oh I believe in yesterday.

Suddenly, I'm not half the man I used to be,
There's a shadow hanging over me,
Oh yesterday came suddenly.

Bridge:
Why she had to go
I don't know, she wouldn't say.
I said something wrong,
Now I long for yesterday.

Yesterday, love was such an easy game to play.
Now I need a place to hide away,
Oh I believe in yesterday.

Repeat From Bridge

Yesterday Once More
Words and Music by John Bettis and Richard Carpenter

recorded by The Carpenters

When I was young I'd listen to the radio
Waitin' for my favorite songs
When they played I'd sing along; it made me smile.
Those were such happy times and not so long ago,
How I wondered where they'd gone.
But they're back again just like a long lost friend,
All the songs I love so well.

Refrain:
Every sha-la-la-la, every wo, wo, wo still shines.
Every shinga-ling-a-ling that they're startin' to sing so fine.

When they get to the part where he's breaking her heart
It can really make me cry just like before.
It's yesterday once more.
(Shoobie do lang lang.)

Lookin' back on how it was in years gone by
And the good times that I had,
Makes today seem rather sad, so much has changed.
It was songs of love that I would sing to them.
And I'd memorize each word.
Those old melodies still sound so good to me,
As they melt the years away.

Refrain

All my best memories come back clearly to me,
Some can even make me cry just like before.

Repeat Refrain and Fade

Yesterday, When I Was Young (Hier Encore)

English Lyric by Herbert Kretzmer
Original French Text and Music by Charles Aznavour

recorded by Charles Aznavour, Roy Clark

Yesterday, when I was young,
The taste of life was sweet as rain upon my tongue,
I teased at life as if it were a foolish game,
The way the evening breeze may tease a candle flame;
The thousands of dreams I dreamed,
The splendid things I planned I always built,
Alas, on weak and shifting sand;
I loved my night and shunned the naked light of day,
And only now I see how the years ran away.

Yesterday, when I was young,
So many drinking songs were waiting to be sung,
So many wayward pleasures lay in store for me.
And so much pain my dazzled eyes refused to see,
I ran so fast that time and youth at last ran out.
I never stopped to think what life was all about,
And every conversation I can now recall,
Concerned itself with me,
And nothing else at all.

Yesterday, the moon was blue,
And every crazy day brought something new to do,
I used my magic age as if it were a wand,
And never saw the waste and emptiness beyond;
The game of love I played with arrogance and pride,
And every flame lit too quickly, quickly died;
The friends I made all seemed somehow to drift away,
And only I am left on stage to end the play.

There are so many songs in me that won't be sung,
I feel the bitter taste of tears upon my tongue,
The time has come for me to pay,
For yesterday when I was young.

You Ain't Seen Nothin' Yet

Words and Music by Randy Bachman

recorded by Bachman-Turner Overdrive

I met a devil woman,
She took my heart away.
She said I had it comin' to me,
And I wanted it that way.
She said that:

Refrain:
Any love is good lovin',
So I took what I could get.
Yes, I took what I could get.
And then she looked at me with those big brown eyes
   and she said:
"You ain't seen nothin' yet.
B-b-b-baby, you just ain't never gonna forget baby.
Ya know, ya know, ya know,
You know, you know you just ain't seen nothin' yet."

And now I'm feelin' better
'Cause I found out for sure.
She took me to her doctor
And he told me of a cure.
He said that:

Refrain

You and I

Words and Music by Stevie Wonder

recorded by Stevie Wonder

Here we are,
On earth together, you and I.
God has made us fall in love, it's true.
I've really found someone like you.
Will it stay,
The love you feel for me?
Will it say,
That you will be by my side to see me through,
Until my life is through?
Well, in my mind,
We can conquer the world.
In love, you and I.
You and I.
You and I.

I am glad,
At least in my life I found someone,
That may not be here forever to see me through.
But I found strength in you.
I only pray,
That I have shown you a brighter day,
Because that's all that I am living for, you see.
Don't worry what happens to me,
'Cause in my mind
You will stay here always.
In love, you and I.
You and I.
You and I.

You and Me Against the World
Words and Music by Paul Williams and Ken Ascher
Copyright © 1974 ALMO MUSIC CORP.

recorded by Helen Reddy

You and me against the world.
Sometimes it feels like you and me against the world.
When all others turn their back and walk away,
You can count on me to stay.
Remember when the circus came to town,
And you were frightened by the clown?
Wasn't it nice to be around someone that you knew,
Someone who was big and strong,
And lookin' out for you and me against the world.

And for all the times we've cried,
I always felt the odds were on our side.
And when one of us is gone,
And one is left alone to carry on,
Well, then remembering will have to do.
Our memories alone will get us through.
Think about the days of me and you,
Of you and me against the world.

Life can be a circus.
They under pay and over work us,
And though we seldom get our due,
When each day is through,
I bring my tired body home,
And look around for me and you against the world.
Sometimes it feels like you and me against the world.
And for all the times we've cried,
I always felt that God was on our side.

And when one of us is gone,
And one is left alone to carry on,
Well, then remembering will have to do.
Our memories alone will get us through.
Think about the days of me and you,
Of you and me against the world.

You Are My Sunshine
Words and Music by Jimmie Davis and Charles Mitchell
Copyright © 1930 by Peer International Corporation
Copyright Renewed

a standard recorded by Tex Ritter, Bing Crosby,
Ray Charles and various other artists

The other night dear as I lay sleeping,
I dreamed I held you in my arms.
When I awoke dear I was mistaken,
And I hung my head and cried:

Refrain:
You are my sunshine, my only sunshine,
You make me happy when skies are gray.
You'll never know dear how much I love you.
Please don't take my sunshine away.

I'll always love you and make you happy,
If you will only say the same.
But if you leave me to love another
You'll regret it all someday:

Refrain

You told me once dear you really loved me,
And no one else could come between.
But now you've left me and love another,
You have shattered all my dreams.

Refrain

You Are So Beautiful
Words and Music by Billy Preston and Bruce Fisher
Copyright © 1973 IRVING MUSIC, INC. and ALMO MUSIC CORP.
Copyright Renewed

recorded by Joe Cocker

You are so beautiful to me.
You are so beautiful to me.
Can't you see you're everything that I hope for
And what's more, you're everything I need.
You are so beautiful, baby, to me.

You're everything that I hope for
And what's more, you're everything I need.
You are so beautiful, baby, to me.

Such joy and happiness you bring.
(I wanna thank you babe.)
Such joy and happiness you bring,
Just like a dream.
You're the guiding light shinin' in the night,
You're heaven still to me.
(Hey baby,)

You are so beautiful.
You are so beautiful.

You Are the Sunshine of My Life

Words and Music by Stevie Wonder

recorded by Stevie Wonder

You are the sunshine of my life,
That's why I'll always be around.
You are the apple of my eye.
Forever you'll stay in my heart.

I feel like this is the beginning,
'Though I've loved you for a million years.
And if I thought our love was ending,
I'd find myself, drowning in my own tears.

You are the sunshine of my life,
That's why I'll always stay around.
You are the apple of my eye.
Forever you'll stay in my heart.

You must have known that I was lonely,
Because you came to my rescue.
And I know that this must be heaven;
How could so much love, be inside of you?

Repeat Verse 1 and Fade

You Brought a New Kind of Love to Me

Words and Music by Sammy Fain, Irving Kahal and
Pierre Norman

from the Paramount Picture *The Big Pond*
a standard recorded by Maurice Chevalier and various
other artists
featured in the film *New York, New York*

If the nightingales could sing like you,
They'd sing sweeter than they do,
For you've brought a new
Kind of love to me.
If the sandman brought me dreams of you,
I'd want to sleep my whole life through;
For you've brought a new kind of love to me.

I know that I'm the slave,
You're the queen, but still you can understand,
That underneath it all,
You're a maid and I am only a man.

I would work and slave the whole day through,
If I could hurry home to you,
For you've brought a new kind of love to me.

You Can't Hurry Love

Words and Music by Edward Holland, Lamont Dozier and
Brian Holland

recorded by The Supremes, Phil Collins

I need love, love to ease my mind;
I need to find, find someone to call mine;
But Mama said;

Refrain:
You can't hurry love,
No you just have to wait,
She said love don't come easy,
It's a game of give and take.

You can't hurry love,
No, you just have to wait,
You gotta trust, give it time,
No matter how long it takes;
But how many heartaches must I stand,
Before I find a love to let me live again.
Right now the only thing
That keeps me hanging on,
When I feel my strength,
Yeah, it's almost gone,
I remember Mama said;

Refrain

How long must I wait
How much more can I take,
Before loneliness will cause
My heart, my heart to break?
No, I can't bear to live my life alone.
I grow impatient for a love to call my own;
But when I feel that I, I can't go on,
These precious words keep me hanging on;
I remember Mama said:

You can't hurry love,
No, you just have to wait,
She said trust, give it time,
No matter how long it takes.

No love, love don't come easy,
But I keep on waiting,
Anticipating for that soft voice
To talk to me at night,
For some tender arms to
Hold me tight.
I keep waiting;
I keep on waiting,
But it ain't easy, it ain't easy
When Mama said:

Repeat Refrain and Fade

You Don't Mess Around with Jim

Words and Music by Jim Croce

recorded by Jim Croce

Uptown got its hustlers,
The Bowery got it's bums.
Forty-Second Street got big Jim Walker,
He a pool shootin' son of a gun.
Yeah, he big and dumb as a man can come
But he stronger than a country hoss.
And when the bad folks all get together at night,
You know they all call big Jim "Boss" just because.
And they say…

Refrain:
"You don't tug on Superman's cape,
You don't spit into the wind,
You don't pull the mask off the old Lone Ranger
And you don't mess around with Jim."

Well out-a south Alabama come a country boy.
He said, "I'm lookin' for a man named Jim,
I am a pool shootin' boy,
My name is Willie McCoy
But down home they call me Slim.
Yeah, I'm lookin' for the king of Forty-Second Street,
He drivin' a drop-top Cadillac.
Last week he took all my money,
And it may sound funny,
But I come to get my money back."
And everybody say,

Refrain

Well a hush fell over the poolroom,
Jimmy come boppin' in off the street.
And when the cuttin' were done
The only part that wasn't bloody
Was the soles of the big man's feet.
Yeah, he were cut in 'bout a hundred places,
And he were shot in a couple more.
And you better believe
They sung a different kind of story
When-a big Jim hit the floor. Oh.
Now they say…

"You don't tug on Superman's cape,
You don't spit into the wind,
You don't pull the mask off the old Lone Ranger
And you don't mess around with Slim."

Spoken:
Yeah, big Jim got his hat,
Find out where it's at,
And not hustling people strange to you.
Even if you do got a two-piece custom-made pool cue.

Repeat Refrain and Fade

You Give Love a Bad Name

Words and Music by Desmond Child, Jon Bon Jovi and Richie Sambora

recorded by Bon Jovi

An angel's smile is what you sell.
You promise me heaven, then put me through hell.
Chains of love got a hold on me.
When passion's a prison, you can't break free.

Refrain:
Oh you're a loaded gun. Yeah.
Oh, there's nowhere to run.
No one can save me, the damage is done.
Shot through the heart and you're to blame.
You give love a bad name.
I play my part and you play your game.
You give love a bad name,
Hey, you give love a bad name.

You paint your smile on your lips.
Blood red nails on your finger tips.
A school boy's dream, you act so shy.
Your very first kiss was your first kiss goodbye.

You Keep Me Hangin' On

Words and Music by Edward Holland, Lamont Dozier and Brian Holland

recorded by The Supremes, Vanilla Fudge, Kim Wilde

Set me free why don't cha baby;
Get out my life why don't cha baby,
'Cause you don't really love me.
You just keep me hangin' on.
You don't really need me
But you just keep me hangin' on.

Why do you keep a comin' around,
Playing with my heart?
Why don't cha get out of my life,
And let me make a new start?
Let me get over you,
The way you've gotten over me.

Set me free why don't cha baby;
Let me be why don't cha baby,
'Cause you don't really love me.
You just keep me hangin' on.
You don't really need me
But you just keep me hangin' on.

You say although we broke up,
You still wanna be just friends.
But how can we still be friends,
When seeing you only breaks my heart again?

Spoken:
And there ain't nothin' I can do about it.

Sung:
Set me free why don't cha baby,
Get out my life why don't cha baby.
Set me free why don't cha baby,
Get out my life why don't cha baby.

You claim you still care for me
But your heart and soul need to be free.
Now that you've got your freedom
You wanna still hold on to me.

You don't want me for yourself,
So let me find somebody else.
Why don't cha be a man about it,
And set me free.

Now you don't care a thing about me,
You're just using me.
Boy, get out, get outta my life
And let me sleep at night,
'Cause you don't really love me,
You just keep me hangin' on.
'Cause you don't really need me,
So let me be,
Set me free.

You Make Me Feel Like Dancing
Words and Music by Vini Poncia and Leo Sayer

recorded by Leo Sayer

You've got a cute way of talking;
You got the better of me.
Just snap your fingers and I'm walking like a dog,
Hanging on your lead.
I'm in a spin, you know;
Shaking on a string, you know.

Refrain:
You make me feel like dancing;
I wanna dance the night away.
You make me feel like dancing;
I'm gonna dance the night away.
You make me feel like dancing.
I feel like dancing, dancing, dance the night away.
I feel like dancing, dancing.

Quarter to four in the morning,
I ain't feeling tired, no. no. no.
Just hold me tight and leave on the light,
'Cause I don't wanna go home.
You put a spell on me;
I'm right where you want me to be.

Refrain

Dance the night away.
I feel like dancing, dancing, dance the night away.
I feel like dancing, dancing, ah.

And if you'll let me stay, we'll dance our lives away.

Repeat and Fade:
You make me feel like dancing;
I wanna dance my life way.
You make me fell like dancing;
I wanna dance my life away.

You Mean the World to Me
Words and Music by Babyface, L.A. Reid and
Daryl Simmons

recorded by Toni Braxton

If you could give me one good reason
Why I should believe you,
Believe in all the things that you tell me,
I would sure like to believe you.
My heart wants to receive you.
Just make me know that you are sincere.
You know I'd love for you to lead me
And follow through completely,
So won't you give me all I ask for,
And if you give your very best
To bring me happiness,
I'll show you just how much I adore you.

Refrain:
'Cause you mean the world to me.
You are my everything,
I swear the only thing that matters,
Matters to me.
Oh, baby, baby, baby, baby, baby,
'Cause you mean so much to me

Now it's gonna take some workin',
But I believe you're worth it,
Long as your intentions are good, so good.
There is just one way to show it,
And boy, I hope you know it,
That no one could love you like I could.

Lord knows I want to trust you
And always how I'd love you.
I'm not sure if love is enough.
And I will not be forsaken
And I hope there's no mistakin'.
So tell me that you'll always be true.

Refrain

There's a feeling in my heart
That I know I know I can't escape.
So please don't let me fall,
Don't let it be too late.
There's a time when words are good
And they just get in the way.
So show me how you feel,
Baby, I'm for real,
Oh, baby, baby, baby, baby, baby.

Repeat Refrain and Fade

You Needed Me
Words and Music by Randy Goodrum

recorded by Anne Murray

I cried a tear, you wiped it dry.
I was confused, you cleared my mind.
I sold my soul, you bought it back for me
And held me up and gave me dignity.
Somehow you needed me.

Refrain:
You gave me strength to stand alone again
To face the world out on my own again
You put me high upon a pedestal
So high that I can almost see eternity.
You needed me. You needed me;

And I can't believe it's you, I can't believe it's true.
I needed you and you were there
And I'll never leave. Why should I leave?
I'd be a fool
'Cause I've finally found someone
Who really cares.

You held my hand when it was cold.
When I was lost, you took me home.
You gave me hope, when I was at the end,
And turned my lies back into truth again.
You even called me friend.

Refrain

You Took Advantage of Me
Words by Lorenz Hart
Music by Richard Rodgers

from the musical *Present Arms*
a standard recorded by various artists

He:
In the spring when the feeling was chronic,
And my caution was leaving you flat,
I should have made use of the tonic,
Before you gave me "that!"
A mental deficient you'll grade me,
I've given you plenty of data.
You came, you saw and you slayed me,
And that-a is that-a!

Refrain:
I'm a sentimental sap, that's all.
What's the use of trying not to fall?
I have no will,
You've made your kill,
'Cause you took advantage of me!
I'm just like an apple on a bough,
And you're gonna shake me down somehow,
So what's the use, you've cooked my goose,
'Cause you took advantage of me!

I'm so hot and bothered that I don't know
My elbow from my ear;
I suffer something awful each time you go,
And much worse when you're near.
Here am I with all my bridges burned,
Just a babe in arms where you're concerned,
So lock the doors and call me your's
'Cause you took advantage of me!

She:
When a girl has the heart of a mother
It must go to someone of course;
It can't be a sister or brother
And so I loved my horse.
But horses are frequently silly,
Mine ran from the beach of Kaluta,
And left me alone for a filly,
So I-a picked you-a.

Refrain

You Wear It Well

Words and Music by Rod Stewart and Martin Quittenton

recorded by Rod Stewart

I had nothing to do on this hot afternoon
But to settle down and write you a line.
I've been meaning to phone you, but from Minnesota,
Hell, it's been a very long time.
You wear it well;

A little old fashioned, but that's all right.
Well, I suppose you're thinkin' how Betty is sinkin',
Or he wouldn't get in touch with me.
Though I ain't beggin' or losin' my head,
I sure do want you to know,
That you wear it well;

Very the lady in the fan so fine.
Oh, my. Remember their basement parties,
Your brothers cavorting,
The all day rock and roll show.
The homesick blues and the radical views
Haven't left a mark on you.
You wear it well;

A little out of time, but I don't mind.
But I ain't forgettin' that you were once mine,
But I'll believe it without even tryin'.
Now I'm eatin' my heart out,
Tryin' to get a letter through.

Since you've been gone, it's hard to carry on.
I'm gonna write about the birthday gown
That I bought in town,
And you sat down and cried on the stairs
You knew it didn't cost the earth,
But, for what it's worth,
You made me feel a millionaire.
And you wear it well.

Madame Onassis got nothin' on you.
No, no.
And when my coffee is cold,
And I'm gettin' told
That I gotta get back to work,
So when the sun goes low and you're home all alone,
Think of me and try not to laugh,
And I'll wear it well.

I don't object if you call collect.
'Cause I ain't forgettin' that you were once mine.
But I feel it without even try'n'.
Now I'm eatin' my heart out,
Trying to get back to you.

You Were Meant for Me

Words and Music by Jewel Kilcher and Steve Poltz

recorded by Jewel

I hear the clock. It's six A.M.
I feel so far from where I've been.
I got my eggs, I got my pancakes, too.
I got my maple syrup, everything but you.
I break the yolks and make a smiley face.
I kinda like it in my brand new place.
Wipe the spots up over me,
Don't leave my keys in the door.
I never put wet towels on the floor anymore

Refrain:
'Cause dreams last so long,
Even after you're gone.
I know that you love me,
And soon you will see,
You were meant for me,
And I was meant for you.

I called my mama, she was out for a walk.
Consoled a cup of coffee, but I didn't want to talk.
So, I picked up the paper, it was more bad news.
My heart's being broken by people being used.
Put on my coat in the pouring rain.
I saw a movie, it just wasn't the same

Refrain

I go about my business. I'm doing fine.
Besides what would I say if I had you on the line?
Same old story, not much to say.
Hearts are broken every day.

I brush my teeth, I put the cap back on.
I know you hate it when I leave the light on.
I pick up a cup and then I turn the sheets down
and then I take a deep breath, a good look around.
Put on my pj's and hop into bed.
I'm half alive, but I feel mostly dead.
I try and tell myself it'll be alright.
I just shouldn't think anymore tonight.

Refrain

Yeah, you were meant for me and I was meant for you.

You'd Be So Nice to Come Home To

Words and Music by Cole Porter

from the musical *Something to Shout About*
a standard recorded by various artists

It's not that you're fairer,
Than a lot of girls just as pleasin',
That I doff my hat as a worshipper at your shrine,
It's not that you're rarer
Than asparagus out of season,
No, my darling, this is reason
Why you've got to be mine:

Refrain:
You'd be so nice to come home to,
You'd be so nice by the fire,
While the breeze, on high, sang a lullaby,
You'd be all that I could desire,
Under stars, chilled by the winter,
Under an August moon,
Burning above,
You'd be so nice,
You'd be paradise to come home to and love.

Refrain:

You'll Be in My Heart (Pop Version)

Words and Music by Phil Collins

from Walt Disney Pictures *Tarzan*™
recorded by Phil Collins

Come stop your crying; it will be all right.
Just take my hand, hold it tight.
I will protect you from all around you.
I will be here; don't you cry.

For one so small you seem so strong.
My arms will hold you, keep you safe and warm.
This bond between us can't be broken.
I will be here; don't you cry.

Refrain:
'Cause you'll be in my heart,
Yes, you'll be in my heart,
From this day on now and forever more.

You'll be in my heart,
No matter what they say.
You'll be here in my heart always.

Why can't they understand the way we feel?
They just don't trust what they can't explain.
I know we're different, but deep inside us,
We're not that different at all.
And...

Refrain

Don't listen to them,
'Cause what do they know?
We need each other to have, to hold.
They'll see in time,
I know.

When destiny calls you
You must be strong.
It may not be with you,
But you've got to hold on.
They'll see in time, I know.
We'll show them together,
'Cause you'll be in my heart.
Believe me, you'll be in my heart.

I'll be there from this day on,
Now and forevermore.
You'll be in my heart,
(You'll be here in my heart.)
No matter what they say.
(I'll be with you.)
You'll be here in my heart,
(I'll be there.)
Always.

I'll be with you.
I'll be there for you always,
Always and always.
Just look over your shoulder.
Just look over your shoulder.
Just look over you shoulder;
I'll be there always.

You'll Never Walk Alone

Lyrics by Oscar Hammerstein II
Music by Richard Rodgers

from the musical *Carousel*

When you walk through a storm, hold your head up high
And don't be afraid of the dark,
At the end of the storm is a golden sky
And the sweet silver song of a lark.

Walk on through the wind,
Walk on through the wind,
Walk on through the rain,
Tho' your dreams be tossed and blown,
Walk on, walk on, with hope in your heart,
And you'll never walk alone,
You'll never walk alone!

You're My Best Friend

Words and Music by John Deacon

recorded by Queen

Ooh, you make me live;
Whatever this world can give to me.
It's you, you're all I see.
Ooh, you make me live now, honey,
Ooh, you make me live.

Ooh, you're the best friend that I ever had.
I've been with you such a long time,
You're my sunshine and I want you to know,
That my feelings are true,
I really love you.

Refrain:
Oh, you're my best friend.
Ooh, you make me live.
Ooh, I've been wanderin 'round,
But I still come back to you.
In rain or shine you've stood by me, girl.
I'm happy at home,
You're my best friend.

Ooh, you make me live
Whenever this world is cruel to me.
I got you to help me forgive.
Ooh, you make me live now, honey,
Ooh, you make me live.

Ooh, you're the first one when things turn out bad.
You know I'll never be lonely,
You're my only one and I love the things,
I really love the things that you do.

Refrain

Ooh, ooh, you're my best friend.
Ooh, you make me live.
Ooh, you're my best friend.

You're Nearer

Words by Lorenz Hart
Music by Richard Rodgers

from the film *Too Many Girls*
a standard recorded by Judy Garland and various other artists

Time is a healer, but it cannot heal my heart.
My mind says I've forgotten you and then I feel my heart.
The miles lie between us, but your fingers touch my own.
You're never far away from me,
For you're too much my own.

Refrain:
You're nearer than my head is to my pillow,
Nearer than the wind is to the willow.
Dearer than the rain is to the earth below,
Precious as the sun is to the things that grow.
You're nearer than the ivy to the wall is.
Nearer than the winter to the fall is,
Leave me, but when you're away
You'll know,
You're nearer, for I love you so.

You're Nobody 'til Somebody Loves You

Words and Music by Russ Morgan, Larry Stock and James Cavanaugh

a standard recorded by Russ Morgan, Dean Martin and other artists

Some look for glory,
It's still the old story,
Of love versus glory,
And when all is said and done:

You're nobody 'til somebody loves you,
You're nobody 'til somebody cares.

You may be king,
You may possess the world and it's gold,
But gold won't bring you happiness
When you're growing old.

The world still is the same,
You'll never change it,
As sure as the stars shine above.

You're nobody 'til somebody loves you,
Do find yourself somebody to love.

You're the Inspiration

Words and Music by Peter Cetera and David Foster

recorded by Chicago

You know our love was meant to be
The kind of love that lasts forever.
And I want you here with me
From tonight until the end of time.
You should know everywhere I go;
Always on my mind, in my heart,
In my soul, baby.

Refrain:
You're the meaning of my life,
You're the inspiration.
You bring feeling to my life,
You're the inspiration.

Wanna have you near me,
I wanna have you hear me saying
No one needs you more than I need you.
(No one needs you more than I.)

And I know (yes, I know)
That it's plain to see;
We're so in love when we're together.
Now I know (now I know)
That I need you here with me
From tonight to the end of time.
You should know everywhere I go;
Always on my mind, you're in my heart,
In my soul.

Refrain

Wanna have you near me,
I wanna have you hear me say yeah,
No one needs you more than I need you.
You're the meaning of my life,
You're the inspiration.
You bring feeling to my life,
You're the inspiration.

When you love somebody:
(Till the end of time;)
When you love somebody
(Always on my mind.)
No one needs you more than I.

You've Changed
Words and Music by Bill Carey and Carl Fischer
Copyright © 1942 by Southern Music Pub. Co. Inc.
Copyright Renewed

a standard recorded by Billie Holiday and various other
artists

You've changed,
The sparkle in your eyes is gone,
Your smile is just a careless yawn.
You're breaking my heart,
You've changed.

You've changed,
Your kisses now are so blasé,
You're bored with me in every way.
I can't understand,
You've changed.

You've forgotten the words, "I love you,"
Each memory that we've shared.
You ignore every star above you,
I can't realize you ever cared.

You've changed,
You're not the angel I once knew,
No need to tell me that we're through.
It's all over now,
You've changed.

You've Got a Friend
Words and Music by Carole King
© 1971 (Renewed 1999) COLGEMS-EMI MUSIC INC.

recorded by James Taylor, Carole King

When you're down and troubled,
And you need some loving care;
(or: And you need a helping hand;)
And nothin' is goin' right
Close your eyes and think of me,
And soon I will be there:
To brighten up even your darkest night.

You just call out my name,
And you know wherever I am
I'll come runnin' to see you again.
Winter, spring, summer or fall,
All you have to do is call,
And I'll be there.
You've got a friend.

If the sky above you
Grows dark and full of clouds;
And that old north wind begins to blow
Keep your head together,
And call my name out loud;
Soon you'll hear me knockin' at your door.

You just call out my name,
And you know wherever I am
I'll come runnin' to see you again.
Winter, spring, summer or fall,
All you have to do is call,
And I'll be there, yes, I will.

Now ain't it good to know that you've got a friend,
When people can be so cold.
They'll hurt you,
Yes, and desert you,
And take your soul if you let them.
Oh, but don't you let them.

You just call out my name,
And you know wherever I am
I'll come runnin' to see you a gain.
Winter, spring, summer or fall,
All you have to do is call,
And I'll be there, yes, I will.

You've got a friend.
You've got a friend.
Ain't it good to know
You've got a friend…

You've Got a Friend in Me

Music and Lyrics by Randy Newman
© 1995 Walt Disney Music Company

from Walt Disney's *Toy Story*
from Walt Disney Pictures' *Toy Story 2* – A Pixar Film

You've got a friend in me.
You've got a friend in me.
When the road looks rough ahead,
And your miles and miles from your nice warm bed,
You just remember what your old pal said:
Son, you've got a friend in me.
Yeah, you've got a friend in me.

You've got a friend in me.
You've got a friend in me.
You got troubles, then I got 'em too.
There isn't anything I wouldn't do for you.
If we stick together we can see it through,
'Cause you've got a friend in me.
Yeah, you've got a friend in me.

Now, some other folks might be a little bit smarter than I am,
Bigger and stronger too.
Maybe. But none of them will ever love you the way I do,
Just me and you, boy.

And as the years go by,
Our friendship will never die.
You're gonna see it's our destiny.

You've got a friend in me.
You've got a friend in me.
You've got a friend in me.

You've Got to Be Carefully Taught

Lyrics by Oscar Hammerstein II
Music by Richard Rodgers
Copyright © 1949 by Richard Rodgers and Oscar Hammerstein II
Copyright Renewed
WILLIAMSON MUSIC owner of publication and allied rights throughout the world

from the musical *South Pacific*

You've got to be carefully taught to hate and fear.
You've got to be taught from year to year.
It's got to be drummed in your dear little ear.
You've got to be carefully taught.

You've got to be taught to be afraid
Of people whose eyes are oddly made,
And people whose skin is a different shade,
You've got to be carefully taught.

You've got to be taught before it's too late,
Before you are six, or seven, or eight,
To hate all the people your relatives hate,
You've got to be carefully taught!
You've got to be carefully taught!

You've Got to Hide Your Love Away

Words and Music by John Lennon and Paul McCartney
Copyright © 1965 Sony/ATV Songs LLC
Copyright Renewed
All Rights Administered by Sony/ATV Music Publishing, 8 Music Square West,
   Nashville, TN 37203

recorded by The Beatles

Here I stand with head in hand,
Turn my face to the wall.
If she's gone I can't go on,
Feeling two foot small.

Everywhere people stare,
Each and every day.
I can see them laugh at me,
And I hear them say,
Hey, You've got to hide your love away.

How can I even try?
I can never win.
Hearing them, seeing them,
In the state I'm in,

How could she say to me?
Love will find a way.
Gather round all you clowns,
Let me hear you say,
Hey, you've got to hide your love away.

You've Made Me So Very Happy

Words and Music by Berry Gordy, Frank E. Wilson,
Brenda Holloway and Patrice Holloway
© 1967 (Renewed 1995) JOBETE MUSIC CO., INC.
All Rights Controlled and Administered by EMI APRIL MUSIC INC. and
   EMI BLACKWOOD MUSIC INC. on behalf of JOBETE MUSIC CO., INC. and
   STONE AGATE MUSIC (A Division of JOBETE MUSIC CO., INC.)

recorded by Brenda Holloway; Blood, Sweat & Tears

I lost at love before,
Got mad and closed the door.
But you said try just once more.
I chose you for the one,
Now I'm having so much fun.
You treated me so kind,
I'm about to lose my mind.
You made me so very happy,
I'm so glad you came into my life.

The others were untrue,
But when it came to lovin' you,
I'd spend my whole life with you.
'Cause you came and you took control,
You touched my very soul.
You always showed me that
Loving you was where it's at.
You made me so very happy,
I'm so glad you came into my life.

I love you so much, it seems
That you're even in my dream.
I hear you calling me.
I'm so in love with you,
All I ever want to do is
Thank you, baby.

Twice:
You made me so very happy,
I'm so glad you came into my life.

Your Cheatin' Heart
Words and Music by Hank Williams

recorded by Hank Williams, Joni James, Frankie Laine

Your cheatin' heart will make you weep,
You'll cry and cry and try to sleep.
But sleep won't some the whole night through,
You're cheatin' heart will tell on you.

Refrain:
When tears come down like fallin' rain,
You'll toss around and call my name.
You'll walk the floor the way I do,
Your cheatin' heart will tell on you.

Your cheatin' heart will pine someday,
And crave the love you threw away.
The time will come when you'll be blue,
You're cheatin' heart will tell on you.

Refrain

Zoot Suit Riot
Words and Music by Steve Perry

recorded by The Cherry Poppin' Daddies

Who's that whispering in the trees?
It's two sailors and they're on leave.
Pipes and chains and swingin' hands;
Who's your daddy?
Yes I am
Fat cat came to play:
Now he can't run fast enough.
You'd best stay away
When the pushers come to shove.

Refrain:
Zoot suit riot (riot),
Throw back a bottle of beer.
Zoot suit riot (riot),
A-pull a comb through your coal black hair.

Zoot suit riot (riot),
Throw back a bottle of beer.
Zoot suit riot (riot),
A-pull a comb through your coal black hair.

Spoken:
Blow, daddy!

Sung:
A whipped up jitterbuggin' brown-eyed man,
A stray cat frontin' out an eight-piece band.
Cut me, Sammy, and you'll understand,
In my veins hot music ran.
You got me in a sway,
And I want to swing you, dove.
Now you sailors know,
Where your women come for love.

Refrain

You're in a zoot suit riot.
You're in a zoot suit riot.
You're in a zoot suit riot.

Za doot, zayow.
Za doot za zoo zee.
Flay abadiya.
Zay zay zay.
Ba doot zayayayow.
Ba doot za zoo zay.
Zay zoo zay ze zoo.
Dey deyt dey.

Oh, you got me in a sway,
And I want to swing you, dove.
Now you sailors know,
Where your women come for love.
Zoot suit riot (riot),
Throw back a bottle of beer.
Zoot suit riot (riot),
A-pull a comb through your coal black hair.

Refrain

You're in a zoot suit riot.
You're in a zoot suit riot.
You're in a zoot suit riot.